Does the Elephant Dance?

Contemporary Indian Foreign Policy

David M. Malone

OXFORD

UNIVERSITY PRESS

OXFORD

UNIVERSITY PRESS

Great Clarendon Street, Oxford OX2 6DP

Oxford University Press is a department of the University of Oxford.
It furthers the University's objective of excellence in research, scholarship,
and education by publishing worldwide in

Oxford New York

Auckland Cape Town Dar es Salaam Hong Kong Karachi
Kuala Lumpur Madrid Melbourne Mexico City Nairobi
New Delhi Shanghai Taipei Toronto

With offices in

Argentina Austria Brazil Chile Czech Republic France Greece
Guatemala Hungary Italy Japan Poland Portugal Singapore
South Korea Switzerland Thailand Turkey Ukraine Vietnam

Oxford is a registered trade mark of Oxford University Press
in the UK and in certain other countries

Published in the United States
by Oxford University Press Inc., New York

British Library Cataloguing in Publication Data
Data available

Library of Congress Cataloging in Publication Data
Data available

Typeset by SPI Publisher Services, Pondicherry, India
Printed in Great Britain on acid-free paper by
MPG Books Group, Bodmin and King's Lynn

ISBN: 978–0–19–955202–3

1 3 5 7 9 10 8 6 4 2

For my Indian friends, who did so much to make my time among them in India a very exciting and happy one.

SOUTH ASIA

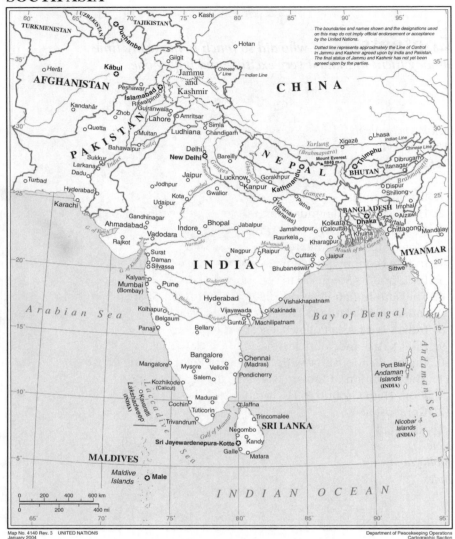

South Asia, Map No. 4140, Rev. 3, January 2004

Source: Reproduced by kind permission from the UN.

Contents

Acknowledgements

Many institutions, friends, and acquaintances have helped make this venture possible.

Independent scholarship is both difficult and lonely. Consequently, I have always sought to anchor my research activity in a high-quality academic or research institution. For this project, I was fortunate to be welcomed into the Centre on International Cooperation (CIC) at New York University. Infused with energy, creativity, and ambition, powered by a terrific young team, and led with great skill by Bruce D. Jones, CIC was entering a phase of new engagement with emerging states in 2007. It generously funded this project's research expenses, including an exciting seminar on Indian foreign policy in New York in October 2009. I am deeply grateful to all those involved at CIC, particularly to Bruce and to Rahul Chandran.

In expanding my knowledge, I wanted to work predominantly with Indians, as I wanted Indian perspectives above all to inform this book. I have benefited from outstanding research assistance that developed into full-fledged research partnerships.

Rohan Mukherjee was recommended to me by two prominent Indians, Pratap Bhanu Mehta, President of the Centre for Policy Research (CPR) in Delhi, and Sam Pitroda, a leading entrepreneur, youthful advisor to the late Prime Minister Rajiv Gandhi, and, during my years in Delhi, Chair of India's Knowledge Commission. From his perch at Princeton University, Rohan and I engaged together on India's security preoccupations, India–USA and India–China relations, and on India's approach to multilateral diplomacy. I have benefited hugely from his sharp mind, his elegant prose, his enthusiasm, and his boundless generosity of spirit.[1]

Taru Dalmia, with whom I explored the links between India's history and the development of its modern foreign policy, returned to Delhi in 2007 from the School of Oriental and African Studies in London with a Masters degree. In Delhi, he somehow combined further study of history, his avocation as a well-known rap artist (under the moniker Delhi Sultanate), and his interest in the martial arts, finding time also for our work together. He is an exceptionally gifted thinker and writer, and I am very grateful to him for kicking off this venture with me in 2007.

Helping shape my ideas on India's immediate neighbourhood was Rajeev Ranjan Chaturvedy, then a doctoral candidate at JNU and a professional development award holder at the International Development Research Centre (IDRC) in Ottawa, whose thesis focuses on China's penetration of India's sphere of influence.[2] We also worked together on the links between India's economy and the changes in its foreign policy since independence.[3] I am very grateful to him for educating me.

Several others proved excellent research partners: Andrew Brunatti, now a doctoral candidate at Brunel University, London, UK, sketched out in depth India's approach to Middle East diplomacy.[4] We also worked together on India's ties with Russia and Western Europe.[5] Andrew tackled these dimensions of India's foreign relations with skill, keen research instincts, and enthusiasm. Poorvi Chitalkar, a very impressive Indian law scholar, helped shape many of my conclusions, provided acute comments on the remainder of the manuscript, and kept the project on track, intellectually and logistically, during its final phases. Archana Pandya, who also helped greatly with manuscript preparation, worked with me on India's 'Look East' policy, bringing order and sharp analysis to a cacophony of relationships all claiming somehow to be 'strategic'.[6] To all three I am most grateful and from each I expect great achievements in years ahead.

My two employers during the years that the book was written, the Department of Foreign Affairs and International Trade of Canada and Canada's IDRC, were tremendously supportive. I am grateful in particular to IDRC Chairman Barbara McDougall, and to Peter Harder and Marie-Lucie Morin, who earlier proved exceptionally helpful within Canada's government, not least in favouring my assignment to India. It is obvious, but I reiterate, that the views advanced in subsequent pages are my own alone, and emphatically not those of either the Canadian government or of IDRC.

My Indian friends did everything they could to help with this project. Professional and personal friends, including many politicians and officials, took time to share with me their views and experience. I shall not name them here, but they know the depth of my gratitude to them. However, I will make an exception to record my heartfelt appreciation to Romila Thapar and Ramachandra Guha, surely among the busiest and most highly regarded historians active anywhere today, for introducing me to Indian history on the page and in person, as well as for their kindness in providing a corrective steer here and there to my thinking.

Two of India's leading Think Tanks, the CPR and the Indian Council for Research on International Economic Relations (ICRIER), each generously organized a round-table in early 2010 to allow me to explore with knowledgeable Indians aspects of their country's multilateral relations. I am very grateful to the respective heads, Pratap Bhanu Mehta and Rajiv Kumar, for taking so much time and trouble to make these very useful sessions happen. Pratap has greatly influenced my thinking on India's international engagement and Rajiv's views on India's international economic relations are always insightful and authoritative.

I had been keen on visiting Pakistan again while working on this book, a wish that came true in February 2010, allowing me to re-acquaint myself with Lahore, still the most beautiful large city of South Asia, after an absence of thirty-five years. There, I was struck by the courage and resiliency of the great Pakistani analyst and scholar Ahmed Rashid, who remains fearless in face of those whom his views antagonize. Islamabad was grim, but still host to many fascinating and impressive Pakistanis. Indians and Pakistanis are such close cousins that one experiences a false sense of sameness. While Indians are confident (if, among themselves, mostly self-critical), Pakistanis today are very worried—not least to see India pulling away from them in terms of economic dynamism and also in the now deep-rooted nature of its democracy. Pakistanis deserve better and will, I hope, achieve in years ahead the society and economy they aspire to.

A conference at Ditchley Park in March 2010 on India as a potential super-power, with a stellar Indian cast of participants, produced useful ideas in a beautiful English country house setting. The Ditchley Foundation has experienced a golden age under the leadership of Sir Jeremy Greenstock, and I am indebted to him and his colleagues for including me in the conference when I had so little to contribute compared to others attending.[7]

One writer on Indian foreign policy who has consistently influenced my thinking is C. Raja Mohan, an enviably talented scholar and commentator, who is also a singularly generous mentor. Kanti Bajpai, who sets standards that the rest of us struggle to meet, not least in the elegance, concision, and clarity of his drafting, is both a friend and a mentor in the study of Indian foreign policy. Prem Shankar Jha is such a fount of knowledge and creativity that his friends often wonder how he manages to contain it all, while sharing so much of it in his books and columns. Others whose commentary I look out for include the great constitutional and political writer A. G. Noorani, who continues to pour forth learned and deliciously tart essays, often in the guise of in-depth book reviews, in the pages of *Frontline* and elsewhere. He has no peer in the West. The Delhi Editor of *The Hindu*, Siddharth Varadarajan, and, when he was still writing in that capacity, his predecessor, Harish Khare—a singularly perceptive constitutional and political analyst now serving the Indian Prime Minister as Media Advisor—superb writers both, have consistently enriched my understanding of the country. Sanjaya Baru, today editor of the *Business Standard*, and a very fine scholar who also served as a close advisor to Dr. Manmohan Singh, has been consistently encouraging, as comes so naturally to him. Mohan Guruswamy, an impressive former classmate, deploys an elegant pen in the service of a sharp mind. The recollections, often pointed and frequently entertaining, of such literate Indian commentators as Inder Malhotra, Kuldip Nayar, and Khushwant Singh, all of whom I was fortunate to know and who had served earlier Indian governments, have provided me with many valued pointers.

Other recent pioneers of Indian scholarship on foreign policy have been very helpful. These include Alka Acharya, long a lonely voice of reason on relations with China and my former colleague at the International Peace Academy, W. P. S. Sidhu, who co-authored exciting volumes on Kashmir and on India–China relations. A raft of Nepali friends enlightened me on India–Nepal ties, not least in connection with a book I am currently co-editing with my long-time confederate Sebastian von Einsiedel and with Suman Pradhan, on the unfolding constitutional and governance crisis there. My friend Thant Myint U has been a constant source of wisdom on Burma and much else. I have also learned tremendously from engaging with Stephen P. Cohen and Christophe Jaffrelot on South Asia.

Among Indian journalists and editors who were particularly helpful in educating me, I should mention Manoj Joshi, Comments Editor of *Mail Today*, who is accessible globally through his excellent blog on Indian foreign and internal policy.[8] Jyoti Malhotra of the exciting new business daily *Mint* always rewards reading as do Pronab Dhal Samata, Deputy Editor of the *Indian Express* and Amit Baruah, head of BBC Hindi and lead BBC editor for India. Over the years, I have learned a lot from the fine historian Rudrangshu Mukherjee, Opinions Editor of the Kolkata-based *Telegraph*.

It is very difficult for a foreigner to be as interesting on India as for an Indian. The terrific historian and essayist, William Dalrymple, rises so far above the challenge as to be in a league of his own. During my years in Delhi, the *International Herald Tribune* was fortunate to feature an extraordinary series of columns, often sad but always fond, by Amelia Gentleman focusing on Indian society rather than on the news. And, joining her in the same newspaper, the tremendously talented Anand Giridharadas, quoted in this book, also provided profound insights into Indian society week after week. Simply reporting on the news from India, astounding as that news often is, must be a less immediately gratifying task, and I admired many of the foreign journalists in India bringing the country into focus daily in their articles. I learned from them all, even as I was learning so much from so many Indians.[9]

Several friends have very helpfully guided my thinking on India's dynamic private sector, notably: Gurcharan Das, author of *India Unbound*, and former CEO of Procter and Gamble India; Tarun Das, the powerhouse behind the Indian Confederation of Industry (CII) over several decades; Suman Dubey, former head of Dow Jones India; and Vikram Mehta, Chairman of Shell India.

Several other friends from my days at or near the United Nations have provided much appreciated encouragement for this project. They include Hamid

Ansari (today India's Vice-President), Chinmaya and Rita Gharekhan, Nitin Desai, Kamalesh Sharma (today Commonwealth Secretary-General) and Babli Sharma, Satish Nambiar (one of the UN's greatest peacekeepers), Vijay Nambiar (today Chief of Staff of the UN Secretary-General) and T. P. Sreenivasan. Their hospitality and company in India did so much to make me feel at home there.

The writing of this book has brought me into contact with several individuals whom I did not know before, but whose writing I had much admired, notably Navroz Dubash, Sumit Ganguly, Devesh Kapur, Sunil Khilnani, Pankaj Mishra, Harsh V. Pant, and Srinath Raghavan. Indeed, through this process, I have made a number of valued new friends, who have all influenced my thinking. Younger writers whose views I look out for include Happymon Jacob, Nitin Pai (who launched the successful monthly *Pragati* several years ago), and Zorowar Daulet Singh.

From within India's impressive civil society and policy research communities, I was influenced by many I met, none more so than R. K. Pachauri, leader of TERI, a think-tank on environmental issues, and co-chair of the International Panel on Climate Change (IPCC). Typically of India, his wife, Saroj, was at least as active and impressive on demographic and population issues.

Among Indian foreign policy professionals, both during my tenure in Delhi and subsequently, I have benefited from great generosity and patience. I am grateful for the frequent access provided to me while in Delhi by M. K. Narayanan, National Security Advisor, 2004–10, and today Governor of West Bengal. He displayed sharp wit and great acumen on regional issues and the global balance of power. My long-time friend, Shashi Tharoor, briefly but with élan Minister of State for External Affairs and himself the author of an excellent book on Indian foreign policy, provided characteristically warm encouragement. Several former Foreign Secretaries went out of their way to be helpful, notably the two most recent, Shiv Shankar Menon (today National Security Advisor) and his predecessor at the Ministry of External Affairs (MEA), Shyam Saran, subsequently a senior advisor to the Prime Minister.[10] They represent the best that the diplomatic profession internationally can offer, and both are, as well, fine writers.

During my assignment in Delhi, I was fortunate that the MEA Secretary responsible for North America, Nalin Surie, earlier his country's Ambassador to China and later its High Commissioner to the UK , was a former counterpart of mine at the UN. Nalin was systematically helpful whenever possible, in both New York and Delhi. So was his predecessor as Secretary (West), the elegant Shashi Tripathi, a superb Indian envoy to the USA and Canada earlier in her career. The MEA Joint Secretary for North America during my time was first the brilliant and engaging S. Jaishankar, later India's envoy to Singapore and China, and thereafter the tremendously effective and warm Gaitri Kumar. Multilateral diplomacy was headed up by a remarkable former envoy to Iran, and later a frequent writer on Indian foreign policy, K. C. Singh. The enviable qualities of his younger colleague, Amandeep S. Gill, then responsible for disarmament issues, suggests that there is striking talent rising within the MEA.

Among the many who offered not just encouragement but also practical assistance, I am most grateful to my exceptional successor in India, Joseph Caron, and his accomplished wife Kumru, for their generous hospitality in Delhi in January 2010. Gita Kwatra of the Canadian High Commission was also characteristically ingenious and helpful. Several colleagues in the IDRC regional office in Delhi provided invaluable assistance, particularly the Regional Director, Stephen McGurk, and also Prabha Sethuraman, a dynamo of enthusiasm and effectiveness. I am very grateful for the hospitality offered me by Pilar and Ed Doe in Kathmandu in April 2010, and by Canada's High Commissioner to Pakistan, Randolph Mank, in Februry 2010.

The Rockefeller Foundation very generously offered me a month-long residency at the Villa Serbelloni in Bellagio, Italy, in July 2010, a terrific opportunity in a glorious location that I devoted to polishing this manuscript. Its wonderful team, notably Pilar Palacia and Elena Ongani, did everything possible to make my stay there both productive and intensely agreeable.

I have for many years now worked with Dominic Byatt, Chief Editor for Social Sciences at the historic headquarters of Oxford University Press (OUP). He is a highly supportive, constructively critical, and tremendously effective editor, whose judgement I trust much more than my own. To him and his colleagues at OUP, notably Elizabeth Suffling and Jennifer Lunsford, I am most grateful, as ever. The manuscript was much improved in its final stages by the singularly helpful Malcolm Todd.

Whenever I undertake new research of a challenging sort, I recall my thesis supervisor, Sir Adam Roberts, today President of the British Academy, and several of his outstanding colleagues in the Centre of International Studies at Oxford, notably Dr. Andrew Hurrell, today Montague Burton Professor of International Relations, with enormous gratitude.[11] They introduced me to in-depth research and taught me that it can prove vastly gratifying.

Finally, I should mention how stimulating I found returning to the New York University School of Law to teach a course on the United Nations during the fall term of the years 2009 and 2010 on a commuting basis from Ottawa. I was drawn into this extraordinary institution over ten years ago by the late Thomas M. Franck, whose influence lives on vibrantly within the School's walls and beyond. It was among the rich diversity of its terrific scholars and students that several ideas for this book occurred to me and that my next research project came to mind one day. To them, and particularly to the School's Dean, Richard L. Revesz, warmest thanks.

Ottawa, September 2010.

Abbreviations

AEC	Asian Economic Community
AIADMK	All India Anna Dravida Munnetra Kazhagam
APEC	Asia-Pacific Economic Cooperation
ASEAN	Association of Southeast Asian Nations
AWACS	Airborne Warning and Control System
BASIC	Brazil, South Africa, India, China
BIMSTEC	Bay of Bengal Initiative for Multi-Sectoral Technical and Economic Cooperation
BJP	Bharatiya Janata Party
BRIC	Brazil, Russia, India, China
BSP	Bahujan Samaj Party
CBMs	Confidence Building Measures
C-DAC	Centre for Development of Advanced Computing of India
CENTO	Central Treaty Organization
CEPA	Comprehensive Economic Partnership Agreement
CLAWS	Center for Land Warfare Studies
CPI (M-L)	Communist Party of India (Marxist-Leninist)
CRPF	Central Reserve Police Force
CTBT	Comprehensive Test Ban Treaty
DMK	Dravida Munnetra Kazhagam
DRDO	Defence Research and Development Organization
EIC	East India Company
EU	European Union
FDI	Foreign Direct Investment
FTA	Free Trade Agreement
GATT	General Agreement on Tariffs and Trade
GCC	Gulf Cooperation Council
GDP	Gross Domestic Product
IAEA	International Atomic Energy Agency

IAS	Indian Administrative Service
IBSA	India, Brazil, South Africa
ICCR	Indian Council for Cultural Relations
IFS	Indian Foreign Service
ILO	International Labour Organization
IMCEITS	India-Myanmar Centre for Development of IT Skill
IMF	International Monetary Fund
IMU	Islamic Movement of Uzbekistan
INC	Indian National Congress
IPI	Iran-Pakistan-India
IPKF	Indian Peacekeeping Force
ISI	Inter Services Intelligence
ITEC	Indian Technical and Economic Cooperation
ITER	International Thermonuclear Experimental Reactor
JKLF	Jammu and Kashmir Liberation Front
JNU	Jawaharlal Nehru University
LCS	Land Customs Stations
LEP	Look East policy
LeT	Lashkar-e-Taiba
LoC	Line of Control
LTTE	Liberation Tigers of Tamil Eelam
MEA	Ministry of External Affairs
MEDO	Middle East Defense Organization
MGC	Mekong Ganga Cooperation
MoD	Ministry of Defence
NAM	Non-Aligned Movement
NATO	North Atlantic Treaty Organization
NHPC	National Hydroelectric Power Corporation Ltd
NMD	Nuclear Missile Defense
NPT	Nuclear Non-Proliferation Treaty
NRIs	Non-resident Indians
NSG	Nuclear Suppliers Group
NSSP	Next Steps in Strategic Partnership
ODA	Official Development Assistance
OECD	Organisation for Economic Co-operation and Development
P-5	Permanent Five

PLA	People's Liberation Army
PMO	Prime Minister's Office
POSCO	Pohang Steel Company
PRC	People's Republic of China
R&D	Research and Development
RAW	Research and Analysis Wing
RBI	Reserve Bank of India
RJD	Rashtriya Janata Dal
SAARC	South Asian Association for Regional Cooperation
SAFTA	South Asia Free Trade Agreement
SCO	Shanghai Cooperation Organization
SEATO	South East Asian Treaty Organization
SEZs	Special Economic Zones
SIMI	Students' Islamic Movement of India
SIPRI	Stockholm International Peace Research Institute
SNIE	Special National Intelligence Estimate
SP	Samajwadi Party
TAPI	Turkmenistan-Afghanistan-Pakistan-India
TCS	Tata Consulting Services
TRIPS	Trade-Related Aspects of Intellectual Property Rights
ULFA	United Liberation Front of Asom
UNCTAD	United Nations Conference on Trade and Development
UNIDO	United Nations Industrial Development Organization
UNSC	United Nations Security Council
UPA	United Progressive Alliance
WTO	World Trade Organization

Preface

Why this book now and by this author?

Both Indian foreign policy and the wider backdrop of international relations in the new century are interesting topics. However, there are more personal answers as well, sketched below.

I came to India in 2006, having travelled in the country, exploring it as much as I could over the years, ever since my youth. My mother unreservedly adored India and everything to do with it. As a boy, I lived for many years in Iran, a country much influenced by several Indian civilizations, particularly after the advent of Islam in both countries. I am deeply grateful to my late parents for offering me the opportunity to discover some of the world beyond Canada in their company when I was a child. I was to return to Iran in my late teens, and again as a university student, and then to travel beyond it to Afghanistan, Pakistan, and India, with friends. We visited Kashmir on both the Pakistani and Indian sides of the line of control, finding each region and its inhabitants enchanting, in spite of the violence to which the Kashmir Valley was prone even in 1975. I have visited no place outside Iran closer in atmosphere, style, and inclination to Persian manners, customs, and outlook than the Kashmir valley, and I loved it on contact, as I still do.

But such a predisposition towards India alone would not have led to this book, particularly by a foreign policy practitioner and occasional scholar having specialized mainly in the multilateral sphere, notably in the study of decision-making in the UN Security Council.

India has played an important role in UN affairs over the years, not least through its shared leadership of the Non-Aligned Movement and its admirable participation in UN peacekeeping. More recently, India, along with several others, has laid claim to a permanent seat on the UN Security Council, about which I had written during the years 2000–6. India has a distinct profile in public international law, my academic field of adoption, one of restrained enthusiasm for legal entanglements enshrined in treaties, but also of respect for those treaties that it does ratify. Thus, its practice of diplomacy was not in all respects *terra incognita* for me. I had worked alongside many skilled and congenial Indian practitioners of the craft, from whom I had learned a good deal.

Perhaps unsurprisingly, much in India reminded me of the United States, a country on whose foreign policy I had often written: the scale, optimism, openness, entrepreneurship, self absorption, and occasional hubris on display were tremendously reminiscent of those of Americans.

But the genesis of my sustained attention to Indian foreign policy was a happy stroke of luck. In early 2006, having returned to the Canadian government after a number of years away directing the International Peace Academy, a non-profit research and policy development institution in New York, I was overseeing Canada's economic and multilateral diplomacy within the Ministry of Foreign Affairs and International Trade when the head of the Foreign Service unexpectedly asked me where I would choose to serve, if I could be assigned anywhere as head of a Canadian diplomatic mission. This did not require any thought: Delhi, I responded instantly. And so, to my delight, some months later, I was appointed my country's envoy to India. I was also fortunate to be accredited as non-resident ambassador to Nepal and Bhutan, two very different but equally compelling smaller neighbours of India, through whose eyes I came to appreciate some of India's regional diplomacy for good and ill.

Knowing parts of India and having already some Indian friends, I threw myself into the assignment with as much energy as I could muster, enjoying every day of my life there tremendously. Much of my assignment was devoted to the usual diplomatic tasks: learning about Indian domestic politics, its economic policies and performance, its history, culture, and much else, in order to be able to interpret the country for my own government, and advocating in India for my country's interests and policies. I was also engaged in formal and informal representations of various sorts, in Delhi and throughout this vast and diverse country. The priority file for Canada, as for most other countries in India, was the promotion of our economic interests there, which, while still modest, were growing fast (although not as quickly as was Indian investment in Canada). I travelled prodigiously in all three of my countries of accreditation – as much as time, health, companions, and hosts would allow. And everywhere, I encountered warm hospitality and much of local interest.

Being a slow reader, it took me some time to survey the field of writing on Indian foreign policy. Among the earlier books, I recalled one by a distant predecessor of mine in Delhi, Escott Reid, titled *Envoy to Nehru*.[1] Although written many years after his departure in 1957 from Delhi, it featured great immediacy, sharp judgements on many Indian personalities and events of that period (borne out by time) and a sense of how personal the formulation of Indian foreign policy then was to Nehru, abetted only by a very few associates. In those days, the small coterie of foreign envoys in Delhi enjoyed access to the highest circles of Indian decision-making when their personal qualities or the importance of their countries commended them, and of this privilege,

Reid, no shrinking violet, took full advantage. I was happy to find his book often cited in the Indian literature of the country's foreign policy.

Since Reid's time, the practice of diplomacy has evolved. While the number and size of diplomatic missions has expanded considerably, the personal importance of ambassadors has withered somewhat as leaders and ministers personally engage with each other more often, through bilateral visits, regional meetings, summitry, and also, of course, the telephone. This is nowhere more true than in Delhi, which today hosts well over 150 diplomatic and multilateral missions. In truth, as the number of embassies worldwide has risen, and the saliency of diplomats to resolution of the key issues of the day has, in the main, waned, so have the relevance, acuity, drive, and personal engagement of many practitioners.

The heads of diplomatic missions routinely involved in goings-on in Delhi are exactly the ones a reader might expect: those of immediate neighbours such as Sri Lanka, Pakistan, and Bhutan; of the great powers; of some countries of regional significance; and also those rare individuals with the force of character and mind—or a sufficiently interesting and charming spouse—to make themselves (if not their country) matter in India. Such was my Chilean colleague, Jorge Heine, a renowned scholar, a former Minister in his country, and an active and admired participant in Delhi's think-tank world, who still contributes extensively to scholarship and commentary in India, notably in the pages of *The Hindu.*[2]

Thus, the practice of diplomacy by its professionals has probably evolved more since Reid's day than in the two preceding centuries, and likely not for the better.

Happily for me, several of my books, obscure tomes on recondite aspects of multilateral diplomacy, had been published (and mostly forgotten) in India. Just as I arrived in 2006, one such book, dealing with the UN Security Council's involvement in Iraq since the outset of the Iran–Iraq war of 1980, came out in Delhi. The local book launch, associated reviews, and the related kindnesses of a number of *Dilliwallahs* drew me away from diplomatic routine and into the life of the mind in Delhi: there is no capital where it is more active or prized excepting Washington, London, and Paris and it is on a par with each of these. And the worlds of reading, writing, debate, and the arts turned out, to a much greater extent than in any other capital I have known, actively to involve many of the country's leading political figures and some of its top business executives. In what other capital would a rapidly rising government Minister take the trouble to pen and deliver a remarkable lecture on a subject as abstruse as the history of India's relations with Canada—as did Jairam Ramesh, then Minister of State for Commerce and Industry (as well as Power), at Delhi University in 2007?[3]

It was this experience of intense policy debate during my assignment in India that emboldened me on the path towards this book. An added incentive to accelerate the work was the difficult decision I took in the summer of 2008 to leave prematurely my diplomatic assignment in a country I had found tremendously congenial and engrossing for a very different position—the one I now hold and also love, as President of Canada's International Development Research Centre.

Thus, the pleasure that I have derived from further exploring on the one hand the impulses, including the historical ones, behind Indian foreign policy and on the other the conduct of its international relations, served to bind me after my departure from India to my Indian friends and colleagues and to console me over my departure from a country I missed very much. (I have made every effort, however, to address my topic unsentimentally.)

Happily, my intuition that the writing of this book would reinforce my ties to India has proved well founded. Indeed, the reserve with which foreign envoys are often treated, and the generous courtesies afforded to them—which can easily be distancing—vanished as soon as I was no longer occupying an official role there, and everyone felt free to engage on my project. Thus, since 2008, I have been discovering aspects of India new to me, and rediscovering other dimensions of it in more relaxed and productive dialogue with Indian colleagues, friends, acquaintances, and those I had admired from a distance while *en poste* in India.

Regular contact with strong and curious students is a wonderful way of having one's certainties challenged. Wherever I had gone in recent years, I had either been associated with or taught at local universities, as I did in New York at Columbia University's School of International and Public Affairs while serving as an ambassador at the United Nations. And, naively, I had hoped to do likewise in Delhi. Reaching that great city, I thought of India's leading graduate teaching and research institution, Jawaharlal Nehru University (JNU). But I was rebuffed, very politely. The relevant Dean there explained to me that several faculty members feared my 'bias', perhaps being comfortable only with their own. Another foreign scholar had spent some time teaching there a few years earlier and his turn of mind had unsettled some in the school. The reserve of JNU may also have related to my status as a foreign diplomat, and, on that score, I am sympathetic, as customs vary from country to country on how foreign envoys should be received.

Disappointed but undeterred, I set about having as much contact with Indian students as I could through casual lectures and seminars in Delhi and as I travelled around the country. I am tremendously grateful to friends at JNU and elsewhere for making those possible. Several of the Vice-Chancellors of Indian universities, including one of its great foreign policy scholars, Amitabh Mattoo, and one of its great international economists, Deepak Nayyar, were also kind enough to take me under their wing and to encourage my active engagement with students and faculty members. At Delhi University, Vice

Chancellor Deepak Pental and the Director of the University's South Campus, Dinesh Singh, were ever welcoming. India, whose universities have suffered a great deal of neglect in recent decades, while the Indian government focused its attention and allocated its resources elsewhere, has nevertheless produced many great scholars. To those who have helped me in so many ways, I am deeply grateful.

Beyond Delhi's think-tanks, universities, the India International Centre, and the non-stop Indian and international conclaves that crowd each other during the city's cooler months, I was fortunate to participate in, contribute to, and learn much from conferences organized by the Indian Law Institute and the Indian Society of International Law. The very active exchange between the Indian and Canadian Supreme Courts, with annual participation of both Chief Justices, allowed me to deepen my acquaintanceship with the Indian judiciary. Serving and retired Indian Supreme Court and High Court justices, as well as many of the leading advocates before the Supreme Court, are a remarkable group, none more so than Fali S. Nariman, president of the Bar Association of India, and in many ways the conscience of India's legal community. One of its Vice-Presidents, Soli Sorabjee, is also a particularly brilliant and frequent intervener in public debate and in landmark cases, and from him I equally learned a great deal. Of the many judges I was fortunate to know, Justice Madan Lokur, of the Delhi High Court, stood out for his generous interest in, and acute knowledge of, the links between Indian and non-Indian justice in all its forms.[4] The admirable retired High Court judge Leila Seth also provided much encouragement. Above all, I am personally indebted to Manoj Kumar Sinha, then Director of the Indian Society of International Law, and now a professor of human rights and refugee law at the National University of Juridical Sciences in Kolkata.

Amartya Sen was kind enough to allow me to trail around behind him in Delhi for a couple of days shortly after my arrival in India. They were perhaps the two richest days of my life in India as I was introduced to so many layers of policy-makers, writers, and activists, and was able to listen in to debates otherwise beyond my reach. Amartya himself was characteristically generous of his time to all comers, agreeing to add to his already packed schedule to accommodate activists keen to capitalize on his presence in town. Much in India is improvised at the last minute, and I learned from observing him on the move that the most memorable events often fall into place in this fashion.

A note on names

Because the colonial and then post-independence capital of New Delhi has today been engulfed in the wider city of Delhi, spilling out in every direction, and having consulted several Indian author friends, whose practice varies, I have used Delhi to denote both India's capital and as a metonym for its government. In referring to historic Calcutta, under the Raj, I have retained the name then in use; the city's official English name was changed to Kolkata in 2001, so any references to contemporary Kolkata conform to the new Indian practice—similarly for Mumbai (formerly Bombay) and Chennai (earlier Madras). Curiously, the new (non-anglicized) Bengaluru has not caught on to the same extent and so, like many Indians, I continue to refer to it as Bangalore.

1

Introduction

Over the past sixty-odd years, much has been written on India's foreign policy by Indians and on occasion by foreigners. Some of the latter, such as Strobe Talbott, have documented with great flair and depth certain episodes of India's recent international relations.[1] Surveys of Indian foreign policy in the form of linked and unlinked essays have been committed to the page quite recently, including that of Rajiv Sikri.[2] But many Indian books on the topic, even those rare surveys, tend to assume a level of knowledge of India's history, its civilizations, its neighbourhood, and its politics that non-Indians, even ones interested in both the country and the topic, do not often possess.[3] Hence, an outside eye to such a subject may be helpful from time to time.

India is a huge, boisterous nation bursting with optimism for its future, and reaping some early fruits of its profitable engagement with globalization, while struggling to reduce the severe poverty afflicting hundreds of millions of its citizens. Like the USA, India is primarily inward-oriented. Goings on within India, of great local interest and often of some international significance given India's growing weight, could readily absorb the sum total of attention that Indians devote to public affairs. Indeed, K. M. Panikkar, an early practitioner and historian of Indian diplomacy following independence, argued that India has, throughout history, had trouble arousing much interest in the world beyond its borders.[4] This self-absorption, if his analysis is correct, arose in part from the Himalayan range that appears to protect India from the north (although several invaders from the north have accessed India through Afghanistan) and perhaps, a sense that India sufficed onto itself.[5]

But today, we witness an India reaching out: its private sector is doing so aggressively, carving out markets for itself globally, investing widely and taking over industrial and service icons abroad. Nonetheless, corporate India faces frustrations within its home country particularly with regard to business conditions and barriers to effective inward investment, as steel magnate Lakshmi Mittal (of Arcelor-Mittal) and Ratan Tata, leader of the Tata conglomerate, often emphasize with asperity.[6]

I was fortunate to be resident in India during the years in which its striking economic success, albeit displaying sharp inequalities (as was the case with economic growth elsewhere during these years), increasingly drew the attention of the world. The joke in foreign policy circles was that India had been emerging for so long that one despaired of it ever completing the process. But the rise of major powers is always a progressive business—as is their decline—accelerated at times by tectonic shifts in relative global power and influence, of which the economic crisis of 2008–10 may prove to be one.

The size and population of India is now complemented by sufficient economic progress as to guarantee it a place at the global high table of influence. With the elevation of the Group of 20 to the level of leaders in 2008 as the key assembly of globally significant countries, India was offered an opportunity to play a major role. Even earlier, it had joined Brazil, China, Mexico, and South Africa as a 'dialogue partner' of the Group of Eight, the forum for policy discussion among leading industrialized countries. While at the G-8, India and the other guests playing a subsidiary role found their unequal status grating, if not insulting. In contrast, at the G-20 they were not only equals, but clearly mattered more than a number of the Western participants in economic global discussions. For India, this was particularly so during the sharp global financial and economic downturn of 2008–9 because the Indian Prime Minister, Manmohan Singh, a distinguished economist, was internationally recognized as the man who had led India's major economic reforms initiated in 1991 that sparked its higher growth. At the G-20 table, when Dr Singh spoke, in his understated manner, all listened.

Thus, it was India's economic significance that lent weight to the country's international profile. Its foreign policy, regional concerns, and geostrategic views were largely unknown to the rest of the world, as they are to most Indians, who remain overwhelmingly preoccupied with the struggle for improved conditions within their own country.[7]

However, as of 2008, its international relations mattered more (at least to non-Indians). In that year India escaped from the partial international purdah into which its 1974 nuclear test and to a lesser extent its 1998 tests had consigned it, thanks to multilateral acceptance of its nuclear cooperation agreement with the USA. Thus, the timing of this volume, and others by authors more accomplished than I, in the months ahead, several of them Indian, might make it somewhat more than normally useful.

Methodology

This volume's methodology is rooted in a review of the literature, both academic and more general. It is informed by an awareness of some of the scholarly theoretical debates of our time in the discipline of International Relations and how they have been applied to India, but this volume offers no theoretical arguments or frameworks of its own. India's development has successfully defied so many historical burdens and challenged so many long- and comfortably held assumptions that theoretical straitjackets are unlikely to fit this particular case. The volume is both historical and empirical in its roots and inquiring in its aims. Its conclusions are tentative (as those of any contemporary chronicler need to be).

Approach to the literature

Much of the Western literature on Indian foreign policy is self-referential: Westerners citing other Westerners, as if most work of value were written outside the region and countries involved. It is a habit of mind in the West that those whose opinions matter are to be found in the leading Western capitals, universities, and publications. Although there are indeed books, chapters, and articles of great relevance and acuity touching or centred on Indian foreign policy authored in the West, the writing most influential in the formulation of Indian foreign policy and in shaping Indian views thereof is, of course, Indian. Most of it is available in fluent, elegant, and lively English. Thus, one of my objectives from the outset has been to draw mainly on Indian authors and policymakers in the drafting of the chapters that follow. Likewise, I sought out research assistance principally from brilliant young Indians, and, of course, was richly rewarded—they not only thought differently from me, but better, and came to different conclusions, often more interesting ones. Engaging my topic mainly through Indians, on the page and in person, has been a tremendous education for me.

The number of Indians writing authoritatively in English on Indian foreign policy is relatively small (perhaps twenty or so, with valuable occasional contributions from others). These include Indian practitioners (nearly always retired ones), Indian scholars teaching in Indian and Western institutions, members of several leading Indian think-tanks, and, to a larger extent than I had anticipated, several Indian editors and scholar-journalists. As well, Indian historians, economists, legal scholars, and practitioners, and some leading private sector voices, have a great deal of value to contribute to the discussion of Indian foreign policy. Many of these are cited in the pages that follow or included in the bibliography (which I have limited for reasons of space to core texts and more recent books of which the reader may not yet be aware). As I was concluding my work on this volume, a tremendous and now indispensable resource for all those interested in the domestic setting for India's international relations was published in the form of the *Oxford*

Companion to Politics in India, edited by Niraja Gopal Jayal and Pratap Bhanu Mehta. It can be warmly recommended to experts and neophytes alike, and contains excellent chapters on India's foreign relations and its defence policy by Kanti Bajpai and Sumit Ganguly respectively.[8]

To this number of persuasive Indian writers on their own foreign policy should be added a number of other non-Indian voices that command a degree of attention within India. But the number is small.[9]

In the era of internet transmission and instantaneous e-mail communication, debate among analysts of Indian foreign policy, some of them dotted around the world, is constant, illuminating, and exciting. They read each other's ideas and riff off them frequently.[10] With these friends, it was a huge relief to be able to discard my diplomatic guise.

Of course, the frenzied pace of information exchange and the immediacy of opinion published the world over today creates a risk that the urgent will trump the important, and that event-driven analysis will displace identification of trends and in-depth ideas developed painstakingly over time. I have tried to circumnavigate these pitfalls by taking my time, over three years, before concluding this manuscript. But it is still much influenced by recent events and doubtless suffers from the myopia of contemporary history.

While many of the ideas and events I cite are drawn from scholarly work, Indian journalism is so astoundingly prolific and its editorial and commentary pages sufficiently stimulating, that I have also drawn on them quite often.[11] India offers the reader a dozen or so high-quality dailies in English and others in the country's many vernacular languages, some national in ambition and distribution, others more regional (such as Chandigarh's excellent *Tribune*). However, as any other, the Indian media also suffers from limitations: it engages only fitfully with the rest of the world and tends towards analysis on issues international strictly in terms of India's perspectives and interests. Raju Narisetti, founding editor of an exciting new economic and business-oriented daily in India, *Mint*, from 2006 to 2008, and earlier Editor of the *Wall Street Journal Europe*, today Managing Editor of the *Washington Post*, comments:

> Much of the coverage, often in editorial pages and columns, is rooted in extreme navel-gazing and significantly influenced by a small coterie of sources among New Delhi bureaucrats and suffers from a lack of dispassionate analysis of India's influence. Even among the few writers based outside India providing copy to major Indian media organizations, much of the sourcing is based on officials at Indian embassies and, in recent years, on Indian trade and advocacy groups. The notion that to be critical of India's foreign policy, with a few obvious exceptions, is to be negative, even downright unpatriotic, is widely shared among correspondents and editors focused on India's foreign affairs.[12]

Despite this, and the fact that quality, aims, political orientation, and presentation of each newspaper vary, several tremendously impressive editors (and perhaps a half-dozen powerful publishers) bestride the profession as a whole. To read a hard copy of *The Hindu*, the *Indian Express*, or the *Asian Age* in the days when M. J. Akbar still held sway there, is to marvel at the creativity, intelligence, and skills that a superb editor can display, as opposed to the more mundane satisfactions available online when merely organized and presented by a web-master. Leading Indian newspaper publishers of ambition allied with editorial flair include Shobhana Bhartia of the *Hindustan Times* and Aveek Sarkar of the Kolkata-based *Telegraph*. Editors of singular achievement include N. Ram at *The Hindu* and Shekhar Gupta at the *Indian Express*, each of whom displays tremendous substantive range.

For this reason, I have gone on subscribing to hard copies of these newspapers and several of India's often very impressive English-language magazines, notably *Frontline*, *Outlook*, and *Tehelka*, the latter an admirable insurgency against the complacencies of the urban elites. As well, many rewards are to be found in India's iconic and historic *Economic and Political Weekly*, to which several of my friends, notably Sanjaya Baru, contribute. But as its impressive editors make few concessions to the casual reader, serious engagement with this publication is reserved mainly for those with time and commitment on their hands. To be distant from India is to miss out on the frequently excellent television talk-shows focused on public policy, and quite often on foreign affairs, with such well-informed hosts as Karan Thapar and Barkha Dutt.

The Relevant Indian actors

This volume draws on the voices of many Indian protagonists, some of them quoted from the media, others consulted directly. During my tenure in Delhi, I was fortunate to have access to many of the country's leading figures in politics, public service, business, the academic world, media, civil society, and the arts, and most remained available to me during the years I was developing this volume. They fall, very broadly, within the following categories.

The politicians

As highlighted in the next few chapters, Indian politics are dominated by domestic concerns, including internal security. Both houses of the Union parliament sometimes participate in major debates on international matters, generally in relation to neighbourhood issues (including often vexed relations with neighbours such as China and Pakistan). Occasionally, they debate issues relating to India's relations with a great power, as was the case, with high drama, in 2008 on India–USA nuclear cooperation.[13] A number of individual parliamentarians, several of them cited in these pages, through inclination or because of current or past professional engagement, are deeply knowledgeable on the world at large, and India's web of ties to it.[14] But they represent a small fraction of India's political class, even more so when state-level politicians are factored in. Only a limited number fully master English, and thus, international interaction is difficult for many.

Most Indian Prime Ministers holding office for more than a few months have stepped on to the world stage, but only the first among them, Jawaharlal Nehru, really bestrode it.

With India's role in international relations growing, this may change. Dr Singh, the current Prime Minister, enjoys significant international credibility on economic issues, and his determination to see through India–USA negotiations on nuclear cooperation between 2005 and 2008 caught many a foreign analyst's eye. But it is too early to pronounce on a tenure not yet completed, and some critics wonder whether his attention to international relations has come at the expense of policy innovation within the country itself.[15] In domestic politics, Dr Singh operates largely in the shadow of the Congress Party leader, Sonia Gandhi, the widow of former Prime Minister Rajiv Gandhi, initially derided by her opponents as an Italian-born neophyte but who has seen them all off with, to date, a sure-footed and consensual style. Doubtless the most powerful woman in the world today, she focuses resolutely on the Indian internal sphere, occasionally receiving visiting foreign dignitaries, sometimes travelling abroad, but always signalling that foreign policy is not her game.[16]

For Indian politicians, by and large, as in other great nations, foreign policy pales relative to domestic political and security concerns.[17] Indeed, the historian and political analyst Mahesh Rangarajan notes that security and identity are the foreign policy issues of greatest resonance in wider Indian politics. This plays out in different ways with respect to relations with two important neighbours:

> In the case of Pakistan, the key ideas in conflict relate to a state constituted along religious lines versus another with a plural idea of nationhood. With China, it is less an issue of identity than one of who will be the premier power in Asia. Rivalries with each involve pride as much as security.[18]

Indian Foreign Service and other officials

Foreign policy professionals in India, like their counterparts abroad, love to believe that they control the foreign policy game, the intricacies of which only they sometimes master completely. In fact, as in most democracies, it is political leaders who rightly make the key decisions. This is nowhere more true than in India, where the knowledge and skills of professionals are a considerable public asset, but where the political class dominates on key files, as was the case with Nehru sixty years ago and as is today, with Sonia Gandhi and Manmohan Singh sharing power, the former preoccupied with domestic politics, the latter more with the realm of policy.

Because India's domestic economic and social concerns are so urgent and daunting, only a small number of other Cabinet members (and occasionally Ministers of State) devote serious time to foreign policy, and generally only do so because their portfolio requires it. The foreign minister, when a strong figure, as so often has been the case, is involved in many key decisions, as are, less frequently, the Defence, Finance, and Commerce ministers.[19]

In recent years, the Prime Minister's Office (PMO) has built up a staff of its own to formulate and conduct, in partnership with the Ministry of External Affairs (MEA) but with more power than the latter, India's foreign policy. A number of the advisors in the PMO, several of them retired MEA mandarins, have achieved enviable influence. Others have hailed from the intelligence agencies or the defence establishment. Neither of India's most recent two Prime Ministers (Singh and Vajpayee) came to office with much experience of foreign policy, although Dr Singh had led a peripatetic and distinguished life abroad as an economist. But both men took key foreign policy decisions and were prepared to stake their reputations thereon (regarding the USA and Pakistan respectively).

The Indian Foreign Service (IFS), a much fabled institution, feared and respected in equal measure—and loathed by some—is, along with the Indian Administrative Service (IAS), perhaps the proudest embodiment of India's public service, both as an ideal and in performance. However, the MEA is comparatively small in its number of authorized positions at home and abroad. Its headquarters staff work punishing hours, not least preparing the visits of the many foreign dignitaries laying siege to Delhi in ever growing numbers as India's importance has expanded. Perhaps because of these pressures and also because even many thoughtful people dislike grand schemes, India's foreign policy has tended to be reactive and formulated incrementally, case-by-case, rather than through high-minded in-depth policy frameworks.

The MEA is one of the world's few foreign ministries to remain genuinely powerful within the wider bureaucracy. It is consulted by other ministries and retains significant blocking power. But due to staffing constraints and the press of daily business, its capacity to mobilize the rest of the Indian senior bureaucracy to support its own goals (where these have been articulated) is limited.

The quality of the IFS personnel is among the highest in the world, along with that of the UK and, increasingly, China.[20] Indian professionals, like their Brazilian counterparts, train hard and compete fiercely for entry into their Foreign Service and must perform spectacularly in order to advance to the greatest heights (although lingering Indian notions of seniority by years in service for intermediate promotions baffle many outsiders). US diplomacy, often supported by remarkable professionals and political appointees alike, is sometimes undermined by appointment of otherwise ill-prepared political campaign contributors, some of whom reflect very little credit on Washington.[21] Russian foreign policy professionals are often breathtakingly knowledgeable, and equally often amusing in private, but their purpose is sometimes less clear than their competence. France has been very well served in India by professionals with a strong sense of French interests and admirable realism about France's place in the Asian world view and how to make the most of it.[22] Australians, more narrowly harnessed to the promotion of economic interests, are often very effective.[23]

Of course, individual personalities vary as much in India as elsewhere. The outside view of Indian diplomats in vogue thirty years ago as hard-working, well-informed, and sometimes brilliant but also often sour, superior, and antagonistic, has given way today to a more cosmopolitan, entertaining, self-deprecating if still highly intelligent and hard-working cadre that is displacing remnants of the earlier order. The MEA, thus, is a microcosm of India at its best, in all of its variety, although innocent bystanders will occasionally be stung by the withering contempt of its denizens for those deemed unworthy of higher consideration.

Warm tribute is paid here to the large and distinguished cadre of retired IFS officers, including former Foreign Secretaries, such as Salman Haidar and Krishnan Srinivasan, who have contributed greatly to scholarship.[24] Many of them are quoted and cited in the pages that follow. Particularly in the absence of a sizeable contingent of younger foreign policy scholars until recently, they have largely shaped the received wisdom on independent India's foreign relations, while greatly enriching the record of events in days gone by.[25]

The defence establishment

India harbours a large and proud defence establishment, in many ways more committed to and successful at defending and upholding their 'corner' of the government apparatus than their IFS counterparts. For one thing, there are many more retirees of the Indian Armed Forces and others with deep knowledge of defence issues. As well, the various Defence colleges and training institutes provide occasional and permanent employment for many younger individuals as well as retirees, often winning them over to Defence and wider security perspectives. India's Armed Forces, admirably and in sharp contrast with those of several neighbouring countries, have always remained under civilian control. However, perhaps in exchange, India's government has allowed the Armed Forces to look after themselves in enviable style. (The military cantonment is generally by far the most impressive quarter of any secondary Indian town, bespeaking the traditions and standards that the Indian military likes to uphold.) The real estate holdings of the Indian Armed Forces, if sold, would raise a pretty penny.

That said, beyond the ceremonial realm and the international peacekeeping in which India has generally distinguished itself, there is much debate about the actual competence and the effective levels of training of junior ranks of India's Armed Forces. Their performance under pressure in India's northeast and in Kashmir has frequently been criticized by the Indian media and by human rights organizations. The Air Force and, particularly, the Navy rather than the Army are seen as the star performers. The Navy displays internationally the best of India's military traditions allied with entrepreneurship, flair, fine training, and a keenness to engage foreign counterparts in friendly (if sometimes competitive) joint manoeuvres. And it is the Navy that is carrying India's standard forward internationally in an ever wider radius.

India's Defence establishment projects its influence into public debate through a number of think-tanks and institutes, frequently onto the commentary pages and into television coverage, in spite of the modest overall resources India devotes to defence. (India's official defence expenditure is restricted to 2.6 per cent of GDP).[26] As elsewhere, many of those commenting on public affairs from a security perspective adopt hawkish views (for example, on Pakistan and China). But this is not universally true, as Commodore (Ret.) Uday Bhaskar and the still youthful Colonel (Ret.) Ajai Shukla, a noted television and print media personality, illustrate in their frequent public interventions. Some security commentators take a dim view of virtually all foreign powers in terms of the compatibility of their policies and interests with those of India. The articulate and incisive Brahma Chellaney, an equal opportunity critic of the USA, China, and Pakistan (with a curious soft spot for Russia), springs to mind under this heading. Others seem mainly to fear that specific threats are being ignored. G. Parthasarathy, an accomplished former Indian envoy to Pakistan and to Myanmar, for example, is a frequent and sharp critic of Delhi's response to security threats from China and Pakistan.[27]

Underpinning much of the commentary is the belief that the Indian government simply does not give enough attention or priority to India's internal and international security. Certainly, most observers would agree that this has been true at least with respect to internal security.

Nevertheless, one significant shift emerges from several chapters of this volume: after years of selective engagement with, and studied indifference to a number of multilateral forums (including several Asian ones thought to be dominated by the USA), India today is engaging on all fronts in all regions.[28]

India's international economic team

Until recently, India's sway in economic diplomacy was mainly on display through the individual efforts of Indians and Indian émigrés providing yeoman service within such multilateral bodies as the International Monetary Fund (IMF), the World Bank, and various agencies and programmes of the United Nations, current Prime Minister Singh being one such in decades past. Now and then, an Indian diplomat would provide strong leadership on a multilateral economic negotiation, as did T. P. Sreenivasan in the run-up to the Earth Summit on the environment in Rio de Janeiro in 1992.

But today, as India spreads its wings in economic as in wider diplomacy, names hitherto familiar only to small bands of specialists are becoming more widely known. Kamal Nath, Minister of Commerce and Industry of India, 2004–9, emerged as one of the key figures of the Doha Round of trade negotiations under the umbrella of the World Trade Organization (WTO), as detailed in Chapter 11. During many of these years, India's Commerce Secretary, Gopal Pillai, was regarded internationally as a model of the self-effacing but tenacious and highly knowledgeable negotiator.[29] Indian Executive Directors at the IMF and the World Bank, while laying claim to a greater role for India, have also increasingly contributed to key policy development processes. For example, the Deputy Governor of India's central Bank (the Reserve Bank of India—RBI), Rakesh Mohan, working with a Canadian colleague, Tiff Macklem, played an important role in fleshing out policy options on issues of regulation and transparency during the depths of the 2008–9 global economic crisis. They produced a report that was much praised by ministers and officials of G-20 countries. India's 'Sherpa' (the personal representative of a national leader) in the G-8 and G-20 processes, unusually one enjoying Ministerial rank, Montek Singh Ahluwalia, was recognized as singularly qualified and effective. Thus, India's profile in multilateral economic diplomacy has already risen and will continue to do so.

Others

Mixing in with the actors above are a number of influential commentators (often either academics, members of India's leading think-tanks, or retired officials), retailing their opinions with flair on editorial pages and on television screens. Many of these are cited in the pages that follow.

Scope and organization of the material

The scope of the topic is vast and daunting. This may explain the few scholarly attempts at surveying Indian foreign policy of late. Most authors, even memoirists, tackle one or a few of the themes of Indian foreign policy of interest to them, often ones that were particularly salient during the period covered. Picking just a few angles is, in many ways, easier than attempting to order the features of Indian foreign policy as a whole. The latter allows for the inclusion of many issues and relationships but requires the exclusion of others, a painful business, particularly for an author having delved into more than can be conveyed in a book of reasonable length.

Inevitably, this volume slights a number of India's partners, in an attempt to avoid the deadening effect that a cataloguing of bilateral relationships or Indian involvement in a myriad of multilateral institutions would produce. Hence, the following chapters, in both what they include and exclude or touch upon only tangentially (for example, my own country Canada), represent a debatable set of choices of the countries, forums, and diplomatic processes that have mattered the most to post-independence India, do so today, or are likely to emerge as dominant in the near future.[30] Accordingly, India's relations with Latin America and the Caribbean as a whole are not discussed at length (in spite of strong Diaspora links with the Commonwealth Caribbean and increasingly meaningful economic links with Brazil, Mexico, and Chile). Likewise, India's relations with much of Africa, long seen through the prism of Indian trading communities spread around the continent, particularly along its shores, are addressed mainly through the prism of India's growing anxiety about its access to the natural resources for which its economy will increasingly hunger.

While the pages of this volume develop only a few major themes, each chapter ends with some conclusions deriving from its earlier paragraphs, a drafting device more helpful perhaps to the author than to the reader.

A discussion of contemporary Indian foreign policy would make little sense without situating it within the wider flow of Indian history (throughout which certain key Indian characteristics relevant to foreign policy emerge), and this is attempted in Chapter 2. Chapters 3 (on Indian domestic politics and security drivers in relation to foreign policy formulation) and 4 (on India's economy and its role in shaping India's contemporary international relations) both contain significant historical sections that cover much of the post-1947 ground, some of which is also attempted in the chapters on individual and regional partners and on India's approach to international organizations and groupings.

Among the basic decisions attending the planning of this book was whether to devote a chapter to Pakistan or to fold Pakistan into a wider discussion of

India's neighbourhood. I chose the latter course. Any country's preoccupations nearly inevitably involve immediate neighbours. The amount of space devoted to Pakistan, in this volume, may slight both the importance of and interest in this subject and, to a degree, the acuity within international relations writ large of its relationship with India. Yet, as India has been growing, particularly in the economic sphere, and as it has trained its aspirations on wider Asian and global ambitions, the place of Pakistan in its preoccupations has shrunk somewhat. Of course, India itself contributed significantly to shrinking Pakistan in 1971 when its military intervention allowed the emergence of an independent Bangladesh from the wreckage of East Pakistan. The cautious nature of India's military engagements with Pakistan since then, particularly India's carefully calibrated and low-key response to Pakistan's adventurism on the Kargil heights in 1999, suggests that an uncontrolled full-scale war between the two countries is today less likely than ever (barring the accession to power in Pakistan of radical individuals or groups).

Three major preoccupations and an important partner

A discussion of Pakistan along with India's other neighbours brings out several characteristic Indian pathologies when dealing with neighbours—some already fading into history, others still topical. This accounts for a long Chapter 5 on India's immediate neighbourhood, the first of its three major foreign policy preoccupations. It raises questions not just about India's management over time of its subcontinental links with such often resentful and sometimes unhelpful neighbours as Pakistan, Bangladesh, Nepal, and Sri Lanka, but also how it has factored in historically and geostrategically important ties with Afghanistan and Burma. The relative paralysis of the South Asian Association for Regional Cooperation (SAARC), a forum created largely by India, suggests the absence of an overall plan and a largely reactive approach to regional developments. However, the chapter notes a much gentler approach to managing regional bilateral relations today than was evident in the 1980s.

Its second major preoccupation, China, warrants a Chapter 6 of its own. It outlines the history of ties and conflicts dating back to the emergence of the Communist regime in China and Nehru's early quest for comity with other developing countries. Against this backdrop it touches on tensions over border issues along the McMahon line in the east and the Aksai Chin area further west that precipitated war in 1962; friction over Tibet; China's support for Pakistan; and the ebb and flow of mutual suspicion and preoccupation with the motives and aims of other powers in the region (notably the Soviet Union and the USA). In doing so, it sketches a relationship defined more by economic cooperation and competition today (although the degree of geostrategic and regional rivalry between them also remains relevant, and at times disturbing).

With reference to Indian policy, M. J. Akbar writes:

The principal element of India's strategic thinking should be built around an analysis of the ideological struggle on the subcontinent against democracy and secularism being waged by those who believe in theocracy and split-personality governance (half obedient to the citizen, and fully obedient to a partisan view of God). The success of the Indian model of nation-building, around democracy, secularism, gender equality and economic equity, will influence events in the region, compelling those who believe in alternative models to work for the destruction of secular democracy by war against its vulnerable aspects. India's wider foreign policy merges seamlessly into such a regional policy, since similar tensions are visible elsewhere too. It is not accidental that China, a party dictatorship, is inimical to the Indian model, and finds a partner in Pakistan, which is trapped in uncertainty between fundamentalism and democracy.[31]

Not only is China a direct neighbour, but it constitutes Delhi's only convincing rival in Asia and is currently more successful economically and more powerful militarily than India. Further, India's unexpected border war with China in 1962 yielded outright defeat for Delhi (unlike its more successful military engagements with Pakistan). The relationship today is complex—growing fast economically, but contentious in other spheres. Outright military conflict of any serious proportions seems highly unlikely, as both governments are focused on economic expansion, and, in any event, quite prudent by nature, but their competition with each other touches on many other countries (and several continents), and spurs policy innovation by both. Nevertheless, Indian resentments linger and may prevent India from 'taking a page out of China's book' on some issues, even where it could do so to its own advantage.[32]

The third major preoccupation of Indian foreign policy decision-makers and analysts of late has been its emergence as a major actor on the global stage, offering a development model that for some years now has been strikingly successful and has achieved sufficient economic heft to matter significantly in the world economy (a judgement reinforced by India's strong performance during the recent global economic and financial crisis).

India's effort to establish a meaningful partnership with two other leading democracies in the developing world, each a dominant actor on its own continent, under the banner of the new IBSA (India, Brazil, South Africa) group, working hard to build content into the concept, is an imaginative way to give practical expression to the idea of South–South cooperation, too long an empty vessel. Its emphasis on democratic kinship within this formation, which might be taken as a dig at China, should perhaps also be seen as an effort by India to develop a 'soft power' component to its diplomacy, moving beyond India's civilizational pull and recent economic success as its principal calling cards in its relations with other developing countries. However, placing many bets on different playing fields, India has also courted the Shanghai Cooperation Organization (SCO), participated in BRIC Summits, and formed groupings of convenience. Indeed, India's international interests suggest that it can be useful, at times, to draw in partners as diverse as Australia and Mexico.[33]

This third preoccupation, with India's wider role in international relations, runs through the book but comes into focus in Chapter 11, which seeks to cover aspects of India's 'emergence', or, more appropriately, re-emergence to the prominence it used to enjoy among key powers in the centuries before colonization. It does so by weaving into the story of India's approach to international organizations since independence an account of its efforts to make a mark on several specific issues, including UN Security Council reform, multilateral trade negotiations, and international discussions on climate change. These themes return also in the volume's conclusions, in Chapter 12.

The India–USA relationship, addressed in Chapter 7, is a historically contentious and counterproductive one that has been largely transformed in recent years, an improvement pregnant with potential implications for both countries and also for other regional and global actors. India today is concerned that the Obama Administration may not be taking it as seriously as did the George W. Bush and Clinton Administrations before it.[34] But, with the relationship having graduated to a new level of mutual understanding (although perspectives and interests still conflict at times), Washington has needed to tend to other, more urgent or disturbing issues. And, while welcoming improved ties with India, some in the Obama team may well consider them yesterday's news, if no less useful for that.

The chapter documents the difficult path towards this rapprochement, marked by a degree of anti-imperialist prickliness on India's part, and a large dose of condescension in Washington during the Cold War. This was further complicated by the US penchant for Pakistan, a puzzling choice in hindsight (although a rational one in the narrow terms in which it was framed during the Cold War). In engineering the unshackling of India from its nuclear pariah status, imposed after its nuclear test of 1974, the USA needed to overcome aspects of the non-proliferation regime it had itself set in place to punish India and to discourage any further proliferation. These were ultimately an unsuccessful set of arrangements as demonstrated by subsequent developments in North Korea and Pakistan—and perhaps soon in Iran. The negotiations were thus difficult on both sides, as India could neither renounce its nuclear capabilities nor its historic decision to seek strategic parity with China after the 1962 war; nor could the USA lightly cast aside non-proliferation arrangements it had earlier deemed essential. Thus, talks first engaged between

Washington and Delhi under President Clinton and Prime Minister Vajpayee in the late 1990s (after further nuclear tests by India, followed by an echoing set in Pakistan) only came to full fruition a decade later, in 2008, at the tail end of the tenure of President Bush and of the first term of Prime Minister Singh. US motivations may have been as much commercial as geostrategic (American companies having taken early note of India's budding economic renewal as of the mid-1990s), but the political rewards for India, and perhaps also for the USA, have significantly altered the positioning of players on the global chessboard, contributing to India's quest for a place among the great powers of the twenty-first century.

Some other relationships

Chapter 8 deals with what is mostly referred to as the Middle East, but which Indians think of as West Asia, a regional designation making clear that this geostrategically critical area also lies in India's own extended region. During the years of non-alignment, India's diplomacy cultivated Iran (not least as a counterweight to Pakistan), and those Arab countries already independent. India's focus on Iran has not wavered, but as economic change and various conflicts in the region reshaped regional alliances (official and *de facto*), India's policy evolved strikingly as of the early 1990s, with the establishment of diplomatic relations with Israel, soon followed by the development of very meaningful economic and military procurement ties with that state. The chapter charts India's nimble adaptation to changes in a region it could do little to affect directly, and concludes with India enjoying positive relations with virtually all countries of the area, no small achievement. For reasons of authorial convenience, this chapter also briefly discusses Indian ties with the Maghreb countries which are both African (rather than Asian) and Arab, as well as its important ties with Egypt, the Gulf, and (historically) Iraq.

On India's other side, Chapter 9 examines India's relationship with the rest of East and Southeast Asia, touching on robust economic ties with South Korea, a cordial but substantively sub-par relationship with Japan in spite of complementary economic strengths, complex and rapidly developing relations with several of the countries of the Association of Southeast Asian Nations (ASEAN), including several Free Trade arrangements and 'strategic partnerships', and occasional references to Australia and New Zealand. In spite of India's 'Look East' policy launched under Prime Minister Narasimha Rao in 1992, the development of substantive ties with its Asian partners to the east for nearly a decade thereafter remained largely episodic and improvised, perhaps due in part to India's cautious approach to multilateral entanglements (for example, initially with respect to ASEAN and to the Asia-Pacific Economic Cooperation forum). Nevertheless, today, Indian diplomacy in Southeast Asia in particular is firing on all cylinders. However, India initiated its serious courtship of ASEAN countries well after China, and is now playing catch-up as best as it can.

Chapter 10 covers India's historically important ties with both the Russian Federation, earlier the Soviet Union, and Western Europe.

The Soviet Union having been India's only ally during the Cold War years, the relationship inevitably had to evolve towards a less exclusive one, more rooted in mutual economic benefit, after the fall of the Berlin Wall. This has happened, with Russia enjoying a significant profile in India (for example, with President Putin invited as Guest of Honour for Delhi's famous Republic Day parade in January 2009) and retaining a strong role in India's defence, science, and some other leading economic sectors. But each side has needed to adjust to the other's reinterpretation of its own economic and foreign policy interests. And the process has not always been smooth, as other economic relationships have grown and outstripped this one. Even in the defence sphere, the Indian Armed Forces clearly hanker after the best that the West (and Israel) have to offer, while accepting that they need to hedge their bets by continuing to deal with Russia on some key procurement items in which it may still be competitive (for example, AWACS aircraft, in a triangular partnership with Israel, the first of which was delivered to India in 2009).[35]

With the exception of the Russian Federation, Europe is a conundrum in Indian foreign policy. Western Europe remains an important economic partner for India, particularly the UK, France, and Germany. It is also to these three countries that India gives clear priority among European Union members, although Germany is dealt with in a less prominent way by India's foreign ministry than are France and the UK (both deemed to warrant Security Council Permanent Member treatment under the direct oversight of India's Foreign Secretary). Italy, and to a degree Spain, are admired as bastions of culture and civilized living. Indeed, overall, Europe is often thought of mostly by India's wealthier middle classes as a holiday destination and by its business community as host to potential corporate acquisitions.

Beyond the sphere of trade policy and multilateral trade negotiations, where its competence is universally recognized, the EU's pretensions to significance privately mystify many Indians, and this even before the rough weather several European economies experienced in 2010. Indeed, the European Commission's insistence on being taken seriously as a dialogue partner by the Indian Government, for now, mostly induces yawns in Delhi. It is hard for Indians to discount the vigorous competition displayed by the leading European countries with each other in vying for Indian favour (mainly in the economic sphere), and the lack of priority these same EU countries accord the EU and its machinery when dealing with India bilaterally. This could change, but only if the EU manages to develop a much more convincing, cohesive, and coherent institutional personality than has been in evidence in India for some years now. With often harsh colonial treatment now largely overtaken in forward-looking Indian minds (if not forgotten), and economic trends promising, it should be possible to develop more meaningful political dialogue in years ahead.

As noted above, the penultimate Chapter 11 addresses India's multilateral diplomacy, which Indian MEA veterans think of as a sphere of particular accomplishment for India over the years. The Non-Aligned Movement (NAM) that Nehru played such a large role in bringing about and shaping was a useful placeholder for India at a time when its leaders needed to devote the bulk of their time to pressing internal challenges. Indeed, Nehru is credited with coining the term 'Third World' to describe those states uninvolved in, indeed seeking to stand apart from, the Cold War ideological conflict—although, as Paul Krugman points out, it rapidly, because of their modest levels of development, morphed into a term connoting backwardness or poverty, hardly Nehru's intent.[36]

Non-alignment, in theory, also allowed India to play the two superpowers and their related blocs off against each other, although after the 1950s, India was not successful in doing so. Moreover, India cut a wide swathe at the UN early on, and subsequently only by fits and starts. The actual achievements of India's multilateral diplomacy are open to question and it is perhaps to this sphere (rather than to that of bilateral diplomacy, in which India has often been remarkably successful) that Indian policymakers and analysts need to devote more thought as India gains access to the most coveted multilateral forums, such as the G-20 and the key negotiating groups in the WTO.

India has innovated creatively by devoting real effort to the new IBSA forum. Chapter 11 explores whether it might want to bring more of this positive, self-confident spirit to bear on multilateral economic and regional forums towards which, in the past, it displayed mainly suspicion. Further, now that resentment is less and less warranted in light of India's economic success, its representatives may want to devote more consistent effort to making friends, rather than impressing the gallery, in the multilateral world. India has been very good at this in world capitals. Why not now on the multilateral stage?

The volume's final Chapter 12, offering some conclusions, reflects on what India's emergence on the global stage requires of the country (including on its internal dispensation, on several key economic challenges that will hamper its rise unless tended to, and in its approach to neighbouring countries)—and to what uses India might put its new status and potential. Whether yet great or not, whether yet fully emerged rather than still emerging, what kind of a world power, with what aims, and in partnership with what others, will India seek to be? And will it need to share global burdens or can it continue for some time as a free rider on issues it is not yet ready to tackle in internationally binding ways? The chapter reverts to India's identity nationally, regionally, and internationally (both in terms of self-image and of the opinion of others). It touches on how an India with global reach can increasingly develop its own 'soft power' beyond the attractions of its culture, including through the Indian Diaspora.[37] Finally, the chapter includes reflections on that perennial chestnut of Indian foreign policy analysis, the country's lack of clear strategic and other conceptual frameworks.

But for now, on to some relevant Indian history.

2

History: A Vital Foundation of India's International Relations

How Indians conceive of their country, its origins, its development through history, and its past relations with others is a vital component of how they imagine, construct, and aspire to develop India's contemporary international relations.

How did India and Indians develop over time?[1] The question of what India and being Indian represented in a pre-nation-state era is far from simple and can be freighted with a variety of interpretations. Readings of the past are always at risk of being viewed through the categories of present-day politics and contemporary approaches to economic and social policy.

No single-chapter survey of Indian history could conceivably translate its rich complexity and diversity. At times, in both north and south India it comprised several (sometimes many) kingdoms and other polities—some resembling republics—each vying for recognition, respect, and space. Rather, the paragraphs that follow attempt to sketch out aspects of Indian experience over the millennia that are relevant to its contemporary self-image as well as some past efforts to project abroad Indian aspirations, values, and power. Inevitably, much more is left out than is included.

The historical overview contained in this chapter will address a number of problematic yet common myths regarding key features of Indian civilization, especially with regard to the nature of religious communities and their inter-action, as well as the nature of processes of immigration and accommodation of diverse ethnic and linguistic groups over the centuries. The spread of multiple faiths in India and the complex nature of cultural exchange that has existed throughout Indian history point to a cosmopolitan development of the modern state that today is India, favouring its essential pluralism, although some within India would dispute this assertion.

Two broad phenomena emerge as constants in the history of India. First, the repeated influx of peoples and ideas from the northwest, at times in the form of invasions, but more often through migration, pastoral circuits, or as traders and missionaries, is striking. Second, barring the colonial period, Indian history is characterized by alternating cycles of imperial consolidation and processes of decentralization, with foreign influences accommodated and assimilated, and 'cultural fusions' occurring throughout.[2] Decentralization did not necessarily portend overall decline but was often characterized by regional economic and cultural growth and assertion. For instance, the disintegration of the Mauryan Empire coincided with the emergence of new states in core regions such as Gandhara and Kalinga that became economically developed. Thus, though the Mauryan Empire lasted only for about 150 years, after which central control declined rapidly, the latter period was nevertheless characterized by regional economic growth.[3] At times, several major dynasties and civilizations (as well as some interesting minor ones) cohabited productively within the subcontinent.

Modern writing on Indian history began with colonial accounts of the Indian past.[4] Much of the colonial historiography was preoccupied with the differentiation between indigenous and alien communities (and later Indian nationalist historiography dwelt on this dimension extensively). Indian civilization came to be seen as essentially Hindu and Sanskritic. Turkish, Afghan, and Mughal chronicles were perceived as alien to Indian civilization, 'even though their contents concerned Indian society and politics and the people whom they wrote about had settled in India to become part of Indian society'.[5] Gradually, canonized European perceptions of Indian culture as uniform influenced the way Indians themselves viewed their past, essentially promoting the idea of an unchanging continuity of society and religion over 3,000 years in a geographic space both well-defined and yet constantly shifting in its contours.[6]

A concept of India defined by religion?

Indian history is often, quite questionably, understood as a succession: first of Hindu civilization, then Muslim rule followed by the British Raj.[7] This organization of Indian history along a clear, simplified timeline and largely along religious lines goes back to James Mill's *History of British India* written in the early nineteenth century.[8] Its perception of the Indian past informs much teaching of history today, in India and beyond, and therefore also informs politics in South Asia to this day.[9]

Initially, Vedic Hindu civilization was thought to begin with the arrival of Aryans on the subcontinent in the second millennium BC. The notion of an Aryan invasion goes back to Max Müller.[10] Müller argued that Aryans originated in Central Asia, with one branch moving to Europe and another reaching India through Iran. According to Müller, Aryans represented a superior civilization and subjugated indigenous populations (and their culture) in northern India.[11] Although historians have now dismissed this theory, it still has a firm grip on wider perceptions. It is now commonly accepted that the Indo-Aryan label refers mostly to language, and that as Indo-Aryans spread over north India, they incorporated into theirs elements of already existing languages.[12]

In the early twentieth century, with the discovery of archaeological sites pointing to the existence of high civilization in the Indian subcontinent much before the arrival of an Aryan language group, some Indian historiography (associated most often with the Hindu faith) shifted from supporting a theory of Aryan invasion, to arguing that Aryans and their language, Sanskrit, were indigenous to India.[13]

> The amended theory became axiomatic to their belief that those for whom the subcontinent was not the land of their ancestors and the land where their religion originated were aliens. This changed the focus in the definition of who were indigenous and who were aliens...the aliens were...Muslims and Christians whose religion had originated in west Asia...According to this theory only the Hindus, as the lineal descendants of the Aryans, could be defined as indigenous and therefore inheritors of the land, and not those whose ancestry was of the subcontinent, but who had been converted to Islam and Christianity.[14]

More generally, for many, history projects not only out of the past, but also into the future: 'Nation-states are widely conceded to be "new" and "historical", the nation to which they give political expression always looms out of an immemorial past, and still more important, glides into limitless future'.[15]

India was not, throughout history, a self-contained unit, either geographically or culturally.[16] In geographical terms, the various kingdoms and regions that preceded the modern Indian nation state had fluctuating borders, and peoples from different parts of the world flowed into the region. Thus, the Indian nation state is best seen as a modern construct—albeit one with a rich past in other forms—that is not grounded in a defined territory (or constant form of society) inherited from a pre-modern past.[17]

Today the cultural and geographical unity of India is usually mapped on the territory covered by terms such as Bharatvarsha, Aryavata, and Jambudvipa in ancient scriptures, which are projected back to the earliest Vedic period.[18] By the nineteenth century these geographical terms came to be seen as coeval with the territory covered by British India and the princely states under its protection. Yet, Bharatvarsha, the term most commonly referred to, is mentioned nowhere in the Vedas, except as the name for one of several Vedic clans.[19] In later literature, the territory denoted by it expands and contracts, often leaving out large tracts of northern India and, by and large, excluding southern India.

The term Hinduism itself is relatively recent. It is not used in Sanskrit in a self-representational way by any religious community before the nineteenth century. The concept of Hindu religion as a monolith seems to have been introduced by missionaries from the west. Major strands of Hinduism such as Vaishnavism, Shaivism, and Shaktism that are today seen as mere sub-sects of Hinduism could have been and still be viewed as autonomous religions no less distinct than Islam, Judaism, and Christianity.[20]

India through the prism of geography

Most historians of India describe, or presume, coherent core regions—that is, areas characterized by stable, long-term political and cultural institutions. Like magnets, the political cores at the heart of these regions give rise to armies and attract scholars, foreign visitors, long-distance merchants, and crucially, court chroniclers. Owing to the considerable data often left behind by such groups, these regions also attract modern historians, explaining why core areas like north India, Bengal, or the Tamil south are comparatively well covered in the historical literature while the Deccan in central India is a relatively understudied region, because it developed no enduring political identity or capital.[21]

Since regions and empires in India have fluctuated greatly it would pose a challenge to write the history of contact between outside civilizations and a nation that has lacked a consistent geopolitical form or even developed a centre of gravity. Of course, in the case of north India a relatively continuous sequence of polities based in or near Delhi evolved, but they featured fluctuating borders contracting and expanding considerably over time, occasionally including Afghanistan, for example.

Similarly, south India does not constitute a homogeneous unit, though it is conventionally identified as the Dravidian area south of the Krishna river, with two macro-ecological zones: the Malabar coast in what is now Kerala to the west, and the wider plains to the east in Tamil Nadu with its Coromandel coast. Historians have focused mostly on the Tamil plain, which produced a succession of 'high civilizations' beginning with the Pallavas in the third century and continued by the remarkably sophisticated mercantile, industrial, and agrarian society under the Cholas between the fifth and thirteenth centuries. The two subregions differed in climate and social organization, but both played a notable role in developing overseas economic ties.

Trade

At various times, the southern part of the Indian subcontinent served as a link in the sea route connecting the Mediterranean region and the Middle East with China and other Asian destinations. While the west coast attracted ships from Africa and Arabia, on the east coast ships from China or the islands and peninsulas of Indonesia, Malaysia, or Thailand found harbour.[22]

Various parts of the regions that now comprise India evolved strong links with other parts of the world millennia ago, the earliest going back to the Indus and Harappan civilization, 2600–1700 BC. As excavations have shown, there were extensive relations in terms of trade, cultural contact, and possibly even the exchange of populations with port cities in ancient Mesopotamia.[23] South India also likely witnessed extensive trade exchanges in the seventh and sixth centuries BC. For example, there is evidence of maritime intercourse between Babylon and south India, with gold, spices, and fragrant woods being received from India.[24]

By the first millennium BC, there were extensive commercial links between the Red Sea and northwest India. Control of this trade may have been captured by Arabs as early as the third century BC. During the 'classic' Hellenic and Roman periods the nature of these contacts becomes better documented. Sophisticated navigation manuals for the sea route to India testify to Europe's long-standing trade with the subcontinent. A number of literary references corroborate this. Petronius in the early first century AD refers disapprovingly to the gossamer cottons adorning Roman women; Pliny in the mid-first century AD provides an account of the sea route to India via Egyptian ports. Ptolemy's geography of the second century AD includes a description of the Malabar coast.[25] Romans imported luxury items such as precious stones, silks, and spices as well as sugar, cotton, and fruits. Trade seems to have weighed heavily in favour of India. Indeed several Roman emperors had to enact laws against the export of bullion from the empire to the East, since Rome produced very few commodities of value for India (the British were to face similar problems in the early phases of trade relations with India).[26]

Soft power: cultural exchange

At various points in time, India occupied an eminent position in the world economy and through the ages attracted peoples from different parts of the world. People from China, Turkey, Persia, sub-Saharan Africa, and Europe settled in India and became a part of its civilization. Many left extensive accounts of their experience and contact with Indian civilization. Some came to India as traders or soldiers, others such as early Chinese pilgrim Fa

Hsien were part of ongoing exchanges of scholars and embassies between their two countries. Likewise, of course, Indian cultural and spiritual influence spread throughout Asia in varying forms of Buddhism in Southeast Asia, China, and Japan, but also of Hinduism, the latter still represented in major archaeological sites as far afield as Indonesia. Buddhism eventually declined in the land of its origin from the thirteenth century AD onwards.

India as a saga of empires?

The concept of 'empire' as a defining category in Indian historiography became fashionable during the colonial period, when a few empires of the past were helpful in presenting the Raj as part of an ongoing legacy.[27] Typically, India was thus presented as a sequence of grand ventures characterized by extensive territory, monumental architecture, and imperial ambitions— followed inevitably by protracted periods of atrophy and disintegration.

The Mauryan Empire

The Mauryan Empire (approximately 321–185 BC) represents the earliest known attempt at imperial government in India, which for the first time brought together many diverse social and cultural systems of the subcontinent under a single highly centralized bureaucracy. The empire was founded by Chandragupta Maurya in 321 BC and centred in the metropolis of Pataliputra (modern-day Patna in Bihar). A series of military campaigns brought the Ganges plains and later the northwestern regions, where the departure of Alexander of Macedon had left a power vacuum, under Chandragupta's control.

The Seleucid region of what are today Afghanistan, Baluchistan, and Makran also devolved to Chandragupta. As the history of this region was characterized throughout by shifts between major states centered on present-day Iran and northern India, it is unlikely that local populations—themselves of varying cultures—would conceive of the dynasties that were ruling them as particularly 'foreign'.[28]

Around the fourth century BC, the Mauryan Empire expanded greatly in the north, though the extent of its presence and influence in the south is not clear. The kingdoms of south India (together with Sri Lanka) are mentioned in the second and thirteenth edicts of Asoka. There appear to have been friendly relations with these kingdoms, with Asoka sending missionaries to preach the *Dhamma* amongst the people of these kingdoms, but there is no indication that he attempted to conquer them.[29] By the time of Bindusara, the second Mauryan emperor, who came to the throne in 297 BC, large parts of the subcontinent had come under Mauryan control although relations with kingdoms of the far south and today's Sri Lanka, that were not a part of the empire remained cordial. But the Mauryan Empire encountered sustained hostility in the kingdom of Kalinga on the east coast (on the territory of what is now Orissa), which was eventually conquered by Bindusara's son Asoka.

The Kalinga war is historically significant since it was said that the brutality and destruction of the campaign filled Asoka with profound remorse and encouraged him to consider the Buddhist social ethic of tolerance and non-violence seriously (although it is unclear whether he actually converted to Buddhism). Furthermore, under Asoka, Buddhism became an actively proselytizing belief system and missions that were sent to various parts of the world eventually led to the propagation of Buddhism all over Asia by the beginning of the Christian era.[30] Nevertheless, like many profoundly Christian leaders in the West, Asoka's Buddhist faith was often practised in the breach: in spite of a commitment to non-violence, he preserved capital punishment for certain crimes and the state still relied on a large army.

Asoka's commitment to defining and propagating a new ideology and social ethic for the empire was unprecedented and unique in Indian history. Many historians have interpreted Asoka's propagation of *Dhamma* as an explicit attempt to make Buddhism the religion of Mauryan India. However, Romila Thapar argues that the numerous rock and pillar edicts spread through the empire were rather 'concerned with using a broader ethic to explore ways of governance and to reduce social conflict and intolerance'.[31] Though one category of inscriptions explicitly proclaims Asoka's adherence to Buddhism, the considerably larger category of inscriptions spread throughout the empire propagates concepts and principles formulated in a manner that would render them acceptable to people belonging to any religious community, though it is possible to discern parallels with key concepts in Buddhist philosophy.

The Mauryan state actively promoted the extension of agriculture and in many cases sponsored extensive irrigation projects. Furthermore the state was instrumental in introducing more wide-ranging systems of commercial exchange and in some instances facilitating the mobility of labour. A meticulous system for the assessment and collection of revenue existed and most commercial and productive activities were taxed, at least in theory. The *Arthasastra*, the text most frequently used to reconstruct Mauryan political and economic practices, lists superintendents of goldsmiths and gold, storehouses, commerce, forest produce, the armoury, measures and weights, tolls, agriculture, weaving, prostitution, liquor, ships, slaughterhouses, cows, horses, elephants, chariots, infantry, passports, and the city.[32]

The Mauryan empire under Asoka was involved in extensive communication with the world beyond the confines of the subcontinent as attested by records of missions sent to the Hellenistic kingdoms, with which there were trade relations.[33]

Despite, or perhaps because of, its expanse and ambition, the Mauryan Empire was short lived. Asoka's reign lasted for thirty-seven years and after his death a period of decline rapidly set in, perhaps because Asoka's propagation of Buddhism alienated politically powerful Brahman communities, while his adhesion to non-violence may have weakened the army and rendered the state vulnerable.

Nonetheless, this period paved the way for other empires by opening up the subcontinent: the extensive building of roads enabled easier contact with more remote areas.[34]

The Kushanas: India, Rome, and China

After the Mauryan period, political developments in India became diffuse—involving a wide variety of polities, people, and time-frames. Romila Thapar speaks of a mosaic of political identities marked by the coexistence of various kinds of political systems: kingdoms, oligarchies, chieftainships, and republic-like tribal organizations. A constant and connecting feature in this diverse political and cultural landscape was the expansion and dynamism of systems of trade and exchange.[35]

In the north, the Kushana State (AD 100–300) covered a vast area extending from the western part of Central Asia to north India. It is not clear whether the ethnic origin of the Kushanas was Turkic, Mongolian, or Iranian, though it is commonly agreed that the empire was founded by the Yueh-Chih people, who had been displaced from Chinese Turkistan by the nomadic Hsiung-nu.[36] Kushana rulers imprinted their coins with images drawn from various religions and cultures, and legends were often bilingual in Greek and Prakrit. Kanishka, the pre-eminent Kushana ruler, used Greek legends, and deities shown on his coins range from Buddha and Shiva to the Persian gods Oado and Atash and the Sumerian goddess Nana.[37] This suggests that the Kushana rulers adopted a tolerant attitude towards religion in order to facilitate commercial exchange across a culturally diverse landscape and with other countries.[38]

Trading centres and connecting routes emerged in many parts of the subcontinent, some reaching into central and western Asia. Some of these were built on roads and networks established in Mauryan times, such as the highway from Taxila to Pataliputra, which was rebuilt and maintained up until the periods of the Afghan ruler Sher Shah, the Mughals, and the British, who referred to it as the Grand Trunk Road. The route is still used today and has been rebranded as India's National Highway No. 1.[39]

The Kushana period was instrumental in linking Indian and Chinese civilizations: the transmission of Buddhism from India to China was paralleled by extensive trade between the two countries. Indian traders also frequently functioned as middlemen in a luxury trade between China and the eastern Mediterranean and Byzantium.

The period saw the rise of a substantial mercantile community and the emergence of frequent and direct trade with Rome during the reign of Augustus (27 BC–AD 15), when various states of India sent envoys to the Roman Emperor. On the Indian side, spices, textiles, semi-precious stones, and ivory were traded primarily for high-value Roman coins as well as wine and coral. The Roman historian Pliny described the trade with India as a considerable drain on the income of Rome.[40] The thriving trade with Rome is believed to have led Indian merchants to expand trade to Southeast Asia, as items sought there were largely spices for the Roman market that were not as easily available in India. Meaningful Southeast Asian contacts with China and India date to the early centuries AD.

It could be said that India, both because of its geographical position and because of its economic enterprise, participated effectively in what was probably viewed in those times as almost a global trade of the early first millennium AD.[41]

Gupta India

The reign of the Gupta dynasty, starting from the accession of Chandra Gupta the first in about AD 319–20, approximated that of the Mauryan Empire in geographical terms up until the sixth century.

The Gupta era is an important reference point for the cultural self-image of Hindus and has often been referred to as the Classical Age of ancient India, due to the exceptionally high standard of living attained among urban upper classes. Advances in science and knowledge were centred either on Brahminical institutions and Buddhist monasteries or guilds specialized in particular crafts, such as metallurgy. Mathematics and astronomy were highly dynamic in this period. The decimal system of numerals had been in regular use among Indian astronomers since the fifth century. It was later introduced in Europe, where it eventually replaced Roman numerals and was known as the Arabic system of numerals.[42] Poetry and prose in Sanskrit were also heavily patronized by the ruling class and reached a high point, exemplified in the writings of Kalidasa, largely regarded as the pre-eminent author of classical Sanskrit literature.

While arts, scientific learning, and urban culture in general reached unprecedented levels in this period, it is nevertheless problematic to speak of a classical age for ancient India as a whole. In the Deccan and southern parts of India it was the post-Gupta period that saw the rise of high civilization. It is the era of the Cholas (particularly around the ninth century AD) that is referred to as the 'classical period' in the south, due to impressive political, economic, cultural, and artistic development of the region during this time.

Having brought northern India under control, the Guptas eventually defeated the Shaka kingdoms in the west and thus gained access to trade with the Mediterranean, conducted from ports on the west coast. The Guptas also are believed to have received tribute from island inhabitants encircling the subcontinent, and possibly as far as Southeast Asia, where large Indian colonies and trading stations had developed. Indeed, Indian merchants in this period increasingly relied on and expanded trade with Southeast Asia, since trade with Rome, which had created considerable fortunes in earlier times, had come to an end in the third century AD with the Hun invasion of the Roman Empire. Though the Gupta Empire was able to withstand initial attacks by the Huns, the empire weakened under successive waves of attacks and Gupta power began to give way to smaller kingdoms by the end of the fifth century when the Huns broke into northern India successfully.

In this period, Buddhism spread to many parts of Asia, largely due to increased trading relationships and commercial networks. Large numbers of Indian Buddhists visited China, where Buddhism was declared the state religion in AD 379. In turn, Chinese Buddhists were interested in gaining access to original Buddhist scriptures and a number of them, most notably Fa Hsien, Hsuang Tsuang, and I Tsing, travelled extensively in India between AD 400 and 700. The cultural exchange developed alongside an expansion of maritime trade between China and south India. Sizeable Indian merchant colonies resided at Canton. Indian influence was also evident in Thailand, Java, and Cambodia.

The Delhi Sultanate, the Mughals, and the emergence of Indo-Islamic culture

The entry of Islam into India gave rise to a unique Indo-Islamic cultural tradition, which represents an impressive process of adjustment and interaction between Islam and local traditions, in the process establishing strong Indian political, economic, and cultural ties to Afghanistan, Persia, Turkey, and the Arabian Peninsula.[43]

Early contact between Islamic and Indic groups developed in northwestern India when the first Ummayid Caliph, Muawiya, and Muhammad bin Qasim conquered Sindh in AD 712. Trade with India was vital for the Islamic world (due to its wealth in gold bullion, its export surplus, and its location at the centre of an early Indian Ocean-wide economy stretching from China to the Levant, or eastern Mediterranean) and large numbers of Arab traders settled on

India's western coast from the eighth century onwards.[44] Their presence being primarily motivated by commercial considerations, early Arab settlers did not attempt large-scale religious conversion.

The large-scale political and economic expansion of Islam in India occurred only from the turn of the eleventh century onwards, when Muhammad Ghuri defeated the Rajput Prithviraj Chauhan, thereby paving the way for the establishment of the first Muslim Sultanate by Qutubuddin Aibak with Delhi as its capital. For the Sultans of Delhi, as later for the Mughals, expansion of Muslim power was aimed primarily at the acquisition of new territories and not at religious conversion. The majority of their subjects throughout remained non-Muslim and their core institutions were not specifically 'Islamic' in nature.[45] 'The sultans themselves were not religious leaders. Like non-Muslim rulers in India, they did not gain their authority through their own holiness or sacred learning but through military prowess and skill in governing.'[46] Though the supremacy of Sharia law was upheld, it was not imposed on the non-Muslim population.

The early court at Delhi was modelled after the Sassanid court of Persia and its military and administrative culture relied on the Turkish institution of elite military slavery.[47] The state structure was composed of a mixture of pre-existing Indian forms and political experiments in West Asia.[48]

At the height of its power by the fourteenth century, the frontiers of the Delhi Sultanate were almost coeval with the contours of the modern nation state.[49] However, in keeping with earlier patterns of political development, by the fifteenth century, independent Sultanates, each with their own wider contact networks, emerged in Kashmir, Bengal, and Gujarat and—in the era following the attack of Timur (Tamerlane) on Delhi in 1398—more widely.[50] Thereafter, Delhi is best viewed as one among a number of regional Sultanates.

Throughout this period, a distinct Indo-Islamic culture developed in northern India, marked by strong Turko-Persian influence.[51] The Delhi Sultanate gave rise to a period of Indian cultural renaissance, leaving lasting monuments in architecture, music, literature, and religion, and innovations in ruling institutions as well as in the fields of political theory, literary and religious styles, and distinctive cultural traditions in law. Urban growth and road networks were developed that encouraged trade within the region as well as with the outside world.[52]

South India too became subject to Islamic influence, after the decline of the Cholas (by the thirteenth century).[53] Under the reign of the sultan of Delhi, Alauddin Khilji, a Muslim polity known as the Bahamani Sultanate was set up in the south, extending to Madurai. However, within a few years of this, an independent Hindu kingdom was founded at Vijayanagar. The Vijayanagar kingdom soon established its hegemony over the whole southern peninsula, making it the most extensive kingdom in the subcontinent.[54] It controlled the spice trade of the south as well as the cotton trade of the southeast and numerous accounts by European travellers speak of the splendour and wealth of this kingdom.[55]

After 1526, the emerging Mughal Empire absorbed the Delhi Sultanate. Its founder Zahiruddin Babar gained control of the Delhi region by defeating Ibrahim Lodi, the last of the Delhi Sultans at Panipat. Babar was a descendent of Timur and of Genghis Khan. (The term Mughal is a reference to Babar's Mongol ancestry and gained currency only in the nineteenth century.) Babar's son Humayun, forced into exile, took refuge in the Safavid court of Persia, and reclaimed his authority with Persian help in 1555. Humayun's son Akbar, the greatest of the Mughals, reinforced the administrative structures he found in place and reigned for half a century, having led successful campaigns against Gujarat and Bengal, thereby gaining control over the richest parts of the subcontinent, agriculturally and commercially. He later extended Mughal control into Kabul, Kashmir, Orissa, and Baluchisthan, creating the Mughal Empire. The territorial expanse of the empire continued to grow under his successors Jahangir (1605–27), Shah Jahan (1627–58), and Aurangzeb (1658–1707).

The expansion and consolidation of the Mughal Empire was roughly coterminous with two other great Muslim empires, the Safavid in Iran and the Ottoman Empire based in Turkey and controlling much of West Asia and northern Africa. The Mughal Empire exceeded both in terms of population, wealth, and power. In 1700, the population of Mughal India is estimated to have been roughly 100 million, five times that of the Ottoman Empire and twenty times that of Safavid Persia.[56] Unlike the Ottoman and Safavid empires, the majority of Mughal India's subjects were non-Muslim. Akbar, who established the structural foundations of the empire, was highly sensitive to this fact and built on the Sultanate policy of encouraging a diverse and inclusive ruling elite. A considerable part of the nobility at the court consisted of Turks, Afghans, Arabs, and Persians as well as locally born Muslims, and powerful non-Muslim indigenous groups, such as the Rajputs, a number of Brahmans, and later the Marathas. In order to build alliance networks and establish links with powerful Rajput clans, Akbar established the custom of taking Rajput wives, who were not expected to convert. Akbar's efforts at constructing an Indo-Islamic empire based on principles of public tolerance are reflected in the flexibility and eclecticism of his private belief system. In 1582 Akbar announced his personal adherence to a new faith that he termed Din-e-Ilahi, or Divine Faith, that drew on strains of both Hindu and Muslim mystical traditions and was also influenced by Zoroastrianism. Nevertheless, Akbar made no attempts to impose it as a state religion.[57]

The political and economic success of Akbar and his successors can be accounted for to a large extent by administrative reforms he initiated, building on precedents set by the Sultans before him. Throughout the empire, nobles and powerful groups were incorporated into the imperial structure through the award of *mansabs*, imperial ranks that were demarcated decimally and that designated the number of armed forces that the individual was to provide to the centre. Accordingly, nobles were assigned *jagirs*, or the right to collect tax revenue over designated pieces of land. Such assignments were not hereditary and were frequently rotated, thus preventing nobles from building regional powerbases that could challenge Mughal authority. Mughal officials typically would negotiate for the delivery of revenue through local chieftains and landholders who homogeneously came to be referred to as zamindars.[58] Thus, the agrarian surplus was distributed amongst various layers of society.

New commercial and political elites emerged, due to the increased monetization and economic expansion under Mughal rule, especially during the seventeenth century. Though the Mughal Empire was primarily agrarian in nature, it was involved in long distance overland and oceanic trade and increasingly relied on revenue from textile exports as much as from rural, essentially agricultural, activities. Indeed, from the mid-seventeenth century onwards the character of the empire became increasingly mercantilist and linked with the international economy. The economic prosperity of the Mughal Empire was heavily reliant on oceanic connections, though unlike the Ottomans, the Mughals never commanded a substantial navy, a circumstance that allowed Europeans gradually to gain control over sea-lanes of the Indian Ocean.

South India

South India is too often slighted in historical accounts, in spite of its varied and rich civilizations and its striking contributions to the subcontinent, including major economic ones today. While glancing references have been made to south India in the paragraphs above, the ones that follow aim to provide some flow to its place in wider India's history at the risk of disrupting the overall chronological nature of this chapter.

Recorded history begins in south India as in the north, with the advent of the Aryans. The process of Aryanization, spread over a long period of seven to eight centuries, saw extensive interaction of south India with lands both to the west and the east. The period of Mauryan Empire in the north was accompanied and followed in the south by the rule of the Satavahanas which lasted until the second century AD. Under the Satavahanas, Buddhism flourished in the south, though Brahminism was favoured by most Satavahana rulers. Their kingdom was eventually partitioned between the Abhiras in the northwest, Chutus in the south, and Ikshvakus in Andhradesa.[59] From the mid-sixth century, for about 300 years the history of south India is that of three major kingdoms in conflict with each other: the Chalukyas of Badami, Pallavas of Kanchipuram (who have attracted the most attention from historians), and Pandyas of Madurai.[60] The Pallavas were involved in naval warfare (at a time of conflict with the Chalukyas) to support their ally, the King of Sri Lanka; this interaction between Tamil Nadu and Sri Lanka was but a continuation of past history and the future pattern of relations.[61] This period saw the settlement on the Malabar and Konkan coasts of Arab traders, who kept the trade with the Roman Empire alive. These traders were welcomed, given land for trading stations, and left free to practise their religion.[62]

Around the ninth century, the Cholas emerged as the dominant power in the south, introducing an era of impressive political, economic, cultural, and artistic development. The Cholas aimed to establish trade supremacy on the high seas and attacked an alliance between the Cheras and Pandyas to break their monopoly on trade with West Asia, bringing Malabar under their control. They also sought to eliminate Arab competition in Southeast Asian trade and launched an ambitious campaign against the kingdom of Shrivijaya, a powerful maritime state that ruled the Malayan peninsula, Sumatra, Java, and controlled the sea routes from India to China.[63] The Chola monarchs sent embassies to China and by the tenth century, merchants in China and south India had established trading relationships.[64]

However, by the latter part of the twelfth century, Chola ascendency had begun to wane. The power of subordinate rulers in the Deccan increased as central control weakened. Frequent military campaigns exhausted Chola resources, and, coupled with a challenge from the Hoysalas in the west and the Pandyas in the south, ultimately led to the fall of the Cholas in the thirteenth century. The region continued to attract foreigners and during this period Jewish traders established settlements on the eastern coast of Kerala for trade. (Subsequent to the persecution of Jews in Europe in later centuries, some would come to Kerala, already familiar from trading contacts.)[65]

The collapse of Vijayanagar in the sixteenth century spelt the end of the south as a separate political arena, with the period following it characterized by extensive warfare among numerous indigenous political entities of the peninsula, culminating in the brilliant expansion of the Mysore state of Haider Ali and Tipu Sultan.[66] The warfare was exacerbated by the intrusion of powers from outside the region such as the Marathas, the Mughals, the Portuguese in the sixteenth and seventeenth centuries, and the French and British in the seventeenth and eighteenth centuries.[67] Despite the continuing struggle for power, between the sixteenth and eighteenth centuries the region lay at the core of an international textile trade, stretching from Southeast Asia to Europe.[68] Eventually, British power in alliance with Hyderabad ruled south India and Mysore was absorbed as a princely State.

Enter the Europeans

Even prior to the establishment of the Mughal Empire, the Portuguese under Vasco da Gama had landed on India's southwestern coast and had begun to establish major settlements in Goa in 1510. Nevertheless, the Portuguese were never able to consolidate a monopoly over Indian Ocean sea trade—the bulk of the trade still being conducted by Arab and Gujarati merchant communities. Even in the latter half of the eighteenth century, Portuguese trading outposts were considerably less important than the Mughal port city of Surat. The Ottoman navy ensured that the Portuguese were never able to close the Red Sea to Persian, Turkish, Arab, and Indian trade. Early on, the English, who had succeeded the Portuguese as the major European sea power in the Indian Ocean, were also supplicants of the Mughal Empire and could only engage in trade with the permission of the Mughal emperor. The East India Company, which was formed in 1600, had to obtain permission from Emperor Jahangir to trade in India in 1619. But this was soon to change.

The Raj in India

Interpretation of the backdrop against which British domination of the Indian subcontinent developed is much disputed. The period prior to the British conquest of large parts of India was seen by nineteenth-century European historians as a period of 'anarchy between the age of Mughal hegemony and the imposition of pax Britannica'.[69] However, it is important 'in any study of India between empires not to confuse the erosion of power of the Mughal court and army with a more general political, economic and societal decline'.[70] Indian politics in the eighteenth century were marked primarily by decentralization rather than decline. The economy was generally buoyant, driven by agriculture, inland trade, and urbanization. Decline in agricultural prosperity due to interstate warfare in some areas of northern India, Punjab, and Maratha-controlled territories was counterbalanced by extensive growth in other regions such as Mysore under Haider Ali and Tipu Sultan. 'States exacted tribute from systems of agricultural commodity production that tied villages to expansive networks of commercial mobility and exchange.' It was 'this vibrant "tributary commercialism"...which made India look attractive to European companies'.[71]

The gradual dismantling of the Mughal successor states and replacement by British domination began in the mid-eighteenth century. Until 1757, European traders had been forced to bring large amount of bullion into India, as Indian cotton and silk products had a well-established market in Europe, whereas no significant Indian demand existed for Western products. This pattern of exchange began to evolve following the British conquest of Bengal between the 1750s and 1760s, when the East India Company, which had initially approached India with a charter to trade, began to set up an elaborate state apparatus to govern the appropriation of land revenue in its Indian territories that was in turn invested in the purchase of products for export to European markets.[72] Thus the East India Company, an organization that had originally been intended to accumulate profits from oceanic trade, came to draw its basic sustenance from land revenue.[73]

British involvement in India and eventually its appropriation of the sub-continent as the crown jewel of its global empire is best viewed as an economic project. From this perspective, British exploitation in India can be divided into three successive phases.[74] These phases often overlapped, with older forms of exploitation never being entirely replaced but rather integrated into newer patterns.[75]

The first 'mercantilist' phase, from 1757 up to 1813, was characterized by direct plunder and the East India Company's monopoly trade. Surplus revenues were used to purchase Indian finished goods (mostly from Bengal) at below market prices for export to England and Europe.

The second phase of exploitation was marked by the establishment of a classical pattern of colonialism, in which India had become a captive market for manufactured goods from the metropolis while exporting, initially mainly to it, a variety of raw materials, such as cotton, jute, tea, coffee, wheat, and oil seeds. The patterns of trade had changed drastically with the Industrial Revolution in England. Between 1813 and 1858 India was converted into a market for Manchester textiles and a source for raw materials. Traditional handicrafts consequently suffered a sharp decline. Between 1870 and 1914, India's export surplus was critical for Britain's balance of payments, since growing protectionism in America and Continental Europe made it increasingly difficult for Britain to sell its manufactured goods in those markets, while it needed to import a variety of agricultural commodities. The export of Indian raw materials to America and Europe was indispensable for financing Britain's deficit with them.[76]

The third phase, beginning from the second half of the nineteenth century, saw the establishment of finance-driven dominance through the export of capital and the establishment of sizeable chains of British-controlled banks, export-import firms, and agency houses. This period also witnessed a dramatic increase in the so-called 'country trade' between India, the Eastern Archipelago, and China, which had first set in towards the end of the eighteenth century, bringing about a 'commercial revolution' in the Indian Ocean.[77] These developments resulted in profound changes in the economic life of lands bordering on the India and China Seas, from Basra and Mocha in the west to Malacca and Canton in the east. The economic orientation of the East

India Company underwent a number of far-reaching changes from the first decades of the nineteenth century onwards.

The Charter Act of 1813 ended the East India Company's monopoly of trade with India due to pressure from a newly emergent industrial capitalist class in Britain, which effectively advocated a doctrine of free trade in order to sell products in Eastern markets. China tea now took the place of Indian textiles as the Company's most profitable item of trade. As in the case of early British trade with India, the Chinese demand for British goods at the time was negligible.[78]

Though British goods did not find a market in China, a solution to Britain's negative balance of trade with China was found when it was discovered that products of British India, mainly raw cotton and later opium, could find a ready market in China. India's resources were now used to finance British investment in China and the purchase of tea and silk at Canton.[79] After 1823, opium replaced Indian cotton as the primary staple commodity in this trade. A considerable part of the surplus of Indian revenues was sent to London in teas from China.[80] In 1830, the Auditor-General of the Company T. C. Melville declared, 'I am prepared to say that India does entirely depend upon the profits of the China trade'.[81] Until the 1920s, 20 per cent of India's revenue was generated through the opium trade. Amitav Ghosh speculates, 'this export of contraband may have incalculably influenced the way the Chinese perceive India'.[82]

Throughout, land revenue remained the single largest source of income for the British East India Company and then the Raj. Receipts increased between 1881 and 1901, despite devastating famines in 1890, due to high and inflexible colonial demands for land revenue.[83] Famines became a frequent feature of life in colonial India, while the first seven decades of the eighteenth century, the period prior to the establishment of British colonial administration, were remarkably free of famines. The great Bengal famine of 1770, in which one-third of the population is thought to have perished, occurred soon after the colonial conquest.

The bureaucratic foundation of the Raj

The Company relied heavily on two institutions of state in India. One was its massive standing army and the other was the centralized civilian bureaucracy in the last decades of the eighteenth century. Though formal control was to be exercised by the Board of Directors of the East Asia Company in London, the Governor General and his bureaucrats enjoyed considerable autonomy. Until well into the twentieth century, the British government in India functioned essentially as an autocracy of hierarchically organized officials headed by the Viceroy in India and the Secretary of State (a member of the Cabinet) in London. Parliamentary control from the metropolis was by and large theoretical.[84]

In spite of a patina of benevolence, on occasion combined with talk of trusteeship and training towards eventual self-governance, the Raj was in reality uncompromisingly white, authoritarian (particularly after the 1857 uprising), and driven by economic considerations for the benefit of Britain. It existed primarily to safeguard colonial exploitation of India's economic and human resources. All higher levels of administration were occupied by Europeans, who held all but sixteen of the 900 posts in the Indian civil service in the early 1880s.[85]

The British Indian Army

The British government in India relied heavily on an army that it frequently employed in campaigns outside India in order to crush resistance movements and consolidate control, such as: the 1882 campaign by Prime Minister Gladstone in Egypt; the campaign against the Mahdi and his movement in Sudan in 1885–6 and again in 1896; and the 'Boxer war' in China in 1900. Army expenditure accounted for 41.9 per cent of the Indian Government budget in 1881–2 and rose to 51.9 per cent by 1904–5.[86]

British military policy provides a number of insights into the nature of colonial rule. After the shock of the rebellion of 1857, the army became one-third white, with a European monopoly over artillery. The Indian sector of the army was equipped with inferior weaponry and was strictly divided along religious and ethnic fault lines, an approach that Sir John Strachey described as a 'policy of water-tight compartments...to prevent the growth of any dangerous identity of feeling from race, religion, caste or local sympathies'.[87] Or, as Sir Charles Wood, the second Secretary of State, put it in 1862: 'I wish to have a different and rival spirit in different regiments, so that Sikh might fire into Hindoo, Goorkha into either, without any scruples in time of need.'[88]

From the 1880s onwards, an ideology of 'martial races' was strictly adhered to under Lord Roberts. Men belonging to particular racial and ethnic communities in India were said to be better suited for soldiering than others, which justified the large scale recruitment of Sikhs and Gorkhas, religiously and ethnically relatively marginal groups who were therefore less likely to be affected by mainstream nationalism.[89]

Similar divisions were encouraged among the civilian population and especially among Indian elite groups, predominantly along religious lines but in many cases along the lines of caste or regional identities. This was partially the result of deliberate efforts by the British administration, with consequences that echo in Indian society and politics up to this day.

The introduction of elected municipalities with separate electorates increased tensions between Hindus and Muslims and forced community leaders to cultivate a constituency among their own religious community. On the whole, colonial administrators regarded communal divisions as politically useful, though at times tensions between religious communities could also pose law and order challenges. Secretary of State Hamilton's confidential letter to Lord Elgin in May 1897 typifies British attitudes in this regard:

> I am sorry to hear of the increasing friction between Hindus and Mohammedans in the North West and the Punjab. One hardly knows what to wish for; unity of ideas and action would be very dangerous politically, divergence of ideas and collision are administratively troublesome. Of the two, the latter is the least risky, though it throws anxiety and responsibility upon those on the spot where the friction exists.[90]

Meanwhile, the economic drain of wealth from India to Britain, as well as the disruption by the British of Indian cultural traditions, helped fuel the rise of nationalism among Indians, as did British racism.[91] Racial discrimination and brutality could on occasion unite higher and lower classes of native society across lines of religion and caste in a shared sense of injustice. The upper echelons of native society frequently encountered discrimination and barriers to promotion in jobs or professions for which they were often well qualified. Compartments of railways and steamers were often reserved exclusively for Europeans. For the less privileged, racism often took on cruder shapes in the form of outright physical violence, sometimes in the guise of 'shooting accidents', with European-dominated courts usually awarding insultingly light sentences to the offenders.[92] Colour played a crucial role in uniting white businessmen in India against potential Indian competition. Innumerable personal and 'club-life' business ties existed between white businessmen and government officials in India. As Lord Curzon pointed out in a speech at Barakar in 1903: 'My work lies in administration, yours in exploitation; but both are aspects of the same question and of the same duty.'[93]

Anti-colonialism, the 1857 uprising, and the birth of nationalism

In 1857, a large-scale military mutiny and civilian uprising seriously challenged colonial rule in India. Colonial officials and historians have described the events of 1857 as a sepoy mutiny,[94] whereas Indian nationalist historiography has often referred to them as 'the first war of independence'. It was both. The revolt was clearly infused with a sense of patriotism, often regionally focused, and aimed at putting an end to colonial rule. Whereas earlier cases of military and civilian revolts had largely been uncoordinated and localized, the 1857 uprising for the first time saw the convergence of multiple strands of resistance. Discontented landed magnates across north India and peasants, tribal communities, as well as artisans, labourers, and rebellious policemen joined forces. The agrarian revolts were thus multi-class in character and at times influenced by religion. Though Hindu religious sentiment did not play a significant role in the rebellion, Muslim religious millenarianism was a constant and crucial factor. However, while many Muslim leaders called for a Jihad against the colonial government, insurgent leaders took care to preserve Hindu and Muslim unity and to emphasize the common threat faced by both.[95]

Though the revolt enjoyed a wide social base, it eventually failed for a number of reasons. Rebel forces were not quick enough to attack British troops advancing from Punjab and further failed to consolidate their control over liberated zones by establishing their own administration that the population could have viewed as legitimate and deserving of support. Furthermore, the politics of the revolt reflected inter-Indian rivalries. Hyderabad, for instance, did not throw its full weight behind the revolt, as it had no interest in seeing rival Maratha power re-establish itself in its immediate neighbourhood.[96]

It took fifty million pounds—and hideous brutality—to quell the mutiny and the East India Company was abolished in its aftermath. India now came under the direct governance of the crown in Britain. Rather typically of India's fate under British influence and then rule, the cost for suppressing the 1857 uprising was included in the Indian debt, which the new crown Raj had to pay back to London as part of its annual Home Charges.

However, these events were pregnant with consequence, some positive, as Ramachandra Guha makes clear:

> To focus on the Raj simply as a vehicle of economic exploitation is one-sided. As Karl Marx pointed out, while the British conquered India through the vilest of motives, they were yet an unconscious tool of history in waking up a moribund civilization. They gave us a wake-up call which was salutary. Indian traditions of nationalism and social reform were a direct product of the provocations and challenges of colonial rule.[97]

Anti-colonial mass mobilization and the emergence of nationalism

The 1857 revolt saw then the convergence of diverse elements of resistance to colonial rule and the emergence of anti-colonial consciousness among broad sections of India's population.

In the past, in discussing the history of anti-colonialism and Indian nationalism, disproportionate attention has often been accorded to the workings of the Western-educated elite. However, anti-colonialism and nationalism in India always had a highly pluralistic character and meant different things to different people. Indeed, the formation of an overarching Indian national movement always had to contend with the need to incorporate a variety of religious communities and linguistic regions and to accommodate a number of contradictory impulses under its umbrella.

While subaltern anti-colonialism clearly predated attempts at mass mobilization against British rule led by urban elites,[98] educated Indians had been forming political associations at regional levels and the Indian National Congress (INC), initially an association of city-based professionals, came into being in 1885.

Until 1920, the Congress remained the preserve of educated groups, predominantly high-caste Hindus.[99] They alone were equipped to engage with the Raj within the existing channels of political manoeuvre and they alone were sufficiently qualified to profit from concessions to place and power in government service or Legislative Councils.[100]

Early INC leadership was moderate in its aims and dedicated to advancing its claims through the path of petitions, with the primary aim of greater Indianization of the administration. On the economic front, it developed a critique of a wide spectrum of colonial policies, ranging from the devastating famines brought about by colonial taxes, to the use of indentured Indian labour at home and on plantations overseas.

Only modest success attended these early attempts to extract concessions from the colonial administration, and by the mid-1890s a new generation of nationalists began to question the moderate approach and call for more assertive measures. The following years saw the beginning of 'no-revenue' campaigns and protests directed against countervailing excise duty imposed on Indian cotton in 1896. The period also saw the first targeted assassinations of colonial officials.

The controversial partition of Bengal in 1905 provided further fuel for various strands of Indian resistance, provoking the beginning of the *swadeshi* (own country) movement, which emphasized the boycotting of British-made goods in favour of Indian ones. The move to partition, a prelude to the 1947 creation of Pakistan and the 1971 emergence of an independent Bangladesh, was aimed at dividing the population along religious lines, since the professed objective was to create a separate Muslim majority province in eastern Bengal with Dhaka as its capital.[101] Due to widespread agitation, the partition of Bengal had to be annulled by 1911 and the British shifted their capital from Calcutta to Delhi, partly in order to operate from a less hostile political environment.

The agitation against the partition of Bengal served to unify moderate and extremist strands around a common cause. The mass nationalist movement that had begun to take shape towards the very end of the nineteenth century gained considerable momentum in the 1920s due to the social and economic dislocation brought about by the First World War, during which Indian manpower and treasure were critical to the British endeavour. The war had impacted upon Indian lives through massive recruitments, heavy taxes, and often semi-compulsory war loans, as well as a sharp increase in prices. This served to extend the national movement to business groups, large sections of the peasantry, and industrial labour.

The war years had witnessed a massive plunder of Indian human and material resources.[102] Large amounts of grain and raw material were extracted and diverted in order to meet army needs. Defence expenditure increased by 300 per cent, bringing about significant changes in the entire financial structure of the Raj. Apart from land revenue and land tax, trade and industry were significantly affected for the first time. It was this that drew large numbers of Indian merchants, companies, and business families to the national movement. The post-war years thus saw a combination of growing grievances with a new mood of self-confidence: 'the classical formula for a potentially revolutionary situation'.[103]

In retrospect, the end of the Raj was largely ordained by the First World War, which weakened Britain and brought about broad challenges to the earlier world order and which also forced significant change on Britain's imperial arrangements in India.

Colonial policy towards Indian industrial development underwent change due to financial demands from London and the realization that a certain amount of Indian economic self-sufficiency was a strategic necessity.[104] As a result, the development of the Indian private sector accelerated and contributed to country-wide nationalist connections. The mass political awakening of the post-war years also owed something to a worldwide upsurge of anti-capitalist and anti-imperialist sentiment. Indian soldiers returning home from campaigns in distant regions are likely to have carried with them a sense of these international currents.[105]

It became increasingly difficult for the colonial state to service the needs of the metropolis while at the same time meeting the political and economic requirements of the administration of India. Furthermore, the Great Depression of the late 1920s and 1930s damaged India's export surplus with the rest of the world, through which the transfer of wealth from the colony to Britain had been channelled.[106] Thus, in order to continue to transfer wealth from the colony to the metropolis, Britain had to resort to tactics, including exchange rate manipulation, that favoured the requirement for the colonial government to meet its obligatory home charges but resulted in British disinvestment within India.[107] The agrarian distress that ensued would prove to be a major impetus to the mass movements of the 1920s and 1930s led by M. K. Gandhi.

Gandhi returned from South Africa (where he had gained valuable political experience through his organization of non-violent protests by South Africa's Indian expatriate community against racist policies) to India in 1915 at a time when the constitutionalism assumed by the moderate leadership in pursuit of its demands for change had not been able to achieve any major concessions, and methods of individual revolutionary violence and armed insurrections during the First World War had been suppressed to a large extent.

According to Partha Chatterjee, it was 'the Gandhian intervention in elite-nationalist politics in India which established for the first time that an authentic national movement could only be built upon organized support of the whole of the peasantry'.[108]

Gandhian ideology and rhetoric situated themselves outside of the nationalist dilemma of the urban elite and drew political and moral authority from a profound moral critique of colonial rule. In 1909, Gandhi published *Hind Swaraj* (Indian Home Rule), which contained a strong critique not only of British rule in India but of modern industrial civilization and the Western conception of civil society as a whole. It was almost instantly banned in British India. Gandhi's critical evaluation of Western industrialism and political institutions resonated deeply among large sections of Indians, ruined as much by factories as by courts of law.[109] Though some have interpreted Gandhi's utopian vision for society as a commonwealth of independent village republics as little more than idealism, they have overlooked the potency of Gandhi as an astute political strategist. He drew immense moral and political authority from his critique of the Raj and it was this that assured success for his nationwide mass agitations around strategic issues. Gandhism was a powerful political weapon.

Widespread disaffection in the second decade of the twentieth century provided Gandhi with a platform to launch his first 'all India' agitation. Initial protests were based on opposition to the Rowlatt Act, which perpetuated wartime ordinances into peacetime, and allowed Indians to be held without trial. This agitation gained considerable momentum when it merged with the Khilafat movement, the latter chiefly concerned with harsh conditions that were to be imposed on the defeated Ottoman Empire and demanding that the Turkish Sultan (*Khalifa*) should retain control over Muslim sacred places, be left with sufficient territory to effectively defend Islamic faith, and that Arabia, Syria, Iraq, and Palestine remain under Muslim sovereignty.[110] Though the Khilafat movement was ostensibly concerned with events that occurred outside India and did not directly affect Indian domestic politics, it effected the large-scale mobilization of India's vast and highly diverse Muslim community. Like the rest of India's population, its Muslim community was divided along regional, linguistic, class, and sectarian fault lines and required a pan-Islamic symbol for effective political mobilization. In its second phase, to a large extent due to Gandhi's efforts and political acumen, the movement reached beyond the Muslim community to become an important symbol in the struggle against imperialism. For Khilafat leaders, Gandhi's support provided an essential link with Hindu politicians, without which any non-cooperation movement and boycott of British institutions and products would have been ineffective.[111] For Gandhi, the support of Khilafat agitation proved helpful in generating popular mobilization that transcended the boundaries of religious communities.[112]

The Rowlatt agitation of 1919 proved to be the largest anti-imperialist movement India had witnessed since 1857 and it was met with brutal repression. On 13 April 1919, an unarmed crowd of villagers that had gathered in Jallianwallah Bagh in Amritsar was fired upon by British soldiers under the command of General Dyer, killing 370 and injuring more than 1,200 men, women, and children. The Jallianwallah Bagh massacre inspired a yet more fervent nationalist response.

The non-cooperation movements led by Gandhi were accompanied by widespread labour unrest and peasant movements occurring between 1919 and 1922, independent of Congress politics.[113] However, at its height the non-cooperation movement was abruptly called off by Gandhi after twenty-two policemen were killed by angry peasants at Chauri Chaura in Gorakhpur district. His decision was deeply resented by the Congress leadership and in the following years, Hindu–Muslim unity at the height of the Khilafat movement gave way to increased tension and cases of violence between religious communities. Its aftermath saw the rise of religiously informed identity politics among Muslims and more aggressive forms of religious nationalism by Hindu organizations. The antecedents of these developments doubtless include the granting of separate electorates by the British for Muslims in 1909. Thus, the 1920s saw a splintering of the nationalist movement into various strands. However, it is important to remember that unlike in Europe, where concepts of nationalism had been inspired by the Enlightenment and Romanticism and had thrived in an economic environment of industrial capitalism to gradually transform dynastic empires into democratic nation states, nationalism in Africa and Asia was essentially a product of anti-colonial resistance movements. Unlike in Europe, sovereignty was not conceptualized as centralized absolute power, but rather as in the Mughal Empire and many Indian ruling structures, shared with the periphery. Borders were often porous and 'generalised cartographic anxiety over territorial possession' was new to the area and was spread only through colonialism.[114] Nevertheless, once religious communities as political entities came into being, this cartographic anxiety was bound to become a constant feature of politics in the subcontinent.

In 1930, the global depression and profound economic crisis provided the basis for a revitalization of the mass nationalist agitations and the launching of Gandhi's Civil Disobedience campaigns. However, a wide range of conflict along the lines of class, caste, and religious communities also gained strength. In 1930, Gandhi selected the tax on the indigenous production of salt as a platform for yet another nationwide agitation and undertook his famous salt march to the coast of central India, triggering large-scale boycotts of British goods and institutions.

Gandhi had been invited to attend a 'Round Table' conference touching on India's future in London, but upon his return without substantial concessions from the British, the Civil Disobedience movement was resumed in 1932 and was once again met with extreme repression by the colonial administration. The hostility and condescension of some of the UK's elite for India and Indians during the first half of the twentieth century, even as India's eventual independence loomed, is encapsulated in Winston Churchill's famously visceral dislike of the country, its people, and its traditions.[115]

The beginning of the Second World War saw unprecedented economic intervention by the British and the diversion, once more, of Indian resources to finance Britain's war effort. Serious shortages developed and prices for essential commodities soared. Large-scale deprivation resulted. Most dramatically, in Bengal a devastating famine occurred in 1943–4 in which between 3.5 and 3.8 million people starved to death in one of the most catastrophic and least publicized hecatombs of the era. According to recent research, no significant decline in aggregate availability of food had occurred in the province. The high rate of mortality was caused by a severe decline in exchange entitlements of vulnerable social groups and the striking absence of relief measures.[116]

In 1942 Gandhi issued a more radical resolution for the British to Quit India and in a sharp contrast to his earlier stance, stated in an interview that he was 'prepared to take the risk of violence' in order to end 'the great calamity of slavery'.[117] The Quit India movement overshadowed the agitations of the 1920s and represented the largest uprising in India since 1857, no less significant for being civilian. Since the entire top leadership of Congress had been imprisoned, the movement was led and coordinated by lower-ranking Congress leaders (who were often of a decidedly socialist bent). In a number of districts, British administration collapsed. A significant political development, though one of only limited military consequence, was the creation in 1942 of the Indian National Army, allied with Japan and dedicated to ending British rule in India.

The political unity of the remarkably successful Quit India movement degenerated into serious divisions among Indian political actors over the political dispensation after independence. Mistrust and tensions grew between Congress and the Muslim League, intermediated erratically by the British colonial administration (which in hindsight seems also to have intentionally created and even encouraged the growing difference). A series of intrigues, policy initiatives, and misfires led to the partition of India along professed religious lines in 1947 at the time of independence, producing one of the most cataclysmic events of the twentieth century. An estimated three million Hindus, Sikhs, and Muslims lost their lives in the violence that ensued. Nine million Hindus and Sikhs were displaced from the region that was to become Pakistan and an estimated six million Indian Muslims migrated to Pakistan. These circumstances were particularly unhappy ones as India sought to assume a leading place at the international level; and their sequelae, notably in Kashmir, would bedevil Indian foreign policy in subsequent decades.

India's foreign relations, while controlled completely by Britain, had increasingly assumed an Indian face since the Versailles peace conference of 1919, at which London was successful in securing a seat for (British) India—in effect providing Britain with a second seat—occupied by the elegant but submissive Maharajah of Bikaner, while Indian nationalists, clamouring for access, were kept at bay from the meeting.[118] This led on to Indian membership in the League of Nations (where India's delegation was headed by a succession of Britons) and to founding membership of the United Nations even before India's independence. Britain also included Indian officials in some of its key diplomatic institutions, notably its embassy in Washington, where Indian economic interests were recognized as relevant.[119]

The following chapters will address the emergence of an independent Indian foreign policy under Jawaharlal Nehru (long a leader of the INC at Gandhi's side, although one with a distinctly more patrician background and outlook), how it was influenced by India's earlier history and the colonial era, and how some steps adopted under colonial rule to provide India with an international identity, albeit largely self-serving ones for London, had prepared the ground for India's emergence as a meaningful player in global diplomacy.

Conclusions

This chapter has sought to highlight the proposition that today's concept of India is not timeless, static, and self-evident. In contrast, it is a product of historical processes, whether with regard to its geographical boundaries, broad political and economic structures, or social categories such as caste and religious identity that continue to have great political import. In interpreting Indian politics, it is helpful to keep the historicity of political categories in mind. Often social and political forces that disguise themselves as traditional are as new and as much a product of modernity as those that self-consciously and overtly assert their modernity. Contending interpretations of the past are a decisive factor in virtually all current political debates especially with regard to economic and also foreign policy.

Thus, India's self-interpretation, its current borders, and its foreign policy preferences, while influenced by previous avatars, cannot be said to descend in a straight line from ancient history. India's borders, particularly in the north, were subject to constant shifts as migrant populations drifted into the region and foreign conquests occurred. Today's dominant religions and philosophies in India, some indigenous while others not, represent a very different mix than they would have one, two, or three thousand years ago. Likewise, the ethnic mosaic of India has undergone constant change. India's civilizational influence within Asia, from antiquity onwards, notably through the spread of both Buddhism and (on a lesser scale) Hinduism, and in many other fields through Persia onwards to the Middle East, has been vast and manifold.

Modern, independent India thus constitutes the core of a region that has interacted with the rest of the world for millennia, extending its cultural, intellectual, and religious influence far and wide, particularly to the east. 'Indianness' is instantly recognizable the world over. Indian trading communities have settled the world over, including along most of Africa's coastline and in the Americas, greatly enriching the make-up of many countries. The British gave India a new territorial unity. Gandhi and others in the national movement imparted a modern purpose to the people of India that continues to evolve in the twenty-first century.

Its colonial experience did much to diminish India relative to its standing in earlier eras. Its economy failed to progress during the two decisive centuries of British dominance, with the industrial revolution nearly entirely bypassing it, by design of London. India's economy represented only a fraction of the relative weight in the global economy in 1947 that it had two centuries earlier.[120]

Not surprisingly, this legacy, in spite of the success of the Quit India movement, left the newly independent state, still smarting from partition, looking for fresh approaches and new departures to establishing an international personality, and harbouring a deep, if sometimes suppressed, distrust for Great Britain (and by extension, much of the West, epitomized by the USA). At the same time, Indians have tended to be generous in their assessment of the more beneficial features of a Raj never primarily designed in their interests. They appreciate the institutions of governance, not least the Westminster parliamentary system, and the independent judiciary, bequeathed to them by the British even as they register the enormous economic depredations of the colonial period.

Partition was to haunt India well into the future, complicating its relations, beyond Pakistan, with many other Muslim countries and also, to a degree, with its own Muslim communities. Further, the distrust of London, and by extension Washington and other Western capitals, combined with Nehru's choice of a broadly socialist model of economic development, precipitated India into an alliance with Moscow, an economic and foreign policy orientation that had turned into a dead end by the late 1980s, as ensuing chapters will explore.

In spite of these challenges, India's centrality in the South Asian subcontinent, its tradition throughout a very long history of engagement with the outside world and mostly of hospitality to inflowing populations (as today with Nepalis and, to a lesser extent, Bangladeshis moving into India in large numbers) have made it a naturally prominent, if not yet a central actor in international relations, with the prospect of emerging in decades ahead as a defining power of the twenty-first century.

3

India's Contemporary Security Challenges: More Internal Than External?

India faces numerous contemporary security challenges, mostly internal, and this is nothing new. Given that domestic politics play a major role in determining which security challenges Indians believe to be the most pressing, this chapter, alongside the immediately following one (on the economic dimensions of Indian foreign policy), lays emphasis on internal factors in shaping Indian foreign policy post-independence. In order to grasp the relative weight of today's security challenges, this chapter first traces the evolution of India's domestic politics and foreign policy since independence. It then discusses various domestic, regional, and global security challenges relevant to India today, and concludes by re-examining the historical trend to determine if India is likely to manage these challenges effectively, as it negotiates its rise to great power status in the foreign policy sphere.

Historical overview: from preacher to pragmatist

India's journey from 1947 till the present day, both in terms of foreign policy and domestic politics, can be seen as a transition from idealism under Nehru, through a period of 'hard realism' (or *realpolitik*) lasting roughly from the mid-1960s to the mid-1980s (coinciding with the dominance of the Indian political scene by Indira Gandhi) to economically driven pragmatism today. These three phases provide an artificial but perhaps useful shorthand (doing little justice to the complexities of Indian policymaking) for understanding the significance of some of the changes India has witnessed, while also highlighting elements of continuity.

1950s and 1960s: unified idealism

The first period, from independence onward through the 1950s and 1960s, was a period in which India's foreign policy stance was framed for international consumption as one of some idealism. Simultaneously, Nehru tackled the tremendous domestic challenges of cohesion and economic revitalization that the British Empire had left as a ticking time bomb of a legacy. The Congress under Nehru, while adhering to democratic practice, essentially enjoyed one-party dominance at home and represented a more or less unified foreign policy ideology to the world, although the domestic political scene was a lively one with several Congress titans astride the political scene even after Mahatma Gandhi's assassination in 1948, and the Communist Party posing serious regionally-based challenges at different times (still reflected in its present-day strength within the important states of West Bengal and Kerala). Within India, the Congress was viewed as the architect of the freedom movement, and hence appealed to a large middle ground of interests and values that coalesced around its project of state nationalism.[1] Internationally too, Nehru chose the middle path of non-alignment in the bipolar order of the Cold War, arguing that India would have to 'plough a lonely furrow'.[2] Indian foreign policy of the time seemed moralistic to outsiders, defining the national interest as congruent with 'world co-operation and world peace'.[3] It was defended as 'the only honourable and right position' for India.[4]

Decision-making, in the Congress Party and hence in the government, was centralized in the office of the Prime Minister. Especially after the deaths of the great domestic politician Sardar Vallabhbhai Patel in 1950 and of the framer of India's constitution, B. R. Ambedkar, in 1956, Nehru increasingly relied on his own instincts in confronting internal challenges as he had all along in formulating foreign policy.[5] Although Nehru extensively debated the ideological moorings of India's foreign policy in Parliament and other public arenas, the Ministry of External Affairs maintained a monopoly on information, resulting in scant public scrutiny and accountability of its policies. In any event, the domestic challenges facing the country were such that few leading national figures wasted much time on the country's international relations and profile.

India's cohesion was severely tested not only by the fall-out of a murderous partition in 1947, but on its heels by the Kashmir crisis, the resistance of several princely states, notably Hyderabad, to joining the Indian union, and some left-over business with respect to decolonization (managed elegantly by France, which negotiated the return of Pondicherry and other minor dependencies to Indian sovereignty, and less so by Portugal, which had to be militarily expelled from Goa in 1961). Even language politics threatened the Indian Union when the state of Tamil Nadu threatened secession rather than contemplate the imposition on it of Hindi as the national language of India—in due course winning its point. Above all, as documented in the next chapter, India's poverty proved the greatest burden passed on to independent India by the colonial era, producing many political implications, real and apprehended.

India's international actions during this period were consonant with its domestic situation and foreign policy outlook, though India's posture regarding various international crises (Indochina, Hungary) was seen by the US-dominated West as inconsistent with its purported idealism. The dissonance was aggravated by the brilliant but often grating (to Western ears) sermonizing of Nehru's preferred envoy and latterly Minister, V. K. Krishna Menon.[6] Wherever possible, India took sides with other 'Third World' countries against imperialist forces of the West, and eschewed those multilateral arrangements that seemed to compromise this objective.[7] This policy of international independence, eventually indistinguishable from that of 'non-alignment' (even though Nehru had not warmed to the latter concept early on), was followed until external events in the form of Chinese aggression in 1962 compelled the Indian establishment to face the realities of power politics in the international system. Even so, upon Nehru's death, Lal Bahadur Shastri upheld India's 'moral duty' to eradicate colonialism and imperialism.[8] Subsequently, having weathered further storms, notably an attack by Pakistan in 1965 and another leadership change in 1966, the domestic scene evolved with splits soon sundering earlier Congress unity, ushering in a new era of Indian foreign policy as well.

1970s and 1980s: intermittent realism

The general election of 1967 was a watershed for India's domestic politics, marking the beginning of the decline of Congress hegemony. The centralized nature of authority within the Congress party and within government, further complicated by the growing antipathy between the government and the Congress party organization, had left little room for the articulation of regional interests in the political system. As a result, the Congress won the 1967 elections, but with a much narrower majority than ever before. It lost control of eight state governments as regionally based actors started to gain significance. The following two decades were characterized by 'the politics of exit', whereby new regional parties were formed by groups breaking away from Congress.[9]

After Nehru's daughter Indira Gandhi came to the helm in 1966, the Congress party by 1969 split into two factions under the government and the party organization respectively. In August 1970, Mrs. Gandhi made a speech at a Congress seminar where, while paying tribute to her father's ideal of non-alignment, she asserted that the problems of developing countries needed to be faced 'not merely by idealism, not merely by sentimentalism, but by very clear thinking and hard-headed analysis of the situation'.[10] This marked the growing realization that India's interests could not be fully protected by its averred international stance.

Domestically, Mrs Gandhi used every method possible—constitutional and unconstitutional—to centralize power and to bring state governments into line. For the latter purpose Article 356 of the Indian Constitution, allowing the centre to suspend state governments in case of constitutional crises, was increasingly used for political ends. The Sarkaria Commission reports that until 1969, this provision had been used on only twelve occasions (generally in truly chaotic circumstances), but was invoked thirty-nine times between 1970 and 1987.[11] It is a tribute to the roots developed by Nehru's democratic outlook that the damage to the democratic process inflicted by the Indira Gandhi government, reaching its nadir during the Emergency years (1975–7), was rewarded by a massive electoral defeat in 1977. As a result, the Congress party split again in 1978.

On the international stage, the realist turn engineered by Mrs. Gandhi in Delhi was evident as it veered away from non-alignment towards alignment with the Soviet Union, marked by the Indo-Soviet treaty of 1971, a few months ahead of India's military intervention in the Bangladesh War, allowing India to shatter Pakistan and halve its size and weight: the first proactive military intervention by India in a neighbouring country (although it was justified publicly by Pakistani atrocities and the influx of Bangladeshi refugees, which had aroused growing international concern). Subsequently, in 1974, India conducted its first nuclear test. In 1975, India intervened during internal unrest in Sikkim (that it had encouraged) and incorporated it into the Union. During this period, India, hitherto thoroughly committed to the Arab world, also began to adjust its view of West Asia with a clandestine visit of the Israeli Foreign Minister during the brief stint of the Janata government following Mrs Gandhi's electoral defeat.

On the home front, an unproductive mix of military and political strategies was deployed to counter the growing agitations in Kashmir, Punjab, and Assam. The Sikh Free Khalistan movement seeking the independence of Punjab, which had been met with fierce opposition by Delhi domestically and internationally, eventually claimed its most famous victim when Mrs. Gandhi was assassinated in 1984 by her Sikh bodyguards, a shocking event that triggered a massive anti-Sikh pogrom in Delhi that claimed up to 2,000 lives. Mrs. Gandhi's assertive style was reflected in Delhi's approach to the Sri Lankan crisis of the mid-1980s under her son, Rajiv Gandhi, who succeeded her as Prime Minister.

In sum, this era dominated by Indira Gandhi was characterized by lip service to anti-imperialism, Third World solidarity, and non-alignment abroad, and secularism, democracy, and socialism at home. However, in both spheres, there was a marked drift in practice toward power politics, in spite of which Mrs. Gandhi remains a tremendously popular, indeed iconic, figure within her own country, remembered more fondly by many Indians than the historically more remote Nehru and Gandhi, who are more admired than loved.

1990s and onward: the birth of pragmatism

The year 1991 was a significant turning point in Indian politics, economic orientation, and foreign policy. It coincided with the collapse of the post-Second World War world order characterized by Cold War confrontation between West and East blocs, giving way to new configurations. The Gulf War that year witnessed the geostrategically significant and economically motivated invasion of one non-aligned country by another. In India, over four decades of socialist economic policy and poor fiscal management culminated in a severe balance of payments crisis. Serious political stress had resulted in three governments in quick succession at the centre between 1989 and 1991. The Mandal Commission in 1980 had brought to light the failures of the state in creating equitable development and unleashed powerful forces for social change. In 1989, the minority government of V. P. Singh sought to implement some of the commission's recommendations involving affirmative action for 'scheduled castes and tribes' and 'other backward classes', resulting in considerable political tension. Shortly thereafter, during the 1991 national election campaign, the Tamil rebels that India had shown sympathy for in Sri Lanka assassinated Rajiv Gandhi, the former prime minister who had sent Indian forces to the island state.

The beginning of the decade ushered in a new era of pragmatism for India, domestically and internationally. Most pretensions to idealized conceptions of India's society, polity, and role in the world were gradually discarded, although reaction against these changes remained lively.

The most remarkable feature of the new ordering of the domestic sphere was the growing pragmatism of political parties, which were compelled to engage in electoral alliances, more often ones of convenience than of ideological sympathy. Alliances were critical for the ascendent Bharatiya Janata Party (BJP), until then the political wing of a relatively marginal cabal of Hindu nationalist organizations, in expanding its geographical base beyond northern India. For the Congress, the days of its national dominance were a distant memory. Although as late as 1998, Sonia Gandhi publicly stated that the party would not form any alliances, by 2001 it had bowed to the exigencies of the new politics and joined with other parties in state-level alliances and sometimes governments in which it was not even a senior partner, for example in Tamil Nadu and in West Bengal.[12] In 2004, the Congress' victory in the national elections hinged entirely upon its ability to form coalitions with regional and identity-based parties. Although the Congress secured a more comfortable minority share of Union parliament seats in the 2009 election, it still fell far short of being able to form a government by itself, resorting again to coalition arrangements.

The change in outlook for political parties ran deeper than the expediency of alliances. At times it drew on conflicting interpretations of national identity. The BJP, in its successful bid at forming a national coalition government in 1998, chose to contest the election on a platform of development and governance, not its religious nationalist ideology of *Hindutva*, though many of its members remained committed to a Hindu nationalist ideology at variance with independent India's mostly secular past. Indeed the media repeatedly reported the growing rift between the *Sangh Parivar* institutions (the 'family of organizations' attached to *Hindutva*) and the BJP as a political entity. The Communist Party of India (Marxist), for decades a bitter opponent of Congress hegemony and policies, in 2004 chose to come out in support of the Congress-led coalition (albeit 'from the outside'), forming with it a loose alliance. Even identity-based parties learned to downplay at times their ideologies and local loyalties in the quest for political power, as was evinced repeatedly in the politics of Uttar Pradesh, where caste issues were manipulated in every conceivable way.

The ideological unmooring of the domestic sphere was reflected also in the international arena. Completing a process that had begun in the time of Indira and Rajiv Gandhi, India shed its non-aligned and anti-Western ideologies in favour of a pragmatic foreign policy. In stark contrast to the Nehruvian years during which India achieved considerable status in the international sphere with barely any achievements on the domestic front, chiefly by taking the moral high ground in foreign affairs, post-1990 India was no longer as convinced of its moral uniqueness and began to think of itself as a nation like several others in the quest of greater power. This favoured the normalization of traditionally antagonistic relationships with neighbouring countries, a greater commitment to international institutions that might legitimize its emerging power status, a positive approach to relations with the world's remaining superpower, and, importantly, greater focus on national defence, including in the nuclear sphere.

These shifts in India's foreign policy manifested themselves in various ways, including better relations with China; India's 'Look East' Policy (launched in 1992) aimed at improved relations with Asia and subsequent involvement with the Association of South East Asian Nations (1995 onwards); the nuclear tests at Pokhran (1998); India's relationship with Israel (after diplomatic relations were established in 1992) and simultaneously enhanced-energy diplomacy with West Asian countries; acquiescence in the US nuclear missile defence programme (2001); support for the US invasion of Afghanistan (2002); the Indo-US nuclear agreements of 2005 and 2008; and India's votes against Iran at the IAEA, all examined later in this volume. The relationship with Pakistan remains vexed, particularly since the potentially dangerous Kargil war of 1999 and with Pakistani stability faltering worryingly at times.

Thus, Indian foreign policy in the twenty-first century is characterized by a marked shift towards pragmatism and a willingness to do business with all, resembling in none of its important specifics that of Indira Gandhi in the mid-1970s, and even less that of her father in the 1950s and 1960s. This radical change paralleled the change in domestic Indian politics sketched above.

Contemporary security challenges

The manner in which India's international relations evolved assisted India in creating higher levels of economic growth and earning greater global influence. However, India still grapples with a number of important security and political challenges at home, in its region, and globally. On the domestic front, while the opening up of the political space to new social groups has deepened democracy in India, it has also led to severe political fragmentation and often creates obstacles to effective policymaking. India's region is fraught with security threats arising out of unstable, often weak states such as Pakistan, Sri Lanka, Nepal, Bangladesh, Myanmar, and Afghanistan, a near-neighbour in which India is much invested.[13] Further afield, India could serve as a pivot in a new triangle (much promoted by geostrategic commentators) involving the USA, China, and India. Beyond the sphere of enjoyable geostrategic speculation, India has in recent times benefited from cooperation with the USA, while it grapples with perennial potential security threats emanating from China. India's regional and global security concerns are reflected in its policies relevant to military modernization, maritime security, and nuclear policy. But domestic security concerns overwhelmingly predominate.

Domestic security challenges

The central aim of post-colonial India's national project has been the accommodation and management of the country's extreme heterogeneity. Diversity is the dominant characteristic of Indian society. Over the centuries, India has been home to innumerable ethnic groups, various cultures, and followers of all the major world religions. Due to Hinduism's assimilative tendencies, the broad cultural trend has been one of coalescence and accommodation, often manifested in religious syncretism. However, the Hindu practice of stratification by caste has played a major role in creating social cleavages in modern India that the state has been at pains to eliminate. The politicization of differences over how a prosperous, socially progressive democracy is to be achieved in modern India has produced or exacerbated a number of security challenges. Similarly, the political rise of Hindu nationalism, or *Hindutva*, since the 1990s has also raised questions about India's identity as a secular nation, at times producing inter-communal clashes, terrorist acts (and retaliations), and other forms of upheaval. While *Hindutva's* appeal today seems to be waning, circumstances could conspire to revive its success in years ahead with unpredictable consequences.

The heterogeneity of Indian society is to a great extent mirrored in the nature of its polity, which is deeply fragmented. After two decades of post-independence Congress-dominated government, in the years following Nehru's death, regional actors began to assert themselves against the excesses of the centre, and eventually mobilized in order to gain access to the resources and power of the state. Differences simmered through the 1970s and 1980s, ultimately boiling over and ushering in an era of coalition governments and political instability from the late 1980s onwards, including a tumultuous period when the nation endured seven successive coalition governments at the centre in the span of just ten years (1989–98). The 1990s also saw the rise of 'identity politics' in which identity, be it of caste, religion, or region, is equated with interest and so projected into the political sphere.[14]

The gradual shift to a more market-based economic policy (or, as Atul Kohli has argued, a pro-business approach) in the 1980s and the liberalization of India's economy precipitated by the balance of payments crisis of 1991 have resulted in high levels of economic growth in contemporary India, although poverty, particularly rural poverty, remains a major problem, with hundreds of millions of Indians adversely affected.[15] India's growth is driven primarily by the services sector (software and information technology in particular), though private-sector manufacturing has also revived significantly. Although a majority of the Indian population is engaged in agriculture, the sector does not enjoy significant growth and suffers from low productivity. Although poverty levels have fallen in the last two decades,[16] economic inequality is on the rise (as elsewhere in the world, including in communist China), but a confounding trend for socially conscious Indians.[17] The uneven nature of development has resulted in significant imbalances between social groups and regions, with potentially destabilizing future consequences.

POLITICAL FRAGMENTATION

The uneven distribution of gains from development is striking in India. These inequalities have provoked the political mobilization of hitherto excluded groups, sometimes through politically motivated violence and forceful struggle. This phenomenon has led to the fragmentation of the political space on the one hand, and changing socio-economic relations on the other. Many parties continue to rely on identity politics, which results in the deepening of social cleavages and the persistence of political fragmentation. The end result has been a multitude of political parties with influence at the centre and mostly two- or three-party arrangements in the states.[18]

Indeed the party system since the early 1990s has seen a proliferation of parties that appeal exclusively to caste, ethnic, or linguistic identities. Chief among them are the Bahujan Samaj Party (BSP) and Samajwadi Party (SP) in Uttar Pradesh, the Dravida Munnetra Kazhagam (DMK) and the All India Anna Dravida Munnetra Kazhagam (AIADMK) in Tamil Nadu, the Rashtriya Janata Dal (RJD) in Bihar, the Shiromani Akali Dal in Punjab, the Shiv Sena in Maharashtra, and the Trinamool Congress in West Bengal. In the 2004 general elections, state-based parties won 30 per cent of seats in the lower house of Parliament (Lok Sabha) with approximately 29 per cent of the vote;[19] up from 7 per cent of seats in the house, with 8 per cent of the vote, in 1951.[20]

The advent of coalition governments has arguably undermined the ability of the state to respond quickly and effectively to security threats. The ability of smaller regional parties to hold national governments hostage on key security issues is a new reality in Indian politics. In the 1980s, this was most evident in Tamil parties using their influence to sway policy on Sri Lanka. Caught between domestic pressure to assist Sri Lankan Tamils and a national imperative not to extend unconditional support to a movement for self-determination (lest it reflect unfavourably for India in Kashmir, and in some other states with secessionist movements), India launched a disastrous peacekeeping effort in the late 1980s that ended up exacerbating the conflict in Sri Lanka and souring India's relations with its neighbour. Similarly, Hindu nationalist parties have exacerbated tensions with Bangladesh over the large-scale illegal entry of Muslim economic migrants into India. Most recently in 2008, domestic political differences threatened to prevent India from capitalizing on the Indo-US nuclear agreement when Prime Minister Manmohan Singh's government was put to a crucial confidence vote in Parliament that it won with a narrow margin.[21]

DOMESTIC INSURGENCY

Uneven development between regions and social groups has created unrest and strife at times; political violence is nowhere starker than in the numerous insurgencies that have arisen on Indian soil in response to the severe neglect of certain regions and communities, and the state's response thereto. India's ethnically diverse northeast, composed of eight states—Arunachal Pradesh, Assam, Manipur, Meghalaya, Mizoram, Nagaland, Sikkim, and Tripura—is home to numerous insurgent groups that at different times emerged due to Delhi's neglect of that vital region.[22] Not only does the northeast collectively provide a sizeable share of India's agricultural output, it is also located strategically in a region surrounded by China, Bangladesh, Myanmar, and Nepal. Yet despite pouring large (though some would still argue insufficient) sums of money into the development of the region, the central government has been unable to focus its policies in a way that might integrate the region better into the Indian Union. A Ministry for the Development of the Northeast Region, established only in 2001, remains relatively sidelined when it comes to regional policy.

As a result, tensions between ethnic groups in the northeastern states and the central government have proliferated and endured, with state governments sometimes caught in the crossfire and at other times turning the politics of ethnicity to their own advantage against Delhi. Various communities in the northeastern region—all more ethnically distinct from the rest of the country than from each other—have been waging war against the Indian state for a number of years with demands ranging from greater autonomy in local decision-making to the formation of new states based on ethnic lines (with a degree of success) to outright separation from India.[23] In 2007 there were an estimated thirty armed insurgent groups operating in the region, including the United Liberation Front of Asom in Assam, the United National Liberation Front in Manipur, and two rival factions of the National Socialist Council of Nagaland in Nagaland.[24] Between 1992 and 2002, insurgency and other types of armed conflict led to 12,175 deaths in the region.[25] Insurgents bordering on Myanmar frequently seek refuge across the international frontier, a densely forested and poorly patrolled one, and resupply themselves with weaponry and munitions.

Delhi has been seeking Naypyidaw's support in cutting off this lifeline and sanctuary for the insurgents—apparently with limited practical success to date, even though Naypyidaw would doubtless like to be helpful. The northeast of India is, in any event, awash with light weapons flowing in from China (without any hint of government support) and from further international trafficking through Myanmar and Bangladesh.[26] As one might expect, there also appears to be some leakage of weaponry and ammunition from the Indian armed forces to insurgents.

More internationally familiar than the insurgencies in the northeast is India's ongoing insurgent problem in its most troubled corner: Kashmir. Its current phase in the Kashmir valley began in the late 1990s, when, in one widely held Indian view, Pakistan, coming to somewhat of a dead end in its attempts to wrest the territory from India through overt military confrontation, stepped up covert support for insurgent groups to inflict 'death by a thousand cuts'[27] by channelling the *mujahideen* trained to fight the Soviets in Afghanistan toward the cause in Kashmir. Originally spearheaded by the Jammu and Kashmir Liberation Front (JKLF), the insurgency in Kashmir has become a multi-pronged threat with new organizations such as the Hizb-ul Mujahideen, the Harkat-ul-Ansar, and the Lashkar-e-Taiba feeding considerable fighting capacity into the valley,[28] which experienced 26,226 fatalities at the height of the insurgency, between 1988 and 2000.[29]

In the aftermath of 9/11 and improving relations between the USA and India, Delhi was gradually able to induce Islamabad into admitting that terrorists were being trained in Pakistan and committing to curbing the cross-border infiltration of terrorists into India. However, progress has been painfully slow; although the incidence of fatalities is lower now than in the 1990s, Indian-occupied Kashmir remains in turmoil.[30] India's purchase on the valley is significantly weakened by the inability of its security forces—both military and police—to establish order without often egregious collateral damage in terms of civilian lives. Counter-insurgency operations have led to numerous civilian fatalities and—in some cases—extra-judicial killings, or 'fake encounters', as they have come to be known in the Indian media.[31] Local protests against the heavy-handedness of the security establishment often turn violent and are met with further brutality, highlighted by a number of incidents of security forces firing into crowds of demonstrators, most recently in mid-2010 when parts of the valley, including the state capital Srinagar, were placed under curfew as tensions rose among protestors, many encouraged by separatist organizations.[32] India's reflexive management of the very real security challenges in the valley have been profoundly unimaginative, essentially ineffective, and corrosive to the standards of its own security forces.

Perhaps India's most insidious insurgent problem, one that was often overlooked until the United Progressive Alliance (UPA) government came to power in 2004, is the Naxalite movement. Originally a student-led left-wing movement launched at Naxalbari in West Bengal in the late 1960s, today the 'movement' is composed of various insurgent groups acting under a loosely defined 'Maoist' ideology and 'Naxal' banner. The original aims of the movement—to bring about 'the physical annihilation of class enemies'[33]—have been superseded by a loose-knit set of grievances revolving primarily around land, unemployment, and socio-economic exclusion of *Dalits* (lower-caste communities) and *Adivasis* (indigenous tribal communities).[34] The cadres of the original Naxalite organization—the Communist Party of India (Marxist-Leninist)—were all but wiped out by police action in West Bengal, or gave up the cause by the early 1970s. Over the following years, however, splinter groups of the CPI(M-L) established themselves in a number of Indian states, especially Bihar (and later Jharkhand), Orissa, Andhra Pradesh, and Madhya Pradesh (and later Chattisgarh). After a lull in the 1980s and 1990s, the new millennium saw the resurgence of Naxalite activity in these states, with the number of annual deaths associated with the movement rising steadily to 721 in 2008 from 482 in 2002.[35]

In 2004, two major Naxalite groups—the People's War Group and the Maoist Communist Centre—merged to form the Communist Party of India (Maoist), and in the process stepped up their attacks on government property and personnel.[36] In 2006, then Home Minister Shivraj Patil declared the Naxalite movement 'an area of serious concern' that had claimed approximately 6,000 lives in the previous two decades.[37] In the second term of the UPA government from 2009 onward, despite the exhortations of Prime Minister Manmohan Singh and Home Minister P. C. Chidambaram, the Indian state and affected state governments have been unable to develop a coherent approach to the Naxal problem, oscillating between heavy-handed military tactics in reaction to specific incidents and approaches based on dialogue.

Perhaps the most intractable feature of the Naxal movement is that aside from being a law and order challenge, it also calls into question, in symbolic and practical terms, the way economic development is progressing in India. By offering a militant response to acute problems of underdevelopment and neglect, the Naxals expose the schizophrenic path of development in India, where the economy registers impressive growth figures while hundreds of millions of individuals continue to live in extreme poverty. Until the government is able to address the stark deprivation characterizing about a third of India's districts (many of them with significant tribal populations), it is not likely to diminish the allure of the Naxal movement among India's disadvantaged youth.

Regional security challenges

By some measures, six of India's neighbours ranked in the top twenty-five dysfunctional states in the world as calculated by the Failed States Index of the Fund for Peace.[38] India is uniquely positioned to be a driver of interstate cooperation in South Asia, which is a 'predominantly Indocentric region' because in terms of religion or culture, or both. 'India has something in common with [each of] its immediate neighbours but the neighbouring states of India do not share similarities of such magnitude or depth among themselves'.[39] Yet India is unable to bring about such cooperation, and despite the great strides it has made in economic growth over the last two decades, it remains mired in security dilemmas in its own region. As Vikram Sood suggests, 'Globally, India is being recognized as a rising economic power but not in the region where economic development has become hostage to security issues.'[40] Another scholar describes India's regional status as one of 'contested dominance', with India dominant because it lacks a convincing regional rival, but not enjoying supremacy because 'its dominance in the region is not accepted and acknowledged by its neighbours'.[41]

As a result, India faces two main regional challenges. The first is a set of what might otherwise be classified as domestic law-and-order problems were it not for the involvement of India's neighbours. Challenges of sub-national ethnic identity, secessionist movements and insurgencies, the creation of new ethnic communities due to migration, and religious conflicts within India fall under this heading. The second relates to bilateral disputes between India and its neighbours over resources, particularly land and water. Territorial disputes (prominently, Kashmir and Siachen with Pakistan, and Arunachal Pradesh and Aksai Chin with China), disputes over the division of water resources, which have become more frequent and more consequential over the decades since India's independence, and other security challenges emanating directly from India's neighbours, conform to this category.

SUB-NATIONAL ETHNIC MOVEMENTS

Indian populations in border regions tend to share common ethnic bonds with populations in adjacent countries. This is true of Tamils and Sri Lanka, Muslims in Kashmir, Punjabis, Indian populations bordering the Tarai region of Nepal, and even Malayalis and their ties to Gulf countries. By corollary, Hindu minorities in Bangladesh and Pakistan share affinities with co-religionists across the border in India. Trafficking of all sorts across mostly pretty open borders (Pakistan's being the exception) presents particular challenges in these circumstances.

The broad territorial division of ethnic groups within India and the strength of regional ethnic identities ensure that Indian policy towards the countries in question is often attentive to the preferences of domestic actors in these regions, as with Sri Lanka, where, at one time, the Indian government acquiesced in the brutal armed tactics of the Liberation Tigers of Tamil Eelam (LTTE).[42] Similarly, there is 'widespread sympathy' in Indian border regions for the Madhesi campaign for autonomy in the Tarai region of Nepal and 'most [Indian] politicians and bureaucrats do not hesitate to express moral support' for it.[43]

SECESSIONIST MOVEMENTS AND INSURGENCIES

Due to India's vast size and heterogeneous society and polity, conflicts have proliferated between sub-national regions and the central government. Scholars have attributed this to the failure of the Indian state to ensure equitable development for large swathes of society. This, they argue, has resulted in the discrediting of state-sponsored nationalism and, *inter alia*, the rise of movements aimed at establishing separate sovereign status from the Union.[44] The history of modern India is replete with such movements, many of which are still in progress.

Movements in border areas are particularly problematic because they become flashpoints with neighbouring countries, mainly for two reasons. First, secessionist movements, especially armed movements, are likely to use the territories of adjacent countries (e.g. Myanmar, Bhutan, Pakistan, Nepal, China, and Bangladesh) to stage their attacks on the Indian state, making it harder to neutralize the insurgents. Second, they allow neighbouring countries with an interest in destabilizing India to interfere in its internal affairs in an adverse manner. (This would apply, in the minds of most Indians, mainly to Pakistan.) These are the considerations that have influenced India's policy toward Pakistan in the case of the Khalistan and Kashmir secessionist movements.[45] But they are also relevant to Burma, Bhutan, China, and Bangladesh in the case of multiple movements in the northeast.[46] And, while somewhat different, they would also apply to Nepal in the case of the widespread Indian Naxalite movement (although not strictly a secessionist movement, but vigorously anti-state nonetheless).

The separatist assertion of regional identities on Indian strategic thinking has sharply accentuated the importance attached by Delhi to territorial integrity of the Indian Union since independence.[47] Indeed, this theme first arose during the early months of independence when Sardar Patel made every effort (including the use of force) to integrate the 536 Princely States of India into the Indian Union.[48] It was echoed in the military action taken by India to wrest control of Goa and Daman and Diu from the Portuguese in the early 1960s; in India's successful efforts to incorporate Sikkim into the Union in 1975; and, ultimately, in the lack of official support given to the LTTE, first and foremost seen as a secessionist movement. It is also reflected in India's long-standing policy of eschewing involvement by non-South Asian nations in its neighbourhood.

The concern with territorial unity runs deep in Indian foreign policy.

NEW ETHNIC GROUPS

The cross-border movement of large populations from neighbouring countries into India over extended periods of time results in the creation of new ethnic groups in the border (and other) regions of India, thus complicating Indian policy towards the originating countries. Two examples stand out—the migration of Tibetans escaping Chinese persecution, and the steady inflow of immigrants (legal and illegal) from Bangladesh into West Bengal and the northeastern region of India (many of them subsequently moving well beyond these regions). These developments have impacted on India's relations with China and Bangladesh respectively.

In the case of China, India has walked a tightrope between official recognition of Tibet as an integral part of China and granting asylum to the Dalai Lama and his followers on Indian territory. Tibetan migrants have integrated relatively well into Indian society, finding geographic and economic niches that do not conflict with local arrangements to a great extent. By contrast, the domestic response to Bangladeshi immigrants has been much less forgiving, possibly due to their purely economic motivation for migration. The reaction has been particularly violent in Assam, where riots against migrant Bengalis date back to the 1960s and 1970s. This has produced a negative impact on Indo-Bangladeshi relations, which are further complicated by a host of other bilateral issues. As a result, India in 1984 initiated construction of a 4,000 km concrete barrier along the Indo-Bangladeshi border, a project that carries on still and has created controversy between the two countries while proving broadly ineffective in stemming the migrant flow.[49]

RELIGIOUS CONFLICT

Religion and its associated customs and practices have a significant impact on social stratification and political mobilization in India. The religious composition of Indian society influences social and economic policy, particularly with regard to minority rights. The frequent occurrence of violence between religious groups—predominantly Hindus and Muslims—in various parts of the country creates major law and order problems as well as a security threat. The latter is evident in the recent radicalization of some sections of India's Muslim population within such groups as the Students' Islamic Movement of India (SIMI). Religiously inspired terrorism took on a new dimension with the arrest of Hindu activists following serial bomb attacks in the predominantly Muslim town of Malegaon in 2006.

The rise of political Hinduism, or *Hindutva*, may be the most significant religious factor influencing Indian politics. The concept pre-dates India's independence, but its salience has increased since then due to the ascent of the Bharatiya Janata Party (BJP) with its deep connections to radical Hindu organizations comprising the *Sangh Parivar*. The ideology of these groups is based on the ideal of Hindu nationalism and is inimical to Christianity and Islam, two religions that did not originate on the Indian subcontinent. Proponents of *Hindutva* initially thrived politically on controversy and benefited electorally, or appeared to, from several incidents of inter-communal violence, most notably the demolition of the Babri Mosque in 1992 and the Gujarat riots of 2002. The growth of Hindu nationalism has somewhat complicated India's relationships with Pakistan, Iran, and other Islamic nations at times. But its current lack of traction owes more to aging leadership and ideological fatigue than to worries over India's image abroad. In spite of some success in Karnataka, it has also been unsuccessful in capturing the imagination of south India.

BILATERAL ISSUES: PAKISTAN

Since independence, India has faced numerous bilateral disputes in its region. The most prominent among them have arisen from disagreements and frequent conflict with Pakistan. The last sixty years have witnessed two major wars (1965 and 1971) between the two countries and two major acts of aggression by Pakistan (1948 over Kashmir and 1999 in Kargil), in addition to numerous small-scale incidents across their borders. During the Cold War, Pakistan was the ally of choice for both the United States and China in South Asia, while India inclined towards friendship, and eventually alliance, with the Soviet Union. Pakistan received billions of dollars' worth of military aid and equipment over the years from its major patrons, much of which was employed in conflicts with India and to sponsor what India termed 'cross-border terrorism' in Indian-occupied Kashmir. Pakistan's abiding alliance with China since the 1950s, even more than Pakistan's erratic relationship of convenience with the USA, causes grave concern for India, especially due to China's transfer of nuclear weapons technology and missile systems to Pakistan.

The Indo-Pakistani rivalry, which had somewhat fallen into a manageable pattern from the mid-1970s to the early 1990s, intensified following India's (and then Pakistan's) nuclear weapon tests of 1998, the Kargil war of 1999, and a 2001 terrorist attack on the Indian parliament, the latter of which led to a tense military stand-off. Prime Minister Vajpayee and President Musharraf subsequently initiated a peace process that led to superficially improved relations between 2003 and 2007. However, internal events in Pakistan that precipitated the end of Musharaff's regime in 2008 created a leadership crisis and the process faltered. The deadly terrorist attacks in Mumbai in November 2008 created fresh challenges in Indo-Pakistani relations. However, the Indian government showed great restraint, initially supported by the BJP-led opposition in Parliament. International pressure eventually forced Pakistan to recognize Pakistani links to the attack, and after a long freeze in bilateral high-level contacts, they resumed in 2009 and intensified in 2010.

Prime Minister Singh was roundly criticized by many in the Indian media and defence and security establishment for his handling of the Mumbai attacks and his post-Mumbai overtures toward Pakistan.[50] However, influential commentators such as Siddharth Varadarajan of *The Hindu* and C. Raja Mohan of the *Indian Express* came out in favour of Singh's actions and the resumption of dialogue with Pakistan. Varadarajan suggested: 'Over time, India has realised the best way to deal with the threat of terror is by strengthening its internal capabilities while utilizing engagement as a lever for influencing Pakistan's behaviour over the long run.'[51] Mohan, while supporting Singh's overtures, worried about Pakistan as an interlocutor: 'Put simply, is Pakistan a country or a grievance? States negotiate with others on the basis of an enlightened self-interest and are open to give and take. But revanchists consumed by real and imagined grievances find it hard to split the difference in a negotiation.'[52]

Indian restraint in this instance was doubtless motivated more by prudence than benevolence, at a time when the USA was increasing its reliance on the Pakistani army to fight its war on terror in Afghanistan and Pakistan, and China was in the process of stepping up nuclear cooperation with Pakistan. Further terrorist attacks credibly linked to Pakistan could, however, force Delhi's hand on targeted retaliation, were Indian opinion to become inflamed.

BILATERAL ISSUES: CHINA

Increasingly, China is more worrying for India than is Pakistan, whatever the provocations launched against India from within the latter's territory. While India has experienced significant economic success over the past twenty years, China initiated its economic reforms well before India did, and has consistently outstripped India's impressive growth by 2–3 per cent each year since then. The result is that China's economy has expanded to roughly three times the size of India's in 2010—which has allowed China to invest significantly in its military sector.[53] Thus, while China and India are often grouped together as 'emerging' countries, China is well on the way to establishing itself as the principal competitor of the USA, while India, for all its recent economic achievements, lags well behind.

If China and India were on comfortable terms with each other, these developments would not need to worry Delhi, but the relationship has been a tense one since the mid-1950s, as explored in greater depth in Chapter 6. Sino-Indian antagonism reached its peak with their border war of 1962, in which India suffered a humiliating defeat at the hands of the People's Liberation Army. The Sino-Indian border dispute remains unresolved and continues to be a thorn in the side of bilateral relations. The alliance between China and Pakistan rankles in India, not least because of continuing Sino-Pakistani cooperation in the realm of nuclear weapons and missile technology.

Tibet overhangs the bilateral relationship. After a tense decade in Lhasa following China's takeover of Tibet in 1950, India gave asylum to the fleeing Dalai Lama in 1959, and the Tibetan refugee population in India has steadily grown since then. Tibet is a hot-button issue for China, at least as worried about territorial integrity as is India, and the Chinese leadership keenly watches the Dalai Lama's activities in India. (Beijing's worries about a seemingly powerless Dalai Lama living in India may not be as irrational as they seem, based on history. In 1910, the thirteenth Dalai Lama, the immediate predecessor of the current incumbent, fled a Chinese Qing dynasty invasion of Tibet, establishing residence in India. Three years later, he triumphantly reclaimed his throne and authority in Tibet, the Qing regime having collapsed in the meanwhile.)

Globally, India and China, while cooperating in a variety of multilateral processes ranging from trade negotiations to discussions on climate change, are increasingly competitors in a global race for wealth, energy, and influence as emerging (or, in China's case, now emerged) powers. Be it in factor and product markets in Africa, or the oil and gas fields of Central Asia, India and China are increasingly rubbing up against each other. To complicate matters, both nations espouse parallel nationalistic mythologies of civilizational great-ness that breed a sense of entitlement to great power status. When these mythologies collide, as they sometimes do on the border issue, it takes careful management and painstaking diplomacy to calm nationalist sentiment in their respective polities.

Indian analysts fear a Chinese strategy of encirclement in Asia. This refers to China's numerous investments in building up port facilities in the Indian Ocean, such as at Bandar Abbas in Iran, Gwadar in Pakistan, Chittagong in Bangladesh, and Hambantota in Sri Lanka.[54] China's booming exports indus-try and hunger for international markets have also led it to develop substantial trading relationships with India's neighbours, especially Pakistan and Bangla-desh. China's rise in India's neighbourhood presents a sensitive challenge to Indian foreign policy, seen by some as deriving from the following calculus: 'Restricting India to the Asian subcontinent remains Chinese policy. The tactics are simple: keep borders with India tranquil but do not solve the [border] dispute, trade with India but arm Pakistan and wean away Nepal, Bangladesh, and Myanmar.'[55]

BILATERAL ISSUES: SRI LANKA, BANGLADESH, NEPAL

India's relationships with other nations in its region are far from settled. India's hegemonic status—or at least perceived aspiration to it—creates threat perceptions among its smaller neighbours. They see India's military (and other) interventions in the neighbouring countries in 'terms of the outward projection and demonstration of military might'.[56]

In the case of the Sri Lankan conflict, India's justifications for military intervention were based on the security imperatives associated with the influx of Tamil refugees, the risk of disrupting commerce in the vital Palk Straits, and the danger of external great powers involving themselves in the conflict, but India's military (formally peacekeeping) action proved counterproductive, alienating the Tamil community, the LTTE, and the Sri Lankan government. Similarly, India's action in 1971 in East Pakistan to relieve West Pakistan's military oppression, while justified in humanitarian terms and on the basis of massive refugee flows to India, was widely viewed as primarily an attempt to dismember an arch-rival. Moreover, contrary to India's expectations, its assistance to Bangladesh did not win it an ally in the region: Bangladesh long provided safe haven for leaders of the United Liberation Front of Asom (ULFA), which operates in India's northeastern region.

While some in India saw the hand of Maoists in Nepal behind the early success of its own thriving multiple Maoist insurgencies, this is today far-fetched. However high-handed India's past approach to Nepal has been, and however hostile Maoists in Nepal may have been towards India, the Naxalite movement in India is home-grown and driven by local factors. It has developed today into the country's foremost internal security challenge.[57]

BILATERAL ISSUES: AFGHANISTAN

Aside from smaller nations such as Bhutan and the Maldives, perhaps the one country in the region where India's involvement has not played against it—to the Pakistani establishment's distress—is Afghanistan. Indians tend to see Delhi's policy as altruistic, in the words of a recent editorial: 'Delhi's partnership with Kabul has thrived because Delhi has neither geographic access to Afghanistan nor a political agenda of its own. What India wants is a moderate and stable Afghanistan that is in harmony with its neighbours.'[58] This assessment glosses over a simple calculus in Delhi's policy toward Afghanistan—to prevent Kabul from tilting excessively towards Pakistan, and allowing itself to be subsumed by Islamabad into its security space. Delhi worries that when the US-led NATO forces begin to pull out, as several NATO members have signalled they wish to do soon, Kabul could submit to the combined influence of Pakistan (supported by China) and the Taliban, leaving India as the loser in a geostrategic tug-of-war. These worries as of mid-2010 are not ill-founded: desperate for an exit strategy of its own, Washington appears to be encouraging a 'negotiated' solution to the conflict that could only strengthen Pakistan's hand locally. India consistently cultivated Prime Minister Hamid Karzai as an ally, but recently is rumoured to have opened up channels of its own with the Taliban, despite maintaining that there is no distinction between 'good' and 'bad' Taliban.[59] A Western withdrawal from Afghanistan would leave numerous Indian assets highly vulnerable; even under present circumstances the Indian embassy was attacked twice in fifteen months in 2008–9.[60] Delhi's remaining option, were that scenario to unfold, of seeking (perhaps with Moscow) to revive the Afghani Northern Alliance, would doubtless prove a disappointing and expensive consolation prize.

Global security challenges

There is a category of security challenges facing India that originate and play out in the international arena, but often overlap with regional issues and actors. These include international terrorism, nuclear proliferation, and India's relations with the USA.

INTERNATIONAL TERRORISM

India has long been a victim of what it calls 'cross-border terrorism' in its territory committed by groups that India alleges to be based in and sponsored by the Pakistani military and intelligence establishment. Most prominent among these groups is the Lashkar-e-Taiba (LeT), which has either claimed responsibility or has been held responsible by the Indian government for numerous incidents including: attacks on civilians and military personnel in Indian-occupied Kashmir, bomb attacks in various Indian cities, and a few high-profile incidents targeting the Red Fort in Delhi, the Indian Parliament, and the 2008 Mumbai attacks. Although Al-Qaeda has not been directly involved in attacks in India, the LeT has established links with the international terrorist network and India is now considered a potential target for further attacks following the incidents in Mumbai.[61] India also worries about links between domestic terrorist groups such as SIMI and like-minded elements in Bangladesh, Nepal, and Pakistan.

India's domestic response to terrorism has been less than satisfactory. Excluding left-wing extremist groups, terrorist activity in India claimed the lives of over 18,000 civilians, 6,700 security personnel, and almost 23,000 terrorists between 1994 and 2005.[62] The 2008 Mumbai attacks were the most visible in a long line of incidents that reveal the overall inability of the Indian state to control its borders, collect and process relevant intelligence and develop security protocols to pre-empt terrorist attacks, and in many cases to react convincingly to terrorist attacks when they occur. Indeed, Indians were furious over the inept security response to the 2008 events in Mumbai, forcing the resignation of the Home Minister and over time a number of shifts in Delhi's machinery of government. Although India has initiated cooperation with other countries on counterterrorism strategies and intelligence sharing, progress has been limited. A stark case in point was that of Pakistani American David Headley, who was instrumental in planning the Mumbai attacks. Until April 2010, Delhi had been unable to convince Washington—a strategic partner—to let Indian officials interrogate Headley, let alone extradite him to India.[63] Quite simply, other powers have little confidence in Delhi's security and intelligence apparatus, a perception Delhi could work harder at addressing. Alas, the Mumbai attack is unlikely to be the last.

INDIA–USA RELATIONS

The tangle over David Headley raises an important global issue for India: its relations with the world's sole superpower, the USA.

For most of the period between India's independence and the end of the Cold War—with the brief exception of the 1962 Sino-Indian war—India and the USA remained at loggerheads over matters of principle and national interest. Like China, but less reliably, the USA used Pakistan as a military ally in the Cold War, especially during the Soviet occupation of Afghanistan in the 1980s. America's 'hyphenated' South Asia policy, which essentially viewed the India–Pakistan relationship as a zero sum game and often came down in Pakistan's favour, was a major problem for India over many decades.[64]

The 1990s were a period of gradual rapprochement between the USA and India through increased trade and private sector ties, encouraged by a growing India lobby in the US Congress. India's nuclear tests of 1998, while sharply criticized and met with sanctions by the USA, were overlooked when the Clinton administration preferred to view India as a growing market for US companies and a potentially helpful player in South Asia soon after Pakistani adventurism at Kargil in 1999 induced a regional rethink in Washington. The upward trend in India–USA relations continued through the fallout of 11 September 2001, which brought Pakistan back into sharp focus in the American view of South Asia. Since then, the USA has provided Pakistan with more than $15 billion in economic and military aid as incentive and resources for fighting its war against the Taliban and Al-Qaeda in Afghanistan and parts of Pakistan.[65] However, this has not significantly hampered India–USA relations.[66] Despite some initial missteps by the Obama administration on the Kashmir issue, the USA–India relationship has progressed on a relatively even keel, though relations are clearly not as warm as they were under George W. Bush, who sought to make radically improved USA–India relations one of his chief foreign policy legacies—indeed it is probably his only significant one.

One of the key motivations of the Bush administration's courting of India with various incentives, especially the game-changing deal on nuclear cooperation, was that it was likely to bolster India as a reliable democratic counterweight to authoritarian China's growing influence in Asia and the world. The USA has supported India's inclusion in restricted elite decision-making groups in various international forums on multilateral trade, climate change, and management of the international economy following the global financial crisis of 2008. India's much improved relationship with Washington has not gone unnoticed by Beijing, and, mostly, Sino-Indian relations began improving noticeably in the new millennium. However, India's relevance to Washington may have diminished somewhat in the wake of the 2008–9 global financial crisis, during which the USA adopted a more conciliatory approach toward China, while prodding it to allow the Renminbi to float up to a more realistic level. Indian commentators have observed with some alarm renewed cooperation between China and the USA in tackling the global economic crisis, as well as increased interdependence of Chinese creditors holding large amounts of US Treasury Bills and the US debtors providing the single largest market for Chinese manufactured goods. This has prompted some Indians to question the logic of picking a side in the unpredictable Sino-US relationship:

> Our strategic gurus were whistling in the dark when they dreamt up India's future as a 'balancer' in the Asian power dynamic. The... government's willingness to be drawn into a 'quadrilateral alliance' against China, it now seems, was an embarrassing goof-up, unprecedented in its naivety.[67]

Another Indian writer has observed less caustically: 'the Bush-Rice doctrine of containing China is being replaced by the Obama-Clinton doctrine of co-opting China to deal with the economic crisis'.[68] The best strategy for India would appear to be an interests-based balancing act between the USA and China. India has much to offer both, actively and passively, even if the USA and China, in the medium term, jointly take on the task of managing the international system.

NUCLEAR PROLIFERATION

While the Bush administration saw and justified the USA–India nuclear deal as a way to draw a troublesome and self-interested conscientious objector into the non-proliferation regime through the back door by imposing various safeguards and monitoring mechanisms on its civilian facilities, Indian leaders viewed it as a vindication of India's clean record on non-proliferation and self-imposed moratorium on nuclear testing after May 1998. Ultimately, the US Congress, the International Atomic Energy Agency (IAEA), and the Nuclear Suppliers Group (NSG, formed after India's first nuclear test in 1974 to ensure that such incidents would not occur again) all voted in favour of amending existing rules to allow India to step out of three decades of nuclear *purdah* in 2008. Having separated its military and civilian facilities and put the latter under IAEA safeguards, India can now access global supply chains of nuclear fuel and technology for civilian purposes (while maintaining an indigenous nuclear weapons programme of its own).

Although India has reason to celebrate the USA-backed global recognition of its status as a responsible nuclear weapons power, it also has reason to worry about nuclear proliferation, particularly in relation to China and Pakistan. China is a known proliferator of nuclear weapons technology to Pakistan,[69] and Pakistan a known proliferator to North Korea, Iran, and Libya. More recently, following the USA–India nuclear deal, China was expected to notify the NSG, which it joined in 2004, of a similar deal between itself and Pakistan for the transfer of civilian nuclear technology. And India can hardly complain about exceptional treatment being provided by a major nuclear power to a non-NPT member. In the context of US–Pakistani nuclear cooperation, Prime Minister Singh was quoted in April 2010 admitting, 'Who am I to interfere with what goes on between the United States and Pakistan?'[70] However, any move that bolsters Pakistan's nuclear weapons capacity worries India as this simply encourages some in Pakistan to pursue a 'sub-conventional war that Delhi is yet to find effective ways to cope with'.[71] In all-out war, which would be damaging to both, India, given its weight and assets, would prevail. But in any conflict less total, relative strength matters in deterring escalation, and India knows this well.

The Bush administration's most important achievement in USA–India relations had a useful kicker—to shake up the international non-proliferation regime. The Obama Administration has picked up the challenge, notably with respect to credible enforcement of the Nuclear Non-Proliferation Treaty (NPT) and promotion of the Comprehensive Test Ban Treaty (CTBT), which the USA has yet to ratify. However, coping as it has had to do throughout 2009 and 2010 with serial financial, economic, and other crises, it is too early yet to predict whether anything meaningful will come of its enthusiasm for reform and strengthening of the global non-proliferation system.

Addressing India's security challenges

Given the evolution of its domestic politics and foreign policy over the past sixty-odd years, what lessons can be drawn on India's ability to manage effectively key domestic and international security challenges? Sumit Ganguly relates the important challenge of 'developing a long-term strategic vision, one that is not subject to the vagaries of regime changes, minor, adverse developments in the country's immediate neighbourhood and periodic crisis' to the development of 'institutional mechanisms...and planning capabilities' he sees as deficient:

[India] has, for the most part, been unable to develop a professional cadre of personnel who are knowledgeable about questions of defence budgeting, acquisitions, capabilities and policymaking. The absence of such a body of skilled personnel has ill-served Indian defence policymaking, and has rendered many decisions subject to political whims and financial constraints.[72]

Institutional resources

As outlined earlier in this volume, the Indian official institutions for foreign policy formulation broadly encompass the Cabinet, the Prime Minister's Office (PMO), the Ministry of External Affairs (MEA), the Indian Foreign Service (IFS), the Ministry of Defence (MoD), the Indian Parliament, and various manifestations of the defence and intelligence establishment (the armed forces, the Defence Research and Development Organization, the nuclear establishment, the Research and Analysis Wing, the Intelligence Bureau etc.). While the defence of India's territorial sovereignty is viewed as paramount by virtually all of these, the defence establishment has historically played a selective role in wider foreign policymaking (except at times of military crisis), instead understandably choosing to focus on immediate threats from within India's neighbourhood. The broader conduct of diplomacy that spans the gamut of interstate relations (and more recently, a range of instruments underpinning India's 'soft' power) has traditionally been the domain of the PMO and MEA, which are accountable to Parliament. With domestic political life ever more fractured and fractious, Parliament's focus on strategic issues has declined over the years, with little attention being devoted to debating the larger goals of Indian diplomacy (a notable exception being the topic of India–USA relations since 2005).

Aside from the traditional concerns of inter-ministerial and intra-ministerial coordination, two main issues stand out with regard to the contemporary foreign policy establishment: the principal–agent problem and institutional capacity.

PRINCIPAL–AGENT PROBLEM
The first pertains to a disjuncture that sometimes exists between the policy-making centres in Delhi and the policy implementers on the international stage. Indian officials, when in international forums, occasionally are observed to pursue outcomes or adopt positions that are contrary to the objectives of Indian foreign policy set at the political level.[73] This was an acute problem soon after the end of the Cold War, when the Indian foreign policy bureaucracy found it hard to shed its ideological baggage and traditional diplomatic attachments and to accept the changed circumstances of the international order. Most desired continuation and rejuvenation rather than a fundamental shift in their historically close relationships with Russia.[74] In contemporary times, it has been exemplified by unseemly turf battles between high-ranking members of the foreign policy establishment whose bureaucratic politics at home at times impact their behaviour abroad.[75]

Likewise, the defence establishment in India writ large (senior civilian and military retirees more than active service personnel) promote a number of their own policy preferences and flog their *bêtes noires* in the media with great skill and tenacity. This is notably the case with China, which they continue to see as the principal threat to India (not least given its friendly ties with Pakistan). The run-up to the visit of Chinese President Hu Jintao to India in November 2006 was marked by near-hysterical attacks from these quarters and their political allies in the media against Beijing's trustworthiness as a neighbour, eventually spilling over into an unattractive debate in Parliament. Unsurprisingly, the visit proved only a moderate success.

INSTITUTIONAL CAPACITY

The second issue is that of bureaucratic capacity. At a time when a degree of specialization is highly prized in the administration of foreign affairs in many capitals, some analysts believe that an abundance of talented generalists are spread (all too thinly) across the spectrum of Indian diplomacy.[76] Indeed, the shortage of Indian government trade negotiators is such that in recent years Delhi has increasingly and sensibly resorted to private sector lawyers and sectoral experts to buttress the bureaucratic cadre. Inevitably, the limited number and capacity of personnel, combined with a plethora of international and multilateral demands and commitments, results in 'the best [having] unbelievable demands placed upon them', yielding an overworked, under-paid, and under-appreciated bureaucracy.[77]

A challenge of a different order arises from the questionable performance of both India's internal intelligence apparatus (mainly, the Intelligence Bureau) and the once-fabled external intelligence operatives of the Research and Analysis Wing (RAW), whose leadership increasingly became an embarrass-ment in the years 2007–8. The failure of Indian intelligence to anticipate a number of murderous terrorist attacks within India, notably in Mumbai in November 2008, or apprehend most of those responsible over the years, speaks not just to weak, under-motivated, and under-equipped police forces but also to dubious intelligence capabilities.

The reputation of India's Armed Forces has fared better, not least because of their controlled response to a number of potentially very dangerous crises (e.g. Kargil), the professionalism of their contributions to UN peacekeeping, and the care they take with training. India's navy has been a great asset in building Indian military ties with partners around the world. That said, even the Armed Forces, never keen on police duties, have not always performed gently, wisely, or effectively in domestic theatres of conflict such as Kashmir and Assam.

Often, confusion relating to organizational roles and jurisdictions between leading institutions (the PMO, the National Security Council, the MEA, and the MoD) exacerbates the challenges of decision-making faced by the foreign policy establishment. These were critically highlighted in its handling of the Kargil crisis with Pakistan.[78] Over time, the disproportionate concentration of authority within a small PMO relative to other actors, a reflection of wider international trends, in India's case may be problematic as Delhi juggles more diplomatic and security-related balls than do all but a very few capitals.[79] That said, the creation of a National Security Adviser providing forward impetus and in a position to arbitrate differences between other foreign policy actors has doubtless been helpful and is indispensable as India emerges as a relevant player on the geostrategic stage.

Nevertheless, bureaucratic factors as well as political distractions are largely responsible for a sense among Indian authors (and some others) that the country lacks effective coordination at the international level. The same factors have also produced a foreign policy that some view as reactive and bereft of strategic vision, highlighted in charges of 'ad hocism' and 'drift'.[80]

Strategic vision

Indian foreign policy following the Cold War has been pragmatic, but it has also been devoid of the kind of strategic vision required for India to achieve great power status.[81] As political fragmentation has progressed in the domestic sphere, foreign policymaking has suffered from the cacophony of voices espousing contrasting ideas of India's place in the world, sometimes at the most senior levels.

A trace of this was evident in the Indian response to the Soviet invasion of Afghanistan in 1979. The Janata government reacted with strong disapproval of Moscow's actions in the United Nations. A month later, Indira Gandhi regained power and, more committed to India's relationship with the USSR, substantially toned down the Indian stand in the UN.[82] Similarly, Rajiv Gandhi's approach to regional cooperation led him to pledge an Indian peacekeeper force (the IPKF) to oversee the devolution of power to the local Tamil government as part of the Indo-Sri Lankan Agreement of 1987. Subsequently, the V. P. Singh government in 1989 ordered the immediate withdrawal of the IPKF from Sri Lanka. This resulted in a power vacuum as India withdrew prematurely, leaving the LTTE rebels to fill the political space vacated by the Indian forces.[83]

India's biggest reversal, however, occurred during the second Gulf crisis of 1990–91. India (under V. P. Singh as Prime Minister and I. K. Gujral as Foreign Minister) initially took a strong stance in the UN in September 1990 counter to the USA's position against Iraq and to the UN's related decision-making. By November, the Singh government had been replaced by another minority coalition, led by Chandra Shekhar. The new government immediately condemned Iraq for its actions and, in a highly controversial decision, allowed American and Australian airplanes to refuel on Indian territory en route to the Gulf.[84]

Arguably, as a result of the incoherence that characterizes a fragmented political system expressing itself in foreign policy (a familiar feature of foreign policy in several Western democracies), Indian foreign policy has become largely reactive in nature. It is criticized at home and abroad for lacking vision and a unified strategy for India's role in the world.[85] But while some Indians argue that the country needs a strategic vision on which to project its power, there is no prospect of wide internal agreement on what such a vision should embody.

THE RISE OF ECONOMIC DIPLOMACY

In the absence of a unifying strategic vision, and with India's economic performance improving significantly each recent decade, economic diplomacy provides the path of least resistance for coalition governments struggling to pull their members along on foreign policy decisions. Difficult strategic decisions, when couched in the language of economic growth and prosperity, are made more palatable to the power elite and a growing Indian middle class reaping the benefits of economic liberalization. This was evident from the USA–India nuclear deal—a hot-button political issue in India— which was sold far less as a strategic alignment with the USA than a quest for energy security that would benefit the Indian economy and the masses.

Political parties of all stripes agree, albeit for different reasons, that economic growth is a good thing for India (although rising inequality is flayed by parties of the left as a national scandal). From a foreign policy perspective, economic prosperity (the 'tide that lifts all boats')[86] is now seen as the key to India's attainment of great power status, and it is the driving argument behind India's current worldview. No longer willing to lead the poor nations of the Third World in a struggle against imperialism, and no longer wishing to project its power merely within the conflicted confines of its own neighbourhood, India is pressing its suit on the world stage. This is evident, not least within the World Trade Organization, in the company of other rising powers such as Brazil, South Africa, and sometimes China.

Indeed trade and bilateral economic cooperation have become the cornerstones of India's relations with the world, even with China, today India's largest trading partner. India no longer discriminates significantly between Russia, America, Israel, Iran, and the ASEAN countries (although restrictions on Chinese investment remain significant, driven by security considerations). It is willing to do business with all. Both moralizing and power politics on the international stage are now viewed as potentially bad for business, whereas economic linkages are seen to promote stability. Thus India is currently engaged in promoting economic development in Africa, securing oil fields in Central Asia, promoting trade and nuclear cooperation with the USA, receiving remittances from its 3.5 million workers in the Gulf and acting as Israel's biggest arms market at times.[87]

This is not to say that ideology and power politics are no longer important. India still accords priority to security issues and retains its nuclear weapons option. However, at the NAM summit in Havana, 2006, Prime Minister Singh's speech focused on anti-terrorism, 'inclusive globalization', nuclear disarmament, energy security, and investing in Africa: issues that are vital to India's global agenda but not necessarily top priorities for developing countries worldwide.[88] On balance, modern India prefers to articulate and prioritize its own national interests over the collective interests of developing countries. In other words, 'the long-sustained image of India as a leader of the oppressed and marginalized nations has disappeared on account of its new-found role in the emerging global order', rather the same metamorphosis China underwent some years earlier.[89]

Conclusion

India's security challenges are mostly structural in nature: Pakistan's griev-ance, the China threat, the US partnership, and other challenges are likely to remain largely beyond India's exclusive control. It is thought that those challenges that are within reach, such as the economic exclusion of certain regions or ethnic groups, can be addressed through better allocation of the gains from economic growth. Prime Minister Singh's repeated words of con-cern about the strength, resiliency, and extent of the Naxalite insurgency seem to have made only a limited impression on public opinion, while the problematic performance of India's internal security forces, particularly the undertrained and poorly led Central Reserve Police Force (CRPF), is both deplored and taken somewhat for granted with a degree of resignation, in spite of the appointment, post-Mumbai 2008, of an energetic Home Minister, P. Chidambaram.

Economic diplomacy does not only provide a way for India to harness global opportunities for the benefit of domestic constituents in the hope of ameliorating poverty (which is how elections are won in India) and alleviating discontentment. It also acts as a pathway to great power status.

Expanding economic relations can also provide a channel of cooperation with potential competitors or rivals, as India has done in securing oil fields in Central Asia with China.[90] By pursuing economic relationships with major powers, some Indians believe the country can progressively build up its own institutional capacity to develop and execute a grander strategy internation-ally and better tend to its burning internal security challenges. However, as the following chapter argues, economic growth alone will not solve all of India's problems. While continuing to remain a useful international calling card, it will not alone secure much greater power status, which will remain a priority for India's security establishment, unhappy with the predominance of eco-nomic themes in the discourse of the Union government.

4

India's Economy: Its Global Calling Card

As outlined in the two chapters immediately before this one, many observers of India now describe the country as an emerging great power with game-changing capabilities. However, such assessments of the country's potential are recent and follow on the launch of India's economic reforms in 1991. These reforms gave impetus to sharp economic growth through liberalization of government policies and the revitalization of the Indian private sector.[1] While India still faces a number of significant challenges, this tectonic shift from slower to high growth rates is important not just for India but also for the developing world, for global institutions, and for great power relationships. This chapter focuses on the impact of India's economy on Indian foreign policy since the country's independence in 1947. The first half deals with India's economic development, and is divided into three periods (broadly parallel to distinct periods in India's political life): desperate times in the wake of the Raj: the search for an autonomous economic policy (1947–66); autocracy and socialism: a toxic mix (1966–90); reforms, globalization, and growing global interdependence (1990 onwards).

Not coincidentally, the three periods coincide with three different phases in the principal drivers and ideology (to the extent there has been one) under-pinning Indian foreign policy. The first phase, one of Nehruvian idealism mostly tempered by prudence and a sense of India's economic fragility, was marked by efforts to keep the superpower conflict and the toxic effects of the Cold War at bay through India's leadership of the Non-Aligned Movement (along with partners such as Indonesia and Egypt). The second, even more than the first, was marked by domestic economic fragility and growing tensions with the West, giving rise to a hard-nosed realism expressed by a large degree of alignment towards Moscow (while the nostrums of non-alignment were still at hand for presentational purposes). Finally, since 1990, the main driver of Indian foreign policy can be seen as support for India's successful break-out from economic stagnation. This largely economic agenda embarrasses those Indians who believe that an emerging power should endow itself with grander aspirations, and a more interesting foreign policy framework. But, for now, most Indians seem content with it.[2]

The second half of the chapter examines how evolving economic patterns and relationships have affected India's foreign policy and its ties with major partners. It addresses the impact of economic factors on India's foreign policy through a variety of prisms, for example, country- and region-specific, and also through cross-cutting factors such as development assistance.

Finally, the chapter concludes that a transition has taken place in Indian foreign policy from the primacy of politics and geostrategic considerations to a new emphasis on economic interests and ties, although economic factors always influenced Indian leaders in their foreign policy choices from Nehru onwards.

Desperate times in the wake of the Raj: the search for an autonomous economic policy (1947–66)

In the pre-colonization period of the early 1700s, India's economy likely accounted for nearly one-quarter of the world's economic output.[3] In the mid-eighteenth century, Britain's East India Company—a formerly trade-oriented colonial entity—reinvented itself from a trading firm into a ruling hierarchy exercising effective sovereignty, buttressed by a significant military capacity. While India's commodities fed the industrial revolution in the United Kingdom, this led to the stagnation of its own economy, which served as a significant market for Britain's manufactured goods. British colonial policy in India deliberately stifled trade with the rest of the world, arrogating to Britain all useful Indian exports. Indeed, the relative weight of India in the world economy plummeted during the two centuries of British colonial domination and the effective economic growth rate of the country was, on average, zero. In brief, the economic benefits of Indian colonization to Britain were very significant, while the Indians themselves bore the costs thereof.

At the chaotic conclusion of colonial rule in 1947, India inherited an economy that was one of the poorest in the world per capita, totally stagnant, with industrial development stalled and agricultural production unable to feed a rapidly growing population.[4] Its economy was a shadow of what it had been before the colonial adventure. The early years of independence were marked by widespread hunger and the threat of famine.[5] At independence, about 60 per cent of India's GDP came from agricultural activities that were mainly dependent on monsoon rains with no significant irrigation systems in place.[6] Although some industry existed in the country at that time, it was designed to serve the interests of the British Empire rather than of India itself—jute mills in and around Calcutta; cotton textiles in and around Bombay; tea plantations;

and railways were well developed. The catastrophic partition of 1947 caused widespread disruption to the economy, for example in relation to industrial raw materials produced in Pakistan whose related factories were located in India. As well, the infrastructural framework for economic activity by way of road, railway, and sea routes was fractured in the country's north.

Jawaharlal Nehru, in a speech at the Constituent Assembly on 4 December 1947, stated his interpretation of the relationship between foreign policy and economic policy:

> But talking about foreign policies, the House must remember that these are not just empty struggles on a chess board. Behind them lie all manner of things. Ultimately, *foreign policy is the outcome of economic policy, and until India has properly evolved her economic policy, her foreign policy will be rather vague, rather inchoate, and will be groping* [emphasis added].[7]

Soon after independence, Prime Minister Nehru and other Indian Congress leaders, faced with this plight, introduced a modified Indian version of state planning and control over the economy.[8] These leaders believed a dominant role of the state would be vital in ensuring rapid industrial and agricultural growth.[9] Simultaneously, in reaction to the British colonial plunder of India, Nehru and his colleagues adopted a strategy of import-substituting industrialization, which completely discouraged foreign investment.

The process of rebuilding the economy started in earnest in 1952 with the first five-year plan for the development of the Indian economy guiding government investment in industries and agriculture. The Industrial Policy Resolutions of 1948 and 1956 gave government a monopoly in armaments, atomic energy, and railroads, and exclusive rights to develop minerals, the iron and steel industries, aircraft manufacturing, shipbuilding, and manufacturing of telephone and telegraph equipment. By the late 1950s, regulatory and licensing structures encouraged private investment into priority areas and discouraged or banned it in others.[10] India's second five-year plan, starting in 1956, adopted a new strategy focused on developing heavy industries. This model was supported by a variety of controls, involving both tariffs and quantitative restrictions.[11]

In the 1950s and 1960s, foreign aid played an important role in India's development process and the need for it influenced foreign policy to an extent. During this period, Nehru sought financial and technical help from nearly all industrialized countries in addition to borrowing from the World Bank for long-term infrastructure development.[12] Much of the assistance was used to import food and other necessary items crucial to India's survival as a fragile and potentially fractious new country.[13] This aid was vital to India at the time.[14] Further, '[t]here is some evidence that during the 1960s, aid helped to increase investment in India'.[15]

Nehru's economic policy has been much criticized in the West. But it may be helpful to see it as a product of its times and of India's unhappy economic history under the British Empire. Moreover, Nehru and his contemporaries were startlingly successful in one respect: while great poverty and hunger continued to stalk India, it never again suffered a famine occasioning mass casualties such as the British had allowed to occur repeatedly when in control of the subcontinent, notably in West Bengal and in India's south during the final decades of their rule.

Autocracy and socialism—a toxic mix (1966–90)

By the mid-1960s India was experiencing discouragement with slow economic progress and suffering from external developments, notably the 1962 border war with China and the 1965 war with Pakistan. In part due to India's economic policies and in part for reasons relating to the Pakistan war—a tremendously expensive one—in 1965, foreign aid from the USA, which had hitherto been a key factor in preventing devaluation of the rupee, was cut off for a year. India was pressured by the USA and other international actors (including the IMF and World Bank) to liberalize its restrictions on trade (its trade deficits having reached unmanageable proportions over some years).[16]

In addition, India's war with Pakistan in 1965 had led to worrying levels of deficit spending (around 24 per cent of total expenditure) and accelerating inflation.[17] Indians mostly interpreted these moves, and their timing, as further evidence that the West favoured Pakistan over India. The response by the Indian government was the unpopular step of devaluation accompanied by some liberalization (a reduction of export subsidization and import tariffs). The devaluation forced on India in 1966 was much needed, but ill timed. It was forced as a condition of the resumption of US aid, against the wishes of the Indian Finance Minister, and it was the subject of major pressure and tensions between the donors and the Government of India. The aid package, designed to support both devaluation and further trade liberalization measures, collapsed after one year when the USA pulled out. Such a degree of leverage over macroeconomic policy was only achieved in conditions of acute economic difficulty for India, and at a cost of chronic disruption to both aid and Indian economic management.

In the medium term, India's response was to diversify its sources of political and economic support. The donors who sought to promote internal changes by strong leverage in fact failed to secure these changes and, in the process, lost the capacity to influence future Indian policy.[18] According to economist T. N. Srinivasan, 'devaluation was seen as capitulation to external pressure which made liberalization politically suspect'.[19] In light of the backlash, Delhi soon reversed most of the liberalization measures.

In spite of early successes with agriculture, food shortages during the 1960s created a sense of insecurity within the country, which was also somewhat unsettled by changes in political leadership (Indira Gandhi became the Prime Minister in 1966 after a brief interlude of Lal Bahadur Shastri as Nehru's successor as of 1964). In these circumstances, the country was particularly sensitive to the threat of foreign 'blackmail'.[20] Indira Gandhi threw her full support behind efforts to overcome the chronic food shortages through experimentation with hybrid grain seeds that could vastly expand production in the country's north (particularly in the Punjab).[21] The ensuing 'Green Revolution', one of the great successes of Indian and global agricultural development, engineered by Indian and some foreign experts, with significant assistance from foreign donors including the Ford and Rockefeller Foundations, extended from roughly 1967 until 1978 and transformed India from a food-deficient country to one of the world's leading agricultural producers (see Box 1).[22]

Box 1 THE GREEN REVOLUTION

India's impressive Green Revolution was brought about under tremendous pressure: disastrous government finances, drought, and Western pressure to tend more effectively to agriculture. As of 1966, Mrs. Gandhi understood that further humiliation at the hands of the West, and specifically of Washington, could only be avoided if India moved beyond the need for short-term food aid. She thus decreed that India must so organize its affairs as to be able to feed itself and provided single-minded and effective support to Indian and foreign researchers (notably, M. S. Swaminathan in India) working to develop high-yield hybrid grain varieties and new approaches both to irrigation and to fertilizers that could achieve this end.

In fact, the input requirements of the Green Revolution also served India well in the short run: areas hosting high-yield crops needed more water, more fertilizer, more pesticides, fungicides, and certain other chemicals. This spurred the growth of some sectors of India's industry. The increase in irrigation created the need for new dams to harness monsoon water. In turn, the water stored was used to create hydroelectric power, available to boost industrial production, create jobs, and improve the quality of life in rural regions. India was able to pay back the multilateral loans it had taken from the World Bank and its affiliates to support the Green Revolution, and this improved India's credibility in the eyes of lending agencies. Meanwhile, talented and energetic farmers from Punjab—rendered redundant by more efficient production methods and by the limit to subdivision of family plots—migrated to the West (notably Canada) and sent significant remittances back to India.

The environmental costs of the Green Revolution, notably those exacted by excessive use of water and chemical fertilizers that eroded the soil and sometimes contaminated ground water supplies, were not well understood for many years. Only early in the new millennium, with agricultural productivity growth stalling and the demand for food rising inexorably as India's population expanded and achieved greater prosperity, did the limitations of earlier policy become clear to all.

In spite of dramatic progress on the agricultural front, external events continued at times to undermine India's development trajectory. The huge cost of the 1971 war with Pakistan had barely registered when the oil price shock of 1973 also contributed to a drop in industrial output. Perforce, Mrs. Gandhi now started to move away from some of the policies adopted by her predecessors. Even though during her early years in power the public sector continued to grow, she later sought to revive the private sector (with only modest success). Populist programmes and policies were now replaced by greater pragmatism. But not all of her new policies were successful. For example her emphasis on growth with equity was supported by policies that did not do enough for either. Consequently, while poverty levels declined between the mid-1960s and the mid-1980s, much of the population continued to struggle for mere survival. Over these decades, the informal economy grew at a faster rate than in the past, and planned economic development was relegated to a secondary position.[23]

Among her notable economic policy planks, beyond support for the Green Revolution, Mrs. Gandhi pursued a vigorous policy of land reform in 1969; placed a ceiling on personal income, private property, and corporate profits; and gave high priority to the promotion of savings. Most large commercial banks were nationalized in 1969. In 1970, the Monopolies and Restrictive Practices Act was introduced. Conspicuous consumption by the rich was discouraged or simply banned through licensing requirements, and princely privileges were abolished.[24] During her tenure, India came to possess a large and diverse skilled scientific and technological sector, building on Nehru's far-sighted commitment to champion indigenous Indian scientific capacity.[25] During these years, India became the world's fifth military power, the sixth overt member of the global nuclear weapons club, the seventh engaged in the race for space, and the tenth industrial power.[26] Nevertheless, the eradication of poverty eluded her grasp and the private sector failed to revive significantly.

After 1984, Mrs. Gandhi's son and successor as Prime Minister, Rajiv Gandhi, attempted greater liberalization of the economy. The government removed price controls and reduced corporate taxes. India once again welcomed foreign businesses and investment inflows in some sectors, and gave priority to modernization of the economy through computerization and telecommunications. It also worked hard to improve relations with western governments. In the seventh plan (1985–89), greater emphasis was placed on the allocation of resources to energy and social spending (at the expense of industry and agriculture).

From 1980 to 1989, the rate of growth of the economy improved to 5.5 per cent annually (or 3.3 per cent on a per capita basis). Industry grew at an annual rate of 6.6 per cent and agriculture at 3.6 per cent. A high rate of investment (up to 25 per cent from about 19 per cent of GDP in the early

1970s) contributed to this significantly improved level of economic growth. But fiscal and current account deficits also increased dangerously. Moreover, most investment was devoted to large, long-gestating, capital-intensive projects, such as electric power, irrigation, and infrastructure, that were marred by delayed completions and cost overruns. Corruption became a major public issue, including the Bofors weapons procurement scandal that tainted Rajiv Gandhi himself. With state resources and private savings tapped out, by the mid-1980s India came to rely increasingly on borrowing from foreign sources. During this time, the central government fiscal deficit increased rapidly, to 8.5 per cent of GDP at its peak in 1986–7.[27]

These macroeconomic imbalances, and a gradual depletion of reserves, threatened the sustainability of growth rates and made the economy particularly vulnerable to shocks.[28] International developments were not favourable: the collapse of the Soviet Union, India's major trading partner, and the first Gulf War in 1991, which cut the level of remittances from Indians working abroad, contributed to a major balance-of-payments crisis for India. A precipitous drop in India's reserve position created a growing perception that it might default on its international obligations. High inflation in 1991 plagued the Indian population.[29]

Reforms, globalization, and growing interdependence (1990 onwards)

After a few unstable coalition governments, a Congress-led coalition under Prime Minister Narasimha Rao faced a serious financial crisis that required drastic measures. The gross fiscal deficit of the government rose from 9.0 per cent of GDP in 1980–1 to 12.7 per cent in 1990–1. The GDP growth rate declined from 6.9 per cent in 1989, to 4.9 per cent in 1990 and to 1.1 per cent in 1991. For the Union government in Delhi alone (leaving aside State-level deficits), the gross fiscal deficit rose from 6.1 per cent of GDP in 1980–1 to 8.4 per cent in 1990–1. As a result, the internal debt of the government accumulated rapidly, rising from 35 per cent of GDP at the end of 1980–1 to 53 per cent of GDP at the end of 1990–1.[30] In March 1991, a financial crisis developed as India's hard currency reserves fell to $2.1 billion—less than the value of six weeks of imports—with $1.5 billion in payments to multilateral financial institutions due at the end of March.[31]

In June 1991, the government launched a series of far-reaching reforms focused on freeing up the investment and trade regime; reforming the financial system; modernizing the tax system; and divesting public enterprises. Over ten years, these reforms, in a controlled way, gradually expanded to other areas—such as agriculture, pensions, insurance, capital markets, and infrastructure—and came to include full-blown privatization. Thus they pro-foundly, if perhaps not sufficiently, transformed the nature of India's econ-omy. The reforms did away with import licensing on all but a handful of intermediate inputs and capital goods items. The new Government an-nounced a floating exchange rate regime in March 1992 that eventually served India well.[32] This proved particularly true during the global financial and economic crisis of 2008–10, when a falling rupee absorbed much of the shock. As a result of the reforms, and accelerating growth, the hitherto limited Indian middle class expanded to somewhere between 50 and 350 million people (depending on the measurements involved).[33]

Less than three years after the reforms were introduced, foreign direct investment (FDI) started pouring in from American companies such as Pepsi Cola, Coca-Cola, General Motors, General Electric, International Business Machines, and McDonald's (several of which had been forced out of India in earlier decades) and from similar companies in Great Britain, Japan, France, and Germany. Mutual funds, investment banks, securities firms, and commer-cial banks increasingly invested in Indian securities. Indian companies raised funds in the world capital markets and began merging with each other as well as with foreign competitors.

In 1998–9, India faced a challenging international economic situation aris-ing from the financial crisis that hit East and Southeast Asia in 1997. As an international slowdown spread, investors shied away from the emerging mar-ket economies, including India and China. But, due to India's limited external sector and large domestic market, as well as prudent management by the Reserve Bank of India (RBI), the direct impact of the slowdown on India was limited. Nevertheless, anxiety arose over India's capacity to sustain its recent export expansion, FDI (and financial inflows), technology transfers, and, more broadly, nascent international confidence in the Indian economy. As India started to gain economic strength, the orientation of India's merchandise trade started to change. On the export side, the major shift was away from Russia and Japan—both troubled economies—towards developing countries in Asia (including, increasingly, China) and the USA.[34] Trade with Western Europe also grew considerably.

Liberalization of trade in services, so important to India during an era of Western 'outsourcing', started during this period. In public sector banks, up to 74 per cent of FDI was permitted—in theory. In reality, the RBI heavily policed where foreign banks were allowed to invest, preferring to channel foreign funds into unprofitable ventures the RBI hoped the international investors could turn around—and they often did. In telecommunications, up to 74 per cent FDI was permitted for many services. Foreign equity was encouraged in software and almost all areas of electronics. In the information technology

---

Box 2 INDIA'S COMPANIES GO GLOBAL: ADITYA BIRLA GROUP[1]

Today, Indian firms are spreading their wings internationally, across many sectors, acquiring foreign rivals and often creating very large groups, of which the takeover of the steel giant Arcelor in 2006 by the Mittal corporation, which created the world's largest steel company, is perhaps the best example. According to the data released by the RBI, the total outward investment from India, excluding that made by individuals and banks, rose 29.6 per cent to US$17.4 billion in 2007–8, largely due to acquisitions. Some of the major acquisitions by Indian companies abroad include Novelis (by Hindalco), Corus (by Tata Steel), Repower (by Suzlon), and Infocrossing (by Wipro).[2]

The Aditya Birla Group was India's first truly multinational corporation. Its origins can be traced back to the nineteenth century, when Seth Shiv Narayan Birla started trading in cotton in the town of Pilani, Rajasthan. In the early part of the twentieth century, the group's founding father, Ghanshyamdas Birla, expanded the group and set up industries in critical sectors such as textiles and fibre, aluminium, cement, and chemicals. In 1969, Aditya Birla, then Chairman, put the group on the global map. He set up nineteen companies outside India, in Thailand, Malaysia, Indonesia, the Philippines, and Egypt. The impetus for international expansion derived from the Indian government's un-favourable regime for Indian private sector companies at the time. Overall, Birla's international ventures prospered remarkably and provided a blueprint for the group's further expansion within India when conditions there for private corporate entities started to improve in the 1980s. Under Aditya Birla's leadership, the group became the world's largest producer of viscose staple fibre, the largest refiner of palm oil, the third largest producer of insulators, and the sixth largest producer of carbon black. After Aditya's demise in 1995, at the age of 52, his son Kumar Mangalam Birla took over.

Today, the Group has an annual turnover of US$24 billion, market capitalization of US $23 billion, over 100,000 employees belonging to over twenty-five different nationalities on its rolls, and a presence in twenty countries. The group has diversified business interests and is a dominant player in all the sectors in which it operates, such as viscose staple fibre, metals, cement, viscose filament yarn, branded apparel, carbon black, chemicals, fertilisers, insulators, financial services, telecom, BPO, and IT services.

[1] See also Joe Leahy and John Reed, 'Troublesome Trophy', *Financial Times*, 31 July 2009 (on Tata's purchase of Jaguar Land Rover).
[2] See 'Indian Investments Abroad', India Brand Equity Foundation, www.ibef.org/economy/indianinvest-mentsabroad.aspx

---

sector, 100 per cent foreign investment was permitted in units set up exclusively for exports.

India's share of world exports, which had declined from 2 per cent at independence to 0.5 per cent in the mid-1980s, bounced back to 0.8 per cent in 2002 and stood at 1.21 per cent in 2010.[35] From 1998 to 2008, the ratio of total goods and services trade to GDP rose from 17.2 per cent to 30.6 per cent. In February 2009, Kamal Nath, then India's Minister of Commerce and Industry, predicted that along with other BRIC and Gulf Cooperation Council economies, India would contribute about 35 to 37 per cent of incremental global GDP growth during the years through 2012.[36]

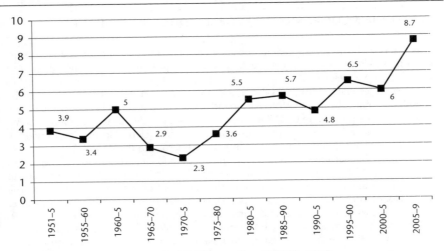

Figure 4.1. India's average annual GDP growth rate 1951–2009

Note: These averages were calculated using the data on annual growth rates at factor cost and at constant prices (at base year 1999–2000).
Source: Reserve Bank of India, *Handbook of Statistics on Economy, 2008–9*.

More broadly, India's reforms led to a meaningful shift in the growth rate of GDP after 1993, which rose at unprecedented rates of 6 to 7 per cent, averaged 8.6 per cent between 2003 and 2007, and peaked at 9 per cent 2007 (see Figure 4.1). Unlike growth in the 1980s, which was fuelled by excessive borrowing at home and abroad, this new growth was largely driven by domestic consumption and continuing high levels of savings and investment.

Gross Domestic Investment (GDI) rates rose from 24.3 per cent of GDP in 2000–1 to 33.8 per cent in 2005–6 and domestic savings from 23.7 per cent in 2000–1 to 32.4 per cent during 2005–6. Over this period, the fiscal management of the country improved, with the combined fiscal deficit of the Union and States declining from 9.5 per cent of GDP in 2000–1 to 6.4 per cent in 2006–7. However, combined public debt as a proportion of GDP remained high at over 70 per cent.[37] Internationally, India came to be ranked the fourth largest economy in terms of purchasing power parity, and at current growth rates could well overtake Japan as the third most significant economic power within ten years.[38] The growth of India's middle class was seen by economists as particularly hopeful (although advocates for the poor rightly point out that the government's social policies too often failed).[39]

Until the global financial and economic crisis of 2008 demonstrated that the notion of 'de-coupling' between major economies had been somewhat of a delusion, there seemed no limit to the ambition (and sometimes overreach) of the Indian private sector as reflected in coverage by India's 'pink' (financial) press, which came to embody the excesses of the 'India Shining' enthusiasms of the early twenty-first century.[40] India's ability to ride out the 2008–9 global economic downturn while racking up growth rates of 6 per cent demonstrated how resilient its domestic market and robust its savings had become, in sharp contrast to Western economies.[41] That said, rising inflation and a deteriorating current account position as of mid-2010 required active management by the government and the RBI.[42]

The face of Indian business changed dramatically. Indian firms were no longer merely seekers of foreign technology, producers of indifferent goods, or providers of low-end services. Their engagement with the world acquired new dimensions. India became the leading nation in software services—Tata Consultancy Services (TCS), Infosys, and Wipro became acknowledged world brands, and Indian companies, as well as Indian professionals, were constantly seeking to move up the value chain.[43] Several Indian oil companies are today part of the Fortune 500 list of top companies worldwide.[44]

Recently, India's more wide-ranging engagement with the rest of the world is also striking: outward FDI by Indian firms, and the rise of Indian multinationals; India's prominence as a platform for R&D with global applications; the cultural influence of books, music, and movies produced in India; and the role of Indian nationals in global corporations, particularly in the fields of science, technology, and finance are now taken for granted—unlike twenty years ago. These four aspects of globalized India extend well beyond the traditional notions of trade and capital flows. Moreover, during the last six or seven years, more than 150 major companies from the USA and Europe have set up larger research, design, and development centres in India. They include big names such as Boeing, Daimler Chrysler, DuPont, General Electric, General Motors, Intel, IBM, Microsoft, Siemens, and Unilever.

India also enjoys, almost uniquely, what many Indians think of as a tremendous demographic advantage as the only very large economy wherein the size of working population is expected to grow over the next twenty years (in sharp contrast with China).[45] However, whether this phenomenon turns into a demographic boon or a demographic bomb will depend very largely on whether India can radically improve public education at every level. Large numbers of unskilled or poorly educated Indians are unlikely to benefit the wider economy greatly in years ahead and could contribute to social instability.[46]

Mostly unnoticed by the rest of the world, in a field where India's geostrategic and economic interests coincide, successive Indian governments have been startlingly effective at developing a credible space programme with the capacity for multiple satellite launches from a single rocket, missile and missile delivery systems, and also, in 2008, the successful launch of a lunar probe, *Chandrayaan 1*. The Indian Space Research Organization (ISRO) in 2009 operated the world's second largest fleet of remote sensing satellites after the USA.[47]

As the balance of economic and geostrategic influence (even power) shifts towards Asia, Indians have increasingly engaged with the idea of a world dominated by Indian and Chinese economic success.[48] But, while Western economic policy mistakes are undeniable, and the USA's geostrategic over-reach following the events of 11 September 2001 are all too easy to document, uncertainties and fragilities abound in the outlook for both the Chinese and Indian economies.[49] For example, Angel Gurria, Secretary-General of the OECD, recalling the 'lost decade' of Latin American economic performance in the 1980s, argues that India needs to reduce both Union and state-level deficits and the national debt in order to protect the impressive 'growth dividend' from its economic reforms.[50] Twenty years ago, nobody forecast the stagnation of Japan in the 1990s, and its continuing relative loss of clout ever since. Thus, while Asian economic successes, including that of South Korea and some of the ASEAN countries, have been tremendously impressive, the crystal ball for global economic handicapping in years beyond the immediate future remains cloudy.

Economic imperatives guiding Indian foreign policy

Economic considerations played a pivotal role in shaping the nation's foreign policy. As emphasized by Nehru when he first articulated his vision of Indian foreign policy in a speech to the Constituent Assembly in December 1947: 'It is well for us to say that we stand for peace and freedom and yet that does not convey much to anybody, except a pious hope . . . What then do we stand for? Well, you have to develop this argument in the economic field.'[51] He added, idealistically, that India's foreign policy was shaped by its commitment to the development of all developing economies. He had in mind the pursuit of an independent foreign policy that would maximize its overall freedom of manoeuvre. He understood that India's role in the world was likely to be achieved less by traditional balance of power politics or through strategic alliances and more by the rapid enhancement of its internal economic capabilities. The primary task of independent India's foreign policy, therefore, in the short run, was to assist in the transformation of India's society and economy in a way that would strengthen the cohesion and viability of the nation. This would help to develop strategic autonomy of choice, and thus, in the longer run, smooth the path of its emergence as a more meaningful global actor.

India's Aid imperative

The urgent need for resources and technology in the early stages of its economic development was a principal factor influencing the direction of Indian foreign policy. Nehru's emphasis was on industrialization, particularly the manufacturing of heavy machinery required to support India's steel, power, fertilizer, and chemical industries.[52] In pursuit of the necessary financial and technical assistance to advance these plans, Indian diplomacy worked hard to cultivate both Moscow and Washington (and, through Washington, the international financial institutions headquartered there).[53] The policy of non-alignment that emerged during the 1950s facilitated the achievement of this objective, allowing Delhi to cultivate cordial relations with the two contending Cold War bloc leaders.[54]

But Nehru may have underestimated the extent to which his asymmetrical interpretation of the concept of non-alignment irritated several capitals in the West. He, in fact, forged much closer relations with Soviet Union, based on what he perceived as a broad convergence of interests. A strategic relationship with India fit well into the Soviet worldview focused on thwarting the geopolitical pretensions of both the USA and China, particularly in wider South Asia.[55]

The Soviet Union was the only major power to support India in developing independent capabilities in heavy industry and cutting-edge technologies. Formal cooperation between the two countries began in 1960 when they agreed on a programme of military cooperation, and by 1965 the Soviet Union was the second largest bilateral contributor to India's development, culminating in the 1971 bilateral treaty. Soviet power and capacities provided India with substantial economic, political, military, and diplomatic support during much of the Cold War.[56] This key bilateral relationship contributed to India's emergence as a significant industrial power.

Soviet aid was extended on the basis of long-term, government-to-government programmes, which provided for generations of technical training for Indians; the supply of raw materials; the integration, where possible, of Indian components and other inputs; and also markets for finished products. These bilateral arrangements were made in non-convertible national currencies, helping to conserve India's scarce foreign exchange. Thus, Indians generally regarded the Soviet contribution to Indian economic development as positive (although private-sector-oriented Indians were alive to the pitfalls of a close economic and political relationship with the USSR). By the late 1970s, the Soviet Union was India's largest trading partner.

Ties with Washington were increasingly strained by Delhi's growing de facto alignment with Moscow. Washington contributed significantly, particularly through food aid (the PL 480 programme), to the development of the Indian economy. By 1964, India depended heavily on aid from the USA.[57] Americans had been much taken by Nehru's flair during his first official visit to the USA in 1949 and continued to entertain a fascination for India. The Kennedy Administration sent John Kenneth Galbraith as US Ambassador to India in 1961, and his arrival in Delhi was soon followed by a highly mediagenic visit by Jackie Kennedy. The positive dimensions of the relationship were critical in sustaining India psychologically at the time of the China–India border war of 1962.

However, the disappointing results of the Indian development model (generating only very limited exports), the huge costs of war with Pakistan in 1965, and a disastrous monsoon together contributed to foreign exchange exhaustion and encouraged the USA to adopt a 'short-tether' policy of doling out food stocks sufficient only to meet requirements a few months at a time, and of explicitly tying the continuation of food aid to the adoption by India of policies aimed at increasing agricultural production and curbing population growth. (Washington adopted similar policies towards Pakistan at the time.) As a result, India devalued its currency in June 1966, despite major dissension in Cabinet and in the Congress Party. Washington resumed its aid programmes ten days later.[58] Washington's 'tough love' approach to India was clearly dictated, at least in part, by irritation with Delhi's criticism of the US role in the Vietnam War, but India's ineffective economic policies also played a central role—and this is often not fully appreciated in India.

India's own foreign aid programme today

Economic diplomacy has been a significant means of achieving broader foreign policy objectives in India. India's foreign aid programme, the Indian Technical and Economic Cooperation programme (ITEC), was established in 1964. ITEC notionally covers 156 countries, together with the Special Commonwealth African Assistance Programme (SCAAP), both managed and run by the Economic Division of the Ministry of External Affairs (MEA). The Technical Cooperation programme, with its emphasis on capacity building, transfer of technology, and sharing of the Indian developmental experience, has become an important element of India's interaction with countries in the developing world. Further, the Investment and Technology Promotion (ITP) Division in the MEA aims to project the image of India as an established economic power with attractive potential for investment and business. A new Energy Security Unit was established in the Ministry in September 2007 to support India's international engagement through diplomatic interventions. The Unit supports the efforts of Indian private and state corporations, in acquiring energy assets overseas, in the transfer of new and emerging technologies to India, and in building strategic partnerships with foreign companies.[59] The MEA also oversees the Indian Council of Cultural

Table 4.1. Principal destinations of India's Aid & Loan Programme (excluding lines of credit)

Aid to countries (in Rupees Crore)	2007–8	2008–9	2009–10
Bhutan	731.00	1205.92	1301.98
Bangladesh	60.00	6.00	3.76
Nepal	100.00	113.00	150.00
Sri Lanka	28.00	30.00	80.00
Maldives	19.50	504.70	3.50
Myanmar	20.00	35.00	55.00
Afghanistan	434.00	418.50	287.00
African Countries	50.00	95.00	125.00
Central Asia	20.00	18.82	–
Latin American Countries	1.53	2.00	2.00
Others	240.08	215.75	205.55

Source: Government of India, Ministry of External Affairs, Annual Report 2007–8, 158; Annual Report 2008–9, 185; Annual Report 2009–10, 199.

Relations, which provides assistance and programmes to improve cultural ties, for instance through student and teacher exchange programmes.

India has been providing substantial military and economic assistance within South Asia since independence with aid to Bhutan alone constituting 42.9 per cent of India's total aid and loan budget (see Table 4.1). Outside India's immediate neighbourhood, Africa is the largest beneficiary of India's foreign aid and related commercial ventures. India has provided credit lines worth $200 million for the New Economic Partnership for Africa's Development (NEPAD), $500 million to the Techno-Economic Approach for Africa-India Movement (TEAM-9) group of countries in West Africa, as well as bilateral lines of credit to Sudan and some other African countries. India has also made lines of credit available to regional banks in Africa.[60]

India's economic growth rates since the 1990s and its own international aid programme call into question its continued need for international assistance beyond multilateral lending (although on this front, India can gain international commercial credit on very favourable terms in light of its economic performance).[61] A decade ago, the issue was a lively one under the National Democratic Alliance (NDA) coalition government, which sought termination of the smaller foreign assistance programmes to India (portrayed as more trouble than they were worth). While the UPA coalition that followed in 2004 reversed the decision, foreign assistance programmes in India are fast winding down.[62]

The 'Hindu rate of growth' and the effects of change elsewhere in Asia

Because the rate of economic growth in independent India was modest in early years, some scholars have been tempted to cast scorn on Nehru's interventionist economic policies, focused on self-sufficiency in food and on industrial development. However, thanks to activist social policy underpinning public health and education programmes, in just forty years following independence, infant mortality was halved, life expectancy nearly doubled, and adult literacy almost tripled.

Even so, four decades of state-directed economic planning under Nehru and his immediate successors brought about decisively slower growth than in many other Asian countries. Compared with East Asia, India fared badly. Its share in world output and exports fell, and social indicators lagged far behind those of others.[63] India's self-imposed isolation from the global trading order, consonant with its strategy of import-substituting industrialization discouraging foreign investment, accrued serious costs. At the same time, the 'license raj' empowered much, and corrupted some, of the public sector while alienating the private sector. Meanwhile, in broad terms, India stagnated and the value of the rupee relative to the US dollar declined by 40 per cent.

During much of the 1980s, when Southeast Asia and even China raced ahead through their steady integration into the global economy, India remained an economic laggard, its rate of growth barely exceeding 3.5 per cent annually—the 'Hindu rate of growth', to borrow the Indian economist Raj Krishna's evocative phrase. Thus, while India's leaders sought to address economic inequalities on a global scale, the outcomes of their domestic economic policies proved increasingly disappointing relative to those elsewhere in Asia.

At times, India's international stance stood in direct contradiction to its interests. For example, India vocally supported the efforts of the Organization of Petroleum Exporting Countries (OPEC) in the early 1970s to extract concessions from the industrialized north by dramatically raising the price of oil, but the price rises compounded India's acute energy needs. Thus, ideology at the time trumped a pragmatic approach to alleviating India's economic plight.

Gradually, with pragmatism creeping into its foreign policy, India was able to play a more assertive and positive role internationally, perhaps encouraged by the success of the 1971 war with Pakistan that fractured its rival and gave birth to Bangladesh. Its bilateral diplomacy became more vigorous and creative, and India increasingly participated in Asian regional discussions, while redoubling its participation in UN peacekeeping. Its strengthening military and its technological successes (not least its controversial nuclear test of 1974) imbued it with greater self-confidence.

But it was internal economic mismanagement rather than foreign policy considerations that forced its hand in introducing significant economic reforms as of 1991, yielding much enhanced economic growth, which provided India with the credibility and room for manoeuvre necessary to play a more central role on the international stage.[64] The simultaneous collapse of the Berlin Wall and of the Soviet bloc also forced a rebalancing of India's positioning at the global level that turned out to be advantageous. India bade farewell to many of the more noxious aspects of socialism without fanfare or much regret, while maintaining at least a strong rhetorical commitment to a large role for the state in combating poverty and regulating the economy.[65] India's excessive external debt of the late 1980s and the balance of payments crisis of 1991 triggered corrective action that put it on a path from which it could hope to compete with China for economic leadership of the continent.[66] Indeed, China's economic rise perhaps proved a more powerful spur to reform impulses within the Indian government than was apparent at the time.

Today, in spite of the still modest share of the external sector within India's economy, both its absolute weight and the emphasis placed on economic factors in its foreign relations suggest that it may be worth reviewing how this shift has altered India's place on the global stage.

Economic ties and their corollaries with major international partners

United States

As outlined above, India's traditional relationship with the USA was marked by considerable development assistance dependency combined with frequent friction over regional and geostrategic issues. With India's economic reforms, its growing success, the decreasing 'pull' of its relationship with Moscow, and a sense in the USA that it needed to cultivate new friends, the relationship, as of the mid-1990s, entered a new phase. On the one hand, the vast potential of India's growing market became clear to American business interests and to the US government. On the other, India's growing openness, vibrant democracy, and increasing international credibility commended it as a more important partner for the USA at a time when Washington's ventures in Iraq after 2003 and Afghanistan after 2001 were generating distress and when American standing internationally was seriously undermined by the excesses of the 'war against terror'.

It is in light of all of these factors that US–Indian negotiations to resume nuclear cooperation (first under President Clinton, then, successfully, under President Bush) may best be understood. For India, the negotiations held out the prospect of breaking India's nuclear isolation and eliminating its 'pariah' status in this field, as well as offering prospects for improved energy supply. For the United States, the stakes also were geostrategic, but perhaps even more so, economic and commercial.

Meanwhile, the US corporate sector connected with India not only through its own market, but also by accessing for its global purposes India's

---

Box 3 BOEING CORPORATION'S INDIA STORY

The signal improvement in USA–India official relations since 1991, as well as the reorientation of the Indian economy away from state control to private-sector-led expansion is vividly illustrated by the Boeing Corporation's India story, and it in turn suggests how inflected US policy can be by commercial opportunities for its private sector.

From the earliest days of the indigenous Indian commercial airline business, Boeing, through its forerunner, de Havilland, was associated with the country. J. R. D. Tata in 1932, having founded Tata Airlines (in 1946 translated into Air India), flew a de Havilland 'Puss Moth' from Karachi to Ahmedabad. In 1960, Air India took delivery of several Boeing 707 jet airliners, over the years expanding its Boeing fleet, eventually to include a number of 747s.

The next major phase in Boeing's relationship with India, constrained by the often touchy relations between the USA and India, including sanctions following the 1974 and 1998 nuclear tests, developed from the emergence as of 1993 of India's private airlines, notably Jet and Kingfisher, which rapidly purchased aircrafts from both Boeing and Airbus in large quantities. This, in turn, for competitive reasons, forced the Indian government to shore up failing Air India and its sister company Indian Airlines (mainly flying domestic routes) by providing the financing for them to renew their fleets. Boeing again benefited royally.

Thomas R. Pickering, who served as US Ambassador to India in 1992–3, recalls USA–India commercial relations in the aircraft sphere to have been limited by a number of factors, both political and economic.[1] For military hardware, India could still rely on barter arrangements with the Soviet Union (although these would soon be shifted to a 'cash and carry' basis by the Russian Federation). President Reagan had allowed some engine sales to India, but the subsequent commercial potential of the Indian market was as yet unanticipated by the USA.

Pickering in January 2001 moved to Boeing as a Senior Vice-President. From the outset he saw Russia, China, and India as critical to Boeing's international prospects—not just as potential competitors but also as clients. Boeing had already sought out commercial partnerships with Indian information technology companies, and would, by late in the decade, set up a major maintenance and repair operation of its own in India. At first, the potential of India was a hard sell at Boeing corporate headquarters, but over time it developed into one of Boeing's largest non-Western markets.

Coinciding with the uptick in Indian commercial aircraft purchases as of 2000, the Indian government sought to renew the fleet of both the Indian Air Force and of the Indian Navy's air arm. Soon, India was in the market for 126 fighter aircrafts, to replace its MIG fleet, and Boeing, together with Indian partners, had placed a bid on what is likely to prove the single largest such contract for some time outside the USA. Meanwhile, as of 2009, it had an order book in India of 100 aircrafts valued at $17 billion and was expanding its footprint in the IT sector and eying space cooperation with India.[2]

---

[1] Interview with Thomas Pickering, 19 June 2009 and correspondence 30 June 2009.
[2] For a fuller account, see David M. Malone and Rajeev Ranjan Chaturvedy, 'Impact of India's Economy on its Foreign Policy since Independence', Research Report (Vancouver, BC: Asia Pacific Foundation, November 2009): www.asiapacific.ca/sites/default/files/Indian__Economic__and__Foreign__Policy.pdf

information technology, business processing, and 'back office' capacities, eventually coming to encompass even legal services. In key sectors where liberalization measures in India had yet to be introduced, many big Indian corporations struck alliances with US companies. In addition, in India, much of the urban upper middle class saw closer ties with the USA as its own passport to greater personal prosperity in an increasingly globalized world. As well, the aspirations of middle class Indians are very close to those of individual Americans. These factors taken together may explain why poll after poll has identified a positive appreciation of the USA among the Indian public, indeed the most positive of any Asian country.[67] Further, the upper echelons of India's bureaucratic and military elite, often featuring personal familiarity (frequently involving higher education) with the USA, increasingly support closer ties, although significant resistance to the trend comes from some academic, think-tank, and political circles fearful of Indian submission to US aims.[68]

The success of the India–USA negotiations on nuclear cooperation in 2008, and the IAEA and the Nuclear Suppliers Group's acceptance of the terms of this agreement, offered India both enhanced economic partnership and geostrategic benefits, not just in relations with the United States but also with the Russian Federation, the European Union, and others. This period was a good one for the USA to announce the scaling back of its bilateral aid programme in India, on the grounds that India's economic success had made it redundant in much of the country.[69]

Russia

Although relations between India and the Russian Federation were never less than cordial following the collapse of the Soviet Union, India's growing international self-confidence and its intensifying ties with the USA introduced a more balanced tone (and the occasional note of mutual irritation) in the relationship with Moscow. The legacy of Soviet economic and military assistance remained an important one, but increasingly Moscow wished India to place the relationship on a strictly commercial footing, while India believed itself over-charged for some Russian military procurement. Notably, as estimates for the cost of a refit of the Russian aircraft carrier *Gorshkov*, which India had purchased, ballooned, India's navy complained pointedly and publicly.[70] Moscow stood on the sidelines of the Indo-US nuclear negotiations, holding in abeyance any active nuclear cooperation of its own until the agreement was sanctioned by the IAEA and NSG. But it had been careful to negotiate the provision of further nuclear reactors to India contingent on these developments (as had France). In 2000, Russia signed a Strategic Partnership of Friendship and Peace with

India at a time when US power seemed at its peak, providing India with a degree of counterweight in its discussions with Washington. Today, the two capitals maintain a good understanding of each other's bilateral and geostrategic concerns while retaining their autonomy of action and expanding their relations with other countries.[71]

Russia's position as an energy superpower—the world's largest gas producer and second-largest oil producer—automatically provides it with Delhi's attention in view of fragile Indian energy security. Moreover, geostrategically, Russia's once again increasing influence in Central Asia and its dominance over most pipeline routes originating in that region suggest that Delhi will take care to maintain friendly ties and economic lifelines with the Russian Federation and its friends.[72] Indeed the emergence in 2001 of the so-called Shanghai Cooperation Organization (SCO), including China and Russia, but not the Indian government, was viewed by Indian analysts with some disquiet.[73]

China

After balmy days during most of the 1950s, India's relationship with Beijing deteriorated sharply in the early 1960s, culminating in the 1962 border war, the outcome of which shocked India. Nevertheless, as China emerged from its Maoist hermeticism and its economic reforms started to bear fruit in the 1980s, India understood it could not afford to ignore China's economic renaissance and the implications thereof for China's geostrategic standing.

India has engaged with China more successfully in the sphere of economic relations than on political and security issues, on which India remains somewhat defensive. As C. Raja Mohan notes, the rise of both countries is likely to lead them to 'rub up against each other' occasionally while simultaneously seeking to manage their differences.[74]

Trade between the two countries has been expanding exceptionally fast since the late 1990s, indeed by as much as 33 per cent in 2008, to nearly $52 billion.[75] Indian investment in China has been welcomed and, although India continues to restrict Chinese investment in a broad range of sectors deemed sensitive from a security perspective, investment flows, while still very modest, are increasing in both directions.[76] The growing economic connections, although not yet leading to meaningful interdependence, make future bilateral strains more likely to be 'managed down' rather than escalated into full-blown rows. Further, both countries are aware, given their populations and economic weight, that their economic and other ties are critical for the future of Asia and the rest of the world. In pursuing closer ties, each country is clearly eager to capitalize on the other's economic strengths—manufacturing and computer hardware in China, services and software in India.

In 2005, India and China announced a new 'strategic partnership', pledging to resolve long-standing border disputes and boost trade and economic co-operation between two countries. As a goodwill gesture, China formally abandoned its claim to the tiny Himalayan state of Sikkim, presenting Indian officials with a map showing the area as part of India. While progress on other border issues can be expected to wax and wane and agreement may prove elusive, such differences could be mitigated eventually by a more comprehensive economic relationship.

West Asia

While India's economic relations with the greater Middle East (commonly referred to in India as West Asia, and sometimes deemed to include northern Africa and the independent republics of Central Asia and the Caucasus) have increased and diversified since the 1990s, India has needed to deal with shifting sands (not least in Iraq and Iran) in circumstances of considerable Indian dependency on the Persian Gulf countries for oil supplies. Likewise, oil- and gas-rich Central Asia is of interest to India primarily in terms of these and other natural resources. India has adapted with great flexibility to various upheavals in the Middle East, introducing a strong economic relationship with Israel (mainly in the area of military procurement) into the mix as of the early 1990s.

In spite of strong ties with Pakistan reinforced by a shared Muslim faith, many Arab countries and Iran have cultivated their ties with India, understanding its systemic importance and appreciating the steady nature of its engagement with them. For India, the Persian Gulf is of great significance as the destination for much Indian migrant labour from Kerala and other states. The resulting remittances are of critical importance to some local economies in India, and the 2008–10 economic downturn in Dubai was keenly felt for those reasons in parts of India. As well, India, always keen on multiplying its options, has looked to the Gulf countries as an attractive source of investment flows.[77] Taken together, these factors have made the Gulf commercial hub of Dubai a symbiotic partner for Mumbai in its role as India's principal financial centre, with Indian nationals playing important roles in a variety of Gulf financial institutions. Overall, India's diplomacy in West Asia, rooted in India's economic interests and buttressed by civilizational links, has been deft, in very challenging circumstances.

East and South Asia

Economic success in much of East and Southeast Asia has been one spur for greater Indian engagement—and China's expanding relationships in those areas another—but India's own immediate neighbourhood on the periphery of South Asia has always claimed more of its attention.[78]

Liberalization and economic growth in India, while likely positively influencing related trends in Pakistan and Bangladesh, have not led to a more economically-oriented Indian diplomacy in the area (with the exception of Bhutan, from which India derives significant hydroelectrical resources). The South Asian regional cooperation forum, SAARC, remains largely inert, with few convincing economic achievements, whereas growing economic prosperity and integration in the region might serve to promote India's security. Unfortunately, other than a useful Free Trade Agreement with Sri Lanka and greater physical connectivity within the region, Indian policy has displayed neither imagination nor much energy in promoting economic ties within the South Asian subregion. As a result, South Asia stands as one of the least integrated regions in the world.

On the other hand, building on a Free Trade agreement with Singapore, India has been engaging more systematically and productively with the countries of Southeast Asia (and with their regional organization, ASEAN).[79] And, beyond China, economic ties with South Korea and Japan, while still well below potential, are valued in India. India's 'Look East' policy launched in 1992 is built on economic rather than primarily geostrategic imperatives as Chapter 9 details.[80]

Western Europe

Europe, which has not played a major role in India's worldview since the colonial era, is nevertheless a major trading and economic partner for India (see Figure 4.2). Britain, Germany, and France are taken seriously as political, economic, and, to a degree, military powers, but the pretensions of the European Union puzzle Indian policymakers at a time when European disunity, rather than commonality of perspective and purpose, is mostly on display. India's view of Europe holds up a mirror to European aspirations and suggests that rhetoric goes only so far when undermined by competition among the major member states for India's favour and contracts.

Indeed, of all of India's potentially significant partners, Europe is the most underperforming today. European companies have been bold in moving into India since liberalization, and have often performed very well. But beyond luxury industries, and as a tourist destination for an increasingly footloose Indian upper middle class, Europe has decisively failed to capture India's imagination (as opposed, notably, to the United States). Europe is the rare case in which very meaningful economic relationships have not translated into a major place in India's geostrategic outlook. In the absence of a genuine European Union with a cohesive and credible foreign policy, individual European capitals are bound to count for less in Delhi even if bilateral economic ties prosper (as the chart in Figure 4.2 suggests they do).

The significance of India's recent economic growth in the multilateral sphere and in the balance of power and influence are considered in Chapters 11 and 12.

Emerging issues and future challenges

Indians have naturally been very taken with the narrative of Western decline and the rise of Asia, as promoted by Kishore Mahbubani and others.[81] The 'India Shining' story was premised largely on assumptions of uninterrupted Indian growth and development, unconnected to wider patterns of international economic performance. The global financial and economic crisis of 2008–10, throughout which India continued to grow economically but at lower rates, put paid to these fantasies, but should not obscure India's assets in the sphere of international economic competition. Its central bank managed India's financial institutions prudently, and India's liberalization and gradual opening to global markets was a relative rather than an absolute process. These factors served it well at a time of global economic downturn.

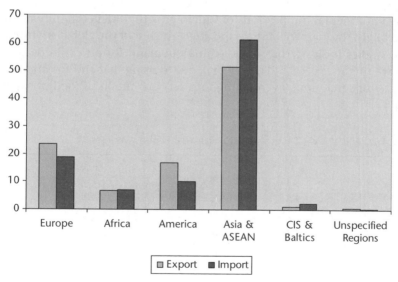

Figure 4.2. India's foreign trade by region (%)
Source: http://commerce.nic.in/ftpa/rgnq.asp

As well, its internal market remained buoyant, with savings and the potential for investment still high.

Thus, whether or not India and China will displace the West as 'action central' for the global economy (as pundits and forecasters were wont to predict early in the millennium), Indian economic progress is likely to continue, and could do so at a very brisk pace if future Indian governments can tackle the challenges of weak public education, health service delivery, and inadequate national infrastructure more effectively.[82] Forecasting firms and specialists tend to advance exciting but questionable projections twenty-five to forty years into the future. For example, based on current trends, by 2025 India's economy can be expected to amount to about 60 per cent the size of that of the USA. One reason statisticians and economists tend to be optimistic for India relates to its demographics, but these are changing fast, so while India can count on a youthful and growing population for some years, the picture could look quite different by 2050.[83] The recent economic and financial crisis makes clear how chancy long-term projections can be, but the trend-lines for India remain hopeful.[84] Indeed, Goldman Sachs (whose strategic guru Jim O'Neill coined the BRIC grouping) has offered a scenario under which India, within a decade, will be outgrowing China by a wide margin (see Table 4.2).[85]

One obvious implication of these projections is that India's need for natural resources, including those required to produce energy, can only increase sharply, barring unforeseen changes in energy technologies. Another is that the environmental implications of Indian growth, unless carefully managed, could blight the country's future and affect the rest of the global environment. Some studies indicate that while China's demand for oil could peak earlier than we might expect, India may experience rising demand for imported oil and gas for some time (even taking into account the likelihood of expanded

Table 4.2. BRICs' real GDP growth (%): Five-Year Period Averages

	Brazil	China	India	Russia
2000–05	2.7	8.0	5.3	5.9
2005–10	4.2	7.2	6.1	4.8
2010–15	4.1	5.9	5.9	3.8
2015–20	3.8	5.0	5.7	3.4
2020–5	3.7	4.6	5.7	3.4
2025–30	3.8	4.1	5.9	3.5
2030–5	3.9	3.9	6.1	3.1
2035–40	3.8	3.9	6.0	2.6
2949–5	3.6	3.5	5.6	2.2
2045–50	3.4	2.9	5.2	1.9

Source: Dominic Wilson and Roopa Purushothaman, 'Dreaming With BRICs: The Path to 2050', *Goldman Sachs Global Economics Paper* No. 99, 1 October 2003, available at: www2.goldmansachs.com/ideas/brics/book/99-dreaming.pdf

internal production).[86] At the same time, as Figure 4.3 indicates, India's domestic ability to produce oil has reached a plateau for now.

Internationally, the economic challenges facing Indian foreign policy are many, including those relating to energy and food security and the unpredictable economic consequences of potential instability in the Middle East. Indians are much preoccupied by China's accelerated economic growth, which provides China with greater means to support its geostrategic aspirations than India can devote to its own. This has led to fears of Chinese encirclement, most often focused on anxieties about China's constructions of naval and air facilities in India's immediate Indian Ocean neighbourhood.[87] Domestically, India's challenges include interregional and urban–rural disparities; a languishing agricultural sector; infrastructure grossly inadequate to the needs of a rapidly growing economic power; and a lack of skilled manpower due to disappointing education opportunities and misaligned training. Failing public service delivery is at the root of slow progress in tackling a number of social challenges, such as illiteracy, malnutrition, and gender inequality.[88] In addition, although it has been declining in relative terms, acute poverty continues to be an overwhelming drag on India, afflicting hundreds of millions.[89] And the local consequences of global warming and climate change, not least in terms of its challenges for water management, are rightly beginning to worry thoughtful Indians seriously.

Nevertheless, it is India's sharply positive economic performance since the mid-1990s that has shifted international perceptions of its potential and that

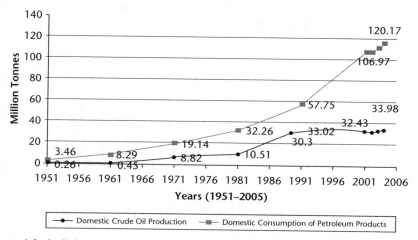

Figure 4.3. India's Domestic Oil Consumption vs. Domestic Production

Source: Government of India, Planning Commission, *Integrated Energy Policy: Report of the Expert Committee* (August 2006)

has fuelled acceptance of its rise on the global stage. And it is these perceptions that create greater opportunity for India in redefining and advancing a foreign policy for a new era, one more strongly marked by Asia than has been the case for many centuries.

India's bilateral diplomacy has mostly been deft beyond its own immediate neighbourhood, and even in the latter it has been improving. However, as India achieves significant economic growth, albeit still struggling with poverty, its multilateral policy (for example, on non-proliferation and trade) has too often been marked by a sense of defiance against an admittedly skewed international economic and political order. India's frustrations are understandable, but its response has been disappointing. It has sought to forge negotiating alliances with other key emerging states but has sometimes been sidelined by them, for example by China in CTBT negotiations in 1996, Brazil at a key moment in the WTO Doha Round in 2008 and again by China on climate change in late 2009 when President Hu Jintao created a positive impression globally with a speech to the UN General Assembly that offered domestic goals to contain emissions growth. More creativity and calculated risk-taking would doubtless yield better results for Delhi as it moves centre-stage internationally. Indeed, it needs to demonstrate, more systematically, a willingness and ability to help manage collectively major global challenges (as Prime Minister Singh and his economic advisors did, gaining considerable credit, in the G-20 during the 2008–9 economic crisis) in order to secure the global recognition it believes is its due.

India's economy provides an opportunity for new beginnings in Indian foreign policy, building on existing strengths. It is now half-way towards being in a position to seize the opportunity, and much will depend on the determination of leadership in Delhi on this front.

5

India and Its South Asian Neighbours

Contemporary Indian foreign policy is focused largely on the promotion of economic interests, India's graduation to the high table of international relations, and, most consistently since its independence, on enhancing its security within its immediate neighbourhood, approaches to which have evolved over the decades. It is on this latter topic that this chapter focuses.

The Indian government has spoken a great deal about the primacy of greater economic cooperation with its neighbours, but on this front, results are meagre and unconvincing, as are the achievements of the South Asian Association for Regional Cooperation (SAARC). That said, India faces the challenges any regional hegemon does in engaging neighbours. A recent editorial essay in the Indian periodical *Seminar* comments:

> Barring an obsession with Pakistan, and for the elite with the Anglo-Saxon West, Indian political imagination and foreign policy has rarely demonstrated the needed knowledge about our near and extended neighbourhood, far less an ability to influence events in pursuance of national interests...The overwhelming presence of India creates an asymmetry that pushes other, smaller countries, into suspecting hegemony in every proposal for greater cooperation, in turn feeding into an incipient irritation within India that its neighbours are united only in their anti-India sentiment.[1]

India shares land and maritime boundaries with eight countries—Bangladesh, Bhutan, China, the Maldives, Myanmar, Nepal, Pakistan, and Sri Lanka. Setting aside China, Maldives, and Bhutan—mostly at peace—six countries in India's immediate neighbourhood have been on the boil on and off for many years.[2] Although India today is not contiguous to Afghanistan, the latter is mostly seen by Indians as an integral part of South Asia, so India's relations with it are discussed in this chapter.

India has close historical, religious, economic, ethnic, and linguistic relationships with all of these states. Unsurprisingly, the complex and dovetailing ties linking up the South Asian subcontinent drive South Asian countries to speak—optimistically—of friendship as a 'geographical imperative'.[3] That they have not succeeded in acting much on it does not condemn them forever to regional dysfunction and friction, but much will depend on how India leads its region and what example it sets in promoting more positive relations with its neighbours.

Since independence in 1947, India's principal challenges have included the promotion of internal cohesion and the management of its often troubled relations with its neighbours, the two often being closely linked. S. D. Muni notes that India's policy towards its immediate neighbours is likely to face serious challenges 'from internal turbulence in those countries and in India itself', as has recently been the case with Pakistan, Nepal, and Sri Lanka. In conceiving of and conducting its South Asia policy, India's tactics have varied, but the trend has been towards a more conciliatory approach, as India reaches beyond its own immediate neighbourhood to establish itself as a global actor.[4]

How do Indians view their own neighbourhood? Raja Mohan argues that without enduring primacy in one's own neighbourhood, no nation can become a credible power on the global stage.[5] He and S. D. Muni argue that for India, 'achieving the objective of becoming one of the principal powers of Asia will depend entirely on India's ability to manage its own immediate neighbourhood'.[6] One of India's leading geostrategic writers, V.P. Dutt, suggests that a country's neighbourhood must enjoy unquestioned primacy in foreign policy making.[7] And former Prime Minister Atal Bihari Vajpayee stated that 'Friends can change but not neighbours who have to live together.'[8] More recently, then Foreign Minister Pranab Mukherjee noted the importance of foreign policy providing 'facilitation of India's developmental processes', a relevant factor in a regional context.[9] But do all of these imperatives and bromides add up to the defining characteristics of India's actual calculus?

This chapter is built around a summary analysis of India's relations with each of its immediate neighbours other than China after first laying out a sense of how India's approach to its neighbours has evolved over the past two decades. It offers some tentative conclusions, suggesting that India's approach to its neighbours is both too often reactive and at times quite dismissive, but also acknowledges that it has been trying much harder in recent years to accommodate and tolerate neighbourly differences. While India's regional rivalry with China as played out in countries abutting India is discussed here, its bilateral relationship with China is discussed separately in Chapter 6.

The challenge of a resentful, dangerous neighbourhood

Unlike the USA, or indeed, the Russian Federation, India is not a fully convincing hegemon within its own subregion. While dwarfed by India's size, population, and subregional weight, several of India's neighbours are consequential states in their own right and reluctant to bow to Indian predominance or pressure. Thus, the challenge of managing asymmetry in its neighbourhood relationships, within its notional 'sphere of influence', is both a real and serious one. India has not always met this challenge impressively, in the past occasionally displaying brusque manners and rough tactics, with indifferent and sometimes counterproductive results.[10]

India's economic liberalization and consequent sharply higher economic growth allowed the country to cast itself as a potential regional economic locomotive. This strand of Indian policy is, in fact, both rational and helpful, but Delhi clearly has not done enough to make greater economic integration politically attractive and administratively feasible. None of its neighbours, except for Bhutan, and possibly the Maldives, in practice accepted India's economic logic (not least given India's feeble efforts at promoting regional economic cooperation within the framework of SAARC).

One feature of India's political life is replicated in several of the neighbouring countries: dynastic rule by one or several political families, in which power passes as readily to matriarchs as to patriarchs. Unlike India, however, periods of often disastrous and corrupt dynastic rule are frequently interrupted by military coups introducing military-led government of equally dismal consequence, but in different ways. When the bankruptcy of the latter becomes clear, some form of electoral consultation leads to a resumption of dynastic rule. Bangladesh has provided a running parody of the model for many years.

India's objectives towards its neighbours

India accepts the reality that it must live with the neighbours it has, preferably peacefully.[11] Translated into the serene cadences of diplomatic communication, the Indian Foreign Ministry couches matters as follows: 'With the objective of a peaceful, stable and prosperous neighbourhood, India continues to attach the highest priority to close and good neighbourly political, economic and cultural relations with its neighbours', also noting that this should be carried out 'on the basis of sovereign equality and mutual respect'.[12]

Hence, one of the cornerstones of India's stated foreign policy, though not a notably successful one to date, has been to build a strategically secure, politically stable, harmonious, and economically cooperative neighbourhood.[13] The ideas are right, as is the notion of India leading an integration of South Asian markets, thus creating a web of regional interdependence, but they are hardly original.[14] Worries in India about maintaining and enhancing its subregional strategic superiority seem, to an outsider, overblown.

Dynamism in India's policy

Though India's first Prime Minister, Jawaharlal Nehru, stressed the importance of keeping foreign powers out of Asia and considered the Indian subcontinent as an exclusive sphere of influence for Delhi, India was in no position, early in its history as an independent country, to keep the great powers at bay. Indeed, it called upon the support of both the United States and the Soviet Union at various times. This has been less true of late, with India able to establish more equal partnerships with Washington and Moscow, as well as Beijing, particularly after the collapse of the Soviet Union. Further, the process of economic globalization forced India to find new anchors for its conduct of external relations.[15] These developments seem to have helped Delhi to take a more benign view of some of its neighbours and also to be better equipped to see its challenges in South Asia against a broader backdrop of rising Indian international influence.

By the 1990s, however tentatively at first, India began to work more closely with other powers (although not necessarily with Beijing) in addressing the political crises in its neighbourhood. Nepal and Sri Lanka provide good examples of this change in approach, in which Delhi was able to reconcile its own drive for subregional leadership with meaningful roles for others. For example a modest but helpful role was established for the United Nations in Nepal, which Delhi had kept firmly out of its orbit since the world body disappointed its aspirations on Kashmir in 1948. India also supported the participation of China, Japan, and the USA as observers in the SAARC.

With respect to cooperation, India sought to engineer a marked improvement in its relations with most of its immediate neighbours as of the 1990s, building on the articulation of the 'Gujral Doctrine' in 1996.[16] The accelerated development of every country in the subcontinent was a key goal of this doctrine. Since then, at the heart of evolving Indian ideas on foreign policy towards the neighbours, a new priority has been at work. 'First establish yourself in your neighbourhood—by privileging the neighbourhood in your foreign policy scheme and strengthening or winning trust and confidence in both areas of strength and areas of problematical, or even bad, relations.'[17]

This new attitude marked a welcome departure for India's regional policy and the development of three clear trends during the 1990s: regular meetings at the level of leaders and of senior officials; a focus on resolving major bilateral issues to build an environment of trust; and an emphasis—at least rhetorically—on the economic dimension of relationships.[18] Indeed, to place India at the heart of the new Asian order, the Indian government in recent years has sought to elevate development discourse over the conventional security debate, highlighting economic globalization and the rejuvenation of long-standing ties with neighbours in line with a pragmatic Indian foreign policy.[19]

Linking geography with strategy

Leaving aside issues of implementation, two overlapping strands emerge clearly in India's contemporary neighbourhood policy: security and development. India is attempting to build a web of 'dense interdependencies'[20] with its neighbours, as was clearly enunciated in a speech by then Foreign Secretary Shyam Saran in February 2005.[21] In another speech, Saran touched on a vulnerability in India's regional policy—reactive decision-making: 'Our effort has been to construct an overarching vision for South Asia, so that we do not deal with neighbours in an ad-hoc and reactive manner, but formulate policies that fit into and promote this larger vision.'[22] He argued for a fresh view of borders in sync with ideas articulated at times by both Prime Ministers Vajpayee and Singh.

India's position in earlier decades had been that neighbours should reciprocate the benefits of relations with India by being sensitive to India's security concerns (a line that naturally found little resonance in most of the neighbouring states). This strand of policy has been retired, at least publicly. The talk now is of India's 'soft power' articulated through its cultural, civilizational, and economic pull. India is thus offering its neighbours a stake in its economic prosperity and much funding of visits by scholars, artists, and others and training of officials from several neighbouring countries. Nevertheless, the formal instruments of regional cooperation, SAFTA (the South Asia Free Trade Agreement) and SAARC, remain anaemic.[23] Indeed, at the April 2010 SAARC summit, Prime Minister Manmohan Singh noted: 'We have created institutions for regional cooperation but we have not yet empowered them adequately to enable them to be more pro-active.'[24]

India's relationship with its South Asian neighbours

Tables 5.1 and 5.2 indicate Gross Domestic Product (GDP) and intraregional and world trade of South Asian countries. This section continues with individual country analyses.[25]

Pakistan

India's relationship with Pakistan is the most intractable and intense of those with neighbours.[26] At the core of animosities lies the question of Kashmir, but

Table 5.1. General information on South Asian countries

Country	GDP per capita (2008)	Total population (2008)	Land area (km²)	Length of border with other countries (km)
Afghanistan	1,103	29,021,099	652,230	China 76 Iran 936 Pakistan 2,430 Tajikistan 1,206 Turkmenistan 744 Uzbekistan 137
Bangladesh	1,335	160,000,128	130,168	India 4,053 Burma 193
Bhutan	4,759	686,789	38,394	India 605 China 470
India	2,946	1,139,964,932	2,973,193	Bangladesh 4,053 Bhutan 605 Burma, 1,463 China 3,380 Nepal 1,690 Pakistan 2,912
Maldives	5,597	305,027	298	–
Myanmar/ Burma	–	49,563,019	653,508	India 1,463
Nepal	1,104	28,809,526	143,351	Bangladesh 193 China 2,185 Laos 235 Thailand 1,800 India 1,690 China 1,236
Pakistan	2,538	166,111,487	770,875	India 2,912 Afghanistan 2,430 China 523
Sri Lanka	4,564	20,156,204	64,630	Iran 909 –

Note: GDP at purchasing power parity in 2008 (current international $).
Sources: The World Bank World Development Indicators Database (GDP and population); and the CIA World Factbook (area and length of border), both consulted in May 2010.

Table 5.2. Intraregional and world trade of South Asian countries, 1991–2006

Year	% share of intra-South Asian imports in total imports of South Asia countries	% share of intra-South Asian exports in total exports of South Asia countries	% share of intra-South Asian trade in total trade of South Asia countries
1991	2.63	3.70	3.11
1992	3.20	4.08	3.59
1993	3.29	3.68	3.47
1994	3.46	3.94	3.68
1995	3.91	4.52	4.18
1996	4.57	4.47	4.53
1997	3.83	4.94	4.32
1998	4.73	4.57	4.66
1999	3.72	4.33	3.97
2000	3.72	4.43	4.03
2001	3.82	4.65	4.18
2002	4.24	5.23	4.69
2003	4.71	6.40	5.46
2004	4.45	6.23	5.20
2005	4.54	6.45	5.32
2006	3.85	6.16	4.73

Note: The above figures do not include the data from Bhutan as it does not report its data. The countries included are Afghanistan, Bangladesh, India, Maldives, Pakistan, Nepal, and Sri Lanka.
Source: IMF DOTS Database.

the relationship today is bedevilled by many further layers of resentment and anxiety. In recent years, Pakistan, rarely a beacon of stability, has been experiencing enhanced political volatility and internal violence, although, happily, in 2008, it returned to democratic rule. Beyond the three major wars that have pitted the two countries against each other, violence has visited India from Pakistan several times, most recently in Mumbai in November 2008. These incidents, with or without the collusion of the government in Islamabad, have sorely tested the patience and the restraint of the Indian nation and its government. Nevertheless, large-scale hostilities have been avoided since 1971 and the nuclear weapons capacity of both countries may, in fact, have rendered all-out war much more unlikely than in past decades. Stephen P. Cohen cites an observation by G. Parthasarathy, a former Indian High Commissioner to Pakistan, that an India–Pakistan reconciliation is like trying to treat two patients whose only disease is an allergy to each other.[27]

For the past sixty years, India–Pakistan relations have been fraught. Theirs is one of 'the most enduring rivalries of the post-World War II era'.[28] Successive Indian and Pakistani governments have attempted to negotiate and resolve outstanding problems, sometimes achieving limited if real success (for example, with World Bank participation and assistance, on the Indus Waters Treaty of 1960), but the overall relationship has never improved fundamentally for long. The two countries have reached numerous agreements since the late 1980s on issues including: the protection of nuclear facilities, bus services between Indian and Pakistani cities, human trafficking, illegal immigration, and the establishment of trading routes.[29] There have also been extensive discussions, both formal and informal, between the two governments over the sensitive Kashmir issue, with each supporting 'track two' discussions among leading scholars, retired officials, and writers.[30] But little ever seems to come of it, due to the lack of trust between the two governments and political risk aversion in tackling their fundamental differences.

TERRORISM

Yet, beyond such Pakistani military adventurism as the ill-advised Kargil operation of 1999, spectacular incidents of terrorism, with proven or suspected links to Pakistan, have all too frequently disrupted efforts to improve ties between the two countries and have repeatedly placed Indian governments at risk of looking 'weak' in the absence of reprisals. Prominent incidents include: the hijacking of an Indian Airlines flight by Pakistan-backed terrorists in December 1999 that compelled the Indian government to release three Islamic militants jailed in India;[31] the December 2001 terrorist attack on the Parliament of India; a suicide car bomb attack on the Indian Embassy in Kabul in July 2008; and the November 2008 terrorist attacks in Mumbai that left nearly 200 dead. In reacting to these incidents, India has established a pattern of considerable restraint if connections to the Islamabad government itself are hard to establish conclusively. However, many other terrorist attacks in India in 2007–8 (e.g. in Hyderabad and Jaipur) were loosely, reflexively, and perhaps inaccurately linked to Pakistan or Bangladesh by the Indian media based on official and semi-official briefings.[32]

Beyond individual incidents, the graver challenge for India is the perception there and elsewhere that to a very large extent, 'Pakistan defines itself in anti-Indian terms'.[33] Rulers in Pakistan, and not just military ones, have all too often played the 'India card' to consolidate their regimes. While Delhi has often been accused domestically of underinvesting in military and intelligence spending, Islamabad has been generous in building up Pakistani military and espionage capabilities, often with sizeable assistance from both the West and China.

On balance, in spite of periods of civilian rule, the Pakistani Army has dominated the political order in Islamabad and always exercises strong influence over civilian governments. It not only sees itself as the ultimate guarantor of the state but has built up vested economic interests at the institutional and personal levels posited on its political role.[34] Thus, despite the civilian government led by President Asif Ali Zardari since 2008, Pakistan remains subject to undue opaque but real influence of its security establishment, exacerbating the country's reputation as an unstable nation state. Pakistani scholar Ahmed Rashid writes: 'The [Pakistani] army...seeks to ensure that a balance of terror and power is maintained with respect to India, and the jihadis are seen as part of this strategy.'[35]

The serial domestic political crises in Pakistan early in the new millennium, coming after the serial failure of democratically elected governments during earlier decades, and the increasing extremism of religious fundamentalists within the country (and spilling out from it) have become much more serious security concerns for India and for much of the rest of the world than is Pakistan's nuclear arsenal. However, India's response to provocations originating in Pakistan, be it the Kargil adventure or the 2008 Mumbai attack, has increasingly involved coercive diplomacy intermediated by Washington (and sometimes, to a degree, by London). While this is sometimes derided as 'weak' by Indians favouring a muscular response, the approach has many benefits: Pakistan's weapons suppliers and financiers are hard to sideline, their intelligence findings hard to duck, and the incentives—positive and negative—that they can offer impossible for Pakistan to ignore. Meanwhile, Washington takes the heat, while the Indian government sits back carefully calibrating varying messages for domestic, international, and Pakistani consumption. Indian novelist Aravind Adiga zeroes in on the dynamic as follows:

> When the strike takes place, it will be found that the local police did not have enough guns, walkie-talkies, training or manpower to fight back quickly. Co-ordination between local security agencies and elite commando forces in Delhi will prove to be poor.... The government will immediately threaten to attack Pakistan, then realise that it cannot do so without risking nuclear war, and finally beg the US to do something. Once it is clear that the government has failed on every front—military, tactical and diplomatic—against the terrorists, senior ministers will appear on television and promise that, next time, they will be prepared.[36]

But delegating the diplomatic heavy lifting to Washington (with a role for the UN Security Council in extreme cases, as with Mumbai), India avoids having to escalate by launching reprisals, which could conceivably lead to an incontrollable tit for tat with lethal (although not likely nuclear) consequences.[37]

KASHMIR AND INDO-PAKISTANI ASYMMETRY

Kashmir remains at the crux of the tortured relationship between India and Pakistan. At different times, both countries have betrayed the aspirations of Kashmiris for independence or at the least meaningful autonomy. But, over the years, in spite of a harsh Indian military occupation of the Kashmir Valley, Pakistan has increasingly come to be seen as the fiercest antagonist bent on upending the status quo. For many Indians, Kashmir is a very distant State of the Union. Nonetheless, India's overall cohesion is strongly supported by most Indians, including its Muslim population, and thus the Indian government has rarely been under domestic pressure to be forthcoming in negotiating with Pakistan. Most Indians are unaware of, or, given the hardships of their own lives, not unduly moved by the severity of conditions in the Valley and the all too frequently brutal military and police presence there. The division of the historical territory of Kashmir between the two countries has stronger emotive resonance in Pakistan, where it is discussed at three levels, as a territorial, ideological, and moral dispute.[38] Fringe elements in Pakistan see it not merely as a just cause, but somewhat quixotically as a key to unravelling the cohesion of India.

How to deal with the 'Line of Control' (LoC) separating Indian and Pakistani forces from each other in Kashmir is contested within India. Some Indians, such as Pankaj Mishra, believe that its defence should be the only key mission of the Indian military in Jammu and Kashmir.[39] Others, such as Chinmaya Gharekhan, believe that for the LoC to become peaceful, it needs to be first recognized by both countries as a legitimate international border.[40] Most outside observers, including friends of India, believe that the nature and overwhelming weight of the security deployment by the Indian armed forces and other security units in the Kashmir valley is not only excessive but increasingly counterproductive, and that significant easing of this security presence in the Kashmir valley (which could partly refocus on the LoC) would help considerably. Chapter 12 provides further thoughts on the matter.

T. V. Paul argues that a crucial, neglected structural factor causing the persistence of an India–Pakistan rivalry is the power asymmetry that has prevailed between the antagonists for over half a century.[41] It may also be that the growing asymmetry in economic performance, as well as in geostrategic significance builds in a powerful structural dimension to Pakistan's resentments. Thus, it is hardly surprising that efforts to engage bilaterally across the border at the level of heads of government have yielded little fruit. Stephen Cohen notes: 'Terrorism' is the core issue for India, 'Kashmir' for Pakistan, and 'nuclear security and stability' for the international community. These tectonic plates crash up against each other, but cannot mesh comfortably.[42]

ECONOMIC AND SOCIETAL RELATIONS
In optimistic times friends of both countries hope for peace through economic cooperation. However, very few items having export potential from India are on the permitted list adopted by the government of Pakistan. Likewise, India imports little from Pakistan.[43] India's main interests in economic cooperation with Pakistan lie in hydropower, water management, gas transportation, tourism, and road-connectivity to Afghanistan and Iran. A proposed 'Iran-Pakistan-India' gas pipeline, a US$7.6 billion tri-nation project, promised to provide market linkages to Iranian natural gas resources and increase the

commercial attractiveness of the natural gas sector. The project, creating a significant economic link with both Pakistan and Iran, one of the world's top three holders of proven oil and natural gas reserves, is also attractive from the perspective of contributing to the reduction of poverty, income disparities, and unemployment in Pakistan, which in turn might discourage radicalism. However, India has been slow to move on this front, partly due to US pressure on Delhi's dealings with Tehran, and partly due to a persistent suspicion in Delhi of Islamabad's reliability as a partner in a venture of this scale.

At the human level, there is intense interest in cross-border visits and exploration of each other's society as it has evolved since 1947. Many touching accounts exist of how well visiting Indians are treated in Pakistan and vice versa (although not always by the security authorities of each). Indian books are read, and films watched, with great enthusiasm in Pakistan and Pakistani maestros of classical music are as much admired in India as in their own country. Indians and Pakistanis share common roots, and there is keen interest in getting re-acquainted among the cultural elite, however high the political and security barriers.

Protocol regimes applying to Indian and Pakistani diplomats assigned in the other country are highly restrictive. Absurdly constraining notification regimes and illiberal authorization patterns for any movements beyond the city of residence, parallel what remain tremendously restricted and tentative efforts to establish cross-border trade, passenger transportation, and more general interaction. Several bus and rail links announced in recent years amount to little in practice, although a murderous bombing of the Delhi-Lahore train in 2007 highlighted the risks involved in any attempt to improve relations.[44]

WESTERN PERSPECTIVES

In Western governments, hope springs eternal that change, virtually any change, in government will be for the better in Pakistan. Military government, it is thought, will bring a measure of stability and less corruption. Civilian rule, it is assumed, will provide better governance more in tune with Western values. Indians are more cynical—they remember the follies of successive Pakistani governments, military and civilian, all of which have played the anti-India card. Thus, when Benazir Bhutto was assassinated in December 2007, the Western media evoked a Greek tragedy calling forth intense emotion, projecting onto the late Ms. Bhutto—an attractive, Western-educated woman particularly skilled at delivering different messages to different audiences—ideals of democratic government she never came close to approximating in power, as Indians all too readily remembered. Indian commentators conceded that she was both admirably brave and articulate but focused mainly on the sorry record of her two spells in power, and her frequent stoking of anti-Indian sentiment.

Pakistani lawyer and columnist Babar Sattar writes:

[In Pakistan a] centrist view is that we have been irresponsible in developing our notions of national security and strategic depth, creating international alliances and pursuing policies dictated by the US. Washington is pointing its finger at us while speaking of terrorism and violence in self-righteous terms. [Meanwhile], it is extremely difficult for the civilian government to renege on Pakistan's traditionally held positions on disputes with India.[45]

Pakistani scholar and analyst, Ahmed Rashid comments:

The relationship between India and Pakistan is becoming more and more complicated as the end game in Afghanistan approaches. Pakistan should...deal with its domestic terrorist threat rather than try to treat the whole issue as India-oriented.[46]

Nevertheless, as the stronger party, the onus is widely seen as being on India to go the extra mile in engaging Pakistan. I agree. Counter-intuitive as this seems to some Indians, given the country's frequent victimization by cross-border terrorism, it makes sense that India should do all in its power to avoid aggravating Pakistan's torment and that it should, whenever circumstances allow, reach out.[47] Indeed, the Indian Government has recently decided to resume multifaceted talks with Pakistan.[48] K. Shankar Bajpai aptly describes dialogue with Pakistan as the 'right, rational choice for a mature power'.[49]

Bangladesh

Either by design or due to drift, relations with Bangladesh, although much more positive than those with Pakistan, are amongst the least cooperative that India has developed in South Asia.[50] A major portion of Bangladesh is surrounded by Indian states, which sometimes makes the country feel 'India locked'.[51] Indeed, India's border with Bangladesh is the longest among all of India's neighbours and all too often, Bangladesh is seen by many Indians as the source of an unending flow of illegal migrants.[52] The Indian High Commissioner in Dhaka comments: 'We have to be circumspect in issuing visas particularly when we know that around 25,000 Bangladeshis do not return after entering India every year. Those who enter unrecorded are many more.'[53] Bangladesh is also thought of prominently as a haven for fundamentalists and terrorists, and a sanctuary for Indian insurgents in the northeast.[54] Hence, with the exception of a brief period in the immediate aftermath of the liberation of Bangladesh in 1971, bilateral relations have been marred by mistrust, disharmony, and suspicion. Sreeradha Datta writes:

The convergences of their cultural links and economic complementarities are apparently not compelling enough for both countries to overcome the growing bilateral problems between the two. Over the years, the differences have deepened while the convergences have got marginalised.[55]

Iftekhar Ahmed Chowdhury, who acted as Foreign Minister with the title of Adviser in the caretaker government of Bangladesh between January 2007 and January 2009, and prior to that a widely respected Ambassador to the United Nations, writes:

India is the preeminent regional power, and Bangladesh has always entertained some wariness of it. Unsurprisingly, 'Indo-centrism' has been a key factor in the processes of policy-formulation. There has, therefore, been a tendency to use the web of other external linkages to make-up for the regional power-gap.[56]

From an Indian perspective, Bangladesh has become increasingly resentful of its economically more successful and larger neighbour, resisting several large Indian-inspired economic projects and related Indian investment and, more generally, all too readily blaming India for ills of its own creation. At first, India seemed to hope that military-backed interim rule instituted in 2007 after several years of government by the Bangladesh Nationalist Party and its Islamist allies, led by Khaleda Zia, the widow of its former leader and no friend of India, would lead to better relations with Delhi. It was, of course, disabused of this view by the time electoral democracy was restored two years later, when Sheikh Hasina, daughter of the founding leader of Bangladesh and head of the Awami League, returned to power. While both women command strong loyalty among their followers, both are tainted by corruption, which the interim government failed to confront convincingly.

The levels of maladministration and corruption in Bangladeshi public life shock even other South Asians, largely inured to a high level of both.[57] Of greater concern to India has been the strength of radical Islam in organized politics as well as the existence of significant Islamist militant groups, some with international links—including to confederates in Pakistan, and, it is widely suspected, in India. The fear of Talibanization of Bangladesh, while seemingly far-fetched to many casual Western observers, remains real and urgent to much of the Indian security establishment.[58]

The issue of illegal migration from Bangladesh into India has at times been a politically salient one for Delhi, not least after terrorist events in India are attributed, not always entirely convincingly, to extremists with Bangladeshi ties. As well, Bangladesh's reported harbouring of separatist movements targeting parts of India's northeast has been a sore point in bilateral relations.[59]

While Bangladeshis are concerned about the potential for Indian domination, India has its own concerns, feeling vulnerable to pressures from

Bangladesh over the narrow Siliguri corridor that links the northeast with the rest of India.[60] Apart from security concerns, many other actual or potential problems mark the relationship between these two countries including issues of border management, problems of water sharing, trade- and transit-related questions, and illegal migration.

The government elected in Bangladesh in December 2008 and its Indian counterpart have projected willingness to improve the bilateral relationship. Bangladesh Prime Minister Sheikh Hasina has welcomed Indian entrepreneurs to invest in Special Economic Zones (SEZs) to double bilateral trade to about $6 billion over two years.[61] Similarly, to boost trade, business, and other economic activities, the two neighbours aim to upgrade existing infrastructural facilities at twenty-seven Land Customs Stations (LCS) in the northeast.[62]

To improve relations and to encourage people-to-people exchanges, India and Bangladesh resumed railway services between Dhaka and Kolkata, which had been suspended during the 1965 Indo-Pakistani conflict (prior to the establishment of Bangladesh), after a gap of over four decades (although, in 1996, a direct bus service linking Kolkata and Dhaka resumed).[63] More recently, during the successful visit to Delhi by Sheikh Hasina in January 2010, five agreements were signed relating to mutual legal assistance in criminal matters, transfers of sentenced persons, fighting terrorism, organized crime, and illegal drug trafficking, power cooperation, and cultural exchange programmes.[64] Moreover, India announced a US$1 billion line of credit to strengthen Bangladesh's infrastructure—the highest credit line India has ever extended to any country.[65]

India's reading of the country is a factor in Bangladesh's politics: during the government led by Khaleda Zia from 2001 to 2007, overt hostility by Dhaka towards India reached an unprecedented peak. Foreign observers thought this was partly designed to divert attention from internal problems in the government and widespread charges of corruption, but also to take advantage of the perception that India was partial to the Sheikh Hasina-led Awami League. While these factors will not be so much at play under Sheikh Hasina, she will nevertheless have to overcome conflicted feelings among Bangladeshis towards their larger, more powerful and economically more successful neighbour. Although one means of achieving greater harmony would be to hitch Bangladesh's economic prospects more clearly to the rising economic star of India, this would not be an easy sell domestically.

Afghanistan

Aside from a shared history and strong bonds of culture, India has a strong security interest in ensuring that Afghanistan remains sovereign, stable, united, and free from outside influence (notably any lasting undue Pakistani, American, or Russian influence).[66] However, India's approach towards Afghanistan has been cautious.[67] Relations have ebbed and waned according to evolving circumstances. But during the twentieth century, many in Afghanistan's elite were educated in India, and both diplomatic and cultural ties were strong until the monarchy in Afghanistan was overtaken by more radical elements during the 1970s.

Partition of India left Afghanistan bordering on Pakistan but separated from India by a narrow band of valleys and mountains in Pakistan's northeast. However, psychologically, India and Afghanistan think of each other as neighbours and friends (their positive relationship deriving added saliency from the difficulties each has experienced with Pakistan).

Nevertheless, India's policy towards Afghanistan demonstrates the dichotomy between its aspiration for a larger role in its north western neighbourhood and the real constraints on it. India's refusal to criticise the Soviet military intervention in Afghanistan at the end of 1979 isolated it from a large segment of the Afghan people. The advent to power of the Islamist Taliban in the 1980s was deeply worrying to India. At the turn of the 1990s, India's first challenge was to pick up the pieces of its shattered Afghanistan policy. Though India's engagement over time increased, the emergence of the Taliban with Pakistan's support limited India's options and India supported anti-Taliban forces in Afghanistan.[68]

The dramatic developments after the 11 September 2001 attack and the ensuing defeat of the Taliban by the US-backed Northern Alliance (with which India also entertained good relations) provided an opportunity for India to re-establish itself in Afghanistan in a radically different international and regional framework. Delhi has provided generous assistance towards Afghanistan's reconstruction and nation building. High-level visits in both directions are routine. Despite security threats and attacks on Indian companies and on its personnel in different projects, India has maintained its commitment to the reconstruction and rebuilding of Afghanistan.

India's direct bilateral commitment to the rebuilding and reconstruction of Afghanistan is US$1.2 billion.[69] Several thousand Indians are engaged in development work in Afghanistan. Funds have been committed to projects spread over a range of sectors, from education to institutional capacity building and strengthening of governance.[70] India is the sixth largest bilateral donor in Afghanistan. In early 2009, the Zaranj–Delaram road, which will provide better access to the country through Iran, was inaugurated.[71] India is also working with other countries such as Germany and Japan in the reconstruction efforts and in capacity-building activities including training courses for diplomats, government officials, policemen, journalists, and doctors.[72]

Nevertheless, tension with Pakistan over India's presence (including five consulates) in Afghanistan—seen as a provocation in Islamabad and as evidence of an Indian strategy of encirclement of its long-time rival—has greatly complicated India's cooperation with Afghanistan and India has needed to emphasize repeatedly that it has provided no military support for the NATO mission in Afghanistan nor sought to engage Pakistani forces from within Afghanistan. While this is true, Pakistani sensitivity to India's activities in Afghanistan is acute and the involvement of Pakistan's ISI in the suicide bombing of the Indian Embassy in Kabul in July 2008 was rumoured with great insistence. On the other hand, Indians recognize that threats internal to Afghanistan affect the region as a whole.[73]

In talks between Mr. Karzai and Dr Singh in April 2010, Delhi reaffirmed its strong commitment to the Afghan government and offered to increase its already considerable reconstruction assistance.[74] India's strong support for Karzai stands in contrast to Washington's wavering over the legitimacy of his re-election as President in 2009. It also follows on leaked suggestions in Washington that India's reconstruction programme in Afghanistan was inconvenient insofar as it was interpreted as provocative in Pakistan, thus complicating Washington's task in securing Islamabad's full cooperation with its policies. Indeed, in 2010, during a visit by Russian Prime Minister Putin to Delhi, he and Prime Minister Singh exchanged notes on their worry over the lack of apparent Western resolve in Afghanistan to resist the Taliban.[75] Indian commentators suggested that were NATO to withdraw from Afghanistan, a revival of the Northern Alliance with Russian, Indian, and possibly Iranian support would be the obvious strategy for preventing a Taliban takeover of the whole country, in effect engineering a partition of the country. Thus, Washington's increasingly fraught relationship with Karzai, mirrored in several other NATO capitals, left India as the Afghan President's sole unqualified major supporter by mid-2010 and in a difficult position when NATO's withdrawal occurs.

Nepal

Nepal is well engaged in a process of transformation, emerging from serious governance challenges in 2006 to strip power from King Gyanendra and to bring the Maoists down from the hills and into government. These developments responded to deep frustrations in society over the previous ineffective and occasionally brutal political order and over the deep poverty with which most of the country continued to be afflicted.[76]

Nepal lies between two powerful neighbours, India and China, 'like a yam between two rocks' and often feels disempowered economically and otherwise by this fact.[77] Relations between India and Nepal, long organized by Raj interests and servants, have, since 1947, experienced the tensions and inter-dependencies that small neighbours typically have with large ones. Links of historical, geographical, economic, political, religious and sociocultural nature, as well as constant flows of population across borders, conspire to create deep attachments but also deep resentments.[78] The open border, national treatment granted to the nationals of the other, and familial links underline the exceptionally intense relations between the two sovereign states—but have also contributed to frequent friction at the political and diplomatic level, including an economic blockade imposed by India against Nepal in 1989.

The Treaty of Peace and Friendship concluded between India and Nepal on 31 July 1950 forms the basis of Indian policy towards Nepal.[79] However, the treaty was driven from an Indian perspective of security considerations. Nepalese resentment of Indian domination impinged directly on India's effort to uphold its special security relations with that country. Indian economic, political, and cultural influence on Nepal was pervasive. For Nepal's government, India was the ultimate guarantor of law and order (through close links between the armed forces of the two countries, which became controversial in 2009 when India appeared to stand by the leader of Nepal's armed forces when he resisted pressure to step down by Nepal's Maoist Prime Minister). Culturally, India's universities, religious and artistic institutions, media, and scientific-technological institutions also exercised a strong influence on Nepal.[80]

Nepal has several concerns vis-à-vis India, beyond worries over excessive Indian interference. Former Indian diplomat Rajiv Sikri writes: 'Indians have taken Nepal too much for granted. India's approach towards Nepal has been dismissive and neglectful. The Indian government and public have never shown adequate sensitivity to Nepali pride and uniqueness.'[81] Thus, as often with a large neighbour of a small and proud country, India justifiably feels at times that it cannot win.

Nepalese also believe that the treaties and agreements between Nepal and India are 'unequal' and not conducive to Nepal's interests. Such perspectives have prevented Nepal from capitalizing on the huge energy-hungry economy next door. Rather than viewing them as opportunities to be replicated, there is resentment in Nepal with regard to agreements on the Kosi and Gandak rivers. Nepal's apprehensions regarding the inadequacy of its arable land and therefore the difficulty of creating large water reservoirs is understandable, as are worries over the challenge of people displaced by hydroelectric development, but Nepal's inability to take constructive action where it could generate income (notably through hydroelectric development) is distressing to its friends.

Since the nadir in bilateral relations in the late 1980s, India has gradually shifted to a more sympathetic approach. In part through the early interventions of the Indian communist (Marxist) party, notably those of Sitaram Yechuri, India shifted from a position of unbridled hostility towards Nepal's Maoists (suspected of links with various Maoist insurgencies in India) towards a willingness to accommodate their participation in talks on Nepal's governance in India from 2006 onwards.[82] India's Communists and other Indian political actors argued strongly that the Maoists needed to renounce armed insurgency and to join the political process, which, to the surprise of many, the Maoists agreed to do in stages in 2005 and 2006.

In a parallel process, India, which had generally been hostile to UN involvement in its neighbourhood, accepted a role for UN monitoring of agreements entered into by political parties in Nepal. India supported the electoral process that brought the Maoists to power in early 2008. Although tensions developed between the Maoists and India (fuelled, in part, by the enhanced relationship the Nepali Maoists seemed keen to build up with Beijing), India has largely avoided overt intervention in the country's recent political affairs. While India can be and frequently is criticized for its 'heavy hand' in Nepal, its current stance and behaviour represent a quantum leap from its earlier outright domination of the country through a dependent Nepali royal family and other allies.

Of course, India also needs a positive agenda in Nepal. It could be more proactive and supportive of economic renewal there and of the strengthening of democracy and civil society. India's approach too often appears reactive to events on the ground, suggesting a lack of actual strategy vis-à-vis this important and troubled neighbour. This is all the more significant in a period marked by the abandonment of power by the Maoists in Kathmandu in early 2009, following parliamentary tensions over their decision to sack the armed forces commander, General Katawal, a decision that also brought them into conflict with Delhi.[83] S. D. Muni suggests:

> The standoff between India and Nepal resulted from a number of factors, principal among them the Maoists deviations from assurances sought by India and given by them on a number of bilateral issues; their propensity to use the China card beyond the 'red lines' drawn by India; [and] their unwillingness or incapacity to give up strong arm methods in dealing with their political opponents. Relevant as well were abrasive diplomatic behaviour of Kathmandu based Indian diplomacy; India's fears that the Maoists were inclined to and capable of changing Nepal's domestic power equations; and finally Delhi's fears that a Constitution drafted under assertive Maoist leadership may not be compatible with the democratic profile of Nepal.[84]

From a Nepali perspective, editor Aditya Adhikari writes:

> There is a pessimistic view of Nepal's place in the world and its future, and India's tremendous economic growth arouses respect and envy. Dislike of India

in Kathmandu has been tempered recently by fear of the Maoists, although Indian interference in domestic politics, real or perceived, is much criticized. Some advocate resort to a 'China card' against India, but this can be done only when politics is stable in Nepal and the centre is cohesive. Even then, however, nobody expects China's influence ever to rival that of India.[85]

Nepali analyst Prashant Jha notes:

One reason why Nepali politicians have not gone too far in playing India off against China is that the Chinese themselves have not shown any real inclination to play this game. But this might be changing now. In the past few years, Chinese investment in business and economic activities; its level of engagement with political parties; the number of high-level visits; and Beijing's public statements on Nepal's situation have increased. Unlike the Indians, Beijing has not yet used its influence to try to substantially influence Nepali domestic political outcomes.[86]

The comments above and the tensions inherent in the relationship between India's government and the Maoists in Nepal point to the wider challenges India faces in influencing developments in neighbouring countries.

Sri Lanka

India and Sri Lanka have deep historical linkages. Buddhism transferred to Sri Lanka from India and so did the Tamils. Unfortunately, the coexistence between the Sinhalese and the Tamils broke down when Sri Lankan nationalism attempted to consolidate itself around a Sinhala Buddhist identity.[87] Tamil discontent led to the demand for an independent Tamil Eelam, which emotionally and sometimes in more concrete ways embroiled India's Tamil population.

Fear of unrest among the Indian Tamil population both galvanized and constrained Indian policy at different times. From 1987 to 1990, India gingerly engaged in a degree of military intervention (in part aimed at addressing the large flows of Tamil refugees accruing to India) under the guise of peacekeeping. This did not work well, however, as, contrary to Indian military expectations, the Indian peacekeeping force was soon engaged in combat with the separatist Tamil LTTE, occasioning significant Indian casualties among its 20,000 troops (at their peak numbers) while failing to nudge the combatants towards compromise.

In 1991, Rajiv Gandhi, who had launched the Indian peacekeeping force, was assassinated by an LTTE suicide bomb squad. India's relationship with Sri Lanka's rulers has not been entirely comfortable ever since, which is why India subsequently moved towards a more 'hands off' policy to the extent that sentiments in the Indian state of Tamil Nadu allowed.[88] This, however, provided space to other players such as Pakistan, China, Israel, and the USA to play a role in promoting various ideas for a negotiated settlement and for economic links with Sri Lanka. With considerable international support, Norway offered its services as a mediator between Colombo and the LTTE, resulting in a cease-fire in 2002. But this agreement soon unravelled, and Norway was never able again to achieve full traction with the belligerents.[89] Following the election of President Mahinda Rajapaksa in 2005, Colombo opted for all-out military confrontation (occasioning many casualties on both sides) that led to the complete defeat of the LTTE and the death of its leader Prabhakaran, announced on 18 May 2009.[90] The Sri Lankan government subsequently espoused reconciliation between the two communities, but because of its hard line in prosecuting the fighting to the finish, high anxiety remained among Tamils in Sri Lanka and abroad.

During recent years, India's views on the Sri Lankan civil war were conflicted. On the one hand, the LTTE's assassination of Rajiv Gandhi left it with few friends in India's body politic and none in the Congress Party, once again leading the Indian government as of 2004. On the other, the Indian government remained convinced that a military 'solution' could never prove permanent without a genuine accommodation of Tamil interests within Sri Lanka. Delhi managed to defuse agitation from the Congress Party's Tamil Nadu ally, the DMK, for more energetic Indian action to protect the Tamils in Sri Lanka by engaging in diplomatic manoeuvres that did little to constrain the Rajapaksa government. In the final days of the civil war, which coincided with the final days of the Indian national election campaign of April–May 2009, Delhi redoubled its diplomatic lobbying in Colombo for the benefit of Tamil Nadu's worried population—quite effectively, as the DMK and Congress carried Tamil Nadu handily in the election results.

More worrying to India's community of geostrategic thinkers and commentators have been the warming ties between China and the Rajapaksa government that could, some Indians fear, result in major Chinese naval assets being developed in Sri Lanka, as part of a strategy centring on India's encirclement.[91] And there are indications that Colombo intends to benefit from playing India and China off against each other whenever possible, especially now that the civil war has ended.

Sri Lanka is the most successful significant state of South Asia in economic terms, with a GDP per capita nearly double India's. The way forward for India may be to forge ever closer and more productive economic relations with Sri Lanka, whose entrepreneurship has been impressive, while also nudging Colombo towards more convincing efforts to achieve reconciliation between Sri Lanka's two leading communities, and the rehabilitation of the many people displaced by the conflict. Sri Lanka has benefited from the rapid growth of the Indian economy (particularly pronounced in India's south). In 1998, the two countries signed a Free Trade Agreement (FTA) that has greatly expanded bilateral trade between them. A new Comprehensive Economic Partnership Agreement (CEPA) is now being discussed. Thus, in spite of tensions over Sri Lanka's civil war, the economic relationship between India and Sri Lanka stands as a model within the region and could serve as a model for other capitals of South Asia.

Sri Lankan scholar and diplomat Dayan Jayatilleka writes:

> India inheres in the very fabric of the island. Sri Lanka is an inverted and miniaturized mirror of India. Even if the Tamil factor did not exist, Sri Lanka's relationship with India would be its most vital external relationship. There is...an existential imperative of dual co-existence: Sri Lanka's co-existence with India, and Sinhala co-existence with the Tamils.
>
> Sri Lankan internal actors can do much less harm to the Sri Lankan state than a potential decision by India, under mounting Tamil Nadu pressure, to tilt against or simply to stop tilting towards Sri Lanka, and a corresponding decision by India's strategic partner, the USA, to mount economic pressure through multilateral institutions and agencies. Under the Obama administration there may be convergence between the positions of the US, EU and India on Sri Lanka.[92]

Bhutan

India and Bhutan enjoyed a cordial but distant relationship until quite recently. While they signed a Treaty of Friendship calling for peace and non-interference in each other's internal affairs on 8 August 1949, the relationship did not gain momentum until Jawaharlal Nehru visited Bhutan in 1958, and was enchanted by it. While formally genuflecting before the principle of non-interference, the essential bargain between India and Bhutan involved considerable Indian assistance in exchange for Bhutanese deference to India's foreign policy and defence concerns, notably as related to China.

Under Indian guidance, Bhutan developed a model of diplomatic engagement with middle powers, but with none of the Permanent Five (P-5) members of the UN Security Council and thus, most significantly, not with China. Indian troops remain stationed in strategic parts of northern Bhutan. Bhutan has subtly expanded the scope of its diplomacy through good working relations with the United States and some others of the P-5 while also engaging in low-key talks with the Chinese on the largely undefined border between them. In spite of clear Indian dominance of its small Himalayan neighbour, the relationship has been a genuinely friendly, positive, and mutually respectful one, with India working hard to keep its own profile in Bhutan as low as possible and the Bhutanese mostly expressing appreciation for India's contributions.

During the years 2006–8, Bhutan engaged in a carefully managed and apparently successful transition from absolute monarchy to a form of parliamentary democracy conjoined with a constitutional monarchy, marked by the abdication of the modernizing fourth King, Jigme Singye Wangchuk, in favour of his partly India-educated son Jigme Khesar Namgyel Wangchuck.[93] The shift was undertaken at the instigation of the monarchy and unfolded against the backdrop of nervousness by much of the population, which trusted the King but was not so sure about politicians. Throughout the process, India kept its inner thoughts to itself, and publicly extolled the vision of the fourth King.

Delhi pulled out all stops for the official visit to India of Bhutan's new King in August 2008, losing no opportunity to mark its regard for him and his country. The King's visit paralleled recent structural changes in the bilateral relationship: India signed a new treaty of friendship in 2007 which ended its guidance on Bhutan's foreign policy (although India's essential security interests are protected).[94]

Bhutan has, in recent years, registered significant economic success, largely due to the hydroelectric resources India has developed on its soil and for which India is the sole client (and one paying well for the privilege). In fact, the export of hydroelectric power to India is Bhutan's most important source of revenue. India has completed three major hydroelectric projects—Chukha, Kurichhu, and Tala—which are a great source of revenue generation for Bhutan, and Thimphu is now encouraging international interest in developing further hydroelectrical resources (for which India would remain the main client).[95] Bhutan enjoys preferential trade and transit facilities and benefits from exceptionally generous Indian aid; India finances nearly three-fifths of Bhutan's budget expenditures. Today, India holds 61 per cent of Bhutan's debt stock, while multilateral agencies hold 28 per cent and other bilateral donors hold 11 per cent.[96]

Indian assistance and aid from other partners, including the Asian development Bank, the World Bank, and several bilateral donors, have allowed Bhutan to leapfrog over many countries that had started their development process earlier, by establishing the infrastructure for a credible knowledge economy and in supporting the emergence, essentially in the span of two generations, of Bhutan's skilled, often English-speaking, modern human capital.

Maldives

The Maldive Islands, India's other 'good' neighbour, are located south of India's Lakshadweep Islands in the Indian Ocean. India and the Maldives enjoy close, cordial, and multidimensional relations. The two countries share ethnic, linguistic, cultural, religious, and commercial links steeped in antiquity. India was among the first to recognize the Maldives after its independence in 1965 and to establish diplomatic relations. It fields the only resident diplomatic mission in the capital, Male. Since 1965, India and the Maldives have developed close strategic, military, economic, and cultural relations. India did little to discomfit increasingly authoritarian President Maumoon Abdul Gayoom during a thirty-year run in power (1978–2008), but also did nothing to interfere with his defeat and replacement in 2008 by the young and dynamic Mohamed 'Anni' Nasheed, whom Gayoom had earlier imprisoned.

Indo-Maldivian relations have been nurtured and strengthened by regular high-level visits between the two countries. India's assistance in developmental work cemented the ties between these two countries. However, India can do little to assist the Maldives with its major concern: climate change that has produced dangerously rising oceans, the threat from which was brought home again at the time of the tsunami of December 2004, which wreaked great havoc on its tourism economy.

The Maldives, along with Bhutan, are the only striking examples of successful Indian relationships with small neighbours.

Myanmar

Myanmar's geographic location largely between China and India endows it with great strategic significance for Delhi. Several of India's northeastern states, afflicted with more or less separatist insurgencies, share a border extending over 1,643 kilometres with Myanmar. The borders are impossible to patrol closely and thus porous, with population, insurgents, and local trade spilling across in both directions. To the north, China's long border with the Indian state of Arunachal Pradesh is a source of tension, as China claims the entire state as its own. Myanmar can connect China with parts of India's northeast beyond Arunachal Pradesh. Myanmar also offers China geographical access to Bangladesh.[97] It is thus the pivot of many forms of actual and potential transit that India could find highly threatening in a part of the country far from its critical mass. There can be little doubt that Delhi's close ties with Myanmar are motivated at least in part by India's desire to discourage and combat insurgencies in its own northeast region.[98] No wonder then that India treads carefully in its relations with the unattractive military regime ensconced in Myanmar's new capital Naypyidaw.

Positive developments in bilateral relations have occurred in all areas since the mid-1990s, especially under the two coalition governments led by Prime Minister Atal Bihari Vajpayee (1998–2004). Bilateral trade has grown strongly although the volume of formal trade remains less than half of that Myanmar conducts with China.[99] Myanmar's exports to India during 2008–9 amounted to US$928.77 million, whereas India's exports to Myanmar for the same period stood at US$221.64 million.[100] Further, both countries have agreed to upgrade border trade at Moreh-Tamu and Zowkhathar-Rhi, and to open a new border trade point at Avangkhung in the states of Nagaland in India and Robermi in Myanmar. The two nations are also emerging as partners in the field of energy, information technology (IT), and power. In September 2008, an MoU was signed between NHPC (India) Ltd. and the Ministry of Power of Myanmar covering development of the Tamanthi Hydro-Power Project in the Chindwin river. The Centre for Development of Advanced Computing of India (C-DAC) has set up an India-Myanmar Centre for Development of IT Skill (IMCEITS), which was inaugurated by the Prime Minister of Myanmar, General Thein Sein, on 16 October 2008.[101]

Prime Minister Thein Sein visited India for the Bay of Bengal Initiative for Multi-Sectoral Technical and Economic Cooperation (BIMSTEC) Summit in November 2008 and the Vice President of India, Hamid Ansari, visited Myanmar 5–8 February 2009. During his visit several agreements in the training field were signed, as well as a Bilateral Investment Promotion & Protection Agreement. Institutional initiatives to check the activities of Indian insurgent groups in Myanmar were also discussed. India remains committed to assistance in developing infrastructure within Myanmar, including the Kaladan Multimodel Transit Transport Project, and to strengthening cooperation in oil and natural gas exploration (among other sectors).[102]

Myanmar is a major exporter to India, mainly of agricultural produce and primarily pulses. In fact between US$50 and US$400 million of pulses get exported to India annually. There generally is no direct trade documentation between Myanmar and India as Myanmar is perceived as high risk and not easy to cover by insurance, especially because of the insurgency activities on both sides of the border. Indian companies also route much of their trade via Singapore in order to avoid tax. Besides the agro-manufacturing and trading which goes via Singapore, there is pharmaceutical distribution through Korean and German companies, rough stones are exported to India and then, once cut, to the Middle East, and there is an increasing volume of tourism.[103]

Myanmar is also India's gateway to ASEAN countries through Thailand and Laos, being the only ASEAN country with which India has both a land and maritime border. Many Indian geostrategists see the relationship with Myanmar as key to preventing China and Pakistan from developing further footholds beyond the Chindwin River. India's Tri-services Command at Andaman (in a group of islands well to the east of India's main coastline) lies alongside Myanmar's maritime boundaries and is separated from Myanmar's Coco islands, where China is believed to be building up its naval infrastructure, by a mere 18–30 km.

India's intelligentsia is hostile to Myanmar's military junta mismanaging the country's economy and oppressing its people. There is much sympathy for opposition leader Aung San Suu Kyi, who received the Jawaharlal Nehru Award for International Understanding in 1995, India's highest honour available to a foreigner.[104] And many Indians, including some prominent politicians such as former Prime Minister I. K. Gujral, believe that their own government should advocate democratic reforms in her country. Indian analysts also worry about spillover effects onto Indian soil and more widely into its neighbourhood, if and when the Naypyidaw regime falls in ways that spawn chaos and fear within the country. But most in government believe that India's strategic interests require it to compete for the favour of any government in Napyidaw, particularly one that has allowed China to gain such a strong foothold in its economy and through Beijing's defence footprint within Myanmar. President Than Shwe visited Delhi without provoking meaningful protest in July 2010. India's privileged relationship with the Naypyidaw generals allowed it quicker humanitarian access than that offered to multilateral agencies following the devastating floods in coastal areas of Myanmar brought about by Cyclone Nargis in May 2008. And it is conceivable that, when the Myanmar regime collapses under its own dead weight at some point in the future, India will be helpful in promoting a more inclusive form of government.

China–South Asia relations and India

As discussed in the next chapter, China's growing influence in South Asia has been an important concern for Delhi. Despite recently booming trade between the two countries, lingering suspicion and mistrust characterize a relationship that can be inflamed at any time by many potential irritants (for example, disputed border claims and the Dalai Lama's residency in India). Their competition for influence in South Asia and neighbouring regions remains a major source of uncertainty at the global level, with commentators far from united over the likely path of their evolving relationship. Neither country is today expansionist in territorial terms (having enough trouble keeping their own existing territory at peace, as demonstrated in China in mid-2009 by violence in the Xinjiang Autonomous Region and in 2008 by clashes between Chinese security authorities and Tibetan communities both within Tibet and beyond, and in India by a plethora of Maoist and separatist insurgencies). But in terms of their international economic interests and their military reach, the scope for friction is very significant, not least through third parties, notably those serving a direct or indirect buffer role.

In nearly every Indian regional relationship outlined above, China has appeared as either an active or potential third party. China is seen by Indians as having systematically sought to counterbalance India in the subcontinent by building up Pakistan and its military capabilities.[105] India watches warily as China expands its military and political roles across the Indian Ocean and South Asian region, fearing that it is sliding into a state of 'strategic encircle- ment' by China, in part through a 'string of pearls' strategy centred on the Indian Ocean.[106] This is the view of Gurmeet Kanwal, Director of a Delhi-based military think-tank, The Center for Land Warfare Studies (CLAWS), who writes:

> China's foreign and defence policies are quite obviously designed to marginalize India in the long term and reduce India to the status of a sub-regional power by increasing Chinese influence and leverage in the South Asian region.[107]

Indian analysts are apprehensive of China's security relations with India's South Asian neighbours. According to Sujit Dutta: 'Unlike China's ties in East Asia, where they are essentially economic, in South Asia ties are primarily political-military in content.'[108] Indeed, the perception of being threatened by China is deeply held in strategic circles in Delhi, and anti-Chinese senti- ment is rarely far from India's editorial and commentary pages, placing India at something of a disadvantage vis-à-vis China, where media commentary can be carefully calibrated in the service of diplomacy.

India is today facing a challenge the United States never faced (irrespective of the Monroe Doctrine). Apart from a brief period in the early 1960s when the Soviet Union challenged Washington's hemispheric hegemony through Cuba, US dominance of the Americas, to the extent that it has cared to pursue and protect it, has not been threatened seriously since the early twentieth century (and probably before). India, on the other hand, sits alongside a powerful neighbour that is growing much faster than it economically and in terms of military capacity, and disposing of the resources necessary to make itself very attractive to other countries in the region.[109]

Whether India can manage its anxieties and develop therapies that soothe rather than exacerbate its fears will be important. It has had the wisdom to signal that it intends to join no alliance against China and that it will never serve as a local pawn for a wider strategy. It has also developed globally, if not regionally, new assets in its competition with China, not least through much warmer and more substantive ties with the USA. But these will not necessarily help it in managing its own neighbourhood.

Challenges and the way forward

No big country is loved by its neighbours. India's neighbourhood policy abounds with ironies. While India has little influence over Pakistan, its policy is thought by many outside observers to be perhaps excessively and unhelp-fully Pakistan-centric.[110] This has prompted other nations to wonder if a belligerent anti-India policy is the best method of attracting Delhi's atten-tion.[111] The irony lies in India's considerable restraint in reacting to security crises believed to have originated from within Pakistan; but the fact remains that while India is considerably less focused on Pakistan than many Pakistanis seem to be on India, the first steps in arranging a lasting détente will probably need to come from the larger, stronger, and more self-confident party in the relationship.

The challenge for Indian diplomacy lies in convincing its neighbours that India is an opportunity, not a threat. Far from being besieged by India, they have through it access to a vast market and to a productive hinterland that could provide their economies far greater opportunities for growth than if they were to rely on their domestic markets alone. For Bangladesh, greater engagement with India could yield major economic dividends, as Sri Lanka has already established. But has India done enough to make this option attractive? Judging from the admittedly narrow prism of its lacklustre leader-ship of SAARC, the answer would have to be not yet. And, as described earlier in this chapter, intra-South Asian trade remains limited. On the other hand, Indian Prime Minister Singh's advocacy of greater economic integration among SAARC partners rings true, as does his positive engagement with global financial and economic challenges in the G-20.[112]

Economic cooperation represents the easiest 'sell' to various constituencies within the countries of the region. Were this to prove successful, cooperation on more divisive and sensitive issues, such as terrorism, separatism, insur-gency, religious fundamentalism, and ethnic strife, could be attempted with greater chances of success.

India's pragmatism on both the Sri Lankan and Nepali civil wars in recent years has served it well. It does not seem to have lost any real (as opposed to imagined) influence in either country, although Nepal's Maoists are quick to see Delhi's hand behind every adverse development befalling them. That India is today, to use an expression of George H. W. Bush in 1988, a 'kinder and gentler' neighbour than it was twenty years ago redounds entirely to its credit. But this still does not amount to much of a strategy.

A strategy for each neighbouring country (and sometimes cross-cutting ones for several neighbours) may require better coordination and more atten-tion among various units of government in Delhi than has been the case to date. As JNU scholar Rajeev R. Chaturvedy comments: 'India must intensify its efforts to improve its internal security conditions and institutional capacity which, through their current deficiencies, are negatively affecting foreign policy formulation and execution by shrinking India's margin for maneuver vis-à-vis cross-border partners.'[113] India also needs to devote more diplomatic

127

and political energy towards tending its relationship with immediate neighbours. The Indian economy is growing at a faster rate than the other South Asian countries, and given the disparity between the size of these economies, India will continue to outpace the others in the years to come. This will give India certain advantages over the other countries but it may also give rise to some difficulties.

For example, migration to India from Bangladesh and Nepal may increase further and create new problems relating to demographic imbalance in certain parts of India, giving rise to friction between communities or simply rises in crime rates. However, if educational and employment opportunities are created in the hilly hinterlands of Nepal or in the outlying districts of Bangladesh, they may act as domestic checks to mitigate pressure for migration.

India may also need to induce greater complementarities of economic production in its region, as many of the South Asian countries today compete with, rather than complement, each other's exports. Some of the neighbouring countries might develop strategies centred on feeding larger industrial input needs or food requirements in India.

South Asia as a whole may have insufficient hydrocarbon energy resources, but it has yet to exploit fully its hydroelectric energy potential available in Nepal and the Indian northeast. There is a very strong case for a pan-South Asian energy grid that can work on the basis of electricity trading—a system that is already in place within India. Greater electricity availability could change the economic face of the whole region.

Finally, India will need a stronger articulation of its vision for South Asia. China, the USA, and Pakistan are the other major actors in the region. In the long run, one key outcome that strategies should be designed to serve is the reversal of the tremendous economic damage inflicted after the 1947 partition: road, rail, and river links that united British India were subject to near-impenetrable barriers. Natural ports were cut off from their hinterlands, as Chittagong was from India's northeast and Kolkata from Bangladesh. Twin commercial cities like Mumbai and Karachi have become distant neighbours. Gradual easing of these barriers could produce significant economic (and eventually security) benefits.

Indian policy in South Asia has improved in tone and quality in recent years. But it is not yet such as to induce either awe or affection amongst those neighbours who matter. India cannot aspire to be a truly convincing 'great power' until it achieves a better handle on its region without the support and active involvement of outsiders. Indeed, India faces a circular challenge: unless its region becomes more cooperative (and prosperous), India is unlikely to develop into more than a regional power, but it is true as well that it cannot be a global power unless it reaches beyond its neighbourhood. This conundrum will arise again, more indirectly, in chapters ahead.

6

The Sino-Indian Relationship: Can Two Tigers Share a Mountain?

Not much has changed in the rhetoric of Sino-Indian relations since 1951, since Mao Zedong declared that 'excellent friendship had existed between the two countries for thousands of years'.[1] Yet few of the lofty proclamations made by leaders on either side are reflected in the reality of relations between China and India.

Being ancient civilizations reincarnated as modern republics around the same time, both countries have lived through tumultuous times domestically and internationally. Today they have emerged as rising powers in Asia, keenly observed by the West and, increasingly, by the rest of the world. Their large populations and rapidly growing economies have, between them, made Asia the rising continent of the global dispensation (along with a stagnating Japan). Yet little attention is paid to the relationship between them beyond their shared border and the limited war fought over it in 1962. Most scholarship on modern Chinese foreign policy has focused on its relations with the United States, Japan, and East Asia. Similarly on the Indian side, the foremost obsessions have been with Pakistan, the South Asian neighbourhood, and the United States. Surprisingly for two states of such growing importance and with such a rich and sometimes fractious history, their relationship seems largely reactive and, more broadly, adrift. Given robustly growing economic ties, a renewed war seems ever less likely. But neither country has apparently developed a grand strategy relating to the other.

An unshakable and largely unprofitable preoccupation with the past on the Indian side and an equally intense preoccupation with domestic consolidation on the Chinese side have left the relationship in many respects undertended. The relationship might best be seen as one of geostrategic competition qualified by growing commercial cooperation. And there is some asymmetry at play. China is a more neuralgic subject in Indian national debates than India is in China. China does not appear to feel threatened in any serious way by India while India at times displays tremendous insecurity in the face of Chinese economic success and military expansion.

The similarities between India and China are striking to many outside observers. Both have nuclear weapons, burgeoning economies, expanding military budgets, and large reservoirs of manpower. Both seem to be vying for influence in the Indian Ocean, the Persian Gulf, Africa, Central Asia, and East Asia. The standard question posed by those who do study Sino-Indian relations is 'cooperation or conflict?' This is no different from the question posed by the many more scholars who study Sino-US relations.[2] The dimensions of the two bilateral relationships, however, are different. Sino-US ties are often seen in terms of a one-to-one contest for global pre-eminence, whereas the Sino-Indian relationship is far less defined by the actions and policies of the two countries themselves than by the interaction of these with extraneous actors such as the United States, Pakistan, and other nations in South Asia. It also is defined in part by strikingly contrasting polities and models of development, each silently competing with the other not just for capital, resources, and markets, but also for legitimacy in the arena of great and emerging global powers.

In what follows, the history of the modern relationship between the two countries is sketched and thematic issues on which India and China have agreed and differed in the past and the present are outlined. Finally, the prospects for future conflict are weighed against the prospects for future cooperation. One conclusion arising from this narrative is that a deeper understanding of each other's domestic compulsions and state–society relations would help India and China to identify and defuse potential sources of sharp conflict before they get out of hand. Meanwhile, each has done a creditable job of avoiding unwarranted antagonism and adventurism in engaging the other.

Historical overview

For analytical convenience, the modern history of Sino-Indian relations can be divided into four distinct periods. The first, from 1950 to 1962, was a period of purported friendship and ideological congruence around anti-imperialist foreign policy objectives. This soon deteriorated into a bitter yet brief border conflict, following which the second period of 1962 to 1976 was described by one pair of scholars as the Sino-Indian 'Cold War'.[3] During this period each aligned with the other's enemy in an effort to augment their own security and undermine that of their adversary, with China cosying up to Pakistan and India to the USSR.[4] After 1976, during the third period, efforts were made by both sides to normalize the relationship, and this led to tentative steps to address differences through careful management and a predictable process of dialogue. This was by no means an easy task, not least because of sensitivities in India, frequently expressed in the media and parliament. Thus Sino-Indian 'normalization' of relations occurred in fits and starts, producing the positive outcome of a gradual build-up of institutional ties between the two countries, and an improved understanding of each other's domestic and regional constraints and priorities.

In 1998, India pointed to China as the justification for its second round of nuclear tests since 1974. Although this could have created significant tensions between the two nations, in retrospect the event was but a blip on the Sino-Indian trend line and economic relations have since intensified. During the fourth period, from 1998 onward, India and China also have increasingly participated alongside each other in a complex web of global economic diplomacy eliciting frequent, if often merely tactical, cooperation, as in multilateral negotiations over strategies to combat climate change. While relations have generally improved in bilateral and international forums, the relationship remains one of uncertainty and occasional antagonism, marked by China's full emergence as a global power and the courting of India by other powers such as the USA, as important not just in its own right but also, potentially, as a counterweight to Chinese power and regional influence.

1950–62: ideological enthusiasms

India and China started off on friendly footing soon after their formation as republics. In 1949, the Indian government under Prime Minister Jawaharlal Nehru was quick to recognize the People's Republic of China (PRC) government even though the latter was officially opposed by the Western powers. In 1950, despite China's military movement into Tibet, India opposed a US-sponsored attempt in the United Nations Security Council to label China an aggressor in the Korean War. In 1951, India boycotted the San Francisco Peace Treaty on the grounds that, *inter alia*, the settlement did not return the island of Formosa (Taiwan) to China.[5] And, in 1954, India officially acquiesced in Chinese dominance over Tibet.

The main source of entente between the two nations, epitomized by the popular Hindi slogan *Hindi Chini Bhai-Bhai* (Indians and Chinese are brothers)[6] in the 1950s, was their shared sense of having cast off the imperialist yoke through long (albeit completely different) struggles. Proclamations by Indian and Chinese statesmen highlighted the shared responsibility that India and China felt in leading the countries newly emerging from colonization in a quest for peace and prosperity against the treacherous backdrop of the US–Soviet superpower rivalry.[7] Moreover, the ideology of anti-imperialism was strongly endorsed by leaders of both nations. Indeed as late as 1962, at the height of the Sino-Indian border dispute, Zhou Enlai reminded Nehru: 'Our two peoples' common interests in their struggle against imperialism outweigh by far all the differences between our two countries. We have a major responsibility for Sino-Indian friendship, Asian-African solidarity and Asian peace.'[8]

Despite the common references to imperialism and Afro-Asian solidarity, there were marked differences in the ideologies of the two great leaders, Mao and Nehru. Mao had led a militant movement that armed and mobilized the peasantry to win a civil war and establish the PRC. On the other hand, alongside Gandhi, Nehru led a movement that won an unlikely victory through non-violent resistance. When Pakistan invaded Kashmir in 1948, he had chosen to refer the matter to the UN. He had refused to allow his country to be dragged into the Korean War, preferring to employ Indian troops in peacekeeping missions. Early in his tenure, he had eschewed violence in favour of diplomacy to deal with the Bengal refugee crisis of 1950 and Pakistani troop movements in Kashmir soon after. Consequently, Nehru chose a foreign policy of non-alignment and Mao one (at least formally, if intermittently) of support for international revolution. Nehru sought to consolidate the principle of sovereignty for newly independent nations, while Mao sought to create class divisions and support communist revolutions in the same countries.[9]

Despite their different approaches, both Nehru and Mao saw an important place for their nations in the future of the international system. Mao was ably supported by Zhou, a sophisticated actor often introducing an element of ambiguity in Chinese policy that helpfully qualified the principles laid down by Mao. However, the mantle of leading the newly independent colonies of Asia and Africa could not be shared by China and India for long. By emphasizing their anti-imperialist credentials and their suffering under imperialist domination, both nations sought to 'build solidarity and gain prestige' among Third World countries.[10] In practice, this created competition between India and China to be viewed as vanguards of the developing world. India under Nehru had acquired somewhat of a head start by hosting the First Asian Relations Conference, held in New Delhi in 1947 while China was still in the throes of a bitter civil war. The Nationalist government of China had sent a representative to this conference, where some tension was evident over India's attempts to project its leadership in Asia.[11]

Subsequently, at the first Afro-Asian Conference at Bandung, Indonesia, in 1955, Nehru took great pride in inviting Zhou and introducing him to other leaders as if India were a 'public mentor and introducer of China into the group of developing nations'.[12] This approach was not well received by Zhou or other PRC leaders. Much later, Zhou would comment to a group of journalists that he had 'never met a more arrogant man'.[13] In their struggle for ideological leadership of the Third World, China and India had already been set at odds by 1955. Indeed at Bandung, China is reported to have reached a 'strategic understanding with Pakistan founded on their convergent interests vis-à-vis India'.[14] This understanding laid the foundation of one of the twentieth century's longest and most stable alliances (despite China being increasingly apprehensive in recent years about the Islamist extremism in Pakistan, that could eventually impact China itself through the Xinjiang Autonomous Region). After Bandung, the emerging ideological competition between India and China contributed to an increasingly strained bilateral relationship that was soon put to the test in addressing a serious irritant: the Sino-Indian border.

The Border War of 1962

While the border dispute can be considered a problematic bequest 'left over by history',[15] its more immediate antecedents lay in the Chinese invasion of Tibet in 1950. This created significant tensions in India, which had strategic interests in Tibet and 'spiritual bonds' with Tibetan civilization stretching back almost two millennia.[16] An Indian analyst writing later at the height of the Sino-Indian border conflict said, 'Any strong expansionist power, entrenched in Tibet, holds in its hands a loaded pistol pointed at the heart of India'.[17] India therefore followed an equivocal policy: on the one hand it lent limited material support to Tibetan rebels during the Chinese occupation (in which it had officially acquiesced); on the other, it declined to support the Tibetans at the UN or expand the scope of conflict in any manner.[18]

It was soon was recognized in Delhi that the Indo-Tibet border in particular, and the Sino-Indian border in general, needed stabilizing. Potential controversy lay in two areas—the eastern sector (56,000 square miles), which the Indians called the North East Frontier Agency (NEFA) and which the Chinese viewed as South Tibet; and the western sector (13,000 square miles), which included most prominently the Aksai Chin plateau, bordering Kashmir, Xinjiang, and Tibet. The year 1959 was somewhat of a watershed in Sino-Indian relations. It had come to be known that Tibetan rebels were being trained and funded by the United States' Central Intelligence Agency (CIA) and Chiang Kai-shek's agents in the Indian hill station of Kalimpong in the state of West Bengal. Although the Chinese had requested that the Indian government suppress these activities and expel the rebels, India had followed through half-heartedly. In March, following an uprising against Chinese rule in Tibet, the Dalai Lama fled to India. In pursuit of the Tibetan rebels, the People's Liberation Army (PLA) came up against the Indian army at Longju and clashes followed. In April 1960, Zhou arrived in New Delhi for talks with Nehru, which 'failed spectacularly' by all accounts.[19]

In November 1961, India launched a more overtly confrontational 'forward policy', which involved establishing military posts north of existing Chinese posts in the disputed territories in an attempt to cut off Chinese supply lines, and force a withdrawal. This approach was reinforced in April 1962 while China was reeling under the disastrous impact of its Great Leap Forward programme of economic reform and facing threats of a military invasion from Taiwan and from US involvement in a proxy conflict through Laos. By July, however, both the Taiwan and Laos challenges had been resolved to China's satisfaction and it focused its energies on countering India's forward policy. China attacked Indian positions in both the eastern and western sectors on 20 October 1962, much to the surprise of an ill-prepared Delhi. Nehru appealed to President John F. Kennedy of the United States seeking assistance, which the USA was quick to provide. Although an American carrier was dispatched to the Bay of Bengal, it was almost immediately recalled when China unilaterally declared a ceasefire and withdrew to the positions it had suggested from the beginning of the dispute. The war had ended in thirty-one days with a comprehensive victory for the Chinese.

1962–76: security dilemma

The Sino-Indian war is often cited as the watershed between Nehruvian idealism in Indian foreign policy and the stirring of pragmatic impulses during the leadership of Indira Gandhi. Nehru's faith in his diplomatic skills and in his ability to bring the Chinese around to a favourable settlement on the border through the forward policy was a drastic miscalculation. It opened the door for an overhaul of India's defence policy, its military planning structure, and an increase in its military expenditure. Nehru himself died in 1964, 'broken' by China's betrayal.[20] The period following the war saw India align more closely with the Soviet Union, which had already begun to split quite noticeably from China within the international Communist movement. China for its part began to follow through on the exploratory discussions it had with Pakistan in the previous decade. A major signal of Pakistani commitment was the settlement of the Sino-Pakistani border early in 1962, through which Pakistan ceded to China territory that India claimed in Kashmir. A modest programme of military transfers from China to Pakistan began in 1964.

The 1965 war between India and Pakistan was a litmus test of the already established USA–Pakistan relationship as well as the new Sino-Pakistani relationship. When the USA declared neutrality and blocked military transfers to both India and Pakistan, the latter turned to China for assistance and received it in generous amounts. Aside from military aid, one scholar also suspects significant Chinese influence on Operation Gibraltar, Pakistan's plan for an attack on Indian Kashmir in 1965.[21] When war broke out, China came down heavily on the Pakistani side and threatened to open a front with India on the Sikkim border. Ultimately it required US intervention and a UN resolution calling for a ceasefire to discourage Chinese involvement.

The year 1964 also saw China conduct its first nuclear test at Lop Nor. This was the motivation behind India's subsequent attempts and success at Pokhran ten years later in conducting a 'peaceful' nuclear explosion. The period from 1965 to 1969 was one of tremendous tumult within China. Following the economic debacle of the Great Leap Forward in the late 1950s, Mao Zedong launched a campaign of social upheaval to consolidate his power within the Chinese Communist Party (CCP). This led to the Cultural Revolution, at the peak of which China's foreign relations with almost all but Pakistan were essentially eliminated.[22] With regard to superpower rivalry, from 'leaning to one side' in the 1950s (i.e. towards the Soviet Union), China adopted a 'dual adversary' foreign policy in the 1960s,[23] starting with the second Taiwan Strait Crisis of 1958. During this period India and China once again exchanged artillery fire in the eastern sector of their disputed border, in 1967.[24] China went to war with the Soviet Union in 1969. That same year China and Pakistan began coordinating the supply of arms, training, and funding to insurgents in the northeastern states of India, particularly in Nagaland, Mizoram, and Manipur—activities that China itself had been engaged in since 1962.[25]

As the Cultural Revolution subsided, the USA began a process of cultivating ties with China through Pakistan. During the 1971 unrest in East Pakistan, India faced tremendous pressure from both the USA and China not to intervene in Pakistan's internal affairs. This in turn drove India to seek a military alliance with the Soviet Union, and the 'so-called America-China-Pakistan versus Soviet-India alliance was established'.[26] From this point until the 1980s when Soviet foreign policies changed, particularly with the rise of Mikhail Gorbachev, India and China were on opposing sides of a global rivalry. Furthermore, superimposed onto this superpower conflict between the USA and the Soviet Union were the Sino-Soviet split and the Indo-Pakistan rivalry. In a world of chessboard diplomacy and geostrategic management, it was logical for China to ally with Pakistan during this time, completing this complex network of antagonisms.

The Sino-US rapprochement brought UN membership and a permanent seat on the UN Security Council for the PRC. India responded to China's new global status with a nuclear test in 1974, and the annexation of Sikkim the following year, provoking loud Chinese protestations. In 1976, China signed an agreement on nuclear cooperation with Pakistan (which was not acted upon until 1981).[27] Looking back at these fourteen years of the Sino-Indian relationship, two things are clear. First, both nations engaged in fairly typical security dilemma behaviour. While India augmented its defence expenditures following the 1962 debacle, China tested a nuclear bomb in 1964, which prompted India to do the same ten years later. Both nations also sought alliances with each other's arch-rivals, Pakistan and the Soviet Union. If there was one actor that benefited from these developments, it was the United States, which was able to discomfit its superpower rival in Moscow by improving ties with China (which also unsettled India).

Second, although India and China engaged in security dilemma behaviour, it is unclear whether the intention behind the Chinese effort was to counter the Indian threat. During this period, China was much more preoccupied with the Soviet Union and the USA and likely saw India neither as a credible threat nor a foreign policy priority. Had it been more preoccupied with India, China would likely have moved sooner to guarantee nuclear weapons for Pakistan. The notion that India does not matter to China as much as China matters to India has been argued by, among others, Susan Shirk, who suggests that even the nuclear test of 1998 barely registered a reaction from China until the Vajpayee government propagated the 'China threat' idea.[28] Therefore, the lesson from the 1962–76 period is that while India and China acted as if they were motivated by the threat each posed to the other, the threat perception was much larger on the Indian side, having suffered a comprehensive and humiliating defeat at the hands of the Chinese in 1962.

1976–98: tentative rapprochement

Although a key Chinese signal to India for rapprochement went back to the 1970 'Mao smile' along with which the Indian chargé d'affaires in Beijing was told warmly by Mao that Sino-Indian relations should improve,[29] events such as the Indo-Pakistan war of 1971, India's nuclear test, and the annexation of Sikkim had to be digested before Indira Gandhi could reciprocate in 1976, when she restored full diplomatic relations between the two countries. Mao died in September 1976 and after a brief leadership struggle Deng Xiaoping replaced him in 1978. Soon after, China made it clear that it would no longer support insurgencies in India's northeastern states.[30]

This policy decision was in keeping with a wider paradigm shift in China's inward and outward orientation following Mao's death. While Deng undertook a programme of economic liberalization and began reversing the economic damage perpetrated at home during the Mao years, internationally China no longer attempted to foment Communist revolutions in developing countries or to antagonize the United States. Deng's new foreign policy, based on the principle of *Tao Guang Yang Hui* ('Hide Brightness, Nourish Obscurity'), prescribed a focus on building up domestic economic strength and disentangling the country from international conflicts. This represented a marked shift from the heady days of Mao's militant internationalism and as a result, the Sino-Indian relationship underwent a slow but real transformation.

The process of rapprochement was, however, rather uneasy and vulnerable to temporary changes in international and bilateral winds, as well as more significant events at home and abroad. Indira Gandhi viewed the Chinese as having betrayed her father and her political predilection was to lean toward the Soviet Union as a counterweight against future challenges on the China front.[31] This naturally made genuine rapprochement difficult. During the brief interlude of the Janata government in 1979, Atal Bihari Vajpayee made a historic visit to China as India's Foreign Minister. Unfortunately, the visit coincided with the Chinese 'Pedagogical War' invasion of Vietnam and caused him much embarrassment. In the same region, India no doubt equated China's support for the Khmer Rouge regime in Cambodia as a counterweight to Vietnam with China's support for Pakistan vis-à-vis India.[32]

Renewed Chinese interest in resolving the border dispute with India was evident in 1980. A long dialogue process was initiated the following year, when Foreign Minister Huang Hua became the first Chinese leader since Zhou Enlai in 1960 to visit India. In 1982 Leonid Brezhnev made an important speech at Tashkent signalling the Soviet Union's desire for a Sino-Soviet rapprochement, thus removing a major potential constraint on the Sino-Indian rapprochement.[33] Around this time, China also decided to adopt a more balanced foreign policy between the two superpowers.[34] While these events created openings for Sino-Indian rapprochement, the border dialogue process initiated in 1981 turned sour during the course of the following six years, culminating in a large-scale military stand-off between India and China in the eastern sector at Sumdurong Chu in 1986–7. New Delhi did not help matters by changing the status of the North East Frontier Agency from a Union Territory to a State of the Indian Union called Arunachal Pradesh, thus providing stronger constitutional protection for the region.

The Sumdurong Chu impasse was eventually resolved and Rajiv Gandhi made a historic visit to China in December 1988. During his visit, he made two unprecedented concessions in Indian policy towards China. First, he reversed the decades-old stance that resolution of the border dispute was a precondition for the normalization of relations between India and China. Second, he admitted that some members of the Tibetan community residing in India were engaged in anti-China activities on Indian soil. This visit was followed by a flurry of high-level diplomatic exchanges during the early 1990s that involved Prime Minister Li Peng in 1991,[35] President R. Venkataraman in 1992, Prime Minister Narasimha Rao in 1993, and President Jiang Zemin in 1996. Cumulatively, these visits resulted in new agreements to cooperate on the border issue and expand cooperation in other areas.

Thus, the period from 1976 to 1998 saw initial steps being taken by India and China to mend their relationship after the fracture of 1962. While domestic changes in China permitted a less hostile and introverted Chinese approach to international relations, India found the growing Sino-Soviet rapprochement to be advantageous in attempting to resolve the border dispute permanently. While this proved too ambitious, the bilateral interactions of the 1980s and early 1990s created a foundation for future cooperation and the institutionalization of efforts to find a permanent settlement to the border dispute.

1998 onwards: the age of uncertainty

Following India's nuclear tests of May 1998, Prime Minister Atal Bihari Vajpayee wrote to US President Bill Clinton in a letter that was leaked by Washington:

> We have an overt nuclear weapon state on our borders, a state which committed armed aggression against India in 1962. Although our relations with that country have improved in the last decade or so, an atmosphere of distress persists mainly due to the unresolved border problem. To add to the distress that country has materially helped another neighbour of ours to become a covert nuclear weapons state.[36]

Ten days prior to the tests, Defence Minister George Fernandes had declared China 'potential threat number one' in an interview.[37] Moreover, as if to exact payback for Vajpayee's embarrassment over China's Vietnam invasion during his visit in 1979, the first tests occurred soon after the New Delhi visit of a senior member of the PLA, General Fu Quanyou, even before he returned to Beijing.[38]

The message to China seemed loud and clear. Nevertheless, after some strident criticisms of the nuclear tests, China did not waste time in resuming relations with India. Unlike the USA, it did not press for sanctions on India.[39] One scholar has argued that this shows China's relative lack of concern about India as a security threat.[40] Another counters this, arguing that the Chinese lack of concern was 'feigned indifference' and that 'China views India very much as a potential challenger, albeit a lower-order threat, but recognizes that only benefits accrue from its consistent refusal to own up to this perception'.[41] An alternative explanation is that China was heavily invested in its domestic affairs and therefore could not afford to antagonize a neighbour (as Deng's philosophy would suggest). Another suggests that China and India simply do not view nuclear weapons as realistic instruments of war and rely on them much more as 'strategic insurance against extreme threats and a symbol of their own aspirations in the international system'.[42] The fact that China's nuclear weapons stockpile far outweighs India's in quantity and reach might also explain China's limited overt concern over India's second round of nuclear tests.

Explanations of China's indifference aside, the relatively subdued reaction to India's nuclear tests (followed by Pakistan's own tests only a few days later) allowed the Sino-Indian rapprochement to continue on an upward swing. A critical test was the Kargil conflict between India and Pakistan in 1999, during which Indian Foreign Minister Jaswant Singh visited China and was assured of Beijing's neutrality in the conflict, much to the satisfaction of Indian leaders.[43] Indeed it has been widely observed that China's statements on the Kashmir issue and on India–Pakistan bilateral conflicts in general since the 1990s advocate their resolution bilaterally. This is a marked change from China's stance during the Indo-Pakistan wars of 1965 and 1971.

The new millennium saw the resumption of high-level diplomatic exchanges despite intermittent flashpoints in the relationship. Indian President K. R. Narayanan, who had been the first Indian ambassador to China in 1976 after the resumption of diplomatic relations, visited Beijing in 2000 to commemorate fifty years of diplomatic relations between the two nations. Early that year, the seventeenth Karmapa, considered the third most senior cleric by many Buddhists, fled from Tibet to India against the wishes of the Chinese Government. Nonetheless, Li Peng visited India again in 2001, followed by Premier Zhu Rongji in 2002. In 2003, Prime Minister Vajpayee visited Beijing, more than two decades after his first visit as Foreign Minister. In 2005, Premier Wen Jiabao made a historic visit to Bangalore (not New Delhi, in pointed recognition of China's desire to partner with India's information technology sector). During this visit, China recognized Sikkim as a part of India and seemed to acquiesce in India's bid for a permanent seat in the United Nations Security Council (although recent events have belied this understanding).[44]

The following year, 2006, was declared 'India–China Friendship Year' and involved a year-long exchange of dignitaries and cultural events between the two nations. A significant symbol of friendship was the reopening of the Nathula trading pass on the Sino-Indian border in Sikkim. Overall, cooperation has steadily increased in trade, growing from US$117 million in 1987 to almost $42 billion in 2008–9,[45] and defence, with India and China hosting their first ever joint military exercises in December 2007. In fact, in 2009, India–China trade overtook India–USA trade in value,[46] making China India's top trading partner. In January 2008, Prime Minister Manmohan Singh visited Beijing and reaffirmed with President Hu Jintao and Premier Wen Jiabao a 'shared vision on the 21st century'.[47] In December 2008, China and India jointly conducted 'Joint Hands-2008', an army counterterrorism exercise.[48] Recently, building on the cooperation witnessed at the December 2009 Copenhagen Climate Change Summit, and coinciding with the sixtieth anniversary of the establishment of diplomatic relations, Indian President Pratibha Patil paid a 'very positive and fruitful' visit to Beijing in May 2010 (the first visit of an Indian head of state to China in a decade).[49]

That said, India–China diplomacy is more easily managed in the highly controlled environment of Beijing than it is in Delhi, where raucous media and parliamentary complaints about comments by the Chinese ambassador on border issues marred the run-up to President Hu Jintao's visit in November 2006.[50] Irritants continue to plague the relationship, notably the border issues (which are often unhelpfully marred by jingoistic media reporting on both the Chinese and Indian sides).[51] In 2007 China refused to grant a visa to a government official from the Indian state of Arunachal Pradesh, which constitutes part of China's territorial claim in the eastern sector, on the grounds that he was already a Chinese citizen. The official was part of a group of 107 officers scheduled to visit China on a study tour. In retaliation, the Indian government cancelled the entire visit.[52] In 2008, Prime Minister Singh invited Chinese displeasure by visiting Arunachal Pradesh and President Pratibha Patil's recent visit to the state and to Tawang, a site of confrontation during the Sino-Indian war of 1962, aroused similar complaints.[53] Chinese opposition to use of an Asian Development Bank loan to India for projects in Arunachal Pradesh revived tension between the two countries in August 2009 that the new Indian Foreign Minister S. M. Krishna sought to diffuse by announcing that India would henceforth raise funds for economic development of that state internally.[54] China also exhibited anxiety over the Dalai Lama's visit to Arunachal Pradesh in late 2009.[55] Moreover, India's concerns regarding the provision of stapled visas by Beijing to passport-holders from Jammu and Kashmir and Chinese-assisted construction in Pakistani Kashmir were subjects of discussions during S. M. Krishna's recent (April 2010) visit to Beijing.[56]

Conflict and cooperation

Starting with a common anti-imperialist bond that led to ideological competition for Third World leadership, the Sino-Indian relationship initially suffered a deeply wounding armed conflict for India, a long period of mutual insecurity, an even longer period of tentative steps towards rapprochement that was very much at the mercy of events, before finally developing into a more stable relationship anchored in expanding economic ties. Engagement between the two nations today is deeper than ever, yet many concerns remain. As mentioned earlier, these concerns coalesce around one central question— will there be conflict or cooperation between India and China in the future? And can there be a relationship that features both?

The prospect of conflict

At base of most conflict-related theories of the Sino-Indian relationship is the notion that two rising powers with rapidly growing economies and global ambitions cannot coexist cooperatively in the close quarters of the Asian region. Measured in yuan, China's estimated military expenditure increased by 14 per cent compounded annually from 1989 till 2007. Measured in rupees, India's military expenditure increased by 11 per cent annually during the same period.[57] It would appear that both are increasingly capable of expanding their regional spheres of influence. Where overlap occurs, there is competition, as in the case of Nepal and Myanmar, where China and India have historically competed for influence and trade ties. India's 'Look East' policy dating back to 1992 is also cited as an attempt to ward off Chinese influence in Southeast Asia (although it can also be interpreted in part or wholly as a policy seeking to make up for lost time with important, neglected neighbours).[58] Ultimately, as their respective regional influence expands, Ashley Tellis argues: 'their power-political capabilities will inevitably compel China and India to interact in other sub-regions [of Asia], either to secure access to resources or to forestall the other from acquiring preponderant influence'.[59]

Standard realist accounts of the relationship view China as unwilling to permit the emergence of India as a power beyond the South Asian region. In the past China has taken the necessary steps to build alliances with countries in the Indian periphery, including Myanmar, Nepal, Sri Lanka, Bangladesh, most notably Pakistan, and most recently Afghanistan.[60] Combined with the Chinese presence in the Indian Ocean region, this has contributed to a significant concern in Indian policymaking circles over perceived strategic 'encirclement' by China.[61] With domestic politics absorbing more of its decision-making bandwidth, India has been cautious, and, in all but naval matters, circumspect about countering this strategy, knowing that China itself worries about potential encirclement—by a configuration of states including the USA, Japan, Australia, and India. India continues to follow a 'one China' policy favouring the PRC over Taiwan, despite growing informal relations with the latter and even reports of greater inter-military exchanges.[62] India rejected membership of ASEAN as early as 1967, accurately seeing it as a US-influenced forum but underestimating its eventual significance. It was only three decades later that India sought to engage seriously with that body, culminating in a limited Free Trade Agreement in 2009. India's Look East policy launched in 1992 translated a serious attempt conceptually to correct the drift in India's approach to Asia beyond China and its immediate neighbourhood, and as a result economic relations with Singapore, Vietnam, and Indonesia have been growing substantially. Yet India has refrained from seeking out strategic alliances in either the East Asian or Southeast Asian regions that could counter or qualify Chinese influence. For example, its relationship with Japan, much touted by Prime Minister Singh, still seems curiously anaemic, both politically and economically.

At the bilateral level, potential conflict could arise under any of the following headings: security, economy, and identity (or perceptions).

Security concerns

Security concerns are numerous. First, the Sino-Indian border dispute is one of the world's longer-running ones. Despite various high-level talks and working groups, occasional actions by either side tend to rake up decades-old grievances. Second, the long-standing relationship between China and Pakistan remains an obstacle to closer ties between China and India. China's unwavering support for Pakistan, despite ideological differences and Pakistan's strategic relationship with the US, has mystified some observers although it offers impeccable logic under balance-of-power principles. Scholars have variously labelled it a 'special case',[63] 'in a category of its own',[64] and a relationship of 'a truly special character'.[65] China's assistance to Pakistan has even entered the realm of nuclear and missile technology.[66] This is of particular concern to India, and overlaps with another security concern—nuclear weapons. It is generally accepted that India's nuclear weapons programme was a response to China's nuclear programme, and Prime Minister Vajpayee's letter to President Clinton in 1998 underscored this assessment. Given Pakistan's covert nuclear ability, likely aided by China, the current situation has the potential to escalate into a mini (albeit highly unequal) nuclear arms race on the subcontinent. That said, following the Mumbai bombings of November 2008 and subsequent setbacks for the civilian Pakistani government in its efforts to contain Islamist influence in the country, it would be surprising if Beijing were not privately developing a degree of wariness vis-à-vis Islamabad, as its own Xinjiang region seethes, and as its fear of terrorism persists.[67]

A fourth and significant issue is Tibet. As pointed out by parliamentarian and author Arun Shourie, 'India's security is inextricably intertwined with the existence and survival of Tibet as a buffer state and to the survival and strengthening of Tibetan culture and religion.'[68] Tibet's role as a buffer state has often been emphasized; without it, China and India brush up directly against each other, with the kinds of results witnessed in 1962, 1967, and 1986. Indian policymakers are particularly concerned about leaving their northern borders exposed.[69] Others have also highlighted the ancient cultural ties between India and Tibet and resentment in India towards the Chinese government's role in the systematic erosion of a culture deeply influenced by Indian traditions.[70] Nonetheless, for India, the Chinese role in Tibet is both a threat and an opportunity. The presence of the Dalai Lama and thousands of

Tibetan refugees in India sometimes offers a lever by which New Delhi can, akin to China's policies toward Pakistan, indirectly apply pressure on Beijing.[71] This lever is not often used, however, as India's position on Tibet over the last six decades has moved firmly toward acknowledging Chinese sovereignty over it. In 2008, the Indian government took great pains to ensure that Tibetan protestors did not cause any embarrassment to Beijing during the passage of the Olympic Torch through New Delhi.[72] Contrastingly, at the height of tensions between both countries over border issues during autumn 2009, a visit by the Dalai Lama to the Buddhist temple community in the disputed Tawang, nestled in northwestern Arunachal Pradesh, could only have been perceived as provocative by Beijing.[73] Thus, although India accepts China's sovereignty in Tibet, future radical action by disaffected Tibetan groups operating from Indian soil could severely complicate the bilateral relationship.[74]

Perhaps the biggest challenge to Sino-Indian rapprochement, but also a source of forward impetus, has come from the rapidly improving US–Indian relationship, particularly during the Bush administration's second term in office between 2005 and 2009. During this time, India and the USA enlarged the scope and depth of their relationship, most notably in the form of the 123 Nuclear Agreement, which legitimized India's nuclear weapons programme and, to a degree, validated in its own case Delhi's long-standing principled opposition to the global non-proliferation regime. While a much improved relationship with the USA has helped India to counter the traditional pro-Pakistan tilt in US foreign policy, it has also made Sino-Indian rapprochement a greater priority for Beijing.[75] This contains echoes of the impulse behind Chinese overtures towards India in the 1970s, which were made partly with an eye to diminishing Indo-Soviet cooperation. As the global contest for power between the United States and China intensifies, India may well become an important factor in this strategic triangle.

In the post-Cold War era, as the USA has attempted to consolidate its status as the lone superpower, China has been poised increasingly as the most significant challenger to US hegemony. Contemporary US approaches to China oscillate between policies of containment and engagement. The former has given birth to 'a new triangle' between the USA, India, and China, whereby the USA cultivates closer ties with India—an established democracy—as a regional bulwark against a potentially aggressive and communist China.[76] On the other hand, the Obama administration's approach to China has fuelled the debate between containment and engagement enthusiasts in the US foreign policy establishment, many arguing that Washington does not have much choice but to engage, given its precarious financial situation, and China's position as holder of significant US sovereign debt (admittedly a two-edged sword). Indian commentators have observed with some alarm renewed cooperation between China and the USA in tackling the global economic crisis, as well as increased interdependence of Chinese creditors holding large amounts of US Treasury Bills and the US debtors providing the single largest market for Chinese manufactured goods. This has prompted some to question the logic of India picking a side in the unpredictable Sino-US relationship.[77]

Sanjaya Baru, for example, writes that: 'the Bush-Rice doctrine of containing China is being replaced by the Obama-Clinton doctrine of co-opting China to deal with the economic crisis.'[78] Indeed, the best-case scenario for the new Indo-US relationship would appear to be an interests-based balancing act for India between the USA and China. At worst, India could be looking at conflict with China in the medium term or being left out in the cold as the USA and China become closer. But geostrategic calculations, like the assertions of pundit economists, generally yield to a messy reality in which clear-cut outcomes are the exception and confident expectations are often confounded. Thus, India's hitherto prudent policy of measured engagement with all of the major powers is more likely to pay off than bold (and consequently risky) moves it can ill afford financially to support at a time when domestic necessities continue to preoccupy its people and its politicians. It may well be that India's rise will occur in relative isolation, as did China's while it tended to its economic priorities, rather than in close partnership with one or several allies among the existing greater powers.

Economic concerns

With regard to economic competition, there are three main areas in which China and India may conflict. The first is their quest for energy security. China and India are both net importers of crude oil that are also looking to diversify their energy supply via natural gas. This has the potential to cast them in direct competition for natural resources from Central Asia and the Persian Gulf. The second is China and India's equal interest in the factor and product markets of developing countries, particularly in Africa. Both nations account for almost 50 per cent of Africa's exports to and imports from Asia.[79] The prospect of economic competition and the struggle for political-economic ties with African governments could set off a frenzy for resources and markets in the region. The third area is international trade. China and India compete in export markets for many products such as textiles, garments, leather goods, and light machinery.[80] China's accession to the WTO could potentially have long-term adverse consequences for the growth of Indian exports in these sectors. Econometric analysis shows that reductions in US tariffs on Chinese imports have led to trade diversion from India.[81] China's better and growing integration into global production networks of manufactured goods could have negative implications for India's exports, although India has excelled mainly at trade in services in the recent past. Between 2002–3 and 2006–7, services contributed to 69 per cent of the overall average growth in GDP.[82] Indeed, Prem Shankar Jha notes, '[w]hereas China has become the manufactory of the world, India is rapidly acquiring a comparable position in the emerging global services industry'.[83]

Identity and perceptions

On issues of identity, there is a very clear sense in both countries that their civilizational greatness contributes to great power status and entitlement thereto. One scholar suggests, 'The relations between China and India in the twenty-first century would seem to have little relevance to the ancient past. Yet leaders in both states since the 1950s...have been convinced of the historic destiny of their own nations to achieve great-power status'.[84] In his budget speech of 1991, then Finance Minister Manmohan Singh borrowed a phrase from Victor Hugo to assert that the emergence of India as a world economic power is 'an idea whose time has come'.[85] China has often been characterized as retaining the Confucian ideal of being 'the Middle Kingdom' around which international relations ought to be ordered.[86] This is compounded to an extent by the 'Century of Humiliation' notion fuelling Chinese nationalist mythology, extending from the First Opium War till the creation of the PRC, and featuring serial national humiliations at the hands of foreign imperialist powers, especially Japan.[87] A significant strand of Chinese foreign policy since 1949 has thus focused on reasserting China's civilizational greatness on the international stage to overcome these distasteful memories.

These parallel discourses of inherent historical and contemporary greatness, often reiterated in public exchanges between leaders of both countries, point to self-perceptions that may prove difficult to reconcile in day-to-day relations: perceptions of each other are somewhat problematic. A 2006 Pew Global Attitudes Survey found that 43 per cent of Chinese had an unfavourable opinion of India, while 39 per cent of Indians had an unfavourable opinion of China; 63 per cent of Indians also said that China's growing military power is a 'bad thing' for their country, while 50 per cent said the same about China's growing economic power. At the same time, 65 per cent of Indians said that China would replace the USA as the dominant power sometime in the next fifty years.[88] China's rise thus seems to pose a threat, as perceived by many Indians. Paranoid public opinion is one thing; more egregious is the Indian foreign policy establishment's perception of the 'China threat'—a self-fulfilling prophecy if carried to its logical conclusion. An eminent Indian foreign policy analyst describes India's China policy as standing on three legs: 'say nice things in public about Sino-Indian friendship, Asian unity and anti-Western solidarity; nurse intense grievances in private; and avoid problem solving because that would need a lot of political courage.'[89] Another author suggests that within government circles, perceptions of China range from 'enemy' to 'challenge',[90] which undoubtedly constricts the space for creative policymaking.

But is conflict likely?

The arguments presented above, when taken together, can seem compelling. There are, however, some equally (if not more) compelling reasons not to support their implication that conflict is likely. On security, while the border issue remains unresolved, both sides have taken meaningful steps to institutionalize the process of its resolution. Most importantly, since 1988 they have managed to de-link the border issues from the overall bilateral relationship.[91] With regards to Pakistan, China has adopted a more even-handed stance. During the Kargil war in 1999, the attack on the Indian Parliament in 2001, and the 2008 terrorist attacks in Mumbai, China asserted neutrality and promoted the resolution of conflict through dialogue. The current Chinese stance can be summed up in the words of Zhang Yan, China's Ambassador to India: 'China hopes India and Pakistan will resolve their differences through dialogue and consultation, which is in the interest of both countries as well as in the interest of peace, stability, and development of the South Asia region.'[92] These apparent palliatives represent a marked change from the pronounced pro-Pakistan tilt in Chinese policy towards South Asia during the 1960s and 1970s. The underlying logic is that Pakistan's growing instability (with domestic consequences for China) and India's growing power compel China to take a middle path: 'It [China] does not want to have to choose between a long term ally... and an increasingly important neighbor.'[93]

Terrorism, notably Islamic terrorism, is an issue on which Indian and Chinese interests have converged, particularly in the sensitive regions of Kashmir and Xinjiang.[94] With regard to military and nuclear issues, the prospect of conflict is diminished by the sheer gap in capabilities between China and India. Although India's military and naval capabilities are rapidly improving, 'India's elite understands profoundly that New Delhi would gain little from direct confrontation with Beijing'.[95] This thought was echoed recently by India's Naval Chief who said it would be 'foolhardy' for India to try to compete with China economically or militarily.[96] Similarly as regards the growing regional influence of both powers, neither China nor India stands to gain from sparking a regional conflict. Both nations are deeply engaged in the domestic sphere: generating economic reform, maintaining state legitimacy, and tackling ethno-nationalism, among other things. International entanglements that distract them from these objectives are not welcome. Even the ostensible machinations of the USA in the region have done little to hamper the current upswing in Sino-Indian relations. Meanwhile, India's growing relationship with the USA has convinced an internally oriented China of India's potential, thus creating an opportunity for India to improve relations with China.[97] In some key international forums, including those addressing climate change, trade, labour laws, arms control, and human rights, China and India have found common ground in countering Western positions.

On the economic front, growing trade relations between India and China are likely to impact relations positively. One analyst sees great potential in the 'low politics' of trade, which often goes unnoticed, in fostering greater coordination between the two nations that might spill over into other realms.[98] On energy, the chances of competition are at present minimal. In sharing the common predicament of being net energy importers, both countries have relied on market mechanisms over temptations of a strategy hinging on exclusive access to supplies.[99] This has allowed them to collaborate in shoring up unstable markets in Central Asia and the Persian Gulf, securing sea-lanes as delivery channels, and participating in consortiums for exploration and extraction rights in certain areas. In January 2006, India's Oil and Natural Gas Corporation (ONGC) and the China National Petroleum Corporation (CNPC) decided to bid jointly for energy projects in some regions. With regard to commercial competition in Africa, currently the major exports from Africa to China and India (oil and natural gas to China, ores and metals to India) are almost mutually exclusive and therefore do not constitute an arena for competition. Similarly in international trade, although China's entry into WTO may negatively impact some of India's export markets, the top twenty-five exports of China and India in 2004 were almost mutually exclusive sets, suggesting that the impact on India would be minimal.[100] A simulated model of China's impact also suggests that other sectors of Indian exports will likely expand to partially offset declines in India's relative economic welfare.[101] Finally, while contemporary reliance on oil and gas for the bulk of energy supplies is an unavoidable preoccupation for governments worldwide, and alternative energy technologies still yield expensive if promising results, India and China both harbour the potential to produce and benefit from significant advances in non-conventional energy generation. Necessity and scientific capacity may well prove mothers to much invention on this front within their borders.

Lastly, on issues of identity, it is possible to misread China's and India's claims to great power status as fertile grounds for regional conflict rooted in nationalism. Although China essentially has achieved great power status, its foreign policy is notably and pointedly oriented towards maintaining regional stability and creating conditions for China's 'peaceful rise'.

According to one scholar, 'China is a revisionist power, but for the foreseeable future it will seek to maintain the status quo.'[102] Chinese elites may be suspicious of multilateral organizations, but they are willing to work within them to advance national interests. Indeed, China's new diplomacy is 'less confrontational, more sophisticated, more confident, and, at times, more constructive' in its approach to regional and international affairs.[103] At the domestic level, modern Chinese nationalism has been called 'pragmatic', it is instrumental and reactive, preoccupied with holding the nation together rather than being hostile to others.[104] China's leaders are acutely aware of the costs of turning the patriotism of their citizens into 'virulent ultranationalism'.[105] Moreover, Chinese nationalism has often been a challenge in its relations with Japan, one of China's largest sources of investment and assistance in the past when it needed it most, and which also harbours a strong nationalist lobby and sentiments.[106]

Contemporary Indian politics and foreign policy evince a similar pragmatic strain. In stark contrast to Nehru's idealism, India today is not as convinced of its uniqueness in the annals of history and prefers to cast itself officially as an ordinary, if significant, nation tending to its economic development imperatives, rather than as one obsessed by the quest for great power status. This approach has favoured the normalization of traditionally antagonistic relationships with neighbouring countries and a greater commitment to international institutions that might legitimize India's emerging power status. Economic prosperity is now seen by most Indians as the key to India's attainment of great power status in the world today, and it is the driving force of India's pragmatic (if excessively lethargic, in the view of its critics) foreign policy. Although India may be an idea whose time has come, even Dr Singh framed India's great power ambitions in strictly economic terms, excluding any aspirations of being an exemplary civilization or paragon of international virtue.

Extrapolating from the past

In assessing the arguments supporting scenarios of conflict and cooperation respectively, the unconnected nature of China and India's rise as great powers is striking. Bilateral trade, while growing fast, still forms a small share of overall trade in both countries. Major strategic partnerships have been made with third parties, including Pakistan and the United States. Societal interaction between the two nations is still negligible although tourism is growing and human interaction relating to the growing trade between the two countries is also increasing. Direct flights between India and China began only in 2002.[107]

In 2007, the two nations with a combined population of over 2 billion exchanged a paltry 570,000 visitors.[108]

Even if China and India truly yearned to be post-imperialist brothers-in-arms and champions of the developing world, two major constraints will hold them back for some time. First, until very recently, there was a remarkably poor overall understanding among their respective foreign policy circles of each other's history and society. Especially with regard to Indian understanding of Chinese foreign policy, many assessments occupy a conceptual space bounded by 1962 with no deeper understanding of (or interest in) the drivers of Chinese policy today. In the words of a former Indian Army Chief, 'though much water has flowed down the Tsangpo since then [the Sino-Indian border war], India's "1962 syndrome" is unaltered'.[109] The bounded rationality of India's China policymakers is compounded by the insufficient academic attention paid to China in India. As Indian foreign policy analyst Raja Mohan states, 'The number of Chinese scholars studying the subcontinent and the reporters based in India is far higher than the pitiful Indian resources devoted to understanding China.'[110] Sophisticated, up-to-date analyses of the China–India relationship are often drowned out in domestic Indian debate on China by revanchist sentiment.[111]

Second, a factor that contributes to the first: the modern history of Sino-Indian relations has been less about China and India than it has been about extraneous actors such as the United States, Soviet Union, and Pakistan, and multilaterally managed issues such as non-proliferation and climate change. There has been little effort until very recently to engage an in-depth widely-gauged Sino-Indian dialogue. And such dialogue needs to eschew fantasies about purported similarities between China and India. India and China are probably today more different than they have ever been as societies and as economies. The main similarity they share is their parallel pursuit of domestic consolidation with international pragmatism tending towards great power status as foreign policy.

Long-term trends in China and India's development are unlikely to bring the two countries closer to conflict with each other relative to the greater risk posed by unpredictable specific events or incidents that might act as triggers. It is important for both to identify and recognize these potential triggers, in order to defuse or at least manage them. From an Indian perspective, a keen sense of history and an understanding of state–society relations in China are important. For example, one important factor is domestic sub-nationalism that afflicts both China and India, but with different characteristics and consequences. India has survived as a polity and society by cobbling together a sometimes conciliatory, often weak political and security response to various insurgencies and separatist movements, but China still very much relies on the heavy hand of the state to suppress such uprisings, as evinced in Tibet in

2008 and Xinjiang in 2009. Ethnic unrest in China's peripheral territories, possibly inviting foreign involvement, has historically been a major vulnerability for the Chinese state, be it in Xinjiang, Tibet, Taiwan, Manchuria, or Mongolia.[112] At times like this, the legitimacy of the Chinese Communist Party (CCP) leadership can be questioned and thus it may perceive itself as modestly threatened, and it has resorted to nationalistic appeals to reassert its hold on the polity. Tibet, therefore, could conceivably (although not likely) ignite a future Sino-Indian conflict, not because of its strategic value but because of the ability of a future well-organized Tibetan revolt to irk the Chinese leadership into demanding unreasonable concessions from India.

Similarly, changes in China's economic fortunes might provoke a nationalistic turn in its foreign policy. Although the leadership since Deng Xiaoping has exhibited pragmatic tendencies, seminal events like the Tiananmen demonstrations or recent events in Xinjiang can always empower nativists, who prefer 'a closed-door foreign policy and a reign of virtue domestically'.[113] Even modest developments in this direction within China could cause major setbacks to bilateral relations with India, and might require only the spark of a serious border incident to ignite larger confrontation (diplomatic and possibly even military).

It is widely thought today that the Chinese state's legitimacy, since Deng Xiaoping's reforms, hinges fundamentally on its economic performance. The state sees its responsibility primarily in satisfying the economic needs of its citizens, and most citizen protests are framed in terms of economic rights.[114] The spectacular performance of the Chinese economy forms a solid foundation for the legitimacy of its political system, which is essentially authoritarian (with some democratic trappings like local elections). Therefore a sustained economic downturn (relative to past performance) or the relatively better economic performance of a developing democratic country nearby might pose a medium-term slow-moving threat to the legitimacy of the Chinese state. Such a threat seems remote today (although sometimes exaggerated in Indian defence establishment analyses of Chinese developments), but, if it materialized, it could seriously undermine relations between India and China.[115]

Conclusion

In August 2010, by some measures, China overtook Japan as the world's second largest economy.[116] The working assumptions of many analysts are rooted in a vision of uninterrupted future rise of both India and China. From his vantage point in Singapore, Simon Tay notes: 'Too many commentators discuss China and India with breathless admiration—extrapolating, for example, that growth will continue at a breakneck pace for decades.'[117] Caution is indeed in order. India in mid-2010 was facing a seriously deteriorating balance of payments and rising inflation (notably in the sensitive sphere of food prices) while China has yet fully to digest the very ambitious recent internal investment in its economy and could be facing serious bottlenecks, not least in the absorptive capacity of its international clients, potentially slowing down its growth in years ahead. Demography could play against rather than in favour of either or both. And each faces challenges of environmental degradation, growing economic inequality, and rising social inequity.

While there can be no certainty with respect to either possible future conflict or sustained cooperation between India and China, the likelihood is a mix of security-related tension and economic cooperation. Outright war is highly unlikely—both sides have too much to lose. But the two nations will continue to rub up against each other, with unpredictable outcomes, as they seek to expand their respective spheres of influence. As the success of India's democratic experiment becomes entrenched and is bolstered by strong economic growth, and as the United States invests more in its new partnership with India, Beijing will increasingly have to factor Delhi into its strategic calculations in Asia and beyond. Similarly, as the Chinese economy grows and the nation's military (especially naval) capacities increase, India will increasingly have to factor a growing Chinese presence in its own neighbourhood into its own strategic calculations.

In 2010, China's controlled, low valuation of the renminbi came under attack from the United States, competing emerging powers, international economic organizations, and myriad commentators as fuelling international economic imbalances and tensions. Beijing's great reluctance to allow more than symbolic adjustments to its exchange rate suggests the risks China's leadership believes the country (and presumably the regime itself) runs were its economic growth rate to slow significantly. At times, China's international messaging was shrill. New perceptions of a China rising arrogantly, rather than mostly in harmony with its neighbours, were compounded by its harsh response to Japanese arrest of the captain of a Chinese trawler near disputed, Japanese-administered islands on 7 September 2010. Fears among less powerful Asian states of a China turned more aggressive in years ahead do not create a strategic advantage for India as much as a reminder of how important an Asian regional actor the United States has been and many Asians hope will remain.[118] But they do remind Asians, at a time when traditional US intentions and capacities in Asia cannot be assumed as constant far into the future, of why they will increasingly wish to engage meaningfully with India, the one resurgent Asian power whose overall weight comes close to rivalling that of China.

Active management of the relationship can help to anticipate and defuse potential sources of conflict. Therefore these important nations need to increase efforts to understand each other's domestic socio-economic and political systems. A dialogue process that acknowledges differences instead of emphasizing imagined similarities is likely to lay the foundations for better mutual understanding. By institutionalizing a bilateral relationship that goes beyond high-level exchanges and diplomatic visits, both sides might be able to transform public perceptions. Patterns of cooperation already established on multilaterally managed issues such as climate change and trade, if further developed by both nations, could help to create new areas of sustained cooperation within an emerging new global multilateral system, in which both have a much greater role to play.

This will be a vital relationship for students of international relations to chart in years ahead. A lot depends internationally on the ability of these 'two tigers to share the same mountain'.[119]

7

India–USA Relations: The Shock of the New

Two comments, uttered almost eighty years apart, mark a contemporary transformation in relations between India and the United States of America. In 1927, Jawaharlal Nehru stated: '[The] great problem of the near future will be American imperialism, even more than British imperialism.'[1] In 2005, Indian Prime Minister Manmohan Singh stated: 'India is today embarked on a journey inspired by many dreams. We welcome having America by our side. There is much we can accomplish together.'[2]

The history of this relationship is as complex as it is varied, and is distinguished by a largely unsuccessful search for common ground. Like the proverbial blind men and the elephant, both nations spent five decades construing their relationship in ways that mystified and displeased the other. Statesmen on both sides have bemoaned this period as 'the lost half century' or 'the fifty wasted years'[3] during which the world's largest democracy and the world's oldest democracy failed to cooperate consistently across a range of issues. Despite his scepticism about America's rise to global hegemony, in a speech to the US Congress in 1949 Nehru had suggested: 'Friendship and co-operation between our two countries are . . . natural.'[4] Yet a full fifty years of India's independent existence would eventually pass before India's sixteenth Prime Minister Atal Bihari Vajpayee could plausibly claim once again that India and the United States are 'natural allies'.[5]

What happened in the intervening decades is the subject of this chapter. The evolution of relations between India and the USA from the early years of the Indian republic till the new millennium is traced. That a fundamental shift has occurred during the past decade is clear. This shift is explored in terms of its motivation and timing, attempting to locate its causes. The analysis rests on a combination of international, regional, and domestic factors that operated jointly to usher in the modern era of India–USA relations.

Historical overview

Three main parameters have played a role in India–USA relations over the years—ideology, strategy, and values. Variously, over time, they have had the effect of creating incentives for divergence or convergence in the relationship. The evolution of these parameters is better understood if, for analytical convenience, we divide modern Indian history into three broad time periods: the Nehruvian era (1947–66), the Indira Gandhi (and post-Indira Gandhi) years (1967–89), and the contemporary period (1990 onwards). In the first period, ideological differences dominated the discourse of India–USA relations. As the Nehru era came to a close, strategic considerations that had been present but not dominant since the 1950s came to the fore and deepened the tension in the relationship. Finally, the period following the end of the Cold War saw a shift in the focus of India's foreign policy from ideology to pragmatism, coloured by India's growing economic success and ambition. This created space for the rediscovery of common interests and shared political values between the USA and India, after fifty years of uneasy relations.

1947–66: ideological differences

In the early years after independence, India viewed the world through a newly forged prism of anti-imperialism, which was seen as an inseparable 'outgrowth of capitalism'.[6] Consequently, to India, the American pursuit of commercial interests in the world and the South Asian region suggested a determination to replace British with American economic hegemony.[7] The Americans on the other hand viewed the world through the prism of emerging anti-Communism. This thinking was crystallized by the hard-nosed maxim of John Foster Dulles: 'Those who are not with us are against us.'[8] Faced with an increasingly bipolar world, India adopted an idealistic yet functionally pragmatic philosophy of non-alignment as the cornerstone of its foreign policy. Non-alignment to Indians was neither neutrality nor alignment. Philosophically it signified 'freedom of action', a concomitant of India's independence. Its application, however, was 'a matter of judgment'.[9] By creating space for morally defensible *ad hoc* foreign policy decisions at a time when the world was bifurcating, non-alignment helped India achieve, with some flair, minimal external objectives while it coped with daunting domestic challenges.

Relations with Washington started off on an uncertain footing, primarily due to the importance of the Anglo-American relationship. This led to less than enthusiastic American support for Indian nationalism in the 1940s,[10] a fact that was duly noted by leaders of India's independence movement. In 1947, the birth of the Indian republic was accompanied by Pakistan's occupation of Kashmir. Nehru's appeal to the United Nations did not garner the kind of support he expected from the great powers, particularly the United States, which declined to label Pakistan an aggressor.[11] In 1949, India was quick to recognize the newly formed People's Republic of China (PRC) and to promote its permanent membership in the UN Security Council, even to the extent of turning down an American offer of taking the PRC's seat in the Council.[12] In 1950, India abstained from a US-sponsored resolution calling for the UN's military involvement in the Korean War. India subsequently voted against UN forces crossing the 38th parallel into North Korea and against labelling China an aggressor in the war. In 1951, India declined an invitation to sign the San Francisco Peace Treaty on grounds of the unfair and unequal treatment of Japan by the Allied Powers. The USA regretted India's inability to 'join this united effort for peace' and observers suggested that even though Nehru's supporters claimed India's absence was designed to avoid linking itself with Russia in opposing the treaty, its statement of reasons 'had much the same effect'.[13]

Amidst the atmosphere of the 1950s, it was but natural for the USA to consider India's non-alignment as 'little more than a sanctimonious cloak' for interests that contradicted its own.[14] Yet the US worldview was no less morally laden than the Indian one. American scholars deplored the Indian tendency to equate the intentions of the USA with those of the Soviet Union, i.e. to believe that the two power blocs were 'equally bad'.[15] Dulles is quoted as saying: 'Neutrality...except under exceptional circumstances...is an immoral conception.'[16] Gaganvihari Mehta, an early Indian Ambassador to the United States commented:

> whereas to the United States the fight against Communism is the supreme issue to which all other problems should be subordinated, India holds that the real enemies of mankind are economic and social evils such as poverty and hunger and disease, racial discrimination, and domination and exploitation of weaker peoples by the powerful nations of the world.[17]

Emerging from over two hundred years of colonialism, India considered imperialism in any form a threat to its freedom. Conversely the United States perceived the growth of Communism as a serious threat to its security. The USA represented to many in the newly decolonized world an emergent imperial power while India, with its planned economy and non-aligned foreign policy, appeared to Americans and others in the West precariously at risk of turning to socialism, and perhaps to alignment with the Soviet bloc. A fundamental ideological divide and much suspicion was thus created and sustained over the years. Non-alignment became somewhat of a moral safety net for India, and continued to influence its foreign policy for many decades, finding an echo in debates even today (though more as a rhetorical device than a fundamental belief). In the post-Wilsonian era of international politics, as the

USA was shedding its 'moralizing tradition' in favour of a realist paradigm, it found India 'cloaking its power plays in moral rhetoric'.[18] This put the purportedly natural allies at odds. India was increasingly viewed as either a fence sitter or a member of the communist bloc, neither of which were complimentary epithets in the Western world.

Beginnings of strategic divergence

This divide between the two nations opened up space for other actors to begin exerting influence on their respective foreign policies. In 1953, after an abortive attempt with the Middle East Defense Organization (MEDO), Pakistan stepped up its efforts to form a defence alliance with the United States. Stalin's death in the same year created a thaw in Soviet policy towards India. Nehru paid his first visit to Moscow in 1954, the year that Pakistan signed a Mutual Defense Assistance Agreement with the USA, which most Indians reportedly viewed as 'essentially an anti-Nehru manoeuvre designed to force his hand'.[19] And, in 1955, top Soviet leaders Nikita Khrushchev and Nikolai Bulganin visited New Delhi for the first time, Pakistan officially aligned with the USA via the South East Asian Treaty Organization (SEATO) and the Central Treaty Organization (CENTO, also known as the Baghdad Pact), and India was a key promoter of the first Afro-Asian conference at Bandung in Indonesia.

India's 'leftward' slant was becoming evident. An American scholar observed that criticisms of the United States in India had become fashionable since the former started aiding Pakistan militarily.[20] A public opinion poll showed a majority of Indians perceiving the USA as 'a foreign government that is willfully preparing for a war of aggression'.[21] The year 1956 saw India criticize the imperialist designs of the Western powers in the Suez Canal while being conspicuously restrained in its reaction to the Soviet invasion of Hungary.[22] It was evident by then that in retaliation to the USA–Pakistan military relationship, Nehru had 'relaxed' his policy of non-alignment to seek support from the Soviet Union.[23] Despite strained relations, in 1959 Eisenhower became the first American President to visit India. That very year, however, India was once again quick to recognize the newly formed communist government in Cuba under Fidel Castro.

As the Cold War gained momentum, America's frustrations with Indian non-alignment mounted. Writing in 1957, Henry Kissinger justified American aid to Pakistan by arguing that America 'cannot permit the balance of power to be overturned for the sake of Allied unity or the approbation of the uncommitted'.[24] At a time when the world was divided among the two power blocs, India's moralizing foreign policy touched a raw nerve in American diplomatic circles. In the absence of cooperation from India, and with a communist government in China, Pakistan became an essential element in the United States' containment of the Soviet Union in Asia.

What began as an ideological gulf between India and the USA was now developing into a strategic complication. This manifested itself in many ways, not least over the issue of the Portuguese colony of Goa in India. Despite repeated counsel to Delhi from the USA against the use of force in liberating the colony (from the hands of a NATO ally, albeit one governed by a military dictator), the Indian military forcibly drove out the Portuguese from Goa in December 1961. Goa was a powerful symbol of the anti-colonial struggle for India, which claimed that it had waited long enough for the USA to exercise diplomatic influence in the face of Portuguese obduracy. The USA saw India's action as a violation of the UN charter and as setting a dangerous international precedent.[25] A US-sponsored UN resolution against India was vetoed by the Soviet Union, and a similar resolution against the Portuguese was vetoed by the USA. Once again the two democracies had locked horns over an issue that challenged the foundations of the international system as each viewed it.[26]

In 1961, the Non-Aligned Movement (NAM), a coalition of developing countries largely from Asia and Africa that subscribed to the ideology of non-alignment with either Cold War power bloc and aimed to carve out a middle path in international politics, was established. Although Nehru was not an enthusiastic supporter of the creation of a third bloc,[27] India was a founding member, and India's foreign policy establishment was soon at the forefront of promoting its tenets.

The Sino-Indian War

Deteriorating relations between India and China culminated in a border war in October 1962, coinciding with the Cuban Missile Crisis and a rapidly escalating Cold War. A growing rift between the Chinese and the Soviets since the mid-1950s prompted the latter to take a pro-India stance in the run up to the conflict. However, since the Cuban Crisis required a semblance of solidarity with China, the Soviet Union initially refrained from coming to India's aid.[28] Lacking alternatives, Nehru turned to Western powers for assistance. Based on a perceived threat in Asia from communist China, the USA was quick to respond.[29] In a key move, the USA prevailed on Pakistan for an assurance that it would not invade Kashmir so that India could redeploy its northern troops towards the front with China.[30] Yet by 20 November 1962 the situation had grown worse for India and Nehru made an 'urgent and open appeal' for, among other things, air strikes by US forces on Chinese troops.[31] An American carrier—the *Enterprise*—was dispatched towards the Bay of Bengal. However, it was withdrawn the next day when the Chinese declared a unilateral ceasefire, possibly influenced by the Soviet decision to revert to its pro-India policy upon the resolution of the Cuban Crisis.[32]

The Sino-Indian war, aside from leaving an indelible impression on India's defence policy planning, marked a significant departure from US policy towards India up till that point. Indian leaders and the public welcomed American assistance but the motives of American intervention—more to ward off the Chinese threat than to genuinely assist the Indians—were not lost on Indian decision-makers. Soon after the war, the Americans along with the British began pressuring India to yield to Pakistan on Kashmir.[33] Soviet assistance, on the other hand, was found to be relatively less loaded with *post hoc* conditions. In a matter of months, controversy erupted between India and the USA over the shared use of an Indian-bought American-supplied radio transmitter for the purpose of countering Chinese propaganda in Southeast Asia. What came to be known as the 'Voice of America' fiasco was a strong reality check for the Americans with regard to India's firm ideological commitment to non-alignment.[34]

India's obstinacy during the 1950s and 1960s came not just from a commitment to an abstract foreign policy principle, but from a strong sense of nationalism and feeling of historical, cultural, and strategic uniqueness. Nehru viewed India as a bridge between the countries of Southeast Asia and those of West Asia and beyond. Accordingly, Indian leaders expected that the USA would recognize India's importance in the international order and confer on it an 'equality of status' if not the 'sharing of common objectives'.[35] America's global objectives, however, were not designed to accommodate Indian greatness. As one observer noted:

> What introduces friction into the ties between India and the United States is that Washington is still unable to find for India a position in its global strategy, which would satisfy India's national self-esteem and ambitions.[36]

American observers often viewed India's 'self-esteem and ambitions' with a sense of irony. Although Indian leaders had a firm belief in their country's greatness, India itself did not yet measure up to most standards of greatness on the world stage. Moreover, despite its moral and ideological leadership of the Third World in the NAM, in strategic terms India's self-importance did not project credibly beyond the South Asian region.

The Sino-Pakistani entente

In 1964 China detonated its first nuclear weapon and significantly tipped the scales of power in the subcontinent. This time India was undiscriminating in its appeal for security guarantees and turned to the United States, England, and the Soviet Union for assistance. None obliged.[37]

A further jolt came the following year when Pakistan attacked India twice in the span of a few months, in the Rann of Kutch and in Kashmir. Of particular concern was Pakistan's use of weapons it had obtained from the USA in the mid-1950s, in contravention of President Eisenhower's guarantee to Nehru at the time that US-supplied arms would not be used by Pakistan in a conflict with India. The American response to the 1965 Indo-Pakistani conflicts was to maintain a position of strict neutrality. Operationally this meant cutting off military aid to both countries, a decision that cost Pakistan more than it did India. The result was counterproductive for the USA on both fronts—it earned the displeasure of India for being neutral in a conflict in which Pakistan was the clear aggressor, and it furthered the process of USA–Pakistan estrangement that began in 1962, in essence driving the latter towards China for military sustenance.[38] Chinese arms transfers to Pakistan, almost non-existent before 1965, shot up by 254 per cent between 1965 and 1966. Indeed from 1964 till 2007, China has been a more reliable and more plentiful supplier of arms to Pakistan (1.5 times more than the USA, in cumulative volume over the period).[39]

The expanding Sino-Pakistani relationship did not, however, prompt a change in India–USA relations. In 1966, responding to India's criticism of the US intervention in Vietnam, President Johnson restricted the supply of grain shipments that had been under way since the mid-1950s under the Public Law 480 programme. This decision, coming at the time of a severe Indian drought, was a very painful reminder to Indian leaders of the divergent nature of interests and values held by the two nations. It seemed that India, by now the vanguard of the post-colonial developing world, might never be able to reconcile its foreign policy with America's global aims. What had begun as ideological divergence had over time declined into antipathy combined with opposing strategic interests in Asia, particularly in the subcontinent.

1967–89: strategic contradictions

If the previous two decades had been about ideological differences between the USA and India, the next two would be about conflicting regional and global strategic interests. Strategic competition between the United States and Soviet Union played an important role in shaping India–USA relations. The USA, faced with an obstinately non-aligned India and the need to develop a strategic presence in Asia against the Soviet and Chinese threats, had subscribed to what one Indian scholar has called the 'Caroe thesis', or the idea that the power vacuum created by the departure of the British from the subcontinent and India's neutrality would greatly impact stability in the Middle East and Southeast Asia unless Pakistan was involved as a key strategic player in the region.[40] India for its part perceived the USA–Pakistan alliance as a direct threat to its regional supremacy and gradually turned to the Soviet Union as a balancing strategy. India's planned economy and its leadership's inclination toward a type of Fabian socialism helped nurture this relationship.

Jawaharlal Nehru died in 1964. An icon of Indian politics and foreign policy, his death left a leadership void that his soft-spoken successor Lal Bahadur Shastri struggled to fill. The short period of Shastri's tenure, from 1964 until his death in early 1966, marked a transition from Nehruvian idealism to the beginnings of Indira Gandhi's brand of *realpolitik* at home and abroad. Mrs. Gandhi's foreign policy maintained a rhetorical commitment to her father's ideology of non-alignment and anti-imperialism, but contained distinctly realist strands of thought and behaviour. Intermittently, India began experimenting with power politics in its region. This conflicted with US interests and exacerbated the emerging strategic disagreements between the two countries.

In 1967 a predominantly anti-American worldview led India to reject founding membership of the Association of Southeast Asian Nations (ASEAN), which it viewed as an attempt at expanding American influence in Asia.[41] A long-standing disagreement with the United States also began in 1968 when India rejected the Non-Proliferation Treaty (NPT) proposed by the world's leading nuclear powers. The NPT was problematic from Delhi's perspective for two main reasons. First, it was viewed by India as an unequal treaty since it did not prevent those with nuclear weapons from acquiring more. Second, it would foreclose any future possibility of an Indian weapons programme to counter the Chinese nuclear threat. The USA reacted to India's obstinacy by ceasing the supply of nuclear fuel to the Indian reactor at Tarapur, a role that France subsequently took over.

The Bangladesh War

In 1971, an internal crisis in Pakistan became a critical test of the India–USA relationship. The Sino-Soviet split had intensified toward the end of the previous decade, as had the warmth between Pakistan and China, both of which (to differing extents) considered India an important factor in their security calculations. India for its part lent ideological and material support to the movement for autonomy in East Pakistan. As the crisis in East Pakistan escalated, precipitated by West Pakistan's unwillingness to recognize the numerical superiority of East Pakistan's ethnically distinct population, India was faced with a considerable refugee problem that became an important pretext for involvement in Pakistan's affairs. In July that year, US Secretary of State Henry Kissinger made his first of many trips to Beijing to leverage the Sino-Soviet divide and lay the groundwork for a rapprochement between the USA and China.[42] Pakistan, already a close ally of China, played a key role in facilitating this relationship. As a result, the USA maintained a studious silence on Pakistan's repressive policies in East Pakistan. Kissinger would later describe events in East Pakistan as 'internal problems of a friendly country'.[43]

On his visit to Beijing, Kissinger made a stop at New Delhi to impress upon Prime Minister Gandhi the importance of not supporting the liberation movement in East Pakistan. Sensing her intransigence, various threats and inducements were subsequently employed by the USA to secure India's compliance.[44] India, however, did not oblige and instead turned once again to the Soviet Union. The month after Kissinger's visit, India and the Soviet Union concluded a Treaty of Peace, Friendship and Cooperation, which was a thinly veiled military pact. The American response was to step up military and economic aid to Pakistan in an effort to contain the East Pakistan situation. In December, India and Pakistan went to war over India's support for East Pakistani militants, and over the large-scale movement of refugees across the border from Bangladesh into India. Soviet and American vetoes in the UN Security Council paralysed the international community's response. Ultimately Nixon chose to explicitly 'tilt' American policy in favour of Pakistan and suspended $87 million worth of economic aid to India.[45] The USA then sent a naval fleet into the Bay of Bengal to send an unambiguous signal to India. The *USS Enterprise*, which had traversed the same route less than a decade earlier in support of an Indian military effort, was now dispatched for quite the opposite purpose.

The outcome of the Indo-Pakistan war was the creation of the state of Bangladesh. Indians considered their victory a major military achievement—one that helped dispel to some extent the ghosts of their defeat at the hands of the Chinese in 1962—and a firm rebuttal of America's efforts to extend its dominion in South Asia. The Americans viewed the outcome as clinching evidence of India's truculence in international matters, and its unmistakable tilt toward the Soviet Union. Yet a prominent Indian politician argued that 'the Americans practically drove us into the arms of the Russians'.[46] In retrospect, the war and the years following it were the lowest point in the history of Indo-US relations. In 1972, Nixon offered to reinstate the economic aid he had withdrawn the previous year, but India refused. In the same year, the Indian government took steps to restrict field research conducted by American social scientists in India.[47]

A major jolt to the USA came in 1974 when India conducted its first nuclear weapon test at Pokhran. It came to light that India had diverted nuclear materials imported for civilian purposes, much of it from the USA, in order to initiate a weapons programme. Although India assured the world that its test was a 'peaceful' one,[48] the event was a blow to not just American influence in South Asia but also the emerging global non-proliferation regime. At almost the same time that India conducted its nuclear test, the USA made plans to upgrade its presence at Diego Garcia, a British-controlled island in India's vicinity in the Indian Ocean leased to the USA. This move rankled the Indian leadership because it brought the arena of US–Soviet competition much closer home. Moreover, it challenged India's objective, supported by both the NAM and the UN, of maintaining the Indian Ocean as a 'region of peace',[49] or in other words, a region of Indian influence.

After Nixon's departure from the Presidency in August 1974, relations began improving somewhat but normalcy was not in sight. The Indian government requested a five-year phase-out of all Western volunteer programmes, primarily the US Peace Corps, which withdrew completely soon after.[50] In June 1975 India faced considerable domestic turmoil and entered a period of Emergency rule under Indira Gandhi. American economic aid, withheld the previous year due to the nuclear test, was again put on hold, and this decision was repeated the following year when Indira Gandhi accused the CIA of trying to undermine her government.[51] The Emergency ended in 1977 and the USA immediately eased restrictions it had placed on World Bank loans to India, and also approved $60 million in direct economic assistance. Relations seemed to improve a little when President Carter and Prime Minister Desai exchanged visits in 1978, resulting in a publicly announced joint emphasis on the importance of democracy and economic development in both countries.

Pakistan and the Afghanistan War

Pakistan (specifically Kashmir) never ceased to be a thorn in the Indian side with regard to US policy towards South Asia. Writing in 1966, Norman Palmer noted that on the whole, 'official and unofficial American views on Kashmir have been more sympathetic with Pakistan than with the Indian case'.[52] Forty years later, Strobe Talbott would observe that for five decades, 'the working assumption in New Delhi had been that the United States was, for reasons of geopolitics, reflexive in its support for Pakistan'.[53] Evidence of this support is strongest when one looks at data on military aid and arms transfers. The USA transferred 9.4 times more arms[54] and 9.9 times more military aid[55] to Pakistan than to India in the period from 1950 to 1990. Indeed, 94 per cent of the military aid supplied by the USA to India was as part of the agreement made during the Sino-Indian war.

The Soviet Union more than made up for this, transferring almost nine times more arms to India in the same period than the USA did to Pakistan (however this gap is less pronounced if one includes arms supplied to Pakistan by China in the same period).[56] US aid to Pakistan was initially conditioned on a non-use policy against India; later, as it became evident that Pakistan could not or would not abide by this condition, it was dropped. Looking back in 1979, Kissinger admitted to having 'misjudged the target of Pakistan's military efforts'.[57] Yet the policy of providing military aid to Pakistan in order to retain a friendly Islamic ally and a counterpoise to the Soviets in

Asia remained unchanged. Although US military aid to Pakistan had been on the decline since the Bangladesh war, the Soviet invasion of Afghanistan at the turn of the decade changed everything. The 1980s saw large amounts of military aid being pumped into Pakistan by the USA in order to fight a proxy war against the Soviets in Afghanistan. This created significant repercussions for internal security in India via the 'arms pipeline' that allowed CIA-supplied weaponry to land in the hands of Pakistan-backed militants in India.[58]

The USA–India relationship in the 1980s was marked by the conflict in nearby Afghanistan and India's own political and economic problems. The Soviet invasion of Afghanistan left India in a difficult position—relations with the Soviets became strained over the issue, yet India was seen by the world as being in the Soviet camp. Indira Gandhi engaged in diplomacy on multiple fronts to improve India's image in this regard. A muted disapproval was conveyed to the Soviets while active efforts were made to develop closer ties with the United States. The latter was complicated in no small measure by the restoration of the USA–Pakistan security relationship as a direct result of the situation in Afghanistan. In June 1981, President Ronald Reagan announced the resumption of arms sales to Pakistan, which had been halted a few years earlier when the latter's nuclear intentions and China-assisted nuclear weapons programme became known. A six-year, $3 billion economic and military aid package was announced for Pakistan, starting in October 1982. This time the USA did not stipulate any restrictions on the use of its arms against India.[59] The Soviets, keen to assuage Indian disapprobation over the Afghanistan issue, were quick to 'more than match'[60] the USA–Pakistan deal in early 1984. The superpowers were now direct competitors in a South Asian arms race.[61]

The conflict in Afghanistan brought the Cold War much closer to India than even Diego Garcia had a few years previously. Concern about its regional autonomy and capacity to resist American global ambitions was one of the motivating factors behind India's involvement in the emerging domestic conflict in Sri Lanka (the other was India's large Tamil population with many ethnic cousins in India's state of Tamil Nadu). As the decade progressed and Soviet policy under Mikhail Gorbachev showed signs of change in Afghanistan and otherwise, India's relations with the USA improved marginally. US arms supplies to India, unheard of since 1962, resumed on a small scale between 1986 and 1988.[62] In 1988, Prime Minister Rajiv Gandhi made a historic visit to China in an attempt to begin the process of normalizing relations between the two neighbours. India seemed to be experimenting with positive diplomacy as a means for resolving long-running disagreements. This was also reflected in India's brief and hesitant spell of logistical support for American military operations in the Gulf War that began in 1990.

In the years since India's independence, the Cold War had negatively affected the regional security environment in South Asia. The US desire for a strategic counterweight in Asia sustained Pakistan's ability to maintain a strategic balance against India for many years. India in turn sought to tip the scales in its favour through a cooperative relationship with the Soviet Union, thus indirectly justifying an unbalanced US policy and an anti-India Pakistani policy. The ultimate outcome was a South Asian arms race and tense relations between India and the United States for most of the 1970s and 1980s. By the end of the 1980s India–USA relations had stagnated, moving little in either direction. The USA considered Pakistan to be a much more reliable ally in its Asian ventures, and India seemed preoccupied with an inability to elect majority governments and a looming balance of payments problem. Things might have remained unchanged were it not for two major events that occurred at this juncture—the end of the Cold War and India's economic crisis.

1990 onwards: rediscovering common interests

The end of the Cold War marked a major shift in world politics and fundamentally restructured a number of relationships around the world, including the India–USA one. Finding itself bereft of Soviet support, India in the 1990s underwent a painful process of orienting itself to a unipolar world order in which it shared a history of acrimony with the only remaining superpower. Indeed, '[t]he story of Indian foreign policy in the 1990s is about the struggle to overcome the sources of opposition to the West.'[63] At the most basic level this meant ideological change. Non-alignment would no longer work in the absence of superpower competition. Enough time had passed to render anti-imperialism an outmoded ideology, particularly as India's own economy began growing with an outward orientation. The USA for its part was confronting the 'end of history' (to quote the famous phrase coined by Francis Fukuyama) and the lack of a global nemesis against which to define its own foreign policy ideology. Strategically it was adapting to an uncertain international system with multiple smaller powers rising fast. The security environment was now vastly different and required new policies. In terms of political values, India and the United States were still democracies, but that fact at the time offered no template for future cooperation.

Looking back to the early 1990s, few would have predicted the depth and breadth of relations between the two countries today. What explains this quantum leap?

Economic factors

On the economic front, 1991 is generally considered a watershed in Indian history. Faced with a severe balance of payments crisis, Prime Minister Rao's government initiated a series of reforms to liberalize the Indian economy under the stewardship of Manmohan Singh, then the Finance Minister. This opened the door to foreign private capital, a significant amount of which was American. Starting from $165 million in 1992, annual Foreign Direct Investment in India shot up to $2.14 billion by 1997, a thirteen-fold increase.[64] As the Indian economy grew in size and openness, so did the participation of American investors, who cumulatively accounted for 19 per cent of Foreign Direct Investment in India between 1991 and 2005.[65] Similarly, trade between India and the USA grew dramatically during this period (despite falling as a share of total global trade) and in 2009 stood at more than $39.7 billion.[66] The growth of India's knowledge economy and the global outsourcing industry brought both countries closer through private sector linkages. Former US Under Secretary of State Nicholas R. Burns points out that 'the big breakthrough in US–India relations was achieved originally by the private sector'.[67] Indian policymakers were aware of the precariousness of the domestic economic situation and the need to guide the Indian economy out of crisis carefully. But, due to the constant internal political argumentation over the nature and impact of the reforms, the initial years were marked by a sense of cautiousness. India did little to upset the status quo in its region and in its bilateral relations with the great powers.

Nowhere was this more evident than on the issue of nuclear testing. Although an Indian nuclear weapons programme had been in the offing since the late 1970s when China's assistance for a Pakistan weapons programme became known, the clearest impetus for its advancement came in 1988 when Rajiv Gandhi initiated a covert nuclear weapons programme based on a potential nuclear threat from Pakistan.[68] This plan was carried forward into the early 1990s and by 1994 the Rao government was ready to test. However the process was stopped short by considerations of the impact of US sanctions on the nascent post-reform Indian economy. Rao, in a conversation with Strobe Talbott, then US Deputy Secretary of State, indicated that India was aware of the importance of integration into the global economy and close relations with the USA. He emphasized that India's economic security would be jeopardized if it 'overplayed its nuclear card'.[69]

Political factors

Economic interdependence more often than not tends to moderate the tone of political differences between nations.[70] Here the role of Indian Americans in the United States deserves mention. The 1990s brought to the fore a number of wealthy Indian Americans who learned to mobilize politically and build relationships with the US Congress in order to influence policy towards India and South Asia. The US Census counted over 2.5 million

Americans of Indian origin in 2007. The median income of a family in this group is almost 79 per cent higher than the national median.[71] This put a significant amount of disposable income in the hands of politically aware and motivated individuals. Indian Americans raised $4 million on behalf of political candidates in the 1992 election, and more than $7 million in the 1998 election.[72] The result of this significant influence was that by the end of the 1990s, there was a high level of interest within Congress in issues pertaining to India, to the extent that more than a quarter of the members of the House of Representatives had joined an informal congressional caucus aimed at fostering India–USA ties.[73] Although the interest of American lawmakers in India was primarily motivated by domestic political and economic concerns, the increased level of interest played an important role in tempering traditional legislative hostility toward India as evinced by the defeat (from 1996 onwards) of the traditionally passed 'Burton amendments' designed to reduce foreign aid to India every year.[74] In 2005 and 2006, Indian Americans also undertook a major lobbying effort to promote the passage of laws allowing civilian nuclear cooperation with India.[75]

Indian policymakers, on the other hand, also began to shed their traditional anti-Americanism and non-aligned rhetoric during this period. The late 1980s witnessed a fundamental transition in Indian electoral politics from a largely one-party-dominant system to a fragmented multiparty system. This created ideological and political space for new voices in the articulation of Indian foreign policy. By 1991, the election manifesto of the Bharatiya Janata Party (BJP) was already dismissing non-alignment as an outdated ideology.[76] The 1990s in retrospect were a period when India gradually shed its anti-imperialist and non-alignment baggage in favour of an approach to foreign policy grounded in *realpolitik*. This was the precursor to the age of 'strategic partnerships' for India. By 2005, India had concluded such partnerships with China, Iran, Japan, and the United States. This signalled a new pragmatism in Indian foreign policy, and a willingness to spread the risks associated with international relations between ties with several friendly powers. India's diplomacy changed in style and content to some extent, with Vajpayee and Indian Foreign Minister Jaswant Singh choosing 'quiet diplomacy' over 'morally laden rhetoric'.[77] Vajpayee's successor, Manmohan Singh, opted for a similar style.

Differences of view with the USA continued over regional security and nuclear issues. In 1995, a Congressional amendment allowed the USA to resume arms supplies to Pakistan that had become attenuated since the Soviet withdrawal from Afghanistan. This was not well received in India, especially in light of a 1994 Human Rights Watch report that traced arms used by militants in Kashmir and Punjab to money and weapons supplied to Pakistan's intelligence agencies by the USA during the Afghanistan war.[78] India found that despite some advances in its relationship with the USA (e.g. the start of modest joint naval exercises in 1991),[79] the USA continued to pursue an unfavourable South Asia policy. While resuming arms supplies to Pakistan, it continued to pressure India to abandon its indigenous Integrated Missile Development Program, blocked the sale of Russian weapons systems to India, and limited India's access to American high technology, fearing that such access would be misused as before.[80] On the nuclear issue, in 1995 the USA pushed through a permanent extension of the NPT, to which India was bitterly opposed. Subsequently, in 1996, India rejected the Comprehensive Test Ban Treaty (CTBT) as a biased arrangement that favoured the major powers which had already enough data and experience in nuclear testing to continue simulating tests without actually conducting them.

The end of the Cold War in some ways liberated India's foreign policy and allowed it to choose its friends without external pressure. The result was a dual approach that emphasized cordial (but not necessarily cooperative) relations with the United States while also building partnerships with countries in the region, particularly China. India, like all other countries in the aftermath of the Cold War, was uncertain about the future shape of the new world order. The USA too was working hard to fill the global power vacuum left by the collapse of the Soviet Union, and was not particularly concerned with matters in South Asia. This was evinced by the continuation of the Pakistan tilt in its policy despite the end of significant Soviet influence in India. This relative indifference towards the region would evaporate a few months into 1998.

Pokhran-II and its impact

In May 1998, India detonated five nuclear devices at Pokhran, the site of its first nuclear test twenty-four years earlier. Barely two weeks later, Pakistan detonated six nuclear devices at the Chagai Hills. Both events sharply focused President Clinton and his administration's attention on South Asia. Although the immediate American response was to place economic sanctions on both countries, the tests precipitated the longest series of high-level bilateral talks in the history of the Indo-American relationship and for the first time, there was an attempt to structure the Indo-American relationship independent of Indo-Pakistani or Indo-Russian concerns.[81] In a paradoxical outcome, C. Raja Mohan argues that the tests of May 1998 were actually the beginning of the end of non-proliferation disagreements between the two countries: 'So long as India remained undecided about what it wanted to do with nuclear weapons, it was natural that the United States would do everything to prevent India from becoming a nuclear weapons power.'[82] In the longer term, Clinton's objectives in South Asia developed along three lines— non-proliferation, progress in relations with India, and continued support for Pakistan as a pro-Western Islamic state.[83] For the first time in the history of India–USA relations, a genuine attempt was made at a balanced approach in American policy towards South Asia. This vindicated the Indian view that 'the world gives respect to countries with nuclear weapons'.[84]

Evidence of American respect for India's concerns came the following year when Pakistan launched an offensive on Indian territory in the Kargil district of Kashmir. Contrary to past experience, India found the USA willing to place responsibility for the aggression squarely on Pakistan's shoulders and subsequently pressuring Prime Minister Nawaz Sharif to withdraw his troops. This marked a change in the American attitude toward Kashmir—previously sympathetic to Pakistan. On the nuclear question, soon after sanctions were imposed domestic lobbies in the USA—mainly Indian-American groups—pressured Congress to ease the sanctions on India.[85] The opposition of many Republican Congressmen to the CTBT also worked in India's favour when a Republican-dominated Congress rejected the CTBT in October 1999. Both these developments weakened the American negotiating position vis-à-vis India and eased the post-Pokhran rapprochement between India and the USA.

In 2000, Clinton became the first US President to visit India in twenty-two years. His trip was a resounding success and a landmark in the ongoing transformation of India–USA relations. The following year, India became one of the first (and few) countries to support President George W. Bush's controversial Nuclear Missile Defense (NMD) initiative. Thereafter, as the events of 11 September 2001 unfolded, India was quick to offer its full operational support for the US war against terrorism. By 22 September, the USA had lifted all sanctions against India and the bilateral Defense Policy Group, suspended since 1998, was revived toward the end of the year. Following a terrorist attack on the Indian Parliament in December 2001, the USA pressured Pakistan into a commitment on curbing cross-border terrorism in India, and put two major organizations—the Jaish-e-Mohammed and Lashkar-e-Taiba—on its list of foreign terrorists. In 2002 the USA initiated a regional security dialogue with India that explored shared interests in India's neighbourhood, including ending the civil war in Sri Lanka, promoting political stability in Bangladesh and reconstructing Afghanistan[86]—a significant break from Cold War difficulties over American influence in the subcontinent. Similarly in Kashmir, for the first time India allowed American observers on the ground during Assembly elections, which were declared free and fair.[87] At the height of fresh India–Pakistan tensions in 2003, Clinton (now a former President) was unofficially brought into the picture as a facilitator and was able to initiate a dialogue between President Musharraf and Prime Minister Vajpayee that paved the way for a rapprochement.[88] Meanwhile Congressmen in the USA passed a resolution making American aid to Pakistan conditional on an annual

Presidential report on Pakistan's cross-border insurgency promotion and nuclear proliferation activities.[89]

Strategic partnership

In 2004, India and the United States formulated the Next Steps in Strategic Partnership (NSSP), which laid the foundations for cooperation in civilian nuclear activities, civilian space programmes, and high-technology trade, along with an expanded dialogue on missile defence. Within the span of a decade the USA had reversed its long-standing policies of nuclear non-cooperation and technology denial toward India. On 18 July 2005 the two countries announced the most wide-ranging partnership in the history of their bilateral relations, covering the economy, energy security, democracy promotion, defence cooperation, and high technology and space cooperation. The most controversial aspect of the agreement was President George W. Bush's commitment to 'work with friends and allies to adjust international regimes to enable full civil nuclear energy cooperation and trade with India'.[90] In effect the USA explicitly recognized and cast itself as prepared to legitimize the nuclear weapons programme of a non-NPT state that had consistently opposed the global non-proliferation regime (though, as India claimed in its defence, it had *de facto* fulfilled the non-proliferation objectives of an NPT state).

A critical test of the new relationship came late in 2005 when India voted along with the United States against Iran at the International Atomic Energy Agency (IAEA) in a resolution on Tehran's nuclear programme, feared to include a weapons component. The double standards inherent in India's stand did not go unnoticed. The following year, India once again cast its lot with the USA at the IAEA on the Iran question, while the USA amended its domestic Atomic Energy Act in order to facilitate civilian nuclear cooperation with India. More recently, however, following a visit to Tehran by India's External Affairs Minister S. M. Krishna in May 2010, during which he praised Iran for 'fighting for its rights', Washington admitted that India and the USA held divergent views on Iran's nuclear programme.[91]

Aside from nuclear cooperation, since July 2005, India and the USA have cooperated in a number of areas such as aviation, trade and investment, business (through a high-powered CEO forum), agriculture, energy, science and technology, defence, disaster relief, democracy promotion, and maritime cooperation.[92] In 2007 India hosted a major round of naval exercises (part of the 'Malabar' series) in the Indian Ocean with twenty-seven warships from five countries including the USA, Japan, Australia, and Singapore.[93]

The end-game on India–USA negotiations toward an agreement governing cooperation in the nuclear sphere came into focus in late 2006. By then, foreign policy achievements of the Bush administration were few, with the

Iraq war widely seen as a strategic disaster for the USA. With developments in Afghanistan also unfavourable, and the NATO alliance coming under some pressure as a result, the President's team identified success on the India front as the most positive potential remaining foreign policy 'legacy' item in the Bush administration's portfolio. Intense negotiations—on the detailed outcome of which India frequently appeared to international observers to have bested the USA (while critics in India bayed about their perception of a Delhi sell-out)— yielded the required so-called '123 Agreement' in July 2007.[94] However, controversy in both countries was such that neither side was able to press for approval of the agreement and its related safeguards clauses at the IAEA or by the Nuclear Suppliers Group (NSG) until mid-2008. Both latter steps were preceded by a raucous debate in the Indian lower house of parliament in July 2008, with the government narrowly winning a no-confidence vote brought against the agreement. The IAEA approved the safeguards agreement on 1 August 2008, and the NSG approved an India-specific waiver from its core terms on 6 September 2008. In the final major step foreseen by the two countries for implementation of their understandings, the US Senate on 1 October 2008 approved the deal by a vote of 86 to 13.

These developments were significant for the India–USA relationship but also for India's global standing and positioning. The USA had helped it off the perch of nuclear pariah status and defiance it had been confined to since 1974, but, through the IAEA and NSG votes, the rest of the world concurred in India's emergence from nuclear purdah. While Indian commentators made much of ambiguous Chinese statements during the IAEA negotiations, neither China nor other countries such as Australia and Canada (which had long adopted an assertive stance in defence of the NPT and the wider non-proliferation regime) stood in the way of IAEA approval. Indian diplomacy contributed significantly to this success, especially the quiet but resolute leadership on this issue of Prime Minister Singh (uncharacteristically tough in staring down domestic critics of the negotiations with the USA, including some within his own Congress Party).[95] Indeed, New Delhi's global diplomatic manoeuvring in relation to the nuclear file during the years 2005–8 suggested just how pragmatic and focused Indian diplomacy had become, given the right incentives.[96] The Obama administration's National Security Strategy and the USA–India Strategic Dialogue of 1–4 June 2010 further reinforce the commitment of both countries to a broad-based partnership, covering a gamut of ties, including non-proliferation.[97]

Rediscovering common values

The post-1990 story of India–USA relations is not just about the end of the Cold War, India's second round of nuclear tests, or economic liberalization. It is also fundamentally a story about rediscovering common political values. For most of the twentieth century American policymakers failed to see the potential in India to be a strong (and democratic) partner in Asia. Instead there was a tendency to see India as 'a revisionist power bent on restructuring the international system at the expense of America's global interests'.[98] Since the early 1990s, however, an increasingly influential school of thought in American foreign policy began recognizing the strategic utility of the common political values espoused by both nations.

Since Indian independence, India's conscious adoption of constitutional liberal democracy had resonated among the American people and at times among its foreign policymakers. As home to a significant section of the world's population, India came to symbolize an important experiment in post-colonial democracy. In this sense both the USA and India always had much to gain from a cooperative relationship.

Indeed, Americans were aware of the importance of promoting democratic stability in India. Data on US economic aid to India and Pakistan confirm a substantial and enduring financial commitment to India in the 1950s and 1960s, likely motivated by this very idea. Especially from 1957 till 1971, the gross amount of economic aid from the USA to India was on average more than twice the amount of aid flowing from the USA to Pakistan. This was repeated from 1977 to 1983, and noticeably from 1991 to 2001, during which the average annual economic aid to India was more than three times the aid to Pakistan.[99] In terms of military aid, with the exception of the Sino-Indian war, Pakistan has uniformly received greater amounts of assistance from the USA than India. However, between 1951 and 2006, more than 84 per cent of American military aid to Pakistan is concentrated in two periods: the decade following the mutual defence agreement of 1955, and the years of intensification of the first Afghanistan war (1983 to 1990).

These data suggest that the USA has always viewed Pakistan as a *military* ally and India as a potential *political* ally. The word 'ally' here must be construed rather loosely, for India was aligned with the USA only in the sense of its domestic political values being somewhat congruent with the latter's. Yet it appears democracy was perceived to be strong enough in India (the aberration of the 1975–7 Emergency notwithstanding) for the USA to be genuinely invested in building up its economy and society through development assistance that helped at different times to avoid famine, launch the Green Revolution, tackle malaria, and expand the educational system. Gary Hess suggests that from the 1950s to the 1980s, the USA maintained a two-pronged strategy of engagement in South Asia that involved 'the simultaneous building of an alliance with Pakistan and promoting close political-economic ties with India'.[100] The focus on shared political values between the United States and India, symbolized by foreign aid, held great potential initially. Yet the momentum was not sustained. The amount of US economic aid was substantially lower after 1971, and continued to decline into the 1990s.

The new millennium saw a resurgence in the value-based approach to India–USA relations through increased interaction that led to a better understanding of each other's domestic priorities. Unsurprisingly, US assistance to India was a declining part of the equation as the Indian government emerged as a donor in its own right. Indeed, early in 2007 the US State Department announced a 35 per cent reduction in aid programmes to India.[101] But increasingly, in the aftermath of 9/11, when democracy promotion became a significant item on the Bush administration's international agenda, a value-based approach complemented by an interests-based economic agenda underpinned the relationship. From being critical of Indian democracy, particularly on human rights issues, during the early years of the Clinton administration, the USA had modified its stance to the extent of involving India as an integral member of both its global democracy promotion initiatives—the Community of Democracies and the UN Democracy Fund.[102] In 2007 Nicholas R. Burns wrote that the promotion of democracy and freedom around the world 'should be an essential component of the new USA–India relationship'.[103] The subtlety of this relationship relies on the American use of democracy promotion as a strategy to 'modernize' the Middle East and other unstable regions of the world. India has been a willing ally in pursuing this value-based foreign policy with strategic overtones. In his speech to the US Congress on 19 July 2005, Manmohan Singh hinted at the coincidence of values and strategy in the new India–USA relationship:

> There are partnerships based on principle and there are partnerships based on pragmatism. I believe we are at a juncture where we can embark on a partnership that can draw both on principle as well as pragmatism. We must build on this opportunity.[104]

Regional power balances

Moving beyond the bilateral relationship, there are a number of longer-term regional and international factors that were fundamental to the warming of India–USA relations. Taken together, a growing India, a declining Pakistan, and an increasingly powerful China all combined to motivate an India–USA entente. On Pakistan, Jaswant Singh, India's former Foreign Minister, reportedly proclaimed to his counterpart Strobe Talbott in 1998 that Pakistan is a 'failed state' while India 'stays together', thus making better relations with India the right strategic choice for the United States.[105] Indeed one of the major features of America's new South Asia policy was the conceptual decoupling of India and Pakistan. No longer did the USA view its actions in the subcontinent as a zero sum game between the region's two most bitter rivals. This allowed the USA to declare Pakistan a major non-NATO ally in 2004 and to sign agreements in 2006 for arms transfers to Pakistan worth $3.5 billion for fighting the war on terrorism. While these moves were criticized in India, the complaints were fairly subdued: 'Particularly striking about the building blocks for the new Indo-US relationship is how little Pakistan figures in them.'[106]

In fact, China, not Pakistan, has gradually emerged as the new third party in the India–USA relationship. Ashutosh Varshney describes this development as 'a new triangle' that is predicated on a simple piece of realist logic: 'when the first- and second-ranked powers fight, the first often ardently courts the third.'[107] This statement captures the new dynamic as many scholars and diplomats see it. China is growing rapidly and is an unpredictable regime— although its stated philosophy is one of peaceful growth, its defence expenditures have been rising and now rank third in the world behind the USA and Russia.[108] It is also a known proliferator of nuclear technology to rogue regimes such as Libya, Pakistan, Iran, and North Korea.[109] Therefore it is hardly surprising that the USA gravitated towards India, growing less rapidly and in a non-threatening manner, in part as a hedge against a potentially revisionist China. Writing in 2000, future National Security Adviser and Secretary of State Condoleezza Rice argued that the USA should pay closer attention to India as 'an element in China's calculation', suggesting a degree of regional rivalry that the USA might have the potential to exploit in its favour.[110]

India itself is growing into the shoes of a meaningful power and is on its way to earning the equality of status it long aspired to with the USA. In the span of just four years, senior officials of the Bush administration went from describing India as having the potential to be a great power[111] to counting it among the 'major powers' along with Russia and China.[112] Indeed President Bush's 2006 *National Security Strategy* claimed that 'India now is poised to shoulder global obligations in cooperation with the United States in a way befitting a major power.'[113] The tendency of the Bush administration to build up Indian power was seen as an effort to groom India into a role where it might effectively support the USA in international affairs, be it against a rising China, in censuring Iran for its nuclear programme, or by being a 'junior partner' in controlling the Indian Ocean.[114]

Indian actions, however, tended to belie this conception. Although the Vajpayee government cited the Chinese threat as one of the main motivators of the Indian nuclear weapons programme in 1998,[115] broader trends contradicted this claim. Rather than take steps to contain China, India steadily (since around 1988) developed a high-level dialogue with China in an attempt to resolve outstanding issues and explore new avenues of cooperation.[116] By the end of 2007 India held its first joint army training exercises with China, and

China hosted the first India–China Annual Defence Dialogue.[117] Indeed India's growing relationship with the USA seemingly convinced an internally oriented China of India's potential, thus creating somewhat of a tentative balance in the region, which India used to improve relations with China.[118] Moreover, a growing India is working on and off to prevent a regional rivalry with China.[119] Many in India consider the predominant foreign problem to be instability in Pakistan. In contrast, China is perceived by some 'as an economic and political opportunity more than a strategic, civilizational, or economic problem'.[120] Hence, in some key international forums, including on climate change, trade, labour laws, arms control, and human rights, India has found common ground with China against Western interests. As regards being a junior partner of the United States, India's deep internal divisions over the India–USA nuclear deal signalled a national unwillingness to play second fiddle. Despite voting against Iran twice in the IAEA, New Delhi sought to maintain positive relations with Tehran through bilateral channels. Moreover, India's pursuit of energy security through a proposed Iran–Pakistan–India gas pipeline continues to be a source of disagreement between India and the United States, as do its friendly policies towards undemocratic regimes in its neighbourhood, notably Myanmar. In these ways, India escapes Washington's control and intends to continue doing so.

A New World Order

Despite considerable disagreement over whether the contemporary international system is unipolar, multipolar, 'uni-multipolar',[121] or even 'nonpolar',[122] a common strand running through most assessments is that the USA is less and less able to 'go it alone' in international affairs. Multilateralism or at least 'coalitions of the willing' are required for the USA to act both legitimately and successfully in the international system. Although the war on terrorism strengthened the American resolve under President Bush to eschew multilateral institutions in favour of a unilateral approach, the long-term results of this policy proved detrimental to US interests, leading to a renewed emphasis on the value of partnerships and alliances in early Obama Administration policy statements.[123]

This logic, when applied to the USA–India relationship, highlights the importance that the USA has placed on secondary powers. In 2008 Condoleezza Rice, then Secretary of State, proclaimed 'investing in strong and rising powers as stakeholders in the international order' as one of two pillars of America's 'unique' realism (the other being support for democracy in weak and poorly governed states).[124] Yet it is not just secondary powers that the USA has focused on, but secondary powers with traditionally perceived revisionist tendencies (particularly China, Russia, and India) that might in future become dissatisfied enough with the global order to engage in balancing behaviour against the United States. A strategy that gives such powers a greater stake in the international system is likely to pre-empt future instability in international relations. Efforts to involve India and China in G-7 meetings, to support China's membership in the Nuclear Suppliers Group despite its proliferation activities, to involve China in the North Korea non-proliferation negotiations, and indirectly to legitimize India's nuclear weapons can all be viewed in this light.[125] In 2006 President Bush's nuclear negotiation team testified to Congress that their intention was to ' "lock in" India to a deal before moving to tie down and restrain the country's nuclear potential in non-proliferation discussions'.[126] It appears therefore that the American strategy has been not just to give emerging powers a greater stake in the system but to involve them in ways that restrict their future margin for manoeuvre. Also important in this context is the emerging salience of Indian democracy in the American worldview. For its part, India has historically been an inactive exporter of democracy, but sensing an opportunity it too has modified somewhat its international stance on the issue.

This form of opportunism has been a key factor in propelling the India–USA relationship. As the USA attempted to restructure international relations in the aftermath of the Cold War and 9/11, India tried to capture as much diplomatic space as possible to articulate its own interests. It did this by supporting the USA on key initiatives, including the war on terrorism and Nuclear Missile Defense (NMD), both of which sought to challenge and modify the 'global rules of the game'.[127] It joined hands with the USA in the name of democracy promotion, and above all it cooperated to a great extent on the nuclear front, placing a number of its nuclear reactors under international safeguards in exchange for almost unconditional entry into the global nuclear club. Although the nuclear deal was a highly contested political topic in India, scholars and politicians in the United States saw it in one of two ways—either as a grave risk to the non-proliferation regime, or as a significant achievement for it.[128] Specifics of the deal aside, its broad thrust once again emphasized the American attempt to reign in a rising power, and India's attempt to maximize the opportunities of a strategic relationship with a hegemonic power.

The Obama Administration's foreign policy orientations at the outset were crafted to emphasize a degree of contrast with those of the previous Washington team. Gone was assertive international democracy promotion. In its place President Obama and Secretary of State Hillary Clinton advanced a wider approach to values, rooted in concepts of 'smart' power, and a greater determination to engage allies and partners.[129] Many in the Indian media and political communities worried that the intensity of the Bush Administration's commitment to improving ties with India would not be replicated by President Obama and his crew. Early signals from the Obama team that it might seek to insert Washington into the Kashmir file, seeing in it a key to unlocking a happy outcome in Afghanistan, worried New Delhi. Ultimately, Obama skated away from that dimension of his transition team's thinking by appointing Richard Holbrooke as Special Envoy for Afghanistan and Pakistan (and noticeably not for India or Kashmir). And while the Administration included more champions of the multilateral non-proliferation regime than had that of President Bush, all official early signals toward India were positive, including during early visits by both Secretary of State Clinton and Special Envoy Holbrooke. Nevertheless, suspicions of Holbrooke's approach and intentions, perceived as favouring Pakistan unduly, remained lively in India throughout 2009.

Although, prior to Obama's visit to India in November 2010, which proved successful, some Indians remained reserved on his commitment to the US relationship with India, Nicholas R. Burns, who negotiated the US–India nuclear cooperation agreement for the previous (Republican) Administration asserts:

> While President Obama was forced to pay more attention to Afghanistan/Pakistan and China in his first year of office, he has made abundantly clear his commitment to continue to build the US–India relationship. As a global power, the US will need to secure close working relations with China, Pakistan and other countries with which India has a difficult relationship. Indians should understand, however, that the US will very likely see India as one of its primary global partners for the next several decades.[130]

Karl F. Inderfurth, who served as Assistant Secretary of State for South Asia under President Clinton, concurs:

> The civilian nuclear agreement with India was a milestone in the relationship and would be a hard act to follow, by any successor US administration. Moreover, as one US South Asia expert has correctly pointed out, the Obama administration is consumed by problems both at home and abroad, and India is simply not a problem.[131]

Conclusion: looking forward

The doctrine John Foster Dulles developed of 'those who are not with us are against us' (echoed in the aftermath of 9/11 by President George W. Bush) is no longer apposite to the USA–India relationship.[132] Today India finds itself 'with' the United States on several key issues when until very recently it was 'against' on most, and Washington is grateful for its support. The interests and values of the two nations converge today much more than they diverge. Yet the stability of this new relationship is not guaranteed. Depending on the circumstances, India might find the USA reluctant to intervene on its behalf. Similarly, the USA cannot always count on India's support for its initiatives, particularly regarding the Islamic world, with which India has strong and ancient cultural and social ties. In the USA, India is often out of focus, neither much better known nor beyond Washington much better liked than fifty years ago. Raju Narisetti, former editor in Delhi of the business daily *Mint*, and today managing editor of the *Washington Post*, writes:

> The sharp shift in India's psyche, to a relatively independent, even arrogant, nation that believes it has come into its own both economically and politically, is not understood widely in the USA. While India's rising economic clout is a matter of much interest, there is very little conviction in the USA that India has matured enough to translate that rising economic clout into any meaningful global political influence, even when India does create the occasional—and very successful—roadblocks, such as its contribution to the deadlock of the WTO Doha round in 2008.[133]

On the nuclear issue, India and the USA are yet to fully resolve their non-proliferation differences and some potential discord in this realm is perfectly conceivable. As well, the issues of energy security and the diversification of energy sources, including natural gas supplies from Iran and other Gulf states, could come to complicate the relationship. India's attempts to obtain a permanent seat in the UN Security Council, endorsed by Obama in Delhi in 2010 but inspiring a sense of international urgency on the issue, may return to haunt the relationship if Delhi were to press hard for Washington to deliver results. Meanwhile, the two countries will likely continue to work cooperatively in the G-20 and several other international forums.[134]

The entente between the two nations is not so much an alliance as a 'selective partnership' based on specific shared interests in some areas and *quid pro quo* arrangements in others, all underscored by strong economic interdependence.[135] As long as their interests are aligned, India and the United States will seem locked in a wider strategic embrace. But perceptions of interests can change rapidly in today's fast-moving and uncertain world. To predicate long-term strategies excessively on systematic cooperation would be hazardous for both nations.

India's ability to overcome its anxieties about and resentment of the United States owes a great deal to its growing self-confidence and to the realization that a policy of non-alignment makes little sense in a world in which several great powers vie with each other and in which India aspires to join them as one of the leading countries of the twenty-first century. American interest in closer relations with India, spurred by its growing market for American goods and the close connections of the two countries in the provision of global services, has been intensified by a very different dynamic—Washington's loss of absolute dominance of international relations in the wake of the Iraq and Afghanistan wars and the US-induced global economic crisis of 2008–9.

Nevertheless, most Indians welcome better ties, as their own economic aspirations exhibit marked affinities with those of Americans, with whom they share many other bonds, not least democratic governance. And Americans, notably in the corridors of power in Washington, often see India as a useful hedge against the rise of China, if not as a reliable ally in all of its global adventures.

This makes clear how far India has come, and perhaps also how US-centred unipolarity proved but a fleeting consequence of the end of the Cold War.

8

India's West Asia Policy: Delicate Manoeuvres

India's ties with its neighbours to the West have traditionally been meaningful. For one thing, as suggested in Chapter 2, most of the non-native conquerors of northern India hailed from the West or, when from Central Asia, penetrated India from the West (through Afghanistan and what is now Pakistan).[1] Afghan invaders were heavily influenced by Persian culture, and most conquerors after the eleventh century were Muslim (the British being the most obvious exception).[2]

During the British Raj, India was closely connected, administratively and otherwise, with West Asia by the British overlords.[3] Under them, Indian army divisions participated in campaigns in Egypt and Palestine in the First World War and in Iran, Syria, and Iraq during the Second World War.[4] As the British colonial role faded, throughout the twentieth century, in South and West Asia (including in Egypt and Palestine), close economic links persisted, particularly with countries of the Persian Gulf, including Iraq and Iran.

These ties were often challenged by the profound antagonisms within West Asia after the Second World War, but also, in the specific case of South Asia, by rivalries in that region also, not least Pakistani attempts to isolate India from the Islamic world. Even if West Asia enjoyed less complex ties with India, it might well be worth surveying the relationships, particularly for Western readers, as the global weight of Western-centric international relations may be declining in importance, relative to the international relations of other regions and countries, particularly Asian ones.

For West Asia, an area with complex, often contradictory impulses towards the United States (hitherto the sole remaining superpower, but now playing more of a *primus inter pares* role), other partners, particularly powerful energy-hungry ones like China and India, are much more important than they were even twenty years ago.[5] Already, the beginnings of a new 'great game' can be detected between rising powers around the world, opening up new possibilities for all involved, but also new dangers, including in relation to energy supplies and to Middle East politics, that perennial tinderbox.

For centuries, West Asia has represented one of the few major regions that empires and superpowers could not fully dominate, although most have tried. Until the discovery of vast oil supplies in the Persian Gulf region, much of the effort exerted by major powers to govern West Asia, directly or indirectly, revolved around its strategic position between Europe and India (or more generally between the north Atlantic and Asia). The constant pursuit of trade routes between these areas has ensured a steady flow of cultures, people, and goods in all directions. The economic rise of India, and the continuing energy riches of West Asia, have ensured that India no longer has merely a diplomatic and neighbourly connection with West Asia, but also an expanding and vital interest in this area, building on a solid foundation of substantive relations with virtually all countries of the region at a time of great geostrategic uncertainty. For example, it has yet to be seen whether the conflict and now political deadlock in Iraq will resolve itself peacefully, or descend into further sectarian violence once US forces largely exit Iraq in 2011.[6] The difference between relative instability as opposed to chaos in Iraq is a critical factor for all its immediate neighbours and the Persian Gulf countries (as well as for naval powers present in the Gulf). Moreover, fears over Iran's nuclear programme, variously pronounced around the globe but most acute in Israel, constitute a wild card in the region and beyond.

In addition, while Israel's campaign to subdue Hamas in Gaza in 2008–9, much decried internationally, was conducted in part with the aim of producing a new deal in the Levant, the Israeli–Palestinian conflict continues to simmer menacingly. And positive relations between Israel and Turkey, one of the few hopeful signposts in the region, were damaged by the flawed interception of a Turkish flotilla carrying pro-Palestinian activists and supplies to Gaza in May 2010.[7] Thus, the Middle East quagmire was no less worrying in the late summer of 2010 than at other times over recent decades.

India has a strong interest in positive outcomes to each of these West Asian challenges, despite not being involved in the 'great power' diplomacy to address them (for example, among the permanent members of the UN Security Council, or within the West Asia 'Quartet' of key international players, i.e. the USA, the EU, Russia, and the UN). India's largely successful approach has been to tend to its various bilateral relationships in West Asia, seeking to maintain friendships (and through them, the promotion of its economic interests) in good order. Indeed, India's diplomacy with West Asian countries stands out as particularly accomplished, despite tense Indian ties with Muslim Pakistan holding the potential to disrupt relationships with other Muslim countries. (This is less true today, with all international actors increasingly willing, often eager, to deal with an increasingly significant India on its own terms.)[8]

India's long shared history with West Asia is a tremendous advantage to it in negotiating the shoals of unpredictable rivalries and hostilities in the region.

West Asian complexity is much better understood in India than in most Western capitals. Further, India's trading relationships in West Asia, dating back to well before European colonialism, are etched into the neighbourhood's DNA.

Throughout the Cold War, India's official policy of non-alignment globally was translated into a policy of 'equidistance' in West Asia, which worked well in the main, although it required constant calibration. This policy largely left the Indian government free to adjust to evolving dynamics at play in the region, and to balance out instability in one state by placing at least temporary, in some cases more long-lasting, emphasis on another. The end of the Cold War, however, brought new (or in some cases rediscovered) complexities to the region, ranging from ethnic tensions to questions of leadership succession and the risk of further proliferation of nuclear weapons. Given these developments, its continuing security concerns and growing energy interests have led India to redouble engagement in the region.

An examination of the dynamics of the relationship between West Asia and India reveals actors on both sides crafting policies that are largely pragmatic. National interests have dominated India's involvement in the region, and the states in West Asia have responded in kind. Also, while trade has historically provided both the incentive and the underpinning for these relationships, security interests are playing an increasing role either by choice, as with Israel, or because of global dynamics over which India has little control, as with Iran.

India's status as a nuclear and economic power is leading to its involvement and participation in global leadership, for example through membership in the G-20. But its new international profile and greater responsibilities are attended by a need to grapple with greater complexity and possibly greater risk. And the expansion of India's interests in West Asia suggests that a policy based mainly on principles of 'equidistance' can no longer alone address its interests, requiring India to make tough decisions in the future in order to maintain the success to date of its West Asian policy.

The past as prologue

The contemporary geostrategic relationship between India and West Asia in its essence dates back to the period of British Empire. West Asia provided key passageways towards Britain's global economic interests, which were primarily anchored in India and parts of the Far East. Testament to this relationship is the fact that responsibility for the Persian Gulf region was delegated from London to the British Viceroy in India, an arrangement that was maintained until India won independence in 1947.[9] During British rule, interaction between Indian and Gulf traders facilitated not only an exchange of ideas between India and the Persian Gulf, but also of commodities, people, and administrative practice.[10] Most of these habits of interaction survived Indian independence and are today a constant for the countries involved.[11]

The fact that West Asia and India share a degree of ethnic and religious heterogeneity has also played a part in India's foreign policy towards the region. India's need to maintain harmony among Hindus and Muslims has played a role in how it approaches the Arab–Israeli conflict and Turkish secularism.[12] For example, although Turkey, like India, is a secular democracy, electoral gains made by political parties with leanings towards Islam have caused tensions, with the military, which is constitutionally the protector of Turkey's secularism. Indians are consequently more interested in Turkey than one might expect. This, coupled with Turkey's geostrategic significance, has led to the quest for closer ties.[13]

While many in the past argued that India's adoption of non-alignment during the Cold War was a moral decision, current scholars and practitioners argue convincingly that the policy of non-alignment for India represented a pragmatic, realist approach to protecting India's international interests through policy independence at a challenging time, and study of India's policy towards West Asia tends to corroborate this conclusion.[14] The advantages of non-alignment as an umbrella ideology for India's foreign policy in its early years of independence included being able to hold a number of international disputes (including ones involving other developing countries) at bay while India focused on essential domestic objectives vital to consolidating the state and tending to the urgent needs of its population.[15] The policy also served India well in fostering a web of bilateral relations with partners of many different persuasions: democratic or authoritarian, Muslim or Christian, Sunni or Shia, and so on, even while instances of West Asian regional cooperation (for example, the Baghdad Pact, CENTO, and the United Arab Republic) proved short-lived or still-born.

This bilateral approach to building and maintaining relationships in West Asia resulted in a policy of equidistance with most of India's partners in the region and enabled India to ensure relatively stable relationships throughout an area long racked with instability. Hamid Ansari writes that some issues touching on religious or other loyalties have affected India's relationship with states in West Asia, specifically citing the Kashmir conflict and the 1971 war in East Pakistan, but Delhi did not allow these to inhibit wider efforts to promote cooperation on interests such as trade.[16]

India's key interests in the region will likely remain similar to what they have been in the past few decades: security and stability in order to guarantee a stable supply of fuel; cooperation and engagement in order to promote trade; and the ability to leverage its position to gain increased access and standing in global forums.

The status quo: India and North Africa[17]

In recent history, the most important focal point for Indian diplomacy in north Africa was Egypt, because of its position of leadership within the Arab world. This was particularly true during the presidency of Gamal Abdel Nasser, whose nationalist, secular, and anti-colonialist rhetoric was very much in line with India's Cold War foreign policy.[18]

The warming of relations between Egypt and India during the 1950s had much to do with personal diplomacy by the leaders in the two states, who saw similar qualities in each other. Bansidhar Pradhan describes how Nehru admired Nasser's condemnation of the US-led Baghdad Pact and the unifying aims of pan-Arabism. Simultaneously, Nasser viewed Nehru as a fellow anti-colonialist who had contributed to forcing the British out of India, much as Nasser was trying to do in the Middle East. These ideas were mirrored in India's support of Egypt during the 1956 Suez Crisis, and the subsequent opposition of each state to the Eisenhower Doctrine, which suggested a greater role for the USA (as the influence of Britain and France faded in the wake of their failure), together with Israel, to impose their will on Egypt over management of the Suez Canal.[19]

While the Indo-Egyptian relationship during this time had a distinct ideological streak, India's interests region-wide were well served by establishing a strong relationship with the most charismatic Arab leader of the age. India's support of Nasser during the Suez Crisis was appreciated throughout the Arab world. This helped to build mutual trust that allowed India to pursue economic interests in the region thereafter.[20] The Indian relationship with Algeria, which at the same time was engaged in its struggle for independence from France, had similar drivers as the Cairo–Delhi relationship, although it was of lesser immediate significance for India as Algiers was less pivotal in the Arab world.

The states in north Africa have taken a back seat in the more recent Indian approach to West Asia. Indeed, in the past two decades, India's West Asian policy has been focused on a new set of key partners: Saudi Arabia, Israel, and Iran.[21] This makes sense in relation to India's pursuit of interests, because India can maintain mutually beneficial relationships with all three of these states (although Iran was an extremely sensitive relationship for India when set against a geopolitical backdrop defined in large part by the George W. Bush Administration's 'war on terror' and 'axis of evil'). In 2008–9, India's exports to Egypt totalled US$1.69 billion and its imports from it US$2.12 billion.[22] By comparison, India's trade in 2008–9 with Israel (linked to India by official diplomatic ties only since 1992) accounted for US$1.45 billion in exports and US$2.09 billion in imports.[23] Notwithstanding Algeria's role as an oil producer, the states in north Africa, save perhaps Egypt because of its political influence, can offer little economic incentive to India to justify more intense bilateral or subregional relationships.

While India has few pressing strategic interests in north Africa, it cannot ignore the area altogether. China, India's primary competitor in many areas, has been increasing its involvement in many African states, specifically in the energy and economic sectors. Although clearly driven by its resource needs, China's policy may also be influenced to a degree by predictions, perhaps more hopeful than imminent, of an African 'renaissance'.[24] With the same view, India will likely maintain its footholds in north Africa so that it can be in a good position there as elsewhere throughout the continent should this happy prospect materialize in the future.

Although India would doubtless support regional integration in north Africa, the dismal history of neighbourly cooperation in this region, notably through the economic Maghreb Union, does not bode well for such a scenario.[25] For now, north Africa will likely remain on the periphery of India's West Asia policy, taking a back seat to others.

India and the Gulf States: economics trump

India's stake—energy needs above all

With an increasing thirst for energy, the centrality of the Gulf states in India's West Asia policy is ever more obvious. India's importing of Gulf oil, however, raises several hard questions for the country regarding its ability to operate alongside potential competitors such as China, and its willingness to invest heavily, in policy terms, in an area which is prone to destabilization.

On all current projections, India's energy consumption will vastly increase over coming decades, barring significant changes in the country itself, in energy technologies, or in the oil market.[26] India has plentiful coal resources and fully intends to draw on them, but thermal energy will not suffice.[27] As discussed in Chapter 4, India's demand for imported oil and gas is only likely to rise as its domestic ability to produce energy stagnates. Juli A. MacDonald and S. Enders Wimbush assert that:

> the strategic reality is that Asian states will become more dependent for energy on the Persian Gulf, not less, as conventional wisdom—which tends to exaggerate the size of energy supplies elsewhere and understate the difficulty of bringing them to market—might suggest.[28]

Thus, the Gulf states will continue to be central in India's foreign policy. In particular, the security of the energy that these states can supply to India will be a key factor, and India's ability to manage it is limited.

Democracy promotion—preferably not in the Gulf

C. Raja Mohan writes that the promotion of democracy was not much of a priority in Indian foreign policy during the Cold War, and the 1990s saw little change even though the demise of the Soviet regime had opened up new margin for manoeuvre in recasting it.[29] However, Washington—the only remaining superpower—itself never pushed democracy promotion in the Persian Gulf countries, with the arguable exception of Iraq, and India saw no need to take the lead. Even in Egypt, where the USA did exert some pressure, Washington's efforts under the George W. Bush administration were episodic and unconvincing. India's response to the Bush Administration's enthusiasm for democracy promotion was to support cross-cutting multilateral initiatives on the topic, often of American design, rather than to engage in bilateral initiatives on this front.[30] Thus, India's principle of non-intervention in the sovereign affairs of other countries (except, occasionally, close neighbours) remained intact. With the Obama Administration mostly playing down the democracy promotion theme, and India sceptical of its relevance to its own foreign policy, Indian energy requirements will likely continue to outweigh local governance factors in India's relations with Gulf capitals and West Asia more generally.

Protecting investments—hard power

A growing stake in the West Asian oil market, and by extension in energy security in the region, is likely to draw India further into West Asia diplomatically and possibly militarily. In his seminal 1836 work *The Influence of Sea Power Upon History*, A. T. Mahan convincingly argues that a nation's status on the global stage is directly linked to its ability to protect trade and commerce routes and project influence through naval capacity.[31] His argument is still broadly valid nearly two centuries later. Even a quick examination of what is known of India's plans, specifically with respect to major military procurements, indicates that India sees its navy as central to projecting its rising military capability (as does China).

India's ability to protect sea-lanes (and thus indirectly project military power) will increase significantly with the addition of new naval and air capabilities including the *Admiral Gorshkov*, a retrofitted ex-Russian aircraft carrier, and long-range SU-33 fighter aircraft. India also has plans to purchase several new diesel-powered submarines, with the top contenders for supply likely being Russian or French export models,[32] and is pursuing an indigenous aircraft carrier design, which is to be constructed by 2011 and to begin operations by 2014.[33] Moreover, it is now conceivable that India will operate at least three aircraft carriers by 2015–20 and finally reach its goal of fielding three operational carrier battle groups.[34]

In 2008–9, India played an active role in policing the Gulf of Aden (alongside several Western powers and the Chinese Navy) to discourage rampant piracy emanating from Somalia, the United Nations Security Council having supplied the necessary mandate.[35] The publication of the first 'Indian Maritime Doctrine' confirms India's new emphasis on a wider mandate beyond the South Asian neighbourhood.[36] Tariq Ashraf addresses the link between the Indian Navy's renewal and the Gulf:

> The emergence of geo-economics as the main determinant of interstate relations requires the availability of adequate naval power to secure sea lines of communication against interference or interdiction by hostile navies. For India, which is predicted to encounter enormous energy shortfalls in the coming years, this is especially relevant; India cannot afford to have its maritime link with the Persian Gulf obstructed or tampered with.[37]

The ability to keep choke points open is dependent on specific systems such as 'blue water' surface and subsurface naval vessels and long-range aviation, and India has recently placed significant emphasis on increasing these capabilities. Overall, as Brunel University scholar Andrew Brunatti notes: 'India's dogged pursuit of naval capacity suggests that power projection in Asia is likely to remain largely a naval project across oceans and sea-lanes that are still of great economic and strategic importance, recalling the earlier colonial period when control of the seas and important ports was paramount in the fierce competition for commercial dominance.'

Furthering investments—soft power

While India's interests in the Persian Gulf are clear, it is unlikely that the use, as opposed to the existence, of 'hard power' will play a predominant role in India's West Asia policy, unless there are serious perceived threats to India's interests there—in which case it would likely prefer to act with others. Diplomacy will continue as the main Indian instrument of policy for the area. While India historically has tended to resort to multilateral institutions to achieve 'diplomatic force multiplication', Ishrat Aziz argues: 'Bilateralism is best pursued when others need you. With its recent political and economic success, India is much better placed to pursue bilateralism today.'[38] India's leverage has indeed increased, and with it, India's bargaining position has improved. Thus, while India will not always prevail (particularly on issues such as better conditions for Indian migrant workers in the Gulf), the pursuit of bilateral agreements between India and Gulf states will likely continue to be an important and effective option. Multilaterally, India will likely continue to contribute troops to UN peacekeeping operations in the West Asian region, sometimes alongside contingents from Pakistan, Bangladesh, or Sri Lanka, in line with its proud peacekeeping history in the area, notably with UNEF 1 (in Sinai, 1956–67) and more recently in UNIFIL (South Lebanon) prior to and following the Israeli-Lebanese border conflict of 2006.[39]

Although the bilateral approach seems well suited to India's objectives in West Asia, it can also prove diplomatically exhausting with a multiplicity of small Persian Gulf actors. The Mumbai Declaration of the First Gulf Cooperation Council (GCC)—India Industrial Conference, issued in February 2004, indicates India's willingness to engage multilateral institutions where this is possible.[40] The 2006 Conference identified not only the energy sector as ripe for joint ventures (involving governments and more so private sectors), but also the petrochemical, communications technology, biotechnology, and tourism sectors.[41] While then Indian Industry and Commerce Minister Kamal Nath strongly supported India–GCC cooperation, talk of a free-trade area has remained just that.[42] It is nowhere near being seriously attempted or achieved. However, save for the GCC (a group of countries sharing many interests), given the relative lack of credibility of regional institutions in West Asia (for example, the Arab League), prospects for regional as opposed to bilateral diplomacy are limited.[43]

Indeed, India's approach to Saudi Arabia is primarily rooted in bilateral arrangements, as recorded in the joint New Delhi Declaration of January 2006, which include efforts to combat terrorism, commitments to Indian assistance in technology sectors, and cultural and educational initiatives.[44] Most importantly for India, the Declaration committed Saudi Arabia to energy initiatives including joint public and private ventures and a guarantee of a cheap and stable supply of oil backed through long-term and flexible contracts. More recently, in the Riyadh Declaration signed during Prime Minister Singh's first visit to Saudi Arabia in February 2010, the two nations re-emphasized the importance of implementing their earlier commitments and upgraded their relationship to a 'strategic partnership covering security, economic, defence and political areas'.[45] If followed up, enhanced cooperation in these fields could prove valuable to both countries.

The conflict in Iraq

India historically maintained close relations with modern Iraq. The two were linked by British influence: and many Indians died under British command in the failed UK effort to subdue Iraq during the 1920s. More recently, close ties have been maintained due to India's energy requirements and significant trade with the region. Until late 1990, trade with Iraq was extensive and much Indian migrant labour was employed there. Nonetheless, the chaos attending and following the US invasion in 2003 has hampered Indian initiatives with Iraq thus far.[46] The economic losses suffered during the first Persian

Gulf War, and Delhi's largely passive diplomacy at the time, resulted in the Indian policy being re-examined in 2002–3 as tensions built up between the USA and Iraq.[47] Some consideration was given to offering troops to the US-led coalition effort, as a multilateral peacekeeping gesture to help stabilize the country and partly in connection with efforts to improve ties with the United States, although Delhi came down against the idea.[48] Subsequent statements by US officials (including military ones) indicated that the USA was not overly concerned with the Indian decision. Significant recent improvement in Indo-US relations, rooted in a breakthrough on nuclear cooperation, suggests Delhi's decision was the right one.[49]

Following the change of government in Delhi in 2004, the notion of serving the UN (or the Coalition) in Iraq did not resurface again. This was partly because of stiff resistance on the home front to any form of military engagement in Iraq. Rejecting the possibility, Amitav Ghosh, a much admired Indian novelist, wrote: 'in many parts of the world Indians are still remembered as Imperial mercenaries, as slaves who allowed themselves to be used without reflection or self-awareness'.[50]

Since then, the self-absorption of state institutions in Iraq in the post-Saddam Hussein era has discouraged economic linkages, and Indian migrant workers there have faced very serious risks. However, if Iraqi politics prove conducive to an orderly draw-down of American troop numbers in 2011 and a degree of reconciliation is engineered among Iraq's leading communities, India would be eager to resume its place as one of Iraq's leading trade partners. But for now Iraq represents, in the short term, a truncated possibility.

Migrant workers

Historic trade relations between South and West Asia have led to a significant flow of people between the two regions. In 2001, the Indian labour force in the Persian Gulf was estimated to be around 3.5 million, and is thought to have remained stable since then, although the figure will have been affected by the economic downturn in the Gulf in 2008–9 temporarily forcing many Indian labourers and even some managers to return home.[51]

One Indian state, Kerala, is particularly dependent on labour flows to the Gulf. Frequent spells of communist rule, which have favoured strong social policy and, in particular, a commendable focus on education, have led to neglect of, and sometimes hostility towards, a vibrant role for the private sector in the state (in contrast to the dispensation in other South Indian states), resulting in a lack of local employment opportunities. This, in turn, has compelled many well-educated Keralites to emigrate in search of employment. Kerala is believed to provide at least half of the Indian labourers in the Gulf who send an estimated US$6 billion back to the state annually.[52]

Table 8.1. Relative magnitude of remittances to Kerala from Persian Gulf migrant workers

Year	Remittances as % of			
	SDP	Govt. expenditure	Value added in manufacture	Value added in industry
1975–6	2	11	16	12
1979–80	7	32	46	34
1989–90	12	47	70	42
1994–5	22	111	179	105
1999–2000	23	113	208	110

Note: SDP refers to 'State Domestic Product'.
Source: K. P. Kannan and K. S. Hari, 'Kerala's Gulf Connection: Emigration, Remittances and Their Macroeconomic Impact, 1972–2000', Center for Development Studies Working Paper No.328 (March 2002).

Table 8.1 shows striking growth in the share of remittances in the make-up of Kerala's economy over the course of twenty-five years from 1975 to 2000.

This high concentration of emigrant labour in a sometimes unstable and at times economically vulnerable area has been a source of concern for India, for example in the run-up to, and during, the Gulf War of 1991.[53] Because India sought to maintain friendly ties with both sides in the lead-up to that war in order to maintain oil supplies and to protect Indian workers, there was criticism in India of the government's hesitant response to the crisis.[54] However, it is hard to see, even with hindsight, what alternative approach would have worked better for India.

More persistent problems have been affecting India's migrant workforce in the Gulf. For example, several Gulf governments are trying to keep worker earnings within their borders rather than allowing them to be mostly repatriated as remittances to the home countries of foreign labour. Furthermore, increasingly some Gulf states have encouraged their own nationals to take on jobs hitherto performed by foreigners—not least because of worries about foreign influence over social and political debates locally.[55] The Indian workforce in the Gulf, like others, is generally treated poorly, and demands by Indian workers that Delhi and its embassies intervene on their behalf create significant challenges for the Indian government, which has generally managed these pressures by responding through 'quiet diplomacy'.[56] (Given that Kerala is a politically influential state within the Indian Union, disproportionately represented within circles of power and influence in Delhi, any Indian government is attentive to its problems, including those faced by its migrant workers in the Gulf.)

Even pressures for change that, at first glance, might seem to undermine Indian interests, hold out opportunities in the Gulf. Greater participation of nationals in the workforce would create pressure for new forms of vocational education, which could create higher-end jobs for Indians in the region, and in which Indian entrepreneurs could invest. The demand for advanced business technologies and software also plays to Indian strong suits.[57] Likewise, the emergence of various Gulf Emirates as tourism hubs opens opportunities for Indian involvement, as picked up in India's joint declarations with the GCC.[58]

The wider, symbiotic, relationship between Gulf countries and India is likely to grow further over time, although the forms it will take are uncertain.

Evolving diplomatic architecture: India and Israel

Full recognition

India recognized Israel as a state in 1950, but did not follow up with diplomatic ties.[59] During the Suez crisis in 1956, India pressed hard for multilateral opposition to the military actions of Britain, France, and Israel. India also reacted strongly against Israel's 1982 invasion of Lebanon, with Prime Minister Indira Gandhi accusing Israel of trying to eliminate the Palestinian cause.[60] Whether driven principally by pragmatism (for example, with its own Muslim population in mind), ideology, India's closeness to the Soviet camp by the 1970s, or a mix of these factors, the outcome was that prior to the 1990s India's West Asia policy was pro-Palestinian and not friendly towards Israel.

The end of a bi-polar world in 1990 opened up diplomatic possibilities in West Asia that were inconceivable during the Cold War years. As a result, India and Israel established full diplomatic relations in January 1992. Lalit Mansingh, then deputy head of India's embassy in Washington (and later Indian ambassador to USA) recalls some nervousness that, based on the sentiments of India's Muslim community, Prime Minister Rao might veto the move, but he did not.[61] Bilateral trade between India and Israel has increased from US$202 million in 1992, to US$3.54 billion in 2008–9.[62] Further, several high-level visits have hinted at close cooperation between the two states, particularly in the security sphere, but also in wider economic cooperation and even in cultural exchange.[63] But in deference to India's close ties to many Arab states, the relationship with Israel remains an ostensibly low-key one.

Security at the forefront

While the 1990s saw steadily increasing Indo-Israeli cooperation, the Vajpayee government emphasized the security dimension in the relationship.[64] Brajesh Mishra, National Security Advisor under the Vajpayee government and a chief architect of its security policy, stated in an address to the American Jewish Committee in 2003 that the USA, Israel, and India 'have to jointly face the same ugly face of modern day terrorism'.[65] Ensuing joint exercises by Indian and Israeli military forces included collaborative training by each state's special forces, and counterterrorism and counter-insurgency operations.[66] Also, India's formation of a new national investigative agency, following the 2008 Mumbai attacks, could provide countries like Israel with a new focal point through which to form closer ties in the intelligence and security field.[67]

The terrorist attack in Mumbai in 2008 was hardly the first terrorist outrage in India, and certainly not the worst.[68] However, because of the capacity of a very small number of terrorists to hold India's security forces at bay for forty-eight hours, the attacks publicly revealed the fractured and, in the aggregate, unsatisfactory nature of the Indian security apparatus, a serious matter in a country dealing with elusive militants hiding among urban millions or holed-up in the Kashmiri mountains and the country's forests.

This tenuous internal security situation is driving one strand of India's relationship with Israel, which has spent decades trying to prevent, counter, and cope with terrorism. Israel has also been looking for stable export markets for its indigenous military and high-tech industries, and in the process of upgrading its military capabilities, India has turned into a major client.[69] While the security relationship is not the only factor driving the Indian-Israeli relationship, it is the most salient one, and likely to remain so as long as terrorist violence threatens both nations.

However, the recent sale of major Israeli weapons systems to India points to Delhi's preoccupation with larger concerns. Pakistan's development of nuclear-capable missile technology has led India to consider ways of defending against such threats, and to address this need, India turned to Israel and its Arrow II theatre missile defence system.[70] Although Washington objected to some elements of the contract,[71] India was still able to purchase the most significant component of the Arrow system, the Green Pine radar, from Israel and is reportedly developing a way of marrying it with a domestically produced interceptor to complete the system.[72]

In addition to ground-based missile defence components, Israel has provided India with the Phalcon airborne warning and control system (AWACS).[73] This sale is significant because it greatly increases India's early warning, command, and coordination capabilities. AWACS are one of the few systems that have been considered 'balance-changing' for states.[74]

These military procurement developments unfolded largely shielded from the glare of public debate and controversy in India (although not in secrecy), suggesting that Indian governments can indirectly discourage some security-related debates considered potentially sensitive.

Despite this evident deepening of relations, Rajan Menon and Swati Pandey advise realism with respect to some limitations in the Indo-Israeli relationship.[75] For one, Israel's strategy and tactics in addressing its own security challenges may not always fit with Indian policy preferences. The December

2008 – January 2009 military action against Gaza, aimed at undermining the capabilities of the militant group Hamas, evoked some sympathy in India for the inhabitants of Gaza (while, typically of India, evoking elsewhere sympathy for Israel's security dilemma).[76] An Israeli strike on Iran would test the limits of flexibility in Indian policy and doubtless provoke widespread criticism in India. Thus, the bilateral relationship, while serving both countries well, could encounter road bumps ahead which would require careful management.

The Palestinian issue

India's independence coincided with another botched British colonial pullout, from Palestine, leaving Jews and Arabs contending with incompatible commitments made by the British, as well as with each other. The outcome was a Jewish state (soon recognized by India), the incorporation of some remaining Palestinian territories into Jordan, and large numbers of Palestinian refugees uprooted within Israel itself, but mostly consigned to camps in Jordan, Syria, Lebanon, and Egypt. These events, which coincided with India experiencing and then beginning to recover from the trauma of partition, created a wellspring of enduring sympathy in India for the Palestinian cause.

Predictably, since the establishment of full diplomatic ties in 1992 and the gradual warming of Indo-Israeli relations, it has become harder for Palestinian authorities to catch India's official ear.[77] However, during the BJP-dominated years, the Congress-led opposition did make token gestures in support of the Palestinian cause, including denunciation of the Israeli military's siege of Arafat's headquarters compound in Ramallah.[78]

Harsh V. Pant believes that India will be careful to avoid allowing its relationship with Israel to be perceived as an anti-Palestinian 'Hindu–Jewish axis'.[79] Indeed, India's intelligentsia is overwhelmingly sympathetic to the Palestinian cause. India is helped here by Israel's quiet recognition of Delhi's quandary, manifest in its willingness to conduct the relationship with a minimum of fanfare and ceremonial visits.

The election of Hamas to political authority in Gaza, which came as a surprise to many, puts India in an awkward position. Hamas ideology and tactics are hardly consonant with the philosophy of the Indian government on both terrorism and secularism. India has not been unduly ideological with its international interlocutors and might well be able to accommodate itself with a Palestinian leadership including moderate elements of Hamas, but to the extent that Hamas casts itself as opposed to peace negotiations with Israel, Delhi will inevitably prefer the more flexible leadership of the Palestinian authority in Ramallah, led by Mahmoud Abbas. In any event, India is not seeking to play a lead role on Israeli–Palestinian relations.

India and Iran: two major regional powers

Historical ties

India's relationship with Iran is rooted in history, yet its salience in India's foreign policy has ebbed and waned over time. Islam was first introduced to north India by Persian Muslims around AD 1000. The sixteenth century saw the beginning of a close relationship between the Shiite communities in what are today Iraq and Iran, and the new Shiite-dominated provinces which arose in India during this time. Some scholars point to the importance of the financial support that Indian Muslims provided for the Shiite shrine in Najaf and Karbala in Iraq as a major factor boosting economic relations between the two areas.[80] Meanwhile, cultural links between Safavid Iran (at its apex in the early seventeenth century) and Mughal India were rich and extensive.

Beginning in the 1960s, Iran's natural resources, particularly its oil and natural gas, became increasingly important for India, and the two states engaged in joint projects to exploit these and other resources.[81] Beyond the energy sector, Iran was a meaningful but somewhat peripheral partner for India through much of the Cold War. But Iran emerged as a more central focus of India's West Asian policy in the new millennium, spurred by trade and energy security preoccupations, India's concerns about nuclear proliferation in its wider neighbourhood, and the risk of friction with the USA over Iran's nuclear programme at a time when Delhi was negotiating with Washington a radically improved relationship centred on nuclear cooperation.[82] India views Iran as a significant partner for other reasons as well: as part of its extended neighbourhood, Iran's important but sometimes vexed relationships with Pakistani and Afghan governments have always been relevant to India, which has sought to enhance its influence in Afghanistan whenever possible, if only in connection with its broader strategy of containing Pakistan. By and large, Indian and Iranian views and actions on Afghanistan have been compatible for at least a couple of decades.

The 1979 Iranian Revolution, which shook up the balance of alliances and partnerships in West Asia, had little overall effect on India's relationship with Iran, a testament to the pragmatism of India's West Asia policy. But the Iran–Iraq War, which began in 1981 with an Iraqi assault on Iran, then distracted both Baghdad and Tehran, which became too preoccupied to focus attention and resources on any but the most vital external relationships. While both Iran and Iraq were unhappy with the neutral stance India adopted during the eight-year conflict, equidistance allowed India to weather the Iran–Iraq war with both relationships largely intact.[83]

The end of the Iran–Iraq War in 1988, followed by the end of the Cold War in the early 1990s, saw India and Iran both looking to renew old friendships.

India was increasingly aware of its energy needs, while Iran's theocratic regime enjoyed being treated by a major regional power as a serious partner rather than a pariah. The relationship proved resilient because it was built on mutual interests. Iran viewed India as helpful in escaping its isolation, as a useful trade partner particularly in the technological sector, and as a reliable source of income because of India's energy requirements. India, in turn, saw Iran as a source of energy, a vital link with Central Asia and the Persian Gulf, and a valuable partner inside the Islamic tent.[84] The Iran–Pakistan–India gas pipeline project mentioned earlier in this volume, while controversial with Washington, and improbable as it would require active Indo-Pakistani cooperation, demonstrates how serious India's quest for diversification of its energy supply has become and also its determination to forge a policy on Iran that serves its own interests, not Washington's. Iran's nuclear programme remains a much more significant source of friction for both the India–USA and Indo-Iranian relationships.

The nuclear issue

Established in the 1950s, Iran's nuclear programme was stated to be for peaceful purposes only, and as such was supported by Western allies including the USA, France, and Germany, who were convinced of the Shah's loyalty towards the West (although his pro-Western orientation was somewhat in question after he raised oil prices considerably in the wake of the 1973 Israeli–Arab war).[85] However, as early as the 1970s, and before the Iranian Revolution, there were concerns that Iranian nuclear development could be used in a weapons programme. Indeed the US intelligence community issued a Special National Intelligence Estimate (SNIE) on 23 August 1974, which raised the possibility, with an Indian twist:

> If [the Shah of Iran] is alive in the mid-1980s, if Iran has a full-fledged nuclear power industry and all the facilities necessary for nuclear weapons, and if other countries have proceeded with weapons development, we have no doubt that Iran will follow suit. Iran's course will be strongly influenced by Indian nuclear programmes.[86]

In 2002, hidden nuclear facilities came to light in Iran.[87] This sparked serious concern, particularly in the West, that Iran had embarked on a parallel secret nuclear weapons programme. The concern was reinforced by Iran's stonewalling of the IAEA's demands for full access to Iranian facilities for inspection.[88] The development of nuclear weapons by Iran would be a destabilizing move in West Asia, and for the global non-proliferation regime, which the earlier government of Iran had accepted in 1968 by signing the Nuclear Non-Proliferation Treaty (NPT). It would doubtless spark further attempts at proliferation in the area.[89]

For India, this challenge raises difficult issues, not least as it introduced nuclear weapons to South Asia itself in 1974, prompting Pakistan to follow suit in 1998. India, which did not sign on to the NPT, has always emphasized adherence to international rules and treaties it does accept. Failure on Iran's part to heed its obligations under the NPT, which it has accepted, places India in the position of having to oppose Iran (as it has in several IAEA votes) or (presumably in an attempt to placate a major oil supplier) attempt to gloss over the serious implications for West Asian and global stability of a nuclear weapons programme there.[90]

For now, India is holding Iran to its NPT obligations. In September 2008, India's Prime Minister Manmohan Singh stated that, 'Iran is a signatory to the Non-Proliferation Treaty (NPT); as such it is entitled to all cooperation in its civilian nuclear programme; at the same time, as NPT signatory, it had undertaken all the obligations.'[91] The Prime Minister also indicated that India was opposed to Iran pursuing nuclear weapons, and would not wish to see the emergence of another nuclear-armed state existing in its region.[92] India's sincerity in wanting to avoid further proliferation in its extended region is beyond question.[93] India has been careful not to engage with the merits of Iran's claims or those of its antagonists mainly in the West, although during its upcoming term on the UN Security Council in 2011–12, it will not be able to duck the core of the challenge to the non-proliferation system that Iran's programme probably represents, and will need to vote on any change in the UNSC-mandated sanctions regime against Iran, most recently strengthened in May 2010.[94] Indeed, India's November 2009 vote against Iran's nuclear programme at the IAEA strained its relations with Tehran at a sensitive time in relation to Delhi's worries about Afghanistan.[95] C. Raja Mohan writes: 'Delhi's diplomatic skills will be tested as the tensions between its regional imperatives and wider interests rise.'[96]

Nevertheless, ever more uncertain prospects for Afghanistan, as NATO countries debate withdrawal and Kabul is encouraged to negotiate with the Taliban by Western capitals that swore only a year previously that they would never contemplate such an expedient, remind students of the region that Tehran and Delhi may well find themselves cooperating actively to salvage their own interests in that war-torn country in light of future decisions by Washington, Kabul, and Islamabad.

Conclusion: different partners, same strategy

As Bansidhar Pradhan suggests, India's West Asia policy has seen a change of focus from the actors who constituted the core of its West Asia policy during much of the Cold War to others, a change more of players than of playbook.[97]

Where once Egypt, the Palestinians, and Iraq were central to India's policy, Saudi Arabia, Iran, and Israel have now taken centre stage. India's energy needs are an increasingly important variable. The Centre for International Security Studies' *South Asia Monitor* states that by 2025, India's energy requirements will have doubled and that 90 per cent of its petroleum will be imported by that time.[98]

The 2008 attacks in Mumbai, as well as many other terrorist successes, indicate the need for India to develop a more sophisticated and effective approach to asymmetrical threats, specifically a more convincing counter-terrorism capacity. Indeed, with national security under such threat, might foreign investors one day take fright?[99] Concern over Pakistan's nuclear arsenal and its continuing development of a long-range missile capability is also on Indian minds.

Taken together, these factors ensure that Saudi Arabia, Iran, and Israel are now central to India's West Asia policy.

During the Cold War, policy was anchored in a pragmatic non-alignment that extended to tactical neutrality in cases of crisis or tension between specific actors. In West Asia, primarily through bilateral channels, India managed to maintain a remarkably stable set of relationships. Since then, Israel has been a very useful addition for India.

But each of India's major relationships in the region operates within certain constraints, which are largely interconnected. India's relationship with Israel is constrained by its reliance on Saudi Arabia and Iran for energy imports, while at the same time, its relationship with these Islamic states is constrained by India's need to acquire military hardware (and conceivably its advice on counterterrorism, as well as intelligence of mutual interest) from Israel. Another factor, if not a constraint, is India's recently deepened relationship with the USA, which could be of interest to Tehran but might also induce suspicion in Iran's official minds.

In West Asia, India has been a brilliant straddler. However, as its international role increases, simultaneous to its reliance on West Asian partners, its strategy may come under strain from unforeseen events. Tension or conflict over Iran's nuclear programme, internal unrest in the Gulf states, or geostrategic brinkmanship focused on the Gulf region could each test India's diplomatic dexterity in the years ahead.

India's National Security Council secretariat produced, in 2002, the initial *National Security Index*, which ranked countries on their ability to ensure the national security of their populations. While the methodological elements of the *National Security Index*, as in other such exercises, are debatable, India's ranking of tenth, following such states as the USA and China (first and third respectively), is suggestive of official thinking in India on its rising security capacity.[100] Mirroring this Indian report is the 2009 effort by the US National

Intelligence Council, entitled *Global Trends 2025: A World Transformed*, which outlines a shifting geopolitical environment as a result of both long-term forces and short-term catalysts.[101] The most significant change identified is a waning of US global dominance and the rise of new regional powers to fill the void.[102]

But in a changing world order, the rise of new players is not always orderly, and their rivalries could either derive from competition in the Gulf, or spill over into it. Thus, while India will want to continue to engage in confidence-building measures with China (as well as, if possible, Pakistan) and other regionally significant emerging powers such as Turkey (with which it entertains a good relationship) it also needs to prepare to, willingly or not, assume a larger role in the various West Asian 'great games' in years ahead.

Such will be the challenges for India in West Asia arising out of the more multipolar world that it has yearned for in recent decades. In West Asia, as of now, India is better equipped than most, by instinct, through its relationships, and due to its growing assets, to tend to its interests.

9

India's East and Southeast Asia Policy: Catching Up

As outlined in Chapter 2, India's ties with the rest of Asia date back many centuries. Indeed, India's civilizational influence to its east has significantly marked many modern Asian nations. During the colonial period, India's long established autonomous ties with Asia were weakened, although many Indians migrated to various other British Asian colonies. And in spite of an early thrust of Nehruvian foreign policy seeking close ties with independent Asian states, notably Indonesia, India's attention to Asia, particularly in the Cold War years, was overwhelmed by its preoccupation with its immediate neighbourhood and with China.

However, the collapse of the Soviet system, as well as the economic success of the 'Asian Tigers', notably during the 1980s, forced a rethink of India's inert Asia policy and refocused India's attention to the east. New Delhi newly remembered again Jawaharlal Nehru's reference to Southeast Asia as a part of 'Greater India'.[1]

This chapter examines India's policy towards Asia east of India encompassing Southeast Asian nations, Japan, South Korea, Australia, and New Zealand, and also China (as an Asian regional actor—rather than as a neighbour, a topic covered in Chapter 6).[2] India's immediate neighbourhood is excluded from our purview here, with the exception of Myanmar, which appears intermittently as a member of the Association of Southeast Asian Nations (ASEAN), and which is addressed in greater detail in Chapter 5.

After a brief discussion of India's historical connections with Asia and the place of Asia in India's foreign policy thinking until the 1990s, this chapter details India's economic, political, geostrategic, and 'soft power' ties with the region since the end of the Cold War before offering some conclusions.

India's historical ties in Asia

India's influence on East and Southeast Asia, as well as some of the Asia-Pacific region, has been extensive. Hinduism and Buddhism spread throughout Asia from India, initially along trading routes. While Hinduism found its way across much of Indonesia, Malaysia, and Thailand, Buddhism reached Japan and Vietnam through China and Korea, and also flourished in countries closer to India, such as Burma, Cambodia, and Thailand.

As Indian trading patterns expanded and religious ties spread throughout Asia so did cultural elements including language (particularly Sanskrit), social customs, styles of art, and architecture.

Great Indianized kingdoms arose over the centuries throughout Asia and particularly Southeast Asia.[3] However, aside from the solitary instance of invasion of the Srivijaya kingdom in Sumatra by the Indian King, Rajendra Chola, in the eleventh century AD to protect Indian commercial interests, India did not show any imperialist ambitions in Southeast Asia.[4] As one non-Indian, former Prime Minister of Singapore Lee Kuan Yew, noted, 'Historically India has had an enormous influence on South-east Asia; economically and culturally too. The Ramayana story is present all over South-east Asia in different versions. The civilizations in the region were really Indian in origin...'[5]

The earliest Indianized kingdoms of Southeast Asia (founded early in the Christian era) were located in the Malay Peninsula, Cambodia, and Annam and on the islands of Java, Sumatra, Borneo, and Bali.[6] Along with the traders that traversed the region, Brahmans (priests) from India introduced Indian rituals, scriptures, and literature among the elite in Southeast Asia. They introduced Indian court customs, administrative organization on the Indian pattern, and laws based on the Code of Manu, the Indian lawgiver.[7] Indianization also included the alphabetical basis of Southeast Asian scripts, the incorporation of Sanskrit in vocabularies along with the adoption of the Hindu-Buddhist religious beliefs, and an Indian concept of royalty.[8]

In maritime Southeast Asia, Srivijaya on Sumatra, between the seventh and thirteenth centuries, was a centre for Buddhist studies and of Sanskrit learning.[9] Moreover, the renowned maritime Southeast Asian dynasty of Sailendra, which became the dominant maritime and land power in Malaysia by the eighth century,[10] is believed to have originated in the Indian state of Orissa.[11] The last Hindu kingdom in the Southeast Asian region was Majapahit, which flourished between the thirteenth and fifteenth centuries on Java.[12] From the fifteenth century onwards, with the rise of the kingdom of Malacca, Islam spread throughout the region. For their part, Indian traders from Gujarat, Malabar, Tamil Nadu, and Bengal helped the spread of Islam in Southeast Asia.[13]

India's connections with Southeast Asia more recently flowed from British colonial expansion in the region. Sir Stamford Raffles arrived in Singapore in 1819 to establish a trading station, ideally located by the Straits of Malacca, as a base from which to protect and resupply East India Company ships carrying cargoes between India and the region, and beyond to China.[14] Later, given this connection, Singapore was governed from Calcutta.

India's interaction with Malaya (today Malaysia) encouraged large-scale migration of Indian (particularly Tamil) labour to Malayan plantations. More than 1.5 million ethnic Tamils from South India were enumerated in 1931 in other British colonies.[15] Today, with over two million persons of Indian origin, Malaysia is home to one of the largest Indian Diaspora communities abroad.[16]

Beyond Southeast Asia, India's interface with China dates back to the second century BC. Even before the advent of Buddhism in China, trade flourished between the two countries, via the famous Silk Routes, and later by sea routes.[17] The transmission of Buddhism from India to China encouraged the travel of Chinese pilgrims to India and vice versa, but it also allowed for Indian cultural influence on art, architecture, music, astronomy, mathematics, and medicine in China, and through it, beyond.[18]

Buddhism entered Korea from China, during the fourth century AD. Korean Buddhist monks visiting India became conduits for cultural currents and not only for Buddhist tenets. The translation of Buddhist texts resulted in the absorption of many Sanskrit words and concepts into the local language.[19] During the medieval period, close cultural interaction declined partly due to the withdrawal of royal patronage from Buddhism in Korea.

Buddhism also travelled into Japan from India (or *Tenjiku*, as it was called in Japan) as a gift from the king of Korea in AD 552.[20] The convert prince of Japan constructed Buddhist temples, monasteries, hospitals, and homes, and sent Japanese students to China for the study of Buddhism.[21] A range of Gods from the Hindu pantheon such as *Lakshmi* and *Saraswati* became a part of Japanese Buddhism as guardian-deities.[22] Indo-Japanese commercial activities were initiated in the late nineteenth century, with a number of Indians immigrating to Japan as temporary servants of the trading relationship.[23]

Although the British colonial period facilitated migration of Indians to the rest of Asia, cultural and civilizational ties between India and the East and Southeast Asian countries were greatly weakened as European interests, values, and methods were promoted by the Raj over local ones. Indeed, '[t]he conquest of India by Europe started a process that disrupted the links between the subcontinent and the rest of Asia. The bountiful subcontinental economy and its prosperous trade was disconnected from ancient and long-standing links with West and Central Asia, China and Indo-China and linked to Europe and to the wider British Empire.'[24] Furthermore, as Indians were frequently the agents for their British colonial masters, they became associated with colonial exploitation and unequal relationships in the minds of many other Asians, with such memories persisting beyond 1947.[25]

Asia in India's foreign policy thinking after independence

At the time of independence, Nehru viewed Asia as a region in which India's new status should endow it with leadership.[26] In the post-independence period, and to some extent even during the years preceding independence, Indian leaders considered the anti-colonial struggles in Southeast Asia (those of Indonesia, Burma, Malaysia, and Vietnam) as indivisible from their own. In March 1947, Delhi organized a Conference on Asian Relations, bringing together delegates from twenty-nine countries, some of which were still under colonial rule, in an attempt to express solidarity with the freedom struggles in other parts of Asia and foster cooperation amongst Asian people.[27] Soon, India proclaimed itself the leader of Asia's march towards independence and confirmed this ambition during both the special 1949 Conference on Indonesia in Delhi and the 1955 Bandung Conference (at which Africa's freedom struggle was also featured).[28]

Delhi also recognized the strategic importance of Southeast Asia and the Indian Ocean for defence of the Indian Peninsula. Several of India's island territories lay barely ninety miles from the Straits of Malacca.[29]

Nevertheless, this Asian 'rediscovery' gradually ground to a halt as India became embroiled in Cold War politics during the 1960s and 1970s and failed to convince other Asians of its non-aligned bona fides. India's interest in Southeast Asia also largely evaporated due to challenges closer to home—the traumatic border war with China in 1962 and conflicts with Pakistan in 1965 and 1971.[30] In the aftermath of the oil shock of the 1970s, India became more concerned about its energy security and consequently West Asia became more of a priority.[31]

From the mid 1950s to the late 1980s, India's attention began to be drawn towards Southeast Asia again. India had developed a strong relationship with North Vietnam, due to its sympathy for the Vietnamese anti-colonial struggle. However, Vietnamese isolation within its own region following its invasion of Cambodia in late 1978 negatively impacted India's aspirations in the region. Several nations, including Indonesia, Singapore, and Thailand, remained profoundly suspicious of communism and friendly towards the USA, with which India continued to entertain strained ties.[32] India was the only non-Communist country to diplomatically recognize the Cambodian Heng Samrin government in 1980, and even though ASEAN offered 'dialogue partnership' to India in the mid-1980s to dissuade it from continuing to extend diplomatic recognition to the sitting government in Cambodia, India did not alter its stance (influenced perhaps by its alliance with Moscow and as rebuff to Beijing which had favoured the earlier Khmer Rouge leadership in Cambodia).[33] Japan, a close ally of the USA during the Cold War, also kept some distance from India beyond its budding commercial opportunities as of the 1980s. In short, India was largely isolated from Southeast Asian nations except for Vietnam, and distant from East Asian ones.

After the collapse of the Soviet bloc, the Indian domestic economic liberalization in 1991 and Asian economic dynamism since the late 1970s prompted a rethink of Delhi's dormant Asian relationships.[34] Hence, 'Indian leaders eagerly invoked their cultural affinities with East Asia in their efforts to join this new pole of growth.'[35]

The 'Look East' policy

Soon after P. V. Narasimha Rao became Prime Minister, he launched the 'Look East' policy (LEP) in 1992.[36] Its implementation during the 1990s focused particularly on engagement with Southeast Asia and ASEAN (although Prime Minister Rao articulated a broader LEP implicitly in Singapore in 1994).[37] Alongside its new efforts to capitalize on Southeast Asia's economic success, India now sought politico-military engagement with the region, in part impelled by the need for new friends and partners after the loss of its superpower patron in 1991, and probably also worrying about China's fast-growing links across Asia.[38] The broad objectives of the LEP during the 1990s were to institutionalize linkages with ASEAN, with its member states, and to prevent Southeast Asia falling under the influence of any one major power.[39]

In its execution, the LEP was characterized by 'stop-and-go' impulses, aggravated by the meagre resources available to India's foreign policy establishment. As well, although impressive relative to earlier Indian practice, Delhi's economic reforms seemed underwhelming to its new ASEAN friends, who were also dismayed by India's parlous infrastructure and the country's sometimes chaotic politics.

Since the turn of the century, the LEP has been reinvigorated, featuring greater consistency and focus of effort. Meanwhile, Southeast Asia woke up to India's increasingly impressive growth rates as of the late 1990s.[40] Yashwant Sinha, then India's Minister of External Affairs, distinguished between the two phases of the LEP in 2003:

> The first phase of India's 'Look East' policy was ASEAN-centred and focussed primarily on trade and investment linkages. The new phase of this policy is characterised by an expanded definition of 'East', extending from Australia to

East Asia, with ASEAN at its core. The new phase also marks a shift from trade to wider economic and security issues, including joint efforts to protect the sea-lanes and coordinate counter-terrorism activities.[41]

Hence, Phase II has been marked not only by attempts to negotiate Free Trade Agreements, but also by more comprehensive defence cooperation, including arrangements for regular access to ports in Southeast Asia. Defence contacts have widened to include Japan, South Korea, and China.[42]

Three other features characterize the so called 'second phase' of the LEP: expanded air and land links to East and Southeast Asia, thus achieving greater physical connectivity with Asian partners; closer political ties through more comprehensive dialogue across a wider range of issues; and the development of regional groupings. As well, with rapidly growing Sino-Indian trade, less Indian nervousness over China's role within Asia is on display.[43]

Today, the LEP broadly encompasses four elements of content: economic and trade, political, geostrategic and soft-power ties. The following sections elaborate on each of these.

Economic ties

In October 1991, then Finance Minister Manmohan Singh chose Singapore as the first foreign venue for an exposition of his economic policy reforms.[44] Foreign direct investment (FDI) and trade between India and its Asian neighbours soon began to expand. But just as the trend of increased economic relations began to pick up steam, the Asian financial crises of 1996–7 and 1998–9 and India's nuclear tests in 1998 interrupted progress. Nevertheless, between 2002 and 2007, the percentage share of India's trade with the Asian region steadily increased, with exports growing from 14.7 per cent of its total to 19.9 per cent in 2008, and imports growing from 11.4 to 18.7 per cent (see Table 9.1).

Table 9.1. India's trade with Asia

	Asia's share in India's total exports and imports (%)						
	2002	2003	2004	2005	2006	2007	2008
Exports	14.7	16.8	16.9	17	16.9	17.9	19.9
Imports	11.4	12.7	13.1	13.4	16.4	17.4	18.7

Note: The calculation of these percentages does not include Japan, Australia, New Zealand, North Korea, Hong Kong, or any West Asian countries.
Source: IMF Direction of Trade Statistics Yearbook 2009.

ASEAN

As India became institutionally more involved with ASEAN (obtaining full dialogue partner status in 1995), the pattern of cross-investment with ASEAN members evolved favourably. Between 1992 and 1997, total FDI from ASEAN-5 (Singapore, Thailand, Malaysia, Indonesia, and Philippines) more than doubled.[45] This period also saw Indian companies investing more in several ASEAN economies such as Thailand, Vietnam, and Indonesia. During the late 1990s and since 2000, the information technology and computer software sector generated considerable outward investment from India towards the ASEAN countries, particularly Singapore.

India and ASEAN have witnessed accelerated trade and investment since 2000. Exports rose from US$2.9 billion to US$19.1 billion in 2009, with imports rising from US$4.1 billion to US$26.2 billion. Singapore has become the largest Asian investor in India, above Japan and China (see Table 9.2).

Complementing the growing trade and investment linkages between India and ASEAN, the first-ever meeting of India and ASEAN economic ministers took place in Brunei in September 2002, marked by India's call for deeper regional economic linkages and a formal Regional Trade and Investment Agreement or a Free Trade Agreement (FTA).[46] After some interim steps, including the creation of an ASEAN–India Economic Linkages Task Force, an agreement was reached on a selective FTA in 2009.[47] It covers only trade in merchandise and excludes services and investments but it will eliminate tariffs on about 4,000 products, agricultural as well as industrial, that account for more than 80 per cent of the trade in goods between the two sides.[48] Work on expanding the agreement to cover services continues.[49] However, while India has been grappling with this FTA, regionally, attention is turning to financial integration, for which India may not be ready.[50]

Table 9.2. FDI inflow to India of selected Asian countries from April 2000 to August 2009

Country	FDI inflows (US$ millions)	% share of total FDI inflows
Singapore	8,667.27	8.72
Japan	3,309.98	3.44
South Korea	501.92	0.51
Australia	272.40	0.28
Malaysia	234.07	0.25
Indonesia	71.55	0.08
Thailand	55.44	0.06
China	14.35	0.02
Myanmar	8.96	0.01
New Zealand	15.21	0.01

Note: Percentage of inflows worked out in terms of rupees and the above amount of inflows received through FIPB/SIA route, RBI's automatic route, and acquisition of existing shares only.

Source: Department of Industrial Policy and Promotion Fact Sheet on Foreign Direct Investment (FDI) from August 1991 to August 2009, Ministry of Commerce and Industry.

Bilaterally, on 9 October 2003 India and Thailand signed an agreement to enhance cooperation in agriculture, tourism, and science. More importantly, given the strong pick-up in economic ties between India and Singapore, the two countries signed a Comprehensive Economic Cooperation Agreement in mid-2005.[51]

Overall, India has established a high comfort level with most ASEAN governments and is working hard on the relevant bilateral as well as multilateral economic agreements. Its more active role today seems widely welcomed within the ASEAN region, if only as a counterweight to China, although it is also valued in and of itself.

Japan

Although Japan was one of the top investors in India during the 1990s, ranking fourth behind the UK, USA, and Mauritius,[52] its performance paled in comparison to that elsewhere in Asia: Japan's direct investment in India in 1998 was one-thirteenth of its direct investment in China.[53] Similarly, between 1990 and 2000, India's total trade with Japan increased from US$3.5 billion to a meagre US$3.8 billion—actually a decrease in inflation-adjusted terms—and the percentage share of its trade with Japan compared to that with the rest of the world decreased from 8.3 to 4.1 per cent.[54] Some of the disincentives to greater Japanese investment in India have included the infrastructure deficit in India, high tariffs, and labour problems.[55]

However, Japanese trade and investment in India have significantly increased in recent years. Indo-Japanese trade rose to US$10.91 billion in 2008–9.[56] Despite this, the balance of trade continues to be consistently in Japan's favour, with India's agricultural exports to Japan declining sharply.[57]

In contrast to India's paltry investment in Japan (see Table 9.4), Japanese FDI in India is continuing to expand and is expected to reach US$5.5 billion by 2010. The number of Japanese business establishments operating in India has increased from 231 in August 2003 to 475 in February 2007.[58] Japanese automobile giant Honda is setting up its second car manufacturing unit in Rajasthan, involving an investment of US$254 million, while the Maruti-Suzuki India Limited partnership is the leading car manufacturer in South Asia.

Official development assistance (ODA) provided to India by Japan is an important aspect of Indo-Japanese economic relations. India has been the largest recipient of Japanese ODA since 2003, largely in the form of loans (as opposed to grants and technical assistance). Moreover, the total quantity of ODA loans has steadily increased since 2002.[59] Focused on infrastructure development (particularly power and transportation), these loans have encouraged private sector development in India.[60] One of the most significant current projects is the Delhi–Mumbai Industrial Corridor, focused largely on

Table 9.3. Indian exports to and imports from Asia 2000–9

Indian exports to Asia (values in US$ million)

Country	2000–1	2001–2	2002–3	2003–4	2004–5	2005–6	2006–7	2007–8	2008–9
Indonesia	400	534	826	1,127	1,333	1,380	2,033	2,164	2,560
Malaysia	608	774	749	893	1,084	1,162	1,305	2,575	3,420
Myanmar	53	61	75	90	113	111	140	186	222
Philippines	203	248	472	322	412	495	581	620	744
Singapore	877	972	1,422	2,125	4,001	5,425	6,054	7,379	8,446
Thailand	530	633	711	832	901	1,075	1,446	1,811	1,938
Vietnam	226	218	337	410	556	691	986	1,610	1,739
ASEAN Total	**2,914**	**3,457**	**4,619**	**5,822**	**8,426**	**10,411**	**12,607**	**16,414**	**19,141**
China	831	952	1,975	2,955	5,616	6,759	8,322	10,871	9,354
Japan	1,794	1,510	1,864	1,709	2,128	2,481	2,868	3,858	3,026
South Korea	451	471	645	765	1,042	1,827	2,518	2,861	3,952
Northeast Asia Total	**6,282**	**5,822**	**7,864**	**9,387**	**13,223**	**16,226**	**19,418**	**26,502**	**25,449**
Australia	406	418	504	584	720	821	925	1,152	1,439
New Zealand	63	62	68	86	93	142	496	159	189
East Asia Total	**494**	**507**	**604**	**704**	**860**	**1,005**	**1,482**	**1,413**	**1,754**

Indian imports from Asia (values in US$ million)

Country	2000–1	2001–2	2002–3	2003–4	2004–5	2005–6	2006–7	2007–8	2008–9
Indonesia	910	1,037	1,381	2,122	2,618	3,008	4,182	4,821	6,666
Malaysia	1,177	1,134	1,465	2,047	2,299	2,416	5,290	6,013	7,185
Myanmar	182	374	336	409	406	526	783	809	929
Philippines	63	95	124	122	187	235	167	205	255
Singapore	1,464	1,304	1,435	2,085	2,651	3,354	5,484	8,123	7,655
Thailand	338	423	379	609	866	1,212	1,748	2,301	2,704
Vietnam	12	19	29	38	87	131	167	174	409
ASEAN Total	**4,147**	**4,387**	**5,150**	**7,433**	**9,115**	**10,884**	**18,108**	**22,675**	**26,203**
China	1,502	2,036	2,792	4,053	7,098	10,868	17,475	27,146	32,497
Japan	1,842	2,146	1,836	2,668	3,235	4,061	4,600	6,326	7,886
South Korea	894	1,141	1,522	2,829	3,509	4,564	4,803	6,045	8,677
Northeast Asia Total	**5,618**	**6,617**	**7,804**	**11,816**	**16,674**	**23,141**	**31,532**	**44,785**	**58,456**
Australia	1,063	1,306	1,337	2,649	3,825	4,948	7,000	7,815	11,098
New Zealand	79	82	76	79	128	217	266	336	424
East Asia Total	**1,182**	**1,394**	**1,423**	**2,751**	**4,050**	**5,281**	**7,575**	**8,356**	**11,788**

Note: ASEAN Total includes: Brunei, Cambodia, Indonesia, Laos, Malaysia, Myanmar, Philippines, Singapore, Thailand, Vietnam; East Asia Total includes: Australia, Fiji Islands, Kiribati, Nauru, New Zealand, Papua New Guinea, Solomon Islands, Tonga, Tuvalu Vanuatu, and Samoa; Northeast Asia Total includes: Taiwan, China, Hong Kong, Japan, North Korea, South Korea, Macao and Mongolia.

Source: Government of India, Department of Commerce, *Export-Import Data Bank* (25 June 2010).

Table 9.4. Approvals of Indian direct investments in joint ventures and wholly owned subsidiaries in Asia from April 2002 to 2009 (US$ million)

Country	2002–3	2003–4	2004–5	2005–6	2006–7	2007–8	2008–9	Total
Singapore	46.8	15.9	239.3	200.5	1085.6	8360.5	4282.6	14231.1
Australia	95.0	92.9	158.8	75.3	174.9	47.9	317.6	962.3
China	29.6	26.6	15.1	52.2	54.6	682.5	50.5	911.1
Thailand	7.7	7.4	3.5	3.4	93.4	21.6	91.3	228.3
Indonesia	0.1	19.3	80.8	7.9	31.3	6.8	59.4	205.7
Malaysia	0.8	1.4	4.9	4.4	14.6	67.5	77.8	171.4
Vietnam	0.06	0.04	0.06	–	76.22	3.38	32.873	112.6
Myanmar	–	4.3	–	–	–	59.1	–	21.2	84.6
Philippines	0.0	0.8	3.3	4.5	1.1	18.4	6.3	34.4
Japan	0.4	0.0	–	0.1	1.3	2.1	12.9	16.9
Cambodia	–	–	0.0	–	14.5	–	–	14.5
New Zealand	0.6	0.0	0.0	0.1	0.6	2.7	0.6	4.7
South Korea	–	–	1.6	–	0.7	–	–	2.3
Laos	–	–	–	–	–	2.0	0.0	2.0

Note: Based on the RBI data for approvals. Data on Brunei was not available.

Source: Ministry of Finance, Government of India, Department of Economic Affairs: IC Section, available at http://finmin. nic.in/the_ministry/dept_eco_affairs/icsection/Annexure_5.html

improved transport links (which will require an estimated total investment of US$50 billion).[61]

Nonetheless, barriers remain, including Japanese concerns about Indian government inefficiency and lack of transparency, lack of infrastructure, and the difficulty in acquisition and utilization of land.[62] In fact, Japan's share of total FDI inflows in India has dropped from 13.15 per cent in 2002–3 to 1.5 per cent in 2008–9 as some other Asian countries, notably Singapore, have dramatically increased their own investments.[63]

Thus, while both polities are rooted in Western-originated democratic structures, the societies of India and Japan, even more than their economies, could not be more different. Japanese visitors to India, including business executives, are sometimes overwhelmed by the apparent chaos, noise, jostling, and the infrastructure deficits that are the antithesis of their own society. Partly for this reason, in spite of official mutual respect and ancient religious ties, the economic relationship has required hard work and is still not performing to its full potential.

South Korea

Although South Korean investment in India was low in 1991, it rose to equal that of Japan thereafter.[64] The South Korean automobile maker Hyundai was able to create a wholly owned subsidiary in India for a total investment of US$700 million. In contrast with most foreign manufacturers, which established plants in India in order to gain access to the domestic market, South Korean firms have localized their production of components and parts and used local labour, resulting in lower labour costs for global production and export.[65] Bilateral trade tripled between 1990 and 2000.[66] This subsequently accelerated further: between 2000 and 2009, Indian imports, particularly of machinery, from South Korea increased from US$451 million to over US$8.6 billion. Several Korean construction companies are currently engaged in highway, power plant, chemical, petrochemical, and metro rail projects in India. In contrast, although in February 2004 Tata Motors acquired Daewoo Commercial Vehicles in South Korea at a cost of US$102 million, India does not figure among the major foreign investors there.[67]

In 2005 the Korean Pohang Steel Company (POSCO), the fifth largest steel maker in the world, agreed to set up a steel plant in Orissa involving the largest foreign direct investment in the country—an estimated US$12 billion.[68] However, to the frustration of POSCO, its implementation has been stymied by challenges pertaining to land acquisition and resettlement of local communities, a reminder that local as well as national politics in India, and issues related to land scarcity, cannot be ignored by foreign economic actors.[69]

South Korea and India signed a Comprehensive Economic Partnership Agreement (CEPA) in August 2009, the first such economic agreement for India with a member of the Paris-based Organization for Economic Cooperation and Development (OECD). It promotes, *inter alia*, the increase in Korean FDI inflows into Indian manufacturing sectors, and inflows of professionals from India to Korea.[70] But Suparna Karmakar notes: 'Unlike Korea's trade with China, where the Chinese bilateral deficit with Korea is compensated by China's trade surplus *vis-à-vis* the rest of the world, Korean exports to India are unlikely to be exported onward. Korean investments into India are... market-seeking as opposed to efficiency-seeking FDI to China.'[71] Therefore, while the middle-class consumer in India will certainly benefit from the CEPA, it is unlikely to improve the trade balance.[72]

Overall, South Korea, with fewer cards to play than Japan, has in many ways been more entrepreneurial in India and is likely to reap the rewards as a result. Potential also exists to increase trade in services between the two countries, a particular opportunity for India.[73] This will require work on both sides to reduce various tariff and non-tariff barriers and further efforts by India to match Korea's success in accessing the Indian market.[74]

China

The economic relationship between India and China has been discussed in Chapters 4 and 6. Suffice it to note here that, of relevance to the rest of Asia, since the turn of the century, China has quietly emerged as India's most important trade partner. In the past decade, particularly since China's entry into the WTO in 2001, Sino-Indian trade has grown from just under US$3 billion in 2001–2 to over US$41.8 billion in 2008–9.[75] China and India are ideally suited as trading partners given India's technology and services-oriented companies complementing China's manufacturing and infrastructure prowess.[76] There is considerably greater potential in the relationship, particularly if India can bring itself to relax investment strictures on Chinese firms in so-called strategic sectors, some of which appear at a distance to be fancifully so labelled. Meanwhile, none of India's IT heavyweights, such as Tata Consulting Services (TCS), Wipro, Infosys, and Satyam have been able to make a dent in the Chinese domestic software market.[77] Nevertheless, Indian and Chinese investment links have been growing, with Indian companies such as TCS and Infosys setting up major global sourcing bases in China, and telecommunications giant Huawei setting up large R&D bases in India.[78] A number of Indian investors have established joint ventures, including Ranbaxy and Aurobindo Pharmaceuticals, while others have set up wholly owned ventures, including Infosys and Essel Packaging.[79]

Controversially, the trading relationship is increasingly tilted in favour of China and is reflected in India's growing trade deficit. Amardeep Athwal writes: 'The fact...that Indian exports, [are] dominated by iron ore exports raises overall doubts about the sustainability of the current high rate of and volume of bilateral trade growth.... There needs to be a move [to]...an increase in the share of manufacturing and low, medium and high technology items.'[80]

On the whole, while the relationship between these two Asian giants is a tense one at the political and security levels, the thriving and rapidly growing trade relationship with, sooner or later, greater cross-investment to follow is a very hopeful development for both countries and for the rest of Asia, helping to build the dynamism of the continent as a whole, which may well prove self-reinforcing over many decades. The big story in Asia involving these two giants of the continent is one of economic and strategic competition which could prove quite beneficial to Asia overall, if played out peacefully, as seems likely into the foreseeable future.

Australia and New Zealand

Since 2000, economic relations between India and Australia have shown a dramatic increase, after a disappointing performance in the 1990s.[81] Trade has grown from just under US$1.5 billion in 2000 to over US$12.5 billion by the end of 2009.[82] In fact, India was Australia's fourth largest merchandise export market and seventh largest merchandise trading partner in 2008–9. Trade between both countries has been rising at 30 per cent annually. However, the trade balance favours Australia due to natural resources and education. Like Indian FDI in Australia, Australian FDI in India remains low at US$281.64 million.[83]

The economic relationship between New Zealand and India has been steady, but lacking momentum.[84] Even though India's 1998 nuclear tests evoked a strong reaction from New Zealand, economic relations remained on track.[85] However, high Indian tariffs on items of interest to New Zealand, particularly value-added products, continue to restrict exports to India. India's employment of non-tariff barriers, particularly sanitary and phytosanitary barriers, have also restricted New Zealand exports to India.[86] Between 1999–2000 and 2008–9 bilateral trade grew from over US$160 million to over US$612 million, but the two countries could do better and know it: they have initiated talks for an FTA to increase investment and trade in services.[87]

India, Australia and New Zealand, all having descended from the British Empire, share many values and structures inherited from London, willingly or otherwise. This creates a level of comfort between them not always present in India's bilateral ties. Australia and India, in particular, have made a success of their economic relationship which should continue to grow. India has for years now been eying Australian uranium supplies, which Australian policy currently precludes Canberra from selling.[88] However, Canada having moved to make uranium available to India in principle, Australia may soon follow suit.

***

In sum, while India's economic integration in Asia has deepened considerably since the 1990s it falls far behind China's and its trade balance remains unfavourable with several key Asian nations. There is further to go in the economic dimension of the LEP.

Political and diplomatic ties

India's rapid economic development and growing economic interaction in Asia have been supported by its political relations in the continent, which have grown significantly since the end of the Cold War and more so since the turn of the century.

In the early 1990s, India's LEP was first initiated in earnest with Myanmar and marked by serious engagement with a military regime there on which it had frowned previously, having earlier supported the democratic aspirations embodied in Aung San Suu Kyi's political movement.[89] This shift in India's policy was the result of interest-based considerations relating to China's growing partnership with Myanmar and also India's need for help in fighting insurgencies in its own northeastern states and hopes for access to Myanmar's energy resources.[90] In 1992, India chose not to oppose Myanmar's readmission to the Non-Aligned Movement.[91] In 1994, the two countries concluded an agreement to maintain peace on their border.[92]

In recent years, Delhi has openly indicated that the development of India's northeast and the containment of the insurgencies there are vital interests, and a pillar of its LEP.[93] Indeed as Carleton University scholar Archana Pandya comments: 'The "Look East" policy, designed to serve national Indian interest, might better integrate the north-eastern Indian states. As orphans of the Union in terms of economic development and Delhi's sustained attention, these states should be on the front lines of a policy seeking greater cooperation to India's East.'

India's new 'realist' approach to ties with Myanmar translated a wider sense in Delhi that its relations with Southeast Asia were now too important to be governed by either sentiment or policy inertia.

Further, during the early 1990s diplomatic exchanges grew between India and Asian countries, marked by many bilateral visits and multilateral engagements in the region.[94] India stepped up its engagement with regional organizations including ASEAN. By the early 1990s, ASEAN, despite having achieved little in terms of regional economic integration, and even less in coordinating foreign policy, had proved strikingly successful in casting itself as the critical regional organization of Asia (in the absence of any other credible ones). It had successfully engaged the major powers in dialogue, a process formalized in 1994 through the ASEAN Regional Forum (ARF) that meets in conjunction with ASEAN Summits and gathers ministers of many significant countries, including the USA, China, Russia, and India.[95] Bilaterally, while India's relations with Indonesia have been important, its stalwart allies within ASEAN have more consistently been Singapore, Malaysia, and Thailand.[96]

India's Pokhran II nuclear tests resulted in varying reactions amongst Asian nations. During the Manila ASEAN Summit of July 1998, two viewpoints emerged among ARF members: those who wanted to impose sanctions against India (Japan, Australia, Canada, Philippines, Thailand, and New Zealand) and those who advocated a more benign attitude (Singapore, Vietnam, Malaysia, and Indonesia). The absence of consensus resulted in a weak resolution deploring the tests.[97] Soon, reflecting the growing confidence between India and ASEAN members, India's relationship with ASEAN was upgraded to Summit-level interaction in 2002. But not much has come of ideas on fostering closer cooperation in reforming international institutions or on an Open Skies Agreement.[98]

Bilaterally, India's ties with Japan were shaken by India's nuclear tests, given Japan's history as the only country against which nuclear weapons have been used: ODA to India was suspended, and Japan opposed financial support for India from the multilateral institutions in which it had a say.[99] Tokyo declared that the normalization of relations could not occur unless India signed the Comprehensive Test Ban Treaty.[100] However, India's spat with Japan was short-lived. In August 2000, Prime Minister Mori Yoshiro made a historic visit to India and there was soon an exchange of visits by Defence ministers.[101]

In 2004, India and Japan launched a joint bid to secure permanent seats on the United Nations Security Council, along with Germany and Brazil, as 'the Group of Four'. However, while the USA supported the Japanese bid, China in effect blocked Japan's accession to a permanent seat and, given the joint nature of the Security Council reform initiative in which Japan and India were both stakeholders, the reform was stymied.[102] Nonetheless, the Indian and Japanese prime ministers have been working to strengthen 'one of the most underdeveloped relationships among Asia's major powers'.[103]

In the south Pacific, Australia reacted to India's nuclear tests by taking stern measures including the suspension of official visits to India. This in turn fuelled a strong response from India, which suspended military cooperation. But, as with Japan, relations soon began to normalize and were cemented by a visit to India by Prime Minister John Howard in July 2000.[104] While Australian uranium sales are still precluded by Canberra, this could, as noted above, soon change. The relationship has also been undermined by attacks on Indian students in Australia during the years 2008–10 seen in India as racist (even though some of them were committed by others of South Asian origin).[105] Another, generally unspoken Indian reservation over Australia relates to scepticism about Australia's claim to be a full Asian player. But a major asset has been the shared passion for cricket.

As noted in Chapter 6, China, after initial irritation over the Indian government's claims that the Pokhran tests were justified by the 'China threat', hardly skipped a beat in working to improve ties with India, including declaring itself neutral in the 1999 Kargil war between India and Pakistan. The Indian President visited Beijing in 2000, and in 2005, China recognized Sikkim as part of India. Bilateral cooperation between India and China in international and regional affairs has been strengthened through close coordination on issues such as climate change, the Doha Round talks, energy and food security, and the international financial crisis (notably in the G-20), a reassuring pattern for other Asians even when they do not agree with the resulting joint positions and strategies.[106] Clashes between India and China, whether in bilateral or multilateral settings, would inevitably be bad for business in Asia.

Regional groupings and forums

Beyond ASEAN, India has joined Asian countries in other regional groupings. One such grouping, launched in 1997, is the Bay of Bengal Initiative for Multisectoral Technical and Economic Cooperation (BIMSTEC). Involving Bangladesh, Myanmar, Sri Lanka, Thailand, Bhutan, Nepal, and India, BIMSTEC aims *inter alia* at promoting subregional cooperation in trade, investment, and technological exchange.[107] For India, the development and integration of its northeast region has been an underlying motivation for its engagement under BIMSTEC.[108] While a proposal for expanded rail links could prove a concrete way of giving expression to such high-minded sentiments, to date, BIMSTEC's achievements remain disappointing.[109]

Another such grouping, through which India engages several Southeast Asian countries, is the Mekong Ganga Cooperation (MGC) forum, launched in 2000 and including as members Myanmar, Thailand, Cambodia, Vietnam, and India. Closer economic cooperation is the main stated objective. Progress under the MGC has been torpid. Thailand, one of the key initiators and funders of the MGC has lost interest in the grouping after it established the Ayeyawady-Chao Phraya-Mekong Economic Cooperation Strategy in 2003 (bringing together the same group of countries minus India).[110] Thus, unsurprisingly, India is not a major player in comparison with the Greater Mekong Sub-region, in which China is the dominant actor.[111]

Looking beyond subregional groupings, in 2003, Indian Prime Minister Atal Bihari Vajpayee proposed an Asian Economic Community (AEC). The concept was refined by Manmohan Singh, who championed the vision of an AEC serving as 'an arc of advantage, peace and shared prosperity in Asia across which there will be large scale movement of people, capital ideas and creativity'.[112] In 2005, a forum for dialogue on broader cooperation within Asia was established when India joined the heads of state or government of fifteen other countries (including ASEAN member countries, Australia, China, Japan, South Korea, and New Zealand) as one of the founding members of the East Asia Summit in Kuala Lumpur.[113] This forum may represent a first step towards the eventual creation of an AEC.[114] However, even if cast as the culmination of the Look East Policy, the AEC concept has made little substantive headway.[115] The future multilateral architecture within Asia remains moot, with rival Chinese, Australian, and US-originated schemes for Asian economic integration being discussed in 2010, and the AEC concept attracting less attention. Such schemes include the Chinese proposal for an East Asian FTA and an American proposal for a Free Trade Area in the Asia-Pacific region (under the aegis of the Asia-Pacific Economic Cooperation forum—APEC), neither of which would include India. Aside from these, a recent Australian proposal for an Asia-Pacific Community, which would include India, has also been the subject of much discussion and debate.[116]

One key multilateral institution of the Asia-Pacific region, to which India was initially indifferent and which it has since then been unsuccessful in joining, is the Asia-Pacific Economic Cooperation forum (APEC), established in 1989 with twelve members aiming to promote trade and strengthen regional economic cooperation.[117] Although APEC is in many ways an ineffective talk-shop, it does gather many global leaders.[118] India has been keen to join since the mid-1990s but, in 1997, a moratorium was placed on new membership for ten years. Australia has championed Indian membership, but could not forestall a further three-year moratorium. As of 2010 Cambodia and Laos seemed best placed to achieve membership.[119] Notwithstanding APEC's identity as primarily a Pacific Rim organization, India's chances of eventually joining seem good given its growing economic clout, although the prize may seem disappointing once secured.[120]

Worth mentioning is India's intense interest in the Shanghai Cooperation Organization, launched in 2001 and including China, Kazakhstan, Kyrgyzstan, Russia, Tajikistan, and Uzbekistan, in which India (along with Iran, Pakistan, and Mongolia) has secured observer status but not full membership. It is centred on a region with which India has rich historic links and one that offers a wealth of natural resources. One expert opines that 'the driving forces for India to engage with this organization are mainly the emerging new security challenges in Afghanistan and Pakistan, and the need to keep watch over developments within this regional organization where China has been increasing its influence', but economic imperatives are at least as compelling.[121] Suffice it here to note that an institution including China and Russia within India's wider neighbourhood but excluding India is of neuralgic sensitivity for Delhi.

India has come a long way in establishing stronger political relations with the nations of Asia, and the growing level of comfort has supported the growth of economic relations. But having started late, it must continue to work hard. However much it is now considered a key player in the Asian continent, India remains excluded from some major regional forums and has yet to achieve much within the regional groupings and organizations in which it is involved.

Geostrategic considerations and defence ties

Impelled by its quest for cooperation on counterterrorism, humanitarian relief, anti-piracy, maritime and energy security, confidence building, and balancing of influence with other powers, particularly China, India has stepped up its political and military engagement with East and Southeast Asia.[122] Most of the countries in Southeast Asia have unsettled maritime boundaries or have articulated claims to offshore assets, islands, or seabed resources. And some of the world's busiest sea-lanes are located in this region.[123] About 20 per cent of the world's oil supply transits through it daily.[124] These factors, combined with China's growing influence in the region, doubtless inspired at least some in ASEAN to regard India as a useful partner to offset China.[125] Although

Singapore had once considered the Indian navy to be a threat, since 1993 it has regularly participated in naval exercises with it, and also used Indian facilities to test some of its armaments. Similarly, Malaysia signed a Memorandum of Understanding with India in 1993 on defence cooperation.[126]

Several security concerns revolve around the Indian Andaman and Nicobar Islands both for India and its Asian neighbours, including the plunder of valuable resources, piracy, narcotics trade, gunrunning, and terrorism. Foreign fishermen poach wildlife of all kinds.[127] And India has been 'particularly concerned about gun-trafficking activities in the Andaman Sea, as the weapons mostly end up in the hands of rebellious ethnic groups running secessionist movements in northeast India through the long permeable borders India shares with Myanmar.'[128] Organized crime elements from the Golden Triangle countries (spanning Thailand, Laos, and Myanmar) have been using the Andaman Sea as a staging area for their operations. Delhi also shares a fear with littoral states of Southeast Asia that terrorist groups could disrupt maritime traffic.[129] India patrols the Andaman Sea jointly with Thailand and Indonesia.[130]

India's concern about terrorism in Southeast Asia further stems from the imperatives of energy and supply chain security. Faced with growing energy requirements, but trying to reduce its dependence on energy sources from the Middle East, India has looked to Asian nations such as Indonesia, Vietnam, and Myanmar for supplies and is interested in energy supplies from Russia that could travel the Asia maritime route. Thus, the security of shipping through these sea-lanes is vital for India.[131]

Aside from terrorist threats at sea, India and Southeast Asian countries have particularly been victims of terrorist attacks by several Islamist militant groups, including Al Qaeda, the Abu Sayyaf Group, and the Moro Islamic Liberation Front (Philippines), and Laskar Jihad and the Free Aceh Movement (Indonesia). Presently, the Jamaah Islamiyah is the largest terrorist organization operating in five countries—Indonesia, Malaysia, Singapore, Thailand, and the Philippines. In recent years it has perpetrated acts of terror in Bali and Jakarta.[132]

India is well positioned to assist in Indian Ocean security given its increasingly strong navy.[133] Despite concerns in the past, a larger role for the Indian navy now appears more acceptable in the region. Indeed, the Indian navy is engaged in multinational exercises at Port Blair to promote confidence-building among several Asian and Pacific countries from as far afield as New Zealand.[134]

Regarding disaster relief, '[t]he Indian navy in particular has been at the cutting edge of India's engagement with the region—as was evident from its ability to deploy quickly to areas hit by the tsunami at the end of 2004'.[135] India, along with the USA, Japan, and Australia formed a coalition to help the

Tsunami affected area—spawning the term 'Tsunami Diplomacy'—that was seen by some as aimed indirectly at China.[136]

ASEAN's approach to external security is primarily 'institutionalist'.[137] The ARF has been the key regional security institution within which India has been able to engage Southeast Asia as a whole. However, its Confidence Building Measures (CBMs) have been unconvincing and serious differences have arisen over moving beyond them to preventive diplomacy. Neither in the case of the East Timor crisis nor the North Korean nuclear imbroglio did the ARF play any role.[138] Understanding these limitations, India is building relationships in Asia through a multiplicity of channels.

Bilaterally, India has cooperative arrangements with several countries stretching from the Seychelles to Vietnam. Since 1991, India has periodically held joint naval exercises with Singapore, Malaysia, and Indonesia in the Indian Ocean and in subsequent years with Vietnam, Thailand, and the Philippines.[139] India is particularly deepening its military ties with Malaysia.[140] The signing of a defence cooperation agreement with Singapore in 2003 has made the city-state India's most important bilateral security partner in Southeast Asia.[141] Indeed, Singapore, with its high quality research institutions and university-based think-tanks, has become an important centre of strategic thinking about India's role in the Indian Ocean and Asia, often drawing on temporarily resident premier Indian scholars and commentators, in recent years including C. Raja Mohan, Sanjaya Baru, and S. D. Muni.[142]

Military contacts between India and Japan have developed significantly in recent years. Their navies and coast guards have engaged in joint exercises.[143] India and Japan elevated their relationship to a 'Strategic and Global Partnership' in August 2007,[144] and subsequently agreed to annual bilateral naval exercises among several other activities.[145] Given that more than 50 per cent of India's trade and more than 80 per cent of Japan's oil imports transit through the Strait of Malacca, both countries share a significant stake in the security of the Indian Ocean.[146] Also, the military build-up undertaken by Beijing in the past decade concerns both. In the near future, China's armed forces could overtake Japan's as the foremost military actors in northeast Asia.[147]

India's defence ties with South Korea have also been deepening as a result of strategic imperatives. South Korea is particularly concerned that China's ongoing military build-up will enable it to dominate the sea-lanes of the South China Sea, which would undercut its political independence from China significantly. Moreover, both nations are also united in their concern about the proliferation of nuclear weapons and missile technology in their respective regions. These worries converge on China, which has aided both Pakistan and North Korea with their nuclear weapons programmes.[148] Thus, South Korean policymakers are open to India's overtures.

An active India–ROK Foreign Policy and Security Dialogue has been established, in part focused on defence cooperation.[149] India and Korea decided to enhance their relationship to a strategic partnership on 25 January 2010.[150]

Following the gradual improvement in Sino-Indian relations and some cross-border confidence-building measures during the 1990s, defence cooperation has expanded in the last decade.[151] Along with increasing exchange between defence officials, the two nations have conducted a number of joint military and naval exercises, sometimes also involving other countries.[152] These efforts are helpful by introducing shock-absorbers into a bilateral security relationship that remains tense and focused to a large extent on worries about strategic encirclement of each by the other. Islamic terrorism is an issue on which Indian and Chinese concerns have converged, particularly in the sensitive regions of Kashmir and Xinjiang.[153] While actual collaboration has been slight, joint counterterrorism training was held in November 2007 and in 2008.[154]

New Zealand has modest defence links with India that have been marked largely by interaction between their navies, with ship visits and naval exercises.[155] In recent years, Australian leaders have recognized India's potential in the security architecture of the wider Asia-Pacific region and the converging interests of both nations in many areas.[156] As a result, a series of agreements in 2006 and 2007 on joint naval exercises, enhanced maritime security cooperation, increased military exchanges, and joint training of the two nations' armed forces were established.[157] In November 2009, the Prime Ministers of India and Australia issued a joint statement upgrading relations to the level of 'Strategic Partnership'.[158]

Overall, with faster economic growth, India's military and strategic capabilities are becoming more consequential for Asia. India is making its presence felt through the expansion of its ties with the region as a whole. Relations between the navies and militaries of India and their Asian counterparts are increasingly institutionalized through a multitude of defence agreements. While the enthusiasm of Asian nations, including Singapore, South Korea, and Japan, is influenced by concern over the growing military capacities of China, C. Raja Mohan emphasizes:

> [t]he important question is not whether India will ever match the power potential of China, nor is it a question of East Asia seeing India as a 'counterweight' to China. So long as Indian economic growth continues at a fast pace, and New Delhi modernises its military capabilities and builds a blue water navy, it will remain a valuable partner for many states of the Asian littoral. A rising India generates options that did not exist before in the Western Pacific . . . [India's] emphasis on pragmatic cooperation rather than ideological posturing and its cooperative maritime strategy make it a valuable security partner for many nations in Pacific Asia.[159]

'Soft power' ties

The power of attraction exerted by cultural affinities and shared values can greatly contribute to international credibility. India's soft-power potential lies, among other things, in its democratic credentials, secular values, pluralistic society, considerable pool of skilled English speaking professionals, varied culture (particularly Bollywood movies), and its food and handicrafts.[160] India, over millennia, has offered refuge and, more importantly, religious and cultural freedom, to Jews, Parsis, several varieties of Christians, and Muslims.[161] In the post-Independence period, India failed to play successfully on its cultural ties to the Asian region. Indeed, its cultural diplomacy then was perceived as somewhat gauche in Asia, insofar as it seemed to suggest that some Southeast Asian countries were India's 'cultural colonies'.[162] Moreover, Indian foreign policy initiatives arguing for Asian solidarity failed to gain traction because East and Southeast Asian nations had no desire to subordinate their national identities to high-minded notions of Asian regional unity; nor did they agree with the claim that India was the 'mother of all civilisations' in Asia.[163]

Recognizing the need to shed these earlier notions of cultural superiority, India's has since the early 1990s engaged pragmatically with Asians on cultural and other issues. Today, India's cultural appeal is evident globally, and particularly in Southeast Asia through the positive resonance of its films, dance, and music: 'India's film stars like Amitabh Bachchan, Aishwarya Rai or Shah Rukh Khan have become icons of India's cultural image. If, today their "presence" in millions of homes across Southeast Asia is a source of joy and fellow feeling, then their contribution to enhancing the comfort level between India and Southeast Asia cannot be insignificant.'[164] Cricket has also fostered strong relations between India and some other Asian nations beyond its immediate neighbourhood. The new Indian 20/20 League, in which New Zealand and Australian players participate, has attracted wide interest in those countries and in some other Asian nations. The October 2010 Commonwealth Games in Delhi (in which the city and country invested tremendously) were intended, in spite of construction delays, rumours of corruption, and many other vicissitudes, to prove a major selling point with the many Asian and Pacific Commonwealth countries as with others.[165] All of these factors generate 'pull' for India, in ways having little to do with economic growth or military might.

India has set up Cultural Centres in Asia to enhance awareness of its rich and diverse cultural heritage and its local relevance.[166] Each year the Indian Council for Cultural Relations (ICCR) sends performing arts groups to participate in festivals around Asia. The year 2007 was declared 'Indian-Japan Friendship Year'. Overall, nearly 400 events were arranged in the two countries throughout that year.[167] 2009 witnessed the Festival of India in Indonesia on a similar scale.[168]

India's youth is a crucial asset, and Asia is sensitive to it. '[The] new, opti-mistic, aspirational India is clearly the India of the young. The entrepreneurs, who are coming into prominence across industries, from telecommunications to banking to manufacturing, are remarkably youthful ... It is the power and energy of our human capital, young and old, that has been central to the Indian transformation.'[169] Thus, unsurprisingly, in Singapore, the finance and IT sectors welcome young Indians with open arms and many companies, banks, and financial institutions have started visiting top Indian campuses for recruitment purposes.[170] Indeed, India has emerged as an important source of skilled workers in much of Asia.[171]

In Southeast Asia, efforts are currently afoot to promote 'networking of universities [by] the linking of Indian higher education institutions with the ASEAN University Network, cooperating on accreditation, joint research, ex-change of professors, and experts and students in information technology, biotechnology, biomedics, and the social sciences, including economics.'[172] Moreover, India provides wide-ranging scholarships for Asian students in India, particularly through the ICCR. The Indian government also helps in the establishment of chairs related to India and its languages in universities of Southeast Asia.[173]

Outside Southeast Asia, growing cooperation on education is taking place through exchanges and recruitment of Indian students in South Korea, New Zealand, Singapore, and, particularly, Australia. For Indians, Australia is the number two destination for overseas study after the USA.[174] In 2009 alone there were over 120,000 Indian students enrolled in Australia and enrolments there have increased at an average annual rate of 41 per cent since 2002.[175]

India's MEA has sought to underpin cooperation with developing countries through its Indian Technical and Economic Cooperation (ITEC) programme, which focuses on technology transfers and capacity building at the bilateral level. For example, around one thousand Indonesian experts and officials have received training under this programme.[176] In recent years the scope of ITEC's activities has increased and it has also engaged with ASEAN, BIMSTEC, and the MGC.[177] In 2008–9, 25 per cent of the total MEA budget was allocated to the programme.[178]

The Indian Diaspora

The Indian Diaspora is a crucial actor in India's influence in Asia. Southeast Asia alone accounts for an estimated 6.7 million people of Indian origin.[179] The significant economic resource represented by Diaspora and migrant labour remittances back to India has guided much of Delhi's effort to engage this large community. Between 2007 and 2008, these remittances increased by nearly 45 per cent, and they proved robust even during the 2008–9 global economic crisis, with the two main sources of remittances being the Gulf and Malaysia.[180] But while the remittances are much welcomed by India, the treatment of Indian citizens (and, in the case of Malaysia, citizens of Indian origin) by host countries can give rise to criticism within India, often with considerable justification. The power struggle between ethnic Indians and indigenous islanders in Fiji over past decades has soured diplomatic relations between the two countries, not least when the ethnic Indian community was adversely affected by the coups of 1999 and 2000 in Suva. In response, the Indian government exerted what diplomatic pressure it could through bilateral and multilateral channels (including the Commonwealth) but was accused by the interim Fijian government of interference, resulting in the closure of the Indian High Commission in Suva.[181] In fact, India has developed scant capacity to guarantee the basic labour rights and promote the interests of its Diaspora communities: 'given its myriad domestic challenges... it is unrealistic to expect that it [India] can influence events in other countries on behalf of its people'.[182]

Similarly, attacks against Indian students in Australia have of late been a source of tension between Canberra and Delhi. With education being Australia's third largest export commodity and Indian students making up 19 per cent of international enrolments, these attacks were worrying for both countries, with Canberra fielding diplomatic damage control visits to India in 2009 and subsequently.[183] Agreement ensued on an annual ministerial exchange between the two countries on education issues.[184] Thus, although the large Indian community in Australia is locally perceived mostly as a positive factor, it has also been one that has heightened tensions between the two nations.

Overall, the people-to-people links that form between Diaspora communities and other countries are important and positive. Ethnic Indians have achieved a great deal in political, business, and professional fields in Asia.[185]

Tourism

Tourism, particularly religious tourism, is another existing but potentially much greater asset in India's relations with Asian nations. Buddhist tourism, already a major draw, has significant potential to generate further arrivals from Asian markets.[186] In mid-2007, the Indian Railway Catering and Tourism Corporation launched a new Buddhist circuit special luxury train and Japanese investors are bankrolling an integrated approach to develop tourism infrastructure along the Buddhist circuit.[187]

The flow of tourists between Asia and India has increased both in absolute numbers and in relative terms in recent years, although not yet dramatically.

Tourist arrivals from East Asia and the Pacific to India increased from over 390,000 in 2003 to more than 820,000 in 2007.[188] Similarly, the percentage share of Indian tourists travelling to Asia has increased in recent years (see Figure 9.1). But the largest markets for Indian inbound tourism remain the US, the UK, and Bangladesh.[189] Worth noting is the negligible flow of visitors between India and China. Although direct flights between India and China began in 2002, in 2007, the two nations with a combined population of over two billion exchanged only 570,000 visitors, with only 60,000 Chinese visitors coming to India.[190]

India can do much better in attracting tourists from Asia, but this will require a better understanding of the value-for-money available in other Asian tourist destinations, and the minimum requirements of comfort and facilities that Asian tourists, including from China, have come to expect during their travels abroad. India's often over-priced, sub-par hotel accommodations, combined with sometimes chaotic local conditions for tourists, and unsympathetic state bureaucracies in charge of many tourist sites, are

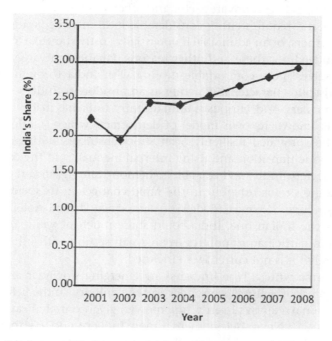

Figure 9.1. Percentage of Indians among international tourist arrivals in Asia and the Pacific

Note: This graph is based on data collected by the United Nations World Tourism Organization (UNWTO). Asia and the Pacific includes all countries in Northeast Asia, Southeast Asia, South Asia, and Oceania.
Source: Government of India, *Incredible India: Tourism Statistics at a Glance, 2008* (New Delhi: Market Research Division, Ministry of Tourism, July 2009).

hardly the Asian ideal for family holidays, even when the archaeological and other attractions themselves are often stupendous. Indeed, if these concerns remain unaddressed, the 'Incredible India!' conveyed in the excellent Indian tourism promotional campaign is destined to remain in reality the 'incredibly inconvenient and expensive' India for many Asians.[191]

Conclusions

India has not yet made the best of its assets in Asia. Its forms of societal organization, occasional unrest, sometimes unfathomable local politics, and sudden spasms of violence—sometimes on a frighteningly large scale—often seem to repel other Asians, particularly East Asians, much more than India's attractive features appeal to them. Even the Indian avatar of corruption, a wider phenomenon present throughout nearly all of Asia in varying degrees, worries Asians insofar as the specifics of the interplay of incentives offered back and forth between private sector and official Indian actors is mysterious to outsiders and requires either considerable local intermediation by Indian business partners, or an admirable if potentially costly stance of 'clean hands' dealings. Indeed, for these and other reasons, Japanese private sector actors find themselves more comfortable dealing with India through Dubai, the latter's antiseptic characteristics acting as an antidote to India's strongly fla-voured particulars. And, curiously, until recently, India has made little effort to make better known its own model of democracy, which, while messy and fractious, has provided resilient social shock-absorbers during a period of rapid economic transition and rising internal inequality in the country. As a pluralistic society, India has been able to demonstrate significant creativity in addressing the strains inherent in the rapid changes in its society. From an Asian perspective, Western models of democracy should not be nearly as relevant as the Indian one. India could share much of value about nation building and participatory politics in an Asian setting with other Asian na-tions, although it is not currently so inclined.

Pavan Varma writes: '[w]e [Indians] are emerging slowly as an important face in the areas of politics, economics and the military. In the field of culture, however, we have always been a superpower, given our civilizational depth and antiquity.'[192] Nevertheless, there is more India can do to enhance its soft power in the Asian region. Sanjaya Baru notes: 'It is ridiculous that India has more diplomats posted in west European capitals than in [E]ast Asian ones! India needs deeper and wider engagement with rising Asia across many fields and on more fronts.'[193]

The new guiding concept of India's Asia policy—the LEP—has certainly evolved since the early 1990s. Born in the context of a dramatically transformed global order and during a time of national economic crisis, India's LEP, though narrowly focused on economic relations in Southeast Asia in its early years, has expanded to encompass multidimensional interaction with all of the major players in the East Asian region. (However, with so many of India's Asian relationships now being elevated to 'Strategic Partnerships', the term may soon cease to impart any real meaning.)

India's concerted push eastward has resulted in a much thicker web of interactions in Asia. India has, however belatedly, established itself in this vast region and is now widely regarded as one of the three major Asian actors, along with China and Japan. Moreover, most of Asia seems eager to engage an increasingly commercially open, diplomatically flexible India that is keen on military (particularly naval) cooperation.

India's medium- and long-term strategy towards the region as a whole and towards individual countries is still tentative. This has also been true of India's approach to the area's regional organizations and arrangements, though India today has dropped its earlier sceptical view in favour of joining as many as seems sensibly possible (including a few formations that have not proved particularly convincing). In part as a legacy of its earlier stand-offish stance, India remains excluded from some important regional forums, which it will doubtless rectify in years ahead.

In all of this, India's unspoken goal, beyond the promotion of its economic interests, seems to be to manage, and, where necessary, counter, rising Chinese influence that might both encircle it and undermine its aspirations to a meaningful leadership role within the Asian continent and globally. Although Indians may sometimes attach more weight to China's differences with their country than seem warranted by the facts to date, in recent years with China growing faster and more self-confident than India in most respects, the China angle remains central for Delhi.

In sum, India enjoys a 'soft power' pull in relations with many Asian nations. But the region is unsentimental and to meet India's expectations will continue to demand more (and more accommodating) Indian engagement than has yet become habitual for Delhi.

10

India's Relationships with Europe and Russia: Fading Glory?

No aspect of Indian foreign policy is more challenging to address than its comparatively underwhelming relationship today with Europe, in spite of dynamic trading ties, and its long-standing, valued, but somewhat shopworn relationship with Russia.

This chapter focuses primarily on Western Europe (sometimes through the lens of the European Union (EU) and Russia. The Nordic countries have mattered to independent India, not least because they were generous providers of assistance in decades past, but their weight in the Indian calculus has probably declined as their identity (with the exception of Norway) became enshrouded in that of the wider EU. Likewise, while a degree of comity was evident with the states of Eastern Europe during the era of India's friendship with the Soviet Union, they are not a major preoccupation for India today. Note deserves to be made of the singular role of Yugoslavia during the era of Marshall Tito, which, together with India, Egypt, and Indonesia, largely forged the concept and the institutional framework for non-alignment in the late 1950s and early 1960s.

India's relationships with Western Europe and Russia evoke history of empire, exploration, and geopolitical tensions. India still reminds many students of history and of international relations of former British colonial global power and reach, with the Raj having served as what British Prime Minister Benjamin Disraeli called the 'jewel in the crown' of the British Empire. For Russia, India played a significant role as Britain's instrument and leaping off territory in the 'Great Game' of the nineteenth century for control of Central Asia and regions stretching from Turkey to Afghanistan. India also serves as a reminder of efforts to grow Russia's own influence and reach (rather successfully) throughout this same region during the Cold War. Largely unnoticed in Western Europe and Russia, India has emerged swiftly as an increasingly equal, and, in terms of forward momentum, a more potent global player than they could have conceived of only twenty years ago. The extent to which India had indeed served as the economic and to some degree security anchor of the British colonial enterprise might have provided a hint of what India could achieve on its own.

Shifting perceptions of relative influence and power among Western Europe, Russia, and India have been influenced by the new saliency of economic growth and weight as a prime indicator within the global pecking order, as has India's centrality in managing current and future global challenges such as climate change and the proliferation of nuclear weapons. On both of these counts, among others, India has a key role to play. Even today, while the United States enjoys a comfortable global lead in political, military, and economic power, new concepts such as human security are increasingly playing a role in the definition of state power. This is leading to a polycentric or multipolar global dynamic in which India can, if and when it wishes to, play an increasingly significant role.[1] Can this assertion be made of Russia or the European Union, today significant actors in international relations, but neither with much wind in their sails?

This chapter first discusses India's pre-colonial and colonial links with Western Europe as well as its relationships with Russia and regions of Russia's near-abroad. It then examines the content of relationships between India and the European Union and its leading member states, addressing the challenges for India of accommodating the twists and turns of the EU 'construction' saga. It thereafter offers an analysis of Indo-Russian ties and the specific successes and challenges attending that relationship. It looks at Europe's geostrategic significance for India, caught as the continent is between the likely dominant powers of the twenty-first century, the USA and China. In its final paragraphs, it offers some brief conclusions on India's relationships with Western Europe and with Russia, marked as they are by India's rise and the relative stagnation of these formerly important and still relevant partners.

The Indo-European relationship

History in brief

India's early encounters with Europe were consistently anchored in maritime trade. While maritime trade was a lifeline for coastal Indian states by 1498, the idea that the sea could be political, a strategic commodity in its own right dominated by a state rather than by commercial competition, was a relatively new concept for Indians.[2] The arrival of Portuguese naval forces in the region, beginning in 1498, changed this and brought European traders, explorers, and soldiers to India for the next 450 years. Among the European powers to hold interests of varying significance at different times in India were the Portuguese, Dutch, French, and British.[3]

The French early on had as much of an interest in India as the British, founding major trading companies to compete in South Asia with Britain's famed East India Company.[4] French aspirations to an Indian jewel in its imperial crown were dashed by the British victory over France that ended the Seven Years' War.[5] While the French devoted some further effort to carving out zones of influence and control in India, the Fourth Mysore War of 1799, culminating in the death of Tipu Sultan, and Napoleon's failure to move any further east than Egypt, ended any plausible scenarios for an India dominated by France (which, in Asia, focused instead on Indochina). France did retain minor dependencies, in such places as Pondicherry in India's south and Chandernagor near Calcutta, so insignificant as to make them acceptable to the British.[6]

The British, by comparison, dominated India from the late 1700s until India's independence in 1947, initially through the expansive paramilitary and economic influence of the British East India Company (EIC). British success in subjugating India was due critically to the ability of the EIC to capitalize on local political divisions and utilize pre-existing local logistical infrastructure to gain political and military dominance over India, establishing territorial control of the Indian peninsula by the early nineteenth century.[7]

Through both World Wars, as noted in Chapter 2, Indian forces operated under the auspices of the British military, with Indian troops being found in nearly all major theatres of war, particularly in Europe and the Middle East during the First World War and in the Pacific and South Asian theatres, as well as in Italy and north Africa, in the Second World War.[8]

In Europe, particularly the UK, a perception lingers that the British did much for India, but the reverse is mostly true. Indians are gracious about those British institutions and modernizations that have proved useful since independence, including the Westminster parliamentary system, adopted both at Union and at State levels throughout the country, a judiciary largely modelled on British conceptions, and the infrastructure such as the Indian railroads. Indeed, a small minority of the country's elite remains determinedly Anglophilic (while many more are drawn to the rougher-hewn charms of the USA). But the experience of British brutality, racism, and expediency (particularly, London's poor planning for Indian independence) have left Indians prepared to believe the worst of Britain at the slightest provocation, for example when Indian film star Shilpa Shetty was insulted during a broadcast of the television reality show Celebrity Big Brother in the UK in 2007, this news completely overshadowed a visit to India at the time by Chancellor of the Exchequer, Gordon Brown. The irony is that many non-resident Indians have built successful lives, a number of them in very prominent national roles, in the multi-cultural and multi-ethnic modern nation that Britain has become in recent decades.

Portuguese colonial rule extended in India until 1961, when Prime Minister Nehru ordered the military takeover of Goa. However, Portuguese culture, cuisine, and art mixed felicitously with those of India's West Coast, and today Goa is one of India's foremost beach holiday playgrounds, with considerable international appeal. The French were wise enough, perhaps spurred on by their local difficulties in Indochina, to negotiate with Delhi the peaceful, staged handover of their Indian colonies between 1954 and 1962, thereby retaining a number of privileges for those holding French nationality in Pondicherry and in their smaller outposts. Like Goa, Pondicherry today retains some of its European flavour, although most of its culture is, of course, Indian.

India's interactions with Europe during the Cold War mainly revolved around the bipolar nature of the global order during the years 1946–89. Much economic assistance was obtained from both Cold War camps. India's attempt to minimize the adverse effects for it of the highly polarized Cold War environment led to its non-aligned position, which allowed it to pursue productive relations with both East and West and served it well during most of the decades involved. But the end of the Cold War heralded many changes for Europe and for India, which required re-engineering of relationships, and, for India, a relative reordering of its partnerships. Prime Minister Rao, coming to power just after the end of the Cold War, recognized a unified Western and Central Europe as a potential major power in the making, and provided it with some profile within his foreign policy.[9] This was significant for the European Union given the pace of growth of India's own economy and of its economic engagement with the rest of the world.

Economics and trade

Since its inception, the Indo-West European relationship has been dominated by trade. However, while historically the trade relationship tended to be Eurocentric in its colonial and immediate post-colonial orientation, the current trend is towards a much more equal dynamic. Figures for 2008–9 put Indian total exports to the EU states at US\$39.3 billion, and total imports at US\$42.7 billion.[10]

However, trade figures show that India's economic interaction with European countries is very much focused on specific players within the EU, with a vast majority of India's trade relationship focused on only a handful of states. Table 10.1 illustrates this focus, with the top ten trading partners for India in the EU listed according to exports and imports in 2007–8.

Table 10.1. Top Trading Partners for India in the EU

EU State	Indian exports 2008–9	EU State	Indian imports 2008–9
UK	6,649.53	Germany	12,006.02
Germany	6,388.54	UK	5,872.32
Netherlands	6,348.69	Belgium	5,776.77
Belgium	4,480.32	France	4,632.48
Italy	3,824.58	Italy	4,428.19
France	3,020.86	Sweden	1,952.50
Spain	2,538.15	Netherlands	1,914.95
Greece	878.43	Finland	1,219.64
Denmark	583.66	Spain	1,023.80
Sweden	566.69	Austria	701.64

Note: All figures in US$ million.
Source: Government of India, Department of Commerce, *Export–Import Data Bank* (consulted June 2010).

More salient than these country-by-country figures, however, is that Europe's position in India's overall global trade is shrinking. The percentage of India's total trade made up by imports and exports from EU states is slowly decreasing as the Indian economy grows. Table 10.2 illustrates this by listing the percentage of Indian trade made up by European imports and exports in the decade from 1998 to 2009. In the case of India's imports from Europe, the relative decline is all the more worrying for European countries in that India's share of the world economy has been growing rapidly.

Not surprisingly, the distressing trends reflected above are also indicative of the increasingly marginal focus accorded to West European states within Indian foreign policy. Thus, India, while still maintaining high priority bilateral relations with a handful of European states, has shaken off any sense

Table 10.2. European Imports and Exports as Percentage of Indian Trade

Year	Imports from Europe (as % of total Indian imports)	Exports to Europe (as % of total Indian exports)
2008–9	14.07	21.23
2007–8	15.28	21.17
2006–7	16.06	21.21
2005–6	17.43	22.53
2004–5	17.31	21.84
2003–4	19.29	14.51
2002–3	20.90	22.55
2001–2	20.71	23.17
2000–1	21.12	24.00
1999–2000	22.39	26.25
1998–9	25.68	27.71
1997–8	26.23	26.83

Note: All figures in US$ million.
Source: Government of India, Department of Commerce, *Export–Import Data Bank* (consulted June 2010).

of Eurocentricity in its worldview, preferring to focus on the USA, East Asian states (particularly China), and sometimes Russia, as truly strategic inter-locutors.

At a formal level, new frameworks have been developed for meaningful engagement, as when India and the EU secured a 'strategic partnership' in 2004.[11] This was followed up by several further negotiated texts such as an India–EU Joint Action Plan, which covers a wide range of fields for cooperation including trade and commerce, security, and cultural and educational exchanges.[12] However, these measures lead mainly to dialogue, commitments to further dialogue, and exploratory committees and working groups, rather than to significant policy measures or economic breakthroughs. Indeed, one wonders whether the all-consuming nature of intra-EU negotiations and the tremendously self-absorbed requirements of Indian domestic politics lend themselves to more than these diplomatic niceties, in the absence of hard facts compelling or inviting closer ties.[13] The major stumbling block to greater Indo-European trade cooperation may be the fact that both parties are so similar in some ways, comfortable with each other but experiencing little compulsion towards closer ties. Pallavi Aiyar writes:

> The EU certainly does not have it easy. Protectionist trade unions, a coalition of 27 member-states with divergent priorities, and a convoluted internal-decision making process do not make for quick results. In this regard, India is Europe's doppelganger. Cumbersome coalitions, powerful civil society organizations and conflicting interests amongst political constituencies are also a hallmark of the decision-making process in New Delhi. But European officials rarely acknowledge these parallels, choosing instead to . . . disparage India for faults the EU itself can be charged with.[14]

While there is substantial room for India and the EU to focus their trade relationship on areas of perceived mutual interest, such as science and technology or the services sector, the relationship will eventually have to breach the dam of current protectionist measures in agricultural trade, not least in the multilateral setting of the multilateral Trade Negotiations, where EU countries were only too happy to watch USA–India differences over agriculture attract the lion's share of attention in 2008 while their own policies and preferences were no less problematic for India.[15]

And which are the countries of the European Union that India takes seriously? Not surprisingly, in view of its own geostrategic concerns, the major former colonial powers that also happen to be the Western European permanent members of the UN Security Council, France and the UK, enjoy pride of place. This is even reflected in how the Indian Ministry of External Affairs allocates country responsibilities among its senior officials—in the case of immediate neighbours and of permanent members of the UN Security Council, this responsibility lies with the Foreign Secretary rather than a subsidiary senior official. This remains true in spite of both France and the UK underperforming relative to potential in their economic links with India. Germany matters as a trading partner (ranking high on both sides of Table 10.1), but also, importantly, as a country like India challenging the established order of states within the UN Security Council, both of them partnering with Japan and Brazil since 2004 in demanding permanent seats of their own in the Council. Several other West European countries register somewhat in India, notably Italy, which shares with India the distinction of having spawned several great civilizations reflected in extraordinary artistic, literary, and other cultural accomplishments.[16] Spain, somewhat in the same vein, is of interest to India, not least because of its privileged links with most of Latin America, a continent whose potential India is only now beginning to explore fully, with major private sector links building up. Finally, Dutch economic entrepreneurship and trading dynamism is recognized in India as impressive.

Defence and security

European and Russian markets have historically provided the answer to India's continuously growing defence procurement needs. Between 2004 and 2008, India was the second largest purchaser of major conventional weapons systems, encompassing 7 per cent of the world's total trade in these systems.[17]

During the early Cold War, Britain was the primary exporter of arms to India, a result largely born out of former colonial ties.[18] France, whose strategic relationship with India did not take off fully until the 1970s, was a significant provider of major weapons systems during the latter half of the Cold War: systems which included the Mirage fighter-bomber and the AMX battle tank.[19] Even recently, from 1999 to 2008, India was Britain's second largest client for major weapons systems, purchasing 14 per cent of its total arms exports.[20]

However, Europe's top companies are finding themselves being increasingly edged out by the sheer volume (and increasing sophistication) of Russia's exports, and particularly by India's increased access to US defence markets.[21] Perhaps the biggest indicator of India's direction in the defence procurement field will be its final decision in the months or years ahead on the Multi-Role Combat Aircraft (MRCA) contract, estimated to be worth US$12 billion.[22] With major US, Russian, and European firms vying for the contract offering some of their best platforms, India's decision on the MRCA aircraft contract will be an important indication of whether Europe is still a major contender for India's defence business.[23] The probability is high that Europe will continue to capture some of the Indian market as Delhi is inclined to spread risk widely amongst suppliers.

Regardless of the major contracts still to be won, there are indications that Europe is playing less of a role in India's defence policy, being replaced by more active bilateral engagement with European states on specialized defence-related fields such as counterterrorism, nuclear non-proliferation, and disarmament. For example, the Indo-French Working Group on Terrorism has met annually since 2001. This may be the best option for both parties, considering that Russia will likely continue to be India's primary supplier of major weapons systems, enjoying residual cost advantages if not always a qualitative edge, and that states such as the UK and Germany have a comparative advantage in specialist functions such as counterterrorism, forensic investigation, and surveillance technology.[24] The ongoing insurgency in Kashmir, the November 2008 Mumbai attacks, and numerous mass-casualty terrorist attacks targeting India's urban centres over the past decade suggest that cooperation in counterterrorism and European remote surveillance technology could be more useful to India in the future than Europe's traditional heavy defence industry.

Energy interests

Energy is a primary concern for India, and will only become more of a priority in future years. India's reliance on energy imports from other states is rising rapidly with the growing Indian population and continued economic growth.[25] Imports accounted for 72 per cent of India's supply of oil in 2004–5.[26] Table 10.3 illustrates that coal is still the dominant energy source for India, but Indian infrastructure for coal production is inefficient and the increasing emphasis on environmental protection standards globally suggests that India will be under increasing pressure domestically and internationally over coming decades to identify cleaner alternatives.[27] This will be doubly true if, as some predict given current rates of consumption, India's coal reserves largely disappear within the next fifty years.[28]

Table 10.3. Main Energy Sources for India

	Mar-02	Apr-03	May-04	Jun-05	Jul-06
Coal	341.3	361.3	382.6	407.0	430.9
Lignite	26.0	28.0	30.3	30.1	31.1
Electricity					
Installed capacity (x1,000 MW)	126.2	131.4	137.5	145.6	157
Generation (bn kWh)	596.5	633.3	665.8	697.4	744.3
Crude petroleum	32.0	33.4	34.0	32.2	34
Petroleum products	100.0	107.8	111.6	113.2	119.6
Natural gas	31.4	n/a	n/a	n/a	n/a

Note: Fiscal years, April–March; millions of tons production unless otherwise indicated.
Source: Economist Intelligence Unit, Country Report 2008: India (London: Economist, 2008), 16.

At the same time, an over-reliance on oil and natural gas imports carries with it significant problems as well, not least of which being that India could be drawn more deeply into the geopolitical quagmire of the West Asian region.[29] Potential instability in West Asia makes further diversification in the sources of Indian oil and gas imports a strategic necessity.

Europe does provide an attractive alternative for India, not only in the form of importable energy, but also for technology and knowledge transfers, especially further to high-tech initiatives such as nuclear, solar, and hydroelectric projects (although Indian science and technology capacity, if harnessed to the challenge, is certainly up to significant innovation of its own in these areas). The India–EU Joint Action Plan emphasizes energy security as a primary concern of both and created a panel to examine matters of mutual interest in this area, stating that the Plan will give priority to 'joint efforts in the development of more efficient, cleaner and alternative energy chains'.[30] It also identifies eight core aspects of energy security for close cooperation including the promotion of energy efficiency, and technology related to the transfer of energy between grid systems and the further development of nuclear power.[31] In addition to this, the EU is cooperating with India and other states in the International Thermonuclear Experimental Reactor (ITER) project.[32]

However, such grand schemes are likely to be the exception rather than the rule, the latter represented by bilateral cooperation and private-sector projects. Significant European energy companies have substantial interests in India, including the British Gas Group, Royal Dutch Shell, Cairn Energy of Scotland, and Gaz de France.[33] On a bilateral basis, European governments that are experienced in energy matters are likely to be favoured by India as partners. A good example is France, whose success with nuclear power and significant defence ties with India have opened doors for deeper bilateral ties on energy issues. Franco-Indian energy cooperation became significantly closer with the signing of the Framework Agreement for Civil Nuclear Cooperation in January 2008 and a follow-up agreement in September 2008 that allows Paris to sell to Delhi French nuclear reactors.[34] And bilateral cooperation does not preclude the EU Council and Commission, as institutions, from projecting a plausible united front on proliferation issues, specifically support of the Nuclear Non-Proliferation Treaty (NPT), while engaging with India as a rising nuclear power.

Political culture

While the drivers of Indian relations with Western Europe mentioned previously are mostly economic, there is a final factor that serves as an asset underpinning their ties: the constitutional arrangements and political culture of the states involved—specifically the electoral democracies that they have in common.

India is rightly proud of its democracy, and playing on genuine values-based convergence where it exists, as well as interests-based considerations, is helpful. Democracy, which has given voice to so many perspectives in India, underpins an essential moderation of its body politic in international relations. In a work examining the philosophical underpinnings of Indian foreign policy, Nalini Kant Jha writes:

> A preference for the middle path is the hallmark of Indian tradition and culture as seen in the Sanskrit saying which goes, *ati sarvatra varjayet*: let us eschew excess at all times. This saying underlines India's philosophical abhorrence of absolutes, of extremes, of the tendency to see things strictly in terms of black and white.[35]

And this factor in Indian political life is sometimes explicitly but more generally tacitly acknowledged in the West (which, nevertheless, would like India to be more open to urging its own political values on, for example, Myanmar). Sunil Khilnani argues that the Indian adoption of democracy was the third act in the great play of liberal democracy, which started with the ideas underpinning the French Revolution and continued with the American Revolution.[36] While the form of democracy varies tremendously across Europe, the Westminster parliamentary system that the Indian Union and its states and to a degree the EU have adopted creates commonality of experience and of constitutional understanding between India and many European nations.

Long-standing educational ties between India and Europe have shaped much of India's elite class over the years, although, particularly after Indian independence, the lure of the top American universities somewhat displaced the earlier focus on Oxford, Cambridge, and other leading UK universities. Indira Gandhi noted the importance of scholars, both Indian and European, in the development not only of Indo-European understanding, but also of Indian self-awareness.[37] Indians and Europeans have worked hard on educational exchanges, with both sides reaping rich benefits.[38] For example, Jawharlal Nehru's political identity emerged in Europe, through his study of the movements of Garibaldi and of Sinn Fein's resistance to British rule in Ireland.[39]

The benefits of shared educational ties run both ways. France, for instance, benefits from the high-quality academic research generated by its *Centre de Sciences Humaines* in Delhi, a hub of social science research on India, which serves as a striking tribute to the significance France attaches to the study of India and its society.[40] Further, partly as a colonial legacy, France can boast of the impressive *Institut Français de Pondichéry*, which engages in multiple scholarly activities relevant to South and Southeast Asia in a wide variety of fields (including environmental ones), not least the painstaking conservation of ancient Indian Sanskrit and other texts.[41] While the work and accomplishments of these French institutions might seem marginal relative to the vibrant bilateral French economic relationships with India, in fact they are complementary thereto and much appreciated in India and Europe alike.

Unlike some other features of the relationship, Indo-European educational links have been marked not just by talk, but also by action. The Asia-Link programme, for instance, provides opportunities for higher-education institutions in both India and Europe to meet and interact on common projects.[42] The India–EU Joint Action Plan also places significant emphasis on furthering educational ties.[43] Statistics in Britain show that Indian students represent the second most numerous group of foreign students in the UK (after Chinese), with Indian rates of enrolment rising steadily (while those of China are falling slightly).[44] There is similar interest in South Asia among European students who are keen to engage in cultural and educational experiences beyond those offered on their own continent, and increasingly European business and science students are recognizing the rising significance of India in these sectors. Advances in communications technology and the availability of cheap international travel have favoured internships and student exchanges in and with India.

The exchange of students is, however, only one aspect of a wider cultural effort by some European states to maintain links with India. Several West European countries devote considerable effort and resources to promoting their own culture and to establishing links with Indian artistic, literary, and performing arts communities. Both France and Germany in recent years— through such institutions as the *Alliance Française*, French cultural centres, and the *Goethe Institut* (operating out of eight Indian cities)—have far out-stripped the effectiveness of the British Council which, to the consternation of many Indians, appears to have abandoned much of its traditional role in promoting the British arts and literature—and creating corresponding connections between India and Britain—for the money-making potential of English-language courses, albeit highly regarded ones.[45]

The Indo-Russian relationship

History in brief: India's Russian interactions

The Indo-Russian relationship does not extend back as far as that of the colonial powers and their forebears. The Himalayas and the Hindu Kush insulated India from meaningful early contact with Russia (although Central Asia played an important role as a passageway to China and as the point of origin for some of the dynasties that dominated northern India after the Muslim conquest). Much of the relevant history is marked by the 'Great Game' in the nineteenth and early twentieth centuries, during which Russia attempted to encroach on Britain's dominance of the South Asian and parts of the Central Asian regions as well as Iran. The inhospitable environment of the Caucasus and Afghanistan, both central to the Great Game, and their distance from home base provided a powerful buffer between India and Russia. Russian expansion, culminating during the Second World War, with a significant Russian presence in Iran and de facto domination of the Caucasus, left India well beyond the Soviet sphere of influence.

However, the beginning of the Cold War, which roughly coincided with India's independence from Britain in 1947, created considerable and sustained Soviet interest in India. As a result of its conflict with China and its experience of the USA as an unreliable partner, India backed into an ever more comprehensive relationship with Moscow, culminating in the 1971 treaty of friendship. Soviet weapons were vital to its successful military campaign in East Bengal in 1971 and, indeed, formed the backbone of Indian military procurement for decades.[46] Christopher Andrew and former KGB officer Vasili Mitrokhin discuss the ease with which the Soviet secret service could operate in India:

> The Asian intelligence successes of which the [KGB] was most proud were in India, the world's second most populous state and largest democracy. It was deeply ironic that the KGB should find democratic India so much more congenial an environment than Communist China, North Korea and Vietnam.[47]

This said, Delhi worked hard to remain independent, and thus could never be included entirely in the Soviet 'camp', however much Washington and some of its allies resented India's close relationship with Moscow.

Economics and trade

While the strategic partnership agreement signed by India and Russia in 2000 offered more substance than the India–EU agreement of 2004–5, economic considerations (leaving aside energy projects) were not central.[48] Instead, the more concrete steps envisaged were in the areas of the political and defence relationships.[49] This is generally true of the overall Indo-Russian relationship since Russia began to recover from post-Cold War economic turmoil. India has focused on its own needs: arms deals, nuclear cooperation and political dialogue.

Table 10.4 illustrates the economic results. While there is growth in the trade relationship in absolute terms, the Russian share of India's booming trade is stagnating.

Table 10.4. India's Trade with Russia

Year	2004–5	2005–6	2006–7	2007–8	2008–9
INDIAN EXPORTS TO RUSSIA	631.26	733.15	903.69	940.61	1,096.34
% growth of exports to Russia	–	16.14	23.26	4.09	16.56
India's total exports	83,535.94	103,090.53	126,414.05	163,132.18	185,295.36
% growth of India's total exports	–	23.41	22.62	29.05	13.59
Exports to Russia as % share of total exports	0.76	0.71	0.71	0.58	0.59
INDIAN IMPORTS FROM RUSSIA	1,322.74	2,022.19	2,409.05	2,478.16	4,328.28
% growth of imports from Russia		52.88	19.13	2.87	74.66
India's total imports	111,517.43	149,165.73	185,735.24	251,654.01	303,696.31
% growth of India's total imports		33.76	24.52	35.49	20.68
Imports from Russia as % share of total imports	1.19	1.36	1.3	0.98	1.43
TOTAL INDO-RUSSIAN TRADE	1,954.01	2,755.33	3,312.73	3,418.77	5,424.62
% growth of total trade		41.01	20.23	3.2	58.67
India's total trade	195,053.37	252,256.26	312,149.29	414,786.19	488,991.67
% growth of India's total trade		29.33	23.74	32.88	17.89
Indo-Russian trade as % share of total Indian Trade	1	1.09	1.06	0.82	1.11
TRADE BALANCE					
India's Trade Balance	−27,981.49	−46,075.20	−59,321.19	−88,521.83	−118,400.95

Notes: All figures in US$ million.
Source: Government of India, Department of Commerce, *Export–Import Data Bank* (consulted June 2010).

Indian President Pratibha Patil's visit to Russia in September 2009 highlighted the limited scope of Indo-Russian bilateral trade. For both, official trade was a paramount concern, with Patil stating 'We need to ponder over why our economies should be satisfied with the current level of trade volumes', and emphasizing that trade levels between the two states were a poor reflection of the 'close political ties'.[50]

The Indo-Russian economic relationship has tended to follow the course of Russia's economic fortunes, marked by a serious partnership throughout much of the Cold War, but a floundering one during the 1990s when Russian mismanagement of the transition to a market economy left the country economically in shock.[51] Russia's recent economic upturn, driven by oil and gas prices, has enabled both states to re-explore a more substantial economic relationship; however, the fragility and unpredictability of Russia's economic performance leaves medium- and long-term future joint endeavours beyond the defence and nuclear sectors uncertain.

This is particularly so as India builds further content into its 'Look East' policy and explores more meaningful ties with Asian partners, and as it capitalizes on strong links with the US private sector. Indeed, India's end-user agreement with the USA provides India easier (although not unlimited) access to the US arms market, a development that might undercut Russia's most lucrative area of cooperation with India.[52] However, while Western partners have proved to be volatile in the past (for example, the sanctions placed by the USA on India after the 1998 Pokhran II nuclear tests), Moscow has proven itself to be a reliable (if sometimes unexciting) weapons supplier, and is likely to remain an attractive partner for India, if only as a hedge against Indian over-reliance on others.[53]

Defence procurement

India's reliance on Russian military hardware has continued over the last two decades since the dissolution of the USSR. And for Russia, India is an important client. Table 10.5 indicates that India is still Russia's second largest customer for conventional weapons exports, after China.

Russia is also, by a vast margin, India's primary supplier of conventional systems, confirming the strength of the weapons procurement relationship. This is illustrated in Table 10.6.

Recently, India has used its long-standing relationship with Russia to acquire weapons platforms intended to bolster India's power projection capability. For instance, India has purchased the *Admiral Gorshkov* (now INS *Vikramaditya*) aircraft carrier and SU-30MK long-range fighter aircraft, and is set to lease an *Akula* class nuclear attack submarine once it is delivered to the Russian Navy.[54] In addition to power projection platforms, India has also purchased two series of Russian T-90 main battle tanks, the first in 2001 for an estimated US$700 million, and the second in late 2007 for US$1.2 billion.[55] These substantial Indian purchases indicate that the Indo-Russian defence relationship continues to be significant for both parties involved.

Russia's position as the dominant supplier of India's weapons is, however, being challenged by the American government, backed by the entrepreneurial US defence industry.[56] Indeed the United States may be slowly changing the Indian arms procurement equation, not least by becoming more involved with the Indian military across the services in joint operations and planning. With this shift, India's procurement of military hardware that is compatible with US systems makes increasing sense, and is a requirement that US companies are perfectly happy to satisfy.[57] Lockheed Martin recently signed a deal with the Indian Air Force to provide six C-130 Hercules transport aircraft, and Northrop

Table 10.5. Suppliers of Major Conventional Weapons

Supplier	Share of global arms exports (%)	Main recipients (share of supplier's transfers)
USA	31	South Korea (15%) Israel (13%) UAE (11%)
Russia	25	China (42%) India (21%) Algeria (8%)
Germany	10	Turkey (15%) Greece (13%) South Africa (12%)
France	8	UAE (32%) Singapore (13%) Greece (12%)
UK	4	USA (21%) India (14%) Chile (9%)

Source: Appendix 7A, SIPRI Yearbook 2009.

Table 10.6. Recipients of Major Conventional Weapons

Recipient	Share of global arms imports (%)	Main supplier (share of recipient's transfers)
China	11	Russia (92%)
India	7	Russia (71%)
UAE	6	USA (54%)
South Korea	6	USA (73%)
Greece	4	Germany (31%)

Source: Appendix 7A, SIPRI Yearbook 2009.

is seeking an export agreement from the US government in order to provide India the E2D Hawkeye airborne early warning and control system (AWACS).[58] European competitors are also challenging Russia on some significant Indian procurement projects. Following a deal signed in 2005, France has provided India with licenses to build six Scorpene class diesel submarines and has transferred a number of SM-39 Exocet missiles.[59]

The most significant albatross in the Indo-Russian defence relationship is the Russian failure to provide India with the refitted *Gorshkov* aircraft carrier on time and for the originally agreed price. The project has gone vastly over both deadline and budget, with the programme now costing India more than if it had acquired a new aircraft carrier from Russian competitors.[60] Indian naval officers and the Indian government have complained about the matter sharply and publicly, and it has done Russia's reputation as a supplier little good in India and beyond.

More subtly, India and Russia tend to have different outlooks on the use of military means to achieve global influence and to project power. Russia has shown an inclination for pre-emptive or first-strike military operations such as those in Chechnya and more recently against Georgia. With the exception of the 1971 war culminating in the independence of Bangladesh, India has mostly responded to attack rather than taking the initiative.

Political values

India's political values evince deep attachment to liberal constitutional democracy, in contrast to Russia's increasingly tenuous rule of law and the unattractive state of its politics to most outsiders (Vladimir Putin's domestic popularity to date notwithstanding). India and Russia might well have clashed at times over political values or over Russia's aggressive tactics against Georgia in South Ossetia in 2008. However, India's strong attachment to classic conceptions of the absolute sovereignty of states and its commitment (in most instances, particularly outside its immediate neighbourhood) to non-interference in the internal affairs of other states—diplomatic predispositions shared by Moscow—have saved the partners from the inconvenience of any public criticism of each other's policies.

Significant efforts were made during the Cold War to promote broad-based ties between the two countries. Typically, these ties took the form of Indo-Soviet 'Societies of Friendship and Cultural Relations'.[61] But, with time and a shifting outlook among Indians (and also Russians), government-driven efforts to promote friendship between the two populations seem both dated and redundant.

The ties of political (and wider) culture between India and Western Europe do not extend in quite the same way to Russia. During the Cold War years, many Indians received high-quality scientific education in Russia, and India benefited significantly. Nowadays, Indians going abroad are more drawn to Western, particularly US, British and Australian universities than Russian ones, with some also favouring leading Asian institutions, including in China and Singapore. Thus, while the habit of political dialogue and the comfort of a long-standing relationship between Delhi and Moscow should not be discounted, at the level of popular culture, Russia is now largely absent from India.

Energy interests

While India looks to Europe for long-term cooperation in reforming its energy sector, it looks to Russia to help satisfy its immediate and growing need for imported oil and natural gas. India increasingly relies on energy imports and Russia possesses a large surplus. The benefits of these complementary circumstances have already begun to be exploited by India. Its US

$1.77 billion investment in the Sakhalin I project yielded its first shipments to India, amounting to over 600,000 barrels of oil, in November 2006.[62] India is vigorously pursuing further measures with Russia such as involvement in the Sakhalin III project and a possible joint exploration venture with Gazprom in exchange for a guarantee to buy 50 million tons of Russian oil per annum.[63]

Russia has also been a valuable partner for India on the nuclear front, helping India to pursue its strategic goal of energy diversity. Russian technical assistance contributed greatly to the completion of two nuclear reactors at Koodankulum, and in late 2008 the two governments signed a further agreement under which Russia will build four more reactors for Indian use.[64] In addition to this, Russia agreed to sell $700 million worth of uranium fuel to India for use in its reactors.[65]

Beyond energy security, a significant geopolitical calculus is involved in India's energy romance with Russia. India hopes that Russia can help it secure greater reach into and political influence in Central Asia (including several former Soviet republics), which, in the future, will likely be the route for several major oil and natural gas pipelines of potential interest to India. Tanvi Madan writes:

> While India wants to be part of the 'new great game', it is being careful not to step on any toes—especially influential Russian ones—in the region. Central Asian countries might view India's entry as the addition of an alternate player. But

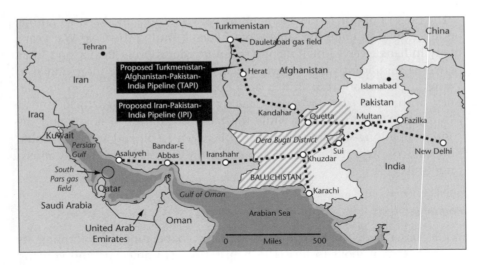

Figure 10.1. Two Proposed Pipelines in South Asia

Source: Ariel Cohen, Lisa Curtis and Owen Graham, 'The Proposed Iran-Pakistan-India Gas Pipeline: An Unacceptable Risk to Regional Security', *Backgrounder #2139* (Washington, DC: The Heritage Foundation, 30 May 2008).

India believes that it needs Russia's cooperation—or at least acquiescence—to be successful in the region.[66]

The geopolitical game over pipelines in India's extended neighbourhood is already a lively one for Delhi. The proposed Iran-Pakistan-India (IPI) pipeline (illustrated in Figure 10.1) that was to have taken natural gas from Iran's plentiful gas fields and pumped it into Pakistan and India has been a confusingly off-and-on affair with India sending many mixed signals over time, some apparently related to its nuclear negotiations with the USA during the years 2005–8.[67]

Indian participation in the project seems to have been put on hold, amongst other reasons, because of India and Iran's inability to find common ground on the price India should pay for Iranian gas and the structure of the deal.[68] Reported Russian interest in the IPI project could relate to its dislike of a possible alternative favoured by the USA.[69] The US-backed competing Turkmenistan-Afghanistan-Pakistan-India (TAPI) pipeline, would cut Iran, currently under mild UN but stringent US sanctions, out of the deal while simultaneously increasing America's influence in the region over Russia's.[70] While US influence will not determine India's policy, increasing Indo-US cooperation on nuclear and defence matters makes the American viewpoint difficult for Delhi to ignore altogether.[71]

As part of its widening geostrategic lens, India has taken an increasing interest in partnerships with Central Asian states outside of the energy sector, and Russia's acquiescence, often for a price, is grudgingly necessary in these manoeuvres. Tajikistan, one of India's important Central Asian partners is home to India's first external military airbase at Ayni.[72] Tajikistan is strategically important for India, sharing borders with two states that raise strategic concerns for India: China and Afghanistan.[73] The relationship was recently highlighted through Indian President Patil's visit to Dushanbe in September 2009.[74] India is also studying the potential of resurrecting a version of the Silk Route to increase trade between Central Asia and the Indian subcontinent.[75]

India and the Central Asian Republics share perspectives and concerns in many areas including counterterrorism, counter-narcotics, and small arms proliferation; these concerns are, of course, aggravated for all parties by the persistence of instability in Afghanistan and the northwestern regions of Pakistan.[76] Pakistan, because of the dominance of Islam in Central Asia, may see the region as an obvious bet for the expansion of its influence.[77] However, several Central Asian governments, fearful of Islamic radicalism and wary of the close ties between Pakistani militants and organizations such as the Islamic Movement of Uzbekistan (IMU), are increasingly turning to India to form a unified front against violent Islamist movements which Pakistan's government currently seems unable to curb. This was attested to by the generally unified front exhibited at the October 2009 meeting of the Shanghai Cooperation Organization consisting of several Central Asian states, Russia, and China, with India and others as observers.[78] India made a point of highlighting the necessity of counterterrorism cooperation, a point with which all of the member governments would have agreed.[79]

Russia and India can establish common cause in promoting stability in Central Asia. Both would benefit from energy pipeline projects through the region that would not be importuned by violence and criminality, and both wish to see the influence of radical Islam diminish. If these actors can build on these shared energy and security interests, India's presence and influence in Central Asia could grow without necessarily irritating China.

Afghanistan

Afghanistan became a prominent topic during summit talks between Indian Prime Minister Singh and Russian Prime Minister Putin in Delhi in March 2010, with India reportedly expressing fears arising from an increasingly possible NATO withdrawal. Some Western voices have suggested that in such an eventuality, India could revive its former relationship with a re-energized 'northern alliance' in Afghanistan, buttressed by Russia and perhaps Iran, leading to a soft or more formal partition of the country in due course. Most Indian geostrategic analysts deplore this line of thinking (not least because it concedes to Pakistani influence at least 40 per cent of Afghanistan, including the capital, Kabul), but it cannot be dismissed given the unpromising alternative options available to Delhi were the Taliban to take power (or meaningfully share it) in Kabul.[80]

Russia and Europe in the middle

The geostrategic positions of India's potential partners

Both the European Union and Russia find themselves in flux in the current global environment, with economic performance, and, in the case of the European Union, a sense of shared purpose, very much in question. How the Europeans and Russians manage these challenges will determine their future relationship with a rising India as much as India's own preferences and policies. India has for some time been pursuing both a closer strategic relationship with the USA, as exemplified by their negotiations towards nuclear cooperation; and, in a less focused way, with China and the Pacific region, as heralded in India's 'Look East' policy. Likewise, India's interests in and engagement with the Middle East have also been growing and hold significant potential, as suggested by a growing Indo-Israeli security partnership and Indian economic relations with the Persian Gulf states.

All this, however, leaves Europe and, to a somewhat lesser extent, Russia in a middle ground between India's regional and global strategic priorities. While Russia has great potential to engage India over energy, its own political and economic roller-coaster, and its strained relations with several of the Central Asian states, leave Russia in a still uncertain position to fulfil India's desiderata in a full strategic partnership of the sort the two countries had enjoyed during earlier decades.

The early twenty-first century is witnessing what is likely the beginning of a role reversal for India and Russia. The transition to a form of democracy and the end of the Soviet Union has been painful for Russia, while increased global integration and the end of a bi-polar global power structure has worked wonders for India in many respects. These developments have produced new ordering in the global power hierarchy for India and Russia, the former rising quite fast but from a limited subregional base, the latter stagnating or, in some views, declining. Russian and Indian interests do not clash. For this reason, the relationship between the two countries should not be unduly affected by the tectonic shifts in geostrategic advantage. But the relationship is not likely to regain the convergence of positioning witnessed in the mid-Cold War years.

Western Europe, while theoretically and to a large degree technically unified through the European Union, is still encumbered by the independent personalities of its leading member States, which have not hesitated to undermine pretensions of a common foreign policy when it suited them to do so (or simply when they wished to demonstrate they could do so). While India has engaged with the EU on several impressive formal diplomatic initiatives, substantive results are few to date.

The position of being caught in the 'middle ground' between India's major foreign policy priorities makes pretty well anything to do with Western Europe less urgent geostrategically for India than much else. Christophe Jaffrelot wrote as early as 2006:

> It is disappointing to find that the European Union hardly figures on the Indian 'radar screen', despite tangible efforts to relaunch cooperation between the two political entities. If remedial action is not undertaken quickly, Europe may well find itself completely sidelined by this new first order Asian—and indeed international—actor.[81]

Meaningful engagement should not be impossible, since both Europe and Russia have significant interests in common with India. And, in the case of Russia, there is much habit of regular high-level consultation. However, the ability of each to achieve a genuine strategic relationship with India (as opposed to an essentially mercantile one) is constrained by the uncertain prospects of Russian economic development and of the European integration process.

India's preference for interest-based bilateralism

Because of the EU's continuing internal incoherence, a factor which slows serious EU diplomatic initiatives to a crawl, India has been most comfortable continuing to engage European states on a bilateral basis, focusing on those capitals that can deliver significant results (for example, Paris in the realm of defence and nuclear issues).[82] An assessment by Eric Gonsalves of Indo-European relations, although written almost two decades ago, still rings generally true today:

> The gradual decline of the role of the European countries in Asia despite the coming into being of the European Community and their gradual reduction to becoming an appendage within the Western alliance... made the interaction between India and Western Europe basically secondary in nature and centred on bilateral concerns...[83]

India may invest even greater effort into strengthening its bilateral ties with major European states (and possibly multilateral ties with the EU, if the latter can prove more agile) should a perception arise that the current US administration is increasingly courting China. Evan Feigenbaum points out that Indian fears of a US–China 'G-2' are based on reasonable concerns in Delhi that such a relationship could embolden China in the still-unresolved border disputes between the two countries and, where possible, to undercut Indian economic influence.[84] Were this to happen, India might well turn to Europe in an effort to maintain balance and diversity in its foreign policy (an option equally applicable to Russia). However, attempts to forge a G-2 power bloc are today highly speculative.[85]

Ratification of the EU's Lisbon Treaty introducing a number of constitutional and structural changes, including the creation of an EU President and of a foreign policy czar, was intended in part to enhance the EU's standing on the global stage. However, the significance of these developments in 2009 for India (and much of the world) was seriously undermined by the appointment of Belgian Prime Minister Herman Van Rompuy, self-described as a 'grey mouse', and the little-known EU Trade Commissioner, Baroness Catherine Ashton, as EU President and High Representative for Foreign Affairs respectively. Both were seen as low-common-denominator compromise candidates who posed little threat to the leading member states. Indian commentators were unimpressed, as were, privately, Indian political figures.[86]

Perhaps the most important multilateral diplomatic engagement of 2009 occurred in Copenhagen on climate change. West European countries had long argued that in view of their rapid economic growth, India and China needed to offer national commitments towards global goals (which the Kyoto Protocol of 1998 had not required of them). However, to the consternation of many Europeans and possibly the quiet satisfaction of Delhi, EU members found themselves marginalized in the key negotiation, involving only Brazil, China, India, South Africa, and the USA on the final day of the meeting. This surprising development and the resulting weak conference outcome were widely interpreted as highlighting the relative eclipse of Western Europe's prominence on this key global issue.[87] Thus, while India could pride itself on having played a leading role, and an unusually conciliatory one at that (allowing China to serve as a punching bag for activists and other critics), the under-performance by the EU was evident to all.[88] Several Indian commentators saw events at Copenhagen as heralding a decline in the multi-lateral fabric, not necessarily to the disadvantage of India's interests.[89] Indian legal scholar Poorvi Chitalkar comments: 'India's often instrumentalist take on multilateral relations rooted in its national interest may in fact equip it well for an enhanced role in major upcoming negotiations on global issues, where give and take among a few key countries likewise disposed will determine the outcome.'

India has unsurprisingly continued to pursue a bilateral relationship with Russia, strongly anchored in India's interests. Delhi has, over the last two decades, pursued Russia as a constantly available supplier of cheap albeit relatively sophisticated weapons systems, and of energy. However, India has increasingly been looking to diversify, especially in defence, to the detriment of Russia's export potential, but potentially to the benefit of West European competitors.[90] As Anuradha Chenoy argues, the 'old model' Indo-Russian relationship is on its way out, yielding to a relationship that is more fluid, one allowing India to design more varied regional and global policies consist-ent with its new global economic position.[91] Thus, Russia's relations with a rising India are similar to those of Western Europe: each partner in these relationships must become accustomed to a new balance in which India plays a more prominent role.

Russia, recently the post-Cold War 'black hole' of global power, appears to be making some sustained progress in restoring its global standing. And, on balance, this very much suits India's vision of a multipolar world where India can engage a number of essentially equal major powers, each with its own particularities, strengths, and weaknesses. During his visit to Delhi in March 2010, Prime Minister Putin emphasized how much in the technological and military procurement fields Russia may still have to offer India, and also high-lighted Russia's significance for Central Asia, an area in which India's interest continues to grow.[92] The history of friendly relations between India and Russia will serve each well in helping Moscow and Delhi to navigate the complexities of a relationship in which a significant realignment of power is occurring.

Conclusions

Although there are substantial differences between the Indo-EU and the Indo-Russian relationships, there are common current and potential interests that act as 'drivers' of India's interactions with each, defence and energy among them. While India's international profile is rising, those of Western Europe and the Russian Federation are stagnating or declining for varying demographic, economic, and geostrategic reasons. For all of Russia's oil and gas reserves, its troubled emergence from the communist era, marked by uncertain rule of law, confounding economic management, and bullying behaviour towards some of its close neighbours, has left it with an international reputation for touchiness, unreliability, and a proclivity for both diplomatic and economic brinkmanship.

Western Europe, home to all of the world's major colonial powers, and very much the 'centre of the world' in the nineteenth century, but then undermined by two devastating world wars in the twentieth century, has increasingly found itself caught in between an American superpower and a rising Asia today encompassing two very significant potential competitors, China and India. However, the ability of the European powers to maintain both internal unity and external effectiveness today on the global stage is, at best, a work in progress. Until a more convincing formula can be devised by EU member states to empower their common institutions, possibly through strong implementation of the Lisbon Treaty over time, the EU's full potential is likely to remain unrealized. And, on an individual basis, it is unlikely that any of the EU member states, with some exceptions in niche issues and products, will be able to play a role comparable to that of China or India globally over the long-term on current trends.

Indeed, by the end of 2009 a new world order seemed to be emerging, with the USA, China, India, and Russia in the vanguard, Brazil near behind, and the West European countries struggling to define how their economic weight might again be translated into international influence and geostrategic power. Although India itself is beyond the reach of such behaviour today, bullying financial policies of the UK and the Netherlands towards non-EU member Iceland between 2008 and 2010 and Germany's less-than-spontaneously generous stance over Greece's financial plight (however self-induced) in early 2010 may conjure up unpleasant memories for a country which spent so many decades under European colonial rule. One prominent ambassador of an EU member state in Delhi remarks:

One would like to believe that India and the European Union should naturally draw close. Ideally, they would see each other as rising powers, each open to supporting the emergence of the other. In reality, however, each has a tendency to look to the most powerful poles in international relations rather than towards each other, and each spends more time deploring the shortcomings of the other rather than building the foundations of future partnership.[93]

Russia remains in a precarious geopolitical and economic position, which inevitably affects its relationship with India. While in recent years economic prospects for Russia have improved (along with rising prices for oil and gas), the collapse of the USSR entailed tremendous costs to self-confidence, geostrategic heft, and national cohesion, as low-level conflicts in Chechnya, Ingushetia, and Ossetia attest. After a brief romance with wildcat capitalism, mainly notable for the rise of the oligarch class, Russia is still in search of a model of economic development that can wean it away from over-reliance on hydrocarbons and provide the quality of life for its citizens that the EU countries deliver for theirs. Less aggressive diplomacy with its Western neighbours in future decades could, in fact, lead to greater influence internationally by creating common cause between the Western European powers and Moscow on a number of issues (as seemed plausible during the Gorbachev and Yeltsin eras). But its domestic political, economic, social, and foreign policy development may yet hold a number of unsettling surprises ahead, much as the rest of the world would prefer otherwise.

Thus, even though the Russian Federation remains a significant military and geostrategic actor, the relatively modest size and questionable management of its economy exert a drag on its overall credibility and influence. Any Russian resurgence is unlikely to restore it fully to superpower status, not least, as with Japan, because of its disastrous demographic profile with a rapidly aging and shrinking population. However, Russia will remain a major regional power, influencing its own vast neighbourhood spanning Europe and Asia, notably in Central Asia and in the Caucasus, and seeking to further its own interests through such influence. Occasionally this will mean rubbing up against the EU and even the USA in the latter region, and possibly against China in some of the former. But friction with India seems unlikely for reasons of geographical distance and broadly compatible foreign policy philosophy.

Overall, the Indo-Russian and Indo-European relationships are in gentle decline compared to some others, not least in the trade sphere, because of India's rise but also because Western Europe to some degree, and certainly Russia, find themselves in a position of some economic uncertainty and of geopolitical flux. And while India also is in flux, it enjoys economic tailwinds producing economic momentum and hence greater international credibility than the absolute figures would argue for.

These relationships will likely continue to be defined by the key interests of India, mainly in private sector development, defence, and energy. Unlike India's relationships with China and the USA, Delhi may well find itself becoming the dominant partner. However, this scenario will take time to unfold and is not pre-ordained, involving as it does a number of currently imponderable factors relating to each of the EU, Russia, and India, not least involving the domestic realities produced by their complex political systems.

11

The Evolution of Indian Multilateralism: From High Ground to High Table

The path to international recognition and respect has not been an easy one for India. A lack of material resources and military capability prevented post-independence India from staking a credible claim to its place in the 'diplomatic sun'.[1] The Cold War offered shelter through alliances but threatened India's newfound independence, which it was unwilling to compromise, at least in principle. During those early years, India turned to multilateral forums as a way of magnifying its influence, *faute de mieux*.

From idealist moralizer to often-pragmatic dealmaker, India's transition within multilateral diplomacy mirrors its rise—second only to China—from the confines of severe poverty and underdevelopment. India's voice carries more weight today in multilateral forums largely due to its enhanced economic performance, political stability, and nuclear capability. Although many of its internal problems—including ethnic separatism, insurgency, poverty, inequality, minority rights, corruption, and poor governance—remain only partially addressed, on the international stage India now exerts real if still tentative geostrategic and economic influence. The assertion that 'the world concludes that India is a "predictable player" with enduring national interests'[2] may be premature, but major powers in the international system are eager today to engage with India.

As India's stature has grown, its stake in some forms of multilateralism has diminished. In several international forums, India increasingly engages with smaller groups of powerful nations to affect outcomes at the expense of the more broad-based universalist approach it traditionally espoused (or claimed to) in multilateral forums. India also today often prefers conducting business bilaterally with major actors such as the United States, China, the EU, Japan, and Russia. In organizations rooted in solidarity between members, such as the Non-Aligned Movement, and even in the Commonwealth (of which

Kamalesh Sharma, an Indian, became Secretary-General in 2009) India of late has seemed somewhat detached.

India's growing predilection for global governance by oligarchy—be it as part of the Five Interested Parties in the World Trade Organization (WTO), the BASIC (Brazil, South Africa, India, China) group at the Copenhagen climate change negotiations of 2009, or the G-4 coalition of countries (Brazil, Germany, India, Japan) demanding permanent membership in the United Nations Security Council (UNSC)—is striking as is its experimentation with a number of new groupings, often excluding the Western powers. Ironically, by eschewing genuine multilateralism in favour of power elites and strategic partnerships, India is buying into a strategy developed largely by the United States, Russia, China, and several West European powers to co-manage international economic and, to a lesser degree, security systems. However, India has not yet displayed that it is willing to assume much responsibility within these systems (as opposed to bilaterally with some states). Further, its shift to adopting the attitudes of a self-interested power focused overwhelmingly on economic prosperity for itself (however it seeks to dress up this position rhetorically) jars with its traditions. Public opinion in India may well be ready for this transition, but it is unclear whether much of India's establishment is.

The rest of this chapter first traces the evolution of India's approach to multilateralism over the last six decades, and then focuses on four substantive fields of foreign policy or forums of significance to India's multilateral stance during this period of global (and Indian) transition and flux: the UNSC; the WTO and its Doha Round negotiations culminating in 2008; international efforts to combat climate change, notably prior to and at the Copenhagen UN conference of late 2009; and some emerging international groupings of states in which India is playing an active role or seeking to.

From High Ground to High Table

Post-independence India immediately became an active participant in the multilateral system, at that time composed largely of the UN and its associated organizations. In spite of its status as a British colony, India had gained original membership of both the United Nations and its predecessor, the League of Nations. It also rapidly adhered to the many institutions associated with the UN, including the IMF and World Bank, and also some others such as the General Agreement on Tariffs and Trade (GATT).

The philosophy embodied in the UN Charter resonated deeply with independent India. In September 1946, Nehru professed 'unreserved adherence, in both spirit and letter' to the UN Charter and committed to 'play that role in [UN] councils to which [India's] geographical position, population and contribution towards peaceful progress entitle her'.[3] Parts of the Indian Constitution that laid out the principles of state policy with regard to international affairs reflected noticeably the principles of the UN Charter extolling the promotion of peace and security, international law, and settlement of international disputes through arbitration.[4]

Kashmir, 1947–8

However, Delhi experienced a major setback at the UN on the issue of Kashmir in the winter of 1947. Faced with the choice of unilaterally repelling the Pakistani attack and militarily consolidating India's hold on the erstwhile princely state, or referring the matter to the UN, Nehru chose the latter option. Much to his disappointment, the United States and Britain—both exercising considerable influence in the UNSC—failed to endorse India's claim to Kashmir, instead insisting on a plebiscite of the state's population. India realized belatedly that 'the Security Council was a strictly political body and that decisions were taken by its members on the basis of their perspective of their national interest and not on the merits of any particular case'.[5]

The Kashmir episode permanently coloured Indian thinking on the United Nations. Since then India has been loath to allow any form of multilateral intervention, not just in Kashmir but in the South Asian region, much of which it regards as its sphere of influence, more generally.[6] Pakistan's consistent efforts to internationalize the Kashmir issue at the UN (and elsewhere) doubtless contributed to India's growing preference for bilateralism over multilateralism.[7] And India's strong attachment to the primacy of state sovereignty in the conduct of its international relations owes much to this early trauma.

Non-alignment

In spite of the UN's position on Kashmir, India recognized two basic advantages offered by multilateralism in the age of superpower rivalry as the Cold War developed. The first is summed up by the proposition that 'the political game must be played in such a manner that India in spite of her political weakness could establish a politically strategic position'.[8] The second was protection of India's independence through the attainment of international influence. Dhiraj Chamling wrote: 'Tensely surrounded by a galaxy of big, industrially-developed powers to one of which interests she could easily fall a prey, the only possible defence for India perhaps was to get vigorously involved in the affairs of the UN.'[9]

Nehru's foreign policy of non-alignment relative to the two power blocs of the Cold War era was a rational response to India's circumstances and the intense polarization of international relations as of the late 1940s. He described it as 'the natural consequence of an independent nation functioning according to its own rights'.[10] The policy was not simply one of neutrality, both Nehru and his foreign policy *eminence grise*, V. K. Krishna Menon, maintained, the latter remarking at the UN, 'there can no more be positive neutrality than there can be a vegetarian tiger'.[11] He asserted that India was not neutral between war and peace, between imperialism and freedom, or on questions of ethics.

For India, non-alignment was therefore a policy that stressed independence in international decision-making above all else. Strategically, non-alignment implied 'adjustment to both sides, all the time, obstinately defending and projecting genuine independence, the real power to choose and not be compelled to accept the policies of other states rooted in their national interests'.[12]

Non-alignment in principle rejected military alliances, especially those with the two superpower blocs, and emphasized friendly relations with all countries.[13] In the UN, this prompted India to push for as broad a membership base as possible (the growth coming from newly decolonized states) and to work to preclude either bloc from appropriating the organization's agenda and resources. This was why India at every opportunity advocated UN membership for the People's Republic of China despite Western reluctance to include a revolutionary communist country. It also explains India's early defence of the veto in the UNSC: 'India prefers an ineffective organization, representing all the major political elements in the international community, to an effective organization which may grow into an instrument of one power bloc.'[14] Thus, India opposed the 1950 Acheson Plan, also known as the 'Uniting for Peace' resolution, which empowered the UN General Assembly to act on security challenges at times when the UNSC was in deadlock.

When war broke out in Korea, India initially endorsed UN intervention but declined to label China an aggressor or support the crossing of UN troops into North Korea. (India committed not troops but a field ambulance unit to the UN effort.) Increasingly, during the 1950s, India was seen as an actively neutral power as between Moscow and Washington. This created new roles for it. At the end of the Korean war, Indian General K. S. Thimayya was Chairman of the UN's Neutral Nations Repatriation Commission that oversaw the repatriation of prisoners of war from both sides. India adopted an equidistant stance at the Geneva Indo-China conference of 1954, eventually serving with Poland and Canada (as the two aligned members) on the International Control Commission monitoring implementation of the undertakings agreed at Geneva.[15] India was a 'champion of pacific settlement of disputes' at the UN, contributing generously to peacekeeping missions in the Suez Canal and the Congo, fielding the highest number of troops in both cases.[16]

However, India was criticized in the West for applying double standards: 'On the one hand, the Government of India intensely desired to bring about a change in the political system of the world by supporting all kinds of anti-colonial and anti-imperialist movements, while on the other when faced with a real situation India supported the maintenance of status quo in the name of peace.'[17] For example, although India was a vociferous critic of Dutch rule in Indonesia, it was (at least overtly) less hostile to the French in Indo-China and the British in Malaysia. Indian decision-makers (essentially Nehru), not unreasonably, reserved to themselves the right to judge each case on its merits, and rhetorically drew a fine distinction between nationalist and communist movements to explain any perceived inconsistency in their positions. (Nehru was sensitive to China's support for communist movements in Indo-China and Malaysia.) Eventually, India's judgement did seem to falter: its failure to condemn the Soviet invasion of Hungary in 1956 (while decrying Western military involvement on the side of Israel in the Suez crisis of the same year) led to perceptions, which were to prove lasting, in the West of Indian duplicity.

Third World leadership

Near-universal decolonization was in many ways the perfect foil for India's international ambitions. As more Asian and African countries gained independence, India, which had blazed a spectacular trail in seeing off Western colonizers, began to assume a leadership role among former colonies and spent considerable diplomatic resources cultivating their support. For example, in 1954, India pressed successfully for special provisions in the GATT for developing countries looking to protect their nascent economies from international competition.[18] Many of these countries found non-alignment to be a useful organizing principle for foreign policy, if not in guaranteeing freedom from foreign influence, at least in leveraging superpower competition for greater economic aid from both blocs.

The Non-Aligned Movement (NAM) emerged out of initial consultations between the leaders of Egypt, India, and Yugoslavia at Brioni, Yugoslavia, in 1956. The first summit of twenty-five non-aligned nations was held in Belgrade in September 1961. However, Nehru himself was never entirely in favour of forming a global movement (or third bloc) based on non-alignment (which to him was primarily India's national policy toward the world).[19] C. Raja Mohan notes: 'The NAM often complemented India's pursuit of its international objectives but never fully supplanted non-alignment', which was India's foreign policy.[20]

By the early 1960s, India began to realize that, through strength in numbers, former colonies of the Third World could exercise considerable sway within international institutions. As a result, it lobbied for the expansion of the

UNSC, and was influential in the creation of the G-77 group of developing countries that remains active to this day on economic and social issues within the UN system alongside the group of NAM countries that address political questions.[21]

India's relationship with the NAM suffered a setback in 1962, with the Sino-Indian War. When China invaded, ostensibly to overturn India's border claims originating from the colonial era, there was little overt support for India from the Third World. Only forty countries responded positively to Nehru's international appeal for China to be declared an aggressor in November 1962, of which only three were from the group of twenty-five non-aligned countries at the time (Ethiopia, Cyprus, and Sri Lanka).[22] Even more disorienting for India's foreign policy inclinations was the immediate support from countries of the Western bloc during this episode. The USA dispatched a fleet to the Bay of Bengal—only to recall it upon China's unexpected withdrawal following a month's fighting. Nevertheless, some observers ironically recalled Nehru's own original thought that the non-aligned should be non-aligned not just with the power blocs, but also with each other.[23] This exasperated Nehru and commentators in India.

Nevertheless, India continued to play an active role in the UN and the NAM. Delhi during the 1960s contributed significantly to the establishment of the United Nations Conference on Trade and Development (UNCTAD) and the United Nations Industrial Development Organization (UNIDO).[24] In 1963, pressure by India and others yielded institutional changes that expanded the UNSC and the Economic and Social Council to give African and Asian countries more representation.[25]

A global and Indian hiatus

The year 1964 was a significant one for India. In October, China conducted its first nuclear test at Lop Nor, prompting India to advocate through the NAM summit in Cairo the inclusion of non-proliferation on the UN's agenda for the first time. But dwarfing all other developments that year for India was the passing of Jawaharlal Nehru, who had scripted and overseen the implementation of the bulk of India's policies toward the world since independence. Following his death, India remained only as engaged in the UN and NAM as to allow it to frustrate Pakistan's attempts to isolate it multilaterally over their bilateral disputes. Commenting on the Nehruvian era, Siddharth Varadarajan recalls that Nehru was not driven by 'abstract principles' alone, but rather was engaged in a quest for 'strategic space' for which he was dealt a very weak hand in 1947.[26] Srinath Raghavan's important recent work on Nehru's strategic thought and foreign policy also severely qualifies a view of Nehru as primarily an idealist.[27]

Nehru's successors, especially his daughter, Indira Gandhi, after 1966, articulated prominent, sometimes forceful, strains of *realpolitik* in their domestic and international dealings. India and Pakistan went to war in 1965, evoking a mixed response from the non-aligned countries, with more of them supporting Pakistan than India in part because of religious affinity. India was once again disappointed (but this time not surprised) by the lack of a response from the non-aligned nations. By 1969 an Indian minister was heard to declare, 'We have no friends, by sermonizing to everybody on what to do or not to do we have alienated all. All the nonaligned countries are afraid to stand up and be counted.'[28] India's profile in international organizations sharply declined in the 1960s.[29]

The relative eclipse of multilateralism in Delhi's worldview and strategies conformed to a broader pattern. Overall, the multilateral system took a back seat for over two decades after the Cold War intensified in the 1960s. Largely sidelined on security issues and in important international crises, the UN turned its attention to socio-economic, environmental, technological, and cultural issues.[30] In the NAM, India's engagement became 'general, rhetorical, and distant'.[31] But India, a champion of technical cooperation for development, contributed the largest number of technical experts under UN auspices of any member state between 1951 and 1967.[32]

Strategic departures

The nadir of India's engagement with the United Nations and some other multilateral groupings came in 1971. As the USA undertook a rapprochement with China, with Pakistan acting as facilitator, India intervened in East Pakistan on humanitarian and strategic grounds, against the atrocities committed by the Pakistani army on their Bengali compatriots. The resulting war brought about the independence of East Pakistan as Bangladesh. India was roundly criticized in the UN and the NAM for intervening in what was legally a matter within the domestic jurisdiction of Pakistan. Despite the millions of Bengali refugees that had crossed the border into India during the conflict, Delhi found itself almost entirely isolated in the international community. With hindsight, India's stance in 1971, while a self-serving one insofar as it allowed the breakup of its enduring antagonist Pakistan, should have evoked more sympathy within the NAM and among Western powers, given the extreme circumstances occasioned by Pakistan's violent repression of the East Bengali provinces ordered by its military leader, Yahya Khan. But in an age unfamiliar with and unsympathetic towards humanitarian intervention, India's actions were seen primarily as aimed at dismembering a member state of the UN. India escaped official censure by the UN solely because of the Soviet veto in the UNSC, further to the Treaty of Friendship signed by Delhi and Moscow earlier in 1971. And because of this treaty India, having aligned itself on the USSR, could expect little support from NAM.[33] For the first time, India had eschewed 'diplomacy by conference' and opted for unilateral military action.

Delhi went on, in 1974, to conduct its first nuclear test, disregarding the non-proliferation regime that India itself had championed just a decade earlier. In defending its action, the Indian government described the test as a peaceful nuclear explosion, and argued it was not in violation of the Non-Proliferation Treaty (NPT), which it had never signed on the grounds that it was unfairly biased toward the established nuclear powers. However, former foreign secretary J. N. Dixit acknowledges that the test was at least in part intended to provide the scientific basis for a future nuclear weapons programme.[34] And the established nuclear powers were entirely unconvinced by India's rationale. This test prompted the establishment by a number of states with nuclear capacities of the Nuclear Suppliers Group (NSG), intending to control export of nuclear materials and technologies to states posing a risk to the Nuclear Non-Proliferation regime. The launch of this group and its subsequent ascendency alongside the International Atomic Energy Agency (IAEA) consigned India to a type of diplomatic *purdah* in the field of arms control and disarmament that was to dog its diplomacy and international image until its successful negotiations with the USA on nuclear cooperation, culminating in 2008. It then also convinced the NSG to approve (unanimously, as required within this forum) a new approach to safeguards on nuclear transfers to India.[35] Nuclear parity with China had been India's unspoken objective in the lead-up to the 1974 test, but, whatever the aim, the international community was wholly unsympathetic at the time.

During the 1980s, the Soviet invasion of Afghanistan, Vietnam's invasion of Cambodia, and the Iran–Iraq war all created divisions in the UN as well as within the NAM. India, which was noticeably ambivalent on Moscow's move into Afghanistan (opposed on substance, but mindful of its alliance with the USSR), grew further estranged from the NAM. In 1987, India intervened in another NAM country's internal affairs by air-dropping food into Tamil areas of Sri Lanka, under domestic political pressure in the Indian state of Tamil Nadu to aid the population there, caught in a rise between the LTTE and Colombo.

By the end of the decade, Cold War tensions eased and rapprochement between the United States and the Soviet Union, as well as China and the Soviet Union, reinvigorated the UN as a forum for multilateral cooperation on security issues.[36] In this spirit, in 1988 at a special session of the UN General Assembly, Rajiv Gandhi put forward an ambitious proposal for nuclear disarmament in a phased manner.[37]

Adjusting to a new world

Post-Cold War, the UNSC became considerably more active than it had been over the previous two decades.[38] The 1990s also saw a major increase in the number of peacekeeping missions, to which India contributed generously.[39] The rest of the multilateral system also thrived, with the exciting 1992 Rio Summit on climate change that agreed on a framework convention, the implementation of the Uruguay Round and establishment of the WTO (succeeding the less ambitious GATT) in 1995, the indefinite extension of the NPT that same year, the adoption of the Comprehensive Test Ban Treaty (CTBT) in 1996, and the adoption of the Kyoto Protocol on climate change in 1997. In all of these discussions India was active and often played a leading role (such as at the Rio conference), but occasionally Delhi opted for a stance perceived by some as that of a 'spoiler', for example in the run-up to agreement on the CTBT in 1996.[40]

In India, the most important development, as of 1991, was a raft of economic reform promoting liberalization and deregulation that accelerated India's economic growth rate considerably and placed India onto the track of 'emerging' nation status. These were opposed strongly at first by the Indian political Left and Right alike, worried respectively about their impact on the poor and the door they might be opening to Western values and cultures.

Meanwhile, the collapse of the Soviet Union hammered the final nail in the coffin of non-alignment as a meaningful instrument. Political fragmentation within India contributed to the emergence of divergent opinions on India's role in the world, while primarily economic objectives began to colour Indian diplomacy. A new, essentially pragmatic, orientation emerged in Indian foreign policy, reflected in the statements of both Congress- and BJP-led coalition governments in Delhi after 1991.[41]

Many in the Indian foreign policy establishment and intelligentsia found these transitions distasteful. But they applauded calls for a multipolar world, a growing leitmotiv in Delhi's global projection of Indian views.[42] More complex, perhaps, was the adjustment to India's shifting stance in international economic negotiations, often bearing little relationship with the priority given earlier to Third World solidarity (although the latter line was revived whenever convenient). However, one set of analysts believed that at the WTO, in the 1990s Indian officialdom retained 'a mindset that had not fully accepted the framework under which a market economy functions'.[43] Rajiv Kumar comments: 'Indian reactions to globalization [through the WTO] cannot be considered independent of Indian reactions to liberalization.'[44] Afro-Asian solidarity had little meaning in WTO negotiations where African agricultural interests could be at odds with those of India, as Amartya Sen tartly pointed out.[45] India could no longer credibly claim to be 'a spokesman of the Afro-Asians, the non-aligned, the under-developed and the small states' and use the UN to enhance its stature in this manner at a time when it had significant economic interests of its own to advance and defend.[46] In any event, the NAM was all but irrelevant on matters of security, being 'politically divided, economically differentiated and ideologically exhausted'.[47]

India had little choice but to re-engage with the multilateral system, as it required stabilization loans from the IMF and wider assistance from the World Bank. In the newly formed WTO, India saw an opportunity for multilateral leadership and in the growing UN debate on humanitarian intervention, the need for active involvement in a key normative debate affecting more than just UN philosophy.

Exploring alternatives: reform of the UN Security Council

Along with pragmatism in its foreign policy came the realization that increasingly India would have to pursue less universal and abstract interests in international forums, rather focusing on the promotion of its own evolving interests. Moreover, as its economy took off, India inevitably started ascending in the global hierarchy of influence and power. India's economic growth on the one hand cast it as a model for many other developing nations keen to emulate its success, but also created a potential rift between it and the poorer nations of the world, the support of whom it still might need on occasion.

Identifying early on an opportunity that India's new economic dispensation could create for it, Prime Minister Narasimha Rao in 1992 made a case for expansion of the UNSC 'to maintain political and moral effectiveness'.[48] Delhi was interested primarily in a permanent seat for itself. The US responded in 1993 with the suggestion that UNSC expansion begin with Germany and Japan only, with indications that any new permanent members might not secure veto power.[49] The American response served as a pointed reminder to India of the cost its long history of anti-Americanism in multilateral institutions could still carry.

In 1991–2, India sat as an elected member in the UNSC during one its busiest periods, at grips as it was with Iraq's invasion of Kuwait; Iraq's subsequent repression of Kurds in the north of the country; the beginnings of the disintegration of Yugoslavia, leading to a succession of wars featuring extensive UN involvement; the humanitarian plight of Somalis; as well as ambitious UN peacekeeping operations in Cambodia, Mozambique, and El Salvador. India sought to temper the enthusiasm of Western powers and some others for armed intervention (as opposed to consent-based peacekeeping), its interventions in Council debates later seeming prophetic of the risks then being courted. Its then Permanent Representative in the Security Council, Chinmaya Gharekhan, wrote:

The Council has acquired the propensity to deal with all kinds of issues by the simple stratagem of defining peace in holistic terms. The developing countries [were], in a manner of speaking, the victims of their own cleverness since it was they who took the initiative in defining peace in such broad terms to squeeze funds from the affluent countries for their development plans. Now, there is practically no restriction on the authority of the Security Council to legislate on any subject.[50]

In 1996, India ran again for an elected seat in the UNSC. It competed with Japan for the single Asian seat available and lost massively. Indian foreign service members spoke privately of the debilitating effects on their campaign of Japanese 'chequebook diplomacy' in the developing world—and doubtless this factor played a role—but it seemed to occur to few in Delhi that the caustic performance of its delegation at the CTBT conference earlier that year might have alienated not a few of its NAM partners as well as many in the West.[51]

After this experience, India increasingly believed that as the world's second most populous (and leading developing) country it should be entitled to a permanent seat. Contention within the Council in 1999 over Kosovo, in 2002–3 over Iraq and its decisive resolution supporting US self-defence after the events of 11 September 2001 were doubtless further elements leading to Indian irritation that it was not part of these systemically important conversations.

Thus, losing patience with the endless and circular discussions among UN member states on whether and how to achieve UNSC reform, in the run-up to the 2005 UN Summit, India banded with Brazil, Germany, and Japan (together known as the G-4) in order to press for the creation of four new permanent seats for them (and another two for Africa, as well as four further elected seats). The G-4 essentially argued their case on the basis of entitlement to the seats given their weight in international relations, their financial share of the UN's bills, and their contributions to aspects of the UN's work such as peacekeeping. Speaking in July 2005 in the US Congress, Manmohan Singh was unequivocal: 'There *must* be comprehensive reform of the United Nations to make it more effective and also more representative...In this context, you would agree that the voice of the world's largest democracy *surely cannot* be left unheard on the Security Council when the United Nations is being restructured'[52] (emphasis added).

In spite of a determined push from the four capitals, the effort failed, ostensibly because of China's hostility to a permanent seat for Japan but actually because most of the existing five permanent members (each of whom could veto the Charter amendment required for reform) had their reservations and because most member states remained unconvinced that they would benefit from these proposed new arrangements, as experience suggested that countries purporting to speak for their regions or other constituencies generally looked after their own interests first. Moreover, some worried more about the UNSC's effectiveness than the additional legitimacy a wider composition could impart, fearing that a much larger Council could become paralysed on key issues.

While disappointment over this failure was keenly felt in some quarters of Indian officialdom, in 2005, India had bigger fish to fry in the form of its negotiations with the USA over nuclear cooperation, initiated in another form by Strobe Talbott and Jaswant Singh in 1999 and 2000. India's then Prime Minister Atal Bihari Vajpayee had delivered a speech at the Asia Society in 2000 in New York claiming that the USA and India were 'natural allies'. In 1999, Washington had demonstrated unprecedented even-handedness when Pakistan attacked India at Kargil. The following year, President Bill Clinton made a successful and highly publicized visit to India. And while the first term of President George W. Bush was taken up with the events of 11 September 2001 and their fallout, during his second term, his administration energetically tackled rapprochement with India.

India's new-found status, and also quiet support from new friends, helped it cope with the renewed interventionism of the United Nations, successfully deflecting Secretary General Kofi Annan's post-1999 efforts to involve the UN in Kashmir, and allowed it to ignore UN calls for Delhi to curb its nuclear weapons and missile programmes.[53] By 2006, Delhi was supporting the candidacy of an Indian candidate, UN Under-Secretary-General Shashi Tharoor, for the position of UN Secretary-General. However, despite consistently placing at least second in the field of candidates, the effort was publicly torpedoed by the USA (doubtless much to the relief of China).

Gradually what fever there was in India for a permanent seat on the UNSC largely dissipated, particularly after the G-20 emerged as the key leader-level forum to address the global 2008–9 financial and economic crisis, with India playing a prominent role. Referring to India's campaign for a UNSC permanent seat, former Foreign Secretary M. K. Rasgotra commented in 2007: 'things of that kind will come to India unasked as its economic and other strengths grow'.[54] In October 2010, India ran for an elected seat at the Council uncontested and secured a two-year term, beginning in 2011.[55]

A more confident India

In 2007, India concluded the '123 Agreement' with Washington that would produce an end to over three decades of nuclear isolation for India. Following intense lobbying by both the USA and India, by October 2008 the deal had been approved by the IAEA, the NSG, and the US Senate, achieving for President Bush his single major foreign policy legacy. The agreement not only legitimized India's civil nuclear programme and recognized its non-proliferation record, but it also opened the channels of nuclear commerce between India and other members of the NSG, most notably Russia and France.[56] While a prominent writer in India expressed alarm at the 'self-conscious revolt in India against multilateralism' that the US–India deal represented, he worried more about 'how much like the US we [Indians] want to become . . . unilateral, oriented towards hegemony more than stability of the world, and besotted with [our] own sense of power'.[57]

From universalism to individualism: the WTO

A more confident India also asserted itself in the multilateral trading regime, as it formed a loose coalition of developing countries.[58] India had spoken up at the 1999 Seattle meeting of the WTO to protest against the inclusion of labour and environmental standards on the WTO agenda.[59] In the run up to the Doha Round of 2001, India challenged the efforts of developed nations to introduce the so-called 'Singapore issues'—competition, investment, trade facilitation, and government procurement—into discussions, and emphasized the need for these countries to fully implement their Uruguay Round commitments (especially in agricultural market access, textiles, and clothing, all priority sectors for India) before launching a new round. India also opposed the strict provisions of the Agreement on Trade-Related Aspects of Intellectual Property Rights (TRIPS) on compulsory licensing for the drug industry, an issue in which Indian pharmaceutical companies had an important stake.[60] Although India acquiesced in the launch of a new trade round at Doha in 2001, it helped secure beneficial outcomes for it on labour standards (which were deflected to the ILO), a substantive discussion on agriculture, and an agreement on TRIPS and public health that reflected its concerns.[61] India's negotiating stance was aided by the fact that India found itself more prepared than other developing countries to meet Uruguay Round commitments (with the exception of intellectual property rights, services, agriculture, and quantitative restrictions) due to its economic reforms that had begun in 1991.[62]

India's multilateral preoccupations had now changed from those of a poor developing nation relying on strength in numbers to those of an emerging power with the ability to hold its own against the major players in the WTO. However, in this forum, India continued to emphasize its developing country credentials in order to form coalitions within the group of developing countries to pressure the industrialized nations for concessions in various forums.

When an opportunity to have a say in the management of the multilateral trading system arose, India was not slow to take it up. In 2004 India was included in a small high-powered group at the WTO called the Five Interested Parties—along with the USA, the EU, Brazil, and Australia—that superseded the traditional 'Quad' of the USA, the EU, Japan, and Canada. India's inclusion (along with Brazil) was a sign, beyond the economic significance of these two

261

countries, of the G-20's significance as a negotiating bloc. It also signalled US acceptance of India as an important player in these negotiations. The EU advocated India's inclusion due to their shared interests in agricultural policy.[63]

India was now also in a better position to confront Western powers in the WTO since its trade portfolio no longer relied on them as much (gradually shifting toward China instead).[64] An important sign of India's transformation was the shift in its position on trade in services between the Uruguay and Doha rounds. Whereas in the past India (and Brazil) had opposed the inclusion of services in trade negotiations, India's services-led growth ensured that by 2004 it was an ardent advocate of some forms of liberalization of trade in services.[65] With the exception of agriculture and TRIPS, India was now more comfortable with international trade liberalization than ever before, although it still maintained greater restrictions and higher tariff barriers than China and Brazil. India's traditional 'deep antipathy toward the global trading system' was gradually being replaced by acceptance that in order to increase its global market share, it would increasingly be to its benefit to cut mutually advantageous deals and to contemplate trade-offs.[66]

Nevertheless, the Doha Round discussions of 2007 and 2008 proved a brass knuckles affair amidst a burgeoning global food security scare (with attendant inflation of basic produce prices in most countries, including India). India and Brazil, speaking 'for' the developing countries, confronted the United States on agricultural issues in the run-up to national elections in the USA in late 2008 and in India in early 2009. While both Washington and Delhi were open to success of the talks, their political bottom lines collided in Geneva in July 2008 largely over a 'Special Safeguard Mechanism' that would have allowed a temporary increase in trade barriers to protect threatened industries. This clash proved fatal for that phase of the talks (which had still not restarted by mid-2010, becalmed by the effects of the global economic and financial crisis of 2008–9 and by the dispiriting Copenhagen conference on climate change in December 2009).

Rather damagingly for India, in the final reel at Geneva, it was abandoned in its hard line by Brazil (which, like many African countries, on balance, wanted an agreement even at the price of greater compromise) and Indian Commerce Minister Kamal Nath stood out in his vehemence within the negotiations. 'I reject everything' he was quoted as saying in response to a compromise paper others seemed to be prepared to swallow.[67] He was alone in seeming to claim credit for the talks' failure, with the EU, US, and Chinese negotiators, who had contributed considerably to the overall deadlock, only too happy to deflect responsibility for failure on to Nath and India. The endgame was—in terms clearly coloured by US official briefings—described as follows in the *Washington Post*:

India's chief negotiator and commerce minister, Kamal Nath, may have played the biggest role in undoing the talks, repeatedly blocking attempts by developed nations to win greater access to India's burgeoning market. Nath's inflexibility was cheered as heroic in India, where his refusal to offer major concessions to rich nations was being portrayed as a classic David vs. Goliath case. 'I kept saying "No, I don't agree" at every point,' Nath said in a telephone interview from Geneva yesterday. 'I come from a country where 300 million people live on 1 dollar a day and 700 million people live on 2 dollars a day. So it is natural for me, and in fact incumbent upon me, to see that our agricultural interests are not compromised. You don't require rocket science to decide between livelihood security and commercial interests.'[68]

India's position was shaped, above all, by domestic politics.[69] On international trade India had faced domestic opposition to its membership of GATT even back in the 1950s.[70] In the 1980s an economic analyst noted, 'India's trade policy is congealed in a mould made by the domestic political interests.'[71] The connection, according to this analyst, was simple—politicians are sustained on the votes of farmers and the money of industrialists. As a result, Indian negotiators have very little space in which to concede anything to other nations. And in 2008 agriculture remained for India the single most sensitive issue, given the 70 per cent of the population that remained rural.[72]

In India, Nath (a highly self-confident, long-time Congress stalwart with a keen eye constantly on domestic political advantage) was largely portrayed in glowing terms coming out of his confrontation with US Trade Representative Susan Schwab in Geneva. Less was said about how the Chinese delegation was only too happy to see Nath in the lead. The contradiction between Nath's raw political motivations and justifications and the Indian Prime Minister's seemingly more ethereal calls for international cooperation, were not fully recognized in India until after the national elections produced a convincing win for the Congress-led UPA. Then, Nath, long rumoured to have been seeking a major portfolio, such as Finance, was shifted to the internationally unglamorous (if domestically important) portfolio of road transport and highways. He was replaced in the commerce portfolio by another Congress party stalwart, Anand Sharma, known for his serene style. India lost no time in calling over thirty leading trade ministers to Delhi for consultations, perhaps in order to allow this change of personnel and style to sink in fully, and, in the words of one commentator, to cast India as a 'pro-active participant in multi-lateral talks rather than a thorn in the flesh as the global media had suggested in 2008'.[73]

Following the collapse of Doha Round negotiations, Delhi, in parallel to the United States, favoured bilateral and regional trade agreements, as illustrated in Chapters 9 and 10.

The shape of things to come: climate change

Although reactions to some of India's actions and positions no doubt over-state the tilt against multilateralism in Indian foreign policy, they do raise two important questions relevant today, as India emerges as a premier global interlocutor. First, what kind of power does India aspire to be, and how will it engage with others in years to come? Second, is the Indian foreign policy establishment attuned to engaging with the multilateral system not just on India's own terms but also on ones that actually will appeal to others and contribute to positive outcomes? On climate change, the signals are positive and, as in the case of India's approach to the WTO (but with opposite results), determined by political leadership rather than bureaucratic preferences.

In 2003, in the run-up to the American invasion of Iraq, the President of the Congress party, Sonia Gandhi, in a rare comment on foreign affairs, wrote: 'the paradox of [America's] power is that it cannot afford to act unilaterally. Many in the United States are impatient with multilateralism, but in today's interdependent world there is simply no alternative to working in concert and collaboration with each other.'[74] In 2004, Manmohan Singh outlined India's global philosophy, which he described as 'cooperative pluralism' enshrined in the Sanskrit phrase and Hindu philosophy of 'Vasudhaiva Kutumbakam'—the whole world is one family. These statements suggest a cooperative outlook ideally suited to multilateral institutions, the desire to transform them con-structively, and a recognition that with greater power and influence comes responsibility in international affairs.

Nonetheless there exists a gap between Prime Ministerial and other Indian aspirations for more genuinely multilateral management of international relations on the one hand, and India's positions and style in a variety of forums and issue-by-issue on the other. Delhi's negotiating posture has been described as 'defensive', 'obstructionist', and a 'spoiler' by Indian and non-Indian observers alike.[75] In early 2010, Minister of State Shashi Tharoor summarized a debate in Delhi by referring to India having 'earned us the negative reputation of running a moralistic commentary on world affairs' that Western diplomats referred to as 'sniping from the sidelines'.[76] Environ-ment minister Jairam Ramesh stated that India needed to drop its traditional 'naysayer' approach, and instead negotiate more constructively.[77] Pratap Bhanu Mehta suggests that India is 'not good at cutting deals' in part because its traditional point of negotiating departure is Indian entitlements.[78] Such assessments surprise some Indians, while they are rejected by others, who believe Delhi is always at risk of conceding too much in multilateral negotiations.

Following the 2009 national elections, and a first term in which environ-mental matters received scant attention within the government, Dr Singh appointed one of India's most talented and mediagenic younger politicians,

Jairam Ramesh, to the environment portfolio. India's position had long been to stick closely to the terms of the Kyoto Protocol, under which industrialized countries committed to specific targets for emission reductions, while developing countries were not required to do so under the 'common but differentiated' responsibilities approach adopted at the UN on the issue since the Rio Conference.[79] Early on in the run-up to the Copenhagen conference of December 2009, Ramesh arranged to establish common cause with China in negotiating strategy (although China's international announcement of significant voluntary emission intensity reductions per economic unit of production at the United Nations in September of that year seemed to take India by surprise).[80]

Ramesh engaged sharply with US Secretary of State Hillary Clinton when she visited India in July 2009, telegraphing that India would concede nothing on emissions targets: 'India's position is clear and categorical that we are simply not in a position to take any legally binding emissions reductions.'[81] Responding to threats within the US Congress to penalize trading partners not matching American measures in this field, he added: 'There is simply no case for the pressure that we, who have been among the lowest emitters per capita, face to actually reduce emissions'. Ms. Clinton mildly replied that the USA would not wish to hamper India's economic growth as 'economic progress in India is in everyone's interest and not just in the interest of Indians'. This exchange made the news all over the world and seemed to suggest an unbending Indian resolve to withstand foreign pressure.

However, it soon transpired that within the government, Ramesh was arguing in favour of flexibility, in line with the reported determination of Prime Minister Singh that, at Copenhagen, India should be 'part of the solution to the problem'.[82] A letter from Ramesh to the Prime Minister, mid-October 2009, leaked to the media, argued for a new negotiating strategy, not least because India needed to curb its own emissions as a matter of national interest. Ramesh was quoted as having argued: 'India must listen more and speak less in negotiations' as its stance is 'disfavoured by the developed countries, small island states and vulnerable countries'.[83] And: 'The position we take on international mitigation commitments only if supported by finance and technology needs to be nuanced simply because we need to mitigate in self-interest.'[84] Ramesh also indicated that engaging the USA was important in terms of securing progress on climate change globally—a controversial stance for any Indian politician to take.[85]

He was soon challenged (as publicized in further leaks) by two of India's long-time negotiators. Specifically, a proposal articulated by Ramesh that India could offer to reduce its carbon intensity by 20–25 per cent of 2005 levels by 2020 was questioned by the negotiators, who queried the prudence of offering unilateral concessions without obtaining reciprocity from other countries.[86] Ramesh was similarly criticized by some civil society commentators for India's concessions (which were in fact not all that far-reaching, particularly in light of China's unilaterally offered targets in September).[87] In the type of tactical bobbing and weaving that Indian democracy tends to require, Ramesh was quick to point out in Parliament that India's concession was not legally binding and would still permit economic growth in future, doubtless a useful tactic in parliament, but one that left India in somewhat of a negotiating quandary.[88]

Ramesh's arguments seemed to recognize on the one hand that India could not stand idly by as its own environment headed toward serious degradation, but also, implicitly, on the other that India needed to be in a position to offer something positive at the negotiating table if it wanted to play in the big leagues. Praful Bidwai offered India an extensive, erudite, and thoughtful agenda for Copenhagen that would aim for a 'strong' accord, in the national and international interest, but he was not widely echoed.[89] In the event, India's offers in the run-up to and at Copenhagen centred on:

> [agreeing] to [voluntary] emissions goals that would be subject to international 'consultation and analysis' but not scrutiny or formal review... [and offering to allow] international monitoring of those of its mitigation activities that are supported by international funds or technologies but not those that are domestically funded.[90]

Although the Copenhagen talks were widely perceived as a fiasco, they served India's diplomatic interests very well. They allowed India to be 'part of the solution', a last-minute truncated accord, offered by the four BASIC powers and the USA, acknowledged—however reluctantly and only by taking 'note' of it—by the conference plenary, and also in underscoring that India was now an indispensable negotiating partner on key global challenges such as climate change. Unlike its posture in Geneva at the WTO in 2008, when China shielded itself behind an assertive India, India allowed China to take the heat for frustrating delegations and NGOs campaigning for an ambitious outcome at Copenhagen.

Further, the results of Copenhagen for India were also perceived by many at home as positive. Some identified 'silver linings', but noted: 'Divisions between the West and China (and its new best friend, India) over how to evaluate domestically chosen mitigation actions haven't been solved. Simply put, without concessions from future large emitters on that, the world's current large emitters have absolutely no incentive to cut.'[91] Others argued that the 'political challenge before the BASIC four, especially India and China, is to redefine the task of drastic emissions reduction globally, led by the developed nations, in a manner that refuses to counterpose the global public good to the development imperative. Climate laggards in the developed as well as the developing world need to be pushed aside in a dialogue that has both the scientific case and the ethical imperative in focus.'[92]

Overall, India demonstrated agility in the run-up to the Copenhagen conference, and dexterity during the meeting, allowing it to emerge as one of the forgers of a compromise. This might suggest the content and style of Indian multilateral approaches in the future.

New diplomacy: new forums

Describing the significance for India of the emergence of the G-20 (at the level of national leaders rather than, as earlier, at the level of finance ministers), Indian planning supremo, Montek Singh Ahluwalia, who has served as India's G-20 'Sherpa', comments: 'The G-20 represents a political induction into a small group which casts itself as the main forum' on global economic and financial issues.[93] The emergence of the G-20 at leader level and India's inclusion represents a politically significant graduation for the country rather than an introduction to serious consultations on global financial issues—India had for long been involved in those at the IMF and at the Bank for International Settlements in Basel, cutting an impressive figure in many instances. Indeed, Delhi's 'finance diplomacy', involving as it has many of India's leading lights over the years, has been one of its strongest contributions to international relations writ large.

Ahluwalia wonders whether the G-20 will turn out to be the key forum in the medium and long term and whether it will be able to tackle issues such as climate change, for example.[94] Unless it is able to provide impetus to progress on this contentious file and to completion of the Doha Round, it will stagnate. As well, its economic and financial mandate, while providing focus, means that political and security challenges will need to be addressed elsewhere, unless it adapts to include them.

If not, the G-20 may well prove a transitional arrangement and another, perhaps smaller, forum will emerge to supersede it. Should this prove to be the case, India is certain to be a member. Meanwhile, the G-20 has been an ideal vehicle for an India led by Manmohan Singh. G-20 insiders report, and US President Obama confirmed after the June 2010 G-20 summit in Toronto, that given his extensive knowledge of international economic issues, Singh has consistently been one of the two or three voices most listened to around the table.[95]

India might prefer to be a 'canny negotiator' that effectively walks the North–South line.[96] However, as Nitin Desai argues, this approach may work less well at a time when India is increasingly seen internationally as advancing its own interests rather than seeking to champion (more than rhetorically) others within a highly differentiated developing world.[97]

India's balancing act is nevertheless on display with respect to the Iran file: India has consistently voted with Washington against Iran's nuclear programme at the IAEA while continuing to maintain friendly bilateral relations with Iran and defending its own nuclear weapons programme. It participates (without much current urgency) in the G-4 to demand a permanent seat on the UNSC, while actively endorsing most of the G-77 and the NAM positions at the UN. India promotes the notion of BRIC (Brazil, Russia, India, China) as a coalition of emerging economies, but Delhi is careful not to antagonize Washington by endorsing an alternative international currency to the dollar, something China and Russia were quite willing to do.[98] At the WTO it is simultaneously a member of the Five Interested Parties and the G-20, attempting to bridge the gap between the developing and developed worlds. At Copenhagen India banded together with China, Brazil, and South Africa to voice the concerns of the developing world, while also displaying awareness of its own environmental vulnerability. In brief, India does not quite sit on the fence between the developed and developing countries but rather seeks to straddle the two camps—exploiting its multiple international identities, including its status as an emerging power, to advance its interests.

While India is happy to play its part in international summits and negotiations, the real Indian foreign policy work is more focused on bilateral relations and regional groupings, as well as small 'caucus' groups within wider institutions and several new forums that have emerged in recent years. India's relationship with the USA has already paid rich dividends in terms of nuclear technology, trade, agriculture, science and technology, military cooperation, and a host of other areas. Buoyed by these successes, Delhi has established strategic partnerships (of varying depth) with other powers, including the EU, Russia, Japan, Israel, Brazil, South Africa, and China.

Today, much of India's diplomacy is organized more around smaller, plurilateral groupings of several meaningful states, and also within regional bodies.[99] In its region, India has actively pursued relationships with ASEAN and the Shanghai Cooperation Organization (SCO), not least because of China's involvement in both organizations and the regions their membership covers. The SCO, because it does not include India among its full members, may actually be of greater concern to India at present, focused as it is on Central Asia, with which north India has long historical and cultural ties.[100]

In 2003 India, Brazil, and South Africa combined to form IBSA, a forum for cooperation along both political and economic lines explicitly presented as composed of the leading democracies of their continents (a rare high-profile opportunity for India to trumpet its affinity for other democracies), and a grouping Montek Singh Ahluwalia describes as a 'natural one'.[101] Initially launched at ministerial level in Brasilia in 2003, with its first official summit in Brasilia in September 2006, this 'dialogue' forum has so far focused mainly on trade (but the three countries emphasize their credentials as multi-ethnic democracies). In 2003, IBSA formed a coalition with China and Argentina in the run-up to the WTO ministerial meeting at Cancun to effectively oppose the North's agricultural protectionism.[102] One analyst describes the forum as 'both a strategic alliance for the pursuit of common interests of developing countries in global institutions but also as a platform for trilateral and inter-regional South-South cooperation'.[103] While the economic content of IBSA is private-sector led, in keeping with the market orientation of all three economies involved, Dr Singh has been an enthusiastic cheerleader. IBSA is for India a first-of-its-kind partnership based partly on political values, though shared democratic values also underpinned India's rapprochement with the USA, its participation in several broader international gatherings of democratic nature, and its repeated upholding of the democratic character and content of the Commonwealth.[104]

One alarm bell triggered by IBSA and other such bodies is whether, rather than representing global outreach, such groupings represent a 'flight from the region', where India's own subregional organization, the South Asian Association for Regional Cooperation (SAARC), is marking time, embarrassingly.[105] All recognize that SAARC's effectiveness as a regional forum is in part undermined by tensions between Pakistan and India, but India's own leadership of the region within which it is, to a degree, a hegemon, has been hesitant, with little credible follow-up between summits and ministerial meetings.[106] Indeed, among students of Indian policy in Delhi, there is a sense that India today would rather 'opt out' of its own region (if it could) than work hard to make something of it.[107] A more positive way of expressing this might be to describe India as reaching beyond, or outgrowing, its own region.

Another reservation over much of the 'variable architecture' available to India in its diplomacy today, a veritable 'alphabetic soup' on each issue, according to economist Shankar Acharya, is that most of the bodies mentioned above are not yet mature, have no secretariats, and may well prove of transitional rather than longer-lasting value.[108] This does not mean that they are irrelevant. Rather, India will need to remain nimble in assessing where it wishes to invest its effort at a time of significant fluidity in plurilateral, regional, and multilateral arrangements.[109]

Reverting to India's wider profile and ambition internationally, David Mulford, US Ambassador in India, 2004–9, and earlier a senior US economic negotiator as Assistant Secretary of the Treasury for International Affairs, comments: 'India could aspire to be much more than a regional power if it were in a frame of mind to do so. This is especially true in the new and highly amorphous grouping of the G-20, where clever coalition building and initiatives with the leading country members could be used to advance Indian ideas and leadership. At present India continues to undersell itself.'[110] This would, of course, require the sort of compromises and give (as well as take) that many Indian commentators would find distasteful and would condemn.

Conclusions: Table manners and domestic politics

A noted denizen of India's Ministry of External Affairs, a keen bilateralist at that, when asked what India does best internationally replied without a moment's hesitation 'multilateral diplomacy'.[111] And yet, queries about Indian performance at the UN and elsewhere in the multilateral sphere hardly validate that judgment: 'arrogant', 'moralistic', and 'confrontational' are terms more invoked by developing and industrialized country counterparts, despite recognition that Indian negotiators are rarely less than 'impressive' and often 'brilliant'.[112] Indeed, there is much about multilateral diplomacy as practised in some of the world that India is not yet attuned to. In discussing the peer review process at the OECD, one Indian economist stated: 'Why would we be interested in peer review? We can afford the best advice commercially available.'[113]

As India continues to seek a greater role in the management of the multilateral system at the high table of international relations alongside actors such as the USA, the EU, China, Brazil, and South Africa, there is a dichotomy between how Indians perceive their engagement with the multilateral system on the one hand, and how India's interventions play out and are at times perceived by its partners on the other.

The gap in perceptions is emphasized by a commentator on the climate change issue: 'In an ironic and to most Indians quite disturbing turn, India is increasingly portrayed as an obstructionist in the global climate negotiations. How did a country likely to be on the frontline of climate impacts—with a vast proportion of the world's poor and a reasonably good record of energy-related environmental policy and performance—reach this diplomatic *cul de sac*?'[114] The story is the same in trade—India holds up its economic liberalization as a major achievement in facilitating the free flow of goods and services across borders, yet gets saddled with the blame for upending the Doha Round. Similarly on nuclear technology, India trumpets its record in non-proliferation and nuclear safety yet is excluded for three decades from multilateral access to nuclear technology and is consistently chided for refusing to sign up to the NPT and CTBT (and even to seriously discuss the possibility until quite recently).

India's stance is influenced by a variety of factors in multilateral forums. As we have seen repeatedly, domestic politics play a key role in determining India's positions on 'hot button' international issues, more so now in the information age than ever before, with accelerated 24/7 news cycles and non-stop internet commentary constraining political initiative. Thus, Indian negotiators have often found themselves on a short leash, for fear they may sell the country out. As well, Jaswant Singh, India's former Foreign Minister (1998–2002) comments: 'Multilaterally, many Indian voices have been very conscious of years of colonial "subjecthood". The result has been excessive Indian touchiness at times. Underlying Indian positions in some international economic negotiations has been a fear of foreign economic looting rooted in our history.'[115]

Climate change provides a case in point. India's representatives are routinely castigated by the domestic political left and the right for caving into US pressure at the slightest hint of a conciliatory stance. In the days preceding Copenhagen, Environment Minister Jairam Ramesh, under pressure in parliament, laid out a clear logic behind the need to make concessions in the climate negotiations. 'We are showing some flexibility because we do not want to become isolated. We do not want to earn a reputation as a deal-breaker', he said.[116] In October 2009 at a conference, Ramesh stated that India shared the responsibility of arriving at an agreement.[117] However, 'on cue, he was torn apart by sections of the domestic constituency, as he [had] been before, for making such utterances'.[118]

At the conclusion of the Copenhagen summit, while Ramesh described the final outcome as a 'good deal' and India's climate envoy agreed that India's 'red lines have been met', an editorial in the *Hindu* described the summit as 'a concerted US strategy to corner the major developing economies in the climate negotiation'.[119] In contrast, another editorially respected major Indian newspaper criticized the G-77 for 'grandstanding and delays', and India and China for their 'dilatory tactics' at the conference.[120] But Indian experts know that a grouping like BASIC works well as long as its central purpose is to counter Western (particularly US or EU) positions—but it hardly creates, at least in its current form, a forum for active cooperation among its members.

While other countries are not immune to the push and pull of domestic politics, India's challenge remains that it is has not yet developed a habit of conciliating domestic pressures with a results-oriented stance in some multilateral institutions. As well, Indian experts point to a wariness of 'multi-motive' gains and a tendency by Indian negotiators to default to zero-sum calculations.[121] Likewise, the organization of Indian arguments around 'principles' largely precludes compromise; whereas advancement of its 'interests' might more greatly favour 'give and take' in order to achieve overall positive outcomes.[122] Despite India's new membership of the multilateral power elite, and running counter to Prime Minister Singh's open and confident stance, the domestic chorus on multilateral deal-making too often remains a resounding 'No'.

India therefore finds itself somewhat disabled, constrained by domestic constituents while not yet endowed with the weight necessary internationally to implement a domestically determined agenda, sometimes improvising counterproductively in a 'spoiler' stance. Delhi's growing drive to break free of the developing country mold and join the major powers in managing the multilateral system thus creates a tension and a degree of unpredictability on India's likely positions in years ahead. An Indian interlocutor comments: 'Indian leaders may yet recognize the difference between perching themselves on a high chair at the high table where they must cooperate with those that really run the show, and sitting at the head of the developing nations' table where they can hold sway and appear to matter.'[123] Nitin Desai, a grandee of UN climate negotiations over many years, colourfully points out that the final Copenhagen agreement was achieved by the two '20% players' (the USA and China in terms of carbon emissions) while India, which was among the '5% players' (with Japan and Russia), was only needed to provide some extra ballast on the Chinese side along with the two '2% players', Brazil and South Africa.[124] Given that the future of the international system is likely to be determined to a significant degree for some years by Sino-US understandings and disagreements, India can keep its options open while its weight in international relations grows. Meanwhile, as India demonstrated on climate change, it is likely to become more rather than less nimble in key negotiations in the future.

Over the years, like many others', Indian practice of multilateralism has been inconsistent relative to the principles it espouses. While India has consistently been a (selective) rule taker in the multilateral system, it likely harboured the desire to be a rule maker and occasionally acted accordingly. Thus while effusively committing itself to the UN Charter and the cause of peace, India forcibly evicted the Portuguese from Goa in 1961, adopted a militarily aggressive posture on the border issue with China in 1962, intervened in the East Pakistan conflict in 1971, annexed the kingdom of Sikkim in 1975, and intervened in the Sri Lankan conflict in 1987. India has consistently championed disarmament at the UN, yet it has conducted nuclear tests twice and refuses to sign non-proliferation and non-testing treaties, advancing a variety of 'principles' that many countries—not just those of the West—find confounding, to justify its actions.

A country that perceives itself as geographically, economically, and culturally entitled to meaningful international power is likely to resent external constraints and rules, as the USA often does. But the USA recognizes that it benefits from most of the multilateral regimes it has done so much to design and develop since the Second World War. As India has gained in international stature, the transition of its foreign policy remains incomplete, but it is increasingly called on to contribute as well. Such are the rules of the high table.

Thus, while India does take its international legal—particularly Treaty—obligations very seriously, pooled or shared sovereignty is, in the words of one Western envoy in Delhi, 'not India's thing'.[125] For many Indian practitioners and analysts, multilateralism is at best a defence against the unilateralism of others, just as arguments for multipolarity have been largely articulated with reference to the unipolar policies of Washington after September 2001. Indeed, in the view of another foreign envoy in Delhi, India's multilateral diplomacy is strikingly 'defensive rather than assertive and creative'.[126] But among other advantages that its current multilateral prominence provides is that it allows India to manage its neighbourhood challenges with greater confidence and serenity. Far from Pakistan being in a position today to outflank India within the NAM, or in the UN General Assembly, it is not even a member of the G-20.

India has not yet thought through the extent to which it must, and can, shoulder domestically costly global burdens. It is not just Western powers that will look to it to do its part; poorer developing countries will as well. The voluntary, non-binding route in defining its commitments, as at Copenhagen, is more attractive for now, but as its economy and weight grow further, it will likely not find it possible to stick to this path. Indeed, the Kyoto Protocol has foundered as an effective tool for burden-sharing because it so blatantly put all of the burden on the industrialized countries while letting large emitters of the South off the hook: a conceivable approach in 1998, but no longer a practicable one in 2010 when both India and China are recording robust growth while the West largely stagnates.

One very attractive feature of Indian foreign policy is that the country's leaders have never obscured the daunting internal challenges that remained their primary task. As the first architect of independent India's foreign policy said, 'I do not pretend to say that India, as she is, can make a vital difference to world affairs. So long as we have not solved most of our own problems, our voice cannot carry the weight that it normally will and should.'[127] And as earlier chapters suggest, India's internal deficits in security, equity, and governance remain daunting. Other countries will need to bear its particular circumstances, many of them admirable, others worrying, in mind, knowing that India possesses the capacity over time to tackle them successfully. In conversation with Indian politicians, business leaders, writers, and civil society figures, the dominant recurring theme is that India must, above all, attack what veteran Congress grandee and former Governor of Jammu and Kashmir, Karan Singh, describes as 'the citadels of poverty'.[128] If India's greater glory internationally needs to take a decidedly secondary place to this objective, so be it for the vast majority of Indians, including a wide range of elites.

Like other large and complex countries, India would prefer the world to adapt to it than to engage in the messy business of give and take required by meaningful engagement with others.[129] But those shaping Indian foreign policy today know that Delhi will increasingly need to meet its international partners half-way, often in multilateral settings.

273

12

Conclusions

On leaving India after six years of working in the private sector and then writing for the *International Herald Tribune* and the *New York Times*, Anand Giridharadas wrote in 2009 that India is 'a country harder to describe than to explain, and easier to explain than to understand', also commenting that 'India is a place for seeking, not concluding'.[1] These are profoundly true but also humbling observations for an author taking leave of a challenging subject.

This concluding chapter seeks to highlight a number of patterns and trends that emerge from the preceding chapters, organizing them somewhat differently, for example some as positive elements of change and others as presenting continuing challenges. It isolates a few specific issues, mostly regional ones (Kashmir, Afghanistan, China) and management of the economy, that are likely to remain troublesome for some time, touching also on the kind of power India might turn into, and whether it can long avoid assuming a share of the burden of managing the global commons and providing other international goods, before bidding farewell to a project and a country which I have loved exploring.

History as prologue

Foreign policy formulation requires a conciliation of ends and means conditioned by the specifics of the country involved and of the wider international situation at any given time. It draws on history, geography, economic performance, regional and global ambition, and many other factors. It is much easier to analyse at the remove of several decades. In the immediate, it generally seems a blur, with key notes lost amidst the white noise. Thus, foreign policy during India's first four decades is more readily captured than its current directions, which are subject to much bobbing and weaving by key actors.

Independent India's early foreign policy, nearly completely dominated by Prime Minister Nehru, sought to create some margin of manoeuvre for the new state, which was still at grips with serious challenges to national cohesion and struggling with abject poverty against the backdrop of the great famines of the final years of the Raj.[2] Nehru believed it was essential for India to maintain a healthy distance from power politics and bloc rivalry soon to crystallize in the East–West Cold War. With hindsight of sixty years, this still seems the best choice at the time. Thus, for India, the non-aligned stance was much more a defensive posture than a challenge to either of the blocs engaged in the superpower conflict. And, as Lakhdar Brahimi, a youthful representative of Algeria's national liberation movement in Indonesia, 1956–61, and former Foreign Minister of Algeria, recalls, India's leadership was as widely welcomed internationally by those still engaged in their own struggle for freedom, as it was by those having recently achieved it.[3]

India's policy was appreciated with much more moderate enthusiasm by the West, which, with overweening superiority, and the assumption that any democracy worthy of the concept should align on it, indulged quite frequently in bullying tactics towards Delhi (while also assisting it economically, particularly with food aid). The Western, particularly US, tactics viewed with hindsight today were distasteful, and, in any event, proved consistently counterproductive in compelling India's compliance.

Russia was eventually able to acquire India as an ally, virtually by default, through a more relaxed projection towards India of its ideological posture, through patience with Indian rhetorical flourishes, and a realist appreciation that India mattered in the balance of power in Asia. Indian needling of the West, particularly of the USA , the fruit of its anti-imperialist sentiment, and the high-minded nature of much Indian speech-making at the UN and elsewhere, was congruent with its eventual alliance with Moscow, but the latter was unable to assist India much with several of its pressing needs.

If India's suffering under the British was the basis of its anti-imperialist and consequently non-aligned stance, the West did not understand it. Ramachandra Guha writes:

> Nehru [believed] past centuries might have belonged to Europe, or to the white races in general, but it was now time for non-white and previously subordinated peoples to come into their own.[4]

Western envoys in India, including Alva Myrdal, John Kenneth Galbraith, Walter Crocker, and Escott Reid, while deploring Delhi's propensity for double speak and morally charged grandstanding, did their best to explain India to their capitals during the 1950s and 1960s, but few were receptive back home.[5] Octavio Paz, the great Mexican writer and poet, and his country's Ambassador to India between 1962 and 1968, adopted a more philosophical tone in his elegant and rich later essays on India.[6]

Incomprehension among the powerful in the West was complete. President Harry Truman of the USA, reacting to Chester Bowles' choice of Delhi for an ambassadorial assignment, stated:

> I thought India was pretty jammed with poor people and cows round streets, witch doctors and people sitting on hot coals and bathing in the Ganges . . . but I did not realize anybody thought it was important.[7]

Truman's reaction to a conversation with Nehru in 1949 was: 'He . . . talked just like a communist'.[8] The relationship did not warm under Eisenhower, whose Secretary of State, John Foster Dulles, was a determined foe of neutrality in the conflict between good (Washington) and evil (Moscow)—and a frequent critic of Delhi.[9]

Nevertheless, although foreign and defence policy may not have been Nehru's strongest suit, competing as it did with often much more urgent domestic challenges, much of his foreign policy writing makes for compelling reading today. It was more in the application of his principles than in their formulation that he stumbled. This was particularly the case towards the end of his life, as India's options grew more constrained. However, such mistakes as he made in foreign as in domestic policy do not, in my view, diminish his greatness overall, which seems to me more evident with each passing decade.

India was no natural ally of the Soviet Union. Indeed, many in India's foreign policy establishment viewed the prospect of Delhi's alignment on Moscow with distress. India's concerns over Washington's systematic support of Pakistan and also its reservations over an unbridled capitalist economic model it did not practise itself were misunderstood or rejected outright by Washington and by some others in the West.[10] Delhi's impatience with the obtuse insistence of Portugal, under a military dictatorship coddled by Washington, to hold on to Goa until India took military action in 1961 to oust this last colonial holdout from Indian soil, was a factor, especially as Western powers at the UN defended Portugal on narrow legal grounds (akin to India's own hypocrisies over Hungary).[11] India backed into its largely unprofitable alliance with Moscow in part due to Western condescension. Indira Gandhi's autocratic nature also fit better with Moscow's ordered view of domestic governance than it did with Washington's. Finally, the readily outstretched hand of friendship from Moscow helped.[12] However, the alliance, in its more exclusive dimensions, did not endure: Prime Minister Rajiv Gandhi worked hard to relaunch a more positive relationship with Western capitals after 1984. And the implosion of the Soviet Union in late 1990 put paid to the Indo-Soviet alliance. But the negative legacy for India in the West lingered until recently.

Independent India, from the outset, saw itself as needing global reach. Indeed, early on, spurred by decolonization elsewhere, it established a global diplomatic footprint few others have rivalled. It also made its mark in the multilateral sphere nearly immediately, participating with rhetorical brilliance in the major international debates of the cold war era, and contributing meaningfully to the growth of the UN's capacity through its frequent provision of military and civilian peacekeepers. Yet, in the absence of widely appreciated economic and social achievements, and with its military might mostly applied to internal conflicts and ones in its immediate periphery, it was viewed as a cantor of the non-aligned countries, but not always a very committed or convincing one given its own great power entanglements. After the Berlin Wall fell, non-alignment became irrelevant, much Western aid was diverted to Eastern Europe, and India's barter trade with Russia was disrupted.[13]

Happily, the sudden end of the Cold War coincided with other tectonic shifts affecting India: the conclusion of the Indira Gandhi years prolonged by her son Rajiv's tenure (the latter marked by early reformist instincts that seemed to subside with time but also an assertiveness in India's neighbourhood that produced a comeuppance in Sri Lanka, and an image of India as regional bully through the prism of its relations with Nepal); the mildly positive but largely inconclusive results from the tentative economic reforms of Rajiv Gandhi's years in power; and, above all, the balance of payments and exchange rate crisis of 1990–1 that produced a quantum leap in economic reform. It was the bold reforms instituted to counter the crisis, and their positive outcomes, that brought about a profound reassessment of India's significance and potential internationally.

In spite of parliamentary turbulence in 1989–91, a sense took hold internationally of India's growing political maturity and the lasting nature of its democracy, the country's institutions having survived the misguided emergency rule of Mrs. Gandhi in 1975–7, and the assassinations of both Indira and Rajiv Gandhi. The levels of political violence in India, exemplified by the anti-Sikh pogrom in Delhi that followed Mrs. Gandhi's assassination in 1984, have found echoes in communally driven rioting since then, at times on a scale that astounds foreign observers. However, such incidents are no longer interpreted as undermining the country's essential cohesion. More worrying for India today are the enduring challenges of the Naxalite (Maoist) and several other insurgencies. While Kashmir continued to fester, often very painfully, India during the 1980s saw off the Free Khalistan movement that contorted the economically critical state of Punjab bordering on Pakistan, though at great cost to the country and to Punjab itself. Thus, the view of India as a cohesive anchor of its subcontinent and wider region, albeit still one afflicted with much poverty, social challenge, and internal violence, is now widely credited internationally.

Indian foreign policy today

Largely for reasons of authorial convenience, as outlined in previous chapters, and without great originality, I have argued that Indian foreign and (to a lesser degree) economic policy can be divided into three broad phases: a Nehruvian period of Indian reinvention as an independent state with idealist overtones in foreign policy; a 'realist' phase accompanied by a starker version of socialism from the mid-1960s to the late 1980s, producing mixed results at best on both foreign policy and economic fronts; and a new phase, extending into the present, inaugurated in the early 1990s and revolving around economic reform and its rewards both for the Indian economy and for India's weight in the world. The latter has increased steadily as the relative dominance of the West, particularly the USA , has faltered and current trend-lines favour the re-emergence of Asia in world affairs.

Naturally, what mattered most in Indian foreign policy during these successive periods varied considerably. Some of what was impossible for India in the 1950s is on offer today, for example, a seat at the high table of international financial and economic diplomacy. These new possibilities displace old stances that were shaped not only by Indian preferences but also by very real constraints at the time.

Positive change

Amongst positive elements of change for India, and accompanying its own transformation at the international level, lies the parallel rise of countries such as Brazil and South Africa. Official India has worked hard to breathe substance into the IBSA (India-Brazil-South Africa) group while its dynamic and globalized private sector engages energetically with these countries. As well, India's re-engagement with East and Southeast Asia over the past decade is a very positive development. Nevertheless these newly invigorated partnerships will not always yield coincidence of interests or agreement on issues of judgement, as Brazil's ultimate decoupling from India at the WTO in 2008 made clear.

Perhaps the most positive development of all has been a fundamental shift in relations with the USA. Even though the USA did much to support India economically in its early years, directly and through the international financial institutions over which it exercised strong influence, the relationship remained contentious from the very early days of Indian independence onwards. This shift represents a victory for both sides.

While some in India still worry that it could abdicate its freedom of manoeuvre and side with the USA reflexively in international affairs, this seems far-fetched. A more realistic concern is that Washington will not always understand India's inability to agree with it, creating a perception of Delhi as a false friend. But even these anxieties seem ill-founded, rooted in fears arising from the past rather than the possibilities of the future. The USA today needs to court Indian support on a range of issues, just as India will value American support in tackling many of its own challenges. And Indians are reassured, in this relationship, to know that the brief unipolar moment, created by the Soviet Union's collapse, that temporarily devolved onto the USA singular global power (which Washington sadly overestimated) has largely passed, allowing for more balanced links with key partners.

It is not unreasonable to anticipate a large degree of mutual accommodation, however frustrated each capital may be at times with the other on individual files. US demand for information technology and other services has been extremely helpful to India, and India's capacity to absorb American exports has greatly strengthened American commerce (at a time when much militates against continued unfettered global US economic dominance).

Although each country will seek to improve and manage its relations with China separately, their challenges in doing so will likely draw them together at times. The outcome of the US-led Western military intervention in Afghanistan, and developments in Pakistan, will influence the tone and content of USA–India ties in ways that are unknowable today but that need not undermine a bilateral relationship that is now more mature and should be mutually confident. The steady, modestly assertive approach of China to relations with Washington may deserve more attention in Delhi than it receives, as pointed out by former Indian Foreign Secretary Maharajakrishna Rasgotra.[14] China's relationship with the USA need create no anxiety in India, but should be viewed as one likely offering opportunities in the future, and as a useful learning experience.

For the USA, its newly improved relationship with Delhi does not make Washington an 'ally' in the classic military sense (although military cooperation is likely to intensify) and for Indians, it does not make the USA a South Asian power. The USA will want to avoid presuming on the relationship, particularly given India's sometimes prickly diplomatic personality. Delhi, meanwhile, must accept that India is not always at the centre of Washington's concerns and refrain from interpreting its every international move and statement as a comment on the US relationship with India. It also needs to accept as a given Pakistan's ability to play Washington as a violin at times, extracting from that relationship much more than Islamabad contributes.

In a review of international developments during the years 1985–2010, Indian commentator John Cherian flags the significance of India's leadership role in the fight against apartheid.[15] Indeed, India has much to be proud of in this respect. Prime Minister Rajiv Gandhi was perhaps the most determined non-African opponent within the Commonwealth and elsewhere of Margaret Thatcher's commercially-minded and tone-deaf rejection of sanctions to combat that abhorrent policy.[16] One of Rajiv Gandhi's associates in this effort, Anand Sharma, then President of the Indian Youth Congress, is today India's Minister of Commerce and Industry. Sharma wears his part in the struggle against apartheid as a badge of honour both privately and publicly. These antecedents and other Indian assets, combined with inevitable mistakes by China in Africa, should be adequate to the challenge of protecting India's economic and other interests on that continent.

Largely unnoticed by the rest of the world, India's attention to the Middle East has paid significant dividends.[17] Many reasons might be adduced for this: ancient and meaningful ties through cultural, dynastic, and other forms of migration; a reluctance to yield influence in the heart of the Islamic world to Pakistan; a desire to accommodate its own large Muslim community by cultivating a region to which it might be assumed to relate (although, beyond the Haj to Mecca, it is not clear how much Indian Muslims care about the Arab world); long-standing trade relations with the region; Indian requirements for energy supplies; and an attempt to ensure the welfare of India's large Diaspora in the Gulf. Nevertheless, this traditionally inhospitable terrain for the diplomacy of non-regional actors has yielded highly successful results for India.

Continuing challenges

Manmohan Singh has doubtless been right repeatedly to describe India's Maoist, Naxalite insurgency as the greatest challenge to India's security today. The insurgents were able to strike several damaging blows against seemingly underequipped and poorly prepared state security forces in mid-2010. While state action to root out the insurgents can be effective, the support of local populations remains the key asset in the struggle for local dominance, and on their needs, Delhi, sometimes contending with venal local politicians courting the popular vote by siding overtly or otherwise with the Naxalites, has not seemed to be able to deliver.[18] Although the insurgency does not currently seem likely to spread much further, having reached a debilitating equilibrium, the existence of such a significant internal challenge to its authority can only sap Delhi's credibility and its ability to tend to other priorities. More broadly, India's impressive former Foreign and Finance Minister, and frequent author, Jaswant Singh comments:

> India needs to reflect on . . . its Maoist presence, and the reality of almost 60% of its population living under the poverty line. Growth needs to be more distributive. Political parties all over the country have become family concerns, resulting in a perversion of parliamentary government and the spread of oligarchy. Consequently, the governance of the States has become unanswerable to the centre and governance in Delhi has become more notional than real. And the economy,

driven by the creative genius of Indian entrepreneurs, can only suffer as essential corrective steps, for example on labour and land acquisition laws, are thwarted.[19]

Relations with Pakistan remain vexed, in spite of recent efforts by Prime Ministers Vajpayee and Singh, and at different times several Pakistani leaders, to move beyond a state of mutual allergic reaction. While India's effort in recent years not to allow individual incidents linked to Pakistan directly or indirectly to drive its policy, future events interacting with domestic Indian political impulsions could cause Pakistan to consume a lot of India's foreign policy bandwidth. This is particularly so as today friction extends well beyond Kashmir (to which this chapter returns later) and individual terrorist acts to include India's reconstruction programme in Afghanistan and suggestions from Islamabad that India might be contributing to undermining Pakistani cohesion through support of nationalist elements in Baluchistan.

Contrary to some foreign perceptions, India does not actually much fear a nuclear war with Pakistan: Pakistan would have everything to lose in such a dire eventuality and, as pointed out by G. Parthasarathy, has been more prudent in arrangements for the storage and maintenance of its nuclear arsenal than is widely supposed.[20] But India's resiliency to provocations is not infinite. M. J. Akbar notes:

> Pakistan's nuclear arsenal has contributed to removing the fear that India can destroy Pakistan: such reassurance is an important basis for normalization. The rationale for continued conflict lies in a Pakistani dream that the status of Kashmir can be changed by persistence and the promotion of 'war by other means'. India has resisted raising the ante, even when the provocation was as serious as in Kargil, but the calmative effect of common sense can, under pressure, surrender to anger. The present stalemate has the potential of becoming toxic as other options fail.[21]

Yashwant Sinha, a respected former Minister of Finance and External Affairs, advocates a two-pronged approach given the current deadlock in the relationship: ignoring Pakistan and equipping India in such a way as to be less vulnerable to terrorist attacks. The restraint displayed by India following both Kargil and 26/11 is, he believes, a sign of a vibrant democracy breeding self-confidence, versus a less democratic and less self-confident neighbour.[22] Mr. Sinha's proposed strategy suggests that India can insulate itself successfully from Pakistan. Currently, this seems unlikely. Thus, attempts to seek an accommodation with Pakistan are likely to continue (and to be strongly supported internationally).

Meanwhile, more pressing for each of India and Pakistan are other challenges they face. Shiv Shankar Menon, during the brief period when he was out of office in 2009, suggested:

Pakistan has allowed an obsession with India and Afghanistan to destroy her own polity and internal balance. India must not allow an obsession with Pakistan to do the same to her foreign and domestic policies. For India (and, I dare say, Pakistan as well though to a lesser extent) the real issues are elsewhere. India's overriding task is her own domestic transformation, as is Pakistan's.[23]

Overall, India's twin instincts of seeking to improve relationships within its own region while simultaneously seeking to exert influence well beyond South Asia are sound. It can and should work harder to persuade neighbours that it wants them to benefit from India's strong economic growth. It is in India's interest to be generous to countries on its periphery in this regard (just as, on balance, it is in India's interest, as the stronger party, to offer generous gestures to Pakistan if only to improve the overall dynamic). This is particularly so as some countries in the region, for example Bangladesh again under the leadership of Sheikh Hasina since 2009, seem to understand that prospects for their own prosperity are strongly linked to those of India. While improved official relations do not make practical challenges, such as the large inflows of Bangladeshi economic migrants into India, go away, they may make them easier to manage vis-à-vis the Indian population and those elements of India's political community inclined towards chauvinism.

Difficult relations with China are also a constant, at least from the late 1950s onward.[24] Were China mired in backwardness and failure, Indians would probably not obsess about the bilateral relationship so much. But China's economic success, its growing ease in international relations, its advantageous position as a permanent member of the UN Security Council, and its increasing self-confidence (or depending on one's view, controlled arrogance) rankle Indians tremendously.[25] While China's presumed brittleness stemming from its totalitarian political system gives its Indian rivals some comfort, and while India's democracy provides its society with political shock-absorbers that China does not possess, most Indians recognize the significance of China's economic success, not only preceding that of India and exceeding it in extent, but also with the gap between them compounding every year. Further, the nature of India's polity, the frequent sensationalism of its free press, and the plethora of its public voices often lead India to overreact to developments that China's highly controlled system can tackle more subtly (however sharp Beijing can decide to sound, on occasion). Reflecting on the unequal state of the relationship, Jaswant Singh argues that, when push comes to shove: 'China can deliver government far more efficiently than either India or the USA.'[26]

Informed Indians worry about access to natural resources and energy in other parts of the developing world, including Africa.[27] India has long-standing trade links with Africa, and Indian communities have for several centuries dotted the African coast, with large numbers in East and South Africa. Some Indians consider that China's determined push into Africa, particularly in countries endowed with natural resources, should be emulated by Delhi. However, worries about China crowding out India in Africa may be misplaced.[28] For one thing, China's African ventures, however much dressed up in diplomatic niceties, are clearly above all a business proposition, and the Chinese modus operandi (relying on home base for most inputs, including often labour) will not make Beijing many friends in Africa beyond self-interested elites.[29] (Their useful and generous offer of scholarships to Chinese universities, on the other hand, may.) India need not replicate all of China's strategies and actions in Africa. Rather, it should identify and reinforce approaches that continue to serve its own interests in its own ways, leaving sometimes risky economic decisions in the hands of its capable private sector whenever possible.

One melancholy shift affecting India's international relations in slow motion has been the decline in relative terms of its relations with Europe. Russia will remain a trusted interlocutor, if only out of habit. Economic relations can be conducted unsentimentally on the basis of mutual interest. But the parties are definitely out of love, if they were ever smitten. As to the European Union, in spite of the extent of its economic and investment ties to India, impetus is deflating gently, while its leading member states vie with each other for Delhi's ear and contracts. The EU as an institution with a formal mandate to speak for its member states has in recent years, and in spite of the ratification in 2009 of the Lisbon Treaty, largely been ignored by countries such as India and China except in the realm of multilateral trade negotiations. On other issues, Beijing and Delhi mostly conduct business with the leading European capitals, which, conveniently, can be played off against each other. It is in Asia that the hollowness of much European rhetoric about unity and integration is most noticeable. Asians have no particular stake in the EU's success, and feel no need to pay it unwarranted tribute.

Multilateral diplomacy

Multilateral relations, often thought of in India as the country's diplomatic strong suit during the heyday of the Cold War, are today more controversial. Where India has performed very well is in financial diplomacy, in forums such as the G-20, at the World Bank, and at the IMF, where it engages with global challenges and trends on merit. Indeed, the competence in this realm of many Indian officials and scholars, as exemplified by the quietly assured Prime Minister Manmohan Singh, is widely recognized and appreciated.

The impatience of India to increase its formal role (as opposed to its substantive profile) in a number of international bodies, including the UN

Security Council, and through greater voting rights in the IMF, have bumped up against the interests of others and, at the IMF, the gross over-weighting of Europe. Entertainingly, if for the moment somewhat mischievously, Martin Wolf has suggested that 'exhausted by the burden of its pretensions, the UK should soon offer its seat [on the Security Council] ... to its former colony'.[30] On these institutional issues, the USA is likely to be India's greatest ally over time. China was careful not to challenge overtly India's candidacy for a permanent seat on the UN Security Council, instead turning all of its ire on Japan, one of India's three partners in its quest to increase the number of permanent seats in 2005. China continues to subscribe to alliances of convenience with India multilaterally where interests largely coincide, as in 2009 on climate change. However, these alliances are probably unstable because of very different styles of national decision-making and diplomacy, and the greater weight of China in the world. Nevertheless, China is unlikely systematically to frustrate India's rise to greater prominence at the various high tables of international diplomacy because it has more vital interests to promote and protect.

Thus, for India, time and its generally prudent policy stance are its greatest assets in attaining its aspirations for international recognition, as exemplified by the emergence of the G-20 at leader level in 2008, and Dr Singh's prominent role therein. This could be hastened by a creative (and cost-free) Indian offer to sign on to the Non-Proliferation Treaty if it can negotiate terms that place it on an equal footing with the existing five legitimate nuclear-weapon states under the treaty framework (as presaged in a statement by India's Prime Minister on 29 November 2009).[31] The path for this step could be paved by Indian accession to the Comprehensive Test Ban Treaty (CTBT), which its public pronouncements and new arrangements with the IAEA and the Nuclear Suppliers Group suggest is no longer in conflict with Indian policy. However, Dr Singh's policy shift on the NPT might be designed in part to fend off US pressure to accept the CTBT, if President Obama is successful in persuading the US Senate to ratify it. Further, India's security establishment is dead set against Indian involvement in a set of treaty obligations it has long seen as unequal, particularly as India possesses 'an unmatched record of restraint and responsibility' in preventing proliferation beyond its borders.[32]

A QUESTION OF STYLE

Indians are mostly brilliant, hard-working, loquacious, fluent, and creative. They generally cleave to engagement with others, and this works wonders at the bilateral level, where the parameters of national interests are perhaps most clearly defined on both sides. In bilateral diplomacy, India has made many friends. Multilaterally, however, while generating for itself a reputation as a country that always needs to be contended with, India has achieved less to date, with its financial diplomacy an honourable exception. The perceived need to outflank all potential or actual rivals and impress all comers sometimes leads Indian practitioners to monopolize attention through rhetorical brilliance and to spend as much time on impressing the gallery as on tending effectively to Indian interests. The cleverest person in the room may win many arguments, but still not win the game, as suggested in the previous chapter. Many of those interviewed for this book in India itself, in South Asia, and beyond have commented that Delhi's negotiating style too often exhibits no 'give' while rarely hesitating to communicate non-negotiable principles and demands.

The previous chapter provides a number of comments from Indians on how grating this style can be. As Edward Luce, a mostly fond and acute observer of India, notes: 'It would be tempting to conclude that India is rising in spite of its diplomacy.'[33] The reason the tone needs to evolve is that the current approach simply will not work at the high table of international relations to which India is acceding. Dr Singh's soft-spoken self-confidence is the antithesis of the sharp-elbowed style mostly associated with India's negotiators and has often served as a foil for it. India's next Prime Minister's equanimity may not be up to the challenge of counteracting the negative fall-out generated by lower-level official pugilists.

This is also why India's often fierce rejection of all criticism of its government action in such forums as the UN Human Rights Council elicit both a weariness and a sense of regret that, for example, India's struggle to advance the status of its *Adivasi* (tribal) communities (fully supported by the Delhi government at home, but largely papered over for international consumption, as if this were possible or credible nowadays) is too often played down by Indian representatives at the UN rather than celebrated.

What kind of a Power will India be?

The scholars of today are sometimes confounded to conclude, as did George Tanham in 1992, that India has no grand plan, no strategic vision for its foreign policy in a post-Cold War world.[34]

For a long time, India was able to cloak interest-based short-term decisions governing its international relations in pronouncements setting itself on a moral plane above the hard calculus of the Cold War's reductive struggle between opposing ideologies. In fact, Nehru improvised thoughtfully and with considerable flexibility as foreign policy challenges claimed his attention, mostly by lucidly assessing the scope of action afforded by available means to shape India's often shifting ends. Indira Gandhi also improvised, but found her margin of manoeuvre constricted by circumstances and some of her own mistakes. Non-alignment did not represent much of an ideology, but it allowed India (and many others, each interpreting the concept in its own way) to multiply its options.

Today, India's voice is sought out and respected but often indistinct. Political scientist Dipankar Gupta notes:

> Much of what India does in terms of diplomacy actually depends on a peculiar combination of memories of hurt and the desire to be recognized. That is why we are usually reacting to issues and rarely ever setting the stage, or the terms of reference, for international relations. There is more 'tactic' than 'strategy'. Indeed, the Indian foreign office's long institutional memory may keep it from thinking imaginatively.[35]

Srinath Raghavan points out that scholarly analysts 'want behaviour to be guided by general principle, and they place a high premium on consistency'.[36] The cacophony of Indian debate, the frequent contradictions in Indian official pronouncements, and the wealth and diversity of Indian commentary defy easy generalizations about either strategic thought or its close cousin, wider foreign policy. This bothers few Indian practitioners: the country's foreign policy is not formulated for the convenience of analysts or of armchair strategists, as noted by Pratap Bhanu Mehta at a recent conference.[37] But it does frustrate foreign policy analysts, as Harsh Pant makes clear:

> The Indian elites do have a growing sense of their country as an emerging power, as an important player on the global stage. Yet, the Indian state seems unable to leverage the opportunities presented by India's economic rise to their full potential.[38]

Is this a bad thing for India? Almost certainly not. Efforts by political leaders the world over to lay out their distinct foreign policy orientations invariably wind up being torpedoed by unexpected events, insufficient resources, short attention spans, and frequently embarrassing incompetence at many levels of government. This was the case for both US presidents Clinton and George W. Bush. Mehta comments on the discrepancy between:

> the 'Grand Strategies' that determine the orientation of the major powers and the instruments they have to achieve them. The strategy is often determined by assumptions about their own power—in reality the power of power is often overestimated. In this sense Grand Strategy can be more a potentially illusory statement of objectives than a feasible plan of action.[39]

Efforts to lay out in great detail a compendium of objectives, policies, and proposed actions in 'foreign policy reviews' and in 'white papers' in Western countries invariably pall within months as fantasy meets hard reality.[40] It is often easier to describe the style of a particular government's foreign policy than its substance, as, on the latter, there is generally a wide gulf between stated intent and actual performance.

In the Indian context, Kanti Bajpai posits three distinct schools of strategic thinking that have been vying for space and dominance: Nehruvians (Left liberals), neoliberals (classical liberals or libertarians), and hyperrealists (conservatives). He goes on to note that 'it is not easy to cast aside deeply held beliefs about political life' in discussion of foreign policy.[41] Consequently, high-minded aspiration to a cross-partisan, nationally unifying foreign policy and strategic framework are doubtless delusional. Nevertheless, there has been considerable continuity of foreign policy in India, described by former Foreign Minister K. Natwar Singh as a 'broad national consensus', between governments since 1991 claiming to have little in common.[42]

The neighbourhood

India's potential global role remains somewhat constrained by its unsatisfactory regional dispensation. The violent end of British Imperial India yielded enduring and corrosive divisions that the region has not yet fully learned to live with, and on which India has, by and large, failed to lead imaginatively or strongly. Most Indian Prime Ministers have inclined more towards domestic consensus-building than bold regional initiatives. As it seeks to reach beyond its own region, an emergence welcomed by most of the world, it runs the risk of leaving its own neighbourhood an orphan lacking for vision and leadership, a risk that is all the greater insofar as its neighbours are all too often hostile. Actively undermining creative approaches to the region has been India's dynamic, knowledgeable, but deeply conservative security establishment. In any event, as Christophe Jaffrelot comments:

> India's aspiration to be recognised as a global player is not only due to an obvious pull factor, global power, but also to a push factor, that of escaping its region, South Asia, where it is surrounded by quasi-failed states, civil war torn countries, guerrilla-plagued societies and overtly antagonistic governments which tend to join hands against New Delhi, making SAARC a non-functioning entity. But neither Pakistan, nor Nepal will allow India to ignore them.[43]

India traditionally has been averse to outside intervention in the region, but it has become more flexible in recent years, reluctantly accepting an active if limited UN political role in Nepal's complex domestic affairs, and essentially welcoming US and NATO involvement in Afghanistan. On Afghanistan, Delhi radiates apprehension. It worries that, in Afghanistan, Pakistan may get the better of the USA, pocketing its financial and military aid while undermining any prospect of a genuinely independent government in Kabul. On Pakistan, it understands that a failed state is not in its own interests but fears a stronger hostile neighbour (even though a stronger, more confident Pakistan might more readily be able to settle its differences with India). Despite Pakistan's provocations, it would doubtless serve India well to reach out, explain itself better to Pakistanis, and take more of the 'risks for peace' of which past leaders in the Middle East used to speak. If India were to do so, perhaps Washington would be more inclined to spend its ultimately limited capital in Islamabad by pressing that capital to meet Delhi halfway. Prime Minister Singh recently spoke again of his desire to settle differences with Pakistan, but did not provide specific ideas on how to do so.[44]

Significant forces favouring inertia are at play. Few politicians publicly advocate accommodation of Pakistan in any concrete form (although some do so in private). Further, the stand-off between the two countries benefits a number of state actors in Pakistan, notably the armed forces and the intelligence community, so Indian advocates of 'no concessions' are echoed loudly by influential voices across the border. Dialogue between the two countries, which is often interrupted by security incidents, should be structured in such a way that it is mostly insulated from incidents of terrorism or other serious 'bumps in the road', rendering it, in the words of former Cabinet Minister and former Consul General of India in Karachi, Mani Shankar Aiyar, a dialogue that is 'uninterrupted and uninterruptable'.[45] An attempt to do so was sketched in the statement issued by India and Pakistan at the conclusion of a meeting between their Prime Ministers in Sharm el Sheikh in July 2009, but a subsequent media and parliamentary uproar in India over a reference to Baluchistan in the same text put paid to any meaningful further high-level dialogue for months.

China has been more helpful than not to India at moments of high tension with Pakistan in recent years, remaining studiedly neutral during the Kargil episode of 1999 and making clear privately at the United Nations that it did not support Pakistan's resistance to international interest in the role of its citizens following the 2008 Mumbai attack. Indeed, China is not in an entirely comfortable position vis-à-vis Pakistan, having empowered it over many years, not least with nuclear technology, only to see the country spawn ever more Muslim extremism, which is hardly to China's taste. Nevertheless, in the complex geostrategic games afoot in Asia, the China–Pakistan alliance is likely to endure, while China also mostly accommodates India's rise.

India's relations with other South Asian states range from the serene (Maldives and Bhutan, both attractive neighbours but hardly major international players) to improving but still marked by a degree of mutual suspicion (Bangladesh) to often tense (Sri Lanka, Nepal). Forward momentum will, in every case, breed rewards. Indeed, India's benign (if economically and geostrategically self-interested) approach to Bhutan could serve as a model, albeit one that is not easily replicated in its specifics, for its relations with others in its periphery.

The difficult challenge India faces in Myanmar of protecting its own relationship with, and interests in, the country, at a time when the weight of China there is increasingly marginalizing all other international actors, evokes sympathy. Nevertheless, India can do more to reflect its own political and societal values in its stance vis-à-vis Naypyidaw rather than seeking to occlude all possible bilateral differences in the relationship. Myanmar, which needs to retain more strings in its international relations fiddle than just Beijing and Thai business interests, needs India nearly as much as Delhi needs it.

Kashmir

Kashmir is widely seen as an international issue in dispute between Pakistan and India on which foreign parties can succeed only in offending one side or the other, if not both. India remains very sensitive to outside intrusion on the issue, as foreign involvement conflicts with its position that the topic must remain a strictly bilateral one between Delhi and Islamabad. It has remained so with dismal results for many years.[46]

Rash as it is for a foreign voice to express any views on the topic, it may suffice to suggest that India could change the game on its own terms by seeking radically to improve the living conditions of the inhabitants of the Kashmir Valley and its environs, much oppressed by an overwhelming Indian military, paramilitary, and police presence that at times has proved both incompetent and brutal.[47] Timid measures to de-escalate India's security deployment in Kashmir were trumpeted in 2009 and 2010, but, on such a scale, little will be achieved. Moreover, impunity for the security forces in Kashmir remains worryingly prevalent.[48]

An effort to re-imagine Indian Kashmir as the proud and prosperous place that it was for so much of its history, rather than as a security problem to be met with overwhelming force, might well prove salutary. M. J. Akbar writes:

> If Kashmir is a part of India, as India insists it must be, then Kashmiris have equal right to the advantages and privileges of economic growth. The greatest attraction for the young Kashmiri is surely the Indian model of a modern nation state, with its freedoms (particularly gender freedom) and economic promise. All a Kashmiri has to do is look west to find India a far more reassuring proposition.[49]

Of course, any relaxation of security control over the Kashmir valley and its surrounding areas could be interpreted as a threat to their *raison d'être* and as an invitation to respond by Pakistan-based militants. Further, Indians are used to thinking of Kashmir as both the central prize up for grabs, and a pawn, in the India–Pakistan relationship. The notion of bold unilateral action—without any reward from Pakistan—to give effect to the autonomy the Indian constitution promises the region strikes a number of Indians as foolish at best.

Nevertheless, such a unilateral step would give Pakistan much to think about at a time when inhabitants of the Kashmir Valley mostly no longer want Pakistani citizenship (they would rather be independent but understand that today this constitutes an impossible dream). Giving priority to the well-being of Indian citizens (as Delhi insists the inhabitants of Indian Kashmir must remain) could place India on the front foot in its dialogue with Pakistan. Further, India could anticipate considerable international sympathy and support if a determined effort were made by Pakistan-based elements to reverse such a process through militant incursions. In any event, as Sushant K. Singh and Rohit Pradhan noted following state elections in Jammu and Kashmir in 2008:

> The security contexts of the Line of Control and Srinagar, for example, are very different. Indeed, the prevalent notion that the army requires a carte blanche to operate across the entire state makes little sense. The army has to be at the forefront of counterterrorism operations on the LoC, but it should play a secondary role to the political leadership in counter-insurgency operations in the Kashmiri heartland.[50]

This is an issue on which India's friends would welcome an Indian stance of exchanging its ever-present 'red lines' for green lights.[51]

Afghanistan

At the time of writing, Afghanistan has become a conundrum for India.[52] The Soviet invasion of the country in 1979, to prop up an unpopular communist regime in Kabul, was an embarrassment for Delhi. Determined US and Saudi support for anti-communist guerrillas fighting the Soviet troops from bases within Pakistan induced long-term mutations that would bedevil the area thereafter. In the late 1980s, it empowered infiltration of militants into Indian Kashmir precipitating a new internal crisis there.

After the Taliban's accession to power in Kabul, the hijacking of Air India flight 814 en route from Kathmandu to Delhi in December 1999, resulting in serial climbdowns by India to secure the release of hostages at Kandahar in Afghanistan, reinforced the conviction in India that a radical Islamist regime in Afghanistan was a dagger pointed at its own heart. It thus welcomed the rout of Al Qaeda and the Taliban following the events of 11 September 2001, and invested heavily in the success of President Hamid Karzai, seen as a friend of India and a moderate force, thereafter.

However, by 2010, the NATO forces propping up Karzai's weak government in Kabul were facing determined opposition from a resurgent Taliban with whom some in NATO, notably the UK, were increasingly inclined to negotiate a degree of power-sharing in Kabul. For India, rarely consulted by NATO countries, the options were unattractive at a time when several NATO capitals were signalling growing impatience to withdraw from the battlefield.

Indians were themselves the target of regular attacks in Afghanistan and adjusted their ambitious and largely successful reconstruction programme there in order better to protect themselves. The Indian embassy in Kabul was twice attacked with devastating consequences at the hands of terrorists thought in India to be acting at the behest of the Pakistani security agencies.

The USA wavered dangerously between praise for the risks India was taking in order to help Afghanistan and its willingness to accommodate Pakistan by signalling that it might be useful for Indian friends to lower their profile in that country.

The medium term looks grim; the likelihood of, at best, a hybrid regime in Kabul with strong links to Islamabad, possibly resisted by a revival of the 'Northern Alliance', raises the possibility in the minds of some Indian and international strategists of a return to the dispensation of the 1990s (with forces in Afghanistan's northern provinces to be supported by India, Russia, and perhaps Iran). Meanwhile, some Indians called for Delhi to commit troops to Afghanistan in support of Karzai to forestall such unhappy contingencies.[53] There were not many takers for this proposed approach, but anxiety over the future of Afghanistan, and Pakistan's role therein, is increasingly rife within India's security establishment. Hence, India compared notes on Afghanistan carefully with Russian Prime Minister Putin during his visit to India in early 2010.[54] Pointing to India's limited options in Afghanistan as of now, Pankaj Mishra writes:

> The reason is the recent history of animosities and suspicions which make India's motives, however altruistic, look suspect to Pakistan and its Afghan proxies, just as Pakistan's role in India's immediate neighbours looks fishy to India and its allies. India may have miscalculated in Afghanistan, now that not only Obama wants it to be discreet but Karzai himself has decided he will have to trust Pakistan to stabilize southern Afghanistan.[55]

China

As Nehru had hoped, India and China today work alongside each other, and frequently partner on multilateral issues such as climate change, more than either country might have expected only a few years ago, and this in spite of their border dispute, and fears of mutual encirclement.[56] Both countries have moved, in the words of Commonwealth Secretary-General Kamalesh Sharma, from the international status of 'demandeurs' to that of 'demandees', from whom the global system wants policy decisions and actions.[57] But as argued by Shyam Saran, India is enjoying 'premature' power, akin to 'being dealt a hand in the geopolitical game, but refusing to play'.[58] The same might be said of China.

The two countries, are, of course, profoundly different in their political and economic systems, and it is the asymmetry between them that is often most striking, not least China's advance on India to date (that some Indians are convinced their country's accelerating growth will reverse in years ahead).[59] In international economic relations, China's model is essentially mercantilist while India mostly allows the impulses of its private sector to predominate.

In the wake of the financial and economic crisis of 2008–9, the notion that power is shifting from West to East became fashionable beyond what prophets of this view, like the fluent and compelling Kishore Mahbubani, had earlier argued.[60] Lost in this new consensus, however, is the reality that India and China will need to accommodate each other and actively cooperate on some issues, rather than compete head-on for power, if the prediction is to come true over time.[61] There are early hints that this may well be possible. Both countries fear Islamic extremism and although each will tackle it in its own way domestically, their shared anxieties could breed deeper cooperation internationally.[62] Both countries have been more 'rule takers' than 'rule makers' internationally, but they share an interest in enforcement of a number of those rules, in areas such as piracy (where each has cooperated further to a UN call for action against attacks on commercial traffic through sea-lanes near Somalia).[63] Their Diasporas cohabit throughout much of the world, including along Africa's shores, and they could develop common views and even action on the defence of Diaspora members in distress. But cooperation will not be instinctive. Former UK High Commissioner to India Michael Arthur sees the relationship as 'fundamentally competitive', and argues that the tension will require active management by both capitals.[64] Princeton University scholar Rohan Mukherjee comments: 'India's competition with China is not just economic or geo-strategic; in a sense it is existential—a clash of two competing political systems, bases of state legitimacy, and ways of ordering state–society relations.'

China and India are likely not just to influence international relations in the abstract but also to change them in practice, and how this occurs will be important to people everywhere. It may be that their perceived responsibility to their own people, and how they act on this, could disrupt international rules. On balance, however, this seems unlikely—both today are straining to advance and protect their interests without upending global rules. At the conclusion of his excellent book *Rivals*, Bill Emmott writes:

> How will the Asian drama end? The answer is that it won't: it is now going to be a permanent feature of world affairs, and arguably the most important single

determinant of whether those affairs proceed peacefully and prosperously or not. The drama will pit new, rising powers against the world's long-established powers in America and Europe; and it will pit Asia's new powers against each other and against the region's first modernizer, Japan. In economics and business, the competition will have overwhelmingly positive results. In politics, we cannot be so sure.[65]

India's economy

India's purchase on international influence today derives from a combination of its size and demographic weight with fast-accelerating economic growth in recent decades. The variable factor is thus its economic momentum, and, as Indians know well, the credibility of its rise internationally hinges on a continued strong economic performance.[66]

India's domestic economy today requires an active national foreign policy.[67] One by-product of economic reform has been much greater openness to and reliance on international markets (while India can also count on a large and robust domestic market offering very high rates of savings for investment purposes). India and China's requirement for growing energy supply, in both cases still largely market-based, demands active diplomacy in order to advance core national resource access interests. Furthermore, India's private sector requires essentially open international markets in order to capitalize on its comparative advantages, not least impressive entrepreneurship.

India's economic growth has been stronger since 2000, in a sustained way, than in all countries other than China and larger than Singapore and the Gulf Emirates (even if the statistical basis for a variety of growth claims, including those of China, is debatable). India not only survived the financial and economic crisis of 2008–9 largely unscathed but grew healthily throughout it, with GDP growth at its lowest in the 5 per cent range—although some sectors of its economy were seriously affected for a few quarters.[68] By mid-2010, growth was again flirting with the 9 per cent level, and India's particular economic model, featuring extraordinary mobility of labour within the country, presented further reasons for optimism. However, future economic and social challenges remain daunting—notwithstanding the resiliency, industriousness, and talent of its human capital.

Demography should play in the country's favour if it can improve education at all levels. Large numbers of educated, skilled young Indians would be a boon not only to their own country but to the world (as so many expatriate Indians today demonstrate daily around the globe). Moreover, a combination of generally respected government secularism and inter-communal tolerance are key bonding factors in India, a country of dizzying diversity. Delhi in 2010 was grappling with a proposed new framework for higher education that implicitly recognizes worrying existing deficits of quality and the need for radical and widespread change. India's small number of elite institutions of learning are not even remotely up to the scale of challenge of pulling the country forward in the ever more competitive international skills-building game, at a time when massive investments in research and higher education are being made elsewhere, not least in China.[69] Weak higher education inevitably impacts innovation, an area in which India has been performing less well than many Indians think (and not just in applications for patent recognition). Successful entrepreneur and senior Indian policy maven Sam Pitroda comments:

> Higher education will be the real engine for growth and prosperity for India in the 21st century. Only through [it] can India hope to address challenges related to disparity, demography and development, focusing on problem solving and new business models. The Indian economy needs substantial skilled human resources to sustain the 8 to 10% growth expected for the next few decades. Today there are significant shortages for qualified managers, engineers, scientists and other professionals at all levels in the business and government.[70]

In the political realm, although identity politics continue to hold sway, coalition governments are more responsive decision-makers, with electors appearing to be more results-oriented and discerning with respect to the effectiveness of government programmes and actions in recent years. Permanent re-election mode for sitting governments produces both promising new initiatives (e.g. the recent rural employment guarantee scheme) but also non-stop pandering (for example, 'a colour television for every home' in Tamil Nadu), the price for today's retail politics. The role of civil society is growing and caste factors, while still important in rural areas, are being eroded in urban India, including in the private sector where previously excluded caste groups have become active and successful.[71] Affirmative action, in the form of reservations (or quotas), has played an important role in advancing disadvantaged groups in society, but India has bumped up against the limits of the policy when carried too far (for example in higher education) and will need to adjust policy to changing social circumstances and economic needs.

The country is adapting to some of the forces of urbanization and modernization that have placed great strain on traditional family practices such as the care of elders by younger generations, while courting risks in others such as gender selection (which, in some parts of the country, has reached alarming proportions and threatens social cohesion a generation hence).

Agriculture can do much better with more sensible water and power policies. But it requires more attention than it has received at the policy level in order to generate the productivity gains that would help feed the country and allow for exports. Indeed, in the long run, India should not be relying on protection of its agricultural sector to the extent it sometimes does, particularly in terms of political posturing. Instead it should focus on making the best of its largely under-tapped potential. Manufacturing could thrive with better infrastructure connecting it to the rest of the country, the immediate region and the world. But progress on infrastructure has been painfully slow, and glowing exceptions, such as the Delhi metro and a raft of new airport terminals, underscore both what is possible with political focus and determination, and the worrying gulf remaining to be bridged in this huge and infrastructurally deficient country—another area of Chinese advantage in the Asian race for dominance.

Siddharth Varadarajan notes that one set of actors rarely discussed in assessing Indian foreign policy is the country's key private sector players.[72] While several of these (for example, Lakshmi Mittal, and the Ambani brothers) have secured for themselves a high international profile, and others such as Ratan Tata are iconic national figures much admired for their philanthropy and public-minded initiatives, the dealings of India's private sector with India's politicians are often opaque at best.

Dynamic outward investment by the Indian private sector, much welcomed internationally, should not just be a source of pride for Indians but also a reason to ponder why internal formal and informal barriers to large-scale investment in manufacturing are encouraging Indian corporations to invest so much abroad. This has been particularly damaging in the infrastructure, large-scale manufacturing, and extractive resource sectors.

When asked about India's economic model, industrialist Analjit Singh, chairman of the Max India conglomerate, points to gaping and rising economic inequalities as the principal challenge.[73] While India, at Union and state levels, struggles and largely fails to provide basic services, such as health and education, to the poor, only few of the country's burgeoning middle class pay meaningful taxes. Veteran Congress politician Mani Shankar Aiyar is scathing on the contribution India's rich make to the country's welfare:

> High growth, which benefits the rich disproportionately, has swollen government revenues and larger expenditure is available for poverty alleviation programmes, but the proportional benefit reaching the poor is a sliver of the humungous benefits of accelerated growth being cornered by the better-off, mostly by the obscenely rich.[74]

International scholar and commentator Ramesh Thakur points to the 200,000 or so estimated farmer suicides in India over the past fifteen years, highlighting how strong the disconnection remains between the dynamic private sector-driven growth of 'India Shining' and the mass of rural poor in India, hundreds of millions of whom survive on 20 rupees (50 US cents) a day or less.[75] Thakur also points to the large-scale criminalization of Indian politics that affects many other dimensions of society.[76]

None of these challenges are insurmountable, but, taken together, they represent a sobering nexus of potential trouble that India's highly fragmented political system, used to muddling through, does not seem ideally suited to address dynamically. Thus, while India has made bold strides economically over the past two decades, much remains to be achieved.

Values and soft power

India's growing belief that the political values enshrined in its constitution, which the country tries hard to live up to within its borders, can make it attractive to others—the 'soft power' of its democracy, multi-ethnic make-up, the vibrancy of its civil society, and the fierce freedom of its press—is well founded. Indeed, the struggle for development, justice, adequate representation, and respect that lies at the heart of Indian politics can be recognized anywhere in the world as both familiar and positive. However, for now, rather like China, it prefers to avoid unnecessary controversy with neighbours, even ones whose behaviour can be repugnant to large numbers of Indians, in order to get on with the country's own development and the gradual rise of its global influence.

It is easy for those at a continental remove and with limited economic and security interests at stake to criticize. But it is potentially more costly for those needing to forge ahead economically in an unforgiving, complex, and often hostile neighbourhood to do so.[77] Might the Indian government have been braver in advocating improved governance in Myanmar? In my view, yes. Having in the late 1980s championed Aung San Suu Kyi (whose mother was Burma's ambassador in India in the early 1960s), Delhi, assessing the weakness of its own position in India's northeast and the growing ties between China and Burma's military rulers, in the 1990s reversed course and sought to deepen and expand its ties with the latter. Its engagement with Naypyidaw is seen in Delhi as a necessity and enjoys a large degree of cross-party support. Should India have condemned Iran's rigged elections and its deliberate slaughter of protesters in 2009? This doubtless represented a tough call for Delhi, particularly after voting against Iran internationally on key nuclear issues.[78] Shrill posturing by Western powers on issues of marginal importance to their economic welfare is not, as seen from Asia, any more attractive than the silence of leaders throughout Asia when faced with Burmese or Iranian government brutality.

Given its noisy democracy, India has found it very challenging to build domestic political support for foreign policy initiatives purely by invoking the argument of power. The argument of national interest is more compelling to

Indians. But Delhi has also continued to need a set of values and norms to justify its actions on the world stage. As a consequence the tension between 'power and principle' remains an enduring one in India's foreign policy.[79] Nevertheless, India's democratic credentials and values are unlikely to be favoured over its key strategic interests—the principal insight of a useful recent volume by S. D. Muni on the democracy dimension of India's foreign policy.[80]

THE DIASPORA

India, along with China and Israel, has generated a significant global Diaspora that has played, and likely will continue to play, a meaningful role in the country's life and self-image.[81] The Indian Diaspora, estimated at twenty-five million, can be found throughout Asia (significantly in Malaysia, Singapore, and Myanmar), in much of the Middle East, particularly the Gulf, around the coasts of Africa (and particularly in South Africa), featuring prominently in the Caribbean, where Kamla Persad-Bissessar in May 2010 was elected the first woman Prime Minister of Trinidad and Tobago, and present in large numbers in Australia, Canada, the UK, and the USA.[82] Non-resident Indians (NRIs), as they are often referred to in India, range across professional categories and play an important role at all levels of international business and increasingly in political life. The role of Indian-Americans in not only creating synergies for trade, investment, and technology transfers between the USA and India but also in mobilizing political support and influencing a positive shift in US policy towards India from the 1990s onwards is one notable example.[83]

Yet, like other Diasporas, their role within their country of origin's wider society is circumscribed, essentially to the economic field. India is the largest recipient of remittances in the world, receiving $43 billion in 2008 (increased from $25 billion in 2006).[84] Despite this, as in Israel, Indians do not wish their domestic or foreign policy dictated from abroad. Thus, while India welcomes the many potential uses of its Diaspora, and in recent years has sought to highlight the value attached to it through annual conferences to draw NRIs back to their country of origin, mostly the influence of even very prominent Diaspora members is slim unless, as is occasionally the case, they retain significant economic assets or develop a discernable political profile in India. Indeed, NRIs are among those who complain most vociferously about the difficulty foreign economic actors face in negotiating the barriers to entry into the Indian market.

As noted in Chapters 8 and 9, India has not always been able to protect or promote the interests of its own citizens (far less NRIs) in Asia to the east and west of the subcontinent. Although on occasion supportive of the concerns of the Indian community (as in the case of attacks on Indians in Australia in 2009), India has by and large preferred not to interfere in the internal affairs of other governments.[85] While seeking to manage the local political fall-out within India of abuse of NRIs abroad, it has not highlighted in its diplomacy their welfare as a principal goal of Indian foreign policy, although a Union Minister for Overseas Indian Affairs (not coincidentally at present from Kerala, which provides so many of the migrant workers) is responsible for their interests in Delhi.

On occasion, such as through support of the Free Khalistan Movement, elements of the Indian Diaspora have threatened Indian interests and national security. For these reasons also, official India is hardly sentimental about long-lost cousins abroad (while making use of them in promoting bilateral relations wherever possible). Nevertheless, it is proud of their successes.

India in the world

Although most countries are nowadays minding their manners when dealing with India, a genuine dialogue with India on potentially contentious subjects need not be disagreeable. However, hectoring India rarely works (just as its own hectoring of others during its early decades produced few results and little good will). A *New York Times* editorial, apparently designed to stiffen the spine of Hillary Clinton before her first visit to Delhi as US Secretary of State, adopted an uncompromising tone: 'It is time for India to take more responsibility internationally. It needs to revive the world trade talks...and—as a major contributor to global warming—to join the developed countries in cutting greenhouse gasses. And it needs to do more to constrain its arms race with Pakistan.'[86] Though perhaps true, these lines suggest that even sophisticated minds in the West have not yet learned how to persuade Asian interlocutors to adopt Western perspectives.

Scoring much better in engaging Indians on the topics of non-proliferation and climate change was Strobe Talbott, who recently wrote:

> The US administration knows it cannot coax or bully India into formally joining the NPT, nor will it renege on the civil nuclear deal it inherited from Mr Bush ... Tightening the verification authorities of the International Atomic Energy Agency, accelerating negotiations to stop the production of fissile material (the stuff at the core of nuclear warheads) and bringing the CTBT into force ... would make India's region safer, since Pakistan might follow suit in a positive direction, just as it did in a negative one when it conducted a nuclear test shortly after India's in 1998. A similar appeal to self-interest might prevail with respect to climate change. Since much of India's population lives in rural and coastal areas, it is acutely vulnerable to the devastation of agricultural lands and rising sea levels that come with global warming.[87]

Put this way, in terms of India's own interests, and bringing into the equation the vacillations of others, many Indians would agree.

India's capacity to play on its power of attraction is significant. Yet, as pointed out in a controversial essay by Barbara Crossette, its international influence and welcome in the halls of power remains tentative.[88] This may have to do with the flip-side of the warmth and intelligence of so many Indians—an overinflated desire, sometimes insistence, on winning every argument, and, if this cannot be achieved, a disposition to obstruct. Domestically, this leads to the Indian government being under much media, parliamentary, and consequently sometimes even public pressure to 'say no', in key negotiations with China, Pakistan, and the USA.

A seeming reluctance a priori to be 'part of the solution', as Prime Minister Singh argued India should be on climate change in 2009, doubtless stems in large part from India's colonial experiences and its weak negotiating position during the early decades of independence. With impressive Indian economic accomplishments in recent decades, the global success of its artists and writers, and much else to its credit, a more self-confident approach by Delhi internationally would now seem in order, with Indian creativity at the service not only of its own interests but also of wider stewardship of international management of global challenges.

India, in much of the world, evokes the glamour of its past, the grandeur of its monuments, the glory of its colours, Himalayan peaks, all of these conveyed to great effect in the country's highly successful 'Incredible India!' promotional campaign. All of these Indian particulars deserve their place in the world's imagination. India has also worked hard to superimpose on these characteristics international understanding of a more modern, private sector-driven country featuring fast growth, ground-breaking service and high tech industries, and a 'can do' spirit among its young professionals and corporate leaders.[89] Although this has worked, up to a point, there is no sense yet of an overall Indian project—as there is with China's relentless drive towards modernization and growth.

How might Indian foreign policy and its establishment reinvent itself for the modern world? Intellectuals, many of them to be found in Delhi's think-tanks, may play a key role. Daniel Markey recently tackled the 'software' of India's foreign policy, producing some helpful suggestions. These include increasing the size of the Indian foreign service, creating greater and more meaningful interaction between official Indian foreign policy actors and India's think-tanks, improving higher education in the field of international studies, and more openness to researchers by India's foreign policy and defence archives, in order that lessons of the past emerge more clearly and systematically.[90]

India's overburdened Foreign Service is, on average, of very high quality, but because it is stretched so thin, its staff spends too much of its time conducting India's international relations through narrow diplomatic channels, managing ministerial and other visits, negotiating memoranda of understanding of no great significance, and by other means that reflect only a fraction of the rich reality of international relations today and of official Delhi's actual international interests.[91] In this, the IFS resembles most of the world's Foreign Services. More investment in this and in other instruments of Indian foreign policy is needed, but so is more thought on how best to use this high-quality instrument.[92]

India's think-tanks are often impressive, having benefited from the decline of the university system. Indeed, they are the envy of many in the developing world, and in number and influence approximate those of London (if not yet Washington): Delhi's Centre for Policy Research, under Pratap Bhanu Mehta's strong leadership, now offers not just depth and excellence on broad strategic analysis of foreign policy (by Srinath Raghavan) and international economic issues (by Navroz Dubash), but also continues to host robust commentary by foreign policy hawks such as Brahma Chellaney and G. Parthasarathy. Its work complements that of several leading economic think-tanks (notably the National Council of Applied Economic Research and the Indian Council on International Economic Relations, both with impressive capabilities on international affairs) and several defence-related institutions with considerable research and advocacy capacity (including the Institute for Defence Studies and Analyses and the National Maritime Foundation). New centres for policy advocacy spring up regularly, most recently the Takshashila Foundation, which publishes the bracing young policy oriented monthly *Pragati*.

The government, including individual ministers, do, in my experience, consult outside experts and analysts more than Markey's admirable survey in Delhi suggests. But it is true that, as with bureaucracies elsewhere, officials are reluctant to part with information, and the policies governing a variety of Indian archives, including the Nehru papers, are confounding. It is only recently that a dynamic new minister responsible for higher education, Kapil Sibal, has outlined concrete ways in which the country can do better in preparing its population to deal with the wider world. Inevitably, these are controversial.

Sophisticated commentary on foreign relations is increasing as some of India's brightest younger scholars choose to return to India rather than to ply their trade in the great universities and research institutions of the West. This yields the added benefit of relieving the excessive weight of retired officials in commenting in the media on policies they helped shape.[93]

While the resources India invests in foreign affairs are more modest in both absolute and relative terms than those of Brazil and China, and even more so when compared with Moscow or Washington, the quality of the human resources involved somewhat makes up for this, as do the contributions to India's wider international relations of many other Indian actors.

Major orientations in foreign policy everywhere are influenced by very few individuals with either the ability or the positioning to do so. India is no different in that regard. The most significant innovation from this perspective has been the growth in the role of the Prime Minister and the Prime Minister's Office in shaping foreign policy relative to that of the MEA, and this shift in India is part of a wider trend, also discernable in Brasilia, London, and Paris, of the leaders in government and their immediate associates seizing the reins of foreign policy. This trend is unlikely to be reversed in any of these or other major capitals.

Global burden-sharing

Now that India is, on the strength of its economic successes, taken quite seriously by other major global players, it will need to grapple with whether, when, how, and in what proportions it can and wants to share global burdens, such as the fight against climate change. This dilemma is at the nub of India's discomfort with discussion of the issue at the international level. As of 2009, Prime Minister Singh and India's Environment Minister, Jairam Ramesh, made clear that India must act for its own reasons to curb pollution of various sorts in India and accept that India (like several of its neighbours) is threatened by global warming patterns. As opposed to the Copenhagen circus that unfolded in 2009, thinking globally and acting locally without engaging in treaty-making and binding international obligations may well be the path forward internationally. At the same time, the complex minuet in which India engaged prior to Copenhagen, seeking to placate domestic nationalists while striking a more open pose internationally, cannot be replicated indefinitely. For an emerging economic power to shelter itself behind appeals to its own poverty and a purported common line with other developing countries is not only ineffective, but also somewhat unworthy.

By underwriting an official assistance programme for neighbouring countries and some other purposes, by volunteering for dangerous peacekeeping duties and, at the policy level, by contributing to G-20 policy commitments, India signals that it is not inherently obstructionist. Rather, it is confident of being able to make a meaningful mark on collective international efforts. The step from here to taking on more ambitious tasks is one that cannot be forced on India by external actors. It is one that India must want to execute. The day when India takes such steps may not be far off.

Envoi

Given India's complexity and scale, in assessing its domestic circumstances and its foreign policy it is easy to get lost in the weeds while seeking to identify the shape of the forest. At root, in the words of Edward Carr, foreign editor of the *Economist*, 'while India's voice in the world is elusive, the economic rise of a democracy of 1.1 billion people can only be a good thing'.[94]

Indians increasingly understand the collective action problem that the refusal of their country and several others among the emerging powers to take on binding responsibilities for nurturing the global commons creates for richer countries and the wider community of nations, despite their compelling complaints about the historic burden of responsibility for economic blight by Western countries. India's diplomacy often has been understandably focused on issues of status. Today, because its growing significance is universally recognized, both its contributions and its objectives are more likely to be rewarded if pragmatically advanced than if done so on the basis of entitlement. Shyam Saran comments:

> India's relative power has outstripped the indices of personal and social well being, unlike in the established industrialized powers where they have historically moved in sync. We will need to overcome the ambivalence this creates and embrace a more proactive regional and global role in line with our national power. A seat at the high table should be sought not as an end in itself, but as an opportunity to negotiate arrangements conducive to our economic and social development...[95]

India today advocates no particular ideology, nor does it operate within a defined foreign policy (or strategic planning) framework, beyond the assertion of national self-interest generally focused on the economic sphere. Given the recent splintering of international relations into a genuinely multipolar system, India will likely organize its multilateral and even some of its bilateral diplomacy in years ahead through issue-driven ad hoc coalitions and in some cases evanescent groupings of countries. While it is often associated as an emerging power with China, Brazil, and South Africa, it will, when its interests dictate, continue to disagree with them publicly. A recent example was its decision in April 2010 to join Brazil in criticizing China's exchange rate policies.[96] More widely, while seeking to advance its interests and increase its influence globally, it is likely to continue to engage in a 'hedging strategy' as between other significant powers.[97]

One welcome by-product of altered global circumstances and of India's own rise is that Delhi is much less likely to indulge in a spoiler role. Sunil Khilnani argues that India's approach, precisely because it is iterative and rests on no particular conception of power, will likely take shape in an unsystematic way (complementing what Prem Shankar Jha sees in the internal sphere as an India that muddles through). Khilnani believes India's greatest asset remains its 'accumulated political legitimacy' rather than any hypothetical or real accumulation of power.[98]

At the strategic level, India is not yet a particularly significant player beyond its own neighbourhood. International experts view only the Indian navy as having developed both a strategy and the political support and resources to implement it in expanding India's global reach. Further, Kanti Bajpai points out that the Indian army is still excessively tied down by internal security duties, in Kashmir and in the country's northeast but also in the fight against Naxalism, 'constraining its ability to project force beyond South Asia'.[99]

Time and history are on India's side as it struggles to recover from several centuries of foreign domination and its consequences. Its re-emergence, particularly if it manages its significant domestic challenges with success, will be one of the major shifts of the twenty-first century. It will have been hard won, and should gladden both students of history and of foreign affairs the world over. Twenty or thirty years from now, the tentative, contingent nature of many of my judgements today may well seem over-cautious. I certainly hope so.

Notes

Acknowledgements

1. Rohan Mukherjee and I have published together, 'India and China: Can two tigers share a mountain?', *Sunday Guardian*, 21 March 2010; 'India and China: Conflict and Cooperation', *Survival*, 52/1 (February/March 2010), 137–58; 'The Shock of the New: India–US Relations in Perspective', *International Journal*, LXIV/4 (Autumn 2009); 'Polity, Security and Foreign Policy in Contemporary India', in T. V. Paul (ed.), *South Asia's Weak States: Understanding the Regional Insecurity Predicament* (Palo Alto, CA: Stanford University Press, 2010). Further articles are planned on security and on India's multilateral diplomacy.

2. See Rajeev Ranjan Chaturvedy and David M. Malone, 'India and Its South Asian Neighbours', *ISAS Working Paper* No. 100 (26 November 2009), Singapore: National University of Singapore—Institute of South Asian Studies, www.isasnus.org/events/workingpapers/99

3. See David M. Malone and Rajeev R. Chaturvedy , 'Impact of India's Economy on its Foreign Policy since Independence', Vancouver, BC: Asia Pacific Foundation, Research Reports (November 2009), http://www.asiapacific.ca/research-report/impact-indias-economy-its-foreign-policy-independence

4. See Andrew Brunatti and David M. Malone, 'India's West Asia Approach: A Triumph of Bilateralism', *Indian Foreign Affairs Journal*, 4/4 (October–December 2009), 43–62.

5. See Andrew Brunatti and David M. Malone , 'Fading Glories? India's Relations with Western Europe and Russia', *International Relations*, 24/3 (September 2010) , 341–70.

6. See Archana Pandya and David M. Malone, 'India's Asia Policy: A Late Look East', *ISAS Special Report* No. 02 (25 August 2010), Singapore: National University of Singapore—Institute of South Asian Studies.

7. The conference report *Is India Ready for Super-Power Status?*, is available at www.ditchley.co.uk

8. mjoshi.blogspot.com

9. A number of publications with global reach cover India seriously, none as consistently well as the *Financial Times*, the *New York Times*, and the *Economist*, all of which devote significant resources to the task. A number of their former India correspondents have risen to great heights, and several have perpetrated interesting books relating to the country. The editor of Canada's *Globe and Mail*, John Stackhouse, is a former long-time Delhi-based correspondent for the paper, and under his leadership, India is now receiving high quality attention in its pages. Perhaps in

emulation, Montreal's *Le Devoir* has recently also fielded outstanding journalism from Delhi.

10. In India, as elsewhere in South Asia, the Foreign Secretary is the senior official of the foreign ministry, heading up the diplomatic service, but always responsible to a senior Cabinet Minister.

11. Dr Hurrell, a noted scholar on international relations broadly and also on Brazil, is currently finishing with a colleague a book relevant to my topic here: Andrew Hurrell and Amrita Narlikar, *Emerging Powers and Global Order* (New York: Oxford University Press, forthcoming 2011).

Preface

1. Escott Reid, *Envoy to Nehru* (Toronto and Delhi: Oxford University Press, 1981).

2. See, for example, Jorge Heine, 'Playing the India card', in Andrew F. Cooper and Jorge Heine (eds.), *Which Way Latin America? Hemispheric Politics Meets Globalization* (New York and Tokyo: United Nations University Press, 2009), 122–39.

3. Jairam Ramesh, 'Managing Diversities—The Canadian and Indian Ways', 13th Lester B. Pearson lecture, 23 April 2007, Delhi University. By the time of writing, he had become India's energetic and influential Minister for the Environment and Forests and a major figure on the international scene.

4. For a useful overview of key issues preoccupying the legal community in India, see *The Indian Advocate* (Journal of the Bar Association of India), Vol. XXXVI, 2008–9, featuring articles by a wide range of jurists, lawyers, political scientists, and philosophers, and some senior government administrators such as Gopalkrishna Gandhi, then Governor of West Bengal.

Chapter 1

1. Strobe Talbott, *Engaging India: Diplomacy, Democracy and the Bomb* (Washington, DC: Brookings Institution Press, 2004).

2. Rajeev Sikri, *Challenge and Strategy: Rethinking India's Foreign Policy* (New Delhi: Sage Publications Ltd, 2009).

3. One of the best surveys was written for grades 11–12 students rather than for adults, as part of the wider high school curriculum, by a committee on which Kanti Bajpai served as convenor: *Contemporary World Politics* (New Delhi: National Council for Education Research and Training (NCERT), for the Central Board of Secondary Education (CBSE), 2007).

4. See his speech to the Indian School of International Studies on 13 February 1961, (*International Studies* 22/2, 1985), excerpted in *Pragati*, 34 (January 2010), 13–15. He contrasts Indian heedlessness beyond its borders with British attentiveness to developments all around India during the Raj: 'They carefully studied the conditions across the borders, developed a large body of experts who studied the geography, language, political conditions, and economic structure of the areas which bordered on India or which were considered to be of vital importance to the defense of India.'

5. Percival Spear comments that British concerns about encroachment on India and its sphere of influence during the colonial period, focused particularly on Russia, turned out to be misplaced. When an active threat to British India came during the Second World War, it arose from a quarter that would have surprised nineteenth-century imperialists—Japan. See Percival Spear, *A History of India*, Vol. II (revised 1978) (New Delhi: Penguin, 1990), 156–7.

6. See, for example, 'LNM says India hasn't been able to handle surge in big investments', *Economic Times*, 8 January 2010. Tata Motors was deeply frustrated that extensive sunk costs into building a plant in West Bengal to produce the inexpensive Nano automobile had to be scrapped when local political skirmishing paralysed the project for months on end, leading to the expensive transfer of operations to Gujarat.

7. See Harsh V. Pant, 'A Rising India's Search for a Foreign Policy', *Orbis*, 53/2 (Spring 2009), 250–64.

8. Niraja Gopal Jayal and Pratap Bhanu Mehta (eds.), *The Oxford Companion to Politics in India* (New Delhi, Oxford, and New York: Oxford University Press, 2010).

9. In the world of policy-relevant scholarship, the July/August 2006 issue of *Foreign Affairs* 85/4, headlined 'The Rise of India', offered four very fine articles by Gurcharan Das ('Unshackling the Economy'), C. Raja Mohan ('India's Global Strategy'), Ashton Carter ('America's New Partner'), and Sumit Ganguly ('The Kashmir Conundrum') that proved highly influential. It followed up in March/April 2010 (Vol. 89, No. 2) with an insightful overview of the India–USA relationship, 'India's Rise, America's Interest' by Evan A. Feigenbaum. Because this journal aims for both accessibility and substantive depth, its articles reach a much wider policy audience than most, at least in the West.

10. And they meet up whenever possible. In January 2009, in Singapore, I was fortunate to be able to sound out a wondrous pod of top Indian foreign policy commentators, scholars, and practitioners then resident there.

11. Among the benefits of the Raj, Amartya Sen credits the British occupation of India with generating its media and with paving the way for the media's importance in India today. See a conversation between Sen and Vinod Mehta, 'I Prefer to Fight Today's Battles', *Outlook*, 17 August 2009.

12. Correspondence with the author, 12 June 2010.

13. In India, the national, or central, government is known as the Union government.

14. One such politician, Shashi Tharoor, a former senior UN official and briefly a Minister of State for External Affairs in 2009–10, quoted elsewhere in this volume, resigned amidst a ruckus over the expansion of the Indian Premier [cricket] League having in equal measure stimulated both public enthusiasm and political opprobrium for reaching out to hundreds of thousands of followers through energetic tweeting on the social networking website Twitter. While Tharoor cut a wide and admired swathe for India on foreign policy, his innovation in political style, doubtless observed closely by other younger politicians with a view to testing the boundaries of Indian politics, proved dangerously provocative to those senior politicians who might have protected him.

15. See Ramachandra Guha, 'Lost on Home Ground', *Hindustan Times*, 16 May 2010.

16. For a recent profile essay on Mrs. Gandhi, see Saba Naqvi, 'The Lady in The Sari: Indira and Sonia, two cogs from a dynastic wheel but seemingly very different', *Outlook*, 22 March 2010, 30–5.

17. Somewhat counteracting this dynamic are respected public figures, often senior civil servants, who join politics mid-career. Of these, Yashwant Sinha and Mani Shankar Aiyar are quoted in this book. Manohar S. Gill, formerly Chief Elections Commissioner of India, a frequent and elegant essayist, later served as Indian Minister of Youth and Sports.

18. Mahesh Rangarajan, correspondence with the author, 2 May 2010 and 20 June 2010.

19. The Home (or interior) Minister is also a key player on neighbourhood security issues spilling over into India's domestic affairs, particularly those involving terrorism.

20. The IFS would also have to be judged one of the most literate foreign services. To name but three, in its current crop of heads of mission: Navtej Sarna, Ambassador to Israel, novelist and frequent non-fiction author; Vikas Swarup, Consul General in Osaka-Kobe and author of *Q & A* (adapted as a script for the film *Slumdog Millionaire*); and Pavan Varma, Ambassador to Bhutan and author, among other books, of *Being Indian*, an indispensable volume on India's psyche and aspirations. They are all fine writers.

   As to the UK, it has a long tradition of sending some of its very best diplomats to Delhi, headed up, in my time, by the very different but equally accomplished Sir Michael Arthur and Sir Richard (Dickie) Stagg successively. While the Chinese Ambassador seeks to and mostly can maintain a low profile in Delhi, the UK High Commissioner is often thrust into the spotlight because of the complex mix of continuing Indian fascination, admiration, resentment, and contempt for its former colonial power, which rears up in unpredictable and complex ways from time to time, while the UK primarily seeks to cultivate business opportunities in India. It is a tough, fascinating assignment for any senior British Foreign Service person.

21. India has been fortunate to host a number of remarkably talented US Envoys in recent decades, including my US colleague there, David Mulford, a highly successful international investment banker and an influential former US Under-Secretary of the Treasury for International Affairs.

22. My excellent French colleague in Delhi recently published a thoughtful essay on the challenges the European Union has faced in being taken seriously by India. See Jérôme Bonnafont (and Guillaume Bazard), 'The European Union seen from India', *Mondes*, 2 (March 2010), 170–7. His predecessor, Dominique Girard, was an exceptionally knowledgeable Asianist.

23. During my assignment, my Australian counterpart, John McCarthy, was the most admired foreign envoy among my Indian connections as he had the knack at the same time of advancing his country's interests and adopting a broad view also open to Indian perspectives. He was the most widely travelled of all the foreign envoys within India and Indians were sensitive to his keen interest in them.

24. See, for example, Krishnan Srinivasan, 'India and China: Similar Challenges, Different Roadmaps', *Indian Foreign Affairs Journal* 4/4 (October–December 2009),

33–42. He also published, with Peter Lyon, an exceptionally perceptive and incisive volume on the Commonwealth, of which he had been Deputy Secretary-General, *The Rise, Decline and Future of the British Commonwealth* (London: Palgrave Macmillan, 2005) and in 2007 a very interesting volume about the Jamdani Revolution in Bangladesh. For a recent example of Haidar's subtle and elegant thought, see Salman Haidar, 'Smoking the Peace Pipeline', *Tehelka*, 26 June 2010, 22–3.

25. Indian IFS officers retire at 60, leaving many years ahead in which to reflect and write. J. N. Dixit, a former Foreign Secretary, and, at the time of his death in 2005, India's National Security Advisor, whose extensive writing displayed a singular ability to take the long view, published a thoughtful history of the Indian Foreign Service: *Indian Foreign Service: History And Challenge* (Delhi: Konark Publishers, 2005).

26. The Stockholm International Peace Research Institute (SIPRI), 'The SIPRI Military Expenditure Database', http://milexdata.sipri.org/ (consulted 9 July 2010).

27. When referring to Burma from a historical perspective, I use that name. However, when referring to the same country in recent years or in the present, I use the name that its current government has given to it, Myanmar. I understand the two names are, in fact, in Burmese closely related.

28. The French scholar, Jean-Luc Racine, discusses the much intensified Indian global engagement in 'Quête de puissance, multipolarité et multilatéralisme', in Christophe Jaffrelot (ed.), *New Delhi et le Monde* (Paris : Éditions Autrement—CERI, 2008), 30–51.

29. He now serves in the sensitive position of Home Secretary.

30. Having been associated with the 1995 Foreign Policy Statement of the Canadian government, I am acutely aware of the costs of politeness—the government, wishing to offend no capital, opted to describe all too many bilateral relationships, often in excessively optimistic terms. The overall effect was to suggest that no choices had been made, and also that infinite resources were available to promote all bilateral relationships and multilateral engagements. Here, being my own master, I can avoid at least this one pitfall. See David M. Malone, 'Foreign Policy Reviews Reconsidered', *International Journal* LVI/4 (Autumn 2001), 555–78.

31. Correspondence with the author, 18 April 2010.

32. Correspondence with Dipankar Gupta, 3 May 2010.

33. Some of these groupings: BRIC (Brazil, Russia, India, China); G-5 (Brazil, China, India, South Africa, Mexico), the G-8's guests for several years; BASIC (Brazil, South Africa, India and China), active at the Copenhagen Climate Change conference of late 2009.

34. Jillian Melchior articulated a sophisticated analysis supporting Indian worries for the Hudson Institute on 1 June 2010, available at www.hudson-ny.org/1352/india-next-under-the-bus

35. 'IAF's first AWACS arrives from Israel, induction on Thursday', *Times of India*, 25 May 2009, http://timesofindia.indiatimes.com/India/IAFs-first-AWACS-arrives-from-Israel/articleshow/4575710.cms

36. Paul Krugman, *The Return of Depression Economics and the Crisis of 2008* (New York: W.W. Norton, 2008), 15–16. More likely, but less famously, the term was introduced by Alfred Sauvy, in an article published in *L'Observateur*, 14 August 1952.

37. Dhruva Jaishankar makes a compelling argument for values alongside interests in Indian foreign policy in 'A uniquely Indian realism: Underlying India's foreign policy framework', *Pragati*, 38 (May 2010), 3–5.

Chapter 2

1. A stimulating contemporary assessment, drawing to a degree on history, can be found in Pavan K. Varma, *Being Indian: Inside the Real India* (London: William Heineman, 2005).
2. See Ayesha Jalal and Sugata Bose, *Modern South Asia: History Culture, Political Economy* (New Delhi: Oxford University Press, 2006), 27.
3. Romila Thapar, *The Penguin History of Early India: From the Origins to AD 1300* (New Delhi: Penguin Books, 2002), 206.
4. Upinder Singh, *A History of Ancient and Early Medieval India* (New Delhi: Pearson Longman, 2008), 7–8.
5. Thapar, 1.
6. Ibid., 4.
7. The historian and indologist Vincent Smith (1848–1920) argued that Indian civilization, which he called Hindu, peaked under the benevolent despots Chandragupta and Asoka Maurya in the third and fourth centuries BC, the Gupta emperors in the fourth and fifth centuries AD and the last great imperial ruler, Harsha, in the seventh century. After that, Indian civilization gradually declined, paving the way for Muslim conquests of the twelfth century. See Ronald Inden, *Imagining India* (Oxford: Bail Blackwell, 1990), 7–8.
8. The most recent re-edition of this seminal text is from Routledge in 1997. While many versions of the original can be found online, the Online Library of Liberty offers the third edition of 1826 (London: Baldwin, Cradock, and Joy, 1826) at oll. libertyfund.org.
9. Thapar, *Early India*, 5–6.
10. See F. Max Müller, *India: What Can It Teach Us* (New Delhi: Rupa and Co., 2003).
11. Thapar, 13.
12. Singh (2008), 186.
13. Thapar, xxiii.
14. Ibid., 14.
15. Benedict Anderson, *Imagined Communities* (London: Verso, 1991), 11.
16. In 1923, V. D. Savarkar, the father of Hindu nationalism, offered his speculative projections of Hindu and Hinduness back to the pre-historical past as proof of the existence of a proto-national community since the dawn of time; Vasudha Dalmia and Heinrich von Stietencron (eds.), *The Oxford India Hinduism Reader* (New Delhi: Oxford University Press, 2007), 3.
17. This reality helps explain why efforts to impose Hindi as *the* national language after independence failed miserably, even threatening the cohesion of the new country.
18. Vasudha Dalmia and Heinrich von Stietencron (eds.), *The Oxford India Hinduism Reader* (New Delhi: Oxford University Press, 2007). 3.
19. Thapar, *Early India*, 4.

20. Dalmia and von Stietencron, 73. A striking articulation of the recent place of Hinduism in the political thought of some Indians is M. S. Golwalkar's *Bunch of Thoughts* (New Delhi: Sahitya Sindhu Prakashana, 2000). Golwalkar from 1938 to 1973 led the Rashtriya Swayamsevak Sangh (RSS) a leading volunteer Hindu nationalist organization with strong connections to national, regional, and (some) municipal politics.

21. Richard M. Eaton, *A Social History of the Deccan, 1300–1761: Eight Indian Lives* (Cambridge: Cambridge University Press, 2005), 1. This is true in spite of the existence in the Marathi language of much writing on the Deccan's history of the late medieval and early modern period, from the time of Shivaji Raje Bhosle (1630–80) onwards, when the region had a capital, Pune, and strong political identity.

22. Janet L. Abu-Lughod, *Before European Hegemony: The World System A.D. 1250–1350* (New York: Oxford University Press, 1991), 261–2.

23. For an excellent discussion on trade in the Harappan civilization see Shereen Ratnagar, 'Harappan Trade in its "World Context",' in Ranabir Chakravarti (ed.), *Trade in Early India* (New Delhi: Oxford University Press, 2001), 102–22; also see Abu-Lughod, 262.

24. K. A. Nilakanta Sastri, *A History of South India* (New Delhi: Oxford University Press, 1966), 71–2.

25. Abu-Lughod, 265.

26. Joan Wardrop, 'The Indian Ocean: the Italian experience', in Giorgio Borsa (ed.), *Trade and Politics in the Indian Ocean: Historical and Contemporary Perspectives* (New Delhi: Manohar, 1990), 16.

27. Abu-Lughod, 174.

28. Ibid., 176.

29. Sastri, 76–7; Thapar, *Early India*, 184. 'Dhamma' is the Prakrit form of the Sanskrit word 'Dharma' meaning the universal law or righteousness, depending on the context.

30. Thapar, *Early India*, 181.

31. Ibid., 201.

32. Ibid., 195. The *Arthasastra* is attributed to Kautilya (also known as Chanakya), who lived *c*.350–283 BC.

33. Ibid., 182.

34. Ibid., 245.

35. Ibid., 234.

36. Liu Xinru, *Ancient India and Ancient China: Trade and Religious Exchanges* (New Delhi: Oxford University Press, 1988), 2–3.

37. Singh, 53, 377.

38. Xinru, 5–6.

39. Ibid., 4.

40. Thapar, *Early India*, 242.

41. Ibid., 244.

42. Romila Thapar, *A History of India*, Vol. I (New Delhi: Penguin Books, 1990), 155.

43. Two variants of Islam existed in India, with related distinct links to the outside world, one through the overland belt reaching from Turkey, Persia, and northern India to the Deccan, the other established by oceanic links between the Arabian Peninsula and coastal southern India, the Bay of Bengal, and Sumatra. See Jalal and Bose, 21.

44. See Abu-Lughod, 270–4. The ports of Cambay and Saymur in Gujarat had absorbed colonies of resident Arab merchants by the early days of Islam, as well as sailors from Siraf, Oman, Basra, and Baghdad.

45. Barbara D. Metcalf and Thomas R. Metcalf, *A Concise History of India* (Cambridge: Cambridge University Press, 2002), 6.

46. Ibid., 4.

47. See Sunil Kumar, 'When Slaves were Nobles: The Shamsi *Bandagan* in the Early Delhi Sultanate', *Studies in History* 10 (1994), 23–52.

48. Jalal and Bose, 17.

49. Sunil Kumar, *The Emergence of the Delhi Sultanate 1192–1286* (New Delhi: Permanent Black, 2007), 2.

50. African slaves were imported by the Muslim dynasties in north and central India, often as warriors, one of whose number, Malik Ambar, eventually ruled in the Deccan after the death of his patron, Chengis Khan. For this interesting episode and others involving Africans in India, see Eaton, 50–2, and several chapters in Kenneth X. Robbins and John McLeod (eds.), *African Elites in India* (Ahmedabad, India: Mapin, 2006). The African connection lives on in the communities of Siddhis, an Indian population of black African descent, present in small numbers (well under 100,000) along India's west coast, from Siddapur in Karnataka to Janjira in Gujarat.

51. Jalal and Bose, 21.

52. Metcalf and Metcalf, 5.

53. Al Basham, *The Wonder that was India* (London: Sidgwick & Jackson, 1954), 77.

54. John Keay, *India: A History* (London: Harper Collins, 1999), 302.

55. Percival Spear, *A History of India*, Vol. II (New Delhi: Penguin Books, 1990), 18; Basham, 77.

56. Metcalf and Metcalf, 1.

57. Jalal and Bose, 31.

58. Metcalf and Metcalf, 20.

59. Sastri, 89.

60. Sastri, 132; Thapar, *Early India*, 328.

61. Thapar, *Early India*, 329–31.

61. Ibid., 332.

62. Ibid., 365.

64. Sastri, 167.

65. Thapar, *Early India*, 369.

66. Keay, 308.

67. Tapan Raychaudhari and Irfan Habib (eds.), *The Cambridge Economic History of India*, Vol. I (Cambridge: Cambridge University Press, 1982), 203.

68. David Washbrook, 'Merchants, Markets and Commerce in Early Modern South India', *Journal of the Economic and Social History of the Orient*, 53 (2010), 266–89.
69. Jalal and Bose, 80.
70. Ibid., 38.
71. Ibid., 43.
72. Ibid., 54.
73. Ibid., 53.
74. This analysis of the British colonial centuries in India was first and most clearly enunciated by Marxist theoretician R. P. Dutt (1896–1974).
75. Sumit Sarkar, *Modern India* (New Delhi: Macmillan, 2001), 24.
76. Jalal and Bose, 80.
77. Om Prakash, *The New Cambridge History of India: European Commercial Enterprise in Pre-Colonial India* (Cambridge: Cambridge University Press, 1998), 287.
78. Michael Greenberg, *British Trade and the Opening of China* (Cambridge: Cambridge University Press, 1951), 8.
79. Holden Furber, *Rival Empires of Trade in the Orient, 1600–1800* (Minneapolis: University of Minnesota Press, 1976), 192.
80. Greenberg, 15.
81. Ibid., 16.
82. Kunal Diwan, 'A seasoned Dilliwallah is back home', *The Hindu*, 18 June 2008.
83. Sarkar, 17.
84. Ibid., 12.
85. Ibid., 1.
86. Ibid., 15; see also Sekhar Bandyopadhyay, *From Plassey to Partition: A History of Modern India* (New Delhi: Orient Blackswan, 2008), 105.
87. Strachey, *India*, 63 cited in Sarkar, 16.
88. Hiralal Singh, 'Problems and Policies of the British in India 1885–1898', 140, cited in Sarkar, 16.
89. Bandyopadhyay, 108.
90. Cited in Sarkar, 21.
91. Colonial writers cast the major cultural disjunction as occurring at the time of Islam's arrival in India, an idea also picked up in some nationalist thinking.
92. Sarkar, 21.
93. J. R. McLane, 'Indian Nationalism and the Early Congress', 37 cited in Sarkar, 21.
94. From the Persian word for soldier.
95. Jalal and Bose, 73–5.
96. Ibid., 73.
97. Correspondence with the author, 16 February 2010.
98. See Ranajit Guha, *Subaltern Studies: Writings on South Asian History and Society*, Vol. I (New Delhi: Oxford University Press, 1997) for extensive historical research on subaltern politics in the South Asian subcontinent.
99. Partha Chatterjee is interesting on the contradictions in the nationalism of colonized peoples. See *The Partha Chatterjee Omnibus* (New Delhi: Oxford University Press, 1999), 11.

100. Judith Brown, 'The Mahatma and Modern India', in Sekhar Bandyopadhyay (ed.), *Nationalist Movement in India: A Reader* (New Delhi: Oxford University Press, 2009), 57.

101. The official rationale behind the partition was administrative efficiency but, as later declassified documents showed, 'our main objective is to split up and thereby weaken a solid body of opponents to our rule' (Sarkar, 95). Also see Bandyopadhyay, *From Plassey to Partition*, 253–4.

102. Though recruitment was theoretically voluntary, in reality coercion was widespread. For instance, in 1918 Michael O'Dwyer, Lieutenant Governor of Punjab, boasted that in the Gujranwala district the proportion of soldiers to the adult male population had been forced up from 1:150 to 1:44 in a single year. See Sarkar, 169.

103. Sarkar, 168–9.

104. Sarkar, 170. For an excellent summary of the role of Indian capital during the national movement see Bandyopadhyay, *From Plassey to Partition*, 358–69.

105. Sarkar, 176.

106. Jalal and Bose, 106.

107. Thus a dramatic outflow of gold ensued that conservative estimates have put at Rs. 3.4 billion between 1931 and 1934.

108. Chatterjee, 124.

109. Jalal and Bose, 110.

110. Bandyopadhyay, *From Plassey to Partition*, 299.

111. Sarkar, 196.

112. Jalal and Bose, 112.

113. Sarkar, 208; see also Bandyopadhyay, *From Plassey to Partition*, 303.

114. Sugata Bose cited by Bandyopadhyay, *Nationalist Movement in India*, xvii.

115. These facets of Churchill are explored in depth in Richard Toye's *Churchill's Empire: The World that Made Him and the World He Made* (New York: Henry Holt & Co, 2010). For an Indian view, see Madhusree Mukherjee, *Churchill's Secret War: The British Empire and the Ravaging of India during World War II* (Delhi: Tranquebar Press, 2010).

116. Jalal and Bose, 130.

117. Ibid., 131.

118. A fascinating account of the efforts of Indian nationalists to break into Western-dominated international diplomacy at the conclusion of the First World War is to be found in Erez Manela's *The Wilsonian Moment* (New York: Oxford University Press, 2007), notably in pages 77–98 and 141–58.

119. Indeed, some of those who were to take on key roles in the early diplomacy of independent India served in such positions, including Sir Girija Shankar Bajpai, Agent-General for India within the British Embassy in Washington and later Secretary-General of the Ministry of External Affairs of India, 1947–52, while a close advisor to Nehru. Bajpai's descendants have formed a distinguished dynasty of foreign policy professionals and academics, including his son, K. Shankar, who served as Indian Ambassador to the USA, China, and Pakistan, and his grandson, Kanti, a professor of international relations at Oxford University, often cited in this volume.

120. According to some estimates, Indian manufacturing as late as 1750 may have been as much as a quarter of the world's output. See David Washbrook, 'India in the Early Modern World Economy: Modes of Production, Reproduction and Exchange', *Journal of Global History* 2 (2007), 87–8: 'there can be no doubting the vast size of Indian textile exports in this era even if we have few means of precisely measuring it . . . India clothed the world from Mexico to the Philippines and from England to Java.'

Chapter 3

1. Zoya Hasan, 'Introduction', in Zoya Hasan (ed.), *Parties and Party Politics in India* (New Delhi: Oxford University Press, 2002).
2. Extracts from Nehru's speech to the Constituent Assembly of India on 4 December 1947, partially reproduced in A. Appadorai, *Select Documents on India's Foreign Policy and Relations 1947–1972*, Vol. I (New Delhi and New York: Oxford University Press, 1982), 10.
3. Ibid.
4. Ibid.
5. Baljit Singh, 'Pandits and Panchsheela: Indian intellectuals and their foreign policy', *Background* 9/ 2 (August 1965), 127–36.
6. A more elegant and agreeable pose, at least to Western eyes, was adopted by Nehru's talented sister, Mrs. Vijaya Lakshmi Pandit, who served as Indian envoy to the Soviet Union, the United States, and the United Kingdom and also served in the high-profile if ceremonial role of President of the UN General Assembly in 1953–4.
7. In 1967, India rejected association with the newly formed ASEAN in the belief that most Southeast Asian countries were aligned with Western powers in the Cold War. Another twenty-five years would pass before India became a dialogue partner of ASEAN and in 1996 a member of ASEAN's Regional Forum (ARF).
8. Extract from Lal Bahadur Shastri's first broadcast to the nation on 11 June 1964, in Appadorai, 59.
9. Pradeep K. Chhibber, *Democracy Without Associations: Transformation of the Party System and Social Cleavages in India* (Ann Arbor: University of Michigan Press, 1999), 90.
10. Appadorai, 62.
11. National Commission to Review the Working of the Constitution (NCRWC), 'A Consultation Paper on Article 356 of the Constitution,' 11 May 2001; Chhibber (p. 97) reports a much higher figure of 72 occasions between 1967 and 1984. Given that the Supreme Court's intervention in the 1990s subsequently led to a decline in the number of times this provision has been invoked, the figure of 72 by 1984 would be more in line with the final report of the NCRWC, which pegs the total figure as of 2002 at 111.
12. Arun R. Swamy, 'India in 2001: A Year of Living Dangerously', *Asian Survey* 42/1, A Survey of Asia in 2001 (January–February 2002), 165–76. Both coalitions subsequently disintegrated.

13. Afghanistan can readily be considered a part of the broader Middle East, of Central Asia, and of South Asia, forming a bridge between these geostrategically sensitive regions.

14. Sudipta Kaviraj, 'The Nature of Indian Democracy', in Veena Das (ed.), *Handbook of Sociology in India* (New Delhi: Oxford University Press, 2004), 451–70.

15. Atul Kohli, 'Politics of Economic Growth in India, 1980–2005, Part I: The 1980s', *Economic and Political Weekly*, 41/13 (1 April 2006), 1251–9.

16. T. N. Srinivasan, 'China and India: Growth and Poverty, 1980–2000', Stanford Center for International Development, Working Paper No. 182 (September 2003).

17. Angus Deaton and Jean Dreze, 'Poverty and Inequality in India: A Re-Examination,' *Economic and Political Weekly*, 37/36 (7 September 2002), 3729–48.

18. As discussed by E. Sridharan in 'The Fragmentation of the Indian Party System, 1952–1999: Seven Competing Explanations', in Hasan (ed.), *Parties and Party Politics in India*, 475–503.

19. Election Commission of India, 'Statistical Report on General Elections, 2004 to the 14th Lok Sabha', Vol. 1, p. 99: http://eci.nic.in/eci_main/SR_KeyHighLights/LS_2004/Vol_I_LS_2004.pdf

20. Election Commission of India, 'Statistical Report on General Elections, 1951 to the First Lok Sabha', Vol. 1, p. 41: http://eci.nic.in/eci_main/statisticalreports/LS_1951/VOL_1_51_LS.pdf

21. That a controversial foreign policy issue should lead to a sharp parliamentary debate and a close vote would not be unusual in many other parliamentary democracies. For example, the Dutch government was defeated through such a process in early 2010 over its military involvement in Afghanistan.

22. To these states should be added the northern reaches of West Bengal, which separate Sikkim from Assam and Nepal from Bhutan, and which host their own agitation, in the Darjeeling Hills, aiming for a separate Indian state of ethnic Nepali identity, so-called Gorkhaland, which has convulsed the affected district on and off for many years. Listless discussions with Delhi and the state capital of Kolkata alternate with *bandhs* (strikes accompanied by demonstrations) and often diffuse violence, at times rendering Darjeeling and other hill communities inaccessible. For a comprehensive survey of terrorism and insurgencies in India's northeast, see Col. Ved Prakash, *Terrorism in India's North-East*, Vols. I–III (Delhi: Kalpaz Publications, 2008).

23. See Kristoffel Lieten, 'Multiple Conflicts in Northeast India', in Monique Mekenkamp, Paul van Tongeren, and Hans van de Veen (eds.), *Searching for Peace in Central and South Asia* (Boulder, CO: Lynne Rienner Publishers, 2002), 407–32.

24. Wasbir Hussain, 'Ethno-Nationalism and the Politics of Terror in India's Northeast', *South Asia: Journal of South Asian Studies*, 30/1 (2007), 93.

25. Ibid., 94.

26. See Subir Bhaumik, 'Insurgencies in India's Northeast: Conflict, Co-option and Change', *East-West Center Working Papers*, 10, 2007; Wasbir Hussain, 'Insurgency in India's Northeast Cross-border Links and Strategic Alliances', South Asia Terrorism Portal, www.satp.org/satporgtp/publication/faultlines/volume17/wasbir.htm

27. This is a popular phrase in the Indian media and policy. For instance, see K. P. S. Gill, 'War of thousand cuts', *Indian Express*, 7 January 2000.

28. D. Suba Chandran, 'Indian and Armed Nonstate Actors in the Kashmir Conflict', in Waheguru Pal Singh Sidhu, Bushra Asif, and Cyrus Samii (eds.), *Kashmir: New Voices, New Approaches* (Boulder, CO and London: Lynne Rienner Publishers, 2006), 50.

29. South Asia Terrorism Portal, 'Jammu and Kashmir Backgrounder', www.satp.org/satporgtp/countries/india/states/jandk/backgrounder/index.html

30. See Navnita Chadha Behera, *Demystifying Kashmir* (Washington, DC: Brookings Institution Press, 2006).

31. See, for a recent example, Press Trust of India, 'Colonel, two majors among 11 chargesheeted in Kupwara "fake encounter" case', *Times of India*, 16 July 2010.

32. This was still an unfolding story at the time of writing. See, for example, *Rediff News*, 'Violence escalates in Srinagar, Army called out', 7 July 2010, http://news.rediff.com/report/2010/jul/07/violence-escalates-in-jk-army-called-out.htm

33. Ajai Sahni, 'Naxalism: The Retreat of Civil Governance', *Faultlines*, http://satp.org/satporgtp/publication/faultlines/volume5/Fault5-7asahni.htm (footnote 1).

34. Suba Chandran and Mallika Joseph, 'The Naxalite Movement', in Mekenkamp et al. (eds.), *Searching for Peace in Central and South Asia*, 384–5.

35. South Asia Terrorism Portal, 'Fatalities in Left-Wing Extremism', www.satp.org/satporgtp/countries/india/maoist/data_sheets/fatalitiesnaxalmha.htm

36. P. V. Ramana, 'The Maoist Movement in India', *Defense & Security Analysis* 22/4 (December 2006), 435–9.

37. Ashok Handoo, 'Naxal problem needs a holistic approach', Press Information Bureau, Government of India, 22 July, 2009, www.pib.nic.in/release/release.asp?relid=50833

38. Vikram Sood, 'India and Regional Security Interests', in Alyssa Ayres and C. Raja Mohan (eds.), *Power Realignments in Asia: China, India, and the United States* (New Delhi: SAGE, 2009), 252.

39. Rajen Harshe, 'South Asian Regional Cooperation: Problems and Prospects', in Rajen Harshe and K. M. Seethi (eds.), *Engaging with the World: Critical Reflections on India's Foreign Policy* (New Delhi: Orient Black Swan, 2009), 321.

40. Sood, 252.

41. Varun Sahni, 'The Agent-Structure Problem and India's External Security Policy', in Navnita Chadha Behera (ed.), *International Relations in South Asia, Search for an Alternative Paradigm* (New Delhi: SAGE, 2008), 212–13.

42. J. N. Dixit, *Across Borders: Fifty Years of India's Foreign Policy* (New Delhi: Picus Books, 1998), 182–93. See also Arun Swamy, 'India in 2000: A Respite from Instability', *Asian Survey* 41/1, A Survey of Asia in 2000 (January/February 2001), 91–103.

43. International Crisis Group, 'Nepal's Troubled Tarai Region', Asia Report No. 136, 9 July 2007, 22. The report goes on to state: 'unless the situation significantly deteriorates, Madhesi issues are unlikely to become a rallying point for Indian parties beyond the immediate border'. However, the significance of the cross-border ethnic bond is evident.

44. Sugata Bose and Ayesha Jalal (eds.), *Nationalism, Democracy and Development* (New Delhi and New York: Oxford University Press, 1997).

45. Dixit, 146. For a brief discussion of Pakistan and the Khalistan movement, see K. Shankar Bajpai, 'India in 1991: New Beginnings', *Asian Survey*, 32(2), A Survey of Asia in 1991: Part II (February 1992), 207–16: 'howsoever limited the extent of Pakistan's physical or logistical support to the Sikh extremists, the Pakistani nexus gave the problem an enlarged dimension; the very fact that they could look to a foreign power made the extremists infinitely harder to deal with'.

46. For a detailed account of the various secessionist movements in the northeast, see Hussain, 'Ethno-Nationalism and the Politics of Terror', 93–110.

47. Sushil Kumar, 'Rethinking Security in South Asia', in Kanti Bajpai and Siddharth Mallavarapu (eds.), *International Relations in India: Theorising the Region and Nation* (New Delhi: Orient Longman, 2005).

48. Dixit, 26.

49. Roland Buerk, 'Villagers left in limbo by border fence', *BBC News*, Dhaka, 28 January 2006, http://news.bbc.co.uk/2/hi/programmes/from_our_own_corre-spondent/4653810.stm

50. See Jim Yardley, 'Balancing Act for India as Talks With Pakistan Resume', *International Herald Tribune*, 25 February 2010.

51. Siddharth Varadarajan, 'Time to end the impasse with Pakistan', *The Hindu*, 26 April 2010.

52. C. Raja Mohan, 'Balancing act in Thimphu', *Indian Express*, 28 April 2010.

53. See The World Bank, *World Development Indicators 2010*, http://data.worldbank.org/data-catalog/world-development-indicators/wdi-2010 According to 2008 figures, China's GDP was $4.327 trillion compared to India's $1.159 trillion. China's GDP per capita at $3,267 was roughly three times that of India's at $1,017; see http://data.worldbank.org/indicator

54. Sood, 260.

55. Ibid., 261.

56. Harshe, 321–2.

57. See Ashok Handoo, 'Naxal problem needs a holistic approach'; See also South Asia Terrorism Portal: www.satp.org/satporgtp/countries/india/maoist/data_sheets/fatalitiesnaxal08.htm Figure comprises deaths of civilians, security forces, and Naxals.

58. 'The good Afghan', *Indian Express*, 26 April 2010.

59. Shishir Gupta, 'India shifts Afghan policy, ready to talk to Taliban', *Indian Express*, 29 March 2010.

60. M. Karim Faiez and Mark Magnier, 'Taliban claims responsibility for Kabul embassy attack', *Los Angeles Times*, 9 October 2009.

61. 'Al-Qaeda planning to target India: Gates', *Indian Express*, 30 January 2010.

62. South Asia Terrorism Portal: www.satp.org/satporgtp/countries/india/database/indiafatalities.htm

63. Stanley A. Weiss, 'The United States, India and the politics of benign neglect', *United Press International*, 28 April 2010.

64. See Ashley J. Tellis, 'India as a New Global Power: An Action Agenda for the United States' (Washington, DC: Carnegie Endowment for International Peace, 2005), 9.
65. Weiss, 'The United States, India and the politics of benign neglect'.
66. President Obama's administration, in a more contemporary twist, has eliminated the need for hyphens by coining the term AfPak, a characteristic American shorthand for its joint and most pressing priorities in the region.
67. M. K. Bhadrakumar, 'Challenges for Indian foreign policy', *The Hindu*, 6 March 2009.
68. Sanjaya Baru, 'India in a changing world', *HT Mint*, 30 March 2009.
69. See Shirley A. Kan, 'China and Proliferation of Weapons of Mass Destruction and Missiles: Policy Issues', *CRS Report for Congress RL31555*, 13 December 2007.
70. Siddharth Varadarajan, 'China, Pakistan and the NSG', *The Hindu*, 24 June 2010.
71. C. Raja Mohan, 'The battle for Pakistan', *Indian Express*, 21 June 2010.
72. Sumit Ganguly, 'Indian Defense Policy', in Niraja Gopal Jayal and Pratap Bhanu Mehta (eds.), *The Oxford Companion to Politics in India* (New Delhi: Oxford University Press, 2010), 550.
73. K. P. Saksena, 'India's Foreign Policy: The Decisionmaking Process', *International Studies* 33/4 (October 1996), 391–405.
74. Sumit Ganguly, 'Indian Foreign Policy Grows Up', *World Policy Journal* 20/2 (Winter 2003/4), 41–7.
75. An example of this was the public turf battle for policymaking authority between the Prime Minister's Principal Secretary (Brajesh Mishra) and the Deputy Chairman of the Planning Commission (Jaswant Singh) that complicated India's diplomatic efforts after the nuclear tests of 1998. See George Iype, 'War in MEA cripples India's battle for world support', *Rediff News*, 14 July 1998, http://www.rediff.com/news/1998/jul/14bomb4.htm
76. Devesh Kapur, 'India in 1999', *Asian Survey*, 40(1) (January/February 2000), 195–207.
77. Pratap Bhanu Mehta, 'Not so credible India', *Indian Express*, 24 April 2008.
78. Kapur, 'India in 1999', 206.
79. Saksena, 398.
80. Harsh V. Pant, 'Four years of UPA: Foreign policy adrift', *Rediff News*, 12 May 2008, http://www.rediff.com/news/2008/may/12guest.htm
81. Retired Admiral Raja Menon and economist Rajiv Kumar, in their book *The Long View From Delhi: Indian Grand Strategy for Foreign Policy* (Delhi: Academic Foundation, 2010) don't so much offer up a strategic framework of their own but rather helpfully outline the considerations such a strategy would need to address, and, in order to stimulate thought, propose four possible scenarios of how the wider world could evolve in years ahead, affecting India's prospects.
82. Dixit, 134–8.
83. Ibid., 87.
84. See J. Mohan Malik, 'India's Response to the Gulf Crisis: Implications for Indian Foreign Policy', *Asian Survey*, 31/9 (September 1991), 847–61.
85. See C. Raja Mohan, 'Peaceful Periphery: India's New Regional Quest', Center for the Advanced Study of India (24 May 2007). Also see Mehta, 'Not so credible India'; and Pant, 'Four years of UPA'.

86. P. C. Chidambaram, 'India Empowered To Me Is', in *A View from the Outside: Why Good Economics Works for Everyone* (New Delhi and New York: Penguin Books, 2007).

87. Ninan Koshy, *Under the Empire: India's New Foreign Policy* (New Delhi: LeftWord Books, 2006), 155.

88. Full text of speech available at http://www.canadaupdates.com/news/text_of_-manmohan_singhs_speech_at_nam_summit-24018.html

89. K. M. Seethi and P. Vijayan, 'Political Economy of India's Third World Policy', in Harshe and Seethi (eds.), *Engaging with the World*, 47.

90. Recently, however, India's global approach to energy security has taken a competitive stance with the establishment of a sovereign fund for the acquisition of energy assets abroad. See Sujay Mehdudia, 'India plans "Sovereign Fund" to seek energy assets abroad', *The Hindu*, 1 April 2010.

Chapter 4

1. I am deeply grateful to Ms. Tejdeep Kaur for early research assistance relative to this chapter.

2. See Rohan Mukherjee and David M. Malone, 'Polity, Security and Foreign Policy in Contemporary India', in T. V. Paul (ed.), *South Asia's Weak States: Understanding the Regional Insecurity Predicament* (Palo Alto, CA: Stanford University Press, 2010).

3. See Angus Maddison, *The World Economy: Historical Statistics* (Paris: OECD Publishing, 2003).

4. Tirthankar Roy, *The Economic History of India, 1857–1947* (Delhi: Oxford University Press, 2000), 1.

5. P. Sainath, 'The Raj and the famines of good governance', *The Hindu*, 16 August 2005.

6. S. Mahendra Dev, 'Agriculture and Rural Development: Policy Issues for Growth and Equity', in Manmohan Malhoutra (ed.), *India: The Next Decade* (New Delhi: Academic Foundation, 2006), 205; see also G. S. Bhalla, *Indian Agriculture Since Independence* (New Delhi: National Book Trust, 2007).

7. Quoted in Sanjaya Baru, *Strategic Consequences of India's Economic Performance* (New Delhi: Academic Foundation, 2006), 58.

8. For about four decades after India's independence, its foreign trade suffered from strict bureaucratic and discretionary controls. Similarly, foreign exchange transactions were tightly controlled by the Government and the Reserve Bank of India. Characteristically for many developing countries, it consistently ran a trade deficit. For details, see Vibha Mathur, *Foreign Trade of India 1947–2007: Trends, Policies and Prospects* (New Delhi: New Century Publications, 2006).

9. Sanjaya Baru, 'Self-Reliance to Dependence in Indian Economic Development', *Social Scientist* 11/11 (November 1983), 34–46.

10. Jerome B. Cohen, 'Problems of Economic Development in India', *Economic Development and Cultural Change*, 1/2 (1953), 196–208.

11. Arvind Virmani, 'The Dynamics of Competition: Phasing of Domestic and External Liberalisation in India', Planning Commission of India Working

Paper No. 4 (April 2006), 6–7, http://planningcommission.nic.in/reports/wrkpapers/wp_dc_pdel.pdf

12. James Heitzman and Robert L. Worden (eds.), *India: A Country Study* (Washington: GPO for the Library of Congress, 1995); Government of India, Ministry of Finance, *Annual Report 1994–95* (New Delhi, 1994), http://www.powermin.nic.in/reports/pdf/ar94-95.pdf Government of India, Planning Commission, *Ninth Five Year Plan*, Vol. I (New Delhi: Yojana Bhavan, 1992).

13. Paul Hallwood, 'The Impact of Foreign Aid Upon India's International Trade 1951–65', *Bulletin of Economic Research*, 25/2 (1973), 129–45.

14. See generally Jagdish Bhagwati, 'The Tying of Aid', in J. Bhagwati and R. S. Eckaus (eds.), *Foreign Aid* (Harmondsworth: Penguin, 1970).

15. Robert Cassen & Associates, *Does Aid Work? Report to an Intergovernmental Task Force* (Oxford: Clarendon Press, 1986), 28.

16. See Praveen K. Chaudry, Vijay L. Kelkar, and Vikash Yadav, 'The Evolution of Homegrown Conditionality in India: IMF Relations', *Journal of Development Studies*, 40/6 (August 2004), 59–81.

17. Defence spending in 1965–6, of around 24.06 per cent of total expenditure, was the highest in the period from 1965 to 1989. See Uma Kapila (ed.), *Indian Economy Since Independence* (New Delhi: Academic Foundations, 2001), 195.

18. Robert Cassen & Associates, *Does Aid Work?*, 88.

19. Devika Johri and Mark Miller, *Devaluation of the Rupee: Tale of Two Years, 1966 and 1991* (Centre for Civil Society, Working Paper, 28), 86: www.ccsindia.org/policy/money/studies/wp0028 see also Surendra K. Kaushik, 'India's Evolving Economic Model: A Perspective on Economic and Financial Reforms', *American Journal of Economics and Sociology*, 56/1 (1997), 69–84.

20. Ashok Gulati, 'Trade Liberalization and Food Security', in Anwarul Hoda (ed.), *WTO Agreement and Indian Agriculture* (New Delhi: Social Science Press, 2002), 39–40. Also see Gurcharan Das, *India Unbound: From Independence to the Global information Age* (New Delhi: Penguin Books India, 2000).

21. I owe to R. K. Pachauri the information that work on seeds by Indian scientists had started as early as the 1930s: 'The whole approach for high yielding hybrid seeds was pioneered by Dr B. P. Pal who was the first Indian to become Director of the Imperial (later Indian) Agricultural Research Institute (IARI) in Pusa and then the very first Director General of the Indian Council of Agricultural Research (ICAR). In fact, Dr Pal conceptualized the project of using high yielding hybrid seeds as early as 1937 when he published a paper called "The search for new genes", *Agriculture and livestock in India* 7/5 (1937), 573–578'; correspondence with the author.

22. See 'The Green Revolution', http://edugreen.teri.res.in/explore/bio/green.htm See also David M. Malone, 'India: Challenges in Agriculture', *The Hindu*, 7 February 2009.

23. See Ashok Bhargava, 'Indian Economy during Mrs. Gandhi's Regime', in Yogendra K. Malik and Dhirendra K. Vajpeyi (eds.), *India: The Years of Indira Gandhi* (Leiden: E. J. Brill, 1988), 42–59.

24. Kangayappan Kumar, 'Some Policy Issues on Mitigating Poverty In India', *Land Economics* 49/1 (1973), 76–81.

25. For a useful outline of India's approach to Science and Technology Development, see a commencement address on 22 February 2003 by Dr R. A. Mashelkar, then Director General of India's Council of Scientific and Industrial Research: http://www.scribd.com/doc/9626774/positivism-by-R-Mashelkar

26. See a brief, incisive and authoritative article by author and prominent newspaper editor Inder Malhotra, a biographer of Indira Gandhi, for the BBC, 'Indira Gandhi's Legacy, 28 October 2004, http://news.bbc.co.uk/2/hi/south_asia/3960877.stm

27. Shankar Acharya, 'India's Macroeconomic Performance in the Nineties', SANEI Distinguished Lecture, 9 November 2001, Colombo: http://www.saneinetwork.net/pdf/shankar.PDF

28. John Williamson and Roberto Zagha, 'From the Hindu Rate of Growth to the Hindu Rate of Reform', *SCID Working Paper* 144 (The Stanford Centre for International Development, Stanford University, 2002), http://scid.stanford.edu/publications-profile/1359

29. Inaugural Address at the 55th Annual Conference of the Indian Society of Agricultural Economics by Montek Singh Ahluwalia, 'New Economic Policy and Agriculture: Some Reflections', http://planningcommission.gov.in/aboutus/speech/spemsa/msa014.doc

30. Government of India, Ministry of Finance, *Economic Survey 1991–92*, Part II: *Sectoral Developments* (New Delhi: Government of India Press, 1992), 13.

31. Shyam J. Kamath, 'Foreign Aid and India: Financing the Leviathan State', (Washington, DC: Cato Institute, May 1992), http://www.cato.org/pubs/pas/pa-170.html

32. Valerie Cerra and Sweta C. Saxena, 'What Caused the 1991 Currency Crisis in India?', *IMF Staff Papers* 49/3 (2002), 395–425, www.imf.org/external/pubs/ft/staffp/2002/03/pdf/cerra.pdf

33. See generally Leela Fernandes, *India's New Middle Class: Democratic Politics in an Era of Economic Reform* (Minneapolis: University of Minnesota Press, 2006).

34. See Cerra and Saxena, 395–425.

35. See *WTO Trade Profile-India 2010*, WTO, http://stat.wto.org/CountryProfile/WSDBCountryPFView.aspxLanguage=E&Country=IN

36. 'Kamal Nath says India remains fastest growing economy in the World', Press Release, 12 February 2009, http://commerce.nic.in/pressrelease/pressrelease_detail.asp?id=2384. BRIC, an acronym that refers to the fast-growing economies of Brazil, Russia, India, and China, was first coined by Goldman Sachs. The Gulf Cooperation Council (GCC) was established on 25 May 1981 to promote stability and economic cooperation among Persian Gulf nations, specifically Bahrain, Kuwait, Oman, Qatar, Saudi Arabia, and the United Arab Emirates.

37. 'Some Perspectives on the Indian Economy', Address by Y. V. Reddy, Governor, Reserve Bank of India, at the Peterson Institute for International Economics, Washington, DC, 17 October 2007, http://rbidocs.rbi.org.in/rdocs/Bulletin/PDFs/81163.pdf

38. Ibid.

39. See Kaushik, 69–84; see also William Nanda Bissell, *Making India Work* (New Delhi: Viking (Penguin), 2009).

40. On enthusiasm over the potential of India's private sector, see Fareed Zakaria, *The Post-American World* (New York: Norton, 2008), particularly 129–66.

41. For a detailed analysis of the impact of the global financial crisis on India's economy, see Sanjaya Baru, 'India: Rising Through the Slowdown', in Asley J. Tellis, Andrew Marble, and Travis Tanner (eds.), *Strategic Asia 2009–10: Economic Meltdown and Geopolitical Stability* (Seattle, WA: The National Bureau of Asian Research, 2009), 198–230.

42. James Lamont, 'India warns about balance of payments', *Financial Times*, 24 August 2010.

43. 'India and Globalisation', speech by P. Chidambaram, Indian Minister of Finance, London, UK, 3 February 2005.

44. For the 2008 compilation, see http://money.cnn.com/magazines/fortune/global500/2008/

45. See Nandan Nilekani, *Imagining India: the Idea of a Renewed Nation* (New York: Penguin, 2009), notably 45–54.

46. India's Knowledge Commission, established in 2005, chaired by Sam Pitroda and with members including Nandan Nilekani, co-founder of INFOSYS, made a number of useful recommendations on education reforms required in India. See www.knowledgecommission.gov.in

47. Ramesh Thakur, a keen observer of developments on the Indian scene, cited these and other science and technology achievements of India in a lecture he delivered at the International Development Research Centre on 5 February 2009 making a strong case for India's too often under-estimated research and development prowess and its significance for the country's future. See http://www.idrc.ca/en/ev-136315-201-1-DO_TOPIC.html

48. Kishore Mahbubani's *The New Asian Hemisphere: The Irresistible Shift of Global Power to the East* (New York: Public Books, 2008) was very well received in India; see also generally B. M. Jain, *Global Power: India's Foreign Policy, 1947–2006* (New Delhi: Lexington Books, 2008); and Shamsi Nayyar, *India: A Global Power* (New Delhi: Anmol Publications Pvt. Ltd, 2004).

49. 'Indian Economy Overview', *Economy Watch*: www.economywatch.com/indianeconomy/

50. Remarks by Angel Gurria delivered at the OECD-India Symposium, New Delhi, December 2009: www.oecd.org/document/0,3343,en_2649_34487_44184122_1_1_1_1,00.html The OECD, in an interesting report on 'The new geography of growth—a structural realignment in the global economy', focuses extensively on India: *Perspective on Global Development: Shifting Wealth* (Paris: OECD, 2010), www.oecd.org/document/8/0,3343,en_2649_33959_45462088_1_1_1_1,00.html

51. 'Indian foreign policy has had a basic consensus', address by the Prime Minister Manmohan Singh on 15 February 2006: www.rediff.com/news/2006/feb/15guest1.htm

52. S. Venkitaramanan, 'The Rediscovery of Jawaharlal Nehru', *The Hindu Business Line*, 10 December 2007: www.thehindubusinessline.com/2007/12/10/stories/2007121050690900.htm

53. See Kaushik, 69–84.

54. See generally Jayantanuja Bandyopadhyaya, *The Making of India's Foreign Policy* (New Delhi: Allied, 1970).

55. See B. M. Jain, 'India and Russia: Reassessing the Time-Tested Ties', *Pacific Affairs* 76/3 (Fall 2003).

56. Zorawar Daulet Singh, 'Reviving the India-Russia Partnership', *AsiaTimes* Online, 14 November 2006: www.atimes.com/atimes/South_Asia/HK14Df01.html

57. Ram Puniyani, 'Nehru and India's Foreign Policy', countercurrents.org, 12 November 2007: www.countercurrents.org/puniyani121107.htm Kumar, Arun, '60 years after partition US de-hyphenates India, Pakistan', *The Indian Star*, 12 August 2007: www.theindianstar.com/index.php?udn=2007-12-11&uan=1310

58. Dietmar Rothermund, *India: The Rise of An Asian Giant* (New Haven and London: Yale University Press, 2008), 77–8; and Deepak Nayyar, *India's Exports and Export Policies in the 1960's* (Cambridge: Cambridge University Press, 2007).

59. Government of India, Ministry of External Affairs, *Annual Report 2007–2008* (New Delhi: Policy and Planning Research Division), 108–12.

60. Rajiv Sikri, *Challenge and Strategy: Rethinking India's Foreign Policy* (New Delhi: Sage India, 2009), 236.

61. Gareth Price, 'India's Aid Dynamics: From Recipient to Donor?', London: Royal Institute of International Affairs, Chatham House, 2004; www.chathamhouse.org.uk/publications/papers/view/-/id/229/

62. The UK aid programme to India, worth over $1 billion during the three years 2008–10, one of the few large survivors, is under some pressure from within the UK's new coalition government. See an essay by new Conservative Member of Parliament and former *Financial Times* correspondent in India Jo Johnson, 'Britain needs to show tough love to India', *Financial Times*, 28 June 2010.

63. Ramesh Thakur, 'India in the World: Neither Rich, Powerful, nor Principled', *Foreign Affairs*, 76/4 (July/August 1997), 16.

64. 'The Indian economy in the global setting', address by Dr Rakesh Mohan, Deputy Governor of the Reserve Bank of India, 8 September 2005: http://rbidocs.rbi.org.in/rdocs/speeches/pdfs/65814.pdf

65. Thakur, 16.

66. See chapter 9 in Heitzman and Worden (eds.), *India: A Country Study*. See also a series of papers (1991–6) by Chakravarti Rangarajan, 'Recent Monetary Policy Measures and the Balance of Payments', in the *Reserve Bank of India Bulletin* (New Delhi: 1991). For an account of the gathering crisis, see C. P. Chandrasekhar, 'India's Balance of Payments under the New Regime', *Social Scientist* 13/9 (September 1985), 31–43; see also Ajai Chopra, Charles Collyns, Richard Hemming, Karen Parker, Woosik Chu, and Oliver Fratzscher, 'India: Economic Reforms and Growth', *IMF Occasional Paper*, 134 (1995); and Arvind Panagariya, 'India in the 1980s and 1990s: A Triumph of Reforms', *IMF Working Paper*, 04/43 (2004); Ashok V. Desai, 'The Economics and Politics of Transition to an Open Market Economy: India', OECD Development Centre *Working Paper*, 155 (1999).

67. For example, Indians registered as the most pro-USA among sixteen populations polled by the Pew Global Attitudes Project in a study released in February 2006,

with 71 per cent expressing a favourable view of the United States. See http://pewglobal.org/commentary/display.php?AnalysisID=1002

68. See C. Raja Mohan, 'India and the Balance of Power', *Foreign Affairs*, 85(4) (July/August 2006), 17–32.

69. 'US slashes aid to India by 35 percent', *Financial Express*, 25 July 2007.

70. 'Rethink Russia ties', *Times of India*, 6 December 2007; 'India to take up Gorshkov, SU-30MKI price hikes with Russia', *Financial Express*, 28 August 2007; 'With Russia hiking Gorshkov price, India goes for indigenous carrier', *The Hindu*, 23 February 2009.

71. Sergei I. Lounev, 'Russia and India Political Cooperation in the sphere of Global, Regional and Bilateral Relations', *China Report*, 381 (2002), 109–11.

72. Singh, 'Reviving the India–Russia Partnership'.

73. India secured observer status of the Shanghai Cooperation Organization, founded in 2001, alongside such countries as Iran and Pakistan.

74. Correspondence with the author, 17 January 2009.

75. Mehul Srivastava, 'India–China Trade Tensions Rise', *Bloomberg Businessweek*, 11 February 2009: www.businessweek.com/globalbiz/content/feb2009/gb20090211_202935.htm.

76. Detailed information about India–China trade and investment is available on the Embassy of India in China website at www.indianembassy.org.cn/

77. C. Raja Mohan, 'India's "Look West" Policy', *The Hindu*, 17 June 2004.

78. Ibid.

79. *A vision for a 21st Century: Economic Powerhouse and Global leader—Asia Society*, 17 March 2005: www.asiasociety.org/publications/21st_century_india.html

80. See Ranjeet Gupta, 'India's 'Look East' Policy', in Atish Sinha and Madhup Mohta (eds.), *Indian foreign Policy: Challenges and Opportunities* (New Delhi: Academic Foundation, 2007), 351–81.

81. See Kishore Mahbubani, *The New Asian Hemisphere: The Irresistible Shift of Global Power to the East* (New York: Public Affairs Books, 2008).

82. 'The Challenges Ahead for India's foreign policy', remarks by Shivshankar Menon, Foreign Secretary of India, 10 April 2007: www.observerindia.com/cms/export/orfonline/modules/orfdiscourse/attachments/menon_1181047978452.pdf

83. Dominic Wilson and Roopa Purushothaman, 'Dreaming with the BRICs: The Path to 2050', *Goldman Sachs Global Economics Paper* No. 99 (1 October 2003): www2.goldmansachs.com/ideas/brics/book/99-dreaming.pdf

84. 'Some Perspectives on the Indian Economy', address by Dr Y. V. Reddy (Governor of the Reserve Bank of India) at the Peterson Institute for International Economics, Washington, DC, 17 October 2007: http://www.iie.com/publications/papers/paper.cfm?ResearchID=823

85. For projected rates of industrialization in India, see Economist Intelligence Unit, *India Country Report* (London: EUI, December 2008).

86. Vibhute Haté, 'India's Energy Dilemma', *South Asia Monitor* (Center for Strategic and International Studies, September 2006), 1; and especially Yasheng Huang, 'The Next Asian Miracle', *Foreign Policy*, 167 (July/August 2008) (throughout).

87. See C. Raja Mohan, 'Sino-Indian Rivalry in the Western Indian Ocean', *ISAS Insights*, 52 (February 2009), 1–6.

88. *A vision for a 21ˢᵗ Century: Economic Powerhouse and Global leader—Asia Society*, 17 March 2005: www.asiasociety.org/publications/21st_century_india.html

89. Arjun K. Sengupta, *Report on Conditions of Work and Promotion of Livelihoods in the Unorganised Sector* (New Delhi: Academic Foundation, 2008).

Chapter 5

1. 'The Problem', *Seminar: Our Troubled Neighbourhood* (web edition), 584 (April 2008): www.india-seminar.com/semframe.html

2. Pranay Sharma, 'Overcoming trust deficit', *Seminar: Our Troubled Neighbourhood* (web edition), 584 (April 2008): www.india-seminar.com/semframe.html

3. This phrase was first used by then President Ershad of Bangladesh in an interview on 7 December 1986, cited in M. S. Rajan, *Recent Essays on India's Foreign Policy* (New Delhi: Kalinga Publications, 1997), 131.

4. S. D. Muni, 'India and Its Neighbour: Persisting Dilemmas and New Opportunities', *International Studies*, 30/2 (1993), 196.

5. C. Raja Mohan, 'India's Neighbourhood Policy: Four Dimensions', *Indian Foreign Affairs Journal*, 2/1 (January/March 2007).

6. S. D. Muni and C. Raja Mohan, 'Emerging Asia: India's Options', *International Studies* 41/3 (2004), 318.

7. V. P. Dutt, *India's Foreign Policy* (New Delhi: Vikas Publishing House Pvt. Ltd., 1984), 136.

8. V. N. Khanna, *Foreign Policy of India* (New Delhi: Vikas Publishing House Pvt. Ltd, 1997), 315.

9. 'Indian Foreign Policy: A Road Map for the Decade Ahead', speech by External Affairs Minister Shri Pranab Mukherjee, 15 November 2006: http://meaindia.nic.in/speech/2006/11/15ss02.htm

10. Soon after taking up office in New Delhi in 2006, I called on one of the most senior members of its security and foreign policy establishment. He mentioned that he was inclined to think of most of India's neighbours as 'thugs and crooks'. He noted, however, that Prime Minister Singh disagreed, arguing that if India's neighbours were all indeed thugs and crooks, India must bear some share of responsibility. Might the truth lie somewhere in between?

11. S. D. Muni, 'Problem Areas In India's Neighbourhood Policy', *South Asian Survey*, 10/2 (2003), 185; U. S. Bajpai, 'Introduction' in U. S. Bajpai (ed.), *India and Its Neighbour* (New Delhi: Lancer International in association with India International Centre, 1986), 4.

12. Government of India, Ministry of External Affairs, *Annual Report 2007–2008* (New Delhi: Policy and Planning Research Division), i.

13. Muni, 'Problem Areas In India's Neighbourhood Policy', 189.

14. Muni and Raja Mohan, 'Emerging Asia: India's Options', 319.

15. C. Raja Mohan, 'India's New Foreign Policy Strategy', paper presented at a seminar in Beijing by China Reform Forum and the Carnegie Endowment for International Peace, 26 May 2006: www.carnegieendowment.org

16. Articulated by former Foreign Minister (and later Prime Minister) I. K. Gujral in a speech in London in September 1996, the doctrine is composed of five points: 'First, with its neighbours like Bangladesh, Bhutan, Maldives, Nepal and Sri Lanka, India does not ask for reciprocity, but gives and accommodates what it can in good faith and trust. Second, we believe that no South Asian country should allow its territory to be used against the interests of another country of the region. Third, that none should interfere in the internal affairs of another. Fourth, all South Asian countries must respect each other's territorial integrity and sovereignty. And finally, they should settle all their disputes through peaceful bilateral negotiations.' See I. K. Gujral, *A Foreign Policy for India* (New Delhi: Ministry of External Affairs, 1998), 69–81. Also see I. K. Gujral, *Continuity and Change: India's Foreign Policy* (New Delhi: Macmillan, 2003), 107–74.

17. John Cherian, 'United Front's Bright Area of Performance', *Frontline* (Chennai), 4 April 1997, 8.

18. Ibid., 66.

19. See for example a speech by Dr Singh, 25 February 2005: http://meaindia.nic.in/speech/2005/02/25ss01.htm

20. This term was used by then Foreign Secretary Shyam Saran during his talk on 'Does India have a Neighbourhood Policy?' at the Indian Council of World Affairs, 9 September 2006: www.meaindia.nic.in/mystart.php?id=290011843

21. Foreign Secretary Shyam Sharan's speech on 'India and its Neighbour' at the India International Centre, New Delhi, 14 February 2005: www.indianembassy.org/Speeches/1.htm

22. Saran, 'Does India Have a Neighbourhood Policy?'

23. See for example, S. D. Muni, 'SAARC at Twenty Five', *ISAS Brief*, 160 (4 May 2010).

24. Prime Minister Singh at SAARC Summit, 28 April 2010: http://meaindia.nic.in/

25. For considerably more country information, see Rajeev Ranjan Chaturvedy and David M. Malone, 'India and Its South Asian Neighbours', *ISAS Working Paper* No. 100 (26 November 2009): www.isasnus.org/events/workingpapers/99

26. For a useful recent history of Pakistan, see Sartaj Aziz, *Between Dreams and Reality: Some Milestones in Pakistan's History* (Oxford: Oxford University Press, 2009).

27. Stephen P. Cohen, *India: Emerging Power* (Washington, DC: Brookings Institution Press, 2001), 62.

28. T. V. Paul, ''Why has the India-Pakistan Rivalry Been so Enduring? Power Asymmetry and an Intractable Conflict', *Security Studies*, 15/4 (October/December 2006), 600–30.

29. Detailed information and timeline on confidence building measures (CBMs) in South Asia is available on www.stimson.org/southasia/?SN=SA20060207948

30. See Steve Coll, 'The Back Channel', *The New Yorker*, 2 March 2009, www.newamerica.net/publications/articles/2009/back_channel_11191 C. Raja Mohan, 'In defence of Track Two diplomacy', *The Hindu*, 4 June 2001.

31. On the incident, see Jaswant Singh, *A Call To Honour: In Service Of Emergent India* (New Delhi: Rupa & Co., 2006), 240 and others.

32. B. Raman, 'Terror's new faces', 19 August 2008: www.rediff.com/news/2008/aug/19raman.htm

33. 'Rising India has a Pakistan Problem', a talk by Stephen P. Cohen, at the International Development Research Centre (IDRC), 9 April 2009. The speech is available at www.brookings.edu/speeches/2009/0409_pakistan_cohen.aspx

34. For an analysis of economic interests of the Pakistani army, see Ayesha Siddiqa, *Military Inc: Inside Pakistani Military Economy* (London: Pluto Press, 2007); also see Hasan Askari Rizvi, *The Military and Politics in Pakistan 1947–86* (Delhi: Konark Publishers, 1988).

35. Ahmed Rashid, 'Pakistan on the Brink', *New York Review of Books*, 56/10 (11 June 2009), 14–15.

36. Aravind Adiga, 'Tips for India's next Premier', *Financial Times*, 12 May 2009.

37. Following the 26 November 2008 attacks against Mumbai, the UN Security Council on 9 December 2008 issued an anodyne Presidential Statement (UN Document S/PRST/2008/45), but held a debate that displayed outrage over the Mumbai attacks. The debate, in which forty-six countries intervened, considerably added to the pressure on Islamabad to cooperate with Indian inquiries and to recognize that the terrorists had originated from Pakistan. See UN Document SC/9524 of 9 December 2008.

38. This view was expressed by eminent Pakistani experts recently in a conference on South Asian Security in Ottawa.

39. Correspondence with the author, 20 June 2010.

40. Chinmaya Gharekhan, 'Kashmir is the issue, LOC the solution', *Sunday Guardian*, 14 February 2010.

41. T. V. Paul, 'Why has the India-Pakistan Rivalry Been so Enduring?', 601.

42. 'Rising India's Pakistan Problem', a talk by Stephen P. Cohen, at IDRC on 9 April 2009.

43. See Nisha Taneja, 'Trade Possibilities and Non-Tariff Barriers to Indo-Pak Trade', *ICRIER Working Papers*, 200 (New Delhi: Indian Council for Research on International Economic Relations, October 2007): www.icrier.org/publication/working_papers_200.html

44. '68 killed as blasts rock Indo-Pak special train', 19 February 2007: www.rediff.com/news/2007/feb/19blast.htm

45. Correspondence with the author, 22 June 2010.

46. Correspondence with the author, 24 May and 22 and 23 June 2010.

47. See Siddharth Varadarajan, 'Time to end the impasse with Pakistan', *The Hindu* (Online Edition), 26 April 2010.

48. Anita Joshua and Sandeep Dikshit, 'Krishna-Qureshi talks in Islamabad on July 15', *The Hindu* (Online Edition), 12 May 2010.

49. K. S. Bajpai, 'Terror is an Event, Peace is a Process', *Outlook*, 22 March 2010, 26–7.

50. Sreeradha Datta, 'India and Bangladesh: Stuck in a Groove?' in Virendra Gupta, Sumita Kumar, and Vishal Chandra (eds.), *India's Neighbourhood: Challenges Ahead* (New Delhi: IDSA and Rubicon Publishers, 2008), 85.

51. Akmal Hussain, 'Geo-politics and Bangladesh Foreign Policy', *CLIO*, 7/2, 99–100, quoted in Sanjay Bhardwaj, 'Bangladesh foreign policy vis-a-vis India', *Strategic Analysis*, 27/2 (2003), 263–78. And to the south lies the Bay of Bengal, heavily patrolled by the Indian navy.

52. An estimated 600,000 Bangladeshis come to India each year. See M. Shamsur Rabb Khan, 'Towards Better India-Bangladesh relations', *IDSA Strategic Comments*, 9 January 2009.

53. 'Indian HC on Illegal Migration', *Daily Star,* Dhaka, 21 July 2009, quoted in Mohd Aminul Karim, 'Bangladesh-India Relations: Some Recent Trends', *ISAS Working Paper*, 96 (12 November 2009).

54. Deb Mukherji, 'Distant Neighbours: India and Bangladesh', in Atish Sinha and Madhup Mohta (eds.), *Indian Foreign Policy: Challenges and Opportunities* (New Delhi: Academic Foundation and the Foreign Service Institute, 2007), 557–8.

55. Sreeradha Datta, 'India and Bangladesh: Stuck in a Groove?', 79.

56. Correspondence with the author, 29 May 2010.

57. Waliur Rahman, 'Bangladesh tops most corrupt list', *BBC News*, 18 October 2005: http://news.bbc.co.uk/2/hi/south_asia/4353334.stm

58. See Bibhu Prasad Routray, 'India—Bangladesh: No Breakthroughs', *South Asia Intelligence Review* 7/12 (29 September 2008): www.satp.org/satporgtp/sair/Archives/7_12.htm#assessment2 For more detail on Islamic resurgence in Bangladesh, see Taj I. Hashmi, 'Islamic Resurgence in Bangladesh: Genesis, Dynamics and Implications' in Satu P. Limaye, Mohan Malik, and Robert G. Wirsing (eds.), *Religious Radicalism and Security in South Asia* (Honolulu: Asia Pacific Centre for Security Studies, 2004): www.apcss.org/Publications/Edited%20Volumes/ReligiousRadicalism/ReligiousRadicalismandSecurityinSouthAsia.pdf also see Harsh V. Pant, 'India and Bangladesh: Will the Twain Ever Meet?', *Asian Survey* 47/2 (March/April 2007), 231–49.

59. See Renaud Egreteau, 'Instability at the Gate: India's Troubled Northeast and its External Connections', *Centre de Sciences Humaines de New Delhi Occasional Paper*, 6 (2006): www.csh-delhi.com/publications/downloads/ops/OP16.pdf

60. 'Siliguri corridor "vulnerable": Security expert', *Indian Express*, 22 July 2007.

61. 'Hasina welcomes Indian investment in Bangladesh', *Business Standard*, 23 July 2009.

62. 'India, Bangladesh to develop border infrastructure', *Hindustan Times*, 27 August 2009.

63. 'Kolkata-Dhaka train on track after 43-yr gap', *Indian Express*, 14 April 2008.

64. 'We won't allow our soil to be used against India: Hasina', *The Hindu*, 12 January 2010.

65. '1$ billion credit line for Bangladesh announced', *The Hindu*, 13 January 2010.

66. I. P. Khosla, 'India and Afghanistan' in Sinha and Mohta (eds.), *Indian Foreign Policy*, 529–55.

67. Rajiv Sikri, *Challenge And Strategy: Rethinking India's Foreign Policy* (New Delhi: Sage Publications Ltd, 2009), 52.

68. For India's support to anti-Taliban forces, see Thomas Withington, 'The early anti-Taliban team', *Bulletin of the Atomic Scientists* (November/December 2001), 13–15.

See also Rahul Bedi, 'India joins anti-Taliban coalition', *Jane's Intelligence Review*, 15 March 2001.

69. Government of India, Ministry of External Affairs, *Annual Report 2008–2009* (New Delhi: Policy and Planning Research Division), 1.

70. See Government of India, Ministry of External Affairs, *Annual Report 2007–2008* (New Delhi: Policy and Planning Research Division).

71. Speech by Pranab Mukherjee at the International Conference on 'Cooperative Development, Peace and Security in South & Central Asia', Kolkata, 1 March 2009.

72. See I. P. Khosla, 'India and Afghanistan' in Sinha and Mohta (eds.), *Indian Foreign Policy*, 529–55.

73. Siddharth Varadarajan, 'US sees rising Indian influence in Afghanistan as problem', *The Hindu*, 22 September 2009.

74. M. K. Bhadrakumar, 'India closes ranks with Hamid Karzai', *The Hindu*, 4 May 2010.

75. James Lamont, 'India tells Putin of Afghan fears', *The Financial Times*, 12 March 2010.

76. Dhruba Kumar, 'What Ails Democracy in Nepal', in Dhruba Kumar (ed.), *Domestic Conflict and Crisis of Governability in Nepal* (Kathmandu: Centre for Nepal and Asian Studies, 2000), 19.

77. R. Shaha, *Nepali Politics: Retrospect and Prospect* (Delhi: Oxford Univerity Press, 1978), 104.

78. Sita Kaushik, 'Indo-Nepal Relations: Some Political and Security Issues', in V. T. Patil and Nalini Kant Jha (eds.), *India in a Turbulent World: Perspectives on Foreign and Security Policies* (New Delhi: South Asian Publishers Pvt. Ltd, 2003), 74.

79. Raj Kumar Jha, *The Himalayan Kingdoms in Indian Foreign Policy* (Ranchi: Maitryee Publications, 1986), 347–50.

80. John W. Garver, *Protracted Contest: Sino-Indian Rivalry in the Twentieth Century* (New Delhi: Oxford University Press, 2001), 139–43.

81. Sikri, *Challenge And Strategy*, 83–4.

82. See Siddharth Varadarajan, 'We want new unity on a new basis with India: without taking cooperation with India forward, we cannot do anything for Nepal, says Prachanda', *The Hindu*, 28 April 2008.

83. Sudeshna Sarkar, 'India asks Nepal not to meddle with army', *Thaindian News*, 26 April 2009, www.thaindian.com/newsportal/politics/india-asks-nepal-not-to-med-dle-with-army_100184871.html also see Kanchan Chandra and Yubaraj Ghimire, 'Why Nepal will stay democratic', *The Indian Express*, 12 May 2009; and S. D. Muni, 'The civil-military crisis in Nepal', *The Hindu*, 6 May 2009.

84. Correspondence with the author, 11 November 2009. Muni also notes the extent to which political actors in Kathmandu connect regularly with counterparts in Delhi, amplifying Indian concerns through their lobbying.

85. Correspondence with the author, 22 and 23 June 2010.

86. Correspondence with the author, 31 May and 22 June 2010.

87. For a detailed analysis on the rise of Tamil nationalism in Sri Lanka see Chelvadurai Manogaran, *Ethnic Conflict and Reconciliation in Sri Lanka* (Hawaii: University of Hawaii Press, 1987).

88. J. N. Dixit, *Assignment Colombo* (New Delhi: Konark Publishers Pvt. Ltd, 1998), 297.

89. John Cherian, 'Changing equations', *Frontline*, 26/12 (6–19 June 2009).
90. B. Muralidhar Reddy, 'The war is over', *Frontline*, 26/12 (6–19 June 2009).
91. China is currently building port facilities at an estimated cost of US$1 billion at Hambantota on Sri Lanka's southern coast. This is interpreted by some geostrategic analysts as one more in China's 'string of pearls' encircling India.
92. Correspondence with the author, 21 June 2010.
93. Aim Sinpeng, 'Democracy from Above: Regime Transition in the Kingdom of Bhutan', *Journal of Bhutan Studies* 17 (Winter 2007): www.bhutanstudies.org.bt/admin/pubFiles/2.JBS17.pdf
94. Amit Baruah, 'India, Bhutan sign a new friendship treaty', *The Hindu*, 10 February 2007.
95. See *Economic and Political Relations between Bhutan and Neighbouring Countries*, Monograph, 12 April 2004, A Joint Research Project of the Centre for Bhutan Studies (CBS) and Institute of Developing Economies, Japan External Trade Organization (IDE/JETRO): www.bhutanstudies.org.bt/ . . . /mono-Ecnmc-Pol-Rel-Bt-Nghbrng.pdf
96. M. Govinda Rao and Anuradha Seth, 'Fiscal Space for Achieving the Millennium Development Goals and Implementing the Tenth Plan in Bhutan', *Economic and Political Weekly*, 44/35 (29 August 2009), 57.
97. See B. S. Malik, 'Myanmar's Strategic Environment" in Gupta et al. (eds.), *India's Neighbourhood: Challenges Ahead*, 89–108.
98. See Udai Bhanu Singh, 'Myanmar Update', in Gupta et al. (eds.), *India's Neighbourhood: Challenges Ahead*, 117–22.
99. Jürgen Haacke, *Myanmar's Foreign Policy: Domestic Influences and International Implications* (London: International Institute for Strategic Studies, Adelphi Paper 381, 2006), 35.
100. Government of India, Ministry of Commerce and Industry, 'Export Import Data Bank', http://commerce.nic.in/eidb/default.asp
101. Government of India, Ministry of External Affairs, *Annual Report 2008–2009*, 9–11.
102. Ibid.
103. Marie Lall, 'India-Myanmar Relations—Geopolitics and Energy in Light of the New Balance of Power in Asia', *ISAS Working Paper*, 29 (2 January 2008), 18.
104. Soe Myint, 'Government to government: The distasteful Burma–India embrace', *Himal Southasian* (February 2007): www.himalmag.com/index.php
105. Steven A. Hoffmann, 'Perception and China Policy in India', in Francine R. Frankel and Harry Harding (eds.), *The India-China Relationship: Rivalry and Engagement* (New Delhi: Oxford University Press, 2004), 41.
106. Garver, *Protracted Contest*, 5–6.
107. Colonel Gurmeet Kanwal, 'China's Long March to World Power Status: Strategic Challenges for India', *Strategic Analysis*, 22/2 (February 1999), 1713–28.
108. Sujit Dutta, 'China's Emerging Power and Military Role: Implications for South Asia', in Jonathan D. Pollack and Richard H. Yang (eds.), *In China's Shadow: Regional Perspectives on Chinese Foreign Policy and Military Development* (Santa

Monica: RAND, 1998), 91–114; see also Brahma Chellaney, 'Dragon designs', *Hindustan Times*, 22 June 2006.

109. See, for example, Shanthi Mariet D'Souza, 'Karzai's Balancing Act: Bringing "China" in?' *ISAS Insights*, 98 (7 May 2010).

110. See Teresita C. Schaffer, *India and the United States in the 21st Century: Reinventing Partnership* (Washington, DC: CSIS, 2009), 211 and 216.

111. Pranay Sharma, 'Adding Enemies', *Outlook*, 25 May 2009, 36.

112. Having, in 2005, described SAARC's economic achievements as a 'modest beginning' (text available at: www.saarc-sec.org/main.php?id=164&t=7.1), Dr Singh at the SAARC Summit in Colombo in August 2008 called for 'Economic cooperation, connectivity and integration' as the cornerstone of SAARC but again recognized that the forum had a long way to go on these issues: 'It is however a fact that South Asia has not moved as fast as we all would have wished. We have only to see the rapid integration within ASEAN and its emergence as an important economic bloc in Asia to understand the opportunities that beckon us all.' The text is available at: www.thaindian.com/newsportal/south-asia/text-of-manmohan-singhs-speech-at-saarc-summit-opening_10079148.html#ixzz0WaQj8i63

113. Correspondence with the author, 1 August 2010.

Chapter 6

1. Shao Chuan Leng, 'India and China', *Far Eastern Survey*, 21/8 (21 May 1952), 73–8.

2. For a comprehensive overview of the different theoretical positions on this question, see Aaron Friedberg, 'The Future of US-China Relations: Is Conflict Inevitable?' *International Security*, 30/2 (Fall 2005), 7–45.

3. Waheguru Pal Singh Sidhu and Jing-dong Yuan, *China and India: Cooperation or Conflict?* (Boulder, CO: Lynne Rienner, 2003), 17.

4. In the words of international relations theorist Joseph Nye, 'If a state feels threatened by its neighbor, it is likely to act in accord with the old adage that "the enemy of my enemy is my friend" ': Joseph S. Nye, Jr., *Understanding International Conflicts: An Introduction to Theory and History*, 4th edn (New York: Longman, 2002), 33.

5. Shao Chuan Leng, 'India and China', 74–5.

6. Today described by an eminent Indian commentator as 'a fake, hypocritical and contrived bonding of an entirely muddled and contradictory ideology' (Shekhar Gupta, 'Stop fighting the 1962 war', *Indian Express*, 19 September 2009).

7. See, for example, Mao Zedong's 26 January 1951 speech in honour of the first anniversary of India's Constitution in Shao Chuan Leng, 'India and China', 73–8.

8. Government of India, *Chinese Aggression in War and Peace: Letters of the Prime Minister of India* (Ministry of Information and Broadcasting, Government of India: 1962), 32.

9. See John W. Garver, *Protracted Contest: Sino-Indian Rivalry in the Twentieth Century* (Seattle: University of Washington Press, 2001), 120.

10. Manjari Chatterjee Miller, 'Scars of Empire: Post-Imperial Ideology, Victimization, and Foreign Policy', Ph.D. Dissertation (Department of Government, Harvard University: August 2007), 98.

11. Kishore C. Dash, *Regionalism in South Asia: Negotiating Cooperation, Institutional Structures* (London/New York: Routledge, 2008), 79.
12. Miller, 'Scars of Empire', 101.
13. Neville Maxwell, *India's China War* (London: Cape, 1970), 261.
14. Garver, *Protracted Contest*, 5.
15. Xuecheng Liu, *The Sino-Indian Border Dispute and Sino-Indian Relations* (Lanham, MD: University Press of America, 1994), 12.
16. Mohan Guruswamy and Zorawar Daulet Singh, *India China Relations: The Border Issue and Beyond* (New Delhi: Viva Books, 2009), 38.
17. P. C. Chakravarti, *India-China Relations* (Calcutta: Firma K. L. Mukhopadhyay, 1961), 'Introduction'.
18. John W. Garver, 'China's Decision for War with India in 1962' (undated), 9–10: www.people.fas.harvard.edu/~johnston/garver.pdf
19. M. Taylor Fravel, 'Regime Insecurity and International Cooperation: Explaining China's Compromises in Territorial Disputes', *International Security*, 30/2 (Fall 2005), 68.
20. Shashi Tharoor, *India: From Midnight to the Millennium* (New York: Harper Perennial, 1998), 30.
21. See Garver, *Protracted Contest*, 197–203.
22. Greg O'Leary, *The Shaping of Chinese Foreign Policy* (London: Croom Helm, 1980), 230–2.
23. Liu, *The Sino-Indian Border Dispute*, 98. See also Harry Harding, 'The Evolution of the Strategic Triangle: China, India, and the United States', in Francine R. Frankel and Harry Harding (eds.), *The India–China Relationship: What the United States Needs to Know* (New York: Columbia University Press, 2004), 321.
24. Sumit Ganguly, 'India and China: Border Issues, Domestic Integration, and International Security', in Frankel and Harding (eds.), *The India–China Relationship*, 119.
25. Garver, *Protracted Contest*, 94.
26. Liu, *The Sino-Indian Border Dispute*, 123.
27. Ashley Tellis, referenced in Susan L. Shirk, 'One-Sided Rivalry: China's Perceptions and Policies toward India', in Frankel and Harding (eds.), *The India–China Relationship*, 79.
28. Shirk, 'One-Sided Rivalry', 85.
29. Ganguly, 'India and China', 120. See also Liu, *The Sino-Indian Border Dispute*, 121.
30. Guruswamy and Singh, *India China Relations*, 93.
31. Steven A. Hoffmann, 'Perception and China Policy', in Frankel and Harding, *The India–China Relationship*, 37.
32. Garver, *Protracted Contest*, 218.
33. Liu, *The Sino-Indian Border Dispute*, 135.
34. Liu, *The Sino-Indian Border Dispute*, 122.
35. The first Chinese Prime Minister to visit India since his foster father Zhou Enlai in 1960, much as Rajiv Gandhi was the first Indian Prime Minister to visit China since his grandfather Jawaharlal Nehru in 1954 (Sidhu and Yuan, *China and India*, 24).
36. Embassy of India, Washington, DC, 'Text of the Prime Minister's letter to US President Bill Clinton', 13 May 1998: www.indianembassy.org/indusrel/pmletter.htm

37. 'China is enemy no 1: George', *Indian Express*, 3 May 1998: www.indianexpress. com/old/ie/daily/19980504/12450024.html

38. Shirk,'One-Sided Rivalry', 82.

39. Sidhu and Yuan, *China and India*, 31.

40. Shirk, 'One-Sided Rivalry', 85.

41. Ashley Tellis, 'China and India in Asia', in Frankel and Harding, *The India–China Relationship*, 139.

42. C. Raja Mohan, *Crossing the Rubicon: The Shaping of India's New Foreign Policy* (New York: Palgrave Macmillan, 2004), 151.

43. Sidhu and Yuan, *China and India*, 32.

44. See Sreeram Chaulia, 'UN Security Council Seat: China Outsmarts India', *Indo-Asian News Service*, 30 May 2008: www.globalpolicy.org/component/content/ article/200/41135.html

45. Former figure from Sidhu and Yuan, *China and India*, 25; latter figure from the Export Import Data Bank of the Department of Commerce, Government of India. Retrieved on 18 June 2010 from http://commerce.nic.in/eidb/iecntq.asp.

46. Ministry of Commerce and Industry, 'India's Trading Partners', Press Release, 27 July 2009: http://pib.nic.in/release/release.asp?relid=51058

47. Zhang Yan, 'India–China relations in one of the best periods in history', *The Hindu*, 9 April 2009: www.hindu.com/2009/04/09/stories/2009040955800900.htm

48. Ibid.

49. Vidya Subrahmaniam, 'A "zhengyou" relationship with China', *The Hindu* (Online Edition), 10 June 2010: www.thehindu.com/2010/06/10/stories/ 2010061062390800.htm 'Understanding sensitivities key to Sino-India friendship: Patil', *Indian Express*, 28 May 2010.

50. Zhang Yan, 'India–China relations'.

51. See A. G. Noorani, 'Jingoism as News', *Frontline*, 7 May 2009, 79–84.

52. 'China denies visa to IAS officer from Arunachal', *Financial Express*, 26 May 2007: www.financialexpress.com/news/China-denies-visa-to-IAS-officer-from-Arunachal/ 200132/

53. 'Now China objects to Prez Patil's visit to Arunachal', *Indian Express*, 7 April 2009: www.indianexpress.com/story-print/444106/

54. Seema Guha, 'Dragon fire makes India give up loan for Arunachal', *Daily News and Analysis*, 17 August 2009: www.dnaindia.com/india/report_dragon-fire-makes-india-give-up-loan-for-arunachal_1283192

55. 'Dalai Lama's Arunachal visit from today', *The Hindu* (Online Edition), 8 November 2009: www.thehindu.com/2009/11/08/stories/2009110855690900.htm

56. 'Krishna visit to consolidate ties with China', *The Hindu*, 4 April 2010.

57. Data are from the Stockholm International Peace Research Institute (SIPRI) Military Expenditure Database. Accessed at http://milexdata.sipri.org/

58. Mark W. Frazier, 'Quiet Competition and the Future of Sino-Indian Relations', in Frankel and Harding (eds.), *The India–China Relationship*, 314.

59. Ashley J. Tellis, 'China and India in Asia', in Frankel and Harding (eds.), *The India–China Relationship*, 135.

60. On Afghanistan, see Thomas Adams and Arnav Manchanda, 'The dragon in the Hindu Kush: China's interests in Afghanistan', *Globe and Mail*, 20 April 2009.

61. Hoffmann, 'Perception and China Policy', in Frankel and Harding, *The India–China Relationship*, 48.

62. On the latter, see Amardeep Athwal, *China-India Relations: Contemporary Dynamics* (London/New York: Routledge, 2008), 64.

63. This is a chapter title in Vinod C. Khanna and C. V. Ranganathan, *India and China: The Way Ahead After 'Mao's India War'* (New Delhi: Har Anand, 2000).

64. Raja Mohan, *Crossing the Rubicon*, 158.

65. Garver, *Protracted Contest*, 187.

66. Shirley A. Kan, 'China and Proliferation of Weapons of Mass Destruction and Missiles: Policy Issues', *CRS Report for Congress RL31555* (13 December 2007).

67. See M. Ehsan Ahrari, 'China, Pakistan, and the "Taliban Syndrome"', *Asian Survey* 40/4 (July/August 2000), 658–71; Tim Luard, 'China's changing views of terrorism', *BBC News*, 15 December 2003; Mohan Guruswamy, 'Birds coming home to roost in Xinjiang!' *The Tribune*, 21 July 2009.

68. Arun Shourie, 'Digging our head deeper in the sand', *Indian Express*, 7 April 2009.

69. Ibid.

70. Garver, *Protracted Contest*, 72.

71. Ibid., 75.

72. 'Olympic torch will be safe here, India assures China', *Indian Express*, 27 March 2008: www.indianexpress.com/news/olympic-torch-will-be-safe-here-india-assures-china/ 288799/

73. The uptick in tension was described most incisively in the Banyan column of *The Economist*, 'Himalayan Histronics', 29 October 2009.

74. However, it seems likely that if the Dalai Lama passes on without any resolution of his differences with Beijing, many of the younger members of the Tibetan community in India will seek to emigrate to Western countries where they think their economic opportunities would be greater. Thus the prospect of a lasting Tibetan threat from within India may not prove convincing over time.

75. Raja Mohan, *Crossing the Rubicon*, 163.

76. Ashutosh Varshney, 'A New Triangle: India, China and the US', *Seminar*, 557 (January 2006). The old triangle for India was between India, Pakistan, and the USA.

77. See, for example, M. K. Bhadrakumar, 'Challenges for Indian foreign policy', *The Hindu*, 6 March 2009.

78. Sanjaya Baru, 'India in a changing world', *HT Mint*, 30 March 2009.

79. Harry G. Broadman, *Africa's Silk Road: China and India's New Economic Frontier* (Washington, DC: The World Bank, 2007), 75.

80. Pradeep Agarwal and Pravakar Sahoo, 'China's Accession to WTO: Implications for China and India', *Economic and Political Weekly* (21 June 2003), 2544–51, cited in Valerie Cerra, Sandra A. Rivera, and Sweta Chaman Saxena, 'Crouching Tiger, Hidden Dragon: What Are the Consequences of China's WTO Entry for India's Trade?' *IMF Working Paper*, May 2005.

81. Cerra, Rivera, and Saxena, 'Crouching Tiger, Hidden Dragon', 4.

82. Mohan Guruswamy and Zorawar Daulet Singh, *Chasing the Dragon: Will India Catch Up with China?* (New Delhi: Dorling Kindersley (India) Pvt. Ltd., 2010), 8.

83. Prem Shankar Jha, *Crouching Dragon, Hidden Tiger: Can China and India Dominate the West?* (New York: Soft Skull Press, 2010), 31.

84. Francine R. Frankel, 'Introduction', in Frankel and Harding (eds.), *The India–China Relationship*, 13.

85. 'Budget 1991–92', speech of Shri Manmohan Singh, Minister of Finance, 24 July 1991, http://indiabudget.nic.in/bspeech/bs199192.pdf This is now an often-quoted remark about India.

86. John Garver, *Foreign Relations of the People's Republic of China* (Englewood Cliffs, NJ: Prentice Hall, 1993), 11.

87. Susan Shirk, *China: Fragile Superpower* (Oxford/New York: Oxford University Press, 2007), 63.

88. All data from the Pew Global Attitudes Project, 'Publics of Asian Powers Hold Negative Views of One Another', 21 September 2006. Accessed at http://pewglobal.org/reports/display.php?ReportID=255

89. C. Raja Mohan, 'The Middle Path', *Indian Express*, 30 September 2009.

90. Giri Deshingkar, *Security and Science in China and India: Selected Essays of Giri Deshingkar*, ed. Manoranjan Mohanty and Mira Sinha Bhattacharjea (Samskriti: 2005), cited in Alka Acharya, *China and India: Politics of Incremental Engagement* (New Delhi: Har-Anand, 2008), 20.

91. On China's border disputes and their management, see M. Taylor Fravel, *Strong Borders, Secure Nation: Cooperation and Conflict in China's Territorial Disputes* (Princeton, NH: Princeton University Press, 2008). An incisive analysis building upon it and focusing on India's relationship with China can be found in A. G. Noorani, "Puzzling Conduct: China's recent conduct with India—unfriendly but just short of being hostile—has been as fuzzy as India's response to it has been calibrated", *Frontline*, 8 October 2010, 82–7.

92. Yan, 'India-China relations'.

93. Sidhu and Yuan, *China and India*, 147.

94. James Clad, 'Convergent Chinese and Indian Perspectives on the Global Order', in Frankel and Harding (eds.), *The India–China Relationship*, 270.

95. J. Mohan Malik, 'China–India Relations in the Post-Soviet Era: The Continuing Rivalry', *The China Quarterly*, 142 (June 1995), 326. See also Ramesh Thakur, 'China and India: growing together or set to collide?' *The Ottawa Citizen*, 15 June 2010.

96. 'China will be one of our primary challenges: Navy Chief', *The Hindu*, 11 August 2009.

97. For a more detailed exposition see George Perkovich, 'The Measure of India: What Makes Greatness?' *Seminar*, 529 (September 2003).

98. Athwal, *China–India Relations*, 11–12.

99. James Clad, 'Convergent Perspectives', in Frankel and Harding, *The India–China Relationship*, 272.

100. Betina Dimaranan, Elena Ianchovichina and Will Martin, 'China, India, and the Future of the World Economy: Fierce Competition or Shared Growth?' *World Bank*

Policy Research Working Paper, 4304 (Washington, DC: World Bank Development Research Group, August 2007), 8.

101. Cerra, Rivera, and Saxena, 'Crouching Tiger, Hidden Dragon', 16.

102. Robert S. Ross, 'Beijing as a Conservative Power', in Guoli Liu (ed.), *Chinese Foreign Policy in Transition* (Howthorne, NY: Aldine de Gruyter Inc., 2004), 142.

103. Even S. Medeiros and M. Taylor Fravel, 'China's New Diplomacy', in Liu (ed.), *Chinese Foreign Policy in Transition*, 387.

104. Suisheng Zhao, 'Chinese Nationalism and Its International Orientations', *Political Science Quarterly* 115/1 (Spring 2000), 2–3.

105. Ibid.

106. Indeed, anti-Japanese agitation in China in 2005, seemingly encouraged at first by the government and ostensibly relating to Japanese textbooks but also aiming to undercut Japanese aspirations for a permanent UN Security Council seat, rapidly got out of hand and required some effort to contain. See Norimitsu Onishi, 'Tokyo Protests Anti-Japan Rallies in China', *New York Times*, 11 April 2005 and David M. Malone, 'The High-Level Panel and the UN Security Council', *Security Dialogue*, 36/3 (September 2005), 371.

107. Alka Acharya, *China and India*, 15.

108. Yan, 'India–China relations'.

109. Shankar Roychowdhury, 'On China, talk softly, but carry a big stick', *Deccan Chronicle*, 22 September 2009.

110. C. Raja Mohan, 'The Middle Path'.

111. In the context of the apparent border tensions between China and India in mid-2009, see M. K. Bhadrakumar, 'Who stands to gain from war hysteria?', *The Hindu*, 21 September 2009; and Shekhar Gupta, 'Stop fighting the 1962 war', *Indian Express*, 19 September 2009.

112. Michael H. Hunt, *The Genesis of Chinese Communist Foreign Policy* (New York: Columbia University Press, 1996), 16.

113. Kenneth Lieberthal, 'Domestic Politics and Foreign Policy', in Harry Harding (ed.), *Chinese Foreign Relations in the 1980s* (New Haven, CT: Yale University Press, 1984), 44–5.

114. See Jeffrey N. Wasserstrom and Elizabeth J. Perry, *Popular Protest and Political Culture in Modern China* (Boulder, CO: Westview Press, 1994).

115. For a recent example, see 'Nervous China may attack India by 2012: Defence expert', *Indian Express*, 12 July 2009.

116. Based on the Japanese Cabinet Office announcement of Japan's GDP for the second quarter of 2010. See David Barboza, 'China Overtakes Japan as the World's Second Largest Economy', *New York Times*, 16 August 2010.

117. Simon Tay, 'Interdependency Theory: China, India and the West', *Foreign Affairs* 89/5 (September/October 2010), 138–43.

118. See Banyan column, *The Economist*, 2 October 2010, 48.

119. An old Chinese proverb holds, 'Two tigers cannot share one mountain.' Applied to the Sino-Indian relationship: see Jim Yardley and Somini Sengupta, 'Two Giants Try to Learn to Share Asia', *New York Times*, 13 January 2008.

Chapter 7

1. Jawaharlal Nehru, 'Report to the All India Congress Committee on the International Congress against Imperialism held at Brussels in February 1927', in Bimla Prasad, *The Origins of Indian Foreign Policy: The Indian National Congress and World Affairs, 1885–1947* (Calcutta: Bookland Pvt. Ltd., 1960), Appendix I, 265.

2. Embassy of India, Washington, DC, 'Prime Minister Dr. Manmohan Singh's Address to Joint Session of the Congress', 19 July 2005: www.indianembassy.org/press_release/2005/July/23.htm

3. The former quote is a chapter title in Strobe Talbott's *Engaging India: Diplomacy, Democracy and the Bomb* (Washington, DC: Brookings Institution Press, 2004). The latter is a quote from Jaswant Singh in the same book, 83.

4. Embassy of India, Washington, DC, 'Prime Minister Jawaharlal Nehru's speech in the US House of Representatives and the Senate', 13 October 1949: www.indianembassy.org/indusrel/india_us/nehru_congress_Oct_13_1949.htm

5. Atal Bihari Vajpayee, 'India, USA and the World: Let us work together to solve the Political-Economic Y2K Problem', speech delivered at the Asia Society, New York, 28 September 1998.

6. Nehru quoted in M. A. Zafar Shah, *India and the Superpowers: India's Political Relations with the Superpowers in the 1970s* (Dhaka: University Press, 1983), 13.

7. Gary R. Hess, 'Global Expansion and Regional Balances: The Emerging Scholarship on United States Relations with India and Pakistan', *The Pacific Historical Review*, 56/2 (May 1987), 263.

8. Quoted in A. Appadorai and M. S. Rajan, *India's Foreign Policy and Relations* (New Delhi: South Asian Publishers, 1985), 216.

9. Both quotes from Nehru in Zafar Shah, *India and the Superpowers*, 9.

10. Hess, 'Global Expansion', 260.

11. Appadorai and Rajan, *India's Foreign Policy and Relations*, 83.

12. J. N. Dixit, *India's Foreign Policy 1947–2003* (New Delhi: Picus Books, 2003), 44.

13. Both quotes from 'San Francisco Conference', *Time*, 3 September 1951.

14. Pratap Bhanu Mehta, '"Natural allies" at odds', *Seminar*, 545 (January 2005).

15. Norman D. Palmer, 'Ups and Downs in Indo-American Relations', *The Annals of the American Academy of Political and Social Science*, 294/1 (1954), 113.

16. E. I. Brodkin, "United States aid to India and Pakistan: The Attitudes of the Fifties," *International Affairs (Royal Institute of International Affairs)*, 43/4 (October 1967), 665.

17. Gaganvihari L. Mehta, 'India and the United States: Democracy East and West', *Annals of the American Academy of Political and Social Science*, 294 (July 1954), 128.

18. William J. Barnds, 'India and America at Odds', *International Affairs (Royal Institute of International Affairs 1944–)*, 49/3 (July 1973), 374.

19. Selig S. Harrison, 'India, Pakistan and the US; Cost of a Mistake', *New Republic* (Washington, DC) 141 (24 August 1954). Quoted in Appadorai and Rajan, *India's Foreign Policy and Relations*, 231.

20. Marshall Windmiller, 'America's Relations with India: A Re-Appraisal', *Far Eastern Survey*, 25/3 (March 1956), 33.

21. Windmiller, 'America's Relations with India', 34.

22. It can be argued that India did not support self-determination for Hungary for fear of creating repercussions for a similar outcome in Kashmir. See Brodkin, 'United States aid to India and Pakistan', 664–77.

23. James Barnard Calvin, *The China–India Border War (1962)*, (Quantico, VA: Marine Corps Command and Staff College, April 1984): www.globalsecurity.org/military/library/report/1984/CJB.htm

24. Henry Kissinger, *Nuclear Weapons and Foreign Policy* (New York: Harper, 1957), 264, quoted in M. J. Vinod, 'Conflicting Strategic Interests of the United States and India: Evaluating US Arms Supply to Pakistan', *International Studies*, 29 (July 1992), 279.

25. Appadorai and Rajan, *India's Foreign Policy and Relations*, 232.

26. For some implications of this episode in public international law, see Simon Chesterman, Thomas M. Franck, and David M. Malone, *The Law and Practice of the United Nations* (Oxford: Oxford University Press, 2008), 444–5.

27. Dixit, *India's Foreign Policy*, 73.

28. Michael Brecher, quoted in Hess, 'Global Expansion', 268.

29. Appadorai and Rajan, *India's Foreign Policy and Relations*, 139.

30. Barnds, 'India and America at Odds', 371–84.

31. For a detailed account of events, see James Barnard Calvin, 'The China–India Border War'.

32. Brecher, quoted in Hess, 'Global Expansion', 268.

33. Dixit, *India's Foreign Policy*, 69.

34. The American precondition for supplying the transmitter was that the Voice of America be broadcast daily during prime time for three hours. This was opposed in India's political circles and media on grounds of non-alignment. Ultimately Nehru, who had signed the agreement, had to nullify it. For a detailed account see Michael Brecher, 'India's Decisions on the Voice of America: A Study in Irresolution', *Asian Survey*, 14/7 (July 1974), 637–50.

35. Brecher, 'India's Decisions on the Voice of America: A Study in Irresolution', 637–50.

36. Zafar Shah, *India and the Superpowers*, 175.

37. Talbott, *Engaging India*, 11.

38. Yaacov Vertzberger in *The Enduring Entente: Sino-Pakistani Relations 1960–1980* (New York: Praeger, 1983), 88, also argued that China, fearing Soviet penetration in Pakistan following the Tashkent conference where Indo-Pakistani peace was brokered, initiated a military assistance programme with Pakistan. Vertzberger is cited in Robert G. Wirsing, 'The Arms Race in South Asia: Implications for the United States', *Asian Survey* 25/3 (March 1985), 265–91.

39. Calculated from Stockholm International Peace Research Institute (SIPRI) Trend Indicator Value (TIV) data on arms transfers. Accessed at: www.sipri.org/contents/armstrad/at_db.html

40. Vinod, 'Conflicting Strategic Interests', 279.

41. Dixit, *India's Foreign Policy*, 93.

42. For similar reasons, this was also the year that the USA reversed its policy on the People's Republic of China's permanent membership in the UN Security Council.

43. Henry Kissinger, *White House Years* (Boston: Little, Brown and Company, 1979), quoted in Appadorai and Rajan, *India's Foreign Policy and Relations*, 243.

44. See Appadorai and Rajan, *India's Foreign Policy and Relations*, 246.

45. Henry Kissinger, 'The Tilt: The India–Pakistan Crisis of 1971', in *White House Years*, 842–918.

46. Morarji Desai quoted in Zafar Shah, *India and the Superpowers*, 163.

47. Surjit Mansingh, 'The United States, China and India: Relationships in Comparative Perspective', *China Report* 35 (1999), 119.

48. It has been suggested that the test was 'more to showcase [India's] advanced scientific capabilities than to develop a nuclear arsenal', see Ashley J. Tellis, 'The Evolution of US–Indian Ties: Missile Defense in an Emerging Strategic Relationship', *International Security*, 30/4 (Spring 2006), 113–51.

49. Hess, 'Global Expansion', 280.

50. Peace Corps Press Release, 'Oldest Known Returned Peace Corps Volunteer Turns 100', 2 June 2006.

51. Zafar Shah, *India and the Superpowers*, 161.

52. Norman D. Palmer, *South Asia and US Policy* (Boston: Houghton Mifflin, 1966), 26. Quoted in Appadorai and Rajan, *India's Foreign Policy and Relations*, 224.

53. Talbott, *Engaging India*, 136.

54. Calculated from Stockholm International Peace Research Institute (SIPRI) Trend Indicator Value (TIV) data on arms transfers. Accessed at: www.sipri.org/contents/armstrad/at_db.html

55. Calculated from the US Overseas Loans and Grants Greenbook. Accessed at http://qesdb.usaid.gov/gbk/

56. Calculated from SIPRI data.

57. Henry Kissinger, *White House Years* (London, 1979), 846. Quoted in M. J. Vinod, 'Conflicting Strategic Interests'.

58. Human Rights Watch, 'Arms and Abuses in Indian Punjab and Kashmir', 1 September 1994: www.hrw.org/en/reports/1994/09/01/arms-and-abuses-indian-punjab-and-kashmir

59. Vinod, 'Conflicting Strategic Interests', 279.

60. Hess, 'Global Expansion', 283.

61. Wirsing, 'The Arms Race in South Asia', 265–91.

62. Determined from Stockholm International Peace Research Institute (SIPRI) Trend Indicator Value (TIV) data on arms transfers. Accessed at: www.sipri.org/contents/armstrad/at_db.html

63. C. Raja Mohan, *Crossing the Rubicon: The Shaping of India's New Foreign Policy* (New York: Palgrave Macmillan, 2004), xv.

64. Government of India, Department of Industrial Policy and Promotion, Ministry of Commerce and Industry, 'FDI in India Statistics'. Accessed at: www.dipp.nic.in/fdi_statistics/india_fdi_index.htm

65. Government of India, Department of Industrial Policy and Promotion, Ministry of Commerce and Industry, 'FDI in India Statistics.'

66. Government of India, Department of Commerce, 'Export Import Data Bank'. Accessed at http://commerce.nic.in/eidb/ecntcomq.asp

67. R. Nicholas Burns, 'America's Strategic Opportunity with India', *Foreign Affairs*, 86/6 (November/December 2007), 145.
68. C. Raja Mohan, *Crossing the Rubicon*, 265–6.
69. Talbott, *Engaging India*, 31.
70. Mansingh, 'The United States, China and India', 119.
71. Website of the US India Political Action Committee (USINPAC). Accessed at: www.usinpac.com
72. Robert M. Hathaway, 'Unfinished Passage: India, Indian Americans, and the US Congress', *The Washington Quarterly*, 24/2 (Spring 2001), 24.
73. Ibid., 21.
74. Ibid., 28.
75. K. A. Kronstadt, *India–US Relations* (Washington, DC: Library of Congress, Congressional Research Service), available at: www.dtic.mil/cgi-bin/GetTRDoc?AD=ADA475269&Location=U2&doc=GetTRDoc.pdf
76. Partha S. Ghosh, 'Foreign Policy and Electoral Politics in India', *Asian Survey*, 34/9 (September 1994), 807–17.
77. George Perkovich, 'The Measure of India: What Makes Greatness?' *Seminar*, 529 (September 2003).
78. Human Rights Watch, *Arms and Abuses in Indian Punjab and Kashmir*.
79. Mansingh, 'The United States, China and India', 125.
80. Thomas A. Timberg, 'The Impact of Indian Economic Liberalization on US–India Relations', *SAIS Review*, 18/1 (1998), 123–36.
81. Arthur G. Rubinoff, 'From Indifference to Engagement: The Role of the US Congress in Making Foreign Policy for South Asia', in Lloyd Rudolph and Susanne Rudolph (eds.), *Making US Foreign Policy Toward South Asia: Regional Imperatives and the Imperial Presidency* (Bloomington: Indiana University Press, 2008).
82. C. Raja Mohan, *Crossing the Rubicon*, 89.
83. Talbott, *Engaging India*, 28.
84. Former Indian Prime Minister and Foreign Minister I. K. Gujral, quoted in Perkovich, 'The Measure of India'.
85. Hathaway, 'Unfinished Passage,' 30–2.
86. C. Raja Mohan, 'Balancing Interests and Values: India's Struggle with Democracy Promotion', *The Washington Quarterly*, 30/3 (Summer 2007), 99–115.
87. C. Raja Mohan, *Crossing the Rubicon*, 199.
88. Talbott, *Engaging India*, 218.
89. Robert M. Hathaway, 'Washington's new strategic partnership', *Seminar*, 538 (June 2004).
90. The White House, 'Joint Statement Between President George W. Bush and Prime Minister Manmohan Singh', 18 July 2005: www.whitehouse.gov/news/releases/2005/07/20050718-6.html
91. 'India hails Iran's fight for right', *Press TV*, 18 May 2010; 'No uniform view with India on Iran: US', *Hindustan Times*, 8 June 2010. See Sinderpal Singh, 'United States-India Strategic Dialogue: Still waiting for Obama?', *ISAS Brief*, 15 June 2010, 164.

92. S. Jaishankar, 'India and USA: New Directions', in Atish Sinha and Madhup Mohta (eds.), *Indian Foreign Policy: Challenges and Opportunities* (New Delhi: Foreign Service Institute, 2007), 767–88.

93. Kronstadt, 'India–US Relations', 6.

94. On the key point of international supervision of Indian nuclear facilities, India yielded much less than US negotiators or many NSG members would have preferred. Increasingly, with time running out for the Bush Administration, and the political imperative of an agreement very strong for the President himself, India had the whip hand in the negotiations. See 'US concerned India stance on nuclear energy could jeopardize deal', *Forbes*, 19 April 2007; 'Dissent Threatens US–India Nuclear Cooperation Deal', *Washington Post*, 26 August 2007; 'As difficult as 123', *Rediff News*, 12 September 2007; and 'Has time run out for the India-US nuclear deal?', *BBC News*, 24 March 2008.

95. The professionalism and discipline of the US negotiating team, mostly under R. Nicholas Burns, was also striking.

96. Perhaps in order to save up its diplomatic freedom of manoeuvre and fire power for this issue, India did not display undue creativity or energy on other files during these years, contenting itself with pressing forward gently on several other fronts: the relationship with China, closer ties with some other Asian partners, a cautious stance on West Asian challenges, and the emergence of its new partnership with Brazil and South Africa in the IBSA formation. New Delhi's calculation was doubtless the right one.

97. The White House, 'National Security Strategy', (May 2010): www.whitehouse. gov/sites/default/files/rss_viewer/national_security_strategy.pdf On how India might reassess its end of the strategic relationship, see Dhruva Jaishankar, 'Relating to defence: Revisiting the India-US defence relationship', *Pragati*, 36 (March 2010), 3–4.

98. Deepa Ollapally and Raja Ramanna, 'US–India Tensions: Misperceptions on Nuclear Proliferation', *Foreign Affairs*, 74/1 (January/February 1995).

99. All ratios calculated from the US Overseas Loans and Grants Greenbook. Accessed at http://qesdb.usaid.gov/gbk/ It must be observed that although gross economic aid to India was higher in these periods, per capita economic aid has been consistently higher to Pakistan since 1952. This should not, however, be considered a reliable metric given India's inordinately large population, which would make any foreign aid commitment look insufficient.

100. Hess, 'Global Expansion', 295.

101. Kronstadt, 'India–US Relations', 62.

102. Website of the UN Democracy Fund: www.un.org/democracyfund/XFinancial-Contributions.htm India made a sizeable financial contribution of $15 million, or 17 per cent, to the endowment of the UN Democracy Fund.

103. Burns, 'America's Strategic Opportunity with India', 144.

104. Manmohan Singh, 'Address to the Joint Session of the United States Congress, Washington, DC, 19 July 2005', reproduced in *Seminar*, 560 (April 2006).

105. Talbott, *Engaging India*, 174.

106. Teresita C. Schaffer, 'Building a New Partnership with India', *Washington Quarterly*, 25/2 (Spring 2002), 41.

107. Ashutosh Varshney, 'A New Triangle: India, China and the US', *Seminar*, 557 (January 2006).

108. Ronald L. Tammen, 'The Impact of Asia on World Politics: China and India Options for the United States', *International Studies Review*, 8 (2006), 563–80.

109. Shirley A. Kan, *China and Proliferation of Weapons of Mass Destruction and Missiles: Policy Issues*, CRS Report for Congress RL31555, 13 December 2007.

110. Condoleezza Rice, 'Promoting the National Interest', *Foreign Affairs*, 79/1 (January/February 2000), 56.

111. Rice, 'Promoting the National Interest', 56.

112. Colin L. Powell, 'A Strategy of Partnerships', *Foreign Affairs*, 83/1 (January/February 2004), 30.

113. Quoted in Kronstadt, 'India–US Relations', 10.

114. Achin Vanaik, 'Post Cold War Indian Foreign Policy', *Seminar*, 581 (January 2008).

115. See www.indianembassy.org/indusrel/pmletter.htm for Prime Minister Vajpayee's justification of the nuclear tests to President Clinton.

116. C. V. Ranganathan, 'The long road to achieving an "India–China strategic and cooperative partnership for peace and development"', in Sinha and Mohta (eds.), *Indian Foreign Policy: Challenges and Opportunities*, 669.

117. Government of India, Ministry of Defence, *Annual Report 2007–2008*.

118. For a more detailed argument along these lines, see George Perkovich, 'The Measure of India: What Makes Greatness?' *Seminar*, 529 (September 2003).

119. Schaffer, 'Building a New Partnership'.

120. Stephen P. Cohen, 'The US and South Asia', *Seminar*, 545 (January 2005).

121. Samuel Huntington, 'The Lonely Superpower', *Foreign Affairs*, 78/2 (March/April 1999). A uni-multipolar world is a world where there is one superpower (the US) with global reach and several major powers (Germany, France, Russia, China, (potentially) Japan, India, Iran, Brazil, South Africa, Nigeria) with regional interests and capabilities.

122. Richard N. Haass, 'The Age of Nonpolarity', *Foreign Affairs*, 87/3 (May/June 2008), 44–56. A nonpolar world is 'a world dominated not by one or two or even several states but rather by dozens of actors possessing and exercising various kinds of power'.

123. Growing disenchantment with the results brought about by its own earlier unilateral style of foreign policy were evident in the statements and policies of the Bush Administration during its late years of 2006–8.

124. Condoleezza Rice, 'Rethinking the National Interest', *Foreign Affairs*, 87/4 (July/August 2008).

125. Some of these instances are mentioned in Daniel W. Drezner, 'The New New World Order', *Foreign Affairs*, 86/2 (March/April 2007).

126. Quoted in Mario E. Carranza, 'From Non-Proliferation to Post-Proliferation: Explaining the US–India Nuclear Deal', *Contemporary Security Policy*, 28/3 (2007), 464–93.

127. This argument is made by C. Raja Mohan in *Crossing the Rubicon*.

128. In spite of the sharp controversies in India and a fierce parliamentary debate on a no-confidence motion in 2008, the issue seems to have played very little role in the 2009 national elections.

129. The concept of 'smart power', seen as a combination of 'hard' and 'soft' power in order to produce positive results, is associated with American scholar Joseph Nye. He and Richard Armitage chaired a commission for the Center for Strategic and International Studies on the concept, which reported in November 2007 (see http://csisbeta.forumone.com/publication/smarter-more-secure-america).

130. Correspondence with the author, 14 June 2010.

131. Correspondence with the author, 13 June 2010.

132. Chalmers Johnson, *The Sorrows of Empire: Militarism, Secrecy, and the End of the Republic* (New York: Metropolitan Books, 2004), 287.

133. Correspondence with the author, 13 June 2010.

134. India's inclusion in the Group of 20 (G-20) leaders, convened to address the crisis in November 2008 and again in April 2009, was not only uncontroversial, but necessary in the circumstances, and further buttressed by Prime Minister Singh's familiarity with, indeed authority on, international economic relations.

135. Schaffer, 'Building a New Partnership', 32.

Chapter 8

1. John Keay, *India: A History* (New York: Harper Perennial, 2000), 181.

2. Ibid., 180–1.

3. While the common name among Western states for the region stretching from Egypt (sometimes even Morocco) in the west to Iran in the east, and from Turkey and Syria in the north, to Yemen in the south is the 'Middle East', Indian policy documents (and common media practice) refer to this area as West Asia. In this book, the area will be referred to as West Asia unless the use of 'Middle East' is clearly indicated by an extraneous factor.

4. See David Omissi, 'The Indian Army in the First World War, 1914–1918', in Daniel P. Marston and Chandar S. Sundaram (eds.), *A Military History of India and South Asia: From the East India Company to the Nuclear Era* (Bloomington: Indiana University Press, 2007), 74–87; and Daniel P. Marston, 'A Force Transformed: The Indian Army and the Second World War', in Marston and Sundaram (eds.), *A Military History of India and South Asia*, 102–22.

5. Although the US star in international relations was much tarnished by Washington's adventures in Iraq and Afghanistan in recent years, its predominance as the leading external power in West Asia has not yet been much affected.

6. The US–Iraq Status of Forces Agreement signed in November 2008 states that all US military forces would withdraw from Iraq no later than 31 December 2011.

7. See, 'Turkey's Fury', *New York Times*, 4 June 2010.

8. Pakistan has sought to needle India through the promotion within the Organization of the Islamic Conference (OIC) of tendentious resolutions on the situation in Kashmir, but these constitute low-grade skirmishing, however much irritation Delhi displays in rebuffing them. For a recent example, in 2009, of

India's reaction to such a move, see Navin Kapoor, 'India snubs OIC's Kashmir Resolution', *Thaindian News*, 29 May 2009.

9. Hamid Ansari, 'India and the Persian Gulf', in Atish Sinha and Madhup Mohta (eds.), *Indian Foreign Policy: Challenges and Opportunities* (New Delhi: Foreign Service Institute/ Academic Foundation, 2007), 277. Also, for an interesting discussion of Indian–Arab interaction far predating colonialism, see Keay, *India*, specifically ch. 9 dealing with Arab expansion into Indian border areas after the Byzantine empire fell.

10. Ansari, 'India and the Persian Gulf', 275.

11. Ibid., 276–7.

12. Rajendra M. Abhyankar, 'India's West Asia Policy: Search for a Middle Ground', in Sinha and Mohta (eds.), *Indian Foreign Policy*, for a discussion of the effect of India's domestic politics on its foreign policy.

13. Atul Aneja, 'India, Turkey to Begin New Phase of Ties', *The Hindu*, 1 April 2000; and Harish Khare, 'India, Turkey Set up JWG on Terrorism', *The Hindu*, 18 September 2003. For a rundown on Turkey's political situation, see Ralph Boulton, 'Tukey's Political Trench Warfare', *Reuters Global News Blog* (Reuters), 19 May 2009, http:// blogs.reuters.com/global/2009/05/19/turkeys-political-trench-warfare/

14. For a discussion of realism in India's West Asia policy, see Ishrat Aziz, 'India and West Asia/North Africa', in *Indian Foreign Policy*, and Bansidhar Pradhan, 'Changing Dynamics of India's West Asia Policy', *International Studies*, 41 (2004), 1–88.

15. Aziz, 'India and West Asia/North Africa', 298–9.

16. Ansari, 'India and the Persian Gulf', 280.

17. While the Maghreb countries can hardly be considered West Asian narrowly defined, they are not strictly African from an Indian perspective. It thus seems useful to include them here.

18. Pradhan, 'Changing Dynamics', 7–10.

19. Ibid.

20. Pradhan, 'Changing Dynamics', 7–10.

21. As suggested convincingly by Pradhan, who has noted a shift based on economic- and security-related interests. This is supported by Ansari's assessment of major initiatives in India's recent West Asia policy.

22. Government of India, Department of Commerce, *Export-Import Data Bank*, http:// commerce.nic.in/eidb/iecntq.asp figures up to date as of June 2010.

23. Ibid.; figures up to date as of June 2010.

24. Gill Bates and James Reilly, 'The Tenuous Hold of China Inc. in Africa', *Washington Quarterly*, 30/3 (Summer 2007). See p. 38 for comments on Chinese feelings of an African renaissance.

25. Political union efforts involving Egypt, Syria, Iraq, and North Yemen in the late 1950s and early 1960s proved equally inconclusive. The most significant multilateral economic forum in West Asia currently would likely be the Gulf Cooperation Council (GCC), with most previous or subsequent attempts at multilateral cooperation falling far short of the GCC.

26. For projected rates of industrialization in India, see Economist Intelligence Unit, *India Country Report* (London: The Economist, December 2008).

27. Coal, up to 2007, accounted for 62.2 per cent of India's energy production, with proven reserves able to satisfy demand for many decades to come. However, increasing environmental concerns suggest the need for cleaner alternatives in the long term. For figures on energy, see Economist Intelligence Unit, *Country Profile: India* (New York: EIU, 2008).

28. Juli A. McDonald and S. Enders Wimbush, 'India's Energy Security', *Strategic Analysis*, 23/5 (August 1999), 821–35.

29. C. Raja Mohan, 'Balancing Interests and Values: India's Struggle with Democracy Promotion', *Washington Quarterly*, 30(3) (Summer 2007), 100–2.

30. Ibid., 107–110.

31. A.T. Mahan, *The Influence of Sea Power Upon History, 1660–1783* (New York, NY: Dover Publications Inc., 1987 reprint of 1894 edition). See specifically the introduction, ch. 1 and ch. 14 for the basis of Mahan's ideas.

32. Rahul Bedi, 'India Launches Submarine-Building Program', *Jane's Defence Weekly*, 27 February 2002; and Jon Grevatt, 'Indian Navy Prepares to Procure Six Foreign Submarines', *Jane's Defence Weekly*, 30 September 2008.

33. Tim Fish, 'India Lays Keel of First Indigenous Aircraft Carrier', *Jane's Defence Weekly*, 3 March 2009.

34. Ibid.

35. 'Indian Navy Foils Another Attack by Somali Pirates', *The Times of India* (Online), 19 November 2008, http://timesofindia.indiatimes.com/Indian_navy_foils_another_attack_by_Somali_pirates/articleshow/3731104.cms Unfortunately, the pirate 'mothership' that was attacked by the INS Tabar turned out to be a Thai fishing trawler; see Rhys Blakely, 'Pirate Mothership was Really Thai Fishing Boat', *Times Online*, 27 November 2008: www.timesonline.co.uk/tol/news/world/africa/article5235404.ece Still, the fact that India's navy took an offensive lead in dealing with pirates in the Gulf of Aden was widely noted, and quietly approved by many, particularly in the merchant shipping community. See also UN Security Council Resolutions 1816 and 1838, respectively adopted on 2 June and 7 October 2008.

36. Tariq M. Ashraf, 'Doctrinal Reawakening of the Indian Armed Forces', *Military Review* (November/December 2004), 60–2.

37. Ibid., 60.

38. Aziz, 'India and West Asia/North Africa', 299.

39. India's participation in UNIFIL did arouse some controversy in Israel, however. See Sudha Ramachandra, 'India Straddles Middle east Divide,' *Asia Times*, 31 March 2007: 'In 2000 . . . Israel accused Indian soldiers of collaborating in the abduction of three Israeli soldiers by Hezbollah guerrillas. Israeli military officials claimed that some Indian soldiers had been aware of Hezbollah's preparations for the abduction but had turned a blind eye. The allegations were not substantiated. . . . India had simply gotten caught in the Israel–Hezbollah crossfire.'

40. For text of the 2004 Mumbai Declaration see Embassy of India, Riyadh: '1st GCC–India Industrial Conference', Mumbai, 17–18 February 2004: www.indianembassy.org.sa/Pages/ComWing/India-GCC(EC)/India-GCC%20Conference.htm

41. Ansari, 'India and the Persian Gulf', 283.

42. Ibid.

43. On a more global scale however, there is incentive for India to try to tie its Persian Gulf interests into a larger framework. Aaditya Mattoo and Arvind Subramanian state that '[a]ll large oil consumers, be they traditional powers (the United States and Europe) or emerging ones (China and India) share an interest in an open energy market without artificial restrictions on supplies': Mattoo and Subramanian, 'From Doha to the Next Bretton Woods', *Foreign Affairs*, 88/1 (February 2009), 15–26; see p. 25 for quote.

44. Subhash Kapila, *India–Saudi Arabia: The Strategic Significance of the Delhi Declaration*, South Asia Analysis Group Paper, 1734 (March 2006): www.southasiaanalysis.org/%5Cpapers18%5Cpaper1734.html

45. Government of India, Press Information Bureau, 'Riyadh Declaration: A New Era of Strategic Partnership', 1 March 2010: www.pib.nic.in/release/release.asp?relid=58617 Vinay Kumar, 'Saudi Arabia visit fruitful, says Manmohan', *The Hindu* (Online Edition), 2 March 2010: www.thehindu.com/2010/03/02/stories/2010030260211000.htm

46. Pradhan, 'Changing Dynamics', 12.

47. India was among the first countries to approach the UN Sanctions Committee created by Security Council Resolution 661 to seek compensation for economic losses sustained due to the Council's decision to impose sanctions. See Chinmaya R. Gharekhan's interesting account of related events in *The Horseshoe Table: An Inside View of the UN Security Council* (New Delhi: Longman, 2006), 44–68; see also David M. Malone, *The International Struggle Over Iraq: Politics in the United Nations Security Council* (Oxford: Oxford University Press, 2006), 65 and fn. 24 at 80–1. By 1996, the UN Compensation Commission awarded $145.2 million as reparations to Indian migrant workers and their families for losses arising out of the Gulf War in 1990–1. For further details, see Thalif Deen, 'Gulf War Victims to get Compensation', *India Abroad*, 12 January 1996: www.highbeam.com/doc/1P1-2390659.html Eventually, the total compensation amounted to US$917,575,243.16 to many of the 151,851 Indian claimants.

48. Fahmida Ashraf, 'US-Iraq War: India's Middle East Policy', *Strategic Studies* (Institute of Strategic Studies, Islamabad), 23/2 (2003): www.issi.org.pk/journal/2003_files/no_2/article/7a.htm John Kifner, 'India Decides Not to Send Troops to Iraq Now', *New York Times*, 15 July 2003.

49. For a good chronology of events relating to Indian decision-making on this matter, see Alan Kronstadt, *India: Chronology of Events*, CRS Report for Congress (Congressional Research Service, September 2008).

50. Amitav Ghosh, 'Lessons of Empire', *The Hindu* (Online Edition), 24 June 2003.

51. For statistics, see the Ministry of Overseas Indian Affairs, 'Estimated Size of the Overseas Indian Community: Country-Wise', in *Report of the High Level Committee on the Indian Diaspora* (December 2001): www.indiandiaspora.nic.in/diasporapdf/part1-est.pdf

52. Yaroslav Trofimov, 'Persian Gulf Slowdown Washes Up on India's Shores', *The Wall Street Journal* (Online), 26 February 2009, http://online.wsj.com/article/SB123561359140377935.html

53. Pradhan, 'Changing Dynamics', 13, identifies several factors governing the Indian reaction to Iraq's invasion of Kuwait, a salient one being the presence of 1.7 million Indian workers in Iraq and Kuwait combined.

54. Ibid.

55. Ansari, 'India and the Persian Gulf', 289. In order to keep numbers under control, Gulf governments resort to a *Kafala* (sponsorship) system, see Anh Nga Logva, 'Keeping Migrant Workers in Check: The *Kafala* System in the Gulf', *Middle East Report*, 211 (Summer 1999), 20–2.

56. Andrezej Kapiszewski, 'Arab Versus Asian Migrant Workers in the GCC Countries', United Nations Expert Group Meeting on International Migration and Development in the Arab Region, Beirut, 15–17 May 2006, 12.

57. Ansari, 'India and the Persian Gulf', 286–7.

58. Ibid., 282–5.

59. Nicolas Blarel, *Inde et Israël: Le Rapprochement Strategique-Pragmatisme et Complementarité* (Paris: L'Harmattan, 2006). See ch. 1, 'Les Relations Indo-Israeliennes 1947–1992'.

60. Pradhan, 'Changing Dynamics', 7–8 for Suez, and 10–11 for the Israeli invasion of Lebanon in 1982.

61. Interview with the author, Ottawa, 27 April 2009.

62. Armand Cucciniello and Parmit Mitra, 'India and Israel Move Closer Together', *South Asia Monitor*, No. 63 (Center for Strategic and International Studies), 1 October 2003. Also, Government of India, Department of Commerce. *Export-Import Data Bank*, http://commerce.nic.in/eidb/iecntq.asp Figures up to date as of June 2010.

63. Many Israeli young people, on completion of their military service, spend time unwinding in India, the closest (and most interesting) point to the east of Israel, beyond Jordan, they are welcome to visit.

64. Pradhan, 'Changing Dynamics', 21–2, and 23, where he states that the National Security Advisors from each country maintain regular dialogue.

65. Address by Shri Brajesh Mishra, National Security Advisor of India at the American Jewish Committee Annual Dinner, Washington, DC, 8 May 2003: www.ajc.org/site/apps/nlnet/content3.aspx?c=ijITI2PHKoG&b=851361&ct=1118743

66. Harsh V. Pant, 'India–Israel Partnership: Convergence and Constraints', *Middle East Review of International Affairs*, 8/4 (December 2004), 63.

67. Vinay Kumar, 'Lok Sabha Passes Anti-Terror Bills', *The Hindu* (Online Edition), 18 December 2008: www.thehindu.com/2008/12/18/stories/2008121860280100.htm

68. Bruce Riedel, *Terrorism in India and the Global Jihad* (Washington, DC: The Brookings Institution, 30 November 2008): www.brookings.edu/articles/2008/1130_india_terrorism_riedel.aspx

69. For a brief outline of the Israeli defence industry, see Globalsecurity.org's *Israel: Military Industry* webpage and links to some of Israel's largest defence contractors: www.globalsecurity.org/military/world/israel/industry.htm

70. Ramtanu Maitra, 'An Arrow to Washington's Heart', *Asia Times Online*, 20 August 2002: www.atimes.com/atimes/South_Asia/DH20Df08.html Also see Efraim Inbar,

'The Indian–Israeli Entente', *Orbis*, 48/1 (2004), 96; and Pant, 'India–Israel Partnership', 65.

71. Inbar, 'The Indian–Israeli Entente', 96.

72. Rahul Singh, 'DRDO Claims to Better US, Russian Missile Defence', *Hindustan Times*, 9 March 2009.

73. Rajan Menon and Swati Pandey, 'An Axis of Democracy? The Uncertain Future of Israeli–Indian Relations', *The National Interest*, Summer 2005, 30.

74. For the political row that can erupt from the sale of AWACS platforms, one need only go back to the US sale of AWACS aircraft to Saudi Arabia in the 1980s, which caused friction in US–Israeli–Saudi relations.

75. Menon and Pandey, 'An Axis of Democracy', 35–6.

76. Amity Shlaes, 'Israel's Gaza Venture Hits Chord in Wounded India', *Bloomberg.com*, (Bloomberg News), 15 January 2009: www.bloomberg.com/apps/news?pid=20601039&sid=aOZwFAGfnokY&refer=home It is also worth noting that the feelings of the Indian public and the Indian elite regarding Israeli actions in the Palestinian territories may not be one and the same. Indeed an editorial in *The Hindu* regarding the Israelis' Gaza offensive suggests that Indian public opinion was far from pro-Israeli. See 'Brutal and Senseless', *The Hindu* (Online Edition), 8 January 2009: www.hindu.com/2009/01/08/stories/2009010853500800.htm

77. Pradhan, 'Changing Dynamics', 17. Yasser Arafat, the PLO Chairman, found it more difficult to gain access to India's decision-makers after 1992. Arafat's difficulties may also have related to his declining credibility as a political leader late in his life.

78. Ibid., 56.

79. Pant, 'India–Israel Partnership', 69.

80. Juan R. I. Cole, '"Indian Money" and the Shi'i Shrine Cities of Iraq, 1786–1850', *Middle Eastern Studies*, 22/4 (1986); see p. 461 on the establishment of Shiite enclaves in India. Cole's entire article is a fascinating look at this phenomenon, particularly in how he addresses the impact of European influence by the mid-1800s on a relationship that was already quite developed.

81. Pradhan, 'Changing Dynamics', 26–9.

82. Pradhan, 'Changing Dynamics', p. 16 for graphic interpretation, but throughout for entirety of argument.

83. Pradhan, 'Changing Dynamics', 26–9.

84. Christine C. Fair, 'India and Iran: New Delhi's Balancing Act', *Washington Quarterly*, 30/3 (2007), 148–53.

85. Greg Bruno, 'Backgrounder: Iran's Nuclear Program', Council on Foreign Relations, 4 September 2008: www.cfr.org/publication/16811/

86. Director of Central Intelligence, 'Prospects for Further Proliferation of Nuclear Weapons', *Special National Intelligence Estimate SNIE-4-1-74*, (Central Intelligence Agency, 23 August 1974), 38.

87. Bruno, 'Backgrounder'.

88. Sharon Squassoni, 'Irans Nuclear Program: Recent Development', CRS Report for Congress (Congressional Research Service, 6 September 2006).

89. Ephraim Kam, 'A Nuclear Iran; What Does it Mean, and What Can be Done', Memorandum 88 (Tel Aviv: Institute for National Strategic Studies, 2007). Kam states that a nuclear Iran could lead regional competitors, specifically Egypt and Saudi Arabia (and potentially Syria), to pursue a nuclear track (see pp. 49–61 for assessment of impact).

90. See India's formal explanation of its vote, as published by India's Ministry of External Affairs, available at http://meaindia.nic.in/pressrelease/2005/09/24pr01.htm

91. Harish Khare, 'India Opposes Iran's "Nuclear Weapon Ambitions"', *The Hindu* (Online Edition), 30 September 2008: www.hindu.com/2008/09/30/stories/2008093060691200.htm

92. Ibid.

93. Any Iranian claims that its arsenal was intended to counter that, all but confirmed, of Israel and deter Israeli nuclear strikes would create further quandaries for India, as Delhi's own nuclear weapons programme was predicated on the need to deter attack by China and, to a lesser extent, Pakistan. Indeed, thoughtful Indians sometimes volunteer that China and India were the early proliferators in Asia and that subsequent events have shown how risky these early decisions in Beijing and Delhi's response have proved to be. On India's nuclear strategy, see Bharat Karnad, *Nuclear Weapons and Indian Security: The Realist Foundations of Strategy* (New Delhi: Macmillan, 2002).

94. See UN Document S/Res/1929 (2010), 9 June 2010, http://daccess-dds-ny.un.org/doc/UNDOC/GEN/N10/396/79/PDF/N1039679.pdf

95. Atul Aneja, 'India and Iran's Afpak policy', *The Hindu*, 7 April 2010.

96. C. Raja Mohan, 'Iran Curbs: What India must do', *Indian Express*, 10 June 2010.

97. Pradhan, 'Changing Dynamics', throughout.

98. Vibhute Haté, 'India's Energy Dilemma', *South Asia Monitor* (Center for Strategic and International Studies, September 2006), 1.

99. Mehul Srivastava and Nandini Lakshman, 'How Risky is India?', *Businessweek*, 15 December 2008, 24–7. Srivastava and Lakshman focus on terrorism, but also allude to more mundane challenges to public safety.

100. See Apurba Kundu, 'The National Democratic Alliance and National Security', in K. Adeney and L. Saez (eds.), *Coalition Politics and Hindu Nationalism* (London: Routledge, 2005) 212–36.

101. Director of National Intelligence, *Global Trends 2025: A World Transformed* (US Office of the Director of National Intelligence, November 2008), NIC 2003-3.

102. Ibid, specifically ch.7.

Chapter 9

1. Jawaharlal Nehru, *The Discovery of India* (New Delhi: Penguin Books, 2004), 213.

2. Australia and New Zealand are included here because, although belonging to the Oceana region, as active members of the broader Asia-Pacific community, both engage a great deal with Asian affairs, as near neighbours and major trading partners.

Australia has played a major role in contributing to the architecture of structures intended to intensify Asian Pacific deliberation and cooperation (such as APEC).

3. See G. Coedès, *The Indianized States of Southeast Asia*, ed. Walter F. Vella, trans. Susan Brown Cowing (Honolulu: East-West Center Press, 1968).

4. D. R. Sardesai, *Southeast Asia: Past and Present*, 6th edn (Boulder, CO: Westview Press, 2010), 17.

5. Sunanda K. Datta-Ray, *Looking East to Look West: Lee Kuan Yew's Mission India* (New Delhi: Penguin Books India, 2009), 13.

6. R. C. Majumdar, *India and South East Asia* (Delhi: B.R. Publishing Corporation, 1979), 16–17.

7. Sardesai, *Southeast Asia*, 17.

8. Coedès, *Indianized States of Southeast Asia*, 15–16.

9. Prabodh Chandra Bagchi, *India and China: A Thousand Years of Cultural Relations*, 2nd edn (Westport, CT: Greenwood Press, 1971), 24; Majumdar, *India and South East Asia*, 19–20.

10. Majumdar, *India and South East Asia*, 18.

11. Nehru, *The Discovery of India*, 216.

12. Sardesai, *Southeast Asia*, 53–4.

13. Prakash Nanda, *Rediscovering Asia: Evolution of India's Look-East Policy* (New Delhi: Lancer Publishers & Distributors, 2003), 59; see also Howard M. Federspiel, *Sultans, Shamans, and Saints: Islam and Muslims in Southeast Asia,* (Honolulu: University of Hawai'i Press, 2007), 33–9.

14. C. Mary Turnbull, *A History of Malaysia, Singapore and Brunei* (Sydney/Boston: Allen & Unwin, 1989), 96–7.

15. Rajsekhar Basu, 'Search for Pasture: Tamil Migration to Malayan Plantations in the 19th and Early 20th Centuries', in Lipi Ghosh and Ramkrishna Chatterjee (eds.), *Indian Diaspora in Asian and Pacific Regions* (Jaipur, Rawat Publications, 2004), 165.

16. Indian High Commission in Malaysia, 'Cultural Relations', http://indianhighcommission.com.my/cult_hfj.php

17. B. R. Deepak, *India–China Relations in the First Half of the 20th Century* (New Delhi: APH Publishing Corporation, 2001), 2–3.

18. See Bagchi, *India and China*, 145–73 ; Deepak, *India–China Relations*, 8–11.

19. Nanda, *Rediscovering Asia*, 81–3.

20. Dwijendra Nath Bakshi, 'Japanese Indianness without the Indian Diaspora in Pre-modern Japan', in Ghosh and Chatterjee (eds.), *Indian Diaspora in Asian and Pacific Regions*, 103.

21. Utpal K. Banerjee, 'Role of Cultural Diplomacy', in Lalit Mansingh (ed.), *Indian Foreign Policy Agenda for the 21st Century*, Vol. I (New Delhi: Foreign Service Institute in association with Konark Publishers, 1997), 400–1.

22. Bakshi, 'Japanese Indianness', 107–8.

23. Mimi Banerjee Dhar, 'Indians in Japan: History and Dimensions of Relations', in Ghosh and Chatterjee (eds.), *Indian Diaspora in Asian and Pacific Regions*, 116–17.

24. Sanajaya Baru, 'How Asian is India?' in *Strategic Consequences of India's Economic Performance* (New Delhi: Academic Foundation, 2006), 223.

25. Ibid.

26. T. A. Keenleyside, 'Nationalist Indian Attitudes towards Asia: A Troublesome Legacy for Post-Independence Indian Foreign Policy', *Pacific Affairs*, 5/2 (Summer 1982), 210–30.

27. A. Appadorai, 'The Asian Relations Conference in Perspective', *International Studies*, 18 (1979), 276–8.

28. Christophe Jaffrelot, 'India's Look East Policy: an Asianist strategy in perspective', *India Review*, 2/2 (April 2003), 42.

29. Mohammed Ayoob, *India and Southeast Asia: Indian Perception and Policies* (London: Routledge, 1990), 9. See also K. M. Pannikkar, *India and the Indian Ocean: An Essay on the Influence of Sea Power on Indian History* (London: George Allen & Unwin, 1945), 21.

30. G. V. C. Naidu, 'Wither the Look East Policy: India and Southeast Asia', *Strategic Analysis*, 28/2 (April–June 2004), 334.

31. Ibid.

32. T. Karki Hussain, 'China, India and Southeast Asia after the Cold War', in Baladas Ghoshal (ed.), *India and Southeast Asia: Challenges and Opportunities* (New Delhi: Konark Publishers Pvt. Ltd, 1996), 46; also see Kripa Sridharan, *The ASEAN Region in India's Foreign Policy* (Aldershot, England: Dartmouth Publishing Company, 1996).

33. Naidu, 'Wither the Look East Policy', 333–4.

34. Ranjit Gupta, 'India's "Look East" Policy', in Atish Sinha and Madhup Mohta (eds.), *Indian Foreign Policy: Challenges and Opportunities* (New Delhi: Foreign Service Institute / Academic Foundation, 2007), 359.

35. Jaffrelot, 'India's Look East Policy', 36. See also Rajiv Sikri, 'India's Foreign Policy Priorities in the Coming Decade', *ISAS Working Paper*, 25 (25 September 2007), 21.

36. Harish Kapur, *Foreign Policies of India's Prime Ministers* (New Delhi/Frankfort, IL: Lancer International, 2009), 308. No official statement elaborated the tenets of this policy; however, it was first mentioned in the Ministry of External Affairs Annual Report (1995–6). See Chak Mun, *India's Strategic Interests in Southeast Asia and Singapore* (New Delhi: MacMillan Publishers, 2009), 2.

37. S. D. Muni and C. Raja Mohan, 'Emerging Asia: India's Options', *International Studies* 41/3 (2004), 321; P. V. Narasimha Rao, 'India and the Asia-Pacific: Forging a New Relationship', *Singapore Lecture 1994* (Singapore: Institute of Southeast Asian Studies, 1994).

38. Sumit Ganguly and Maneet S. Pardesi, 'Explaining Sixty Years of India's Foreign Policy', *India Review*, 8/1 (January 2009), 13–14.

39. Naidu, 'Wither the Look East Policy', 332. In practice, this by then meant China—the saliency of the USA in the Indian Ocean and even to a degree in the South China Sea faded somewhat after its adventures in Indochina in the 1960s and 1970s, its air base at Diego Garcia—of use mainly in relation to the Persian Gulf—notwithstanding.

40. Muni and Raja Mohan, 'Emerging Asia', 321.

41. 'Resurgent India in Asia', speech by Indian External Affairs Minister Yashwant Sinha at Harvard University, Cambridge, MA, 29 September 2003, http://meaindia.nic.in/

42. C. Raja Mohan, 'Look East Policy: Phase Two', *The Hindu*, 9 October 2003.

43. Ibid.

44. Sunanada K. Datta-Ray, 'Rediscovering Suvarnabhumi: India and South-East Asia', in Sinha and Mohta (eds.), *Indian Foreign Policy*, 409.

45. Sanjaya Baru, 'India and ASEAN: The emerging economic relationship towards a Bay of Bengal community', in *Strategic Consequences of India's Economic Performance*, 247.

46. D. Gopal and Sailaja Gullapalli, 'India's Diplomacy of Regional Trading Groups: A Case of India-ASEAN Free Trade Area and Sub-Regional Agreements', in Yagama Reddy (ed.), *Emerging India in Asia-Pacific* (New Delhi: New Century Publications, 2007), 74.

47. 'Framework Agreement on Comprehensive Economic Cooperation Between the Republic of India and the Association of Southeast Asian Nations', Bali, Indonesia, 8 October 2003: www.aseansec.org/20188.htm Suparna Karmakar, 'India-ASEAN FTA—A realistic assessment', *The Hindu Business Line*, 11 September 2009.

48. Vani Archana, 'Look Southeast Policy: The ASEAN FTA could propel India's trade to another level', *Indian Express*, 22 August 2009; Baladas Ghoshal, 'India, Southeast Asia and the FTA: Strengthening Economic Integration', *Policy Brief*, 114 (New Delhi: Institute of Peace and Conflict Studies, August 2009), 3; http://se1.isn.ch/serviceengine/Files/ISN/105190/ipublicationdocument_singledocument/5BB661CC-765E-496E-B5FD-05DB040C7058/en/IB114-SEARP-Ghoshal.pdf

49. 'India–ASEAN FTA on services soon: Shashi Tharoor', *The Hindu*, 14 February 2010.

50. Sanjaya Baru, 'It's time for a "Look Further East" Policy', *Business Standard*, 7 December 2009.

51. Gopal and Gullapalli, 'India's Diplomacy of Regional Trading Groups', 76–8.

52. K. V. Kesavan, 'Economic Liberalization in India and Japan's Wavering Response', *Ritsumeikan Annual Review of International Studies*, 2 (2003), 133.

53. 'India and Japan: A Japanese perspective on India—Interview with Hiroichi Yamaguchi', *Frontline*, 15/9 (25 April – 8 May 1998).

54. Nagesh Kumar, 'India's Economic Engagement with East Asia: Trends and Prospects', in K. Kesavpany, A. Mani, and P. Ramasamy (eds.), *Rising India and Indian Communities in East Asia* (Singapore: ISEAS, 2008), 119–20.

55. Kesavan, 'Economic Liberalization', 136.

56. Government of India, Department of Commerce, Export-Import Data Bank (25 June 2010), http://commerce.nic.in/eidb/default.asp

57. Tan Chung, *Rise of the Giants: The Dragon-Elephant Tango*, ed. Patricia Uberoi (New Delhi: Anthem Press, 2008), 269.

58. Ibid., 270.

59. Ministry of Foreign Affairs of Japan, 'Outline of Japan's ODA to India' (September 2009): www.mofa.go.jp/POLICY/oda/region/sw_asia/india_o.pdf

60. Geethanjali Nataraj, 'India Japan Investment Relations: Trends and Prospects', *ICRIER Working Paper*, 245 (January 2010), 8–10.

61. The Delhi–Mumbai Industrial Corridor is a mega-infrastructure project covering an overall length of 1,483 kilometres between the political and business capitals of India, Delhi and Mumbai respectively.

62. Nataraj, 'India Japan Investment Relations', 13.

63. Government of India, Ministry of Commerce and Industry, 'India FDI Factsheets', (October 2005 and December 2009), http://dipp.nic.in/fdi_statistics/india_fdi_index.htm

64. Jaffrelot, 'India's Look East Policy', 51.
65. Nataraj, 'India Japan Investment Relations', 14.
66. Kumar, 'India's Economic Engagement with East Asia,' 119.
67. Rajan Jha, 'Recent Technical Advancements in India-Korea Trade, Research and Development', in Sushila Narsimhan and Kim Do Young (eds.), *India and Korea: Bridging the Gaps* (New Delhi: Manak Publications, 2008), 143.
68. Netrananda Sahu, 'Posco Deal: A Major Economic Breakthrough for the Government of Orissa', in Narsimhan and Do Young (eds.), *India and Korea: Bridging the Gaps*, 127–8; POSCO-India, 'Investment', http://posco-india.com/website/project/investment.htm
69. Posco-India, 'Rehabilitation and Resettlement,' http://posco-india.com/website/sustainability/rehabilitation-&-resettlement.htm
70. Pravakar Sahoo, 'India-Korea CEPA: A step in right direction', *East Asia Forum*, 15 September 2009: www.eastasiaforum.org/2009 /09/15/india-korea-cepa-a-step-in-right-direction/
71. Suparna Karmakar, 'India-Korea CEPA—Gains likely to be non-commercial', *The Hindu Business Line*, 28 August 2009.
72. Ibid.
73. Pravakar Sahoo, Durgesh Kumar Rai, and Rajiv Kumar, 'India-Korea Trade and Investment Relations', *ICRIER Working Paper*, 242 (December 2009), 35: www.icrier.org/publication/working_papers_242.html
74. Ibid., 9.
75. Government of India, Ministry of Commerce and Industry, 'Export Import Data Bank' (25 June 2010).
76. Sumit Ganguly, 'The Rise of India in Asia', in Devesh Shambaugh and Michael Yahuda (eds.), *International Relations of Asia* (Lanham, MD: Rowman and Littlefield Publishers, 2008), 158.
77. Ji Ping, 'China: Indians' New-Found Land', in K. Kesavpany, A. Mani and P. Ramasamy (eds.), *Rising India and Indian Communities in East Asia*, 202–3.
78. Kumar, 'India's Economic Engagement with East Asia: Trends and Prospects', 117.
79. Ping, 'China: Indians' New-Found Land', 198.
80. Amardeep Athwal, *China–India Relations: Contemporary dynamics* (London/New York: Routledge, 2008), 93. See also Jonathan Holslag, *China and India: Prospects for Peace* (New York: Columbia University Press, 2010), 77.
81. Madhu Bala, 'India Australia Trade and Investment Relations in the 1990s', in D. Gopal (ed.), *Australia in the Emerging Global Order: Evolving Australia–India Relations* (New Delhi: Shipra Publications, 2002), 242–3.
82. Government of India, Ministry of Commerce and Industry, 'Export Import Data Bank', (25 June 2010).
83. Australian Government, Department of Foreign Affairs and Trade, 'India country Brief': www.dfat.gov.au/GEO/india/india_brief.html Government of India, Ministry of Commerce and Industry, 'India FDI Factsheets' (December 2009), http://dipp.nic.in/fdi_statistics/india_FDI_December2009.pdf
84. Kumar, 'India's Economic Engagement with East Asia', 119–20.

85. Sekhar Bandyopadhyay, 'India and New Zealand: A Sixty Year Roller Coaster', *New Zealand International Review*, 32/4 (July/August 2007), 13–14.

86. New Zealand Ministry of Foreign Affairs and Trade, 'Republic of India': www.mfat. govt.nz/Countries/Asia-South-and-Southeast/India.php#facts

87. Sujay Mehdudia, 'India, New Zealand start FTA talks', *The Hindu*, 4 February 2010, http://beta.thehindu.com/business/article100892.ece

88. See 'Australia keen to export uranium to India', *Financial Express*, 24 April 2010: www.financialexpress.com/news/australia-keen-to-export-uranium-to-india/ 610702/

89. Kapur, *Foreign Policies*, 308–9.

90. See Ranjit Gupta, 'The Myanmar Conundrum: The Way Forward for India', *Indian Foreign Affairs Journal*, 3/2 (April/June 2008), 51–67; see also Anindya Batabyal, 'Balancing China in Asia: A Realist Assessment of India's Look East Strategy', *China Report*, 42/2 (2006), 183–4.

91. Gilles Boquérat, 'India's Confrontation with Chinese Interests in Myanmar', in Frédéric Grare and Amitabh Mattoo (eds.), *India and ASEAN: The Politics of India's Look East Policy* (New Delhi: Manohar Publishers & Distributors, 2001), 177.

92. S. D. Muni, *India's Foreign Policy: The Democracy Dimension* (New Delhi: Foundation Books, 2009), 80–2.

93. Manjeet S. Pardesi, 'Southeast Asia in Indian Foreign Policy: Positioning India as a Major Power in Asia', in Sumit Ganguly (ed.), *India's Foreign Policy: Retrospect and Prospect* (New Delhi: Oxford University Press, 2010), 123.

94. Sushila Narsimha, 'India's 'Look East' Policy: Past, Present, and Future', in K. Raja Reddy (ed.), *India and ASEAN: Foreign Policy Dimensions for the 21st Century* (New Delhi: New Century Publications, 2005), 34–6.

95. Naidu, 'Wither the Look East Policy', 337.

96. Ibid., 337–8.

97. ASEAN, 'Chairman's Statement: The Fifth Meeting of the ASEAN Regional Forum', Manila, 27 July 1998: www.aseansec.org/707.htm.

98. See ASEAN, 'Plan of Action to Implement the ASEAN–India Partnership for Peace, Progress and Shared Prosperity': www.aseansec.org/16842.htm; and ASEAN, 'Chairman's Statement of the 6th ASEAN-India Summit', Singapore, 21 November 2007: www.aseansec.org/21133.htm

99. Jaffrelot, 'India's Look East Policy', 53.

100. Jyoti Malhotra, 'Jaswant to visit Japan on November 23', *Indian Express*, 10 November 1999: www.indianexpress.com/ie/daily/19991110/ige10014.html

101. Aftab Seth, 'India and Japan', in Sinha and Mohta (eds.), *Indian Foreign Policy*, 815.

102. N. V. Subramanian, 'Bridging the China-India gap', *The Japan Times*, 1 November 2008, http://search.japantimes.co.jp/cgi-bin/eo20081101a1.html see also, Pranab Dhal Samanta, 'Revealed: How Pak and China didn't want India at UN high table', *The Indian Express*, 15 June 2008: www.indianexpress.com/news/revealed-how-pak-and-china-didnt-want-india-at-un-high-table/322949/0

103. C. Raja Mohan, 'Out of the Ordinary: Building another Asia: Delhi must welcome Tokyo's leadership', *Indian Express*, 28 December 2009.

104. Chandrakant Yatanoor, 'Indo-Australian Relations in the Emerging World Order', in Reddy (ed.), *Emerging India in Asia-Pacific*, 324–6.

105. Ashutosh Misra, 'Friendly southern face: India's strategic partnership with Australia will depend on public diplomacy', *The Indian Express*, 13 November 2009.

106. Zhang Yan, 'India–China relations in one of the best periods of history' (Interview), *The Hindu*, 9 April 2009: www.hindu.com/2009/04/09/stories/2009040955800900.htm

107. BIMSTEC, 'About BIMSTEC': www.bimstec.org/about_bimstec.html

108. Chak Mun, *India's Strategic Interests*, 86.

109. Man Mohini Kaul, 'Regional Groupings: an Overview of BIMSTEC and MGC', *South Asian Survey*, 13/2 (2006), 316.

110. Sikri, 'India's Foreign Policy Priorities', 119.

111. Kaul, 'Regional Groupings', 316.

112. Nagesh Kumar, 'India in 21st Century Asia-Pacific', in Reddy (ed.), *Emerging India in Asia-Pacific*, 11.

113. P. S. Suryanarayan, 'East is watching', *Frontline*, 19 June 2009, 59.

114. Kumar, 'India in 21st Century Asia-Pacific', 11.

115. Kumar, 'India's Economic Engagement with East Asia', 118.

116. Banyan, 'Come Together', *Economist*, 12 December 2009. See also Peter Drysdale, 'Rudd in Singapore on the Asia Pacific Community idea', *East Asia Forum*, 31 May 2009: www.eastasiaforum.org/2009/05/31/rudd-in-singapore-on-the-asia-pacific-community-idea/

117. Shankari Sundararaman, 'APEC and Chindia', *Asian Age*, 24 November 2009.

118. See, for example, Mukul G. Asher and Rahul Sen, 'India's Membership: APEC's Relevance', *Faculty Working Papers* (Lee Kuan Yew University School of Public Policy, National University of Singapore, 2007): www.spp.nus.edu.sg/Handler.ashx?path=Data/Site/SiteDocuments/wp/wp0707.pdf

119. 'India APEC membership may be years away', *Financial Times*, 26 December 2007.

120. Bhanoji Rao, 'Does APEC membership really matter for India?' *The Hindu Business Line*, 23 January 2007.

121. Meena Singh Roy, 'The 9th Shanghai Cooperation Organisation Summit: An Assessment', *IDSA Comment* (24 June 2009): www.idsa.in/strategiccomments/The9thShanghaiCooperationOrganisationSummit_MSRoy_240609 A dissenting view is offered by Emilian Kavalski in his book *India and Central Asia: The Mythmaking and International relations of a Rising Power* (London/New York: I.B. Tauris, 2010), particularly 79–109.

122. Chietigj Bajpaee, 'India rediscovers East Asia', *Asia Times*, 31 October 2007: www.atimes.com/atimes/South_Asia/IJ31Df02.html

123. G. V. C. Naidu, 'Southeast Asian Security Dynamics', in N. S. Sisodia and Sreeradha Datta (eds.), *Changing Security Dynamics in Southeast Asia* (New Delhi: Magnum Books, 2008), 95.

124. Nanda, *Rediscovering Asia*, 19–20.

125. G. V. C. Naidu, *Indian Navy and Southeast Asia* (Delhi: Knowledge World, 2000), 182.

126. G. V. C. Naidu, 'India's Strategic Relation with Southeast Asia', in Baladas Ghoshal (ed.), *India and Southeast Asia* (New Delhi: Konark Publishers, 1996), 32–3.

127. Kishore Kumar, 'Andaman and Nicobar Islands: Our Gateway to the East', in Raja Reddy (ed.), *India and ASEAN: Foreign Policy Dimensions of the 21st Century* (New Delhi: New Century Publications, 2005), 48.

128. Frédéric Grare, 'In Search of a Role: India and the ASEAN Regional Forum', in Grare and Mattoo (eds.), *India and ASEAN*, 135.

129. Kumar, 'Andaman and Nicobar Islands', 48; See also Gurpreet Khurana, 'Cooperation among Maritime Security Forces', *Strategic Analysis*, 29/2 (April/June 2005), 297–8.

130. C. Raja Mohan, 'There's a new game in Asia', *The Indian Express*, 31 May 2005.

131. Arabinda Acharya, 'India and Southeast Asia in the Age of Terror: Building Partnerships for Peace', *Contemporary Southeast Asia*, 28/2 (2006), 310–11; Khurana, 'Cooperation among Maritime Security Forces', 304.

132. Sudhir Deware, *India and Southeast Asia: Towards Security Convergence* (Singapore: ISEAS, 2006), 58.

133. Robert D. Kaplan, 'Center Stage for the Twenty-first Century', *Foreign Affairs*, 88/2 (March/April 2009).

134. Government of India, Ministry of Defence, *Annual Report 2008–2009*, 37, http://mod.nic.in/reports/welcome.html

135. C. Raja Mohan, 'India and the Balance of Power', *Foreign Affairs*, 85/4 (July/August 2006).

136. See Gurpreet S. Khurana, 'China-India Maritime Rivalry', *India Defence Review*, 23/4 (April 2009): www.indiandefencereview.com/2009/04/china-india-maritime-rivalry.html

137. Mak Joon Num, 'ASEAN-India Defence Interactions', in Grare and Mattoo (eds.), *India and ASEAN*, 156.

138. Naidu, 'Southeast Asian Security Dynamics,' 90–91.

139. Walter C. Ludwig III, 'Delhi's Pacific Ambition: Naval Power, "Look East," and India's Emerging Influence in the Asia-Pacific', *Asian Security*, 5/2 (2009), 95.

140. P. S. Suryanarayan, 'New Partnerships: India's growing engagement with Japan, South Korea and Malaysia opens new possibilities of cooperation', *Frontline*, 26 February 2010.

141. See Government of India, Ministry of Defence, *Annual Report 2003–2004*, 193–4 and throughout, http://mod.nic.in/reports/welcome.html

142. Teresita Schaffer, *India and the United States in the 21st Century: Reinventing Partnership* (Washington: Centre for Strategic and International Studies, 2009), 147.

143. Seth, 'India and Japan', 815.

144. Ministry of Foreign Affairs of Japan, 'Joint Statement on the Advancement of the Strategic and Global Partnership between Japan and India', Tokyo, 22 October 2008: www.mofa.go.jp/region/asia-paci/india/pmv0810/joint_s.html

145. K. V. Prasad, 'India, Japan finalize action plan to advance security cooperation', *The Hindu*, 30 December 2009; Ministry of Foreign Affairs of Japan, 'Action Plan to advance Security Cooperation based on the Joint Declaration on Security Cooperation between Japan and India', 29 December 2009: www.mofa.go.jp/region/asia-paci/india/pmv0912/action.html

146. Uttara Dukkipati, 'India-Japan Relations: A Partnership for Peace and Prosperity', *South Asia Monitor*, 134 (Center for Strategic and International Studies, 1 October 2009).

147. Ludwig, 'Delhi's Pacific Ambition', 99.

148. See Mohan Malik, 'The Proliferation Axis: Beijing-Islamabad-Pyongyang', *The Korean Journal of Defense Analysis*, 15/1 (Spring 2003), 57–98.

149. Lakhvinder Singh, 'New Direction of Korea-India Ties', *Korea Times*, 21 January 2010: www.koreatimes.co.kr/www/news/opinon/2010/06/198_59420.html

150. 'Strategic Partnership', *Korea Times*, 26 January 2010: www.koreatimes.co.kr/www/news/opinon/2010/01/202_59705.html

151. Swaran Singh, *China–South Asia: Issues, Equations, Policies* (New Delhi: Lancer's Books, 2003), 131–41.

152. Bajpaee, 'India rediscovers East Asia'.

153. James Clad, 'Convergent Chinese and Indian Perspectives on the Global Order', in Francine R. Frankel and Harry Harding (eds.), *The India–China Relationship: What the United States Needs to Know* (New York: Columbia University Press, 2004), 270.

154. Yan, 'India–China relations'.

155. New Zealand Ministry of Foreign Affairs and Trade, 'Republic of India'.

156. See 'Australia and India: A Convergence of Interests', speech by Minister for Foreign Affairs Stephen Smith at *The Asia Society*, Mumbai, 15 October 2009: www.foreignminister.gov.au/speeches/2009/091015_asia_society.html

157. Mark Dodd, 'India Defence ties to be tightened', *Australian*, 4 June 2007: www.theaustralian.com.au/news/nation/india-defence-ties-to-be-tightened/story-e6frg6nf-1111113672689 'Australia inks first defence pact with India, maritime ties focus', *Indian Express*, 7 March 2006: www.indianexpress.com/oldStory/89139/

158. 'India-Australia Joint Declaration on Security Cooperation', New Delhi, 12 November 2009, http://pmrudd.archive.dpmc.gov.au/node/6324

159. C. Raja Mohan, 'Is India an East Asian Power? Explaining New Delhi's Security Politics in the Western Pacific', *ISAS Working Paper*, 81 (Singapore: ISAS, 2009) , 20–1: www.isasnus.org/events/workingpapers/80.pdf

160. Rajeev Ranjan Chaturvedy, 'Making the Case for Soft Power', *ICRIER Think Ink*, 1 November 2008: www.icrier.org/page.asp?MenuID=24&SubCatId=177&SubSubCatId=326

161. Shashi Tharoor, 'Indian Strategic Power: Soft', *Global Brief*, 13 May 2009, http://globalbrief.ca/blog/2009/05/13/soft-is-the-word/

162. C. Raja Mohan, 'Soft Power, Hard Facts', *The Indian Express*, 19 November 2007.

163. Ibid.

164. Deware, *India and Southeast Asia*, 171.

165. See an excellent analysis: Syeda Sana Rahman, 'The 2010 Commonwealth Games: India's Triumph or Disaster?', *ISAS Brief*, 166 (8 July 2010), Singapore: Institute of South Asian Studies, National University of Singapore, www.isas.nus.edu.sg

166. See the Indian Council for Cultural Relations (ICCR) website at http://iccrindia.net/index.html

167. Embassy of Japan in India, 'Grand Success of Japan-India Friendship Year': www. in.emb-japan.go.jp/Friendship_Year2007/join.html

168. Veeramalla Anjaiah, 'Relations between RI and India reach "historic high" in 2009', *Jakarta Post*, 4 January 2010: www.thejakartapost.com/news/2010/01/04/relations-between-ri-and-india-reach-'historic-high'-2009.html

169. Nandan Nilekani, *Imagining India: The Idea of a Renewed Nation* (New York: Penguin, 2009), 26–7.

170. Ishani Duttagupta, 'Skilled Indians shop for jobs in Singapore', *Economic Times*, 26 June 2008.

171. Amarjit Kaur, 'Indians in Southeast Asia: Migrant Labour, Knowledge workers and the new India', in Rajesh Rai and Peter Reeves (eds.), *The South Asian Diaspora: Transnational Networks and Changing Identities* (New York: Routledge, 2009), 84.

172. Deware, *India and Southeast Asia*, 172.

173. See 'Chairs' and 'Scholarships' on the ICCR website at: www.iccrindia.org/chairs.htm

174. Janelle Bonner, 'Australia and India: An Important Partnership', in *South Asian Survey*, 15/1 (2008), 166–7.

175. Australian Government, Department of Foreign Affairs and Trade, 'India country Brief'.

176. Baladas Ghoshal, 'India's Soft power approach can contribute to Indonesia's growth', *Jakarta Post*, 28 November 2008.

177. Government of India, Ministry of External Affairs, *Annual Report 2008–2009* (New Delhi: Policy and Planning Research Division, 2009), 132.

178. For sectoral allocations in the 2008–9 budget of the Ministry of External Affairs, see MEA *Annual Report 2008–2009*, 184.

179. Kripa Sridharan, *The ASEAN Region in India's Foreign Policy* (Aldershot: Dartmouth Publishing Company, 1996), 79–80.

180. Government of India, Ministry of Overseas Indians, *Annual Report 2008–2009*, 5–6, http://moia.gov.in/writereaddata/pdf/Annual_Report_2008-09.pdf

181. Sridharan, 'India and Southeast Asia in the Context of India's Rise', 83.

182. Ibid.

183. 'Indian Students shunning Australia', *BBC News*, 1 January 2010, http://news.bbc.co.uk/go/pr/fr/-/2/hi/asia-pacific/8444870.stm Rahul Mishra, 'India-Australia Relations: Off Again, On Again?' *IDSA Comment*, 16 November 2009: www.idsa.in/idsacomments/IndiaAustraliaRelations_rmishra_161109

184. Australian Government, Department of Foreign Affairs and Trade, 'India country Brief'.

185. Deware, *India and Southeast Asia*, 175.

186. John Koldowski and Oliver Martin, 'Emerging Market Segments: Religious and Medical Tourism in India', in Roland Conrady and Martin Buck (eds.), *Trends and Issues in Global Tourism 2008* (Berlin: Springer, 2008), 128.

187. Ibid., 128–9.

188. United Nations World Tourism Organization, *Yearbook of Tourism Statistics (2009 Edition)* (Madrid: World Tourism Organization, 2009), 358.

189. Shekhar Niyogi, 'New Growth Sectors for Indian Tourism', *Travel Daily News*, 7 October 2009: www.traveldailynews.com/pages/show_page/33438-New-growth-sectors-for-Indian-tourism

190. Alka Acharya, *China and India: Politics of Incremental Engagement* (New Delhi: Har-Anand, 2008), 15; Yan, 'India–China relations'.

191. Pallavi Aiyar, 'Tourism in India and China, a study in striking contrast', *The Hindu*, 14 April 2008: www.thehindu.com/2008/04/14/stories/2008041454911100.htm

192. Pavan Varma, 'Culture as an instrument of diplomacy', in Sinha and Mohta (eds.), *Indian Foreign Policy*, 1137.

193. Sanjaya Baru, 'Sanjaya Baru: It's time for a "Look Further East" Policy', *Business Standard*, 7 December 2009.

Chapter 10

1. On India's place in the changing definition of power, see Chandrashekhar Dasgupta, 'India and the Changing Balance of Power', in Atisha Sinha and Madhup Mohta (eds.), *Indian Foreign Policy: Challenges and Opportunities* (New Delhi: Academic Foundation, 2007), 91–111.

2. John Keay, *India: A History* (London: Harper Collins, 2000), 305–6.

3. Even the Danes established a foothold in India, of which scenic remains can be found at Tranquebar on the Tamil Nadu coast.

4. Dilip Lahiri, 'India and France', in Sinha and Mohta (eds.), *Indian Foreign Policy*, 711–12.

5. Ibid., 712.

6. Ironically, when the French withdrew from Indochina after 1954, they relocated part of one of their principal centres of Asian learning, the École française d'Extrême-Orient, in Pondicherry, where it can still be found today in association with the Institut Français de Pondicherry.

7. Kaushik Roy, 'The Armed Expansion of the English East India Company: 1740s–1849', in Daniel P. Marston and Chandar S. Sundaram (eds), *A Military History of India and South Asia: From the East India Company to the Nuclear Era* (Bloomington: Indiana University Press, 2007), 15.

8. For good overviews of Indian involvement in both conflicts, see the following in Marston and Sundaram, *A Military History of India and South Asia*: David Omissi, 'The Indian Army and the First World War', 74–87, and Daniel P. Marston, 'A Force Transformed: The Indian Army and the Second World War', 102–22. During the Second World War up to 50,000 Indians, under the banner of the Indian National Army, for reasons of anti-imperial nationalism, made common cause with Japanese forces in the Asian theatre of conflict, fighting in Burma and India's northeast against the British imperial army, eventually under the leadership of Subhas Chandra Bose (who died in an air crash in 1945), still today a hero in his native Calcutta.

9. See Harish Kapur, *Foreign Policies of India's Prime Ministers* (Frankfort, IL: Lancer Publishers, 2009), 304–8.

10. Statistics are drawn from the Government of India, Department of Commerce, *Export-Import Data Bank* and are up to date as of June 2010.

11. Council of the European Union, 'Fifth India-EU Summit: Joint Press Statement', 8 November 2004: www.consilium.europa.eu/ueDocs/cms_Data/docs/pressData/en/er/82635.pdf see also for analysis K. Gajendra Singh, 'India and the Europe Union: New Strategic Partnership', *South Asia Analysis Group Paper*, 1163 (2004): www.southasiaanalysis.org/papers12/paper1163.html

12. 'India-EU Strategic Partnership: Joint Action Plan (2005)' (revised 2008). This document can be found at http://ec.europa.eu/external_relations/india/index_en.htm along with several other documents relating to the India–EU relationship.

13. On EU politics see Biswajit Choudhury, 'Emerging Divisions in Europe', *Frontline* 20/10 (10–23 May 2003): www.hinduonnet.com/fline/fl2010/stories/20030523000805800.htm; and Vaiju Naravane, 'Turbulent Times Ahead for European Union', *The Hindu* (Online), 10 August 2005, www.hinduonnet.com/2005/08/10/stories/2005081002051000.htm

14. Pallavi Aiyar, 'Bilateral Agreements are New Messiah for World Trade', *Business Standard* (Online), 27 August 2009: www.business-standard.com/india/news/bilateral-agreementsnew-messiah-for-world-trade/367916/

15. R. Ramachandran, 'An Emerging Partner', *Frontline*, 24/4 (24 February – 9 March 2007): www.hinduonnet.com/fline/fl2404/stories/20070309004904400.htm Regarding the ongoing agricultural trade battles, see 'Protectionism Hurting India's Trade with the EU: FICCI', *The Hindu* (Online), 2 August 2009: www.hindu.com/thehindu/holnus/006200908021453.htm See also Paul Blustein's excellent account of Doha Round trade negotiations, *Misadventures of the Most Favored Nations: Clashing Egos, Inflated Ambitions and the Great Shambles of the World Trading System* (New York: Public Affairs, 2009).

16. See Antonio Armellini, *L'elefante ha messo le ali* (Milan: EGEA editore-Università Bocconi, 2008).

17. 'Appendix 7A', *SIPRI Yearbook 2009* (Stockholm International Peace Research Institute, 2009). These statistics can be found online at: www.sipri.org/yearbook/2009/07/07A

18. G.S Ramesh, 'French Arms Trade Policy and Indian Sub-Continent', in Verinder Grover (ed.) *International Relations and Foreign Policy of India*, Vol. IX: *Europe and India's Foreign Policy* (New Delhi: Deep and Deep Publications, 1992), 357–8.

19. Lahiri, 'India and France', 711.

20. 'Appendix 7A', *SIPRI Yearbook 2009*.

21. Teresita C. Schaffer, in her excellent book *India and the United States in the 21st century* (Washington, DC: CSIS, 2009) discusses both the drivers of and remaining impediments to the defence trade between India and the United States on pages 65–88.

22. Siddharth Srivastava, 'India's Fighter Wars', *Asia Sentinel* (Online), 24 August 2009, http://asiasentinel.com/index.php?option=com_content&task=view&id=2021&Itemid=225.

23. Advanced F-16 and F-18 models from the US, Mig-31s from Russia, the Eurofighter Typhoon from the UK/Italy/Spain/Germany, and the Saab Gripen from Sweden.

24. UK Scotland Yard counterterrorism police assisted the Indian authorities with their investigation of the November 2008 Mumbai attacks. On this, see Laura King, 'Mumbai Attacks put Spotlight on Lashkar-e-Taiba', *Los Angeles Times* (Online), 5 December 2008, http://articles.latimes.com/2008/dec/05/world/fg-lashkar5?pg=1 and 'FBI, Scotland Yard Teams Visit Terror Attack Sites in Mumbai', *The EconomicTimes* (Online), 1 December 2008, http://economictimes.indiatimes.com/LATEST_NEWS/FBI_Scotland_Yard_teams_visit_terror_attack_sites_in_Mumbai/articleshow/3781479.cms

25. Government of India, Planning Commission, *Integrated Energy Policy: Report of the Expert Committee* (Government of India, August 2006), 55.

26. Ibid.

27. Carin Zissis, 'Backgrounder: India's Energy Crunch', Council on Foreign Relations, 23 October 2007: www.cfr.org/publication/12200/indias_energy_crunch.html

28. Tanvi Madan, *Energy Security Series: India* (Brookings Institute, November 2006). Madan states that the exhaustion of Indian coal reserves may occur within as little as forty years.

29. For the importance of these and other major chokepoints, see Energy Information Administration, *World Oil Transit Chokepoints*, Country Analysis Briefs (US Department of Energy, January 2008).

30. 'India-EU Strategic Partnership: Joint Action Plan (2005)' (revised 2008), 14.

31. Ibid. The eight areas are: Promoting energy efficiency and energy conservation; development of affordable clean energy technologies; identification of new technologies in the field of new, renewable, conventional, and non-conventional energy sources; oil and gas, with a view to promoting security of supplies and stability in prices; nuclear energy; technology and expertise in exchange of energy between different grid systems and development of energy markets; development of hydrogen and fuel cells; methane recovery and use.

32. Madan, *Energy Security Series: India*, 85; and on the ITER project, see Dr Karan Singh's address, 'India and Europe: The Way Ahead', presented at the EGMONT Institute-RIIR Conference, 1 June 2006: www.irri-kiib.be/speechnotes/06/060601-India.Singh.htm

33. Madan, *Energy Security Series: India*, 73. Madan also gives a good breakdown of each company's interests in India.

34. 'France, India Sign Major Nuclear Deal', *ABC News* (Online), 30 September 2008:   www.abc.net.au/news/stories/2008/09/30/2378538.htm?section=world and 'India and France in Nuclear Deal', *BBC News* (Online), 30 September 2008, http://news.bbc.co.uk/2/hi/south_asia/7644377.stm

35. Nalini Kant Jha, 'The Cultural and Philosophical Roots of India's Foreign Policy', *International Studies*, 26(1) (1989), 46.

36. Sunil Khilnani, *The Idea of India* (New York: Farrar, Straus and Giroux, 1997), 4, 17. Khilnani further writes: 'India became a democracy without really knowing how, why, or what it meant to be one. Yet the democratic idea has penetrated the Indian political imagination and has begun to corrode the authority of the social order and of a paternalist state' (p. 17).

37. Indira Gandhi, 'Europe and India', in Grover (ed.), *International Relations and Foreign Policy of India*, 87–92.

38. Indira Gandhi, 'Towards a New Synthesis in Civilization', in Grover (ed.), *International Relations and Foreign Policy of India*, 348.

39. Kapur, *Foreign Policies*, 25.

40. See www.csh-delhi.com India remains acutely, excessively sensitive to foreign research findings its government believes damage India's image, leading to unseemly wrangling over research visas, notably with French and American scholars, which sometimes escalate into diplomatic tensions, as prior to President Chirac's visit to India in 2006. The notion that research findings affecting India's image can be managed through the expedient of visa non-issuance is nearly farcical in the current day and age, and unworthy of a country like India with such tremendously open debate and such a dynamic research tradition within its own borders.

41. See www.ifpindia.org

42. For further information on the Asia-Link project, see its website at www.asia-link.eu/

43. 'India-EU Strategic Partnership: Joint Action Plan (2005)' (revised 2008).

44. Donald MacLeod, 'UK Universities Continuing to Attract Indian Students', *Guardian* (Online), 26 March 2007: www.guardian.co.uk/education/2007/mar/26/highereducation.uk; and John Gill, 'UK Sees 24% Rise in Indian Students', *Times Higher Education* (Online), 27 March 2008: www.timeshighereducation.co.uk/story.asp?storyCode=401182&sectioncode=26

45. For activities in India of these various organizations, see www.afindia.org, www.goethe.de/Ins/in/lp/enindex.htm, and www.britishcouncil.org/india

46. See Christopher Andrew and Vasili Mitrokhin, *The Mitrokhin Archive II: The KGB and the World* (London: Allen Lane, 2005), 320–1 for arms and Indo-Pakistani conflict.

47. Ibid., 266

48. Gulshan Sachdeva, 'Reviving Economic Interests', *Frontline* 17/21 (14–27 October 2000): www.hinduonnet.com/fline/fl1721/17210170.htm

49. John Cherian, 'A Strategic Partnership', *Frontline* 17/21 (14–27 October 2000): www.hinduonnet.com/thehindu/fline/fl1721/17210100.htm

50. Vidya Subrahmaniam and Vladimir Radyuhin, 'India-Russia Trade does not Reflect Close Political Ties, Says President', *The Hindu* (Online), 4 September 2009.

51. Sumit Ganguly, 'India in 2007: A Year of Opportunities and Disappointments', *Asia Survey*, 48/1 (January/February 2008), 173. Ganguly explains this trend succinctly by stating that after the Cold War: 'The Russians evinced scant interest in maintaining the rupee-ruble trade arrangement; they were loath to sell high-technology weaponry at bargain basement prices, and above all, they were unwilling to serve as a strategic guarantor against possible PRC revanchism.'

52. On the End User Monitoring Agreement (EUMA), see 'EUMA Brings India into Nuclear Non-proliferation Mainstream: US', *Express India* (Online), 23 July 2009: www.expressindia.com/latest-news/EUMA-brings-India-into-nuclear-non-proliferation-mainstream-US/493086/. The EUMA was not all-encompassing, however. On this aspect, see 'No Blanket EUMA with US on Cards', *The Hindu* (Online), 14 August 2009: www.thehindu.com/2009/08/14/stories/2009081460981100.htm

53. See Vijay Sen Budhraj, 'Major Dimensions of Indo-Soviet Relations', in Grover (ed.), *International Relations and Foreign Policy of India*, 122–4; and Tom Lansford, 'The Great Game Renewed?: US-Russian Rivalry in the Arms Trade of South Asia', *Security Dialogue*, 33/2 (2002), 129.

54. On the *Akula* lease, see Jon Grevatt, 'Indian Navy to take Delivery of Russian Submarine by End of 2009', *Jane's Defence Industry*, 3 June 2009.

55. Keri Wagstaff-Smith, 'Indian Army Receives First 10 T-90 MBTs', *Jane's Defence Industry*, 25 August 2009.

56. Lansford, 'The Great Game Renewed?', 133–4.

57. For instance, see Ravi Khanna, 'India-US Military Relations Growing Rapidly', *Voice of America News* (Online), 8 October 2009: www.voanews.com/english/2009-10-08-voa15.cfm

58. See Jon Grevatt, 'Lockheed Martin Discusses Hercules Sale with India', *Jane's Defence Industry*, 31 July 2009; and Gareth Jennings, 'Aero India 2009: Northrop Grumman Negotiates E2D Clearance for India', *Jane's Defence Industry*, 12 February 2009.

59. Rahul Bede and Nick Brown, 'India Commissions Armaris to Build Six Scorpenes', *Jane's Defence Industry*, 1 November 2005.

60. For a full breakdown of the *Gorshkov* carrier saga, see 'INS Vikramaditya: Waiting for Gorshkov...', *Defense Industry Daily*, 17 August 2009; see also 'Second-Hand Gorshkov to Cost More than New Carrier, India Told', *Jane's Defence Industry*, 27 July 2009. The carrier was originally supposed to be delivered by 2008, and the cost of refit has risen from US$975 million to US$2.2 billion.

61. N. M. Pegov, 'Economic and Cultural Relations of USSR and India', in Grover (ed.), *International Relations and Foreign Policy of India*, 613.

62. Madan, *Energy Security Series: India*, 75.

63. Siddharth Srivastava, 'India's Quest for Russian Energy', *Asia Times* (Online), 7 November 2006: www.atimes.com/atimes/South_Asia/HK07Df02.html

64. 'India, Russia sign Accord for 4 Nuke Reactors', *India Express* (Online), 5 December 2008: www.indianexpress.com/news/india-russia-sign-accord-for-4-nuke-reactors/394667/ Also see T. S. Subramanian, 'Koodankulam Calling', *Frontline* 17/21 (14–27 October 2000), for earlier developments on Indo-Russian nuclear cooperation.

65. 'Russia Agrees India Nuclear Deal', BBC (Online), 11 February 2008, http://news.bbc.co.uk/2/hi/south_asia/7883223.stm

66. Madan, *Energy Security Series: India*, 48. For an interesting look at the strategic implications of the Central Asian pipelines and the politics around them, see Gawdat Baghat, 'Pipeline Diplomacy: The Geopolitics of the Caspian Sea Region', *International Studies Perspectives*, 3/3 (2002). Energy diplomacy is a major driver of India's interest in the Shanghai Cooperation Organization, within which India has Observer status and whose Summit in October 2009 Indian Prime Minister Manmohan Singh attended.

67. On this strategic manoeuvring, see the following coverage: Maha Atal, 'IPI vs. TAPI', *Forbes* (Online), 31 July 2008: www.forbes.com/global/2008/0721/028.html 'No Bowing to Pressure on IPI Pipeline Project: Deora', *The Hindu* (Online),

21 July 2009: www.thehindu.com/2009/07/21/stories/2009072155921100.
htm 'Washington Links Pakistani Aid to IPI', *UPI Asia* (Online), 18 August 2009:
www.upiasia.com/Energy_Resources/2009/08/18/Washington-links-Pakistani-aid-
to-IPI/UPI-91101250614232/

68. Bill Samii, 'Iran-Pakistan-India Gas Pipeline Imperiled', *Pars Times* (RFE/RL), 2005:
www.parstimes.com/news/archive/2005/rfe/iran_india_pipeline.html While Iran
prefers a 'take-or-pay' structure in which India would pay for contracted amounts
regardless of whether it takes delivery, India for obvious reasons rejects this in
favour of a 'supply-or-pay' structure in which Iran must deliver the contracted
amount or pay the difference.

69. On Russian participation, see: 'Russia Keen to Participate in Iran-Pak-India Pipeline
Project', *Hindu Business Line* (Online), 25 November 2005: www.thehindubusiness-
line.com/2005/11/26/stories/2005112603560300.htm

70. Maha Atal, 'IPI vs. TAPI', *Forbes* (Online), 31 July 2008. For American views regarding the IPI project, see Ariel Cohen, Lisa Curtis, and Owen Graham, *The Proposed
Iran-Pakistan-India Gas Pipeline: An Unacceptable Risk to Regional Security*, Backgrounder 2139 (Washington, DC: Heritage Foundation, 30 May 2008).

71. 'New Delhi Considers IPI Talks', *UPI* (Online), 19 August 2009: www.upi.com/Ener-
gy_Resources/2009/08/19/New-Delhi-considers-IPI-talks/UPI-90731250700880/ For a
recent analysis of the pipeline competition and the associated international maneu-
vering, see Tariq Fatemi, 'The Politics of Pipelines', *DAWN* (Online), 13 August 2009:
www.dawn.com/wps/wcm/connect/dawn-content-library/dawn/news/pakistan/16-
the-politics-of-pipelines-hs-05

72. Sudha Ramachandran, 'India's Foray into Central Asia', *Asia Times* (Online),
12 August 2006: www.atimes.com/atimes/South_Asia/HH12Df01.html Neither
the Tajiks nor the Indians are very forthcoming about the arrangements governing
the Ayni airbase. However it is estimated that about 150 Indian personnel and an
IAF unit are based there. See Ramakrishna Upadhya, 'India Reaches Out to Tajikistan', *Deccan Herald* (Online), 8 September 2009: www.deccanherald.com/content/
23972/india-reaches-tajikistan.html

73. Ibid.

74. Vidyam Subrahmaniam, 'First-ever Visit by an Indian President Recognizes Tajikistan's Importance', *The Hindu* (Online), 7 September 2009, http://beta.thehindu.
com/news/national/article16150.ece

75. 'India Seeks to Restore Silk Route', *Daily Times* (Online), 25 September 2009: www.
dailytimes.com.pk/default.asp?page=2009\09\25\story_25-9-2009_pg7_41

76. Meena Singh Roy, 'India's Interests in Central Asia', *Strategic Analysis*, 24/12 (March
2001).

77. Poonam Mann, 'Fighting Terrorism; India and Central Asia', *Strategic Analysis*,
26/11 (2001).

78. Ananth Krishnan, 'SCO Meet's Focus on Economics, Terror', *The Hindu* (Online),
14 October 2009, http://beta.thehindu.com/news/international/article34071.ece

79. 'India Calls for Zero Tolerance to Terrorism at SCO Meeting,' *NetIndian News
Network* (Online), 14 October 2009, http://netindian.in/news/2009/10/14/
0003733/india-calls-zero-tolerance-terrorism-sco-meeting

80. Perhaps because it was now facing a range of unpalatable options, Delhi by May 2010 was signalling quietly that it was open, in principle, to some form of dialogue with the Taliban.

81. Christophe Jaffrelot, *India and the European Union: The Charade of a Strategic Partnership* (Paris: Centre for International Studies and Research, March 2006): www.ceri-sciencespo.com/archive/mars06/art_cj.pdf Similar statements have been made by Indian observers. See Rajendra M. Abhyankar, 'India and the European Union: Non-Associable to Strategic Partner', in Sinha and Mohta (eds.), *Indian Foreign Policy*, 464.

82. On Indo-EU dialogue see Emilian Kavalski, 'Venus and the Porcupine: Assessing the India-European Union Strategic Partnership', *South Asian Survey*, 15/1 (2008), 63–81.

83. Eric Gonsalves, 'India and Western Europe', in A. K. Damodaran and U. S. Bajpai (eds.), *Indian Foreign Policy, the Indira Gandhi Years* (New Delhi: Radiant Publishers, 1990).

84. Evan A. Feigenbaum, 'India's Rise, America's Interest: The Fate of the US–Indian Partnership', *Foreign Affairs*, 89/2 (March/April 2010), 76–91.

85. For a discussion of the debates in Washington over US–China relations, see John Lee, 'An Insider's Guide to Washington's China War', *Foreign Policy* (Online), 28 July 2009: www.foreignpolicy.com/articles/2009/07/28/an_insiders_guide_to_washingtons_china_war

86. See Jorge Heine, 'Is the European Union in Decline?', *The Hindu*, 3 December 2009; and Alia Allana, 'Personnel Issues', *Indian Express*, 23 November 2009.

87. For one Indian view of the outcome, see Praful Bidwai, 'Fouling Up the Air', *Frontline*, 29 January 2010.

88. See T. Jayaraman, 'Taking stock of Copenhagen', *The Hindu*, 24 December 2009, in which he described the EU as 'currently smarting from being sidelined in the US end-run at Copenhagen'. Several detailed Indian media round-ups of the Copenhagen conference and its results barely mentioned the EU.

89. See M. K. Venu, 'Among Ourselves—G-20 to Copenhagen: Behold the Waning of the Multilateral Era', *Indian Express*, 28 December 2009.

90. India has been looking favourably at French as well as Russian designs for its future submarine purchases.

91. Anuradha M. Chenoy, 'India and Russia: Allies in the International Political System', *South Asian Survey*, 15/1 (2008), 49–62.

92. See 'Soviet Diplomacy: Russia seeks to rebuild an old alliance with India', *Financial Times*, 12 March 2010.

93. Confidential interview, Delhi, February 2010.

Chapter 11

1. T. Ramakrishna Reddy, *India's Policy in the United Nations* (Cranbury, NJ: Associated University Presses, 1968), 30, quoting Jawaharlal Nehru.

2. Sanjaya Baru, 'India in a changing world', *HT Mint*, 30 March 2009.

3. *The Indian Annual Register: July–December 1946* (Calcutta: N.N. Mitra, 1947), 252–3, cited in The Indian Council of World Affairs, *India and the United Nations* (New York: Manhattan Publishing Company, 1957), 28.

4. Dhiraj R. Chamling, *India and the United Nations* (New Delhi: Associated Publishing House, 1978), 9.

5. Chinmaya R. Gharekhan, 'India and the United Nations', in Atish Sinha and Madhup Mohta (eds.), *Indian Foreign Policy: Challenges and Opportunities* (New Delhi: Foreign Service Institute/ Academic Foundation, 2007), 200.

6. See C. Raja Mohan, 'India and the New World Order', *Seminar* 529, 29 August 2003.

7. See Muchkund Dubey, 'Reform of the UN system and India', in Sinha and Mohta (eds.), *Indian Foreign Policy*, 186.

8. Werner Levi, 'Necrology on Indian Neutralism', *Eastern World*, 17/2 (1963), 10, cited in Reddy, *India's Policy*, 26.

9. Chamling, *India and the United Nations*, 116.

10. *Asian Recorder*, 3 (1957), 1531, cited in Priyankar Upadhyaya, *Nonaligned States and India's International Conflicts* (New Delhi: South Asian Publishers, 1990), 7.

11. United Nations, General Assembly, Fifteenth Session, part 1, *Official Records*, Vol. 1, 906th plenary meeting, agenda item 9 (17 October 1960) (New York, 1961), 751, cited in Reddy, *India's Policy*, 34.

12. A. K. Damodaran, *Beyond Autonomy: Roots of India's Foreign Policy* (New Delhi: Somaiya Publications, 2000), 116.

13. A. Appadorai and M. S. Rajan, *India's Foreign Policy and Relations* (New Delhi: South Asian Publishers, 1985), 38–9.

14. Indian Council of World Affairs, *India and the United Nations*, 209.

15. Appadorai and Rajan, *India's Foreign Policy*, 488. Western countries perceived the Indian members of the commission to be mostly partial to communist actors in Indochina battling Western influence and troops. Indian sympathies indeed lay with anti-imperialist local actors, quite understandably (if not commendably) so given India's recent colonial experiences.

16. Charles P. Schleicher and J. S. Bains, *The Administration of Indian Foreign Policy Through the United Nations* (New York: Oceana, 1969), 108.

17. Chamling, *India and the United Nations*, 155.

18. Indian Council of World Affairs, *India and the United Nations*, 185–8.

19. A. K. Damodaran, 'Non-aligned movement and its future', in Sinha and Mohta (eds.), *Indian Foreign Policy*, 130.

20. C. Raja Mohan, *Crossing the Rubicon: The Shaping of India's New Foreign Policy* (New York: Palgrave Macmillan, 2004), 30.

21. The G-77 in early 2010 numbered 130 states, including India. The NAM as of early 2010 had 118 members, including India, having lost a dozen members since its inception.

22. Upadhyaya, *Nonaligned States*, 55.

23. Upadhyaya, *Nonaligned States*, 14.

24. J. N. Dixit, *India's Foreign Policy 1947–2003* (New Delhi: Picus Books, 2003), 260.

25. Reddy, *India's Policy*, 22–5.

26. Conversation, New Delhi, February 2010.

27. Srinath Raghavan, *War and Peace in Modern India: A Strategic History of the Nehru Years* (London: Palgrave Macmillan, 2009).

28. Kuldip Nayar, *Between the Lines* (New Delhi, 1969), 169, cited in Upadhyaya, *Nonaligned States*, 56.

29. Appadorai and Rajan, *India's Foreign Policy*, 495.

30. See Erik Voeten, 'Why no UN Security Council reform? Lessons for and from institutionalist theory', in Dimitris Bourantonis, Kostas Ifantis, and Panayotis Tsakonas (eds.), *Multilateralism and Security Institutions in an Era of Globalization* (Abingdon and New York: Routledge, 2008), 292. Also see Dixit, *India's Foreign Policy*, 263–4.

31. Damodaran, *Beyond Autonomy*, 169, 175.

32. See for example, Schleicher and Bains, *The Administration of Indian Foreign Policy*, 5, 110.

33. See, for example, Dubey, 'Reform of the UN system', in Sinha and Mohta (eds.), *Indian Foreign Policy*, 186.

34. Dixit, *India's Foreign Policy*, 286.

35. See Ian Anthony, Christer Ahlstrom, and Vitaly Fedchenko, *Reforming Nuclear Export Controls: The Future of the Nuclear Suppliers Group*, SIPRI Research Report No. 22 (Oxford: Oxford University Press, 2007), 41–56.

36. See David M. Malone (ed.), *The UN Security Council, from Cold War to 21st Century*, (Boulder, CO and London: Lynne Rienner, 2004), particularly 4–13, 617–49, and the chapter by Peter Wallensteen and Patrick Johansson, 'Security Council Decisions in Perspective', 17–33.

37. See Dixit, *India's Foreign Policy*, 203.

38. Voeten, 'Why no UN Security Council reform?' in Bourantonis et al. (eds.), *Multilateralism and Security Institutions*, 292.

39. For an interesting essay on how UN peacekeeping and monitoring has evolved, substantively and numerically, since 1947, see Michael W. Doyle and Nicholas Sambanis, 'Peacekeeping Operations', in Thomas G. Weiss and Sam Daws (eds.), *The Oxford Handbook on the United Nations* (Oxford/ New York: Oxford University Press, 2007), 323–48. For current UN peacekeeping deployments, see: www.un.org/en/peacekeeping In March 2010, 117,000 UN personnel were deployed in seventeen peacekeeping missions across four continents.

40. Amitav Mallik, *Technology and Security in the 21st Century: A Demand-Side Perspective*, SIPRI Research Report No. 20 (Oxford: Oxford University Press, 2004), 74.

41. See C. Raja Mohan, *Crossing the Rubicon*, for a fuller exposition of these ideas.

42. See, for example, Sitaram Yechury, 'Back to basics', *Seminar*, 1 January 2007.

43. Dipankar Sengupta, Debashis Chakraborty, and Pritam Banerjee (eds.), *Beyond the Transition Phase of WTO* (New Delhi: Academic Foundation, 2006), 21.

44. Rajiv Kumar, 'Introduction', in Suparna Karmakar, Rajiv Kumar, Bibek Debroy (eds.), *India's Liberalisation Experience: Hostage to the WTO?* (New Delhi: Indian Council for Research on International Economic Relations, 2007), 26.

45. See Sen's comments in P. S. Suryanarayana, 'India will continue to grow, says Amartya Sen', *The Hindu*, 19 February 2009: 'When the last Doha Round [of global trade talks] got busted, basically, the Chinese, the Indians, and the Brazilians didn't

like what was being proposed . . . And, they wanted a bigger concession [on agriculture] . . . The Chinese, the Indians, and the Brazilians were right to demand it. On the other hand, the Europeans and Americans had put on the table some concessions which would have been very good for Africa. Now, when China, India, and Brazil busted the Doha Round, it served their interests quite well. It did not serve the interests of Africa.'

46. Reddy, *India's Policy*, 45.
47. Raja Mohan, *Crossing the Rubicon*, 46.
48. Tad Daley, 'Can the UN Stretch to Fit its Future?' *The Bulletin of the Atomic Scientists*, 48/3 (1992), 41.
49. Dixit, *India's Foreign Policy*, 273. Later, the George W. Bush Administration, which had clashed with Germany in the UNSC over Iraq in 2003, limited itself to explicit support for Japan, while remaining open, in principle, to the possibility of other permanent members.
50. Chinmaya R. Gharekhan, *The Horseshoe Table: An Inside view of the UN Security Council* (New Delhi: Longman, 2006), 3. Gharekhan's book is a remarkable dispassionate and insightful account of events and dynamics at the UN roughly covering the 1990s.
51. Extensive interviews of UN delegates in New York by the author in December 1996, after the election, suggested that the CTBT conference was a factor for a number of developing countries in the election.
52. Prime Minister Manmohan Singh's Address to the Joint Session of United States Congress, Washington, DC, 19 July 19, 2005: www.indianembassy.org/press_release/2005/July/23.htm Emphasis added.
53. C. Raja Mohan, 'India and the New World Order', *Seminar*, 29 August 2003.
54. Maharajakrishna Rasgotra, 'Foreign policy must meet the needs of the 21st century', *The Tribune* (Chandigarh), India at Sixty—Special Supplement, 15 August 2007.
55. Yoshita Singh, 'India to be elected as non-permanent member of UNSC', *Business Standard*, 11 May 2010.
56. BBC News, 'India-Russia nuclear deal signed', 5 December 2009.
57. Pratap Bhanu Mehta, 'Five Balancing Acts', *Seminar*, 560, 1 January 2007.
58. Paul Blustein, *Misadventures of the Most Favored Nations: Clashing Egos, Inflated Ambitions, and the Great Shambles of the World Trade System* (New York: Public Affairs, 2009), 67, 96.
59. Sengupta et al., *Beyond the Transition*, 29.
60. See Aaditya Mattoo and Arvind Subramaniam, 'India and the Multilateral Trading System Post-Doha: Defensive or Proactive?' in Aaditya Mattoo and Robert M. Stern (eds.), *India and the WTO* (Washington, DC: World Bank and Oxford University Press, 2003), 328.
61. Sengupta et al., *Beyond the Transition*, 31.
62. Bibek Debroy, 'India's Economic Liberalisation and the WTO', in Suparna Karmakar, Rajiv Kumar, and Bibek Debroy (eds.), *India's Liberalisation Experience: Hostage to the WTO?* (New Delhi: Indian Council for Research on International Economic Relations, 2007), 40–1.

63. Blustein, *Misadventures*, 183.
64. Debashis Chakraborty and Amir Ullah Khan, *The WTO Deadlocked: Understanding the Dynamics of International Trade* (New Delhi: SAGE, 2008), 2.
65. Chakraborty and Khan, *The WTO Deadlocked*, 5.
66. Blustein, *Misadventures*, 111.
67. Ibid., 267.
68. Anthony Faiola and Rama Lakshmi, 'Trade Talks Crumble in Feud Over Farm Aid', *Washington Post*, 30 July 2008.
69. Confidential interviews, New Delhi, February 2010.
70. Indian Council of World Affairs, *India and the United Nations*, 185–6.
71. Ashok Desai, 'India and the Uruguay Round', *Economic and Political Weekly*, 23/45–7 (November 1988), 2383.
72. One leading Indian economist noted during a confidential interview that if India's agricultural sector is such a 'mess', then surely successive governments rather than the WTO have a great deal to do with this. Other experts note that India's interest in expanding internationally its services sector was barely mentioned in the WTO rows, suggesting that official decision-making is driven much more by political impulses than the totality of India's actual economic and social needs, setting up a conflict between 'principles and outcomes'. And, in spite of enthusiasm over Nath's theatrics in the short term, his performance today is assessed more critically even by a number of strong Indian nationalists as 'too abrasive'. (Conversations in Delhi, January and February 2010.)
73. Rituparna Bhuyan, 'WTO meet: Taking the Doha Round forward', *Indian Express*, 4 September 2009. Anwarul Hoda, a multilateral trade veteran in the Indian government and former Deputy Director General of the WTO, in conversation in Delhi in February 2010 pointed out that during the 1980s, the USA argued in favour of 'free trade' while developing countries called for 'fair trade', while today it is the reverse.
74. Sonia Gandhi, 'Conflict and Coexistence in Our Age', *Seminar*, 521 (7 February 2003).
75. On trade, see Mattoo and Subramaniam, 'India and the Multilateral Trading System', 327; Sengupta et al., *Beyond the Transition*, 24; and Blustein, *Misadventures*, 111. On climate change, see Prem Shankar Jha, 'Indian Public Perceptions of the International Climate Negotiations', in David Michel and Amit Pandya (eds.), *Indian Climate Policy: Choices and Challenges* (Washington, DC: The Henry L. Stimson Center, 2009), 30; 'Silver Linings', *Indian Express*, 21 December 2009; and Saubhik Chakrabarti, 'The us-versus-us debate', *Indian Express*, 21 December 2009.
76. James Lamont, 'An appetite to lead on climate and trade', *Financial Times*, 29 January 2010.
77. Ibid.
78. Conversation, February 2010.
79. A useful discussion of the 'common but differentiated responsibilities' principle by the Centre on International Sustainable Development Law of McGill University is to be found at: www.cisdl.org/pdf/brief_common
80. For President Hu's speech to the UN Climate Change Summit in New York on 23 September 2009, see www.china-un.org/eng/xnyfgk/t606111.htm

81. See One India news story, 'India not in a position to pledge emission cuts', http://news.oneindia.in/2009/07/20/india-carbon-emission-targets-hillary-clinton.html

82. See text of a conversation between Dr. Singh and Council on Foreign Relations President Richard Haas, the transcript of which is dated 22 November 2009 and is available at: www.cfr.org/publication/20840/conversation_with_prime_minister_dr_manmohan_singh.html

83. Nitin Sethi, 'Jairam for major shift at climate talks', *Times of India*, 19 October 2009.

84. Ibid.

85. On concerns in India over acting under any perceived outside pressure, see Lola Nayar, 'Charcoal Sam was here: is India shifting its stand on climate change under US pressure?', *Outlook*, 2 November 2009.

86. Aarti Dhar, 'Jairam irons out differences with negotiators', *The Hindu*, 7 December 2009.

87. For example, see D. Raghunandan, 'India's offer on emissions: Each nation for itself', *Economic Times*, 7 December 2009.

88. For an analysis of India's negotiating quandary going into the Copenhagen conference, see Dhruva Jaishankar, 'Taking the Heat: Where India stands on climate change', *Pragati*, 33 (December 2009), 3–5.

89. Praful Bidwai, *An India That Can Say Yes: A Climate-Responsible Development Agenda for Copenhagen and Beyond* (New Delhi: Heinrich Boll Foundation, 2009). For a thoughtful critique of Bidwai's volume see Lawrence Surendra, 'Posturing as Policy: A Critique of India's Position on Climate Change', *Frontline*, 16 July 2010, 73–6.

90. Evan A. Feigenbaum, 'India's Rise, America's Interest', *Foreign Affairs*, 89/2 (March/April 2010), 90.

91. 'Silver linings', *Indian Express*, 21 December 2010.

92. 'Far from inspiring', *The Hindu*, 21 December 2009.

93. Interview, New Delhi, February 2010.

94. Interview, New Delhi, February 2010.

95. Confidential interviews, 2009 and 2010. See also 'Obama Praises PM: When he talks at G-20, people listen', *The Indian Express*, 29 June 2010.

96. David Michel, 'Introduction', in Michel and Pandya (eds.), *Indian Climate Policy*, 1.

97. Conversation, Delhi, 2010.

98. 'India reluctant to join de-dollarization chorus at BRIC', *Asian News International*, 15 June 2009. India also does not hold as much in US Treasuries as China and Russia do, and this might add to its reluctance to join their chorus. The BRIC acronym, coined by Goldman Sachs global research chief Jim O'Neill in 2001, may be the least convincing of the new forums for diplomacy insofar as the characteristics of its members vary greatly. While China, India, and Brazil are genuinely emerging and fast-growing powers, including demographically, Russia is a country that spent much of the 1990s in steep decline,is buoyed economically only by its oil and gas sector, and is afflicted with serious demographic atrophy.

99. G. Parthasarathy points out, rightly, that the West was very slow to notice this evolution of Indian foreign policy, in particular its growing engagement with ASEAN and other Asian actors. (Conversation, February 2010).

100. A particular perspective on India and Central Asia is offered by Emilian Kavalski in *India and Central Asia: The Mythmaking and International Relations of a Rising Power* (London/New York: I.B. Tauris, 2010), which interprets India's claim to emerging power status as rooted in its nuclear capability rather than in its sustained economic growth pattern of the last two decades. He rejects a vision of India as a 'model' for Central Asia, and views its power of attraction as verging on nil. While some of the analysis is sharp, and the point of view is bracing (see in particular 195–211), overall his interpretation of India is highly questionable.

101. Interview, February 2010.

102. Gladys Lechini, 'Middle Powers: IBSA and the New South-South Cooperation', *NACLA Report on the Americas* (September/October 2007), 29.

103. Daniel Flemes, '"Emerging Middle Powers" Soft Balancing Strategy: State and Perspectives of the IBSA Dialogue Forum', *Working Paper*, 57 (Hamburg: German Institute of Global and Area Studies, August 2007), 6.

104. S. D. Muni in an interesting volume, *India's Foreign Policy: The Democracy Dimension* (New Delhi: Foundation Books, 2009) on page 35 cites Prime Minister Manmohan Singh on his discussions with president Bush in Washington on 19 July 2005, during which he invoked shared democracy, endorsed a Global Democracy Initiative and spoke of India's decision to contribute $10 million to the UN Democracy Fund.

105. Conversation with Rajiv Kumar, Delhi, February 2010.

106. At its 2007 Summit in Delhi, the most exciting feature of the meeting in some respects was the flagging off of a regional car rally.

107. Conversations, Delhi, January and February 2010.

108. Shankar Acharya consulted in conversation in Delhi, February 2010.

109. I am grateful to economist Anwarul Hoda for sparking these thoughts during a conversation in Delhi, February 2010.

110. Correspondence with the author, 10 August 2010.

111. Confidential interview, May 2008.

112. Multiple interviews, 2007–10.

113. Confidential discussion, April 2008.

114. Navroz K. Dubash, 'Climate Politics in India: How Can the Industrialized World Bridge the Trust Deficit?' in Michel and Pandya (eds.), *Indian Climate Policy*, 49.

115. Interview, January 2010 and correspondence with Mr. Singh, February 2010.

116. Sandeep Joshi, 'Jairam Ramesh: India will not accept legally binding emission cuts', *The Hindu*, 25 November 2010.

117. Sindhu Manjesh, 'Talking Past Each Other', *Times of India*, 25 November 2009.

118. Ibid.

119. 'Jairam to make statement on Copenhagen accord today', *The Hindu*, 21 December 2009 and (for the editorial) 'Far from inspiring', also 21 December 2009.

120. 'Silver Linings', *Indian Express*, 21 December 2009.

121. Conversations, Delhi, February 2010.

122. Conversation, Delhi, February 2010.

123. Confidential correspondence, January 2010.

124. Nitin Desai, 'When two's company', *Times of India*, 4 January 2010.
125. Confidential Interview, Delhi, February 2010.
126. Confidential Interview, Delhi, February 2010. This judgement was also related to one of 'reactiveness' in India's policy on Afghanistan.
127. Jawaharlal Nehru, *Jawaharlal Nehru's Speeches 1949–53* (Delhi, 1954), 144, cited in Appadorai and Rajan, *India's Foreign Policy and Relations*, 494.
128. Interview, February 2010.
129. Confidential interview, Delhi, February 2010.

Chapter 12

1. Anand Giridharadas, 'Once-Clear Thoughts Are Clouded', *International Herald Tribune*, 19 June 2009. Giridharadas comments more extensively on change in India in *India Calling: An Intimate Portrait of a Nation's Remaking* (New York, NY: Times Books, 2011 (forthcoming)).
2. On Nehru's approach to foreign policy, see Srinath Raghavan, *War and Peace in Modern India: A Strategic History of the Nehru Years* (New Delhi: Permanent Black, 2010), 12–25.
3. Conversation with the author, 19 March 2010, and then correspondence, 4 April 2010.
4. Ramachandra Guha, *India After Gandhi: The History of the World's Largest Democracy* (New York: Harper Collins, 2007), 153.
5. See John Kenneth Galbraith, *Ambassador's Journal* (London: H. Hamilton, 1969). Canada's Escott Reid, in *Envoy to Nehru*, was more frustrated with Indian officialdom than the urbane Galbraith, but also sought to convince Ottawa, throughout much of the 1950s, of the need to assess Indian policies from the perspective of India's own interests and experiences, although he was highly critical of New Delhi's pro-Hanoi tilt in Indochina and the hash New Delhi made of the Hungary crisis in 1956. See Escott Reid, *Envoy to Nehru* (Delhi/Toronto: Oxford University Press, 1981). See also Walter Crocker, *Nehru, A Contemporary's Estimate* (New York: Oxford University Press, 1966). (The book was reissued in India in 2008 by Random House, with an introduction by Ramachandra Guha.) Crocker, twice Australia's envoy to India between 1952 and 1962, was sympathetic to India's dilemma in crafting foreign policy during an unforgiving decade and wrote favourably of Nehru, but believed he over-indulged the theatrical Krishna Menon, who eventually, as Defence Minister, assumed much of the blame for the calamitous border war with China in 1962. Nehru seemed amused by Menon's histrionics but probably underestimated how thoroughly Menon alienated Western capitals. Nobel prize winner Alva Myrdal, Sweden's Ambassador to India (1955–61), according to her daughter, the moral philosopher Sissela Bok, 'found [Menon] unprincipled and manipulative'. See Sissela Bok, *Alva Myrdal: A Daughter's Memoir* (New York: Perseus Books, 1991), 252. Harish Kapur, who produced a severe assessment of Nehru as a foreign policy actor, quotes a cable from the UK High Commission in India describing him as 'over-idealistic,

inexperienced in foreign affairs, and far too vain'. See Harish Kapur, *Foreign Policies of India's Prime Ministers* (New Delhi: Lancer, 2009), 74.

6. Octavio Paz, *In Light of India* (New York: Harvest Books, 1995). Like Myrdal, Octavio Paz was a Nobel Prize winner in due course.

7. Robert L. Beisner, *Dean Acheson: A Life in the Cold War* (Oxford/New York: Oxford University Press, 2006), 508.

8. Ibid.

9. His grandfather, John Welsh Dulles, had been a missionary in India.

10. Guha, *India After Gandhi*, 527.

11. See Simon Chesterman, Thomas M. Franck, and David M. Malone, *The Law and Practice of the United Nations* (Oxford: Oxford University Press, 2008), 444–5.

12. An excellent analysis of Indian foreign policy under Indira Gandhi can be found in Shashi Tharoor, *Reasons of State: Political Development and India's Foreign Policy under Indira Gandhi, 1966–1977* (New Delhi: Vikas, 1982), particularly 342–426. With India's international standing on the wane after 1971, he ends with a withering summation on p. 363, incorporating a comment by Mrs Gandhi during an interview with him on 15 July 1977: 'It was a measure of the lack of imagination and flexibility of India's application of its dogmas that Mrs Gandhi could complacently declare at the end of her first tenure: "I have had no change in my views in these years. I think that what has been happening [in the world] has only confirmed my original views . . ." She cited the West's changed views towards the Arabs and China as her vindication. Therein lay the essential weakness of Indian foreign policy: in the last analysis the Prime Minister justified it not because of results, but because, in some abstract conception, it was right.'

13. On the latter two points, see Sunil Khilnani, *The Idea of India* (New Delhi: Penguin, 1998), 96.

14. Maharajakrishna Rasgotra, 'Foreign policy must meet the needs of the 21st century', *The Tribune* (Chandigarh), *India at Sixty*—Special Supplement, 15 August 2007.

15. John Cherian, 'A different world', *Frontline*, 15 January 2010.

16. Brian Mulroney, Canadian Prime Minister from 1984 to 1993, worked hardest among international leaders, alongside Rajiv Gandhi, to combat the apartheid regime.

17. See Pranay Gupta, 'Music in the Desert: India warms up to the Arab world—vital in itself and in its effects', *Outlook*, 15 March 2010.

18. A 32-page essay by author and activist Arundhati Roy ('Walking with the comrades', *Outlook*, 29 March 2010) recounting several days spent among Naxalite insurgents on the march provoked a furore in India nearly as large as that following the massacre days later of seventy-four Indian security officers by Naxalites on 7 April 2010, following on several other massacres, notably on 17 February 2010 in Phulwari, Bihar. All served to remind Indians that this insurgency, while unfolding far from the major Indian cities, remains potent.

19. Interview, January 2010, and correspondence, 18 February 2010.

20. G. Pathasarathy, 'Afpak for Dummies: A Primer', *World Affairs*, 172/3 (January/February 2010), 72.

21. Correspondence with the author, 18 April 2010.
22. Interview with the author, February 2010, and correspondence, 23 March 2010.
23. Shiv Shankar Menon, 'Hostile Relations India's Pakistan dilemma', *Harvard International Review* (22 September 2009): www.allbusiness.com/government/government-bodies-offices/13490404-1.html
24. A. G. Noorani provides an incisive analysis of early China–India relations through the prism of a summit meeting between Nehru and Chinese Prime Minister Zhou En Lai in April 1960. See 'Fateful Handshakes', *Frontline*, 4 June 2010, 85–7.
25. See an interesting essay on Asian, particularly Chinese, economic prospects and likely challenges in years to come: Shahid Javed Burki, 'Asia in the "Catch-Up" Game', *ISAS Working Paper*, 106 (9 April 2010).
26. Interview, January 2010, and correspondence, 18 February 2010.
27. See John Cherian, 'Grabbing Africa', *Frontline*, 7 May 2010.
28. See, for example, Alex Vines, Lillian Wong, Markus Weimer, and Indira Campos, *Thirst for African Oil: Asian National Oil Companies in Nigeria and Angola*, a Chatham House Report (London: Royal Institute of International Affairs, August 2009): www.chathamhouse.org.uk.
29. See Yazeed Fakier and Adekeye Adebajo (eds.), *Crouching Tiger, Hidden Dragon? China and Africa*, Policy Seminar Report (Cape Town: Centre for Conflict Resolution, 2009).
30. Martin Wolf, 'India's elephant charges on through the economic crisis', *Financial Times*, 3 March 2010.
31. This possible course of action is discussed helpfully by M. Vidyasagar in 'A Nuclear Power by any name', *Pragati*, 34 (January 2010), http://pragati.nationalinterest.in/2010/01/a-nuclear-power-by-any-name See also David Fidler and Sumit Ganguly, 'Singh's shrewd move: a shift on India's nuclear policy', *Newsweek*, 4 December 2009.
32. Shyam Saran, 'Delink Indo-Pak: The NPT Review Conference and Its Likely Implications for India', *Times of India*, 26 March 2010.
33. Edward Luce, *In Spite of the Gods: The Strange Rise of Modern India* (London: Abacus Books, 2007), 288. See Luce more extensively on Indian diplomacy, 266–8 and 287–9.
34. See George K. Tanham, *Indian Strategic Thought: An Interpretive Essay* (Santa Monica, CA: Rand, 1992).
35. Correspondence with the author, 3 May 2010.
36. Srinath Raghavan, 'Virtues of being vague', *Asian Age*, 8 January 2010.
37. 'Emerging Powers, Global Security and the Middle East', organized by New York University's Centre on International Cooperation and the Abu Dhabi Institute, 8–10 February 2010. For the conference report, see www.cic.nyu.edu
38. Harsh V. Pant, 'Indian Foreign and Security Policy: Beyond Nuclear Weapons', *The Brown Journal of World Affairs*, 15/2 (Spring/Summer 2009), 236.
39. Correspondence with the author, 6 April 2010.
40. See David M. Malone, 'Foreign Policy Reviews Reconsidered', *International Journal*, 56/4 (Autumn 2001), 555–78.

41. Kanti Bajpai, 'India in the World', in Niraja Gopal Jayal and Pratap Bhanu Mehta (eds.), *The Oxford Companion to Politics in India* (New Delhi: Oxford University Press, 2010), 538.

42. Correspondence with the author, 23 March 2010.

43. Correspondence with the author, 20 June 2010.

44. Sandeep Dikshit, 'India and Pakistan put dialogue back on track', *The Hindu*, 30 April 2010.

45. Correspondence with the author, 24 June 2010.

46. For an excellent, dispassionate recent account of conditions in Kashmir, see Basharat Peer, *Curfewed Night: One Kashmiri Journalist's Frontline Account of Life, Love, and War in His Homeland* (New York: Scribner, 2010).

47. See Gautam Navlakha, 'Shooting Down Slogans: Treating protest as terror in Kashmir is a gross error of proportion', *Outlook*, 24 May 2010, 24.

48. See Siddharth Varadarajan, 'This is not zero tolerance, Mr. Prime Minister', *The Hindu*, 4 June 2010. Impunity would be much greater without brave Indian investigative media reporting.

49. Correspondence with the author, 18 April 2010.

50. Sushant K. Singh and Rohit Pradhan, 'Fewer troops in the Kashmiri heartland', *Pragati*, 28 (July 2009), http://pragati.nationalinterest.in/2009/07/fewer-troops-in-the-kashmiri-heartland/

51. 'Green lights rather than red lines' was a recurring theme of the excellent Ditchley Foundation conference on India in March 2010, 'Is India ready for super-power status?', of which a summary can be found at www.ditchley.co.uk/page/365/india.htm

52. See Gautam Mukhopadhaya, 'India', in A. J. Tellis and A. Mukharji (eds.), *Is A Regional Strategy Viable in Afghanistan* (Washington, DC: Carnegie Endowment for International Peace, 2010), 27–37.

53. See Nitin Pai and Rohit Pradhan, 'Why India Must Send Troops to Afghanistan', *Pragati*, 34 (January 2010), http://pragati.nationalinterest.in/2010/01/why-india-must-send-troops-to-afghanistan/

54. See John Cherian, 'Stronger Ties: Vladimir Putin signs a slew of defence and civil nuclear deals during his recent visit to India', *Frontline*, 9 April 2010, 44–6. See also Dmitri Trenin and Alexei Malashenko, *Afghanistan: A View from Moscow*, a research paper for the Carnegie Endowment for International Peace, 2010, particularly p. 22.

55. Correspondence with the author, 20 June 2010. See also Pankaj Mishra, 'The India & Pakistan Connection', *New York Review of Books*, 57/1 (14 January 2010); and see, in the same issue of the NYRB, Rory Stewart, 'Afghanistan: What Could Work'. Equally relevant to Afghanistan and Pakistan, see Ahmed Rashid, 'A Deal with the Taliban?', *New York Review of Books*, 57/3 (25 February 2010).

56. For an Indian perspective on the great encirclement debate, see P.S. Das, 'India and the Indian Ocean Littoral: Opportunities and Challenges', *Indian Foreign Policy Journal*, 4/4 (October–December 2009), 1–32.

57. Correspondence with Kamalesh Sharma, 16 July 2010.

58. Shyam Saran, 'Premature Power', *Bussiness Standard*, 17 March 2010.

59. See a presentation by Arvind Virmani, then Chief Economic Advisor in India's Finance Ministry, on 19 March 2009, available at: www.cprindia.org/semiid.php? s=82 with further data and arguments on 10 March 2010 available at http://info. worldbank.org/etools/docs/WBIvideos/avirmani/avirmani.html

60. See Kishmore Mahbubani, *Can Asians Think? Understanding the Divide Between East and West* (Hanover, NH: Steerforth Press, 2001); and *The New Asian Hemisphere: The Irresistible Shift of Global Power to the East* (New York: Public Affairs Books, 2008).

61. Discussion of Asia's rise nowadays generally ignores Japan's role even though it remains a powerful economic actor that, with more effective political leadership and a less hidebound bureaucracy, might well emerge again as a key player in a triangle of economic power relationships on the continent, with South Korea, Indonesia, and Australia exerting some influence on their periphery. Of course, at present, both India and China enjoy tremendous momentum, while Japan's economy is becalmed and deflation has been eroding it alarmingly for extended periods.

62. Correspondence with Dimitri Streltsov of the Moscow State Institute of International Relations, 3 April 2010.

63. The idea of Asians as 'rule takers' rather than 'rule makers' is one that Ramesh Thakur has frequently developed. See, for example, a presentation available at: http://apcd.anu.edu.au/pdf/Thakur_Diplomatic_Update.pdf

64. Correspondence with Sir Michael Arthur, 12 April 2010.

65. Bill Emmott, *Rivals: How the Power Struggle between China, India and Japan will Shape Our Next Decade* (London/New York: Allen Lane, 2008), 274.

66. In China, the argument that India's international status today hinges mainly or solely on its economic growth is not accepted by everyone. Li Li of the China Institutes of Contemporary International Relations believes that India's nuclear weapons status is, in its case, equally relevant. Correspondence with the author on 6 April 2010.

67. This point is made repeatedly and in different ways in two remarkable books on India's economy: Arvind Panagariya, *India: The Emerging Giant* (Oxford/New York: Oxford University Press, 2008); and Shankar Acharya and Rakesh Mohan (eds.), *India's Economy: Performance and Challenges* (New Delhi: Oxford University Press, 2010), including excellent chapters by Martin Wolf (on India in the world) and Anne Krueger (on India's trade), 369–429.

68. See Sanjaya Baru, 'Economic Meltdown and Geopolitical Stability', in Ashley Tellis, Andrew Marble and Travis Tanner (eds.), *Strategic Asia 2009–2010* (Seattle, WA: The National Bureau of Asian Research, 2009), 199–230.

69. The appointment of Kapil Sibal, one of the more impressive, dynamic, younger Congress Party politicians, as Human Resources Development Minister in 2009 is encouraging for reform of this sector, but the challenge is sufficiently large that actual optimism would seem premature. Efforts to attract foreign universities to India, which at best could only represent a partial response to the country's pressing needs, may not be successful given the balance of incentives being offered by India in legislation tabled mid-2010. See Arunadha Raman, 'Shadows of the Dreamy Spires', *Outlook*, 5 April 2010.

70. Correspondence with the author, 4 April 2010.

71. See Harish Damodaran, *India's New Capitalists: Caste, Business, and Industry in a Modern Nation* (New York: Palgrave Macmillan, 2008).

72. Conversation, Delhi, February 2010.

73. Interview with Analjit Singh, 2 February 2010.

74. Correspondence with the author, 24 June 2010.

75. See Ramesh Thakur, 'India is the solution', *The Ottawa Citizen*, 3 July 2010. This startling figure may be less stark than it looks. A nominal income of 50 cents (US) translates into a purchasing power parity income of $2 per day, considerably above the World Bank-researched international poverty line of $1.25 a day. Nevertheless, the Indian state-run National Commission for Enterprises in the Unorganised Sector (NCEUS) found in 2007 that 77 per cent of Indians, or 836 million people, lived on less than this sum, a finding that, while contested, highlighs the extent of poverty in the country.

76. For example, in 'India's dysfunctional police', *The Hindu*, 26 January 2007.

77. A compelling version of the argument that India should do more to promote democracy is offered by James Purnell, 'India Should Be More Like Google', *New Statesman*, 19 April 2010.

78. On India's delicate Iran diplomacy, see Pranay Sharma, 'A Dear Old Isotope: Side-lined in Af-Pak, India Warms to Iran, Rehearses an Old Role', *Outlook*, 3 May 2010, 58–9.

79. C. Raja Mohan, 'India's New Foreign Policy Strategy', paper presented at a seminar in Beijing by China Reform Forum and the Carnegre Endowment for International Peace, Beijing, 26 May 2006, available at http://www.carnegreendowment.org

80. S. D. Muni, *India's Foreign Policy: The Democracy Dimension* (New Delhi: Foundation Books, 2009), *passim* but particularly 125–39.

81. See J. C. Sharma, 'India Around the World', in Atish Sinha and Madhup Mohta (eds.), *Indian Foreign Policy: Challenges and Opportunities* (New Delhi: Academic Foundation of India, 2007), 1111–34.

82. Government of India, Ministry of Overseas Indian Affairs, *Annual Report 2008–2009* (New Delhi: MOIA, 2009), 5. Of these, the largest number of overseas Indians reside in South East Asia (32 per cent) and the Gulf (19 per cent). See International Migration and Diaspora Studies Project, Binod Khadria (ed.), *India Migration Report 2009: Past, Present and the Future Outlook* (New Delhi: JNU, 2009).

83. *Report of the High Level Committee on the Indian Diaspora* (Commissioned by the Ministry of External Affairs, 2001): www.indiandiaspora.nic.in/contents.htm

84. Government of India, Ministry of Overseas Indian Affairs, *Annual Report* 2008–9.

85. Sudhir Devare, *India and South-East Asia: Towards Security Convergence* (Singapore: ISEAS Publications, 2006), 175.

86. 'Secretary Clinton Goes to India', *New York Times*, 17 July 2009.

87. Strobe Talbott, 'A Tough Message to India on Climate Change, Non-proliferation', *Financial Times*, 16 July 2009.

88. Barbara Crossette, 'The Elephant in the Room', *Foreign Policy* (January/February 2010).

89. While India's private sector continues to project a positive imagine of Indian entrepreneurship abroad, notions of 'India Shining' are seriously undermined by

inept government management of large-scale projects such as preparations for the Commonwealth Games of October 2010 that seemed to disintegrate into chaos in the immediate run-up to this international event that India had been long been preparing for. That the Games themselves came off quite well is unlikely to erase memories abroad of the shambolic final days of preparation before the opening ceremony. While there is much more the private sector can do in India, the state must continue to play a central role in the country's future, and the quality of government and wider governance needs to improve significantly. On this score, any sober prognosis must remain guarded at best for now, given recent trends discussed particularly in Chapter 3.

90. Daniel Markey, 'Developing India's Foreign Policy "Software"', *Asian Policy*, 8 (July 2009), 73–96. See also Muthiah Alagappa, 'Galvanizing international studies: India's rising profile demands investment in intellectual foundations', *Pragati*, 30 (September 2009), 11–16.

91. The MEA's staffing by mostly very talented generalists has served it well in the past in an era of resource scarcity. As India's interests become ever more entwined with the global economy, and negotiations in global forums of an essentially technical nature proliferate, the ministry would probably do well to encourage a greater extent of specialization alongside the basic skills required of all diplomats.

92. On this point, see Arun Shourie, 'India and its Neighbours', in Tan Tai Yong (ed.), *Challenges of Economic Growth, Inequality and Conflict in South Asia* (Singapore: World Scientific Press, 2010), 21.

93. Several retired officials render admirable public service by commenting sharply on policy. K. Subrahmanyam, India's foremost strategic thinker, often cited in this book, comes to mind. Among foreign policy dynasties in India, including the Bajpais and the Menons, Subramanyam's, including his son S. Jaishankar, currently India's Ambassador to China, and his grandson Dhruva Jaishankar, a denizen of the Washington think-tank world and Indian op-ed pages, constitutes a remarkable one.

94. Correspondence with the author, 13 June 2010.

95. Shyam Saran, 'Premature Power', *Financial Standard*, 17 March 2010.

96. Geoff Dyer, 'Brazil and India join renminbi protests', *Financial Times*, 22 April 2010, the headline story of the day in this newspaper. Questioning the cohesion of the BRIC grouping, see 'The BRICs: The Trillion-dollar club', *Economist*, 17 April 2010, 59–61.

97. The idea of a 'hedging strategy' is drawn from a speech by Shyam Saran at the India Habitat Centre on 26 April 2010, available at: www.defenceforum.in/forum/showthread.php/9839-Geopolitical-Consequences-of-the-Global-Financial-and-Economic-Crisis-A-Reassessment

98. Correspondence with the author, 6 April 2010.

99. Correspondence with the author, 13 April 2010.

Bibliography

Books

Indian history

Abu-Lughod, J. L. (1991). *Before European Hegemony: The World System A.D. 1250–1350.* New York: Oxford University Press.

Anderson, B. (1991). *Imagined Communities.* London: Verso.

Bagchi, P. C. (1971). *India and China: A Thousand Years of Cultural Relations.* 2nd edn. Westport, CT: Greenwood Press.

Baker, D. E. U. (2007). *Baghelkhand, or the Tiger's Lair: Region and Nation in Indian History.* New Delhi: Oxford University Press.

Bandyopadhyay, S. (2008). *From Plassey to Partition: A History of Modern India.* New Delhi: Orient Blackswan.

—— (ed.) (2009). *Nationalist Movement in India: A Reader.* New Delhi: Oxford University Press.

Basham, A. L. (1954). *The Wonder that was India.* London: Sidgwick & Jackson.

Borsa, G. (ed.) (1990). *Trade and Politics in the Indian Ocean: Historical and Contemporary Perspectives.* New Delhi: Manohar.

Chakravarti, R. (ed.) (2001). *Trade in Early India.* New Delhi: Oxford University Press.

Chandra, B., Mukherjee, M., and Mukherjee, A. (2000). *India After Independence 1947–2000.* New Delhi: Penguin.

Chatterjee, P. (1999). *The Partha Chatterjee Omnibus.* New Delhi: Oxford University Press.

Dalmia, V. and von Stietencron, H. (eds.) (2007). *The Oxford India Hinduism Reader.* New Delhi: Oxford University Press.

Devadas, D. (2007). *In Search of a Future: The Story of Kashmir.* New Delhi: Viking/ Penguin.

Eaton, R. M. (2005). *A Social History of the Deccan, 1300–1761: Eight Indian Lives.* Cambridge: Cambridge University Press.

Furber, H. (1976). *Rival Empires of Trade in the Orient, 1600–1800.* Minneapolis: University of Minnesota Press.

Guha, R. (1997). *Subaltern Studies: Writings on South Asian History and Society,* Vol. I. New Delhi: Oxford University Press.

—— (2007). *India After Gandhi: The History of the World's Largest Democracy.* New York: Harper Collins.

Jalal, A. and Bose, S. (2004). *Modern South Asia: History, Culture, Political Economy.* New Delhi: Oxford University Press.

Kapila, U. (ed.) (2001). *Indian Economy Since Independence.* New Delhi: Academic Foundations.

Karlekar, H. (1998). *Independent India: The First fifty Years.* Delhi: Oxford University Press.

Keay, J. (2000). *India: A History.* London: Harper Collins.

Khan, Y. (2007). *The Great Partition: The Making of India and Pakistan.* New Delhi: Viking/Penguin.

Kumar, S. (2007). *The Emergence of the Delhi Sultanate 1192–1286.* New Delhi: Permanent Black.

Marston, D. P., and Sundaram, C. S. (eds.) (2007). *A Military History of India and South Asia: From the East India Company to the Nuclear Era.* Bloomington: Indiana University Press.

Mathur, V. (2006). *Foreign Trade of India 1947–2007: Trends, Policies and Prospects.* New Delhi: New Century Publications.

Metcalf, B. D. and Metcalf, T. R. (2002). *A Concise History of India.* Cambridge: Cambridge University Press.

Misra, M. (2007). *Vishnu's Crowded Temple: India Since the Great Rebellion.* London: Allen Lane.

Mukherjee, M. (2010). *Churchill's Secret War: The British Empire and the Ravaging of India during World War II.* Delhi: Tranquebar Press.

Müller, F. M. (2003). *India: What Can It Teach Us.* New Delhi: Rupa & Co.

Nilakanta Sastri, K. A. (1966). *A History of South India.* New Delhi: Oxford University Press.

Noorani, A. G. (2010). *India–China Boundary Problem, 1846–1947.* New Delhi: Oxford University Press.

Pannikkar, K. M. (1945). *India and the Indian Ocean: An Essay on the Influence of Sea Power on Indian History.* London: George Allen & Unwin.

Prakash, O. (1998). *The New Cambridge History of India: European Commercial Enterprise in Pre-Colonial India.* Cambridge: Cambridge University Press.

Raghavan, S. (2009). *War and Peace in Modern India: A Strategic History of the Nehru Years.* London: Palgrave Macmillan.

Raju, S., Kumar, M. S., and Corbridge, S. (eds.) (2006). *Colonial and Post-Colonial Geographies of India.* New Delhi: Sage.

Raychaudhari, T. and Habib, I. (eds.) (1982). *The Cambridge Economic History of India,* Vol. I. Cambridge: Cambridge University Press.

Robbins, K. X. and McLeod, J. (eds.) (2006). *African Elites in India.* Ahmedabad, India: Mapin.

Roy, T. (2000). *The Economic History of India, 1857–1947.* Delhi: Oxford University Press.

Sardesai, D.R. (2010). *Southeast Asia: Past and Present.* 6th edn. Boulder, CO: Westview Press.

Sarkar, S. (2001). *Modern India.* New Delhi: Macmillan.

Singh, U. (2008). *A History of Ancient and Early Medieval India: From the Stone Age to the 12th Century.* New Delhi: Pearson Longman.

Spear, P. (1990). *A History of India,* Vol. II. New Delhi: Penguin Books.

Talbot, P. (2007). *An American Witness to India's Partition.* New Delhi: Sage.

Thapar, R. (1990). *A History of India,* Vol. I. New Delhi: Penguin Books.

—— (2002). *The Penguin History of Early India: From the Origins to AD 1300*. New Delhi: Penguin Books.

Toye, R. (2010). *Churchill's Empire: The World that Made Him and the World He Made*. New York: Henry Holt & Co.

Von Tunzelman, A. (2007). *Indian Summer*. New York: Henry Holt and Sons.

Xinru, L. (1988). *Ancient India and Ancient China: Trade and Religious Exchanges*. New Delhi: Oxford University Press.

Indian's Society economy, and union

Acharya, S. and Mohan, R. (eds.) (2010). *India's Economy: Performance and Challenges*. New Delhi: Oxford University Press.

Aziz, J., Dunaway, S. V., and Prasad, E. (2006). *China and India Learning From Each Other: Reforms and Policies for Sustained Growth*. Washington, DC: IMF.

Baru, S. (2006). *Strategic Consequences of India's Economic Performance*. New Delhi: Academic Foundation.

Bhalla, G. S. (2007). *Indian Agriculture Since Independence*. New Delhi: National Book Trust.

Bissell, W. N. (2009). *Making India Work*. New Delhi: Viking (Penguin).

Chan, W. K. (2006). *Economic liberalization and India's foreign policy*. Delhi: Kalpaz Publications.

Chidambaram, P. C. (2007). *A View from the Outside: Why Good Economics Works for Everyone*. New Delhi/New York: Penguin Book.

Damodaran, H. (2008). *India's New Capitalists: Caste, Business, and Industry in a Modern Nation*. New York: Palgrave Macmillan.

Das, G. (2000). *India Unbound: From Independence to the Global information Age*. New Delhi: Penguin Books India.

Das, V. (ed.) (2004). *Handbook of Sociology in India*. New Delhi: Oxford University Press.

Dev, S. M. (2008). *Inclusive Growth in India: Agriculture, Poverty, and Human Development*. New Delhi: Oxford University Press.

Guha, R. (2006). *How Much Should A Person Consume?: Environmentalism In India And The United States*. New Delhi: Permanent Black.

Gupta, D. (2009). *The Gaged Phoenix: Can India Fly?* New Delhi: Penguin Viking.

Hoda, A. (ed.) (2002). *WTO Agreement & Indian Agriculture*. New Delhi: Social Science Press.

Inden, R. (1990). *Imagining India*. Oxford: Bail Blackwell.

—— (ed.) (2009). *Emerging States: The Wellspring of a New World Order*. New York: Columbia University Press.

Jahanbegloo, R. (2008). *India Revisited: Conversations on Contemporary India*. New Delhi: Oxford University Press.

Karmakar, S., Kumar, R., and Debroy, B. (eds.) (2007). *India's Liberalisation Experience: Hostage to the WTO?* New Delhi: Indian Council for Research on International Economic Relations.

Khalidi, O. (2006). *Muslims in the Indian Economy*. Gurgaon, India: Three Essays Collective.

Khanna, T. (2008). *Billions of Entrepreneurs: How China and India are Reshaping Their Futures—and Yours*. Cambridge, MA: Harvard University Press.

Kumar, N., Mohapatra P., and Chandrasekhar, S. (2009). *India's Global Powerhouses: How They Are Taking On the World*. Cambridge, MA: Harvard Business Press.

Malhoutra, M. (ed.) (2006). *India: The Next Decade*. New Delhi: Academic Foundation.

Mattoo, A. and Stern, R. M. (eds.) (2003). *India and the WTO*. Washington, DC: World Bank and Oxford University Press.

Murthy, N. R. N. (2009). *A Better India, A Better World*. Delhi: Allen Lane.

Nayyar, D. (2007). *India's Exports and Export Policies in the 1960s*. Cambridge: Cambridge University Press.

Nayyar, S. (2004). *India: A Global Power*. New Delhi: Anmol Publications Pvt. Ltd.

Nilekani, N. (2009). *Imagining India: the Idea of a Renewed Nation*. New York: Penguin.

Panagariya, A. (2008). *India: The Emerging Giant*. Oxford/New York: Oxford University Press.

Rothermund, D. (2008). *India: The Rise of an Asian Giant*. New Haven and London: Yale University Press.

Schaffer, T. C. (2005). *Kashmir: The Economics of Peace Building*. Washington, DC: The Center for Strategic and International Studies.

Sengupta, N. (ed.) (2006). *Building A Better Future*. New Delhi: Lotus Collection, Roli Books.

Tharoor, S. (1998). *India: From Midnight to the Millennium*. New York: Harper Perennial.

Varma, P. K. (2005). *Being Indian: Inside the Real India*. London: William Heineman.

Indian Foreign Policy

Abhyankar, R. M. (ed.) (2008). *West Asia and the Region: Defining India's Role*. New Delhi: Academic Foundation.

Alam, A. (ed.) (2008). *India and West Asia in the Era of Globalisation*. New Delhi: New Century Publications.

Appadorai, A. (1982). *Select Documents on India's Foreign Policy and Relations 1947–1972*, Vol. I. New Delhi: Oxford University Press.

—— and Rajan, M. S. (1985). *India's Foreign Policy and Relations*. New Delhi: South Asian Publishers.

Ayoob, M. (1990). *India and Southeast Asia: Indian Perception and Policies*. London: Routledge.

Ayres, A., and Raja Mohan, C. (eds.) (2009). *Power Realignments in Asia: China, India, and the United States*. New Delhi: SAGE.

Bajpai, K. and Mallavarapu, S. (eds.) (2005). *International Relations in India: Theorising the Region and Nation*. New Delhi: Orient Longman.

Bajpai, K. S. (2007). *Democracy and Diversity: India and the American Experience*. New Delhi: Oxford University Press.

Bandyopadhyaya, J. (1970). *The Making of India's Foreign Policy*. New Delhi: Allied.

Basu, P. K., Chellaney, B., Khanna, P., and Khilnani, S. (2005). *India as a New Global Leader*. London: The Foreign Policy centre.

Bidwai, P. (2009). *An India That Can Say Yes: a Climate-Responsible Development Agenda for Copenhagen and Beyond*. New Delhi: Heinrich Boll Foundation.

Blarel, N. (2006). *Inde et Israël: Le Rapprochement Strategique-Pragmatisme et Complementarite*. Paris: L'Harmattan.

Chak Mun, S. (2009). *India's Strategic Interests in Southeast Asia and Singapore*. New Delhi: MacMillan Publishers.

Chakravarti, P. C. (1961). *India–China Relations*. Calcutta: Firma K. L. Mukhopadhyay.

Chamling, D. R. (1978). *India and the United Nations*. New Delhi: Associated Publishing House.

Chari, P. R., Cheema, P. I., and Cohen, S. P. (2008). *Four Crises and a Peace Process: American Engagement in South Asia*. New Delhi: Harper Collins.

Chaudhry, P. K. and Vanduzer-Snow, M. (eds.) (2008). *The United States and India: A History through Archives; The Formative Years*. New Delhi: Sage Publications India Pvt. Ltd.

Cohen, S. P. (2001). *India: Emerging Power*, Washington, DC: Brookings Institution Press.

Damodaran, A. K. (2000). *Beyond Autonomy: Roots of India's Foreign Policy*. New Delhi: Somaiya Publications.

—— and Bajpai, U. S. (eds.) (1990). *Indian Foreign Policy, The Indira Gandhi Years*. New Delhi: Radiant Publishers.

Datta-Ray, S. K. (2009). *Looking East to Look West: Lee Kuan Yew's Mission India*. New Delhi: Penguin Books India.

Dixit, J. N. (1998). *Across Borders: Fifty Years of India's Foreign Policy*. New Delhi: Picus Books.

—— (2003). *India's Foreign Policy 1947–2003*. New Delhi: Picus Books.

—— (2005). *Indian Foreign Service: History and Challenge*. Delhi: Konark Publishers.

Dutt, V. P. (1984). *India's Foreign Policy*. New Delhi: Vikas Publishing House Pvt. Ltd.

—— (1999). *India's Foreign Policy in a Changing World*. New Delhi: Vikas.

Emmott, B. (2008). *Rivals: How the Power Struggle Between China, India and Japan Will Shape Our Next Decade*. London: Allen Lane.

Gaens, B., Jokela, J., and Limnell, E. (eds.) (2009). *The Role of the European Union in Asia: China and India as Strategic Partners*. Surrey: Ashgate.

Ganguly, S. (ed.) (2010). *India's Foreign Policy: Retrospect and Prospect*. New Delhi: Oxford University Press.

Ghosh, A., Chakraborti, T., Majumdar, A. J., and Chatterjee, S. (eds.) (2009). *India's Foreign Policy*. Delhi: Pearson.

Ghosh, L. and Chatterjee, R. (eds.) (2004). *Indian Diaspora in Asian and Pacific Regions*. Jaipur: Rawat Publications.

Ghoshal, B. (ed.) (1996). *India and Southeast Asia: Challenges and Opportunities*. New Delhi: Konark Publishers Pvt. Ltd.

Gordon, S. (1995). *India's Rise to Power in the 21st Century and Beyond*. Houndmills: Macmillan.

Government of India (1962). *Chinese Aggression in War and Peace: Letters of the Prime Minister of India*. Ministry of Information and Broadcasting, Government of India.

Grare, F. and Mattoo, A. (eds.) (2001). *India and ASEAN: The Politics of India's Look East Policy*. New Delhi: Manohar Publishers & Distributors.

Grover, V. (ed.) (1992). *International Relations and Foreign Policy of India*, Vol. IX: *Europe and India's Foreign Policy*. New Delhi: Deep and Deep Publications.

Gujral, I. K. (1998). *A Foreign Policy for India*. New Delhi: Ministry of External Affairs.

—— (2003). *Continuity and Change: India's Foreign Policy*. New Delhi: Macmillan.

Gupta, K. R. and Shukla, V. (2009). *Foreign Policy of India*. New Delhi: Atlantic Publishers and Distributors (P) Ltd.

Harshe, R. and Seethi, K. M. (2005). *Engaging with the World: Critical Reflections on India's Foreign Policy*. New Delhi: Orient Longman.

Indian Council of World Affairs, The. (1957). *India and the United Nations*. New York: Manhattan Publishing Company.

Jaffrelot, C. (ed.) (2008). *New Delhi et le Monde*. Paris: Editions Autrement – CERI.

Jain, B. M. (2008). *Global Power: India's Foreign Policy 1947–2006*. New Delhi: Lexington Books.

Kapur, A. (2006). *India: From Regional to World Power*. New York: Routledge.

Kapur, H. (2009). *Foreign Policies of India's Prime Ministers*. New Delhi: Lancer International.

Karat, P. (2007). *Subordinate Ally: The Nuclear Deal and India–US Strategic Relations*. New Delhi: LeftWord Books.

Kavalski, E. (2010). *India and Central Asia: The Mythmaking and International Relations of a Rising Power*. London/New York: I.B. Tauris.

Kesavpany, K., Mani, A., and Ramasamy, P. (eds.) (2008). *Rising India and Indian Communities in East Asia*. Singapore: ISEAS.

Khanna, P. (2008). *The Second World: Empires and Influence in the New Global Order*. London: Allen Lane.

Khanna, V. N. (1997). *Foreign Policy of India*. New Delhi: Vikas Publishing House Pvt Ltd.

Koshy, N. (2006). *Under the Empire: India's New Foreign Policy*. New Delhi: LeftWord Books.

Kumar, S. and Kapur, P. K. (eds.) (2008). *India of My Dreams*. New Delhi: Foreign Service Institute/Academic Foundation.

Kumaraswamy, P. R. (2010). *India's Israel Policy*. New York: Columbia University Press.

Majumdar, R. C. (1979). *India and South East Asia*. Delhi: B.R. Publishing Corporation.

Mansingh, L. (ed.) (1997). *Indian Foreign Policy Agenda for the 21st Century*, Vol. I. New Delhi: Foreign Service Institute in association with Konark Publishers.

McLeod, D. (2008). *India and Pakistan: Friends, Rivals or Enemies?* Aldershot: Ashgate Publishing Limited.

Mehta, J. S. (2006). *Negotiating for India: Resolving Problems Through Diplomacy; Seven Case Studies, 1958–1978*. New Delhi: Manohar.

—— (2008). *Rescuing the Future: Bequeathed Misperceptions in International Relations*. New Delhi: Manohar.

Menon, R. and Kumar, R. (2010). *The Long View From Delhi: Indian Grand Strategy for Foreign Policy*. Delhi: Academic Foundation.

Michel, D. and Pandya, A. (eds.) (2009). *Indian Climate Policy: Choices and Challenges*. Washington, DC: The Henry L. Stimson Center.

Mishra, A. D. and Prasad, G. (eds.) (2003). *India and Canada: Past, Present and Future*. New Delhi: Mittal Publications.

Mohan, C., Raja (2004). *Crossing the Rubicon: The Shaping of India's New Foreign Policy*. New York: Palgrave Macmillan.

—— (2007). *Impossible Allies: Nuclear India, United States, and the Global Order*. New Delhi: India Research Press.

Muni, S. D. (2009). *India's Foreign Policy: The Democracy Dimension*. New Delhi: Foundation Books.

Nafey, A. and Raj, C. S. (eds.) (2007). *Canada's Global Engagements and Relations with India*. New Delhi: Manak Publications.

Nair, K. S. (2007). *Inside IB and RAW: The Rolling Stones that Gathered Moss*. New Delhi: Manas Books.

Nanda, P. (2003). *Rediscovering Asia: Evolution of India's Look-East Policy*. New Delhi: Lancer Publishers & Distributors.

Narsimhan, S. and Do Young, K. (eds.). *India and Korea: Bridging the Gaps*. New Delhi: Manak Publications.

Nehru, J. (1946). *The Discovery of India*. New Delhi: Penguin Books.

Pant, G. (2008). *India: The Emerging Energy Player*. New Delhi: Dorling Kindersley (India) Pvt. Ltd.

Pant, H. V. (2008). *Contemporary Debates in Indian Foreign Policy: India Negotiates its Rise in the International System*. New York: Palgrave Macmillan.

—— (2008). *Indian Foreign Policy in a Unipolar World*. London: Taylor and Francis.

Paz, O. (1995). *In Light of India*. New York: Harvest Books.

Prasad, B. (1960). *The Origins of Indian Foreign Policy: The Indian National Congress and World Affairs, 1885–1947*. Calcutta: Bookland Pvt. Ltd.

Raj, C. S. and McAndrew, M. (2009). *Multiculturalism: Public Policy and Problem Areas in Canada and India*. New Delhi: Manak Publication.

Raja Reddy, K. (ed.) (2005). *India and ASEAN: Foreign Policy Dimensions for the 21st Century*. New Delhi: New Century Publications.

Rajan, M. S. (1997). *Recent Essays on India's Foreign Policy*. New Delhi: Kalinga Publications.

Ramakrishna Reddy, T. (1968). *India's Policy in the United Nations*. Cranbury, NJ: Associated University Presses.

Rana, K. S. (2007). *Asian Diplomacy: The Foreign Ministries of China, India, Japan, Singapore and Thailand*. Geneva: The Diplomatic Foundation.

Reddy, Y. Yagama (ed.) (2007). *Emerging India in Asia-Pacific*. New Delhi: New Century Publications.

Reid, E. (1981). *Envoy to Nehru*. Delhi/Toronto: Oxford University Press.

Rothermund, D. (2008). *India: The Rise of an Asian Giant*. New Haven, CT: Yale University Press.

Schaffer, T. C. (2009). *India and the United States in the 21st Century: Reinventing Partnership*. Washington, DC: The CSIS Press.

Schleicher, C. P. and Bains, J. S. (1969). *The Administration of Indian Foreign Policy Through the United Nations*. New York: Oceana.

Shankar, K. (2007). *India and the United States: Politics of the Sixties*. New Delhi: Macmillan.

Sikri, R. (2009). *Challenge and Strategy: Rethinking India's Foreign Policy*. New Delhi: Sage Publications Ltd.

Singh, J. (2006). *A Call To Honour: In Service Of Emergent India*. New Delhi: Rupa & Co.

Sinha, A. and Mohta, M. (eds.) (2007). *Indian Foreign Policy: Challenges and Opportunities*. New Delhi: Academic Foundation.

Sridharan, K. (1996). *The ASEAN Region in India's Foreign Policy*. Aldershot: Dartmouth Publishing Company.

Sudarshan, V. (2008). *Anatomy of an Abduction: How the Indian Hostages in Iraq Were Freed*. New Delhi: Penguin.

Talbott, S. (2004). *Engaging India: Diplomacy, Democracy and the Bomb*. Washington, DC: Brookings Institution Press.

Tharoor, S. (1982). *Reasons of State: Political Development and India's Foreign Policy under Indira Gandhi, 1966–1977*. New Delhi: Vikas.

Wadhva, C. D. and Yuen Pau Woo (eds.) (2005). *Asian Regionalism, Canadian and Indian Perspectives*. New Delhi: A P H Publishing Corporation.

Winters, A. and Yusuf, S. (2007). *Dancing With Giants: China, India, and the Global Economy*. Washington, DC: World Bank.

Yahya, F. B. (2008). *Economic Cooperation between Singapore and India: An Alliance in the Making?* New York: Routledge.

Zafar Shah, M. A. (1983). *India and the Superpowers: India's Political Relations with the Superpowers in the 1970s*. Dhaka: University Press.

Indian Politics

Advani, L. K. (2008). *My Country, My Life*. New Delhi: Rupa.

Aiyar, M. S. (2006). *Confessions of a Secular Fundamentalist*. New Delhi: Penguin Books.

Bhargava, R. (ed.) (2008). *Politics and Ethics of the Indian Constitution*. New Delhi: Oxford University Press.

Bose, S. and Jalal, A. (eds.) (1997). *Nationalism, Democracy and Development: State and Politics in India*. New Delhi: Oxford University Press.

Brown, J. M. (2003). *Nehru: A Political Life*. New Delhi: Oxford University Press.

Chhibber, P. K. (1999). *Democracy Without Associations: Transformation of the Party System and Social Cleavages in India*. Ann Arbor: University of Michigan Press.

Crocker, W. (1966). *Nehru, A Contemporary's Estimate*. New York: Oxford University Press.

Fernandes, L. (2006). *India's New Middle Class: Democratic Politics in an Era of Economic Reform*. Minneapolis: University of Minnesota Press.

Hasan, Z. (ed.) (2002). *Parties and Party Politics in India*. New Delhi: Oxford University Press.

Jaffrelot, C. (ed.) (2007). *Hindu Nationalism: A Reader*. New Delhi: Permanent Black.

Jayal, N. G. and Mehta, P. B. (eds.) (2010). *The Oxford Companion to Politics in India*. New Delhi: Oxford University Press.

Kakar, S. (2007). *Indian Identity*. New Delhi: Penguin Books.

Kamdar, M. (2008). *The Turbulent Rise of the Largest Democracy and the Future of Our World*. New York: Scribner.

Khilnani, S. (1998). *The Idea of India*. New Delhi: Penguin.

Malik, Y. K. and Vajpeyi, D. K. (eds.) (1988). *India: The Years of Indira Gandhi*. Leiden: E J Brill.

Nath, K. (2008). *India's Century*. Delhi: Tata McGraw-Hill.

Nayar, B. R. (ed.) (2007). *Globalization and Politics in India*. New Delhi: Oxford University Press.

Nussbaum, M. C. (2007). *The Clash Within: Democracy, Religious Violence and India's Future*. Cambridge, MA: Bellknap Press/Harvard University Press.

Sinha, Y. (2007). *Confessions of a Swadeshi Reformer: My Years as Finance Minister*. New Delhi: Viking.

Thakurta, P. G. and Raghuraman, S. (2007). *Divided We Stand: India in a Time of Coalitions*. New Delhi: Sage Publications.

Verghese, B. G. (2008). *Rage, Reconciliation and Security*. New Delhi: Penguin.

Whitehead, A. (2007). *A Mission in Kashmir*. New Delhi: Viking/Penguin.

India's Neighbours *(relevant to Indian foreign policy)*

Acharya, A. (2008). *China and India: Politics of Incremental Engagement*. New Delhi: Har-Anand Publications.

Aiyar, P. (2008). *Smoke and Mirrors: An Experience of China*. New Delhi: Harper Collins.

Athwal, A. (2008). *China–India Relations: Contemporary Dynamics*. New York: Routledge.

Bajpai, U. S. (ed.) (1986). *India and Its Neighbourhood*. New Delhi: Lancer International in association with India International Centre.

Baruah, Amit (2007). Dateline Islamabad. New Delhi: Penguin.

Behera, N. C. (ed.) (2008). *International Relations in South Asia, Search for an Alternative Paradigm*. New Delhi: SAGE.

Broadman, H. G. (2007). *Africa's Silk Road: China and India's New Economic Frontier*. Washington, DC: The World Bank.

Chung, T. (2008). *Rise of the Giants: The Dragon–Elephant Tango*. Ed. Patricia Uberoi. New Delhi: Anthem Press.

Coedès, G. (1968). *The Indianized States of Southeast Asia*, ed. Walter F. Vella, trans. Susan Brown Cowing. Honolulu: East-West Center Press.

Cohen, S. P. (2004). *The Idea of Pakistan*. Washington, DC: Brookings.

Dash, K. C. (2008). *Regionalism in South Asia: Negotiating Cooperation, Institutional Structures*. London/New York: Routledge.

Deepak, B. R. (2001). *India–China Relations in the First Half of the 20th Century*. New Delhi: APH Publishing Corporation.

Dixit, J. N. (1998). *Assignment Colombo*. New Delhi: Konark Publishers Pvt. Ltd.

—— (2001). *India and its Neighbours*. New Delhi: Gyan.

Frankel, F. R. and Harding, H. (eds.) (2004). *The India–China Relationship: What the United States Needs to Know*. New York: Columbia University Press.

Fravel, M. T. (2008). *Strong Borders, Secure Nation: Cooperation and Conflict in China's Territorial Disputes*. Princeton, NH: Princeton University Press.

Garver, J. (1993). *Foreign Relations of the People's Republic of China*. Englewood Cliffs, NJ: Prentice Hall.

—— (2001). *Protracted Contest: Sino-Indian Rivalry in the Twentieth Century*. New Delhi: Oxford University Press.

Gilles, B. and Grare, F. (ed.) (2004). *India–China–Russia: Intricacies of an Asian Triangle*. New Delhi: India Research Press.

Grygiel, J. J. (2006). *Great Powers and Geopolitical Change*. Baltimore: The Johns Hopkins University Press.

Gupta, V., Kumar, S. and Chandra, V. (eds.) (2008). *India's Neighbourhood: Challenges Ahead*. New Delhi: IDSA and Rubicon Publishers.

Guruswamy, M. and Singh, Z. D. (2009). *India China Relations: The Border Issue and Beyond*. New Delhi: Viva Books.

—— —— (2010). *Chasing the Dragon: Will India Catch Up with China?* New Delhi: Dorling Kindersley (India) Pvt. Ltd.

Harding, H. (ed.) (1984). *Chinese Foreign Relations in the 1980s*. New Haven, CT: Yale University Press.

Holslag, J. (2010). *China and India: Prospects for Peace*. New York: Columbia University Press.

Hunt, M. H. (1996). *The Genesis of Chinese Communist Foreign Policy*. New York: Columbia University Press.

Jha, P. S. (2010). *Crouching Dragon, Hidden Tiger: Can China and India Dominate the West?* New York: Soft Skull Press.

Jha, R. K. (1986). *The Himalayan Kingdoms in Indian Foreign Policy*. Ranchi: Maitryee Publications.

Kapur, A. and Wilson A. J. (ed.) (1996). *Foreign Policies of India and Her Neighbours*. London: Macmillan.

Kaul, T. N. (2000). *A Diplomat's Diary (1947–1999): China, India and USA, the Tantalizing Triangle*. New Delhi: Macmillan.

Khanna, V. C. and Ranganathan, C.V. (2000). *India and China: The Way Ahead After 'Mao's India War'*. New Delhi: Har Anand.

Kumar, D. (ed.) (2000). *Domestic Conflict and Crisis of Governability in Nepal*. Kathmandu: Centre for Nepal and Asian Studies.

Lall, M. (ed.) (2009). *The Geopolitics of Energy in South Asia*. Singapore: ISEAS Publications.

Latif, A. I. (2007). *Between Rising Powers: China, Singapore and India*. Singapore: ISEAS Publishing.

Liu, G. (ed.) (2004). *Chinese Foreign Policy in Transition*. Howthorne, NY : Aldine de Gruyter Inc.

Liu, X. (1994). *The Sino-Indian Border Dispute and Sino-Indian Relations*. Lanham, MD: University Press of America.

Manogaran, C. (1987). *Ethnic Conflict and Reconciliation in Sri Lanka*. Hawaii: University of Hawaii Press.

Maxwell, N. (1970). *India's China War*. London: Cape.

Mekenkamp, M., van Tongeren, P. and van de Veen, H. (eds.) (2002). *Searching for Peace in Central and South Asia*. Boulder, CO: Lynne Rienner.

Meredith, R. (2007). *The Elephant and the Dragon: The Rise of India and China and What it Means for All of Us*. New York: W.W. Norton.

Muni, S. D. (ed.) (2010). *The Emerging Dimensions of SAARC*. New Delhi: Cambridge University Press India.

Nawaz, S. (2008). *Crossed Swords: Pakistan, Its Army and the War Within*. New York: Oxford University Press.

Pollack, J. D. and Yang, R. H. (eds.) (1998). *In China's Shadow: Regional Perspectives on Chinese Foreign Policy and Military Development*. Santa Monica, CA: Rand.

Preeg, E. H. (2008). *India and China: An Advanced Technology Race and How the United States Should Respond*. Arlington, TX: Manufacturers Alliance/MAPI.

Raju, A. S. (2007). *India–Sri Lanka Partnership in the 21st Century*. New Delhi: Kalpaz Publications.

Ramesh, J. (2005). *Making Sense of Chindia: Reflections on China and India*. New Delhi: India Research Press.

Rizvi, H. A. (1988). *The Military and Politics in Pakistan 1947–86*. Delhi: Konark Publishers.

Shaha, R. (1978). *Nepali Politics: Retrospect and Prospect*. Delhi: Oxford University Press.

Shambaugh, D. (ed.) (2005). *Power Shift: China's and Asia's New Dynamics*. Berkeley/Los Angeles/London: University of California Press.

—— and Yahuda, M. (eds.) (2008). *International Relations of Asia*. Lanham, MD: Rowman and Littlefield Publishers.

Shirk, S. (2007). *China: Fragile Superpower*. Oxford/New York: Oxford University Press.

Shourie, A. (2008). *Are We Deceiving Ourselves Again? Lessons the Chinese Taught Pandit Nehru but which We Still Refuse to Learn*. New Delhi: Rupa.

Siddiqa, A. (2007). *Military Inc: Inside Pakistani Military Economy*. London: Pluto Press.

Sidhu, W. P. S. and Yuan, J. (2003). *China and India: Cooperation or Conflict?* Boulder, CO: Lynne Rienner.

Srinivasan, K. (2007). *The Jamdani Revolution*. Kolkata: Har-Anand Press.

Tai Yong, T. (ed.) (2010). *Challenges of Economic Growth, Inequality and Conflict in South Asia*. Singapore: World Scientific Press.

Tan, C. (2008). *Rise of the Asian Giants: Dragon-Elephant Tango*, ed. P. Uberoi. New Delhi: Anthem Press.

Tellis, A. J., Marble, A. and Tanner, T. (eds.) (2009). *Strategic Asia 2009–10: Economic Meltdown and Geopolitical Stability*. Seattle, WA: The National Bureau of Asian Research.

Thant, M. (2007). *The River of Lost Footsteps: Histories of Burma*. London: Faber and Faber.

Tow, W. T. and Chin, K. W. (eds.) (2009). *ASEAN, India, Australia: Towards Closer Engagement in a New Asia*. Singapore: ISEAS Publications.

Van Praagh, D. (2003). *The Greater Game: India's Race with Destiny and China*. Montreal: McGill-Queen's University Press.

Wasserstrom, J. N. and Perry, E. J. (1994). *Popular Protest and Political Culture in Modern China*. Boulder, CO: Westview Press.

Indian Security

Behera, N. C. (2006). *Demystifying Kashmir*. Washington, DC: Brookings Institution Press.

Devare, S. (2006). *India and Southeast Asia: Towards Security Convergence*. Singapore: ISEAS.

Holmes, J. R., Winner, A. C., and Yoshihara, T. (2009). *Indian Naval Strategy in the Twenty First Century*. New York: Routledge.

Jamal, A. (2009). *Shadow War: The Untold Story of Jihad in Kashmir*. Brooklyn, NY: Melville.

Karnad, B. (2002). *Nuclear Weapons and Indian Security: The Realist Foundations of Strategy.* New Delhi: Macmillan.

Lama, M. P. (2010). *Human Security in India: Discourse, Practices and Policy Implications.* Dhaka: University Press Limited.

Levy, A. and Scott-Clark, C. (2007). *Deception: Pakistan, the United States and the Global Nuclear Weapons Conspiracy.* New Delhi: Penguin.

Limaye, S. P., Malik, M. and Wirsing, R. G. (eds.) (2004). *Religious Radicalism and Security in South Asia.* Honolulu: Asia Pacific Centre for Security Studies.

Naidu, G. V. C. (2000). *Indian Navy and Southeast Asia.* Delhi: Knowledge World.

Patil, V. T. and Jha, N. K. (eds.) (2003). *India in a Turbulent World: Perspectives on Foreign and Security Policies.* New Delhi: South Asian Publishers Pvt Ltd.

Paul, T. V. (ed.) (2010). *South Asia's Weak States: Understanding the Regional Insecurity Predicament.* Palo Alto, CA: Stanford University Press.

Prakash, V. (2008). *Terrorism in India's North-East*, Vols. I–III. Delhi: Kalpaz Publications.

Sidhu, W. P. S., Asif, B., and Samii, C. (eds.) (2006). *Kashmir: New Voices, New Approaches.* Boulder, CO/London: Lynne Rienner.

Singh, S. (2003). *China–South Asia: Issues, Equations, Policies.* New Delhi: Lancer's Books.

Tanham, G. K. (1992). *Indian Strategic Thought: An Interpretive Essay.* Santa Monica, CA: Rand.

Upadhyaya, P. (1990). *Nonaligned States and India's International Conflicts.* New Delhi: South Asian Publishers.

Other

Andrew, C. and Mitrokhin, V. (2005). *The Mitrokhin Archive II: The KGB and the World.* London: Allen Lane.

Ansari, H. (2005). *Iran Today: Twenty–five Years after the Islamic Revolution.* New Delhi: Rupa.

—— (2008). *Travelling Through Conflict: Essays in the Politics of West Asia.* New Delhi: Pearson Education.

Armellini, A. (2008). *L'elefante ha messo le ali.* Milan: EGEA editore-Università Bocconi.

Aziz, S. (2009). *Between Dreams and Reality: Some Milestones in Pakistan's History.* Oxford: Oxford University Press.

Beisner, R. L. (2006). *Dean Acheson: a life in the Cold war.* Oxford/New York: Oxford University Press.

Bhagwati, J. and Eckaus, R. S. (eds.) (1970). *Foreign Aid.* Harmondsworth: Penguin.

Blustein, P. (2009). *Misadventures of the Most Favored Nations: Clashing Egos, Inflated Ambitions, and the Great Shambles of the World Trade System.* New York: Public Affairs.

Bok, S. (1991). *Alva Myrdal: A Daughter's Memoir.* New York: Perseus Books.

Bourantonis, D., Ifantis, K., and Tsakonas, P. (eds.) (2008). *Multilateralism and Security Institutions in an Era of Globalization.* Abingdon/New York: Routledge.

Cassen, R. and Associates (1986). *Does Aid Work? Report to an Intergovernmental Task Force.* Oxford: Clarendon Press.

Chakraborty, D. and Khan, A. U. (2008). *The WTO Deadlocked: Understanding the Dynamics of International Trade.* New Delhi: SAGE.

Chesterman, S., Franck, T. M., and Malone, D. M. (2008). *The Law and Practice of the United Nations*. Oxford: Oxford University Press.

Conrady, R. and Buck, M. (eds.) (2008). *Trends and Issues in Global Tourism 2008*. Berlin: Springer.

Federspiel, H. M. (2007). *Sultans, Shamans, and Saints: Islam and Muslims in Southeast Asia*. Honolulu: University of Hawai'i Press.

Furber, H. (1976). *Rival Empires of Trade in the Orient, 1600–1800*. Minneapolis: University of Minnesota Press.

Galbraith, J. K. (1969). *Ambassador's Journal*. London: H. Hamilton.

Gharekhan, C. R. (2006). *The Horseshoe Table: An Inside View of the UN Security Council*. New Delhi: Longman.

Giridharadas, A. (2011). *India Calling: An Intimate Portrait of a Nation's Remaking*. New York: Times Books.

Greenberg, M. (1951). *British Trade and the Opening of China*. Cambridge: Cambridge University Press.

Harel-Shalev, A. *The Challenge of Sustaining Democracy in Deeply Divided Societies: Citizenship, Rights, and Ethnic Conflicts in India and Israel*. Lanham, MD: Lexington Books.

Hurrell, A. and Narlikar, A. (2011). *Emerging Powers and Global Order*. New York: Oxford University Press, forthcoming.

Johnson, C. (2004). *The Sorrows of Empire: Militarism, Secrecy, and the End of the Republic*. New York: Metropolitan Books.

Kissinger, H. (1957). *Nuclear Weapons and Foreign Policy*. New York: Harper.

—— (1979). *White House Years*. Boston: Little, Brown and Company.

Luce, E. (2007). *In Spite of the Gods: The Strange Rise of Modern India*. London: Abacus Books.

Maddison, A. (2003). *The World Economy: Historical Statistics*. Paris: OECD Publishing.

Mahan, A. T. (1987). *The Influence of Sea Power Upon History, 1660–1783*. New York: Dover Publications Inc. (reprint of 1894 edition).

Mahbubani, K. (2001). *Can Asians Think? Understanding the Divide Between East and West*. Hanover, NH: Steerforth Press.

—— (2008). *The New Asian Hemisphere: The Irresistible Shift of Global Power to the East*. New York: Public Affairs Books.

Malone, D. M. (ed.) (2004). *The UN Security Council, from Cold War to 21st Century*. Boulder, CO and London: Lynne Rienner.

—— (2006). *The International Struggle Over Iraq: Politics in the United Nations Security Council*. Oxford: Oxford University Press.

Manela, E. (2007). *The Wilsonian Moment*. New York: Oxford University Press.

Nye, Jr., J. S. (2002). *Understanding International Conflicts: An Introduction to Theory and History*, 4th edn. New York: Longman.

O'Leary, G. (1980). *The Shaping of Chinese Foreign Policy*. London: Croom Helm.

Peer, B. (2010). *Curfewed Night: One Kashmiri Journalist's Frontline Account of Life, Love and War in His Homeland*. New York: Scribner.

Rashid, A. (2008). *Descent into Chaos: The United States and the Failure of Nation Building in Pakistan, Afghanistan, and Central Asia*. New York: Viking.

Rudolph, L. and Rudolph S. (eds.) (2008). *Making US Foreign Policy Toward South Asia: Regional Imperatives and the Imperial Presidency*. Indiana: Indiana University Press.

Sengupta, D., Chakraborty, D., and Banerjee, P. (eds.). (2006). *Beyond the Transition Phase of WTO*. New Delhi: Academic Foundation.

Toye, R. (2010). *Churchill's Empire: The World that Made Him and the World He Made*. London: Pan Macmillan.

Turnbull, C. M. (1989). *A History of Malaysia, Singapore and Brunei*. Sydney/Boston: Allen & Unwin.

Weiss, T. G. and Daws, S. (eds.) (2007). *The Oxford Handbook on the United Nations*. Oxford/New York: Oxford University Press.

Zakaria, F. (2008). *The Post-American World*. New York: Norton.

Chapters in edited volumes

Abhyankar, R. M. (2007). 'India and the European Union: Non-Associable to Strategic Partner'. In A. Sinha and M. Mohta (eds.). *Indian Foreign Policy: Challenges and Opportunities*. New Delhi: Foreign Service Institute/ Academic Foundation.

Ansari, H. (2007). 'India and the Persian Gulf'. In A. Sinha and M. Mohta (eds). *Indian Foreign Policy: Challenges and Opportunities*. New Delhi: Foreign Service Institute/ Academic Foundation.

Aziz, I. 'India and West Asia/North Africa'. In A. Sinha and M. Mohta (eds). *Indian Foreign Policy: Challenges and Opportunities*. New Delhi: Foreign Service Institute/ Academic Foundation.

Bajpai, K. (2010). 'India in the World'. In N. G. Jayal and P. B. Mehta (eds.). *The Oxford Companion to Politics in India*. New Delhi: Oxford University Press.

Bajpai, U. S. (1986). 'Introduction'. In U. S. Bajpai (ed.). *India and Its Neighbourhood*. New Delhi: Lancer International in association with India International Centre.

Bakshi, D. N. (2004). 'Japanese Indianness without the Indian Diaspora in Pre-modern Japan'. In L. Ghosh and R. Chatterjee (eds.). *Indian Diaspora in Asian and Pacific Regions* (Jaipur, Rawat Publications.

Bala, M. (2002). 'India Australia Trade and Investment Relations in the 1990s'. In D. Gopal (ed.). *Australia in the Emerging Global Order: Evolving Australia-India Relations*. New Delhi: Shipra Publications.

Banerjee, U. K. (1997). 'Role of Cultural Diplomacy'. In L. Mansingh (ed.). *Indian Foreign Policy Agenda for the 21st Century*, Vol. I. New Delhi: Foreign Service Institute in association with Konark Publishers.

Basu, R. (2004). 'Search for Pasture: Tamil Migration to Malayan Plantations in the 19th and Early 20th Centuries'. In L. Ghosh and R. Chatterjee (eds.). *Indian Diaspora in Asian and Pacific Regions*. Jaipur: Rawat Publications.

Baru, S. (2009). 'India: Rising Through the Slowdown'. In A. J. Tellis, A. Marble, and T. Tanner (eds.). *Strategic Asia 2009–10: Economic Meltdown and Geopolitical Stability*. Seattle, WA: The National Bureau of Asian Research.

Bhagwati, J. (1970). 'The Tying of Aid'. In J. Bhagwati and R. S. Eckaus (eds.). *Foreign Aid*. Harmondsworth: Penguin.

Bhargava, A. (1988). 'Indian Economy during Mrs. Gandhi's Regime'. In Y. K. Malik, and D. K. Vajpeyi (eds.). *India: The Years of Indira Gandhi*. Leiden: E J Brill.

Boquérat, G. (2001). 'India's Confrontation with Chinese Interests in Myanmar'. In F. Grare and A. Mattoo (eds.). *India and ASEAN: The Politics of India's Look East Policy*. New Delhi: Manohar Publishers & Distributors.

Budhraj, V. S. (1992). 'Major Dimensions of Indo-Soviet Relations'. In V. Grover (ed.). *International Relations and Foreign Policy of India*, Vol. IX: *Europe and India's Foreign Policy*. New Delhi: Deep and Deep Publications.

Chandran, D. S. (2006). 'Indian and Armed Nonstate Actors in the Kashmir Conflict'. In W. P. S. Sidhu, B. Asif, and C. Samii (eds.). *Kashmir: New Voices, New Approaches*. Boulder, CO, and London: Lynne Rienner.

Chidambaram, P. C. (2007). 'India Empowered To Me Is'. In *A View from the Outside: Why Good Economics Works for Everyone*. New Delhi and New York: Penguin Books.

Clad, J. (2004). 'Convergent Chinese and Indian Perspectives on the Global Order'. In F. R. Frankel and H. Harding (eds.). *The India–China Relationship: What the United States Needs to Know*. New York: Columbia University Press.

Damodaran, A. K. (2007). 'Non-aligned movement and its future'. In A. Sinha and M. Mohta, (eds.). *Indian Foreign Policy: Challenges and Opportunities*. New Delhi: Foreign Service Institute/ Academic Foundation.

Dasgupta, C. (2007). 'India and the Changing Balance of Power'. In A. Sinha and M. Mohta, (eds.) *Indian Foreign Policy: Challenges and Opportunities*. New Delhi: Foreign Service Institute/ Academic Foundation.

Datta, S. (2008). 'India and Bangladesh: Stuck in a Groove?'. In V. Gupta, S. Kumar, and V. Chandra, (eds.). *India's Neighbourhood: Challenges Ahead*. New Delhi: IDSA and Rubicon Publishers.

Datta-Ray, S. K. (2007). 'Rediscovering Suvarnabhumi: India and South-East Asia'. In A. Sinha and M. Mohta (eds.). *Indian Foreign Policy: Challenges and Opportunities*. New Delhi: Foreign Service Institute/ Academic Foundation.

Debroy, B. (2007). 'India's Economic Liberalisation and the WTO'. In S. Karmakar, R. Kumar, and B. Debroy (eds.). *India's Liberalisation Experience: Hostage to the WTO?* New Delhi: Indian Council for Research on International Economic Relations.

Dev, S. M. (2006). 'Agriculture and Rural Development: Policy Issues for Growth and Equity'. In M. Malhoutra (ed.). *India: The Next Decade*. New Delhi: Academic Foundation.

Dhar, M. B. (2004). 'Indians in Japan: History and Dimensions of Relations'. In L. Ghosh and R. Chatterjee (eds.). *Indian Diaspora in Asian and Pacific Regions*. Jaipur: Rawat Publications.

Doyle, M. W. and Sambanis, N. (2007). 'Peacekeeping Operations'. In T. G. Weiss and S. Daws (eds.). *The Oxford Handbook on the United Nations*. Oxford/ New York: Oxford University Press.

Dubash, N. K. (2009). 'Climate Politics in India: How Can the Industrialized World Bridge the Trust Deficit?'. In D. Michel and A. Pandya (eds.). *Indian Climate Policy: Choices and Challenges*. Washington, DC: The Henry L. Stimson Center.

Dubey, M. (2007). 'Reform of the UN system and India'. In A. Sinha and M. Mohta (eds.). *Indian Foreign Policy: Challenges and Opportunities*. New Delhi: Foreign Service Institute/ Academic Foundation.

Dutta, S. (1998). 'China's Emerging Power and Military Role: Implications for South Asia'. In J. D. Pollack and R. H. Yang (eds.). *In China's Shadow: Regional Perspectives on Chinese Foreign Policy and Military Development*. Santa Monica, CA: RAND.

Frazier, M. W. (2004). 'Quiet Competition and the Future of Sino-Indian Relations'. In F. R. Frankel and H. Harding (eds.). *The India–China Relationship: What the United States Needs to Know*. New York: Columbia University Press.

Gandhi, I. (1992). 'Europe and India'. In V. Grover (ed.). *International Relations and Foreign Policy of India*, Vol. IX: *Europe and India's Foreign Policy*. New Delhi: Deep and Deep Publications.

—— (1992). 'Towards a New Synthesis in Civilization'. In V. Grover (ed.). *International Relations and Foreign Policy of India*, Vol. IX: *Europe and India's Foreign Policy*. New Delhi: Deep and Deep Publications.

Ganguly, S. (2004). 'India and China: Border Issues, Domestic Integration, and International Security'. In F. R. Frankel and H. Harding (eds.). *The India-China Relationship: What the United States Needs to Know*. New York: Columbia University Press.

—— (2008). 'The Rise of India in Asia'. In D. Shambaugh and M. Yahuda (eds.). *International Relations of Asia*. Lanhamm, MD: Rowman and Littlefield Publishers.

—— (2010). 'Indian Defence Policy'. In N. G. Jayal and P. B. Mehta (eds.). *The Oxford Companion to Politics in India*. New Delhi: Oxford University Press.

Gharekhan, C. R. (2007). 'India and the United Nations'. In A. Sinha and M. Mohta (eds.). *Indian Foreign Policy: Challenges and Opportunities*. New Delhi: Foreign Service Institute/ Academic Foundation.

Gonsalves, E. (1990). 'India and Western Europe'. In A. K. Damodaran and U. S. Bajpai (eds.). *Indian Foreign Policy, the Indira Gandhi Years*. New Delhi: Radiant Publishers.

Gopal, D. and Gullapalli, S. (2007). 'India's Diplomacy of Regional Trading Groups: A Case of India-ASEAN Free Trade Area and Sub-Regional Agreements'. In Y. Yagama Reddy (ed.). *Emerging India in Asia-Pacific*. New Delhi: New Century Publications.

Grare, F. (2001). 'In Search of a Role: India and the ASEAN Regional Forum'. In F. Grare and A. Mattoo (eds.). *India and ASEAN: The Politics of India's Look East Policy*. New Delhi: Manohar Publishers & Distributors, 2001.

Gulati, A. (2002). 'Trade Liberalization and Food Security'. In A. Hoda (ed.). *WTO Agreement and Indian Agriculture*. New Delhi: Social Science Press.

Gupta, R. (2007). 'India's "Look East" Policy'. In A. Sinha and M. Mohta (eds.). *Indian Foreign Policy: Challenges and Opportunities*. New Delhi: Foreign Service Institute/ Academic Foundation.

Harding, H. (2004). 'The Evolution of the Strategic Triangle: China, India, and the United States'. In F. R. Frankel and H. Harding (eds.). *The India-China Relationship: What the United States Needs to Know*. New York: Columbia University Press.

Harshe, R. (2009). 'South Asian Regional Cooperation: Problems and Prospects'. In R. Harshe and K. M. Seethi (eds). *Engaging with the World: Critical Reflections on India's Foreign Policy*. New Delhi: Orient BlackSwan.

Hoffmann, S. A. (2004). 'Perception and China Policy in India'. In F. R. Frankel and H. Harding (eds.). *The India-China Relationship: Rivalry and Engagement*. New Delhi: Oxford University Press.

Hussain, T. K. (1996). 'China, India and Southeast Asia after the Cold War'. In B. Ghoshal (ed.). *India and Southeast Asia: Challenges and Opportunities*. (New Delhi: Konark Publishers Pvt. Ltd).

Jaishankar, S. (2007). 'India and USA: New Directions'. In A. Sinha and M. Mohta (eds.). *Indian Foreign Policy: Challenges and Opportunities*. New Delhi: Foreign Service Institute/ Academic Foundation.

Jha, P. S. (2009). 'Indian Public Perceptions of the International Climate Negotiations'. In D. Michel and A. Pandya (eds.). *Indian Climate Policy: Choices and Challenges*. Washington, DC: The Henry L. Stimson Center.

Jha, R. (2008). 'Recent Technical Advancements in India-Korea Trade, Research and Development'. In S. Narsimhan and K. Do Young (eds.). *India and Korea: Bridging the Gaps*. New Delhi: Manak Publications.

Kaur, A. (2009). 'Indians in Southeast Asia: Migrant Labour, Knowledge workers and the new India'. In R. Rai and P. Reeves (eds.). *The South Asian Diaspora: Transnational Networks and Changing Identities*. New York: Routledge.

Kaushik, S. (2003). 'Indo-Nepal Relations: Some Political and Security Issues'. In V. T. Patil and N. K. Jha (eds.). *India in a Turbulent World: Perspectives on Foreign and Security Policies*. New Delhi: South Asian Publishers Pvt Ltd.

Khosla, I. P. (2007). 'India and Afghanistan'. In A. Sinha and M. Mohta, (eds.). *Indian Foreign Policy: Challenges and Opportunities*. New Delhi: Foreign Service Institute; Academic Foundation.

Kissinger, H. (1979). 'The Tilt: The India–Pakistan Crisis of 1971'. In *White House Years*. Boston: Little, Brown and Company.

Koldowski, J. and Martin, O. (2008). 'Emerging Market Segments: Religious and Medical Tourism in India'. In R. Conrady and M. Buck (eds.). *Trends and Issues in Global Tourism 2008*. Berlin: Springer.

Lieten, K. (2002). 'Multiple Conflicts in Northeast India'. In M. Mekenkamp, P. van Tongeren, and H. van de Veen (eds.). *Searching for Peace in Central and South Asia*. Boulder, CO: Lynne Rienner.

Kumar, D. (2000). 'What Ails Democracy in Nepal'. In D. Kumar (ed.). *Domestic Conflict and Crisis of Governability in Nepal*. Kathmandu: Centre for Nepal and Asian Studies.

Kumar, K. (2005). 'Andaman and Nicobar Islands: Our Gateway to the East'. In R. Reddy (ed.). *India and ASEAN: Foreign Policy Dimensions of the 21st Century*. New Delhi: New Century Publications.

Kumar, N. (2007). 'India in 21st Century Asia-Pacific'. In Y. Yagama Reddy (ed.). *Emerging India in Asia-Pacific*. New Delhi: New Century Publications.

—— (2008). 'India's Economic Engagement with East Asia: Trends and Prospects'. In K. Kesavpany, A. Mani, and P. Ramasamy (eds.), *Rising India and Indian Communities in East Asia*. Singapore: ISEAS.

Kumar, R. (2007). 'Introduction'. In S. Karmakar, R. Kumar, and B. Debroy (eds.). *India's Liberalisation Experience: Hostage to the WTO?* Indian Council for Research on International Economic Relations.

Kundu, A. (2005). 'The National Democratic Alliance and National Security'. In K. Adeney and L. Saez (eds.). *Coalition Politics and Hindu Nationalism*. London: Routledge.

395

Lahiri, D. (2007). 'India and France'. In A. Sinha and M. Mohta (eds.). *Indian Foreign Policy: Challenges and Opportunities*. New Delhi: Foreign Service Institute/ Academic Foundation.

Lieberthal, K. (1984). 'Domestic Politics and Foreign Policy'. In H. Harding (ed.). *Chinese Foreign Relations in the 1980s*. New Haven, CT: Yale University Press.

Malik, B. S. (2008). 'Myanmar's Strategic Environment'. In V. Gupta, S. Kumar, and V. Chandra, (eds.). *India's Neighbourhood: Challenges Ahead*. New Delhi: IDSA and Rubicon Publishers.

Marston, D. P. (2007). 'A Force Transformed: The Indian Army and the Second World War'. In D. P. Marston and C. S. Sundaram (eds). *A Military History of India and South Asia: From the East India Company to the Nuclear Era*. Bloomington: Indiana University Press.

Mattoo, A. and Subramaniam, A. (2003). 'India and the Multilateral Trading System Post-Doha: Defensive or Proactive?'. In A. Mattoo and R. M. Stern (eds.). *India and the WTO*. Washington, DC: World Bank and Oxford University Press.

Medeiros, E. S. and Fravel, M. T. (2004). 'China's New Diplomacy'. In G. Liu (ed.). *Chinese Foreign Policy in Transition*. Howthorne, NY: Aldine de Gruyter Inc.

Michel, D. (2009). 'Introduction'. In D. Michel and A.Pandya (eds.). *Indian Climate Policy: Choices and Challenges*. Washington, DC: The Henry L. Stimson Center.

Mukherjee, R. and Malone, D. M. (2010). 'Polity, Security and Foreign Policy in Contemporary India'. In T. V. Paul (ed.). *South Asia's Weak States: Understanding the Regional Insecurity Predicament*. Palo Alto, CA: Stanford University Press.

Mukherji, D. (2007). 'Distant Neighbours: India and Bangladesh'. In A. Sinha and M. Mohta (eds.). *Indian Foreign Policy: Challenges and Opportunities*. New Delhi: Academic Foundation and the Foreign Service Institute.

Naidu, G. V. C. (1996). 'India's Strategic Relation with Southeast Asia'. In B. Ghoshal (ed.). *India and Southeast Asia*. New Delhi: Konark Publishers.

—— (2008). 'Southeast Asian Security Dynamics'. In N. S. Sisodia and S. Datta (eds.). *Changing Security Dynamics in Southeast Asia*. New Delhi: Magnum Books.

Narsimha, S. (2005). 'India's "Look East" Policy: Past, Present, and Future'. In K. Raja Reddy (ed.). *India and ASEAN: Foreign Policy Dimensions for the 21st Century*. New Delhi: New Century Publications.

Num, M. J. (2001). 'ASEAN-India Defence Interactions'. In F. Grare and A. Mattoo (eds.). *India and ASEAN: The Politics of India's Look East Policy*. New Delhi: Manohar Publishers & Distributors.

Omissi, D. (2007). 'The Indian Army in the First World War, 1914–1918'. In D. P. Marston and C. S. Sundaram (eds.). *A Military History of India and South Asia: From the East India Company to the Nuclear Era*. Bloomington: Indiana University Press.

Pardesi, M. S. (2010). 'Southeast Asia in Indian Foreign Policy: Positioning India as a Major Power in Asia'. In S. Ganguly (ed.). *India's Foreign Policy: Retrospect and Prospect*. New Delhi: Oxford University Press.

Pegov, N. M. (1992). 'Economic and Cultural Relations of USSR and India'. In V. Grover (ed.). *International Relations and Foreign Policy of India*, Vol. IX: *Europe and India's Foreign Policy*. New Delhi: Deep and Deep Publications.

Ping, J. (2008). 'China: Indians' New-Found Land'. In K. Kesavpany, A. Mani and P. Ramasamy (eds.). *Rising India and Indian Communities in East Asia*. Singapore: ISEAS.

Racine, J. (2008). 'Quete de puissance, multipolarité et multilatéralisme'. In C. Jaffrelot (ed.). *New Delhi et le Monde*. Paris: Editions Autrement – CERI.

Ramesh, G. S. (1992). 'French Arms Trade Policy and Indian Sub-Continent'. In V. Grover (ed.). *International Relations and Foreign Policy of India*, Vol. IX: *Europe and India's Foreign Policy*. New Delhi: Deep and Deep Publications.

Ranganathan, C.V. (2007). 'The long road to achieving an "India-China strategic and cooperative partnership for peace and development"'. In A. Sinha and M. Mohta (eds.). *Indian Foreign Policy: Challenges and Opportunities*. New Delhi: Foreign Service Institute/ Academic Foundation.

Ratnagar, S. (2001). 'Harappan Trade in its "World Context"'. In R. Chakravarti (ed.). *Trade in Early India*. New Delhi: Oxford University Press.

Ross, R. S. (2004). 'Beijing as a Conservative Power'. In Guoli Liu (ed.), *Chinese Foreign Policy in Transition*. Howthorne, NY: Aldine de Gruyter Inc.

Roy, K. (2007). 'The Armed Expansion of the English East India Company: 1740s–1849'. In D. P. Marston and C. S. Sundaram (eds.). *A Military History of India and South Asia: From the East India Company to the Nuclear Era*. Bloomington: Indiana University Press.

Rubinoff, A. G. (2008). 'From Indifference to Engagement: The Role of the US Congress in Making Foreign Policy for South Asia'. In L. Rudolph and S. Rudolph (eds.). *Making US Foreign Policy Toward South Asia: Regional Imperatives and the Imperial Presidency*. Bloomington: Indiana University Press.

Sahu, N. (2008). 'Posco Deal: A Major Economic Breakthrough for the Government of Orissa'. In S. Narsimhan and K. Do Young (eds.). *India and Korea: Bridging the Gaps*. New Delhi: Manak Publications.

Seethi, K. M. and Vijayan, P. (2009). 'Political Economy of India's Third World Policy'. In R. Harshe and K. M. Seethi (eds.). *Engaging with the World: Critical Reflections on India's Foreign Policy*. New Delhi: Orient BlackSwan.

Seth, A. (2007). 'India and Japan'. In A. Sinha and M. Mohta (eds.). *Indian Foreign Policy: Challenges and Opportunities*. New Delhi: Foreign Service Institute/ Academic Foundation.

Sharma, J. C. (2007). 'India Around the World', In A. Sinha and M. Mohta (eds.). *Indian Foreign Policy: Challenges and Opportunities*. New Delhi: Foreign Service Institute/ Academic Foundation.

Shirk, S. L. (2004). 'One-Sided Rivalry: China's Perceptions and Policies toward India'. In F. R. Frankel and H. Harding (eds.). *The India–China Relationship: What the United States Needs to Know*. New York: Columbia University Press.

Shourie, A. (2010). 'India and its Neighbours'. In T. T. Yong (ed.). *Challenges of Economic Growth, Inequality and Conflict in South Asia*. Singapore: World Scientific Press.

Singh, U. B. (2008). 'Myanmar Update'. In V. Gupta, S. Kumar, and V. Chandra (eds.). *India's Neighbourhood: Challenges Ahead*. New Delhi: IDSA and Rubicon Publishers.

Sridharan, E. (2002). 'The Fragmentation of the Indian Party System, 1952–1999: Seven Competing Explanations'. In Z. Hasan (ed.). *Parties and Party Politics in India*. New Delhi: Oxford University Press.

Sudipta, K. (2004). 'The Nature of Indian Democracy'. In V. Das (ed.). *Handbook of Sociology in India*. New Delhi: Oxford University Press.

Tellis, A. (2004). 'China and India in Asia'. In F. R. Frankel and H. Harding (eds.). *The India–China Relationship: What the United States Needs to Know.* New York: Columbia University Press.

Varma, P. (2007). 'Culture as an instrument of diplomacy'. In A. Sinha and M. Mohta (eds.). *Indian Foreign Policy: Challenges and Opportunities.* New Delhi: Foreign Service Institute / Academic Foundation.

Voeten, E. (2008). 'Why no UN Security Council reform? Lessons for and from institutionalist theory'. In D. Bourantonis, K. Ifantis, and P. Tsakonas (eds.). *Multilateralism and Security Institutions in an Era of Globalization.* Abingdon and New York: Routledge.

Yatanoor, C. (2007). 'Indo-Australian Relations in the Emerging World Order'. In Y. Yagama Reddy (ed.). *Emerging India in Asia-Pacific.* New Delhi: New Century Publications.

Journal and Periodical Articles

Acharya, A. (2006). 'India and Southeast Asia in the Age of Terror: Building Partnerships for Peace', *Contemporary Southeast Asia*, 28(2): 297–321.

Ahrari, M. E. (2000). 'China, Pakistan, and the "Taliban Syndrome"', *Asian Survey*, 40(4): 658–71.

Alagappa, M. (2009). 'Galvanizing International Studies: India's Rising Profile Demands Investment in Intellectual Foundations', *Pragati*, 30: 11–16.

Appadorai, A. (1979). 'The Asian Relations Conference in Perspective', *International Studies*, 18: 275–85.

Asher, M. G. (2010). 'A Strategic Approach to Trade Agreements: Getting the Most out of PTAs and Economic Agreements', *Pragati—The Indian National Interest Review*, 36: 13–16.

Ashraf, T. M. (2004). 'Doctrinal Reawakening of the Indian Armed Forces', *Military Review* (November/December), 53–62.

Ashton Carter, A. (2006). 'America's New Partner', *Foreign Affairs*, 85(4): 33–44.

Baghat, G. (2002). 'Pipeline Diplomacy: The Geopolitics of the Caspian Sea Region', *International Studies Perspectives*, 3(3): 310–27.

Bajpai, K. (2006/7). 'The US and Us', India 60, *IIC Quarterly*, 33(3 & 4): 94–105.

Bajpai, K. S. (1992). 'India in 1991: New Beginnings', *Asian Survey*, 32(2): 207–16.

Bandyopadhyay, S. (2007). 'India and New Zealand: A Sixty Year Roller Coaster', *New Zealand International Review*, 32(4): 10–14.

Barnds, W. J. (1973). 'India and America at Odds', *International Affairs (Royal Institute of International Affairs 1944–)*, 49(3): 371–84.

Baru, S. (2009). 'The Influence of Business and Media on Indian Foreign Policy', *India Review*, 8(3): 266–85.

—— (2002). 'Strategic Consequences of India's Economic Performance', *Economic and Political Weekly*, 37 (26): 2583–5; 2587–92.

Batabyal, A. (2006). 'Balancing China in Asia: A Realist Assessment of India's Look East Strategy', *China Report* 42(2): 179–97.

Bhardwaj, S. (2003). 'Bangladesh foreign policy vis-à-vis India', *Strategic Analysis*, 27(2): 263–78.

Bonnafont, J. and Bazard, G. (2010). 'The European Union seen from India', *Mondes*, 2: 170–7.

Bonnor, J. (2008). 'Australia India: An Important Partnership', *South Asian Survey*, 15(1): 165–77.

Brecher, M. (1974). 'India's Decisions on the Voice of America: A Study in Irresolution', *Asian Survey*, 14(7): 637–50.

Brodkin, E. I. (1967). 'United States aid to India and Pakistan: The Attitudes of the Fifties', *International Affairs (Royal Institute of International Affairs 1944–)*, 43(4): 664–77.

Broinowski, R. (2000). 'India, China and Australia: The Fractured Triangle', *South Asia: Journal of South Asian Studies*, 23(1): 141–50.

Brunatti, A. and Malone, D. M. (2009). 'India's West Asia Approach: A Triumph of Bilateralism', *Indian Foreign Affairs Journal*, 4(4): 43–62.

—— —— (2010). 'Fading Glories?: India's Relations with Western Europe and Russia', *International Relations*, 24/3: 341–70.

Burns, R. N. (2007). 'America's Strategic Opportunity with India', *Foreign Affairs*, 86(6): 131–46.

Buzan, B. (2002). 'South Asia Moving Towards Transformation: Emergence of India as a Great Power', *International Studies*, 39(1): 1–24.

Carranza, M. E. (2007). 'From Non-Proliferation to Post-Proliferation: Explaining the US–India Nuclear Deal', *Contemporary Security Policy*, 28(3): 464–93.

Chakravarti, R. (2007). 'India's middle class failure', *Prospect Magazine*, 138 (September).

Chandrasekhar, C. P. (1985). 'India's Balance of Payments under the New Regime', *Social Scientist*, 13(9): 31–43.

Chaudry, P. K., Kelkar, V. L., and Yadav, V. (2004). 'The Evolution of Homegrown Conditionality in India: IMF Relations', *Journal of Development Studies*, 40(6): 59–81.

Chenioy, K. M. and Chenoy, A. M. (2007). 'India's Foreign Policy Shifts and the Calculus of Power', *Economic and Political Weekly*, 42(35): 3547–53.

Chenoy, A. M. (2008). 'India and Russia: Allies in the International Political System', *South Asian Survey*, 15(1): 49–62.

Cohen, J. B. (1953). 'Problems of Economic Development in India', *Economic Development and Cultural Change*, 1(2): 196–208.

Cohen, S. P. (2005). 'The US and South Asia', *Seminar*, 545.

Cole, J. R. I. (1986). '"Indian Money" and the Shi'i Shrine Cities of Iraq, 1786–1850', *Middle Eastern Studies*, 22(4): 461–480.

Crossette, B. (2010). 'The Elephant in the Room', *Foreign Policy* (January/February).

Crow, B. and Singh, N. (2009). 'The Management of International Rivers as Demands Grow and Supplies Tighten: India, China, Nepal, Pakistan, Bangladesh'. *India Review*, 8(3): 306–39.

Daley, T. (1992). 'Can the UN Stretch to Fit its Future?' *The Bulletin of the Atomic Scientists*, 48(3): 38–42.

Das, G. (2006). 'The India Model,' *Foreign Affairs*, 85(4): 2–16.

Bibliography

Das, P. S. (2009). 'India and the Indian Ocean Littoral: Opportunities and Challenges', *Indian Foreign Policy Journal*, 4(4): 1–32.

Deaton, A. and Dreze, J. (2002). 'Poverty and Inequality in India: A Re-Examination,' *Economic and Political Weekly*, 37(36): 3729–48.

Desai, A. (1988). 'India and the Uruguay Round', *Economic and Political Weekly*, 23(45/47), 2371–84.

Drezner, D. W. (2007). 'The New New World Order', *Foreign Affairs*, 86(2): 34–45.

Dukkipati, U. (2009). 'India-Japan Relations: A Partnership for Peace and Prosperity', *South Asia Monitor*, 134 (Center for Strategic and International Studies, 1 October).

Feigenbaum, E. A. (2010). 'India's Rise, America's Interest: The Fate of the US–Indian Partnership', *Foreign Affairs*, 89(2): 76–92.

Fravel, M. T. (2005). 'Regime Insecurity and International Cooperation: Explaining China's Compromises in Territorial Disputes', *International Security*, 30(2): 46–83.

Friedberg, A. (2005). 'The Future of US–China Relations: Is Conflict Inevitable?' *International Security*, 30(2): 7–45.

Gandhi, S. (2003). 'Conflict and Coexistence in Our Age', *Seminar*, 521.

Ganguly, S. (2003/4). 'Indian Foreign Policy Grows Up', *World Policy Journal*, 20(2): 41–7.

—— (2006). 'The Kashmir Connection', *Foreign Affairs*, 85(4): 45–57.

—— (2008). 'India in 2007: A Year of Opportunities and Disappointments', *Asia Survey*, 48(1): 164–76.

—— and Pardesi, M. S. (2009).'Explaining Sixty Years of India's Foreign Policy', *India Review*, 8(1): 4–19.

Ghosh, P. S. (1994). 'Foreign Policy and Electoral Politics in India', *Asian Survey*, 34(9): 807–17.

Gupta, R. (2008). 'The Myanmar Conundrum: The Way Forward for India', *Indian Foreign Affairs Journal*, 3(2): 51–67.

Haass, R. N. (2008). 'The Age of Nonpolarity', *Foreign Affairs*, 87(3): 44–56.

Hallwood, P. (1973). 'The Impact of Foreign Aid Upon India's International Trade 1951–65', *Bulletin of Economic Research*, 25(2): 129–45.

Hathaway, R. M. (2001). 'Unfinished Passage: India, Indian Americans, and the U.S. Congress', *The Washington Quarterly*, 24(2): 24–34.

—— (2004). 'Washington's new strategic partnership', *Seminar*, 538.

Hess, G. R. (1987). 'Global Expansion and Regional Balances: The Emerging Scholarship on United States Relations with India and Pakistan', *The Pacific Historical Review*, 56(2): 259–95.

Hilali, A. Z. (2001). 'India's Strategic Thinking and Its National Security Policy', *Asian Survey*, 41(5): 737–64.

Huang, Y. (July/August 2008). 'The Next Asian Miracle', *Foreign Policy*, 167: 32–40.

Huntington, S. (1999). 'The Lonely Superpower', *Foreign Affairs*, 78(2): 35–49.

Hussain, W. (2007). 'Ethno-Nationalism and the Politics of Terror in India's Northeast', *South Asia: Journal of South Asian Studies*, 30(1): 93–110.

Hymans, J. E. C. (2009). 'India's Soft Power and Vulnerability', *India Review*, 8(3): 234–65.

Jaffrelot, C. (2003). 'India's Look East Policy: an Asianist Strategy in Perspective', *India Review*, 2(2): 35–68.

Jaishankar, D. (2009). 'Taking the Heat: Where India stands on climate change'. *Pragati–The Indian National Interest Review*, 33: 3–5.

—— (2010). 'A Uniquely Indian Realism: Underlying India's Foreign Policy Framework', *Pragati*, 38: 3–5.

Jha, N. K. (1989). 'The Cultural and Philosophical Roots of India's Foreign Policy', *International Studies*, 26(1): 45–67.

Kanwal, Col. G. (1999). 'China's Long March to World Power Status: Strategic Challenges for India', *Strategic Analysis*, 22(2): 1713–28.

Kaplan, R. D. (2009). 'Center Stage for the Twenty-first Century', *Foreign Affairs*, 88(2): 16–32.

Kapur, D. (2000). 'India in 1999', *Asian Survey*, 40(1): 195–207.

—— (2009). 'Public Opinion and Indian Foreign Policy', *India Review*, 8(3): 286–305.

—— (2009). 'Introduction: Future Issues in India's Foreign Policy: Ideas, Interests and Values', *India Review*, 8(3): 200–8.

Kaul, M. M. (2006). 'Regional Groupings: an Overview of BIMSTEC and MGC', *South Asian Survey*, 13(2): 313–22.

Kaushik, S. K. (1997). 'India's Evolving Economic Model: A Perspective on Economic and Financial Reforms', *American Journal of Economics and Sociology*, 56(1): 69–84.

Kavalski, E. (2008). 'Venus and the Porcupine: Assessing the India-European Union Strategic Partnership', *South Asian Survey*, 15(1): 63–81.

Keenleyside, T. A. (1982). 'Nationalist Indian Attitudes towards Asia: A Troublesome Legacy for Post-Independence Indian Foreign Policy', *Pacific Affairs*, 5(2): 210–30.

Kesavan, K. V. (2003). 'Economic Liberalization in India and Japan's Wavering Response', *Ritsumeikan Annual Review of International Studies*, 2: 129–42.

Khurana, G. (2005). 'Cooperation among Maritime Security Forces', 29(2): 295–316.

Khurana, G. S. (2009). 'China-India Maritime Rivalry', *India Defence Review*, 23(4): www.indiandefencereview.com/2009/04/china-india-maritime-rivalry.html.

Kohli, A. (2006). 'Politics of Economic Growth in India, 1980–2005, Part I: The 1980s', *Economic and Political Weekly*, 41(13): 1251–9.

Kudaisya, M. (2009). ' "A Mighty Adventure": Institutionalising the Idea of Planning in Post-colonial India, 1947–60', *Modern Asian Studies*, 43: 939–78.

Kumar, K. (1973). 'Some Policy Issues on Mitigating Poverty In India'. *Land Economics*, 49(1): 76–81.

Kumar, S. (1994). 'When Slaves were Nobles: The Shamsi *Bandagan* in the Early Delhi Sultanate', *Studies in History*, 10: 23–52.

Lansford, T. (2002). 'The Great Game Renewed?: US-Russian Rivalry in the Arms Trade of South Asia', *Security Dialogue*, 33(2): 127–40.

Leng, S. C. (1952). 'India and China', *Far Eastern Survey*, 21(8): 73–8.

Levi, W. (1963). 'Necrology on Indian Neutralism', *Eastern World*, 17(2): 9–11.

Lounev, S. I. (2002). 'Russia and India Political Cooperation in the sphere of Global, Regional and Bilateral Relations', *China Report*, 381: 109–11.

Ludwig III, W. C. (2009). 'Delhi's Pacific Ambition: Naval Power, "Look East," and India's Emerging Influence in the Asia-Pacific', *Asian Security*, 5(2): 87–113.

Ma, J. (2000). 'Striving to Establish a Constructive and Cooperative Partnership between India and China', *China Report*, 36(3): 375–81.

Malik, J. M. (1991). 'India's Response to the Gulf Crisis: Implications for Indian Foreign Policy', *Asian Survey*, 31(9): 847–61.

—— (1995). 'China–India Relations in the Post-Soviet Era: The Continuing Rivalry', *The China Quarterly*, 142: 317–55.

Malik, M. (2003). 'The Proliferation Axis: Beijing-Islamabad-Pyongyang', *The Korean Journal of Defense Analysis*, 15(1): 57–98.

Malone, D. M. (2001). 'Foreign Policy Reviews Reconsidered', *International Journal* 56(4): 555–78.

—— (2005). 'The High-Level Panel and the UN Security Council', *Security Dialogue*, 36(3): 370–72.

—— and Mukherjee, R. (2010). 'India and China: Conflict and Cooperation', *Survival*, 52(1): 137–58.

Mansingh, S. (1999). 'The United States, China and India: Relationships in Comparative Perspective', *China Report* 35: 119–42.

Markey, D. (2009). 'Developing India's Foreign Policy "Software" ', *Asian Policy*, 8: 73–96.

Mattoo, A. and Subramanian, A. (2009). 'From Doha to the Next Bretton Woods', *Foreign Affairs*, 88(1): 15–26.

McDonald, J. A. and Wimbush, S. E. (1999). 'India's Energy Security', *Strategic Analysis*, 23(5): 821–35.

Mehta, G. L. (1954). India and the United States: Democracy East and West', *Annals of the American Academy of Political and Social Science*, 294: 124–30.

Mehta, P. B. (2005). ' "Natural allies" at odds', *Seminar*, 545.

—— (2007). 'Five Balancing Acts', *Seminar*, 560.

—— (2009). 'Still Under Nehru's Shadow? The Absence of Foreign Policy Frameworks in India', *India Review*, 8(3): 209–33.

Menon, S. S. (September 22, 2009). 'Hostile Relations India's Pakistan dilemma', *Harvard International Review*: www.allbusiness.com/government/government-bodies-offices/13490404–1.html

Mohan, C. Raja (2003). 'India and the New World Order', *Seminar*, 529.

—— (2006). 'India and the Balance of Power', *Foreign Affairs*, 85(4): 17–32.

—— (2007). 'India's Neighbourhood Policy: Four Dimensions', *Indian Foreign Affairs Journal*, 2(1).

—— (2007). 'Balancing Interests and Values: India's Struggle with Democracy Promotion', *The Washington Quarterly*, 30(3): 99–115.

—— (2008). 'India's Geopolitics and Southeast Asian Security', *Southeast Asian Affairs*, Volume 2008: 43–60.

—— (2009). 'The Re-making of Indian Foreign Policy', *International Studies*, 46(1–2): 147–63.

—— (2009). 'Sino-Indian Rivalry in the Western Indian Ocean', *ISAS Insights*, 52: 1–6.

Mukherjee, R. and Malone, D. M. (2009). 'The Shock of the New: India–US Relations in Perspective', *International Journal*, 64(4).

—— —— (2010). 'India and China: Can two tigers share a mountain?', *Sunday Guardian*, 21 March.

Mukherji, R. and Kale, S. S. (2009). 'Introduction: India, Sixty Years on', *India Review*, 8(1): 1–3.

Muni, S. D. (1993). 'India and Its Neighbour: Persisting Dilemmas and New Opportunities', *International Studies*, 30(2): 189–206.

—— (2003).'Problem Areas In India's Neighbourhood Policy', *South Asian Survey*, 10(2): 186–96.

—— and Raja Mohan, C. (2004). 'Emerging Asia: India's Options', *International Studies*, 41(3): 313–33.

Naidu, G. V. C. (2004). 'Wither the Look East Policy: India and Southeast Asia', *Strategic Analysis*, 28(2): 331–46.

Ollapally, D. and Ramanna, R. (1995). 'U.S.–India Tensions: Misperceptions on Nuclear Proliferation', *Foreign Affairs*, 74(1): 13–18.

Pai, N. (2009). 'The Capacity to Engage', *Pragati—The Indian National Interest Review*, 33: 7–12.

—— and Pradhan, R. (2010). 'Why India Must Send Troops to Afghanistan', *Pragati*, 34: 3–5, http://pragati.nationalinterest.in/2010/01/why-india-must-send-troops-to-afghanistan/

Pal, B. P. (1937). 'The Search for New Genes', *Agriculture and Livestock in India*, 7(5): 573–8.

Palmer, N. D. (1954). 'Ups and Downs in Indo-American Relations', *The Annals of the American Academy of Political and Social Science*, 294(1): 113–23.

Pant, H. V. (2004). 'India–Israel Partnership: Convergence and Constraints', *Middle East Review of International Affairs*, 8(4): 60–73.

—— (2004). 'India and Iran: An "Axis" in the Making?', *Asian Survey*, 44(3): 369–83.

—— (2009). 'Indian Foreign and Security Policy: Beyond Nuclear Weapons', *The Brown Journal of World Affairs*, 15(2): 236.

—— (2009). 'A Rising India's Search for a Foreign Policy', *Orbis*, 53(2): 250–64.

Pathasarathy, G. (2010). 'Afpak for Dummies: A Primer', *World Affairs*, 172(3): 64–74.

Paul, T. V. (2006). 'Why has the India-Pakistan Rivalry Been so Enduring? Power Asymmetry and an Intractable Conflict', *Security Studies*, 15(4): 600–30.

Perkovich, G. (2003). 'The Measure of India: What Makes Greatness?' *Seminar*, 529.

Powell, C. L. (2004). 'A Strategy of Partnerships', *Foreign Affairs*, 83(1): 22–34.

Pradhan, B. (2004). 'Changing Dynamics of India's West Asia Policy', *International Studies*, 41: 1–88.

Rajamani, L. (2009). 'The Copenhagen Agreed Outcome: Form, Shape and Influence', *The Economic and Political Weekly*, 44(48): 30–35.

—— (2009). 'India and Climate Change: What India Wants, Needs, and Needs to Do', *India Review*, 8(3): 340–74.

Ramana, P. V. (2006). 'The Maoist Movement in India', *Defense & Security Analysis*, 22(4): 435–9.

Rao, M. G. and Seth, A. (2009). 'Fiscal Space for Achieving the Millennium Development Goals and Implementing the Tenth Plan in Bhutan', *Economic and Political Weekly*, 44(35): 51–60.

Rice, C. (2000). 'Promoting the National Interest', *Foreign Affairs,* 79(1): 45–62.

—— (2008). 'Rethinking the National Interest', *Foreign Affairs*, 87(4): 2–27.

Rusko, C. J. and Sasikumar, K. (2007). 'India and China: From Trade to Peace?', *Asian Perspective*, 31(4): 99–123.

Sagar, S. (2007). 'Global Hypocrisy on Myanmar', *Economic and Political Weekly*, 42(40): 4027–9.

Saksena, K. P. (1996). 'India's Foreign Policy: The Decision Making Process', *International Studies*, 33(4): 391–405.

Sasikumar, K. (2009). 'India's Debated Nuclear Policy', *India Review*, 8(3): 375–84.

Schaffer, T. C. (2002). 'Building a New Partnership with India', *Washington Quarterly*, 25(2): 41.

Scott, D. (2006). ''India's ''Grand Strategy'' for the Indian Ocean: Mahanian Visions'. *Asia-Pacific Review*, 13(2), 97–129.

—— (2009). 'India's ''Extended Neighborhood'' Concept: Power Projection for a Rising Power', *India Review*, 8(2): 107–43.

Singh, B. (1965).'Pandits and Panchsheela: Indian intellectuals and their foreign policy', *Background* 9(2): 127–36.

Sinha, A. and Dorschner, J. P. (2010). 'India: Rising Power or a Mere Revolution of Rising Expectations?', *Polity*, 42(1): 74–99.

Srinivasan, K. (2009). 'India and China: Similar Challenges, Different Roadmaps', *Indian Foreign Affairs Journal*, 4(4): 33–42.

Swamy, A. (2001). 'India in 2000: A Respite from Instability', *Asian Survey* 41(1): 91–103.

—— (2002). 'India in 2001: A Year of Living Dangerously', *Asian Survey*, 42(1): 165–76.

Tammen, R. L. (2006). 'The Impact of Asia on World Politics: China and India Options for the United States', *International Studies Review*, 8: 563–80.

Tay, S. (2010). 'Interdependency Theory: China, India and the West', *Foreign Affairs*, 89(5): 138–43.

Tellis, A. J. (2006). 'The Evolution of U.S.-Indian Ties: Missile Defense in an Emerging Strategic Relationship', *International Security*, 30(4): 113–51.

Thakur, R. (1997). 'India in the World: Neither Rich, Powerful, nor Principled', *Foreign Affairs*, 76(4): 15–22.

Timberg, T. A. (1998). 'The Impact of Indian Economic Liberalization on U.S.–India Relations', *SAIS Review* 18(1): 123–36.

Vanaik, A. (2008). 'Post Cold War Indian Foreign Policy', *Seminar*, 581.

Varshney, A. (2006). 'A New Triangle: India, China and the US', *Seminar*, 557.

Vinod, M. J. (1992).'Conflicting Strategic Interests of the United States and India: Evaluating US Arms Supply to Pakistan', *International Studies*, 29: 253–79.

Washbrook, D. (2007). 'India in the Early Modern World Economy: Modes of Production, Reproduction and Exchange', *Journal of Global History*, 2: 87–111.

—— (2010). 'Merchants, Markets and Commerce in Early Modern South India', *Journal of the Economic and Social History of the Orient*, 53: 266–89.

Windmiller, M. (1956). 'America's Relations with India: A Re-Appraisal', *Far Eastern Survey*, 25(3): 33–8.

Wirsing, R. G. (March, 1985). 'The Arms Race in South Asia: Implications for the United States', *Asian Survey*, 25(3): 265–91.

Xavier, C. (2010). 'Beyond Borders: Governing the Diaspora; Time to Review the Policy on Overseas Indian Affairs', *Pragati—The Indian National Interest Review*, 36: 11–12.

Zhao, S. (2000). 'Chinese Nationalism and Its International Orientations', *Political Science Quarterly*, 115(1): 1–33.

Extended Articles

Jane's Defence Industry

'Second-Hand Gorshkov to Cost More than New Carrier, India Told', *Jane's Defence Industry*, 27 July 2009.

Bede, R. and Brown, N., 'India Commissions Armaris to Build Six Scorpenes', *Jane's Defence Industry*, 1 November 2005.

Bedi, R., 'India joins anti-Taliban coalition', *Jane's Intelligence Review*, 15 March 2001.

Grevatt, J., 'Indian Navy to take Delivery of Russian Submarine by End of 2009', *Jane's Defence Industry*, 3 June 2009.

Grevatt, J., 'Lockheed Martin Discusses Hercules Sale with India', *Jane's Defence Industry*, 31 July 2009.

Jennings, G., 'Aero India 2009: Northrop Grumman Negotiates E2D Clearance for India', *Jane's Defence Industry*, 12 February 2009.

Wagstaff-Smith, K., 'Indian Army Receives First 10 T-90 MBTs', *Jane's Defence Industry*, 25 August 2009.

New York Review of Books

Mishra, P., 'Impasse in India', *New York Review of Books*, 54(11), 28 June 2007: 48–51.

Pankaj Mishra, O., 'The India & Pakistan Connection', *New York Review of Books*, 57(1), 14 January 2010.

Rashid, A., 'A Deal with the Taliban?', *New York Review of Books*, 57(3), 25 February 2010.

—— 'Pakistan on the Brink', *New York Review of Books*, 56(10), 11 June 2009: 14–15.

Stewart, R., 'Afghanistan: What Could Work', *New York Review of Books*, 57(1), 14 January 2010.

Economist

'The BRICs: The Trillion-dollar club', *Economist*, 17 April 2010: 59–61.

Banyan, 'Does the elephant dance?', *Economist*, 6 June 2009.

Banyan, 'Himalayan Histronics', *Economist*, 29 October 2009.

Banyan, 'Come Together', *Economist*, 12 December 2009.

New Yorker

Coll, S., 'The Back Channel', *New Yorker*, 2 March 2009: www.newamerica.net/publications/articles/2009/back_channel_11191

Mishra, P., 'Exit Wounds: The legacy of Indian partition', *New Yorker*, 13 August 2007: 78–84.

Newsweek

Fidler, D. and Ganguly, S., 'Singh's shrewd move: a shift on India's nuclear policy', *Newsweek*, 4 December 2009.

Other news media

Domestic: *Deccan Chronicle; Deccan Herald; Economic Times; Financial Express; Financial Standard; Financial Times; Frontline; Hindustan Times; HT Mint; Indian Express; NetIndian News Network; Newsweek; Outlook; Rediff News; Sunday Guardian; Asian Age;*

Business Standard; Daily Star; Guardian; The Hindu; The Hindu Business Line; Hindustan Times; Pioneer; Times of India; Tribune.

International: *ABC News; Asia Sentinel; Asia Times; Asian News International; AsiaTimes Online; BBC News; Bloomberg Businessweek; Daily Times; DAWN; Defense Industry Daily; Forbes; India Abroad; Indo-Asian News Service; International Herald Tribune; Los Angeles Times; New Statesman; New York Times; Press TV; Thaindian News; Australian; Globe and Mail; Jakarta Post; Japan Times; Korea Times; Ottawa Citizen; Wall Street Journal; Time; Travel Daily News; United Press International; UPI Asia; Voice of America News; Washington Post.*

Official Government Documents

'Kamal Nath says India remains fastest growing economies in the World', Press Release, 12 February 2009, http://commerce.nic.in/pressrelease/pressrelease_detail.asp?id=2384

Election Commission of India, 'Statistical Report on General Elections, 2004 to the 14th Lok Sabha', Vol. 1, http://eci.nic.in/eci_main/SR_KeyHighLights/LS_2004/Vol_I_LS_2004.pdf

Election Commission of India, 'Statistical Report on General Elections, 1951 to the First Lok Sabha', Vol. 1, http://eci.nic.in/eci_main/statisticalreports/LS_1951/VOL_1_51_LS.PDF

Government of India, Ministry of Commerce and Industry, 'India FDI Factsheets' (October 2005 and December 2009), http://dipp.nic.in/fdi_statistics/india_fdi_index.htm

Government of India, Ministry of Commerce and Industry, 'India's Trading Partners', Press Release, 27 July 2009, http://pib.nic.in/release/release.asp?relid=51058

Government of India, Ministry of Defence, *Annual Report 2003–2004*, http://mod.nic.in/reports/welcome.html

Government of India, Ministry of Defence, *Annual Report 2007–2008*, http://mod.nic.in/reports/welcome.html

Government of India, Ministry of Defence, *Annual Report 2008–2009*, http://mod.nic.in/reports/welcome.html

Government of India, Ministry of External Affairs, *Annual Report 2007–2008*. New Delhi: Policy and Planning Research Division.

Government of India, Ministry of External Affairs, *Annual Report 2008–2009*. New Delhi: Policy and Planning Research Division.

Government of India, Ministry of Finance (1992), *Economic Survey 1991–92*, Part II: *Sectoral Developments*. New Delhi: Government of India Press.

Government of India, Ministry of Finance (1994), *Annual Report 1994–95*: www.powermin.nic.in/reports/pdf/ar94–95.pdf

Government of India, Ministry of Overseas Indian Affairs (2001), *Report of the High Level Committee on the Indian Diaspora*: www.indiandiaspora.nic.in/contents.htm

Government of India, Ministry of Overseas Indians, *Annual Report 2008–2009*, http://moia.gov.in/writereaddata/pdf/Annual_Report_2008–09.pdf

Government of India, Planning Commission (1992). *Ninth Five Year Plan*, Vol. I. New Delhi: Yojana Bhavan.

Government of India, Planning Commission (2006). *Integrated Energy Policy: Report of the Expert Committee*.

Government of India, Press Information Bureau, 'Riyadh Declaration: A New Era of Strategic Partnership', 1 March 2010: www.pib.nic.in/release/release.asp?relid=58617

Handoo, A., 'Naxal problem needs a holistic approach', Press Information Bureau, Government of India, 22 July 2009, http://www.pib.nic.in/release/release.asp?relid=50833

Reports and Other

Anthony, I. Ahlstrom, C., and Fedchenko, V. (2007). *Reforming Nuclear Export Controls: The Future of the Nuclear Suppliers Group*. SIPRI Research Report, 22. Oxford: Oxford University Press.

Asher, M. G. and Sen, R. (2007). 'India's Membership: APEC's Relevance', *Faculty Working Papers*. Singapore: Lee Kuan Yew University School of Public Policy, National University of Singapore.

Bhaumik, S. (2007). 'Insurgencies in India's Northeast: Conflict, Co-option and Change'. *East-West Center Working Papers*, 10. Hawaii: East West Center.

Bruno, G. (2008). *Backgrounder: Iran's Nuclear Program*. New York/Washington: Council on Foreign Relations.

Burki, S. J. (2010). 'Asia in the "Catch-Up" Game'. *ISAS Working Paper*, 106. Singapore: ISAS.

Calvin, J. B. (1984). *The China–India Border War (1962)*. Quantico, VA: Marine Corps Command and Staff College.

Centre for Bhutan Studies and Institute of Developing Economies, Japan External Trade Organization (IDE/JETRO). (2004). *Economic and Political Relations between Bhutan and Neighbouring Countries*.

Cerra, V., Rivera, S. A., and Saxena, S. C. (2005). 'Crouching Tiger, Hidden Dragon: What Are the Consequences of China's WTO Entry for India's Trade?'. *IMF Working Paper*, Washington, DC: IMF.

—— and Saxena, S. (2002). 'What Caused the 1991 Currency Crisis in India?', *IMF Staff Papers*, 49(3): 395–425.

Chaturvedy, R. R. (2008). 'Making the Case for Soft Power'. *ICRIER Think Ink*. New Delhi: Indian Council for Research on International Economic Relations.

Chaturvedy, R. and Malone, D. (2009). 'India and Its South Asian Neighbours', *ISAS Working Paper*, 100 (26 November). Singapore: National University of Singapore—Institute of South Asian Studies, www.isasnus.org/events/workingpapers/99

Chopra, A. Collyns, C. Hemming, R. Parker, K. Chu, W. and Fratzscher, O. (1995). 'India: Economic Reforms and Growth', *IMF Occasional Paper*. 134. Washington, DC: IMF.

Cohen, A., Curtis, L., and Graham, O. (2008). *The Proposed Iran-Pakistan-India Gas Pipeline: An Unacceptable Risk to Regional Security*. Backgrounder 2139. Washington, DC: Heritage Foundation.

Bibliography

D'Souza, S. M. (May 7, 2010). 'Karzai's Balancing Act: Bringing "China" in?' *ISAS Insights*, 98: 1–9.

Desai, A. (1999). 'The Economics and Politics of Transition to an Open Market Economy: India', *Working Paper*, 155. Paris: OECD Development Centre.

Dimaranan, B., Ianchovichina, E., and Martin, W. (2007). 'China, India, and the Future of the World Economy: Fierce Competition or Shared Growth?' *World Bank Policy Research Working Paper*, 4304. Washington, DC: World Bank Development Research Group.

Director of Central Intelligence. (1974). *Prospects for Further Proliferation of Nuclear Weapons*. Special National Intelligence Estimate SNIE-4-1-74. Central Intelligence Agency.

Director of National Intelligence. (2008). *Global Trends 2025: A World Transformed*. US National Intelligence Council.

Egreteau, R. (2006). 'Instability at the Gate: India's Troubled Northeast and its External Connections', *Occasional Paper*, 6. New Delhi: Centre de Sciences Humaines de New Delhi.

Fakier, Y. and Adebajo, A. (eds.). (2009). *Crouching Tiger, Hidden Dragon? China and Africa*. Policy Seminar Report. Cape Town: Centre for Conflict Resolution.

Flemes, D. (2007). '"Emerging Middle Powers" Soft Balancing Strategy: State and Perspectives of the IBSA Dialogue Forum'. *Working Paper*, 57. Hamburg: German Institute of Global and Area Studies.

Ghoshal, B. (2009). 'India, Southeast Asia and the FTA: Strengthening Economic Integration', *Policy Brief*, 114. New Delhi: Institute of Peace and Conflict Studies.

Haacke, J. (2006). 'Myanmar's Foreign Policy: Domestic Influences and International Implications'. *Adelphi Paper 381*. London: International Institute for Strategic Studies.

Heitzman, J. and Worden, R. (eds.). (1995). *India: A Country Study*. Washington, DC: Library of Congress.

Human Rights Watch, (1994). *Arms and Abuses in Indian Punjab and Kashmir*. www.hrw.org/en/reports/1994/09/01/arms-and-abuses-indian-punjab-and-kashmir

Johri, D. and Miller, M. (2002). *Devaluation of the Rupee: Tale of Two years, 1966 and 1991*. *Working Paper*, 28. New Delhi: Centre for Civil Society.

Kan, S. (2007). *China and Proliferation of Weapons of Mass Destruction and Missiles: Policy Issues*. Washington, DC: CRS Report for Congress RL31555.

Kapila, S. (2006). *India–Saudi Arabia: The Strategic Significance of the Delhi Declaration*. South Asia Analysis Group Paper, 1734.

Khan, M. (2009). 'Towards Better India-Bangladesh relations', *IDSA Strategic Comments*. New Delhi: IDSA.

Kronstadt, A. (2008). *India: Chronology of Events*. Washington, DC: CRS Report for Congress.

Kronstadt, K. A. (2006). *India–US Relations*. Washington, DC: Library of Congress, Congressional Research Service.

Lall, M. (2008). 'India-Myanmar Relations—Geopolitics and Energy in Light of the New Balance of Power in Asia', *ISAS Working Paper*, 29. Singapore: ISAS.

Mallik, A. (2004). *Technology and Security in the 21st Century: A Demand-Side Perspective*. SIPRI Research Report, 20. Oxford: Oxford University Press.

Malone, D. and Chaturvedy, R. (2009). *Impact of India's Economy on its Foreign Policy since Independence*. Vancouver, BC: Asia Pacific Foundation.

Miller, M. C. (2007). *Scars of Empire: Post-Imperial Ideology, Victimization, and Foreign Policy*. Ph.D. Dissertation. Boston: Department of Government, Harvard University.

Mishra, R. (2009). 'India-Austral Relations: Off Again, On Again?'. *IDSA Comment*. New Delhi: IDSA.

Mukhopadhaya, G. (2010). 'India'. In A. J. Tellis and A. Mukharji (eds.). *Is A Regional Strategy Viable in Afghanistan*. Washington, DC: Carnegie Endowment for International Peace, 27–37.

Muni, S. D. (2010). 'SAARC at Twenty Five', *ISAS Brief*, 160 (4 May): 1–5.

Nataraj, G. (2010). 'India Japan Investment Relations: Trends and Prospects'. *ICRIER Working Papers*, 245. New Delhi: ICRIER: Indian Council for Research on International Economic Relations.

Panagariya, A. (2004). 'India in the 1980s and 1990s: A Triumph of Reforms'. *IMF Working Paper*. 04/43. Washington, DC: IMF.

Pandya, A. and Malone, D. M. (2010). 'India's Asia Policy: A Late Look East'. *ISAS Special Report*, 02 (25 August). Singapore: National University of Singapore—Institute of South Asian Studies.

Price, G. (2004). *India's Aid Dynamics: From Recipient to Donor?* London, UK: Royal Institute of International Affairs, Chatham House.

Rahman, S. S. (2010). 'The 2010 Commonwealth Games: India's Triumph or Disaster?', *ISAS Brief*, 166: 1–7.

Raja Mohan, C. (2007). *Peaceful Periphery: India's New Regional Quest*. Pennsylvania: Center for the Advanced Study of India.

—— (2009). 'Is India an East Asian Power? Explaining New Delhi's Security Politics in the Western Pacific'. *ISAS Working Paper*. 81. Singapore: ISAS.

Rangarajan, C. (1991). 'Recent Monetary Policy Measures and the Balance of Payments' *Reserve Bank of India Bulletin*. New Delhi.

Research and Information System for Developing Countries. (2004). 'Future Directions of BIMST-EC: Towards A Bay of Bengal Economic Community (BoBEC)'. *RIS Policy Brief*, 12.

Research and Information System for Developing Countries. (2006). 'Facilitating India's Overland Trade in the Eastern Neighbourhood'. *RIS Policy Brief*. 29.

Research and Information System for Developing Countries. (2007). 'Restoring Afghanistan-Pakistan-India-Bangladesh-Myanmar (APIBM) Corridor: Towards a New Silk Road in Asia'. *RIS Policy Brief*. 30.

Roy, M. S. (2009). 'The 9th Shanghai Cooperation Organisation Summit: An Assessment'. *IDSA Comment*. New Delhi: IDSA.

Sahoo, P. (2009). *India–Korea CEPA: A Step in Right Direction*. East Asia Forum: www.eastasiaforum.org/2009/09/15/india-korea-cepa-a-step-in-right-direction/

—— Rai, D. K., and Kumar, R. (2009). 'India–Korea Trade and Investment Relations'. *ICRIER Working Papers*, 242. New Delhi: Indian Council for Research on International Economic Relations.

Sengupta, A. (2008). *Report on Conditions of Work and Promotion of Livelihoods in the Unorganised Sector*. New Delhi: Academic Foundation.

Sikri, R. (2007). 'India's Foreign Policy Priorities in the Coming Decade'. *ISAS Working Paper*, 25. Singapore: Institute of South Asian Studies.

Singh, K.G. (2004). 'India and the Europe Union: New Strategic Partnership', *South Asia Analysis Group Paper*, 1163. Noida, India: South Asia Analysis Group.

SIPRI. (2009). *SIPRI Yearbook 2009*. Stockholm: Stockholm International Peace Research Institute.

Squassoni, S. (2006). *Iran's Nuclear Program: Recent Development*. Washington, DC: CRS Report for Congress.

Srinivasan, T. N. (2003). 'China and India: Growth and Poverty, 1980–2000', *Stanford Center for International Development Working Paper*, 182.

Taneja, N. (2007). 'Trade Possibilities and Non-Tariff Barriers to Indo-Pak Trade', *ICRIER Working Papers*, 200. New Delhi: Indian Council for Research on International Economic Relations.

Tharoor, S. (2009). 'Indian Strategic Power: Soft'. *Global Brief*. http://globalbrief.ca/blog/2009/05/13/soft-is-the-word/

Economist Intelligence Unit. (2008). *Country Profile: India*. New York: EIU.

—— (2008). *India Country Report*. London: EUI.

Organization for Economic Co-operation and Development (2010). *Perspective on Global Development: Shifting Wealth*. Paris: OECD.

The White House. (2005). *Joint Statement Between President George W. Bush and Prime Minister Manmohan Singh*, 18 July 2005: www.whitehouse.gov/news/releases/2005/07/20050718–6.html

—— (2010). *National Security Strategy*, May 2010: www.whitehouse.gov/sites/default/files/rss_viewer/national_security_strategy.pdf

The World Bank (2010). *World Development Indicators 2010*. http://data.worldbank.org/data-catalog/world-development-indicators/wdi-2010

The World Trade Organization (2010). *WTO Trade Profile-India 2010*.

Trenin, D. and Malashenko, A. (2010). *Afghanistan: A View from Moscow*. Washington, DC: Carnegie Endowment for International Peace.

Vines, A., Wong, L., Weimer, M. and Campos, I. (2009). *Thirst for African Oil: Asian National Oil Companies in Nigeria and Angola*. London: Royal Institute of International Affairs, Chatham House.

Virmani, A. (2006). 'The Dynamics of Competition: Phasing of Domestic and External Liberalisation in India'. *Planning Commission of India Working Paper*, 4. New Delhi: Planning Commission of India.

Williamson, J. and Zagha, R. (2002). 'From the Hindu Rate of Growth to the Hindu Rate of Reform', *Working Paper* 144. Stanford, CA: The Stanford Centre for International Development.

Wilson, D. and Purushothaman, R. (2003). 'Dreaming with the BRICs: The Path to 2050', *Goldman Sachs Global Economics Paper*, 99.

Zissis, C. (2007). *Backgrounder: India's Energy Crunch*. Council on Foreign Relations.

Index